International Economics

International Economics

FIFTEENTH EDITION

ROBERT J. CARBAUGH

Professor of Economics, *Central Washington University*

CENGAGE
Learning·

Australia · Brazil · Japan · Korea · Mexico · Singapore · Spain · United Kingdom · United States

International Economics, Fifteenth Edition

Robert J. Carbaugh

Vice President, General Manager, Social Science & Qualitative Business: Erin Joyner

Product Director: Michael Worls

Product Manager: Steven Scoble

Content Developer: Jeffrey Hahn

Product Assistant: Mary Umbarger

Marketing Manager: Katie Jergens

Media Developer: Leah Wuchnick

Manufacturing Planner: Kevin Kluck

Art and Cover Direction, Production Management, and Composition: Integra Software Services Pvt. Ltd.

Cover Image: Ian McKinnell/ Photographer's Choice/Getty Images

Intellectual Property

  Analyst: Jennifer Nonenmacher

  Project Manager: Sarah Shainwald

For product information and technology assistance, contact us at
Cengage Learning Customer & Sales Support, 1-800-354-9706

For permission to use material from this text or product, submit all requests online at **www.cengage.com/permissions**
Further permissions questions can be e-mailed to
permissionrequest@cengage.com

Library of Congress Control Number: 2014940617

ISBN: 978-1-285-85435-9

Cengage Learning
20 Channel Center Street
Boston, MA 02210
USA

Cengage Learning is a leading provider of customized learning solutions with office locations around the globe, including Singapore, the United Kingdom, Australia, Mexico, Brazil, and Japan. Locate your local office at: **www.cengage.com/global**

Cengage Learning products are represented in Canada by Nelson Education, Ltd.

To learn more about Cengage Learning Solutions, visit **www.cengage.com**.

Purchase any of our products at your local college store or at our preferred online store **www.cengagebrain.com**

Printed in the United States of America
Print Number: 01   Print Year: 2014

Brief Contents

Contents

CHAPTER 3

Sources of Comparative Advantage 69

CHAPTER 4

Tariffs. 107

CHAPTER 7

Trade Policies for the Developing Nations 227

CHAPTER 8

Regional Trading Arrangements 267

CHAPTER 9

International Factor Movements and Multinational Enterprises 295

Preface

I believe the best way to motivate students to learn a subject is to demonstrate how it is used in practice. The first fourteen editions of *International Economics* reflected this belief and were written to provide a serious presentation of international economic theory with an emphasis on current applications. Adopters of these editions strongly supported the integration of economic theory with current events.

The fifteenth edition has been revised with an eye toward improving this presentation and updating the applications as well as including the latest theoretical developments. Like its predecessors, this edition is intended for use in a one-quarter or one-semester course for students having no more background than principles of economics. This book's strengths are its clarity, organization, and applications that demonstrate the usefulness of theory to students. The revised and updated material in this edition emphasizes current applications of economic theory and incorporates recent theoretical and policy developments in international trade and finance.

INTERNATIONAL ECONOMICS THEMES

This edition highlights five current themes that are at the forefront of international economics:

- **GLOBALIZATION OF ECONOMIC ACTIVITY**
- Wooster, Ohio bears brunt of globalization—Ch. 2
- Japan fades in the global electronics industry—Ch. 3
- Comparative advantage and global supply chains—Ch. 2
- Caterpillar bulldozes Canadian locomotive workers—Ch. 9
- Apple uses tax loopholes to dodge taxes—Ch. 9
- Diesel engines and gas turbines as engines of growth—Ch. 1
- Waves of globalization—Ch. 1
- Has globalization gone too far?—Ch. 1
- Putting the H-P Pavilion together—Ch. 1
- Is the United States losing its innovation edge?—Ch. 1
- Rising transportation costs hinder globalization—Ch. 3
- iPhone's complex supply chain highlights limitations of trade statistics—Ch. 10
- Constraints imposed by capital flows on the choice of an exchange rate system—Ch. 15

- **FREE TRADE AND PROTECTIONISM**
- Whirlpool wins dumping case—Ch. 5
- Wage increases and China's trade—Ch. 3
- Should shoe tariffs be stomped out?—Ch. 4
- Natural gas boom fuels trade debate—Ch.2
- Element Electronics brings TV manufacturing back to the United States—Ch. 1
- Carbon tariffs—Ch. 6
- Averting trade barriers during the Great Recession—Ch. 6
- Bangladesh's sweatshop reputation—Ch. 7

- Does the principle of comparative advantage apply in the face of job outsourcing?—Ch. 2
- Boeing outsources work, but protects its secrets—Ch. 2
- Does trade make the poor even poorer?—Ch. 3
- WTO rules against subsidies to Boeing and Airbus—Ch. 3
- Does wage insurance make free trade more acceptable to workers?—Ch. 6
- China's hoarding of rare earth metals declared illegal by WTO—Ch. 6
- The environment and free trade—Ch. 6

■ TRADE CONFLICTS BETWEEN DEVELOPING NATIONS AND INDUSTRIAL NATIONS

- U.S.-Mexico tomato dispute—Ch. 8
- Is state capitalism winning?—Ch. 7
- Canada's immigration policy—Ch. 9
- Is international trade a substitute for migration?—Ch. 3
- Economic growth strategies–import substitution versus export led growth—Ch. 7
- Does foreign aid promote the growth of developing countries?—Ch. 7
- The globalization of intellectual property rights—Ch. 7
- How to bring in developing countries from the cold—Ch. 7
- Microsoft scorns China's piracy of software—Ch. 6
- The Doha Round of multilateral trade negotiations—Ch. 6
- Wage increases work against China's competitiveness—Ch. 7
- China's export boom comes at a cost: How to make factories play fair—Ch. 7
- Will emerging economies soon outstrip the rich ones?—Ch. 7
- Do U.S. multinationals exploit foreign workers?—Ch. 9

■ LIBERALIZING TRADE: THE WTO VERSUS REGIONAL TRADING ARRANGEMENTS

- Does the WTO reduce national sovereignty?—Ch. 6
- Regional integration versus multilateralism—Ch. 8
- Is Europe really a common market?—Ch. 8
- The U.S.-South Korea Free Trade Agreement—Ch. 8
- NAFTA and the U.S.-Mexico trucking dispute—Ch. 8
- Will the euro survive?—Ch. 8

■ TURBULENCE IN THE GLOBAL FINANCIAL SYSTEM

- Yen's depreciation drives Toyota's profits upward—Ch. 11
- People's Bank of China punishes speculators—Ch. 11
- Can the euro survive?—Ch. 8
- Does currency depreciation give weak countries a way out of crisis?—Ch. 14
- Currency manipulation and currency wars—Ch. 15
- Paradox of foreign debt: how the United states borrows at low cost—Ch. 10
- Mistranslation of news story roils currency markets—Ch. 12
- Why a dollar depreciation may not close the U.S. trade deficit—Ch. 14
- Japanese firms send work abroad as yen makes its products less competitive—Ch.14
- Preventing currency crises: Currency boards versus dollarization—Ch. 15
- Should Special Drawing Rights replace the dollar as the world's reserve currency?—Ch. 17
- Should the United States return to the gold standard?—Ch. 17

Besides emphasizing current economic themes, the fifteenth edition of this text contains many new topics such as outsourcing and the U.S. auto industry, U.S. safeguards limiting imports of textiles from China, why Italian shoemakers strive to give the euro the boot, bike imports that forced Schwinn to downshift, and how currency markets draw day traders. Faculty and students will appreciate how this edition provides a contemporary approach to international economics.

ORGANIZATIONAL FRAMEWORK: EXPLORING FURTHER SECTIONS

Although instructors generally agree on the basic content of the international economics course, opinions vary widely about what arrangement of material is appropriate. This book is structured to provide considerable organizational flexibility. The topic of international trade relations is presented before international monetary relations, but the order can be reversed by instructors choosing to start with monetary theory. Instructors can begin with Chapters 10–17 and conclude with Chapters 2–9. Those who do not wish to cover all the material in the book can easily omit all or parts of Chapters 6–9, and Chapters 15–17 without loss of continuity.

The fifteenth edition streamlines its presentation of theory to provide greater flexibility for instructors. This edition uses online *Exploring Further* sections to discuss more advanced topics. By locating the *Exploring Further* sections online rather than in the textbook, as occurred in previous editions, more textbook coverage can be devoted to contemporary applications of theory. The *Exploring Further* sections consist of the following:

- Comparative advantage in money terms—Ch. 2
- Indifference curves and trade—Ch. 2
- Offer curves and the equilibrium terms of trade—Ch. 2
- The specific-factors theory—Ch. 3
- Offer curves and tariffs—Ch. 4
- Tariff-rate quota welfare effects—Ch. 5
- Export quota welfare effects—Ch. 5
- Welfare effects of strategic trade policy—Ch. 6
- Government procurement policy and the European Union—Ch. 8
- Economies of scale and NAFTA—Ch. 8
- Techniques of foreign-exchange market speculation—Ch. 11
- A primer on foreign-exchange trading—Ch. 11
- Fundamental forecasting–regression analysis—Ch. 12
- Income adjustment mechanism—Ch. 13
- Exchange-rate pass-through—Ch. 14

To access the *Exploring Further* sections, go to www.cengagebrain.com.

SUPPLEMENTARY MATERIALS

For Students

International Economics CourseMate (www.cengagebrain.com)

In this age of technology, no text package would be complete without Web-based resources. An international economics CourseMate product is offered with the fifteenth edition.

Within the online study tool CourseMate, students will find a vast amount of resources for self-study including access to the eBook, glossary, online quizzes, videos, graphing workshop games, EconApps, and flashcards. Students can purchase Course-Mate at www.cengagebrain.com.

Study Guide

To accompany the fifteenth edition of the *International Economics* text, Jim Hanson (Professor Emeritus at Willlamette University) has prepared an online Study Guide for students. This guide reinforces key concepts by providing a review of the text's main topics and offering practice problems, true–false, multiple choice, and short–answer questions. The Study Guide is available online only and students can purchase it at www.cengagebrain.com.

For Instructors

International Economics CourseMate (www.cengagebrain.com)

Through CourseMate, instructors have access to Engagement Tracker that is designed to assess that students have read the material or viewed the resources that you've assigned. Engagement Tracker assesses student preparation and engagement. Using the tracking tools enables you to see progress for the class as a whole or for individual students, identify students at risk early in the course, and uncover which concepts are most difficult for your class.

Aplia

Aplia is another feature of the fifteenth edition. With Aplia, international economics students use interactive chapter assignments and tutorials to make economics relevant and engaging. Students complete online assignments to improve their proficiency in understanding economic theory and they receive immediate, detailed explanations for every answer. Math and graphing tutorials help students overcome deficiencies in these crucial areas.

PowerPoint Slides

The fifteenth edition also includes PowerPoint slides created by Syed H. Jafri of Tarleton State University. These slides can be easily downloaded from the Carbaugh Website available for instructors-only at http://login.cengage.com. Slides may be edited to meet individual needs. They also serve as a study tool for students.

Instructor's Manual

To assist instructors in the teaching of international economics, there is an *Instructor's Manual with Test Bank* that accompanies the fifteenth edition. The manual contains: (1) brief answers to end-of-chapter study questions; (2) multiple choice; and (3) true–false questions for each chapter. The *Instructor's Manual with Test Bank* is available for download for qualified instructors from the Carbaugh Website for instructors-only at www.cengagebrain.com.

Study Guide

To accompany the fifteenth edition of the *International Economics*, Jim Hanson (Professor Emeritus at Willlamette University) has prepared an online Study Guide for students. This guide reinforces key concepts by providing a review of the text's main topics and offering practice problems, true–false, multiple choice and short–answer questions. The

Study Guide is only available online and students can purchase it at www.cengagebrain.com. Instructors can view the online Study Guide through http://login.cengage.com.

Compose

Compose is the home of Cengage Learning's online digital content. Compose provides the fastest, easiest way for you to create your own learning materials. South–Western's Economic Issues and Activities content database includes a wide variety of high-interest, current event/policy applications as well as classroom activities designed specifically to enhance economics courses. Choose just one reading or many—even add your own material—to create an accompaniment to the textbook that is perfectly customized to your course. Contact your South–Western/Cengage Learning sales representative for more information.

ACKNOWLEDGMENTS

I am pleased to acknowledge those who aided me in preparing the current and past editions of this textbook. Helpful suggestions and often detailed reviews were provided by:

- Sofyan Azaizeh, University of New Haven
- J. Bang, St. Ambrose University
- Burton Abrams, University of Delaware
- Abdullah Khan, Kennesaw State University
- Richard Adkisson, New Mexico State University
- Richard Anderson, Texas A&M
- Brad Andrew, Juniata College
- Richard Ault, Auburn University
- Mohsen Bahmani-Oskooee, University of Wisconsin—Milwaukee
- Kevin Balsam, Hunter College
- Kelvin Bentley, Baker College Online
- Robert Blecker, Stanford University
- Scott Brunger, Maryville College
- Jeff W. Bruns, Bacone College
- Roman Cech, Longwood University
- John Charalambakis, Asbury College
- Mitch Charkiewicz, Central Connecticut State University
- Xiujian Chen, California State University, Fullerton
- Miao Chi, University of Wisconsin—Milwaukee
- Howard Cochran, Jr., Belmont University
- Charles Chittle, Bowling Green University
- Christopher Cornell, Fordham University
- Elanor Craig, University of Delaware
- Manjira Datta, Arizona State University
- Ann Davis, Marist College
- Earl Davis, Nicholls State University
- Juan De La Cruz, Fashion Institute of Technology
- Firat Demir, University of Oklahoma
- Gopal Dorai, William Paterson College
- Veda Doss, Wingate University
- Seymour Douglas, Emory University
- Carolyn Fabian Stumph, Indiana University—Purdue University Fort Wayne

- Farideh Farazmand, Lynn University
- Daniel Falkowski, Canisius College
- Patrice Franko, Colby College
- Emanuel Frenkel, University of California—Davis
- Norman Gharrity, Ohio Wesleyan University
- Sucharita Ghosh, University of Akron
- Jean-Ellen Giblin, Fashion Institute of Technology (SUNY)
- Leka Gjolaj, Baker College
- Thomas Grennes, North Carolina State University
- Darrin Gulla, University of Kentucky
- Li Guoqiang, University of Macau (China)
- William Hallagan, Washington State University
- Jim Hanson, Willamette University
- Bassam Harik, Western Michigan University
- Clifford Harris, Northwood University
- John Harter, Eastern Kentucky University
- Seid Hassan, Murray State University
- Phyllis Herdendorf, Empire State College (SUNY)
- Pershing Hill, University of Alaska—Anchorage
- David Hudgins, University of Oklahoma
- Ralph Husby, University of Illinois—Urbana/Champaign
- Robert Jerome, James Madison University
- Mohamad Khalil, Fairmont State College
- Wahhab Khandker, University of Wisconsin—La Crosse
- Robin Klay, Hope College
- William Kleiner, Western Illinois University
- Anthony Koo, Michigan State University
- Faik Koray, Louisiana State University
- Peter Karl Kresl, Bucknell University
- Fyodor Kushnirsky, Temple University
- Daniel Lee, Shippensburg University
- Edhut Lehrer, Northwestern University
- Jim Levinsohn, University of Michigan
- Martin Lozano, University of Manchester, UK
- Benjamin Liebman, St. Joseph's University
- Susan Linz, Michigan State University
- Andy Liu, Youngstown State University
- Alyson Ma, University of San Diego
- Mike Marks, Georgia College School of Business
- Michael McCully, High Point University
- Neil Meredith, West Texas A&M University
- John Muth, Regis University
- Al Maury, Texas A&I University
- Tony Mutsune, Iowa Wesleyan College
- Jose Mendez, Arizona State University
- Roger Morefield, University of St. Thomas
- Mary Norris, Southern Illinois University
- John Olienyk, Colorado State University
- Shawn Osell, Minnesota State University—Mankato
- Terutomo Ozawa, Colorado State University
- Peter Petrick, University of Texas at Dallas

- Gary Pickersgill, California State University, Fullerton
- William Phillips, University of South Carolina
- John Polimeni, Albany College of Pharmacy and Health Sciences
- Rahim Quazi, Prairie View A&M University
- Chuck Rambeck, St. John's University
- Elizabeth Rankin, Centenary College of Louisiana
- Teresita Ramirez, College of Mount Saint Vincent
- Surekha Rao, Indiana University Northwest
- James Richard, Regis University
- Suryadipta Roy, High Point University
- Daniel Ryan, Temple University
- Manabu Saeki, Jacksonville State University
- Nindy Sandhu, California State University, Fullerton
- Jeff Sarbaum, University of North Carolina, Greensboro
- Anthony Scaperlanda, Northern Illinois University
- Juha Seppälä, University of Illinois
- Ben Slay, Middlebury College (now at PlanEcon)
- Gordon Smith, Anderson University
- Sylwia Starnawska, Empire State College (SUNY)
- Steve Steib, University of Tulsa
- Robert Stern, University of Michigan
- Paul Stock, University of Mary Hardin—Baylor
- Laurie Strangman, University of Wisconsin—La Crosse
- Hamid Tabesh, University of Wisconsin–River Falls
- Manjuri Talukdar, Northern Illinois University
- Nalitra Thaiprasert, Ball State University
- William Urban, University of South Florida
- Jorge Vidal, The University of Texas Pan American
- Adis M. Vila, Esq., Winter Park Institute Rollins College
- Grace Wang, Marquette University
- Jonathan Warshay, Baker College
- Darwin Wassink, University of Wisconsin—Eau Claire
- Peter Wilamoski, Seattle University
- Harold Williams, Kent State University
- Chong Xiang, Purdue University
- Elisa Quennan, Taft College
- Afia Yamoah, Hope College
- Hamid Zangeneh, Widener University

I would like to thank my colleagues at Central Washington University—Tim Dittmer, David Hedrick, Koushik Ghosh, Roy Savoian, Peter Saunders, Toni Sipic, and Chad Wassell—for their advice and help while I was preparing the manuscript. I am also indebted to Shirley Hood who provided advice in the manuscript's preparation.

It has been a pleasure to work with the staff of Cengage Learning, especially Steven Scoble, who provided many valuable suggestions and assistance in seeing this edition to its completion. Thanks also to Jeffrey Hahn who orchestrated the development of this book in conjunction with Tintu Thomas, project manager at Integra Software Services. I also appreciate the meticulous efforts that Hyde Park Publishing Services did in the copyediting of this textbook. Finally, I am grateful to my students, as well as faculty and students at other universities, who provided helpful comments on the material contained in this new edition.

I would appreciate any comments, corrections, or suggestions that faculty or students wish to make so I can continue to improve this text in the years ahead. Please contact me! Thank you for permitting this text to evolve to the fifteenth edition.

Bob Carbaugh
Department of Economics
Central Washington University
Ellensburg, Washington 98926
Phone: (509) 963-3443
Fax: (509) 963-1992
E-mail: Carbaugh@cwu.edu

The International Economy and Globalization

In today's world, no nation exists in economic isolation. All aspects of a nation's economy—its industries, service sectors, levels of income and employment, and living standard—are linked to the economies of its trading partners. This linkage takes the form of international movements of goods and services, labor, business enterprise, investment funds, and technology. Indeed, national economic policies cannot be formulated without evaluating their probable impacts on the economies of other countries.

The high degree of **economic interdependence** among today's economies reflects the historical evolution of the world's economic and political order. At the end of World War II, the United States was economically and politically the most powerful nation in the world, a situation expressed in the saying, "When the United States sneezes, the economies of other nations catch a cold." But with the passage of time, the U.S. economy has become increasingly integrated into the economic activities of foreign countries. The formation in the 1950s of the European Community (now known as the European Union), the rising importance in the 1960s of multinational corporations, the market power in the 1970s enjoyed by the Organization of Petroleum Exporting Countries (OPEC), the creation of the euro at the turn of the twenty-first century, and the rise of China as an economic power in the early 2000s have all resulted in the evolution of the world community into a complicated system based on a growing interdependence among nations.

The global recession of 2007–2009 provides an example of economic interdependence. The immediate cause of the recession was a collapse of the U.S. housing market and the resulting surge in mortgage loan defaults. Hundreds of billions of dollars in losses on these mortgages undermined the financial institutions that originated and invested in them. Credit markets froze, banks would not lend to each other, and businesses and households could not get loans needed to finance day-to-day operations. This shoved the economy into recession. Soon the crisis spread to Europe. European banks were drawn into the financial crisis in part because of their exposure to defaulted mortgages in the United States. As these banks had to write off losses, fear and uncertainty spread regarding whether banks had enough capital to pay off their debt obligations. The financial crisis also spread to emerging economies such as Iceland and Russia that generally lacked the resources to restore confidence in their economic systems. It is no wonder that "when the United States sneezed, other economies caught a cold."

Recognizing that world economic interdependence is complex and its effects uneven, the economic community has taken steps toward international cooperation. Conferences devoted to global economic issues have explored the avenues that cooperation could be fostered between industrial and developing nations. The efforts of developing nations to reap larger gains from international trade and to participate more fully in international institutions have been hastened by the impact of the global recession, industrial inflation, and the burdens of high priced energy.

Over the past 50 years, the world's market economies have become increasingly interdependent. Exports and imports as a share of national output have risen for most industrial nations, while foreign investment and international lending have expanded. This closer linkage of economies can be mutually advantageous for trading nations. This link permits producers in each nation to take advantage of the specialization and efficiencies of large scale production. A nation can consume a wider variety of products at a cost less than what could be achieved in the absence of trade. Despite these advantages, demands have grown for protection against imports. Protectionist pressures have been strongest during periods of rising unemployment caused by economic recession. Moreover, developing nations often maintain that the so called liberalized trading system called for by industrial nations serves to keep the developing nations in poverty.

Economic interdependence also has direct consequences for a student taking an introductory course in international economics. As consumers, we can be affected by changes in the international values of currencies. Should the Japanese yen or British pound appreciate against the U.S. dollar, it would cost us more to purchase Japanese television sets or British automobiles. As investors, we might prefer to purchase Swiss securities if Swiss interest rates rise above U.S. levels. As members of the labor force, we might want to know whether the president plans to protect U.S. steelworkers and autoworkers from foreign competition.

In short, economic interdependence has become a complex issue in recent times, often resulting in strong and uneven impacts among nations and among sectors within a given nation. Business, labor, investors, and consumers all feel the repercussions of changing economic conditions and trade policies in other nations. Today's global economy requires cooperation on an international level to cope with the myriad issues and problems.

GLOBALIZATION OF ECONOMIC ACTIVITY

When listening to the news, we often hear about globalization. What does this term mean? **Globalization** is the process of greater interdependence among countries and their citizens. It consists of the increased interaction of product and resource markets across nations via trade, immigration, and foreign investment—that is, via international flows of goods and services, people, and investments in equipment, factories, stocks, and bonds. It also includes noneconomic elements such as culture and the environment. Simply put, globalization is political, technological, and cultural, as well as economic.

In terms of people's daily lives, globalization means that the residents of one country are more likely now than they were 50 years ago to consume the products of another country, invest in another country, earn income from other countries, talk by telephone to people in other countries, visit other countries, know that they are being affected by economic developments in other countries, and know about developments in other countries.

What forces are driving globalization?[1] The first and perhaps most profound influence is technological change. Since the industrial revolution of the late 1700s, technical innovations have led to an explosion in productivity and slashed transportation costs. The steam engine preceded the arrival of railways and the mechanization of a growing number of activities hitherto reliant on muscle power. Later discoveries and inventions such as electricity, telephone, automobile, container ships, and pipelines altered production, communication, and transportation in ways unimagined by earlier generations. More recently, rapid developments in computer information and communications technology have further shrunk the influence of time and geography on the capacity of individuals and enterprises to interact and transact around the world. For services, the rise of the Internet has been a major factor in falling communication costs and increased trade. As technical progress has extended the scope of what can be produced and where it can be produced, and advances in transport technology have continued to bring people and enterprises closer together, the boundary of tradable goods and services has been greatly extended.

Also, continuing liberalization of trade and investment has resulted from multilateral trade negotiations. For example, tariffs in industrial countries have come down from high double digits in the 1940s to about 4 percent by 2014. At the same time, most quotas on trade, except for those imposed for health, safety, or other public policy reasons, have been removed. Globalization has also been promoted through the widespread liberalization of investment transactions and the development of international financial markets. These factors have facilitated international trade through the greater availability and affordability of financing.

Lower trade barriers and financial liberalization have allowed more companies to globalize production structures through investment abroad that in turn has provided a further stimulus to trade. On the technology side, increased information flows and the greater tradability of goods and services have profoundly influenced production location decisions. Businesses are increasingly able to locate different components of their production processes in various countries and regions and still maintain a single corporate identity. As firms subcontract part of their production processes to their affiliates or other enterprises abroad, they transfer jobs, technologies, capital, and skills around the globe.

How significant is production sharing in world trade? Researchers have estimated production sharing levels by calculating the share of components and parts in world trade. They have concluded that global production sharing accounts for about 30 percent of the world trade in manufactured goods. Moreover, the trade in components and parts is growing significantly faster than the trade in finished products, highlighting the increasing interdependence of countries through production and trade.[2]

WAVES OF GLOBALIZATION

In the past two decades, there has been pronounced global economic interdependence. Economic interdependence occurs through trade, labor migration, and capital (investment) flows such as corporation stocks and government securities. Let us consider the major waves of globalization that have occurred in recent history.[3]

---

[1]World Trade Organization, *Annual Report*, 1998, pp. 33–36.

[2]A. Yeats, *Just How Big Is Global Production Sharing?* World Bank, Policy Research Working Paper No. 1871, 1998, Washington, DC.

[3]This section draws from World Bank, *Globalization, Growth and Poverty: Building an Inclusive World Economy*, 2001.

TRADE CONFLICTS FEDERAL RESERVE POLICY INCITES GLOBAL BACKLASH

Economic interdependence is part of our daily lives. When domestic economic policies have spillover effects on the economies of other countries, policymakers must take these into account. This why major countries frequently meet to discuss the impacts of their policies on the world economy. Consider the effects of the Federal Reserve's policies on other economies as discussed below.

For decades, the Federal Reserve (Fed) has attempted to fulfill its mandate to promote full employment, price stability, and economic growth for the U.S. economy. Pursuing these objectives can impose adverse spillover effects on economies of other nations, as seen in the following example.

Facing a sluggish economy in 2010, the Fed enacted a controversial decision to pursue economic growth by purchasing $600 billion of U.S. Treasury bonds. The idea was to pump additional money into the economy that would cause long-term interest rates to fall. This would encourage Americans to spend more on investment and big ticket consumption items, thus stimulating the economy. However, critics doubted that the program would work and maintained that it might cause an increase in inflationary expectations that could destabilize the economy.

Also, the Fed's program was criticized by U.S. trading partners such as Germany and Brazil, as an attempt to improve American competitiveness at their expense.

They noted that printing more dollars, or cutting U.S. interest tends to cause depreciation in the dollar's exchange value, that will be explained in Chapter 11 of this text. If the value of the dollar decreases, other countries' exports become more expensive for American consumers, thus reducing the amount of goods the United States imports from the rest of the world. The accompanying rise in the exchange value of other countries' currencies makes American goods cheaper for foreign consumers to purchase that should increase the amount of exports leaving the United States. This would benefit U.S. producers who would likely increase hiring to meet the increased production requirements of the increased global demand for their exports. What's more, the rest of the world's producers would see their exports fall, resulting in job losses for their workers. Producers in the United States would gain at the expense of producers abroad.

However, Federal Reserve officials challenged this argument by stating that the purpose of their program was not to push down the dollar in order to disadvantage America's trading partners. Instead, it was an attempt to grow the economy that is not just good for the United States, but for the world as a whole. A depreciation of the dollar was only a side effect of a growth oriented policy, not the purpose of the policy. This argument did not dampen the fears of foreigners regarding the Fed's monetary policy, and their criticism continued.

iStockphoto.com/photosoup

First Wave of Globalization: 1870–1914

The first wave of global interdependence occurred from 1870 to 1914. The interdependence was sparked by decreases in tariff barriers and new technologies that resulted in declining transportation costs, such as the shift from sail to steamships and the advent of railways. The main agent that drove the process of globalization was how much muscle, horsepower, wind power, or later on, steam power a country had and how creatively it could deploy that power. This wave of globalization was largely driven by European and American businesses and individuals. Therefore, exports as a share of world income nearly doubled to about 8 percent while per capita incomes, which had risen by 0.5 percent per year in the previous 50 years, rose by an annual average of 1.3 percent. The countries that actively participated in globalization, such as the United States, became the richest countries in the world.

However, the first wave of globalization was brought to an end by World War I. Also, during the Great Depression of the 1930s, governments responded by practicing protectionism: a futile attempt to enact tariffs on imports to shift demand into their domestic markets, thus promoting sales for domestic companies and jobs for domestic workers.

For the world economy, increasing protectionism caused exports as a share of national income to fall to about 5 percent, thereby undoing 80 years of technological progress in transportation.

Second Wave of Globalization: 1945–1980

The horrors of the retreat into nationalism provided renewed incentive for internationalism following World War II. The result was a second wave of globalization that took place from 1945 to 1980. Falling transportation costs continued to foster increased trade. Nations persuaded governments to cooperate to decrease previously established trade barriers.

However, trade liberalization discriminated both in terms of which countries participated and which products were included. By 1980, trade between developed countries in manufactured goods had been largely freed of barriers. Barriers facing developing countries had been eliminated for only those agricultural products that did not compete with agriculture in developed countries. For manufactured goods, developing countries faced sizable barriers. For developed countries, the slashing of trade barriers between them greatly increased the exchange of manufactured goods, thus helping to raise the incomes of developed countries relative to the rest.

The second wave of globalization introduced a new kind of trade: rich country specialization in manufacturing niches that gained productivity through **agglomeration economies**. Increasingly, firms clustered together, some clusters produced the same product and others were connected by vertical linkages. Japanese auto companies, for example, became famous for insisting that their parts manufacturers locate within a short distance of the main assembly plant. For companies such as Toyota and Honda, this decision decreased the costs of transport, coordination, monitoring, and contracting. Although agglomeration economies benefit those in the clusters, they are bad news for those who are left out. A region can be uncompetitive simply because not enough firms have chosen to locate there. Thus, a divided world can emerge, in which a network of manufacturing firms is clustered in some high wage region, while wages in the remaining regions stay low. Firms will not shift to a new location until the discrepancy in production costs becomes sufficiently large to compensate for the loss of agglomeration economies.

During the second wave of globalization, most developing countries did not participate in the growth of global trade in manufacturing and services. The combination of continuing trade barriers in developed countries and unfavorable investment climates and antitrade policies in developing countries confined them to dependence on agricultural and natural resource products.

Although the second globalization wave succeeded in increasing per capita incomes within the developed countries, developing countries as a group were being left behind. World inequality fueled the developing countries' distrust of the existing international trading system that seemed to favor developed countries. Therefore, developing countries became increasingly vocal in their desire to be granted better access to developed country markets for manufactured goods and services, thus fostering additional jobs and rising incomes for their people.

Latest Wave of Globalization

The latest wave of globalization that began in about 1980 is distinctive. First, a large number of developing countries, such as China, India, and Brazil, broke into the world markets for manufacturers. Second, other developing countries became increasingly marginalized in the world economy and realized decreasing incomes and increasing poverty. Third, international capital movements, which were modest during the second wave of globalization, again became significant.

Of major significance for this wave of globalization is that some developing countries succeeded for the first time in harnessing their labor abundance to provide them with a competitive advantage in labor intensive manufacturing. Examples of developing countries that have shifted into manufacturing trade include Bangladesh, Malaysia, Turkey, Mexico, Hungary, Indonesia, Sri Lanka, Thailand, and the Philippines. This shift is partly because of tariff cuts that developed countries have made on imports of manufactured goods. Also, many developing countries liberalized barriers to foreign investment that encouraged firms such as Ford Motor Company to locate assembly plants within their borders. Moreover, technological progress in transportation and communications permitted developing countries to participate in international production networks. However, the dramatic increase in manufactured exports from developing countries has contributed to protectionist policies in developed countries. With so many developing countries emerging as important trading countries, reaching further agreements on multilateral trade liberalization has become more complicated.

Although the world has become more globalized in terms of international trade and capital flows compared to 100 years ago, there is less globalization in the world when it comes to labor flows. The United States had a very liberal immigration policy in the late 1800s and early 1900s and large numbers of people flowed into the country, primarily from Europe. As a large country with abundant room to absorb newcomers, the United States also attracted foreign investment throughout much of this period, which meant that high levels of migration went hand in hand with high and rising wages. However, since World War I, immigration has been a disputed topic in the United States, and restrictions on immigration have tightened. In contrast to the largely European immigration in the 1870–1914 globalization waves, contemporary immigration into the United States comes largely from Asia and Latin America.

Another aspect of the most recent wave of globalization is foreign outsourcing, when certain aspects of a product's manufacture are performed in more than one country. As travel and communication became easier in the 1970s and 1980s, manufacturing increasingly moved to wherever costs were the lowest. U.S. companies shifted the assembly of autos and the production of shoes, electronics, and toys to low wage developing countries. This shift resulted in job losses for blue collar workers producing these goods and cries for the passage of laws to restrict outsourcing.

When an American customer places an order online for a Hewlett-Packard (HP) laptop, the order is transmitted to Quanta Computer Inc. in Taiwan. To reduce labor costs, the company farms out production to workers in Shanghai, China. They combine parts from all over the world to assemble the laptop that is flown as freight to the United States, and then sent to the customer. About 95 percent of the HP laptop is outsourced to other countries. The outsourcing ratio is close to 100 percent for other U.S. computer producers including Dell, Apple, and Gateway. Table 1.1 shows how the HP laptop is put together by workers in many different countries.

By the 2000s, the Information Age resulted in the foreign outsourcing of white collar work. Today, many companies' locations hardly matter. Work is connected through digitization, the Internet, and high speed data networks around the world. Companies can now send office work anywhere, and that means places like India, Ireland, and the Philippines where workers are paid much less than American workers. A new round of globalization is sending upscale jobs offshore, including accounting, chip design, engineering, basic research, and financial analysis as shown in Table 1.2. Analysts estimate that foreign outsourcing can allow companies to reduce costs of a given service from 30 to 50 percent.

TABLE 1.1

Manufacturing an HP Pavilion, ZD8000 Laptop Computer

Component	Major Manufacturing Country
Hard disk drives	Singapore, China, Japan, United States
Power supplies	China
Magnesium casings	China
Memory chips	Germany, Taiwan, South Korea, Taiwan, United States
Liquid-crystal display	Japan, Taiwan, South Korea, China
Microprocessors	United States
Graphics processors	Designed in United States and Canada; produced in Taiwan

Source: From "The Laptop Trail," *The Wall Street Journal*, June 9, 2005, pp.B1 and B8.

TABLE 1.2

Globalization Goes White Collar

U.S. Company	Country	Type of Work Moving
Accenture	Philippines	Accounting, software, office work
Conseco	India	Insurance claim processing
Delta Air Lines	India, Philippines	Airline reservations, customer service
Fluor	Philippines	Architectural blueprints
General Electric	India	Finance, information technology
Intel	India	Chip design, tech support
Microsoft	China, India	Software design
Philips	China	Consumer electronics, R&D
Procter & Gamble	Philippines, China	Accounting, tech support

Source: From "Is Your Job Next?" *Business Week*, February 3, 2003, pp. 50–60.

Boeing uses aeronautics specialists in Russia to design luggage bins and wing parts for its jetliners. Having a master's degree or doctorate in math or aeronautics, these specialists are paid $700 per month in contrast to a monthly salary of $7,000 for an American counterpart. Similarly, engineers in China and India, earning $1,100 a month, develop chips for Texas Instruments and Intel; their American counterparts are paid $8,000 a month. However, companies are likely to keep crucial research and development and the bulk of office operations close to home. Many jobs cannot go anywhere because they require face-to-face contact with customers. Economists note that the vast majority of jobs in the United States consist of services such as retail, restaurants and hotels, personal care services, and the like. These services are necessarily produced and consumed locally, and cannot be sent offshore.

Besides saving money, foreign outsourcing can enable companies to do things they simply couldn't do before. A consumer products company in the United States found it impractical to chase down tardy customers buying less than $1,000 worth of goods. When this service was run in India, however, the cost dropped so much the company could profitably follow up on bills as low as $100.

Although the Internet makes it easier for U.S. companies to remain competitive in an increasingly brutal global marketplace, is foreign outsourcing good for white collar workers? A case can be made that Americans benefit from this process. In the last two decades, U.S. companies have imported hundreds of thousands of immigrants to ease engineering shortages. Now, by sending routine service and engineering tasks to nations with a surplus of educated workers, U.S. labor and capital can be shifted to higher value industries and cutting-edge research and development.

However, a question remains: What happens if displaced white collar workers cannot find greener pastures? The truth is that the rise of the global knowledge industry is so recent that most economists have not begun to figure out the implications. People in developing nations like India see foreign outsourcing as a bonus because it helps spread wealth from rich nations to poor nations. Among its many other virtues, the Internet might turn out to be a great equalizer. Outsourcing will be discussed at the end of Chapter 2.

TRADE CONFLICTS DIESEL ENGINES AND GAS TURBINES AS MOVERS OF GLOBALIZATION

When you consider internal combustion engines, you probably think about the one under the hood of your car or truck—the gasoline powered engine. Although this engine is good for moving you around, it is not adequate for moving large quantities of goods and people long distances; global transportation requires more massive engines.

What makes it possible for us to transport billions of tons of raw materials and manufactured goods from country to country? Why are we able to fly almost anywhere in the world in a Boeing or Airbus jetliner within twenty-four hours? Two notable technical innovations that have driven globalization are diesel engines, which power cargo ships, locomotives, and large trucks, and natural gas-fired turbines that power planes and other means of transportation.

The diesel engine was first developed to the point of commercial success by Rudolf Diesel in the 1890s. After graduating from Munich Polytechnic in Germany, Diesel became a refrigerator engineer, but his true love lay in engine design. He developed an engine that converted the chemical energy available in diesel fuel into mechanical energy that could power trucks, cargo ships, and so on. Today, more than 90 percent of global trade in manufactured goods and raw materials is transported with the use of diesel engines.

The natural gas-fired turbine is another driver of globalization. A gas turbine is a rotary engine that extracts energy from a flow of combustion gas. This energy produces a power thrust that sends an airplane into the sky. It also turns a shaft or a propeller that moves locomotives and ships. The gas turbine was invented by Frank Whittle, a British engineer, in the early 1900s. Although Wilbur and Orville Wright are the first fathers of flight, Whittle's influence on global air travel should not be underestimated.

These two engines, diesels and turbines, have become important movers of goods and people throughout the world. They have reduced transportation costs to such an extent that distance to the market is a much smaller factor affecting the location of manufacturers or the selection of the origin of imported raw materials. Indeed, neither international trade nor intercontinental flights would have realized such levels of speed, reliability, and affordability as have been achieved because of diesel engines and gas turbines. Although diesels and turbines have caused environmental problems, such as air and water pollution, these machines will likely not disappear soon.

Source: Vaclav Smil, *Prime Movers of Globalization*, MIT Press, Cambridge, Massachusetts, 2010 and Nick Schulz, "Engines of Commerce," *The Wall Street Journal*, December 1, 2010.

THE UNITED STATES AS AN OPEN ECONOMY

It is generally agreed that the U.S. economy has become increasingly integrated into the world economy (become an open economy) in recent decades. Such integration involves a number of dimensions that include the trade of goods and services, financial markets, the labor force, ownership of production facilities, and the dependence on imported materials.

Trade Patterns

To appreciate the globalization of the U.S. economy, go to a local supermarket. Almost any supermarket doubles as an international food bazaar. Alongside potatoes from Idaho and beef from Texas, stores display melons from Mexico, olive oil from Italy, coffee from Colombia, cinnamon from Sri Lanka, wine and cheese from France, and bananas from Costa Rica. Table 1.3 shows a global fruit basket that is available for American consumers.

The grocery store isn't the only place Americans indulge their taste for foreign made products. We buy cameras and cars from Japan, shirts from Bangladesh, DVD players from South Korea, paper products from Canada, and fresh flowers from Ecuador. We get oil from Kuwait, steel from China, computer programs from India, and semiconductors from Taiwan. Most Americans are well aware of our desire to import, but they may not realize that the United States ranks as the world's greatest exporter by selling personal computers, bulldozers, jetliners, financial services, movies, and thousands of other products to just about all parts of the globe. International trade and investment are facts of everyday life.

As a rough measure of the importance of international trade in a nation's economy, we can look at that nation's exports and imports as a percentage of its gross domestic product (GDP). This ratio is known as **openness**.

$$Openness = \frac{(Exports + Imports)}{GDP}$$

Table 1.4 shows measures of openness for selected nations as of 2013. In that year, the United States exported 14 percent of its GDP while imports were 18 percent of GDP; the

TABLE 1.3

The Fruits of Free Trade: A Global Fruit Basket

On a trip to the grocery store, consumers can find goods from all over the globe.

Fruit	Country	Fruit	Country
Apples	New Zealand	Limes	El Salvador
Apricots	China	Oranges	Australia
Bananas	Ecuador	Pears	South Korea
Blackberries	Canada	Pineapples	Costa Rica
Blueberries	Chile	Plums	Guatemala
Coconuts	Philippines	Raspberries	Mexico
Grapefruit	Bahamas	Strawberries	Poland
Grapes	Peru	Tangerines	South Africa
Kiwifruit	Italy	Watermelons	Honduras
Lemons	Argentina		

Source: From "The Fruits of Free Trade," *Annual Report*, Federal Reserve Bank of Dallas, 2002, p. 3.

TABLE 1.4

Exports and Imports of Goods and Services as a Percentage of Gross Domestic Product GDP), 2013

Country	Exports as a Percentage of GDP	Imports as a Percentage of GDP	Exports Plus Imports as a Percentage of GDP
Netherlands	87	79	166
South Korea	56	54	110
Germany	52	46	98
Norway	41	27	68
United Kingdom	32	34	66
Canada	30	32	62
France	27	30	57
United States	14	18	32
Japan	15	16	31

Source: From The World Bank Group, *Country Profiles,* 2014, available at http://www.worldbank.org.

openness of the U.S. economy to trade equaled 32 percent. Although the U.S. economy is significantly tied to international trade, this tendency is even more striking for many smaller nations, as shown in the table. Large countries tend to be less reliant on international trade because many of their companies can attain an optimal production size without having to export to foreign nations. Therefore, small countries tend to have higher measures of openness than do large ones.

Figure 1.1 shows the openness of the U.S. economy from 1890 to 2013. One significant trend is that the United States became less open to international trade between 1890 and 1950. Openness was relatively high in the late 1800s because of the rise in world trade resulting from technological improvements in transportation (steamships) and communications (trans-Atlantic telegraph cable). However, two world wars and the Great Depression of the 1930s caused the United States to reduce its dependence on trade, partly for national security reasons and partly to protect its home industries from import competition. Following World War II, the United States and other countries negotiated reductions in trade barriers that contributed to rising world trade. Technological improvements in shipping and communications also bolstered trade and the increasing openness of the U.S. economy.

The relative importance of international trade for the United States has significantly increased during the past century, as shown in Figure 1.1. But a fact is hidden by these data. In 1890, most U.S. trade was in raw materials and agricultural products, today, manufactured goods and services dominate U.S. trade flows. Therefore, American producers of manufactured products are more affected by foreign competition than they were a hundred years ago.

The significance of international trade for the U.S. economy is even more noticeable when specific products are considered. We would have fewer personal computers without imported components, no aluminum if we did not import bauxite, no tin cans without imported tin, and no chrome bumpers if we did not import chromium. Students taking a 9 a.m. course in international economics might sleep through the class (do you really believe this?) if we did not import coffee or tea. Moreover, many of the products we buy from foreigners would be more costly if we were dependent on our domestic production.

With which nations does the United States conduct trade? Canada, China, Mexico, and Japan head the list, as shown in Table 1.5.

FIGURE 1.1

Openness of the U.S. Economy, 1890–2013

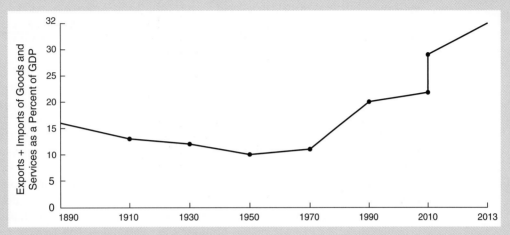

The figure shows that for the United States the importance of international trade has significantly increased from 1890 to 2013.

Source: Data from U.S. Census Bureau, Foreign Trade Division, *U.S. Trade in Goods and Services*, at http://www.census.gov/foreign-trade/ statistics and *Economic Report of the President*, various issues.

TABLE 1.5

Top Ten Countries with Whom the U.S. Trades, 2012

Country	Value of U.S. Exports of Goods (in billions of dollars)	Value of U.S. Imports of Goods (in billions of dollars)	Total Value of Trade (in billions of dollars)
Canada	292.5	323.9	616.4
China	110.5	425.6	536.1
Mexico	215.9	277.6	493.5
Japan	70.0	146.4	216.4
Germany	48.8	108.7	157.5
United Kingdom	54.9	55.0	109.9
South Korea	42.3	58.9	101.2
France	30.1	41.7	71.8
Brazil	43.8	32.1	75.9
Taiwan	24.4	38.9	63.3

Source: From U.S. Department of Commerce, U.S. Census Bureau, *Foreign Trade: U.S. Trade in Goods By Country*, 2013.

Labor and Capital

Besides the trade of goods and services, movements in factors of production are a measure of economic interdependence. As nations become more interdependent, labor and capital should move more freely across nations.

However, during the past 100 years, labor mobility has not risen for the United States. In 1900, about 14 percent of the U.S. population was foreign born. But from the 1920s to the 1960s, the United States sharply curtailed immigration. This curtailment resulted in the foreign born U.S. population declining to 6 percent of the total population. During the 1960s, the United States liberalized restrictions and the flow of immigrants increased. By 2014, about 12 percent of the U.S. population was foreign born while foreigners made up about 14 percent of the labor force. People from Latin America accounted for about half of this figure while Asians accounted for another quarter. These immigrants contributed to economic growth in the United States by taking jobs in labor scarce regions and filling the types of jobs native workers often shun.

Although labor mobility has not risen for the United States in recent decades, the country has become increasingly tied to the rest of the world through capital (investment) flows. Foreign ownership of U.S. financial assets has risen since the 1960s. During the 1970s, OPEC recycled many of their oil dollars by making investments in U.S. financial markets. The 1980s also witnessed major flows of investment funds to the United States as Japan and other nations, with dollars accumulated from trade surpluses with the United States, acquired U.S. financial assets, businesses, and real estate. By the late 1980s, the United States was consuming more than it produced and became a net borrower from the rest of the world to pay for the difference. Increasing concerns were raised about the interest cost of this debt to the U.S. economy and the impact of this debt burden on the living standards of future U.S. generations. This concern remains at the writing of this book in 2014.

Globalization has also increased in international banking. The average daily volume of trading (turnover) in today's foreign exchange market (where currencies are bought and sold) is estimated at about $4 trillion, compared to $205 billion in 1986. The global trading day begins in Tokyo and Sydney and, in a virtually unbroken 24-hour cycle, moves around the world through Singapore and Hong Kong to Europe and finally across the United States before being picked up again in Japan and Australia. London remains the largest center for foreign exchange trading, followed by the United States; significant volumes of currencies are also traded in Asia, Germany, France, Scandinavia, Canada, and elsewhere.

In commercial banking, U.S. banks have developed worldwide branch networks for loans, payments, and foreign exchange trading. Foreign banks have also increased their presence in the United States, reflecting the multinational population base of the United States, the size and importance of U.S. markets, and the role of the U.S. dollar as an international medium of exchange and reserve currency. Today, more than 250 foreign banks operate in the United States; in particular, Japanese banks have been the dominant group of foreign banks operating in the United States. Like commercial banks, securities firms have also globalized their operations.

By the 1980s, U.S. government securities were traded on virtually a 24-hour basis. Foreign investors purchased U.S. treasury bills, notes, and bonds, and many desired to trade during their own working hours rather than those of the United States. Primary dealers of U.S. government securities opened offices in such locations as Tokyo and London. Stock markets became increasingly internationalized with companies listing their stocks on different exchanges throughout the world. Financial futures markets also spread throughout the world.

WHY IS GLOBALIZATION IMPORTANT?

Because of trade, individuals, firms, regions, and nations can specialize in the production of things they do well and use the earnings from these activities to purchase from others those items for which they are high-cost producers. Therefore, trading partners can produce a larger joint output and achieve a higher standard of living than would otherwise be possible. Economists refer to this as the law of comparative advantage that will be further discussed in Chapter 2.

According to the **law of comparative advantage**, the citizens of each nation can gain by spending more of their time and resources doing those things where they have a relative advantage. If a good or service can be obtained more economically through trade, it makes sense to trade for it instead of producing it domestically. It is a mistake to focus on whether a good is going to be produced domestically or abroad. The central issue is how the available resources can be used to obtain each good at the lowest possible cost. When trading partners use more of their time and resources producing things they do best, they are able to produce a larger joint output that provides the source for mutual gain.

International trade also results in gains from the competitive process. Competition is essential to both innovation and efficient production. International competition helps keep domestic producers on their toes and provides them with a strong incentive to improve the quality of their products. Also, international trade usually weakens monopolies. As countries open their markets, their monopoly producers face competition from foreign firms.

With globalization and import competition, U.S. prices have decreased for many products like TV sets, toys, dishes, clothing, and so on. However, prices increased for many products untouched by globalization, such as cable TV, hospital services, sports tickets, rent, car repair and others. The gains from global markets are not restricted to goods traded internationally. They extend to such non-traded goods as houses that contain carpeting, wiring, and other inputs now facing greater international competition.

During the 1950s, General Motors (GM) was responsible for about 60 percent of all passenger cars produced in the United States. Although GM officials praised the firm's immense size for providing economies of scale in individual plant operations, skeptics were concerned about the monopoly power resulting from GM's dominance of the auto market. Some argued that GM should be divided into several independent companies to inject more competition into the market. Today, stiff foreign competition has resulted in GM's current share of the market to stand at less than 24 percent.

Not only do open economies have more competition, but they also have more firm turnover. Being exposed to competition around the globe can result in high-cost domestic producers exiting the market. If these firms are less productive than the remaining firms, then their exit represents productivity improvements for the industry. The increase in exits is only part of the adjustment. The other part is new firms entering the market unless there are significant barriers. With these new firms comes more labor market churning as workers formerly employed by obsolete firms must now find jobs in emerging ones. Inadequate education and training can make some workers unemployable for emerging firms creating new jobs that we often cannot yet imagine. This is probably the key reason why workers find globalization to be controversial. The higher turnover of firms is an important source of the dynamic benefits of globalization. In general, dying firms have falling productivity, and new firms tend to increase their productivity over time.

Economists have generally found that economic growth rates have a close relation to openness to trade, education, and communications infrastructure. Countries that open their economies to international trade tend to benefit from new technologies and other sources of economic growth. As Figure 1.2 shows, there appears to be some evidence of an inverse relation between the level of trade barriers and the economic growth of nations. Nations that maintain high barriers to trade tend to realize a low level of economic growth.

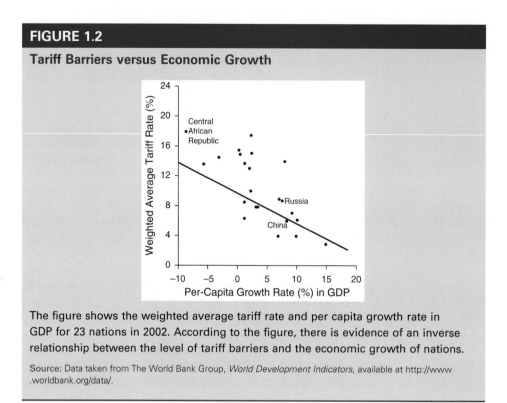

FIGURE 1.2

Tariff Barriers versus Economic Growth

The figure shows the weighted average tariff rate and per capita growth rate in GDP for 23 nations in 2002. According to the figure, there is evidence of an inverse relationship between the level of tariff barriers and the economic growth of nations.

Source: Data taken from The World Bank Group, *World Development Indicators*, available at http://www .worldbank.org/data/.

International trade can also provide stability for producers, as seen in the case of Invacare Corporation, an Ohio based manufacturer of wheelchairs and other health care equipment. For the wheelchairs it sells in Germany, the electronic controllers come from the firm's New Zealand factories; the design is largely American; and the final assembly is done in Germany with parts shipped from the United States, France, and the United Kingdom. By purchasing parts and components worldwide, Invacare can resist suppliers' efforts to increase prices for aluminum, steel, rubber, and other materials. By selling its products in 80 nations, Invacare can maintain a more stable workforce in Ohio than if it was completely dependent on the U.S. market. If sales decline anytime in the United States, Invacare has an ace up its sleeve—exports.

On the other hand, rapid growth in countries like China and India has helped to increase the demand for commodities like crude oil, copper, and steel. Thus, American consumers and companies pay higher prices for items like gasoline. Rising gasoline prices, in turn, have spurred governmental and private sector initiatives to increase the supply of gasoline substitutes like biodiesel or ethanol. Increased demand for these alternative forms of energy has helped to increase the price of soybeans and corn that are key inputs in the production of chicken, pork, beef, and other foodstuffs.

Moreover, globalization can make the domestic economy vulnerable to disturbances initiated overseas, as seen in the case of India. In response to India's agricultural crisis, some 1,200 Indian cotton farmers committed suicide during 2005–2007 to escape debts to money lenders. The farmers borrowed money at exorbitant rates, so they could sink wells and purchase expensive biotech cotton seeds. But the seeds proved inadequate for small plots resulting in crop failures. Farmers suffered from the low world price of their cotton crop that fell by more than a third from 1994 to 2007. Prices were low partly because cotton was heavily subsidized by wealthy countries, mainly the United States.

According to the World Bank, cotton prices would have risen about 13 percent if the subsidies had been eliminated.

Although India's government could impose a tariff on imported cotton to offset the foreign subsidy, its textile manufacturers, who desired to keep production costs low, welcomed cheap fibers. India's cotton tariff was only 10 percent, much lower than its tariffs on most other commodities.

The simple solution to the problem of India's farmers would be to move them from growing cotton to weaving it in factories. India's restrictive labor laws discouraged industrial employment and the lack of a safety net resulted in farmers clinging to their marginal plots of land.

There is great irony in the plight of India's cotton farmers. The British developed India's long-fiber cotton in the1800s to supply British cotton mills. As their inexpensive cloth drove India's weavers out of business, the weavers were forced to work the soil. By the early 2000s, India's textile makers were enjoying a revival but its farmers could not leave the soil to work in factories.[4]

GLOBALIZATION AND COMPETITION

Although economists recognize that globalization and free trade can provide benefits to many firms, workers, and consumers, they can inflict burdens on others. Consider the cases of Eastman Kodak Company, the Schwinn Bicycle Company and Element Electronics Inc.

Kodak Reinvents Itself under Chapter 11 Bankruptcy

Vladimir Lenin, a Russian politician, once said, "A capitalist will sell you the rope to hang him." That quote may contain an element of truth. Capitalists often invest in the technology that ruins their business, as seen in the case of Eastman Kodak Company.

Kodak is a multinational imaging and photographic equipment company headquartered in Rochester, New York. Its history goes back to 1889 when it was founded by George Eastman. During much of the 1900s, Kodak held a dominant position in the photographic equipment market. In 1976 it had a 90 percent market share of film sales and an 85 percent share of camera sales in the United States. Kodak's slogan was "You press the button and we do the rest." However, Kodak's near monopoly position resulted in a culture of complacency for its management who resisted changing their strategy as global competition and new technologies would emerge.

In the 1980s, Japanese competitor Fuji Photo Film Co. entered the U.S. market with lower priced film and supplies. However, Kodak refused to believe that American consumers would ever desert its popular brand. Kodak passed on the opportunity to become the official film of the 1984 Los Angeles Olympics. Fuji won these sponsorship rights that provided it a permanent foothold in the American market. Fuji opened up a film manufacturing plant in the United States and its aggressive marketing and price cutting began capturing market share from Kodak. By the mid-1990s, Fuji held a 17 percent share of the U.S. market for photo film while Kodak's market share plunged to 75 percent. Meanwhile, Kodak made little headway in Japan, the second largest market for its photo film and paper after the United States. Clearly, Kodak underestimated the competitiveness of its Japanese rival.

---

[4]"Cotton Suicides: The Great Unraveling," *The Economist*, January 20, 2007, p. 34.

Another factor that contributed to Kodak's decline was the development of digital cameras and smart phones that operate as cameras. Strange as it may seem, Kodak built one of the first digital cameras in 1975 but Kodak was slow in launching the production of digital cameras. Because Kodak's competitors did not have this technology at that time, Kodak faced no pressure to change its strategy of selling cheap cameras to customers who would buy lots of its expensive film. All of this changed in the 1990s with the development of digital cameras by companies like Sony. With its lucrative film sales dropping, Kodak launched the production of digital cameras. By 2005, Kodak ranked at the top of the digital camera market in the United States. Despite high growth, Kodak failed to anticipate how fast these digital cameras became commodities with low profit margins, as more companies entered the market. Kodak's digital camera sales were quickly undercut by Asian competitors who could produce their cameras more cheaply. Also, smart phones were developed to replace cameras. Kodak also failed to understand emerging markets correctly. Kodak hoped the new Chinese middle class would purchase lots of film. They did for a short while, but then decided that digital cameras were preferable.

Kodak provides a striking example of an industrial giant that faltered in the face of global competition and advancing technology. By 2012 Kodak was running short of cash. As a result, Kodak filed for Chapter 11 bankruptcy under which it would undergo reorganization under the supervision of a bankruptcy court judge. Following its filing, Kodak sold off many of its businesses and patents while shutting down the camera unit that first made it famous. Many of Kodak's former employees lost retirement and health care benefits as a result of the bankruptcy. In 2013, Kodak received court approval for its plan to emerge from bankruptcy as a much smaller digital imaging company. It remains to be seen how Kodak will perform in the years ahead.

Bicycle Imports Force Schwinn to Downshift

The Schwinn Bicycle Company illustrates the notion of globalization and how producers react to foreign competitive pressure. Founded in Chicago in 1895, Schwinn grew to produce bicycles that became the standard of the industry. Although the Great Depression drove most bicycle companies out of business, Schwinn survived by producing durable and stylish bikes sold by dealerships that were run by people who understood bicycles and were anxious to promote the brand. Schwinn emphasized continuous innovation that resulted in features such as built-in kickstands, balloon tires, chrome fenders, head and taillights, and more. By the 1960s, the Schwinn Sting Ray became the bicycle that virtually every child wanted. Celebrities such as Captain Kangaroo and Ronald Reagan pitched ads claiming that "Schwinn bikes are the best."

Although Schwinn dominated the U.S. bicycle industry; the nature of the bicycle market was changing. Cyclists wanted features other than heavy, durable bicycles that had been the mainstay of Schwinn for decades. Competitors emerged such as Trek, which built mountain bikes and Mongoose which produced bikes for BMX racing.

Falling tariffs on imported bicycles encouraged Americans to import from companies in Japan, South Korea, Taiwan, and eventually China. These companies supplied Americans with everything ranging from parts and entire bicycles under U.S. brand names, or their own brands. Using production techniques initially developed by Schwinn, foreign companies hired low wage workers to manufacture competitive bicycles at a fraction of Schwinn's cost.

As foreign competition intensified, Schwinn moved production to a plant in Greenville, Mississippi in 1981. The location was strategic. Like other U.S. manufacturers, Schwinn relocated production to the South in order to hire nonunion workers at lower wages. Schwinn also obtained parts produced by low wage workers in foreign countries. The Greenville plant suffered from uneven quality and low efficiency and it produced bicycles no better than the ones imported from the Far East. As losses mounted for Schwinn, the firm declared bankruptcy in 1993.

Eventually Schwinn was purchased by the Pacific Cycle Company that farmed the production of Schwinn bicycles out to low wage workers in China. Most Schwinn bicycles today are built in Chinese factories and are sold by Walmart and other discount merchants. Cyclists do pay less for a new Schwinn under Pacific's ownership. It may not be the industry standard that was the old Schwinn, but it sells at Walmart for approximately $180, about a third of the original price in today's dollars. Although cyclists may lament that a Schwinn is no longer the bike it used to be, Pacific Cycle officials note that it is not as expensive as in the past either.[5]

Element Electronics Survives by Moving TV Production to America

Few American industries have faltered as much as television manufacturing. During the 1950s–1960s, there were about 150 domestic producers and employment stood at about 100,000 workers. Imports began arriving, first from Japan and later from China, South Korea, and other Asian countries. The introduction of flat panel televisions tipped the scales further in favor of Asia, because their lighter weight and sleek styling made shipping costs cheaper than the heavier and more bulky tube televisions that formerly dominated sales. By the early 2000s, American television manufacturing was virtually nonexistent.

Costs in China have recently been going up as workers' wages and other expenses, such as transportation, have increased. Meanwhile, sluggish wage increases in the United States and rapid productivity gains have reshaped many U.S. factories into more robust competitors.

Once such competitor is Element Electronics Inc. headquartered in Eden Prairie, Minnesota. In 2012, Element Electronics became the only company assembling televisions in the United States. All of the parts of its televisions are imported. On an assembly line located in Detroit, Michigan, the firm produces a variety of flat screen models that are sold by Walmart, Target, and other retailers. Element Electronics made the decision to manufacture products in America to shorten its supply chain and related lead times, thus becoming more responsive to American consumers. This would allow the firm to get the right products, at the right price, to the right place at the right time as well as reduce waste and increase the quality of the consumer's out-of-box experience.

Element Electronics' locating a factory in Detroit provided advantages in terms of a qualified labor pool and distribution efficiencies based on population across the United States. Also, the firm said that by producing in Detroit rather than in Asia, it could avoid a 5 percent tariff on imported televisions and the higher cost of shipping televisions to American retailers. In 2013, the firm estimated that the average savings on tariffs was $27 for a 46-inch television, enough to account for the higher cost workers of Detroit. Moreover, the firm automated the assembly of its televisions to reduce the amount of labor required to build a television.

Officials of Element Electronics said that locating production in the United States was an emotional decision. Rather than being a contributor to jobs leaving America for other countries, they wanted to pioneer a resurgence of creating quality manufacturing jobs in the United States. Element Electronics televisions are shipped in boxes painted with a colorful

---

[5]Judith Crown and Glenn Coleman, *No Hands: The Rise and Fall of the Schwinn Bicycle Company, an American Institution.* (New York, Henry Holt and Co., 1996) and Jay Pridmore, *Schwinn Bicycles.* (Osceola, WI: Motorbooks International, 2002). See also Griff Wittee, "A Rough Ride for Schwinn Bicycle," *The Washington Post,* December 3, 2004.

red, white, and blue flag on the side to portray a "Made in America" image. The boxes also display American workers assembling televisions at the Detroit factory.[6]

COMMON FALLACIES OF INTERNATIONAL TRADE

Although gains from international trade are apparent, misconceptions prevail.[7] One misconception is that trade results in a zero-sum game—if one trading partner benefits, the other must suffer. It turns out that both partners can benefit from trade.

Consider the example of trade between Colombia and Canada. These countries can produce more combined output when Canadians supply natural gas and Colombians supply bananas. The larger output allows Colombians to benefit by using revenues from their banana exports to buy Canadian natural gas. Canadians benefit by using revenues from their natural gas exports to buy Colombian bananas. Therefore, the larger combined production yields mutual benefits for both countries. According to the principle of comparative advantage, if countries specialize in what they are relatively best at producing, they will import products that their trading partners are most efficient at producing, yielding benefits for both countries.

Another misconception is that imports result in unemployment and burden the economy, while exports enhance economic growth and jobs for workers. The source of this misconception is a failure to consider the connections between imports and exports. American imports of German machinery will result in losses of sales, output, and jobs in the U.S. machinery industry. However, as Germany's machinery sales to the United States increase, Germans will have more purchasing power to buy American computer software. Output and employment will thus increase in the U.S. computer software industry. The drag on the U.S. economy caused by rising imports of machinery tends to be offset by the stimulus on the economy caused by rising exports of computer software.

People sometimes feel tariffs, quotas, and other import restrictions result in more jobs for domestic workers. However, they fail to understand that a decrease in imports does not take place in isolation. When we impose import barriers that reduce the ability of foreigners to export to us, we are also reducing their ability to obtain the dollars required to import from us. Trade restrictions that decrease the volume of imports will also decrease exports. As a result, jobs promoted by import barriers tend to be offset by jobs lost due to falling exports.

If tariffs and quotas were that beneficial, why don't we use them to impede trade throughout the United States? Consider the jobs that are lost when, for example, Wisconsin purchases grapefruit from Florida, cotton from Alabama, tomatoes from Texas, and grapes from California. All of these goods could be produced in Wisconsin, although at a higher cost. Thus, Wisconsin residents find it less expensive to "import" these products. Wisconsin benefits by using its resources to produce and "export" milk, beer, electronics, and other products it can produce efficiently. Indeed, most people feel that free trade throughout America is an important contributor of prosperity for each of the states. The conclusions are the same for trade among nations. Free trade throughout America fosters prosperity; so, too, does free trade among nations.

---

[6]Ashok Bindra, "Element Electronics Brings TV Manufacturing Back to the United States," *TMCNet*, January 11, 2012; "Element Electronics: USA Made TV is Bringing Jobs Back Home," *American Made Insider*, February 17, 2013; Timothy Aeppel, "Detroit's Wages Take on China's," *The Wall Street Journal*, May 23, 2012; Matt Roush, "Element Electronics: America Matters," *CBS Detroit*, January 11, 2012.

[7]This section is drawn from James Gwartney and James Carter, *Twelve Myths of International Trade*, U.S. Senate, Joint Economic Committee, June 2000, pp. 4–11.

TRADE CONFLICTS IS THE UNITED STATES LOSING ITS INNOVATION EDGE?

The next time that you are at an electronics store, pick up an iPhone. Open the box and you will find that the device was designed by Apple Inc. in California. Next look at the back of the iPhone and you will see that it was assembled in China.

In the past, the United States has seen numerous industries disappear from its shores and locate in other countries. Industries ranging from smart phones to wind turbines, from solar panel technology to highly advanced computer circuitry born in the United States, now exist elsewhere. Moreover, when abandoning an industry, the United States may also lose technologies that would foster the development of future industries.

Consider the case of the Amazon Kindle. In 2007 in a Silicon Valley research facility, Amazon engineers and designers developed the Kindle electronic reader, a device that enables users to download and read newspapers, magazines, textbooks, and other digital media on a portable computer screen. Amazon first released the Kindle in November, 2007, for $399 and was sold out in five and one half hours; the device remained out of stock for five months, until late April 2008. By 2011, the Kindle sold for less than $140 as competition from other manufacturers intensified.

To produce the electronic ink for the Kindle, Amazon initially partnered with E-Ink Co., a U.S. based firm. Because E-Ink did not have the technology to produce the computer screen for the Kindle, Amazon had to look for another partner. The search initially began in the United States, but it was not successful since American firms lacked the expertise and capability to produce the Kindle screen. Eventually, Amazon turned to Prime View, a Taiwanese manufacturer, to produce the screen. Soon thereafter, Prime View purchased E-Ink and moved its production operations from the United States to Taiwan. Even though the Kindle's key innovation, its electronic ink was invented in the United States, most of the value added in producing the Kindle wound up being captured by the Taiwanese.

Some economists maintain that the United States has been losing its innovation edge as American manufacturers locate abroad. They note that manufacturing is a key driver of research and development that generates inventions that fuel economic growth. The United States cannot sustain the level of economic growth it needs without a strong manufacturing sector. According to these economists, to promote a stronger manufacturing sector, the United States needs investment friendly public policies.

Other economists disagree. They contend that from the perspective of America's competitiveness, all of the key technologies and high-value added activities are still captured on American soil and that the United States leads the world in scientific and technological development. They also note that trade and comparative advantage foster an evolution in a country's industries over time. In the television market, the manufacturing of televisions initially began in the United States. As technologies became standardized, television production moved offshore to countries with much lower wages and manufacturing costs and prices continued to fall, to the benefit of consumers.

The global economy is dynamic and the firms that have survived have been the ones able to transform their business models to match their competitors. U.S. firms will continue to face strong competition as other countries master next generation production techniques and accrue expertise in innovation. In Chapter 2, we will learn more about the outsourcing of production and jobs to other countries.

Source: Andrew Liveris, *Make It In America: The Case for Re-Inventing the Economy*, John Wiley & Sons, Inc., Hoboken, New Jersey, 2011 and James Hagerty, "U.S. Manufacturers Gain Ground," *The Wall Street Journal*, August 18, 2013.

iStockphoto.com/photosoup

DOES FREE TRADE APPLY TO CIGARETTES?

When President George W. Bush pressured South Korea in 2001 to stop imposing a 40 percent tariff on foreign cigarettes, administration officials said the case had nothing to do with public health. Instead, it was a case against protecting the domestic industry from foreign competition. However, critics maintained that nothing is that simple with tobacco. They recognized that free trade, as a rule, increases competition, lowers prices, and makes better products available to consumers, leading to higher consumption. Usually, that's a good thing. However, with cigarettes, the result can be more smoking, disease, and death.

Globally, about four million people die each year from lung cancer, emphysema, and other smoking related diseases, making cigarettes the largest single cause of preventable death. By 2030, the annual number of fatalities could hit 10 million according to the World Health Organization. That has antismoking activists and even some economists arguing that cigarettes are not normal goods but are, in fact, "bads" that require their own set of regulations. They contend that the benefits of free trade do not apply to cigarettes and that they should be treated as an exception to trade rules.

This view is finding favor with some governments, as well. In recent talks of the World Health Organization, dealing with a global tobacco control treaty, a range of nations expressed support for provisions to emphasize antismoking measures over free trade rules. The United States opposed such measures. In fact, the United States, that has sued tobacco companies for falsifying cigarettes' health risks, has promoted freer trade in cigarettes. President Bill Clinton demanded a sharp reduction in Chinese tariffs, including those on tobacco, in return for U.S. support of China's entry into the World Trade Organization. Those moves, combined with free trade pacts that have decreased tariffs and other barriers to trade, have helped stimulate the international sales of cigarettes.

The United States, first under President Clinton and then President Bush, has only challenged rules imposed to aid local cigarette makers, not nondiscriminatory measures to protect public health. The United States opposed South Korea's decision to impose a 40 percent tariff on imported cigarettes because it was discriminatory and aimed at protecting domestic producers and not at protecting the health and safety of the Korean people, according to U.S. trade officials. However, antismoking activists maintain that this is a false distinction and anything that makes cigarettes more widely available at a lower price is harmful to public health. Cigarette makers oppose limiting trade in tobacco. They maintain that there is no basis for creating new regulations that weaken the principle of open trade protected by the World Trade Organization.

Current trade rules permit countries to enact measures to protect the health and safety of their citizens as long as all goods are treated equally, tobacco companies argue. A trade dispute panel notified Thailand that, although it could not prohibit foreign cigarettes, it could ban advertisements for both domestic and foreign made smokes. But tobacco control activists worry that the rules could be used to stop governments from imposing antismoking measures. They contend that special products need special rules, pointing to hazardous chemicals and weapons as goods already exempt from regular trade policies. Cigarettes kill more people every year than AIDS. Anti-tobacco activists think it's time for health concerns to be of primary importance in the case of smoking, too.

IS INTERNATIONAL TRADE AN OPPORTUNITY OR A THREAT TO WORKERS?

- Tom lives in Chippewa Falls, Wisconsin. His former job as a bookkeeper for a shoe company that employed him for many years was insecure. Although he earned $100 a day, promises of promotion never panned out and the company eventually went bankrupt because cheap imports from Mexico forced shoe prices down. Tom then went to a local university, earned a degree in management information systems, and was hired by a new machine tool firm that exports to Mexico. He now enjoys a more comfortable living even after making the monthly payments on his government subsidized student loan.

- Rosa and her family recently moved from a farm in southern Mexico to the country's northern border where she works for a U.S. owned electronics firm that exports to the United States. Her husband, Jose, operates a janitorial service and sometimes crosses the border to work illegally in California. Rosa and Jose and their daughter have improved their standard of living since moving out of subsistence agriculture. Rosa's wage has not increased in the past year; she still earns about $3 per hour with no future gains in sight.

Workers around the globe are living increasingly intertwined lives. Most of the world's population now lives in countries that either are integrated into world markets for goods and finance or are rapidly becoming so. Are workers better off as a result of these globalizing trends? Stories about losers from international trade are often featured in newspapers: how Tom lost his job because of competition from poor Mexicans. But Tom currently has a better job and the U.S. economy benefits from his company's exports to Mexico. Producing goods for export has led to an improvement in Rosa's living standard and her daughter can hope for a better future. Jose is looking forward to the day when he will no longer have to travel illegally to California.

International trade benefits many workers. Trade enables them to shop for the cheapest consumption goods and permits employers to purchase the technologies and equipment that best complement their workers' skills. Trade also allows workers to become more productive as the goods they produce increase in value. Producing goods for export generates jobs and income for domestic workers. Workers in exporting industries appreciate the benefits of an open trading system.

Not all workers gain from international trade. The world trading system, for example, has come under attack by some in industrial countries where rising unemployment and wage inequality have made people feel apprehensive about the future. Cheap exports produced by lower cost foreign workers threaten to eliminate jobs for some workers in industrial countries. Others worry that firms are relocating abroad in search of low wages and lax environmental standards or fear that masses of poor immigrants will be at their company's door, offering to work for lower wages. Trade with low wage developing countries is particularly threatening to unskilled workers in the import-competing sectors of industrial countries.

As an economy opens up to international trade, domestic prices become more aligned with international prices; wages tend to increase for workers whose skills are more scarce internationally than at home and to decrease for workers who face increased competition from foreign workers. As the economies of foreign nations open up to trade, the relative scarcity of various skills in the world marketplace changes still further, harming those countries with an abundance of workers who have the skills that are becoming less scarce. Increased competition also suggests that unless countries match the productivity gains of their competitors, the wages of their workers will deteriorate. It is no wonder that workers in import-competing industries often lobby for restrictions on the importation of goods so as to neutralize the threat of foreign competition. Slogans such as "Buy American" and "American goods create American jobs" have become rallying cries among many U.S. workers.

Keep in mind that what is true for the part is not necessarily true for the whole. It is certainly true that imports of steel or automobiles can eliminate American jobs. It is not true that imports decrease the total number of jobs in a nation. A large increase in

U.S. imports will inevitably lead to a rise in U.S. exports or foreign investment in the United States. In other words, if Americans suddenly wanted more European autos, eventually American exports would have to increase to pay for these products. The jobs lost in one industry are replaced by jobs gained in another industry. The long run effect of trade barriers is not to increase total domestic employment, but to reallocate workers away from export industries and toward less efficient, import-competing industries. This reallocation leads to a less efficient utilization of resources.

International trade is just another kind of technology. Think of it as a machine that adds value to its inputs. In the United States, trade is the machine that turns computer software that the United States makes very well, into CD players, baseballs, and other things that it also wants but does not make quite so well. International trade does this at a net gain to the economy as a whole. If somebody invented a device that could do this, it would be considered a miracle. Fortunately, international trade has been developed.

If international trade is squeezing the wages of the less skilled, so are other kinds of advancing technology, only more so. "Yes," you might say, "but to tax technological progress or put restrictions on labor saving investment would be idiotic: that would only make everybody worse off." Indeed it would, and exactly the same goes for international trade—whether this superior technology is taxed (through tariffs) or overregulated (in the form of international efforts to harmonize labor standards).

This is not an easy thing to explain to American textile workers who compete with low wage workers in China, Malaysia, etc. Free-trade agreements will be more easily reached if those who might lose by new trade are helped by all of the rest of us who gain.

BACKLASH AGAINST GLOBALIZATION

Proponents of free trade and globalization note how it has helped the United States and other countries prosper. Open borders permit new ideas and technology to flow freely around the world, fueling productivity growth and increasing living standards. Moreover, increased trade helps restrain consumer prices, so inflation becomes less likely to disrupt economic growth. Without trade, coffee drinkers in the United States would pay much higher prices because the nation's supply would depend solely on Hawaiian or Puerto Rican sources.

Critics maintain that U.S. trade policies primarily benefit large corporations rather than average citizens—of the United States or any other country. Environmentalists argue that elitist trade organizations, such as the World Trade Organization, make undemocratic decisions that undermine national sovereignty on environmental regulation. Unions maintain that unfettered trade permits unfair competition from countries that lack labor standards. Human rights activists contend that the World Bank and International Monetary Fund support governments that allow sweatshops and pursue policies that bail out governmental officials at the expense of local economies. A gnawing sense of unfairness and frustration has emerged about trade policies that ignore the concerns of the environment, American workers, and international labor standards.

The noneconomic aspects of globalization are at least as important in shaping the international debate as are the economic aspects. Many of those who object to globalization resent the political and military dominance of the United States. They also resent the influence of foreign (mainly American) culture, as they see it, at the expense of national and local cultures.

Public opinion surveys note that many Americans are aware of both the benefits and costs of interdependence with the world economy, but they consider the costs to be more than the benefits. In particular, less skilled workers are more likely to oppose freer trade and immigration than their more skilled counterparts who have more job mobility. While concerns about the effect of globalization on the environment, human rights, and other issues are an important part of the politics of globalization, it is the tie between policy liberalization and worker interests that forms the foundation for the backlash against liberalization in the United States.

Some critics point to the terrorist attack on the United States on September 11, 2001, as what can occur when globalization ignores the poor people of the world. The terrorist attack resulted in the tragic loss of life for thousands of innocent Americans. It also jolted America's golden age of prosperity and the promise it held for global growth that existed throughout the 1990s. Because of the threat of terrorism, Americans have become increasingly concerned about their safety and their livelihoods. Table 1.6 summarizes some of the pros and cons of globalization.

The way to ease the fear of globalization is to help people move to different jobs as comparative advantage shifts rapidly from one activity to the next. This process implies a more flexible labor market and a regulatory system that fosters investment. It implies an education system that provides people with the skills that make them mobile. It also implies removing health care and pensions from employment, so that when you move to a new job, you are not risking losing everything. For those who lose their jobs, it implies strengthening training policies to help them find work. These activities are expensive, and they may take years to work. But an economy that finds its national income increasing because of globalization can more easily find the money to pay for it.

TABLE 1.6

Advantages and Disadvantages of Globalization

Advantages	Disadvantages
Productivity increases faster when countries produce goods and services in which they have a comparative advantage. Living standards can increase more rapidly.	Millions of Americans have lost jobs because of imports or shifts in production abroad. Most find new jobs that pay less.
Global competition and cheap imports keep a constraint on prices, so inflation is less likely to disrupt economic growth.	Millions of other Americans fear getting laid off, especially at those firms operating in import-competing industries.
An open economy promotes technological development and innovation, with fresh ideas from abroad.	Workers face demands of wage concessions from their employers, which often threaten to export jobs abroad if wage concessions are not accepted.
Jobs in export industries tend to pay about 15 percent more than jobs in import-competing industries.	Besides blue collar jobs, service and white collar jobs are increasingly vulnerable to operations being sent overseas.
Unfettered capital movements provide the United States access to foreign investment and maintain low interest rates.	American employees can lose their competitiveness when companies build state-of-the-art factories in low wage countries, making them as productive as those in the United States.

Source: "Backlash Behind the Anxiety over Globalization," *Business Week*, April 24, 2000, p. 41.

THE PLAN OF THIS TEXT

This text is an examination of the functioning of the international economy. Although the emphasis is on the theoretical principles that govern international trade, there also is considerable coverage of the empirical evidence of world trade patterns and trade policies of the industrial and developing nations. The book is divided into two parts. Part One deals with international trade and commercial policy; Part Two stresses the balance-of-payments and the adjustment in the balance-of-payments.

Chapters 2 and 3 deal with the theory of comparative advantage, as well as theoretical extensions and empirical tests of this model. This topic is followed by Chapters 4 through 6, a treatment of tariffs, nontariff trade barriers, and contemporary trade policies of the United States. Discussions of trade policies for the developing nations, regional trading arrangements, and international factor movements in Chapters 7 through 9 complete the first part of the text.

The treatment of international financial relations begins with an overview of the balance-of-payments, the foreign exchange market, and the exchange rate determination in Chapters 10 through 12. The balance-of-payments adjustment under alternate exchange rate regimes is discussed in Chapters 13 through 15. Chapter 16 considers macroeconomic policy in an open economy, and Chapter 17 analyzes the international banking system.

SUMMARY

1. Throughout the post-World War II era, the world's economies have become increasingly interdependent in terms of the movement of goods and services, business enterprise, capital, and technology.

2. The United States has seen growing interdependence with the rest of the world in its trade sector, financial markets, ownership of production facilities, and labor force.

3. Largely owing to the vastness and wide diversity of its economy, the United States remains among the countries that exports constitute a small fraction of national output.

4. Proponents of an open trading system contend that international trade results in higher levels of consumption and investment, lower prices of commodities, and a wider range of product choices for consumers. Arguments against free trade tend to be voiced during periods of excess production capacity and high unemployment.

5. International competitiveness can be analyzed in terms of a firm, an industry, and a nation. Key to the concept of competitiveness is productivity, or output per worker hour.

6. Researchers have shown that exposure to competition with the world leader in an industry improves a firm's performance in that industry. Global competitiveness is a bit like sports: You get better by playing against folks who are better than you.

7. Although international trade helps workers in export industries, workers in import-competing industries feel the threat of foreign competition. They often see their jobs and wage levels undermined by cheap foreign labor.

8. Among the challenges that the international trading system faces are dealing with fair labor standards and concerns about the environment.

KEY CONCEPTS AND TERMS

Agglomeration economies (p. 5)   Globalization (p. 2)   Openness (p. 9)
Economic interdependence (p. 1)   Law of comparative advantage (p. 13)

STUDY QUESTIONS

1. What factors explain why the world's trading nations have become increasingly interdependent, from an economic and political viewpoint, during the post-World War II era?
2. What are some of the major arguments for and against an open trading system?
3. What significance does growing economic interdependence have for a country like the United States?
4. What factors influence the rate of growth in the volume of world trade?
5. Identify the major fallacies of international trade.
6. What is meant by international competitiveness? How does this concept apply to a firm, an industry, and a nation?
7. What do researchers have to say about the relation between a firm's productivity and exposure to global competition?
8. When is international trade an opportunity for workers? When is it a threat to workers?
9. Identify some of the major challenges confronting the international trading system.
10. What problems does terrorism pose for globalization?

PART 1

International
Trade Relations

Foundations of Modern Trade Theory: Comparative Advantage

The previous chapter discussed the importance of international trade. This chapter answers the following questions: (1) What constitutes the **basis for trade**—that is, why do nations export and import certain products? (2) At what **terms of trade** are products exchanged in the world market? (3) What are the **gains from international trade** in terms of production and consumption? This chapter addresses these questions, first by summarizing the historical development of modern trade theory and next by presenting the contemporary theoretical principles used in analyzing the effects of international trade.

HISTORICAL DEVELOPMENT OF MODERN TRADE THEORY

Modern trade theory is the product of an evolution of ideas in economic thought. In particular, the writings of the mercantilists, and later those of the classical economists—Adam Smith, David Ricardo, and John Stuart Mill—have been instrumental in providing the framework of modern trade theory.

The Mercantilists

During the period 1500–1800, a group of writers appeared in Europe who were concerned with the process of nation building. According to the **mercantilists**, the central question was how a nation could regulate its domestic and international affairs to promote its own interests. The solution lay in a strong foreign trade sector. If a country could achieve a *favorable trade balance* (a surplus of exports over imports) it would realize net payments received from the rest of the world in the form of gold and silver. Such revenues would contribute to increased spending and a rise in domestic output and employment. To promote a favorable trade balance, the mercantilists advocated government regulation of trade. Tariffs, quotas, and other commercial policies were proposed by the mercantilists to minimize imports in order to protect a nation's trade position.[1]

---

[1]See E. A. J. Johnson, *Predecessors of Adam Smith* (New York: Prentice-Hall, 1937).

By the eighteenth century, the economic policies of the mercantilists were under strong attack. According to David Hume's **price-specie-flow doctrine**, a favorable trade balance is possible only in the short run for over time it would automatically be eliminated. To illustrate, suppose England achieves a trade surplus that results in an inflow of gold and silver. Because these precious metals constitute part of England's money supply, their inflow increases the amount of money in circulation. This leads to a rise in England's price level relative to that of its trading partners. English residents would therefore be encouraged to purchase foreign-produced goods, while England's exports would decline. As a result, the country's trade surplus would eventually be eliminated. The price-specie-flow mechanism thus shows that mercantilist policies could provide at best only short-term economic advantages.[2]

The mercantilists were also attacked for their *static view* of the world economy. To the mercantilists, the world's wealth was fixed. This view meant that one nation's gains from trade came at the expense of its trading partners; not all nations could simultaneously enjoy the benefits of international trade. This view was challenged with the publication in 1776 of Adam Smith's *The Wealth of Nations*. According to Smith (1723–1790) the world's wealth is not a fixed quantity. International trade permits nations to take advantage of specialization and the division of labor that increase the general level of productivity within a country and thus increase world output (wealth). Smith's dynamic view of trade suggested that *both* trading partners could simultaneously enjoy higher levels of production and consumption with trade. Smith's trade theory is further explained in the next section.

Although the foundations of mercantilism have been refuted, mercantilism is alive today. However, it now emphasizes employment rather than holdings of gold and silver. Neo-mercantilists contend exports are beneficial because they result in jobs for domestic workers, while imports are bad because they take jobs away from domestic workers and transfer them to foreign workers. Trade is considered a zero-sum activity in which one country must lose for the other to win. There is no acknowledgment that trade can provide benefits to all countries, including mutual benefits in employment as prosperity increases throughout the world.

Why Nations Trade: Absolute Advantage

Adam Smith, a classical economist, was a leading advocate of **free trade** (open markets) on the grounds that it promoted the international division of labor. With free trade, nations could concentrate their production on the goods that they could make the most cheaply, with all the consequent benefits from this the division of labor.

Accepting the idea that *cost differences* govern the international movement of goods, Smith sought to explain why costs differ among nations. Smith maintained that *productivities* of factor inputs represent the major determinant of production cost. Such productivities are based on natural and acquired advantages. The former include factors relating to climate, soil, and mineral wealth, whereas the latter include special skills and techniques. Given a natural or acquired advantage in the production of a good, Smith reasoned that a nation would produce that good at a lower cost and become more competitive than its trading partner. Smith viewed the determination of competitiveness from the *supply side* of the market.[3]

Smith founded his concept of cost on the **labor theory of value** that assumes within each nation, labor is the only factor of production and is homogeneous (of one quality) and the cost or price of a good depends exclusively on the amount of labor required to

---

[2]David Hume, "Of Money," *Essays*, Vol. 1, (London: Green and Co., 1912), p. 319. Hume's writings are also available in Eugene Rotwein, *The Economic Writings of David Hume* (Edinburgh: Nelson, 1955).

[3]Adam Smith, *The Wealth of Nations* (New York: Modern Library, 1937), pp. 424–426.

produce it. For example, if the United States uses less labor to manufacture a yard of cloth than the United Kingdom, the U.S. production cost will be lower.

Smith's trading principle was the **principle of absolute advantage**: in a two-nation, two-product world, international specialization and trade will be beneficial when one nation has an absolute cost advantage (uses less labor to produce a unit of output) in one good and the other nation has an absolute cost advantage in the other good. For the world to benefit from specialization, each nation must have a good that is absolutely more efficient in producing than its trading partner. A nation will *import* goods in which it has an absolute cost *disadvantage* and *export* those goods in which it has an absolute cost *advantage*.

An arithmetic example helps illustrate the principle of absolute advantage. Referring to Table 2.1, suppose workers in the United States can produce five bottles of wine or 20 yards of cloth in an hour's time, while workers in the United Kingdom can produce 15 bottles of wine or ten yards of cloth in an hour. Clearly, the United States has an absolute advantage in cloth production; its cloth workers' productivity (output per worker hour) is higher than that of the United Kingdom, and leads to lower costs (less labor required to produce a yard of cloth). In like manner, the United Kingdom has an absolute advantage in wine production.

According to Smith, each nation benefits by specializing in the production of the good that it produces at a lower cost than the other nation, while importing the good that it produces at a higher cost. Because the world uses its resources more efficiently as the result of specializing, an increase in world output occurs that is distributed to the two nations through trade. All nations can benefit from trade, according to Smith.

The writings of Smith established the case for free trade that is still influential today. According to Smith, free trade would increase competition in the home market and reduce the market power of domestic companies by lessening their ability to take advantage of consumers by charging high prices and providing poor service. Also, the country would benefit by exporting goods that are desired on the world market for imports that are cheap on the world market. Smith maintained that the wealth of a nation depends on this division of labor that is limited by the extent of the market. Smaller and more isolated economies cannot support the degree of specialization needed to significantly increase productivity and reduce cost, and thus tend to be relatively poor. Free trade allows countries, especially smaller countries, to more fully take advantage of the division of labor, thus attaining higher levels of productivity and real income.

Why Nations Trade: Comparative Advantage

In 1800, a wealthy London businessman named David Ricardo (1772–1823) came across *The Wealth of Nations* while on vacation and was intrigued. Although Ricardo appreciated the persuasive flair of Smith's argument for free trade, he thought that some of

---

TABLE 2.1

A Case of Absolute Advantage when Each Nation is More Efficient in the Production of One Good

World output possibilities in the absence of specialization

	OUTPUT PER LABOR HOUR	
Nation	**Wine**	**Cloth**
United States	5 bottles	20 yards
United Kingdom	15 bottles	10 yards

© Cengage Learning®

TRADE CONFLICTS DAVID RICARDO

David Ricardo (1772–1823) was the leading British economist of the early 1800s. He helped develop the theories of *classical economics* that emphasize economic freedom through free trade and competition. Ricardo was a successful businessman, financier and speculator, and he accumulated a sizable fortune.

Being the third of 17 children, Ricardo was born into a wealthy Jewish family. His father was a merchant banker. They initially lived in the Netherlands and then moved to London. Having little formal education and never attending college, Ricardo went to work for his father at the age of 14. When he was 21, Ricardo married a Quaker despite his parents' preferences. After his family disinherited him for marrying outside the Jewish faith, Ricardo became a stockbroker and a loan broker. He was highly successful in business and was able to retire at 42, accumulating an estate that was worth more than $100 million in today's dollars. Upon retirement, Ricardo bought a country estate and established himself as a country gentleman. In 1819, Ricardo purchased a seat in the British Parliament and held the post until the year of his death in 1823. As a member of Parliament, Ricardo advocated the repeal of the Corn Laws that established trade barriers to protect British landowners from foreign competition. However, he was unable to get Parliament to abolish the law that lasted until its repeal in 1846.

Ricardo's interest in economics was inspired by a chance reading of Adam Smith's *The Wealth of Nations* when he was in his late twenties. Upon the urging of his friends, Ricardo began writing newspaper articles on economic questions. In 1817 Ricardo published his groundbreaking *The Principles of Political Economy and Taxation* that laid out the theory of comparative advantage as discussed in this chapter.

Like Adam Smith, Ricardo was an advocate of free trade and an opponent of protectionism. He believed that protectionism led countries toward economic stagnation. However, Ricardo was less confident than Smith about the ability of a market economy's potential to benefit society. Instead, Ricardo felt that the economy tends to move toward a standstill. Yet Ricardo contended that if government meddled with the economy, the result would be only further economic stagnation.

Ricardo's ideas have greatly affected other economists. His theory of comparative advantage has been a cornerstone of international trade theory for almost 200 years and has influenced generations of economists in the belief that protectionism is bad for an economy.

Source: Mark Blaug, *Ricardian Economics.* (New Haven, CT: Yale University Press, 1958), Samuel Hollander, *The Economics of David Ricardo*, (Cambridge: Cambridge University Press, 1993), and Robert Heilbronner, *The Worldly Philosophers*, (New York: Simon and Schuster, 1961).

Smith's analysis needed improvement. According to Smith, mutually beneficial trade requires each nation to be the *least-cost producer* of at least one good it can export to its trading partner. But what if a nation is more efficient than its trading partner in the production of *all* goods? Dissatisfied with this looseness in Smith's theory, Ricardo developed a principle to show that mutually beneficial trade can occur whether countries have an absolute advantage. Ricardo's theory became known as the **principle of comparative advantage**.[4]

Like Smith, Ricardo emphasized the supply side of the market. The immediate basis for trade stemmed from the cost differences between nations that their natural and acquired advantages supported. Unlike Smith, who emphasized the importance of absolute cost differences among nations, Ricardo emphasized *comparative* (relative) cost differences. Indeed, countries often develop comparative advantages, as shown in Table 2.2.

---

[4]David Ricardo, *The Principles of Political Economy and Taxation* (London: Cambridge University Press, 1966), Chapter 7. Originally published in 1817.

TABLE 2.2

Examples of Comparative Advantages in International Trade

Country	Product
Canada	Lumber
Israel	Citrus fruit
Italy	Wine
Jamaica	Aluminum ore
Mexico	Tomatoes
Saudi Arabia	Oil
China	Textiles
Japan	Automobiles
South Korea	Steel, ships
Switzerland	Watches
United Kingdom	Financial services

According to the principle of comparative advantage, even if a nation has an absolute cost disadvantage in the production of *both* goods, a basis for mutually beneficial trade may still exist. The *less efficient* nation should specialize in and export the good in which it is relatively less inefficient (where its absolute disadvantage is least). The *more efficient* nation should specialize in and export that good in which it is relatively more efficient (where its absolute advantage is greatest).

To demonstrate the principle of comparative advantage, Ricardo formulated a simplified model based on the following *assumptions*:

1. The world consists of two nations, each using a single input to produce two commodities.
2. In each nation, labor is the only input (the labor theory of value). Each nation has a fixed endowment of labor and labor is fully employed and homogeneous.
3. Labor can move freely among industries within a nation but is incapable of moving between nations.
4. The level of technology is fixed for both nations. Different nations may use different technologies, but all firms within each nation utilize a common production method for each commodity.
5. Costs do not vary with the level of production and are proportional to the amount of labor used.
6. Perfect competition prevails in all markets. Because no single producer or consumer is large enough to influence the market, all are price takers. Product quality does not vary among nations, implying that all units of each product are identical. There is free entry to and exit from an industry, and the price of each product equals the product's marginal cost of production.
7. Free trade occurs between nations; that is, no government barriers to trade exist.
8. Transportation costs are zero. Consumers will thus be indifferent between domestically produced and imported versions of a product if the domestic prices of the two products are identical.
9. Firms make production decisions in an attempt to maximize profits, whereas consumers maximize satisfaction through their consumption decisions.

10. There is no money illusion; when consumers make their consumption choices and firms make their production decisions, they take into account the behavior of all prices.
11. Trade is balanced (exports must pay for imports), thus ruling out flows of money between nations.

Table 2.3 illustrates Ricardo's principle of comparative advantage when one nation has an absolute advantage in the production of both goods. Assume that in one hour's time, U.S. workers can produce 40 bottles of wine or 40 yards of cloth, while U.K. workers can produce 20 bottles of wine or ten yards of cloth. According to Smith's principle of absolute advantage, there is no basis for mutually beneficial specialization and trade because the U.S. workers are more efficient in the production of both goods.

However, the principle of comparative advantage recognizes that U.S. workers are four times as efficient in cloth production $(40/10 = 4)$ but only twice as efficient in wine production $(40/20 = 2)$. The United States thus has a *greater absolute advantage* in cloth than in wine, while the United Kingdom has a *smaller absolute disadvantage* in wine than in cloth. Each nation specializes in and exports that good in which it has a *comparative* advantage—the United States in cloth, the United Kingdom in wine. Therefore, through the process of trade, the two nations receive the output gains from specialization. Like Smith, Ricardo asserted that both nations can gain from trade.

Simply put, Ricardo's principle of comparative advantage maintains that international trade is solely due to international differences in the productivity of labor. The basic prediction of Ricardo's principle is that countries tend to export those goods in which their labor productivity is relatively high.

In recent years, the United States has realized large trade deficits (imports exceed exports) with countries such as China and Japan. Some of those who have witnessed the flood of imports coming into the United States seem to suggest that the United States does not have a comparative advantage in anything. It is possible for a nation not to have an absolute advantage in anything; but it is not possible for one nation to have a comparative advantage in everything and the other nation to have a comparative advantage in nothing. That's because comparative advantage depends on *relative* costs. As we have seen, a nation having an absolute disadvantage in all goods would find it advantageous to specialize in the production of the good in which its absolute disadvantage is *least*. There is no reason for the United States to surrender and let China produce all of everything. The United States would lose and so would China, because world output would be reduced if U.S. resources were left idle. The idea that a nation has nothing to offer confuses absolute advantage and comparative advantage.

Although the principle of comparative advantage is used to explain international trade patterns, people are not generally concerned with which nation has a comparative advantage when they purchase something. A person in a candy store does not look at Swiss

TABLE 2.3

A Case of Comparative Advantage when the United States Has an Absolute Advantage in the Production of Both Goods

World output possibilities in the absence of specialization

Nation	OUTPUT PER LABOR HOUR	
	Wine	**Cloth**
United States	40 bottles	40 yards
United Kingdom	20 bottles	10 yards

© Cengage Learning®

chocolate and U.S. chocolate and ask, "I wonder which nation has the comparative advantage in chocolate production?" The buyer relies on price, after allowing for quality differences, to tell which nation has the comparative advantage. It is helpful, then, to illustrate how the principle of comparative advantage works in terms of money prices, as seen in *Exploring Further 2.1* that can be found at www.cengage.com/economics/Carbaugh.

PRODUCTION POSSIBILITIES SCHEDULES

Ricardo's law of comparative advantage suggested that specialization and trade can lead to gains for both nations. His theory, however, depended on the restrictive assumption of the labor theory of value, in which labor was assumed to be the only factor input. In practice, labor is only one of several factor inputs.

Recognizing the shortcomings of the labor theory of value, modern trade theory provides a more generalized theory of comparative advantage. It explains the theory using a **production possibilities schedule**, also called a transformation schedule. This schedule shows various alternative combinations of two goods that a nation can produce when *all* of its factor inputs (land, labor, capital, entrepreneurship) are used in their most efficient manner. The production possibilities schedule thus illustrates the maximum output possibilities of a nation. Note that we are no longer assuming labor to be the only factor input, as Ricardo did.

Figure 2.1 illustrates hypothetical production possibilities schedules for the United States and Canada. By fully using all available inputs with the best available technology

FIGURE 2.1

Trading Under Constant Opportunity Costs

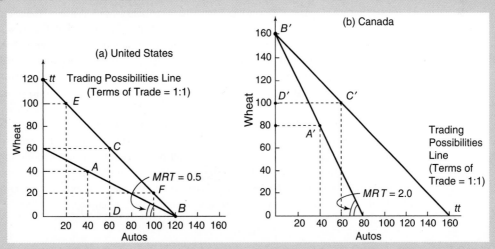

With constant opportunity costs, a nation will specialize in the product of its comparative advantage. The principle of comparative advantage implies that with specialization and free trade, a nation enjoys production gains and consumption gains. A nation's trade triangle denotes its exports, imports, and terms of trade. In a two-nation, two-product world, the trade triangle of one nation equals that of the other nation; one nation's exports equal the other nation's imports, and there is one equilibrium terms of trade.

during a given time period, the United States can produce either 60 bushels of wheat or 120 autos or certain combinations of the two products. Similarly, Canada can produce either 160 bushels of wheat or 80 autos or certain combinations of the two products.

Just how does a production possibilities schedule illustrate the concept of comparative cost? The answer lies in the slope of the production possibilities schedule, which is referred to as the **marginal rate of transformation (MRT)**. The MRT shows the amount of one product a nation must sacrifice to get one additional unit of the other product:

$$MRT = \frac{\Delta Wheat}{\Delta Autos}$$

This rate of sacrifice is sometimes called the *opportunity cost* of a product. Because this formula also refers to the slope of the production possibilities schedule, the MRT equals the absolute value of the production possibilities schedule's slope.

In Figure 2.1, the MRT of wheat into autos gives the amount of wheat that must be sacrificed for each additional auto produced. Concerning the United States, movement from the top endpoint on its production possibilities schedule to the bottom endpoint shows that the relative cost of producing 120 additional autos is the sacrifice of 60 bushels of wheat. This sacrifice means that the relative cost of each auto produced is 0.5 bushel of wheat sacrificed $(60/120 = 0.5)$; the MRT = 0.5. Similarly, Canada's relative cost of each auto produced is two bushels of wheat; that is, Canada's MRT = 2.0.

TRADING UNDER CONSTANT-COST CONDITIONS

This section illustrates the principle of comparative advantage under **constant opportunity costs**. Although the constant-cost case may be of limited relevance to the real world, it serves as a useful pedagogical tool for analyzing international trade. The discussion focuses on two questions. First, what are the *basis for trade* and the *direction of trade*? Second, what are the potential *gains from trade*, for a single nation and for the world as a whole?

Referring to Figure 2.1, notice that the production possibilities schedules for the United States and Canada are drawn as straight lines. The fact that these schedules are linear indicates that the relative costs of the two products do not change as the economy shifts its production from all wheat to all autos or anywhere in between. For the United States, the relative cost of an auto is 0.5 bushels of wheat as output expands or contracts; for Canada, the relative cost of an auto is 2 bushels of wheat as output expands or contracts.

There are *two reasons* for constant-costs. First, the factors of production are perfect substitutes for each other. Second, all units of a given factor are of the same quality. As a country transfers resources from the production of wheat into the production of autos, or vice versa, the country will not have to resort to resources that are inadequate for the production of the good. Therefore, the country must sacrifice exactly the same amount of wheat for each additional auto produced, regardless of how many autos it is already producing.

Basis for Trade and Direction of Trade

Let us examine trade under constant-cost conditions. Referring to Figure 2.1, assume that in **autarky** (the absence of trade) the United States prefers to produce and consume at point *A* on its production possibilities schedule, with 40 autos and 40 bushels of wheat. Assume also that Canada produces and consumes at point *A'* on its production possibilities schedule, with 40 autos and 80 bushels of wheat.

The *slopes* of the two countries' production possibilities schedules give the *relative cost* of one product in terms of the other. The relative cost of producing an additional auto is only 0.5 bushels of wheat for the United States but it is 2 bushels of wheat for Canada. According to the principle of comparative advantage, this situation provides a basis for mutually favorable specialization and trade owing to the differences in the countries' relative costs. As for the direction of trade, we find the United States specializing in and exporting autos and Canada specializing in and exporting wheat.

Production Gains from Specialization

The law of comparative advantage asserts that with trade, each country will find it favorable to specialize in the production of the good of its comparative advantage and will trade part of this for the good of its comparative disadvantage. In Figure 2.1, the United States moves from production point *A* to production point *B*, totally specializing in auto production. Canada specializes in wheat production by moving from production point *A'* to production point *B'* in the figure. Taking advantage of specialization can result in **production gains** for both countries.

We find that prior to specialization, the United States produces 40 autos and 40 bushels of wheat. But with complete specialization, the United States produces 120 autos and no wheat. As for Canada, its production point in the absence of specialization is at 40 autos and 80 bushels of wheat, whereas its production point under complete specialization is at 160 bushels of wheat and no autos. Combining these results, we find that both nations together have experienced a net production gain of 40 autos and 40 bushels of wheat under conditions of complete specialization. Table 2.4(*a*) summarizes these production gains. Because these production gains arise from the reallocation of *existing* resources, they are also called the *static gains* from specialization: through specialization, a country can use its current supply of resources more efficiently and thus achieve a higher level of output than it could without specialization.

Japan's opening to the global economy is an example of the static gains from comparative advantage. Responding to pressure from the United States, in 1859 Japan opened its ports to international trade after more than two hundred years of self-imposed economic isolation. In autarky, Japan found that it had a comparative advantage in some products

TABLE 2.4

Gains from Specialization and Trade: Constant Opportunity Costs

(a) Production Gains from Specialization

	BEFORE SPECIALIZATION		AFTER SPECIALIZATION		NET GAIN (LOSS)	
	Autos	**Wheat**	**Autos**	**Wheat**	**Autos**	**Wheat**
United States	40	40	120	0	80	−40
Canada	40	80	0	160	−40	80
World	80	120	120	160	40	40

(b) Consumption Gains from Trade

	BEFORE TRADE		AFTER TRADE		NET GAIN (LOSS)	
	Autos	**Wheat**	**Autos**	**Wheat**	**Autos**	**Wheat**
United States	40	40	60	60	20	20
Canada	40	80	60	100	20	20
World	80	120	120	160	40	40

and a comparative disadvantage in others. For example, the price of tea and silk was much higher on world markets than in Japan prior to the opening of trade, while the price of woolen goods and cotton was much lower on world markets. Japan responded according to the principle of comparative advantage: it exported tea and silk in exchange for imports of clothing. By using its resources more efficiently and trading with the rest of the world, Japan was able to realize static gains from specialization that equaled eight to nine percent of its gross domestic product at that time. Of course the long-run gains to Japan of improving its productivity and acquiring better technology were several times this figure.[5]

However, when a country initially opens to trade and then trade is eliminated, it suffers static losses, as seen in the case of the United States. In the early 1800s, Britain and France were at war. As part of the conflict, the countries attempted to prevent the shipping of goods to each other by neutral countries, notably the United States. This policy resulted in the British and French navies confiscating American ships and cargo. To discourage this harassment, in 1807 President Thomas Jefferson ordered the closure of America's ports to international trade: American ships were prevented from taking goods to foreign ports and foreign ships were prevented from taking on any cargo in the United States. The intent of the embargo was to inflict hardship on the British and French, and discourage them from meddling in America's affairs. Although the embargo did not completely eliminate trade, the United States was as close to autarky as it had ever been in its history. Therefore, Americans shifted production away from previously exported agricultural goods (the goods of comparative advantage) and increased production of import-replacement manufactured goods (the goods of comparative disadvantage). The result was a less efficient utilization of America's resources. Overall, the embargo cost about eight percent of America's gross national product in 1807. It is no surprise that the embargo was highly unpopular among Americans and, therefore, terminated in 1809.[6]

Consumption Gains from Trade

In the absence of trade, the consumption alternatives of the United States and Canada are limited to points *along* their domestic production possibilities schedules. The exact consumption point for each nation will be determined by the tastes and preferences in each country. But with specialization and trade, the two nations can achieve post-trade consumption points *outside* their domestic production possibilities schedules; that is, they can consume more wheat and more autos than they could consume in the absence of trade. Thus, trade can result in **consumption gains** for both countries.

The set of post-trade consumption points that a nation can achieve is determined by the rate at which its export product is traded for the other country's export product. This rate is known as the **terms of trade**. The terms of trade defines the relative prices at which two products are traded in the marketplace.

Under constant-cost conditions, the slope of the production possibilities schedule defines the domestic rate of transformation (domestic terms of trade) that represents the relative prices that two commodities can be exchanged at home. For a country to consume at some point *outside* its production possibilities schedule, it must be able to exchange its export good internationally at terms of trade more favorable than the domestic terms of trade.

[5]D. Bernhofen and J. Brown, "An Empirical Assessment of the Comparative Advantage Gains from Trade: Evidence from Japan," *The American Economic Review*, March 2005, pp. 208–225.

[6]D. Irwin, *The Welfare Cost of Autarky: Evidence from the Jeffersonian Trade Embargo, 1807–1809* (Cambridge, MA) Working Paper No. W8692, December 2001.

TRADE CONFLICTS BABE RUTH AND THE PRINCIPLE OF COMPARATIVE ADVANTAGE

Babe Ruth was the first great home run hitter in baseball history. His batting talent and vivacious personality attracted huge crowds wherever he played. He made baseball more exciting by establishing home runs as a common part of the game. Ruth set many major league records, including 2,056 career walks and 72 games in which he hit two or more home runs. He had a .342 lifetime batting average and 714 career home runs.

George Herman Ruth (1895–1948) was born in Baltimore. After playing baseball in the minor leagues, Ruth started his major league career as a left-handed pitcher with the Boston Red Sox in 1914. In 158 games for Boston, he compiled a pitching record of 89 wins and 46 losses, including two 20-win seasons—23 victories in 1916 and 24 victories in 1917.

On January 2, 1920, a little more than a year after Babe Ruth had pitched two victories in the Red Sox World Series victory over Chicago, he became violently ill. Most suspected that Ruth, known for his partying excesses, simply had a major league hangover from his New Year's celebrations. The truth was, Ruth had ingested several bad frankfurters while entertaining youngsters the day before, and his symptoms were misdiagnosed as being life-threatening. The Red Sox management, already strapped for cash, thus sold its ailing player to the Yankees the next day for $125,000 and a $300,000 loan to the owner of the Red Sox.

Ruth eventually added five more wins as a hurler for the New York Yankees and ended his pitching career with a 2.28 earned run average. Ruth also had three wins against no losses in World Series competition, including one stretch of 29 2/3 consecutive scoreless innings. At the time, Ruth was one of the best left-handed pitchers in the American league.

Although Ruth had an absolute advantage in pitching, he had even greater talent at the plate. Simply put, Ruth's comparative advantage was in hitting. As a pitcher, Ruth had to rest his arm between appearances and thus could not bat in every game. To ensure his daily presence in the lineup, Ruth gave up pitching to play exclusively in the outfield.

In his 15 years with the Yankees, Ruth dominated professional baseball. He teamed with Lou Gehrig to form what became the greatest one-two hitting punch in baseball. Ruth was the heart of the 1927 Yankees, a team regarded by some baseball experts as the best in baseball history. That year, Ruth set a record of 60 home runs. At that time, a season had 154 games compared to 162 games today. He attracted so many fans that Yankee Stadium that opened in 1923,was nick-named "The House that Ruth Built." The Yankees released Ruth after the 1934 season and he ended his playing career in 1935 with the Boston Braves. In Ruth's final game, he hit three home runs.

The advantages to having Ruth switch from pitching to batting were enormous. Not only did the Yankees win four World Series during Ruth's tenure, but they also became baseball's most renowned franchise. Ruth was elected to the Baseball Hall of Fame in Cooperstown, New York, in 1936.

Source: Edward Scahill, "Did Babe Ruth Have a Comparative Advantage as a Pitcher?" *Journal of Economic Education*, Vol. 21, 1990. See also, Paul Rosenthal, "America at Bat: Baseball Stuff and Stories," *National Geographic*, 2002, Geoffrey Ward and Ken Burns, *Baseball: An Illustrated History*, (Knopf, 1994), and Keith Brandt, *Babe Ruth: Home Run Hero*, (Troll, 1986).

iStockphoto.com/photosoup

Assume that the United States and Canada achieve a terms of trade ratio that permits both trading partners to consume at some point outside their respective production possibilities schedules (Figure 2.1). Suppose that the terms of trade agreed on is a 1:1 ratio, whereby 1 auto is exchanged for 1 bushel of wheat. Based on these conditions, let line *tt* represent the international terms of trade for both countries. This line is referred to as the **trading possibilities line** (note that it is drawn with a slope having an absolute value of one).

Suppose now that the United States decides to export 60 autos to Canada. Starting at post-specialization production point *B* in the figure, the United States will slide along its trading possibilities line until point *C* is reached. At point *C*, 60 autos will have been exchanged for 60 bushels of wheat, at the terms of trade ratio of 1:1. Point *C* then represents the U.S. *post-trade consumption point*. Compared with consumption point *A*, point *C* results in a consumption gain for the United States of 20 autos and 20 bushels of wheat. The triangle *BCD* that shows the U.S. exports (along the horizontal axis), imports (along the vertical axis), and terms of trade (the slope) is referred to as the **trade triangle**.

Does this trading situation provide favorable results for Canada? Starting at post-specialization production point *B′* in the figure, Canada can import 60 autos from the United States by giving up 60 bushels of wheat. Canada would slide along its trading possibilities line until it reaches point *C′*. Clearly, this is a more favorable consumption point than point *A′*. With trade, Canada experiences a consumption gain of 20 autos and 20 bushels of wheat. Canada's trade triangle is denoted by *B′C′D′*. In our two-country model, the trade triangles of the United States and Canada are identical; one country's exports equal the other country's imports that exchange at the equilibrium terms of trade. Table 2.4(*b*) on page 37 summarizes the consumption gains from trade for each country and the world as a whole.

One implication of the foregoing trading example is that the United States produced only autos, whereas Canada produced only wheat—that is, **complete specialization** occurs. As the United States increases and Canada decreases the production of autos, both countries' unit production costs remain constant. Because the relative costs never become equal, the United States does not lose its comparative advantage, nor does Canada lose its comparative disadvantage. The United States therefore produces only autos. Similarly, as Canada produces more wheat and the United States reduces its wheat production, both nations' production costs remain the same. Canada produces only wheat without losing its advantage to the United States.

The only exception to complete specialization would occur if one of the countries, say Canada, is too small to supply the United States with all of its need for wheat. Canada would be completely specialized in its export product, wheat, while the United States (large country) would produce both goods; however, the United States would still export autos and import wheat.

Distributing the Gains from Trade

Our trading example assumes that the terms of trade agreed to by the United States and Canada will result in both benefiting from trade. But where will the terms of trade actually lie?

A shortcoming of Ricardo's principle of comparative advantage is its inability to determine the actual terms of trade. The best description that Ricardo could provide was only the *outer limits* within which the terms of trade would fall. This is because the Ricardian theory relied solely on domestic cost ratios (supply conditions) in explaining trade patterns; it ignored the role of demand.

To visualize Ricardo's analysis of the terms of trade, recall our trading example of Figure 2.1. We assumed that for the United States the relative cost of producing an additional auto was 0.5 bushels of wheat whereas for Canada the relative cost of producing an additional auto was 2 bushels of wheat. Thus, the United States has a comparative advantage in autos, whereas Canada has a comparative advantage in wheat. Figure 2.2 illustrates these domestic cost conditions for the two countries. However, for each country, we have translated the domestic cost ratio, given by the negatively sloped production possibilities schedule, into a *positively sloped* cost-ratio line.

According to Ricardo, the domestic cost ratios set the **outer limits for the equilibrium terms of trade**. If the United States is to export autos, it should not accept any terms of trade less than a ratio of 0.5:1, indicated by its domestic cost-ratio line. Otherwise, the U.S. post-trade consumption point would lie inside its production possibilities schedule. The United States would clearly be better off without trade than with trade. The U.S.

FIGURE 2.2

Equilibrium Terms of Trade Limits

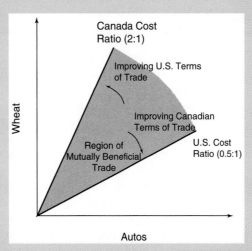

The supply-side analysis of Ricardo describes the outer limits within which the equilibrium terms of trade must fall. The domestic cost ratios set the outer limits for the equilibrium terms of trade. Mutually beneficial trade for both nations occurs if the equilibrium terms of trade lies between the two nations' domestic cost ratios. According to the theory of reciprocal demand, the actual exchange ratio at which trade occurs depends on the trading partners' interacting demands.

© Cengage Learning®

domestic cost-ratio line therefore becomes its **no-trade boundary**. Similarly, Canada would require a minimum of 1 auto for every 2 bushels of wheat exported, as indicated by its domestic cost-ratio line; any terms of trade less than this rate would be unacceptable to Canada. Thus, its domestic cost-ratio line defines the no-trade boundary line for Canada.

For gainful international trade to exist, a nation must achieve a post-trade consumption location at least equivalent to its point along its domestic production possibilities schedule. Any acceptable international terms of trade has to be more favorable than or equal to the rate defined by the domestic price line. Thus, the **region of mutually beneficial trade** is bounded by the cost ratios of the two countries.

Equilibrium Terms of Trade

As noted, Ricardo did not explain how the actual terms of trade would be determined in international trade. This gap was filled by another classical economist, John Stuart Mill (1806–1873). By bringing into the picture the intensity of the trading partners' demands, Mill could determine the actual terms of trade for Figure 2.2. Mill's theory is known as the **theory of reciprocal demand**.[7] This theory asserts that within the outer limits of the terms of trade, the actual terms of trade is determined by the relative strength of each country's demand for the other country's product. Simply put, production costs determine the outer limits of the terms of trade, while reciprocal demand determines what the actual terms of trade will be within those limits.

Referring to Figure 2.2, if Canadians are more eager for U.S. autos than Americans are for Canadian wheat, the terms of trade would end up close to the Canadian cost

---

[7]John Stuart Mill, *Principles of Political Economy* (New York: Longmans, Green, 1921), pp. 584–585.

ratio of 2:1 Thus, the terms of trade would improve for the United States. However, if Americans are more eager for Canadian wheat than Canadians are for U.S. autos, the terms of trade would fall close to the U.S. cost ratio of 0.5:1 and the terms of trade would improve for Canadians.

The reciprocal-demand theory best applies when both nations are of equal economic size, so that the demand of each nation has a noticeable effect on market price. However, if two nations are of unequal economic size, it is possible that the relative demand strength of the smaller nation will be dwarfed by that of the larger nation. In this case, the domestic exchange ratio of the larger nation will prevail. Assuming the absence of monopoly elements working in the markets, the small nation can export as much of the commodity as it desires, enjoying large gains from trade.

Consider trade in crude oil and autos between Venezuela and the United States before the rise of the Organization of Petroleum Exporting Countries (OPEC). Venezuela, as a small nation, accounted for only a very small share of the U.S.–Venezuelan market, whereas the U.S. market share was overwhelmingly large. Because Venezuelan consumers and producers had no influence on market price levels, they were in effect price takers. In trading with the United States, no matter what the Venezuelan demand was for crude oil and autos, it was not strong enough to affect U.S. price levels. As a result, Venezuela traded according to the U.S. domestic price ratio, buying and selling autos and crude oil at the price levels that existed in the United States.

The example just given implies the following generalization: If two nations of approximately the *same size* and with similar taste patterns participate in international trade, the gains from trade will be shared about *equally* between them. However, if one nation is significantly larger than the other, the *larger* nation attains *fewer* gains from trade while the *smaller* nation attains *most* of the gains from trade. This situation is characterized as the **importance of being unimportant**. What's more, when nations are very dissimilar in size, there is a strong possibility that the larger nation will continue to produce its comparative-disadvantage good because the smaller nation is unable to supply all of the world's demand for this product.

Terms of Trade Estimates

As we have seen, the terms of trade affect a country's gains from trade. How are the terms of trade actually measured?

The **commodity terms of trade** (also referred to as the *barter terms of trade*) is a frequently used measure of the international exchange ratio. It measures the relation between the prices a nation gets for its exports and the prices it pays for its imports. This is calculated by dividing a nation's export price index by its import price index, multiplied by 100 to express the terms of trade in percentages:

$$Terms\ of\ Trade = \frac{Export\ Price\ Index}{Import\ Price\ Index} \times 100$$

An *improvement* in a nation's terms of trade requires that the prices of its exports rise relative to the prices of its imports over the given time period. A smaller quantity of export goods sold abroad is required to obtain a given quantity of imports. Conversely, *deterioration* in a nation's terms of trade is due to a rise in its import prices relative to its export prices over a time period. The purchase of a given quantity of imports would require the sacrifice of a greater quantity of exports.

Table 2.5 gives the commodity terms of trade for selected countries. With 2005 as the base year (equal to 100), the table shows that by 2013 the U.S. index of export prices rose to 124, an increase of 24 percent. During the same period, the index of U.S. import prices rose by 27 percent, to a level of 127. Using the terms of trade formula, we find

TABLE 2.5			
Commodity Terms of Trade, 2013 (2005 = 100)			
Country	Export price index	Import price index	Terms of trade
Australia	194	143	136
Argentina	166	153	108
Canada	132	125	106
Switzerland	148	142	104
United States	124	127	98
China	127	130	98
Brazil	156	184	85
Japan	108	145	74

Source: From International Monetary Fund, *IMF Financial Statistics*, Washington, DC, December 2013.

that the U.S. terms of trade *worsened* by 2 percent $[(124/127) \times 100 = 98]$ over the period 2005–2013. This means that to purchase a given quantity of imports, the United States had to sacrifice 2 percent *more* exports; conversely, for a given number of exports, the United States could obtain 2 percent *fewer* imports.

Although changes in the commodity terms of trade indicate the direction of movement of the gains from trade, their implications must be interpreted with caution. Suppose there is an increase in the foreign demand for U.S. exports, leading to higher prices and revenues for U.S. exporters. In this case, an improving terms of trade implies that the U.S. gains from trade have increased. However, suppose that the cause of the rise in export prices and terms of trade is the falling *productivity* of U.S. workers. If these result in reduced export sales and less revenue earned from exports, we could hardly say that U.S. welfare has improved. Despite its limitations, however, the commodity terms of trade is a useful concept. Over a long period, it illustrates how a country's share of the world gains from trade changes and gives a rough measure of the fortunes of a nation in the world market.

DYNAMIC GAINS FROM TRADE

The previous analysis of the gains from international trade stressed specialization and reallocation of *existing* resources—the so called static gains from specialization. However, these gains can be dwarfed by the effect of trade on the country's growth rate and the volume of additional resources made available to, or utilized by, the trading country. These are known as the **dynamic gains from international trade** as opposed to the static effects of reallocating a fixed quantity of resources.

We have learned that international trade tends to bring about a more efficient use of an economy's resources that leads to higher output and income. Over time, increased income tends to result in more saving and, thus, more investment in equipment and manufacturing plants. This additional investment generally results in a higher rate of economic growth. Moreover, opening an economy to trade can lead to imported investment goods such as machinery that fosters higher productivity and economic growth. In a roundabout manner, gains from international trade grow larger over time. Empirical evidence shows that countries that are more open to international trade tend to grow faster than closed economies.[8]

Free trade also increases the possibility that a firm importing a capital good will be able to locate a supplier who will provide a good that more closely meets its specifications. The better the match, the larger the increase in the firm's productivity, which promotes economic growth.

Economies of large-scale production represent another dynamic gain from trade. International trade allows small and moderately sized countries to establish and operate many plants of efficient size that would be impossible if production were limited to the domestic market. For example, the free access that Mexican and Canadian firms have to the U.S. market, under the North American Free Trade Agreement (NAFTA), allows them to expand their production and employ more specialized labor and equipment. These improvements have led to increased efficiency and lower unit costs for these firms.

Also, increased competition can be a source of dynamic gains in trade. For example, when Chile opened its economy to global competition in the 1970s, its exiting producers with comparative disadvantage were about eight percent less efficient than producers that continued to operate. The efficiency of plants competing against imports increased three to ten percent more than in the domestic economy where goods were not subject to foreign competition. A closed economy shields companies from international competition and permits them to pull down overall efficiency within an industry. Open trade forces inefficient firms to exit the industry and allows more productive firms to grow. Therefore, trade results in adjustments that raise average industry efficiency in both exporting and import-competing industries.[9]

Simply put, besides providing static gains rising from the reallocation of existing productive resources, trade can also generate dynamic gains by stimulating economic growth. Proponents of free trade note the many success stories of growth through trade. However, the effect of trade on growth is not the same for all countries. In general, the gains tend to be less for a large country such as the United States than for a small country such as Belgium.

How Global Competition Led to Productivity Gains for U.S. Iron Ore Workers

The dynamic gains from international trade can be seen in the U.S. iron ore industry, located in the Midwest. Because iron ore is heavy and costly to transport, U.S. producers supply ore only to U.S. steel producers located in the Great Lakes region. During the early 1980s, depressed economic conditions in most of the industrial world resulted in a decline in the demand for steel and thus falling demand for iron ore. Ore producers throughout the world scrambled to find new customers. Despite the huge distances and the transportation costs involved, mines in Brazil began shipping iron ore to steel producers in the Chicago area.

The appearance of foreign competition led to increased competitive pressure on U.S. iron ore producers. To help keep domestic iron mines operating, American workers agreed to changes in work rules that increased labor productivity. In most cases, these changes involved an expansion in the set of tasks a worker was required to perform.

---

[8]D. Dollar and A. Kraay, "Trade, Growth, and Poverty," *Finance and Development*, September 2001, pp. 16–19 and S. Edwards, "Openness, Trade Liberalization, and Growth in Developing Countries," *Journal of Economic Literature*, September 1993, pp. 1358–1393.

[9]Nina Pavcnik, "Trade Liberalization, Exit, and Productivity Improvements: Evidence from Chilean Plants," *Review of Economic Studies*, Vol. 69, January 2002, pp. 245–276.

For example, the changes required equipment handlers to perform routine maintenance on their equipment. Before, this maintenance was the responsibility of repairmen. Also, new work rules resulted in a flexible assignment of work that required a worker to occasionally do tasks assigned to another worker. In both cases, the new work rules led to the better use of a worker's time.

Prior to the advent of foreign competition, labor productivity in the U.S. iron ore industry was stagnant. Because of the rise of foreign competition, labor productivity began to increase rapidly in the early 1980s; by the late 1980s, the productivity of U.S. iron ore producers had doubled. Simply put, the increase in foreign competitive pressure resulted in American workers adopting new work rules that enhanced their productivity.[10]

CHANGING COMPARATIVE ADVANTAGE

Although international trade can promote dynamic gains in terms of increased productivity, patterns of comparative advantage can and do change over time. In the early 1800s, the United Kingdom had a comparative advantage in textile manufacturing. Then that advantage shifted to the New England states of the United States. Then the comparative advantage shifted once again to North Carolina and South Carolina. Now the comparative advantage resides in China and other low-wage countries. Let us see how changing comparative advantage relates to our trade model.

Figure 2.3 illustrates the production possibilities schedules for computers and automobiles, of the United States and Japan under conditions of constant opportunity cost. Note that the MRT of automobiles into computers initially equals 1.0 for the United States and 2.0 for Japan. The United States thus has a comparative advantage in the production of computers and a comparative disadvantage in auto production.

FIGURE 2.3

Changing Comparative Advantage

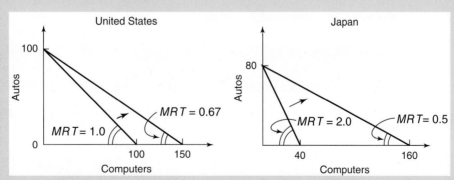

If productivity in the Japanese computer industry grows faster than it does in the U.S. computer industry, the opportunity cost of each computer produced in the United States increases relative to the opportunity cost of the Japanese. For the United States, comparative advantage shifts from computers to autos.

© Cengage Learning®

---

[10]Satuajit Chatterjee, "Ores and Scores: Two Cases of How Competition Led to Productivity Miracles," *Business Review*, Federal Reserve Bank of Philadelphia, Quarter 1, 2005, pp. 7–15.

Suppose both nations experience productivity increases in manufacturing computers but no productivity change in manufacturing automobiles. Assume that the United States increases its computer manufacturing productivity by 50 percent (from 100 to 150 computers) but that Japan increases its computer manufacturing productivity by 300 percent (from 40 to 160 computers).

Because of these productivity gains, the production possibilities schedule of each country rotates outward and becomes flatter. More output can now be produced in each country with the same amount of resources. Referring to the new production possibilities schedules, the MRT of automobiles into computers equals 0.67 for the United States and 0.5 for Japan. The comparative cost of a computer in Japan has thus fallen below that in the United States. For the United States, the consequence of lagging productivity growth is that it loses its comparative advantage in computer production. But even after Japan achieves comparative advantage in computers, the United States still has a comparative advantage in autos; the change in manufacturing productivity thus results in a change in the direction of trade. The lesson of this example is that producers who fall behind in research and development, technology, and equipment tend to find their competitiveness dwindling.

It should be noted, however, that all countries realize a comparative advantage in some product or service. For the United States, the growth of international competition in industries such as steel may make it easy to forget that the United States continues to be a major exporter of aircraft, paper, instruments, plastics, and chemicals.

To cope with changing comparative advantages, producers are under constant pressure to reinvent themselves. Consider how the U.S. semiconductor industry responded to competition from Japan in the late 1980s. Japanese companies quickly became dominant in sectors such as memory chips. This dominance forced the big U.S. chip makers to reinvent themselves. Firms such as Intel, Motorola, and Texas Instruments abandoned the dynamic-random-access-memory (DRAM) business and invested more heavily in manufacturing microprocessors and logic products, the next wave of growth in semiconductors. Intel became an even more dominant player in microprocessors, while Texas Instruments developed a strong position in digital signal processors, the "brain" in mobile telephones. Motorola gained strength in microcontrollers and automotive semiconductors. A fact of economic life is that no producer can remain the world's low-cost producer forever. As comparative advantages change, producers need to hone their skills to compete in more profitable areas.

TRADING UNDER INCREASING-COST CONDITIONS

The preceding section illustrated the comparative-advantage principle under constant-cost conditions. In the real world, a good's opportunity cost may *increase* as more of it is produced. Based on studies of many industries, economists think the opportunity costs of production increase with output rather than remain constant for most goods. The principle of comparative advantage must be illustrated in a modified form.

Increasing opportunity costs give rise to a production possibilities schedule that appears bowed outward from the diagram's origin. In Figure 2.4, with movement along the production possibilities schedule from *A* to *B*, the opportunity cost of producing autos becomes larger in terms of wheat sacrificed. Increasing costs mean that the MRT of wheat into autos *rises* as more autos are produced. Remember that the MRT is measured by the absolute slope of the production possibilities schedule at a given point. With movement from production point *A* to production point *B*, the respective tangent lines

TRADE CONFLICTS NATURAL GAS BOOM FUELS DEBATE

Natural gas provides an example of comparative advantage, as discussed below. Natural gas is nothing new. Its origins date back to about 1000 B.C. when a goat herdsman in Greece came across a flame rising from a fissure in rock on Mount Parnassus. The Greeks, believing it was divine origin or supernatural, built a temple on the flame. It wasn't until about 500 B.C. that the Chinese discovered that the source of the flame was natural gas seeping to the earth's surface. The Chinese made crude pipelines out of bamboo shoots to transport the gas, where it was used to boil sea water, separating the salt and making the water drinkable. Around 1785 Britain became the first country to commercialize the use of natural gas that was produced from coal and could be used to light houses and streetlights.

In the United States, the natural gas industry has existed for over 100 years. The United States has exported some natural gas during this period of time, but has generally imported more than it has exported, mostly from Canada. However, this trend began to change around 2010 when new sources of natural gas were found in the United States, particularly from shale gas. Technologies were developed (hydraulic fracturing and horizontal drilling) that allowed water, sand, and chemicals to create fissures in shale, allowing trapped natural gas to be cost-effectively extracted. Suddenly the United States increased its ability to produce natural gas.

The natural gas bonanza helped lower U.S. energy prices and resulted in U.S. producers being poised to ship vast quantities of gas overseas. However, federal law requires the U.S. Department of Energy to determine that natural gas projects are in the public interest before granting export permits to countries that do not have free-trade agreements with the United States. As producers such as Exxon Mobil sought federal permits for export projects, a debate ensued over whether they should be allowed to expand their exports.

Industry proponents argue that natural gas exports provide a much needed source of energy to American trading partners and foster economic growth and jobs in the United States. They are eager to take advantage of large price differentials between the United States and foreign markets. For example, U.S. prices are about $3 per million metric British thermal units (MMBtus), while prices in Europe are $11 to $13 per MMBtu and as high as $18 per MMBtu in Southeast Asia. Industry experts acknowledge that although many countries are endowed with large shale reserves, most countries are several years behind the United States in extraction and exploration. Moreover, proponents maintain that expanded exports of natural gas are a boost to key U.S. allies, especially Japan, as it transitions away from nuclear power.

However, environmentalists contend that natural gas still leaves a significant carbon footprint: A global interest in U.S. natural gas means an extended reliance on fossil fuels and the delay of the shift to clean-tech energy such as solar power or wind power. They also are concerned about the environmental damage from drilling techniques used in the extraction of natural gas from shale that can harm drinking water.

What effect exporting natural gas will have on U.S. prices is another vital question in the debate over whether to export. A significant increase in U.S. natural gas exports would likely impose upward pressure on domestic prices, but the extent of any rise is unclear. There are a variety of factors that affect prices, such as economic growth rates, differences in local markets, and government regulations. Producers contend that increased exports will not increases prices significantly because there is ample supply to meet domestic demand, and there will be the extra benefits of increased revenues, trade, and jobs. Consumers of natural gas who are helped by low prices, fear prices will rise if natural gas is exported.

At the writing of this text, it remains to be seen how the effects of increased natural gas exports will play out.

Source: Michael Ratner, and others, *U.S. Natural Gas Exports: New Opportunities, Uncertain Outcomes*, Congressional Research Service, Washington, DC, April 8, 2013; Gary Hufbauer, Allie Bagnall, and Julia Muir, *Liquified Natural Gas Exports: An Opportunity for America*, Peterson Institute for International Economics, February 2013; and Robert Pirog and Michael Ratner, *Natural Gas in the U.S. Economy: Opportunities for Growth*, Congressional Research Service, Washington, DC, November 6, 2012.

iStockphoto.com/photosoup

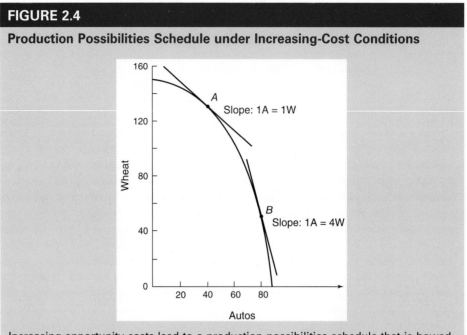

FIGURE 2.4

Production Possibilities Schedule under Increasing-Cost Conditions

Increasing opportunity costs lead to a production possibilities schedule that is bowed outward, viewed from the diagram's origin. The MRT equals the (absolute) slope of the production possibilities schedule at a particular point along the schedule.

© Cengage Learning®

become *steeper*—their slopes increase in absolute value. The MRT of wheat into autos rises, indicating that each additional auto produced requires the sacrifice of increasing amounts of wheat.

Increasing costs represent the typical case in the real world. In the overall economy, increasing costs result when inputs are imperfect substitutes for each other. As auto production rises and wheat production falls in Figure 2.4, inputs that are less adaptable to autos are introduced into that line of production. To produce more autos requires more of such resources and thus an increasingly greater sacrifice of wheat. For a *particular product*, such as autos, increasing cost is explained by the principle of diminishing marginal productivity. The addition of successive units of labor (variable input) to capital (fixed input) beyond some point results in decreases in the marginal production of autos that is attributable to each additional unit of labor. Unit production costs thus rise as more autos are produced.

Under increasing costs, the slope of the production possibilities schedule varies as a nation locates at different points on the schedule. Because the MRT equals the production possibilities schedule's slope, it will also be different for each point on the schedule. In addition to considering the *supply factors* underlying the production possibilities schedule's slope, we must also take into account the demand factors (tastes and preferences) for they will determine the point along the production possibilities schedule at which a country chooses to consume.

Increasing-Cost Trading Case

Figure 2.5 shows the production possibilities schedules of the United States and Canada under conditions of increasing costs. In Figure 2.5(*a*), assume that in the absence of

FIGURE 2.5

Trading Under Increasing Opportunity Costs

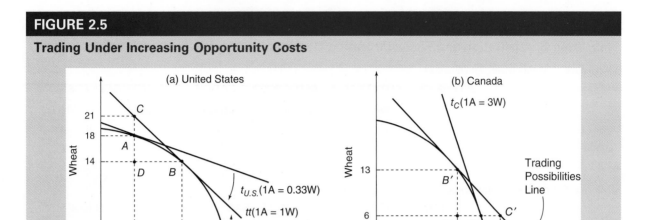

With increasing opportunity costs, comparative product prices in each country are determined by both supply and demand factors. A country tends to partially specialize in the product of its comparative advantage under increasing-cost conditions.

© Cengage Learning®

trade the United States is located at point A along its production possibilities schedule; it produces and consumes 5 autos and 18 bushels of wheat. In Figure 2.5(b), assume that in the absence of trade Canada is located at point A' along its production possibilities schedule, producing and consuming 17 autos and 6 bushels of wheat. For the United States, the relative cost of wheat into autos is indicated by the slope of line $t_{U.S.}$ tangent to the production possibilities schedule at point A (1 auto = 0.33 bushels of wheat). In like manner, Canada's relative cost of wheat into autos is indicated by the slope of line t_C (1 auto = 3 bushels of wheat). Because line $t_{U.S.}$ is *flatter* than line t_C, autos are relatively cheaper in the United States and wheat is relatively cheaper in Canada. According to the law of comparative advantage, the United States will export autos and Canada will export wheat.

As the United States specializes in auto production it slides downward along its production possibilities schedule from point A toward point B. The relative cost of autos (in terms of wheat) rises, as implied by the increase in the (absolute) slope of the production possibilities schedule. At the same time, Canada specializes in wheat. As Canada moves upward along its production possibilities schedule from point A' toward point B', the relative cost of autos (in terms of wheat) decreases, as evidenced by the decrease in the (absolute) slope of its production possibilities schedule.

The process of specialization continues in both nations until the relative cost of autos is identical in both nations and U.S. exports of autos are precisely equal to Canada's imports of autos, and conversely for wheat. Assume that this situation occurs when the domestic rates of transformation (domestic terms of trade) of both nations converge at the rate given by line *tt*. At this point of convergence, the United States produces at point B, while Canada produces at point B'. Line *tt* becomes the international terms of trade line for the United States and Canada; this point coincides with each nation's domestic terms of trade. The international terms of trade are favorable to both nations because *tt* is steeper than $t_{U.S}$ and flatter than t_C.

TABLE 2.6

Gains from Specialization and Trade: Increasing Opportunity Costs

(a) Production Gains from Specialization

	BEFORE SPECIALIZATION		AFTER SPECIALIZATION		NET GAIN (LOSS)	
	Autos	**Wheat**	**Autos**	**Wheat**	**Autos**	**Wheat**
United States	5	18	12	14	7	−4
Canada	17	6	13	13	−4	7
World	22	24	25	27	3	3

(b) Consumption Gains from Trade

	BEFORE TRADE		AFTER TRADE		NET GAIN (LOSS)	
	Autos	**Wheat**	**Autos**	**Wheat**	**Autos**	**Wheat**
United States	5	18	5	21	0	3
Canada	17	6	20	6	3	0
World	22	24	25	27	3	3

© Cengage Learning®

What are the *production gains* from specialization for the United States and Canada? Comparing the amount of autos and wheat produced by the two nations at their points prior to specialization with the amount produced at their post-specialization production points we see that there are gains of 3 autos and 3 bushels of wheat. The production gains from specialization are shown in Table 2.6(*a*).

What are the *consumption gains* from trade for the two nations? With trade, the United States can choose a consumption point along international terms of trade line *tt*. Assume that the United States prefers to consume the same number of autos as it did in the absence of trade. It will export 7 autos for 7 bushels of wheat, achieving a post-trade consumption point at *C*. The U.S. consumption gains from trade are 3 bushels of wheat, as shown in Figure 2.5(*a*) and also in Table 2.6(*b*). The U.S. *trade triangle*, showing its exports, imports, and terms of trade, is denoted by triangle *BCD*.

In like manner, Canada can choose to consume at some point along international terms of trade line *tt*. Assuming Canada holds constant its consumption of wheat, it will export 7 bushels of wheat for 7 autos and wind up at post-trade consumption point *C'*. Its consumption gain of 3 autos is also shown in Table 2.6(*b*). Canada's *trade triangle* is depicted in Figure 2.5(*b*) by triangle *B'C'D'*. Note that Canada's trade triangle is identical to that of the United States.

In this chapter, we discussed the autarky points and post-trade consumption points for the United States and Canada by assuming "given" tastes and preferences (demand conditions) of the consumers in both countries. In *Exploring Further 2.2 and 2.3*, located at ww.cengage.com/economics/Carbaugh, we introduce indifference curves to show the role of each country's tastes and preferences in determining the autarky points and how gains from trade are distributed.

Partial Specialization

One feature of the increasing cost model analyzed here is that trade generally leads each country to specialize only partially in the production of the good in which it has a comparative advantage. The reason for **partial specialization** is that increasing costs constitute a mechanism that forces costs in two trading nations to converge. When cost differentials are eliminated, the basis for further specialization ceases to exist.

Figure 2.5 assumes that prior to specialization the United States has a comparative cost advantage in producing autos, whereas Canada is relatively more efficient at producing wheat. With specialization, each country produces more of the commodity of its comparative advantage and less of the commodity of its comparative disadvantage. Given increasing-cost conditions, unit costs rise as both nations produce more of their export commodities. Eventually, the cost differentials are eliminated, at which point the basis for further specialization ceases to exist.

When the basis for specialization is eliminated, there exists a strong probability that both nations will produce some of each good. This is because costs often rise so rapidly, that a country loses its comparative advantage vis-à-vis the other country before it reaches the endpoint of its production possibilities schedule. In the real world of increasing-cost conditions, partial specialization is a likely result of trade.

Another reason for partial specialization is that not all goods and services are traded internationally. For example, even if Germany has a comparative advantage in medical services, it would be hard for Germany to completely specialize in medical services and export them. It would be very difficult for American patients who require back surgeries to receive them from surgeons in Germany.

Differing tastes for products also result in partial specialization. Most products are differentiated. Compact disc players, digital music players, automobiles, and other products provide a variety of features. When purchasing automobiles, some people desire capacity to transport seven passengers while others desire good gas mileage and attractive styling. Thus, some buyers prefer Ford Expeditions and others prefer Honda CRVs. Simply put, the United States and Japan have comparative advantages in manufacturing different types of automobiles.

THE IMPACT OF TRADE ON JOBS

As Americans watch the evening news on television and see Chinese workers producing goods that they used to produce; the viewers might conclude that international trade results in an overall loss of jobs for Americans. Is this true?

Standard trade theory suggests that the extent to which an economy is open influences the *mix* of jobs within an economy and can cause dislocation in certain areas or industries, but has little effect on the *overall* level of employment. The main determinants of total employment are factors such as the available workforce, total spending in the economy, and the regulations that govern the labor market.

According to the principle of comparative advantage, trade tends to lead a country to specialize in producing goods and services at which it excels. Trade influences the mix of jobs because workers and capital are expected to shift away from industries in which they are less productive relative to foreign producers and toward industries having a comparative advantage.

The conclusion that international trade has little impact on the overall number of jobs is supported by data on the U.S. economy. If trade is a major determinant on the nation's ability to maintain full employment, measures of the amount of trade and unemployment would move in unison, but in fact, they generally do not. As seen in Figure 2.6, the increase in U.S. imports as a percentage of GDP over the past several decades has not led to any significant trend in the overall unemployment rate for Americans. Indeed, the United States has been able to achieve relatively low unemployment while imports have grown considerably.

FIGURE 2.6

The Impact of Trade on Jobs

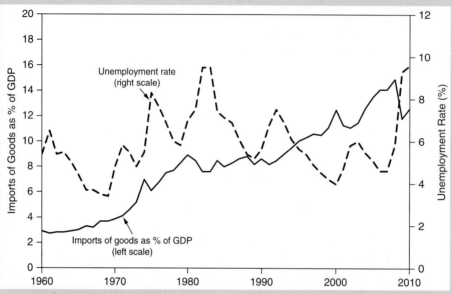

Increased international trade tends to neither inhibit overall job creation nor contribute to an increase in the overall rate of unemployment. As seen in the figure, the increase in U.S. imports of goods as a percentage of GDP over the past several decades has not led to any significant trend in the overall unemployment for Americans.

Simply put, increased trade has neither inhibited overall job creation nor contributed to an increase in the overall rate of unemployment. This topic will be further examined in Chapter 10 in the essay entitled "Do Current Account Deficits Cost Americans Jobs?"

WOOSTER, OHIO BEARS THE BRUNT OF GLOBALIZATION

According to the principle of comparative advantage, although free trade tends to move resources from low productivity to high productivity, some people can be left behind. Consider the case of Rubbermaid's exit from Wooster, Ohio.

Rubbermaid is an American producer of household items such as food storage containers, trash cans, laundry baskets, and the like. The company was founded in 1933 in Wooster when James Caldwell received a patent for his red rubber dustpan. Soon the company was producing a variety of rubber and plastic kitchen products under the name Rubbermaid.

A solid corporate citizen, Rubbermaid donated to the arts, initiated a downtown revitalization by opening a retail store and led a drive to convert an old movie theater into a cultural center. Also, it was designated as one of America's most admired companies. Although workers on Rubbermaid's factory floors were not getting wealthy, work was plentiful and it was common to find three generations of a family on the payroll.

However, trouble began for Rubbermaid in 1995 when the firm was dealing with sky-rocketing prices for resin, a key ingredient in plastic products. In that year, the firm lost $250 million, mainly because of resin price hikes. When Rubbermaid tried to pass a higher price for its plastic products onto Walmart, which accounted for about 20 percent of its business, Walmart warned that if prices rose it would pull Rubbermaid's products from its shelves. When negotiations failed, Walmart terminated the relationship and turned to other suppliers; generally foreign companies with lower labor costs. This resulted in Rubbermaid's profits plunging by 30 percent in 1995, the closing of 9 of its manufacturing plants, and laying off 10 percent of its workers, the first major downsizing in its history.

In 1999, Rubbermaid was purchased for $6 billion by Newell Corporation, a multinational consumer product corporation known for cost cutting; the newly merged firm was called Newell Rubbermaid Inc. Newell Rubbermaid transferred manufacturing work from Wooster's rubber division to Mexico to take advantage of lower labor costs. Rubbermaid had established manufacturing plants in Poland, South Korea, and Mexico, but most of its production remained in America. Also, the corporate staff was transferred to Atlanta, Georgia, the headquarters of Newell Rubbermaid. As a result, the work force in Wooster was cut by 1,000, while remaining workers toiled at a distribution center for Newell Rubbermaid products. As former Rubbermaid workers depleted their modest severance packages, they tried to find new employment. Some succeeded in landing jobs, often temporary and without benefits that paid 30–40 percent less than they were earning.

The middle class workers of Wooster believed in the American dream that if you work hard and adhere to the rules you will prosper in America and your children would enjoy a better life than yours. However, they were shaken by the loss of their major employer in a globalized economy.[11]

COMPARATIVE ADVANTAGE EXTENDED TO MANY PRODUCTS AND COUNTRIES

In our discussion so far, we have used trading models in which only two goods are produced and consumed and trade is confined to two countries. This simplified approach has permitted us to analyze many essential points about comparative advantage and trade. The real world of international trade involves more than two products and two countries; each country produces thousands of products and trades with many countries. To move in the direction of reality, it is necessary to understand how comparative advantage functions in a world of many products and many countries. As we will see, the conclusions of comparative advantage hold when more realistic situations are encountered.

More Than Two Products

When two countries produce a large number of goods, the operation of comparative advantage requires that the goods be ranked by the degree of comparative cost. Each country exports the product(s) in which it has the greatest comparative advantage. Conversely, each country imports the product(s) in which it has the greatest comparative disadvantage.

Figure 2.7 illustrates the hypothetical arrangement of six products—chemicals, jet planes, computers, autos, steel, and semiconductors—in rank order of the comparative

---

[11]Donald Barlett and James Steel, *The Betrayal of the American Dream*, Public Affairs–Perseus Books Group, New York, 2012; Huang Qingy, et. al., "Wal-Mart's Impact on Supplier Profits," *Journal of Marketing Research*, Vol. 49, No. 2, 2012; Richard Freeman and Arthur Ticknor, "Wal-Mart Is Not a Business: It's An Economic Disease," *Executive Intelligence Review*, November 14, 2003.

FIGURE 2.7

Hypothetical Spectrum of Comparative Advantages for the United States and Japan

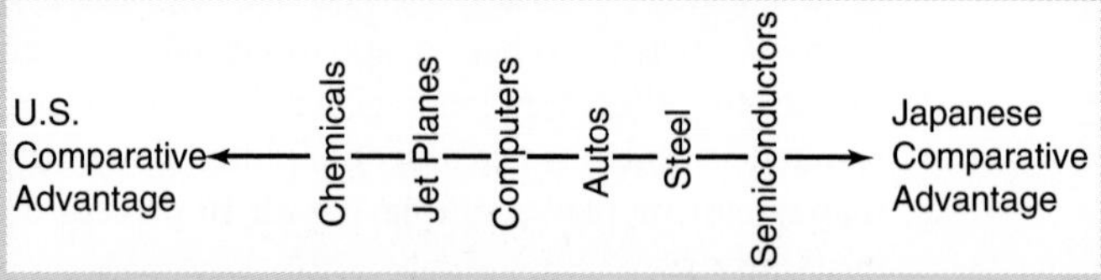

When a large number of goods is produced by two countries, operation of the comparative-advantage principle requires the goods to be ranked by the degree of comparative cost. Each country exports the product(s) in which its comparative advantage is strongest. Each country imports the product(s) in which its comparative advantage is weakest.

© Cengage Learning*

advantage of the United States and Japan. The arrangement implies that chemical costs are lowest in the United States relative to Japan, whereas the U.S. cost advantage in jet planes is somewhat less. Conversely, Japan enjoys its greatest comparative advantage in semiconductors.

This product arrangement clearly indicates that with trade, the United States will produce and export chemicals and that Japan will produce and export semiconductors. Where will the cutoff point lie between what is exported and what will be imported? Between computers and autos? Or will Japan produce computers and the United States produce only chemicals and jet planes? Will the cutoff point fall along one of the products rather than between them—so that computers, for example, might be produced in both Japan and the United States?

The cutoff point between what is exported and what is imported depends on the - relative strength of international demand for the various products. One can visualize the products as beads arranged along a string according to comparative advantage. The strength of demand and supply will determine the cutoff point between U.S. and Japanese production. A rise in the demand for steel and semiconductors, for example, leads to price increases that move in favor of Japan. These increases lead to rising production in the Japanese steel and semiconductor industries.

More Than Two Countries

When a trading example includes many countries, the United States will find it advantageous to enter into *multilateral trading relations*. Figure 2.8 illustrates the process of multilateral trade for the United States, Japan, and OPEC. The arrows in the figure denote the directions of exports. The United States exports jet planes to OPEC, Japan imports oil from OPEC, and Japan exports semiconductors to the United States. The real world of international trade involves trading relations even more complex than this triangular example.

This example casts doubt upon the idea that *bilateral balance* should pertain to any two trading partners. The predictable result is that a nation will realize a trade surplus (exports of goods exceed imports of goods) with trading partners that buy a lot of the things that it supplies at low cost. Also, a nation will realize a trade deficit (imports of goods exceed exports of goods) with trading partners that are low-cost suppliers of goods that it imports intensely.

FIGURE 2.8

Multilateral Trade Among the United States, Japan, and OPEC

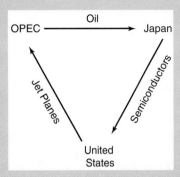

When many countries are involved in international trade, the home country will likely find it advantageous to enter into multilateral trading relationships with a number of countries. This figure illustrates the process of multilateral trade for the United States, Japan, and OPEC.

© Cengage Learning®

Consider the trade "deficits" and "surpluses" of a dentist who likes to snow ski. The dentist can be expected to run a trade deficit with ski resorts, sporting goods stores, and favorite suppliers of services like garbage collection and medical care. Why? The dentist is highly likely to buy these items from others. On the other hand, the dentist can be expected to run trade surpluses with his patients and medical insurers. These trading partners are major purchasers of the services provided by the dentist. Moreover, if the dentist has a high rate of saving, the surpluses will substantially exceed the deficits.

The same principles are at work across nations. A country can expect to run sizable surpluses with trading partners that buy a lot of the things the country exports, while trade deficits will be present with trading partners that are low-cost suppliers of the items imported.

What would be the effect if all countries entered into bilateral trade agreements that balanced exports and imports between each pair of countries? The volume of trade and specialization would be greatly reduced and resources would be hindered from moving to their highest productivity. Although exports would be brought into balance with imports, the gains from trade would be lessened.

EXIT BARRIERS

According to the principle of comparative advantage, an open trading system results in a channeling of resources from uses of low productivity to those of high productivity. Competition forces high-cost plants to exit, leaving the low-cost plants to operate in the long run. In practice, the restructuring of inefficient companies can take a long time because they often cling to capacity by nursing along antiquated plants. Why do companies delay plant closing when profits are subnormal and overcapacity exists? Part of the answer lies in the existence of **exit barriers**, various cost conditions that make a lengthy exit a rational response by companies.

Consider the case of the U.S. steel industry in which overcapacity has often been a key problem. Overcapacity has been caused by factors such as imports, reduced demand for steel, and installation of modern technology that allows greater productivity and increases output of steel with fewer inputs of capital and labor.

Traditional economic theory envisions hourly labor as a *variable* cost of production. However, the U.S. steel companies' contracts with United Steelworkers of America, the labor union, make hourly labor a *fixed* cost instead of a variable cost, at least in part. The contracts call for many employee benefits such as health and life insurance, pensions, and severance pay when a plant is shut down, as well as unemployment benefits.

Besides employee benefits, other exit costs tend to delay the closing of antiquated steel plants. These costs include penalties for terminating contracts to supply raw materials and expenses associated with the writing off of undepreciated plant assets. Steel companies also face environmental costs when they close plants. Owners are potentially liable for environmental costs at their abandoned facilities for treatment, storage, and disposal costs that can easily amount to hundreds of millions of dollars. Furthermore, steel companies cannot realize much income by selling their plants' assets. The equipment is unique to the steel industry and is of little value for any purpose other than producing steel. What's more, the equipment in a closed plant is generally in need of major renovation because the former owner allowed the plant to become antiquated prior to closing. Exit barriers hinder the market adjustments that occur according to the principle of comparative advantage.

EMPIRICAL EVIDENCE ON COMPARATIVE ADVANTAGE

We have learned that Ricardo's theory of comparative advantage implies that each country will export goods for which its labor is relatively productive compared with that of its trading partners. Does his theory accurately predict trade patterns? A number of economists have put Ricardo's theory to empirical tests.

The first test of the Ricardian model was made by the British economist G.D.A. MacDougall in 1951. Comparing the export patterns of 25 separate industries for the United States and the United Kingdom for the year 1937, MacDougall tested the Ricardian prediction that nations tend to export goods in which their labor productivity is relatively high. Of the 25 industries studied, 20 fit the predicted pattern. The MacDougall investigation thus supported the Ricardian theory of comparative advantage. Using different sets of data, subsequent studies by Balassa and Stern also supported Ricardo's conclusions.[12]

A more recent test of the Ricardian model comes from Stephen Golub who examined the relation between relative unit labor costs (the ratio of wages to productivity) and trade for the United States vis-à-vis the United Kingdom, Japan, Germany, Canada, and Australia. He found that relative unit labor cost helps to explain trade patterns for these nations. The U.S. and Japanese results lend particularly strong support for the Ricardian model, as shown in Figure 2.9. The figure displays a scatter plot of U.S.–Japan trade data showing a clear negative correlation between relative exports and relative unit labor costs for the 33 industries investigated.

---

[12]G.D.A. MacDougall, "British and American Exports: A Study Suggested by the Theory of Comparative Costs," *Economic Journal*, 61 (1951). See also B. Balassa, "An Empirical Demonstration of Classical Comparative Cost Theory," *Review of Economics and Statistics*, August 1963, pp. 231–238 and R. Stern, "British and American Productivity and Comparative Costs in International Trade," *Oxford Economic Papers*, October 1962.

FIGURE 2.9

Relative Exports and Relative Unit Labor Costs: U.S./Japan, 1990

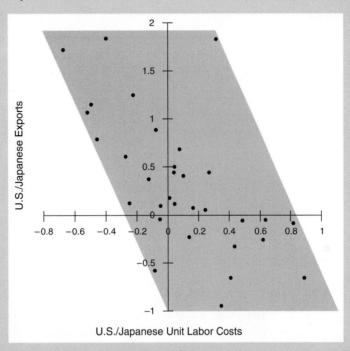

The figure displays a scatter plot of U.S./Japan export data for 33 industries. It shows a clear negative correlation between relative exports and relative unit labor costs. A rightward movement along the figure's horizontal axis indicates a rise in U.S. unit labor costs relative to Japanese unit labor costs; this correlates with a decline in U.S. exports relative to Japanese exports, a downward movement along the figure's vertical axis.

Source: Stephen Golub, *Comparative and Absolute Advantage in the Asia-Pacific Region*, Center for Pacific Basin Monetary and Economic Studies, Economic Research Department, Federal Reserve Bank of San Francisco, October 1995, p. 46.

Although there is empirical support for the Ricardian model, it is not without limitations. Labor is not the only input factor. Allowance should be made where appropriate for production and distribution costs other than direct labor. Differences in product quality also explain trade patterns in industries such as automobiles and footwear. We should therefore proceed with caution in explaining a nation's competitiveness solely on the basis of labor productivity and wage levels. The next chapter will discuss this topic in more detail.

COMPARATIVE ADVANTAGE AND GLOBAL SUPPLY CHAINS

For decades, most economists have insisted that countries generally gain from free trade. Their optimism is founded on the theory of comparative advantage developed by David Ricardo. The theory states that if each country produces what it does best and allows trade, all will realize lower prices and higher levels of output, income and consumption than could be achieved in isolation. When Ricardo formulated his theory, major factors of production could not move to other nations. Yet in today's world, important resources—labor, technology, capital, and ideas—often shift around the globe.

From electronics and automobiles to clothing or software development, many goods today are provided by global supply chains. Rather than carrying out everything from research and development to delivery and retail sales within a particular country, many industries have separated this process into stages or tasks that are undertaken in many countries. The international production networks that allow firms to move goods and services efficiently across national borders are known as global supply chains.

Global supply chains employ the practice of **outsourcing** (off shoring) which refers to the subcontracting of work to another firm or the purchase of components for a product rather than manufacturing them in order to save on production costs. The location of production near customers is another motivation of outsourcing.

Over time, several factors have contributed to the development of global supply chains—technological changes that allow production processes to be fragmented, falling trade barriers, lower transportation costs, improved telecommunications, more secure intellectual property rights, and improved contract enforcement. As countries have become more integrated into these chains, they become more specialized in specific tasks based on comparative advantage.

Concerning comparative advantage, global supply chains foster new patterns of trade, as firms in a country specialize in a particular stage or task. In electronics, for example, intermediate goods are often produced in South Korea, Japan, Taiwan, and Hong Kong, while final assembly activities are contracted to Chinese companies. Apple's iPhone, iPod and iPad are familiar examples of goods produced via a global supply chain.[13]

The ability to separate the production process into tasks that can be done in different locations has implications for the pattern of world trade. First, it means a change in the nature of specialization. Traditionally, a country's exports were concentrated in final goods or services in which it had a comparative advantage. However, with global supply chains, specialization is more narrowly defined, with countries specializing in tasks or stages within products, based on comparative advantage. Also, the nature of trade flows are affected by global supply chains. As supply chains expand, trade between industrial and developing countries tends to increase, since the location of tasks depends on differences in comparative advantage. Moreover, the pattern of trade becomes more dominated by trade in intermediate goods and services—such as parts, components, and computer services—as supply chains expand.

The semiconductor industry provides an example of these effects. In the past, the United States would have exported finished semiconductors to China. Now, the United States performs research and development and also the design and front-end fabrication of a semiconductor. It then exports the semi-finished semiconductor to a Southeast Asian country, such as Malaysia, that performs the back-end testing, assembly, and packaging of that semiconductor. Malaysia then exports the packaged semiconductor to China where it is incorporated into various electronic products, such as television sets, and then exported to consumers throughout the world. Therefore, global supply chains enhance a country's gains from trade because they allow a good to be produced more efficiently than if the entire process had to take place in a single location.

[13]U.S. International Trade Commission, "Global Supply Chains." In *The Economic Effects of Significant U.S. Import Restraints*, August 2011; Judith Dean and Mary Lovely, "Trade Growth, Production Fragmentation and China's Environment." In *China's Growing Role in World Trade*, edited by R. Feenstra and S. Wei, National Bureau of Economic Research and University of Chicago Press, 2010; Premachandra Athukorala and Nobuaki Yamashita, "Production Fragmentation and Trade Integration: East Asia in a Global Context," *North American Journal of Economics and Finance*, Vol. 17, 2006.

Global supply chains may also provide gains for developing countries because of opportunities to participate in one or more stages in the production of technology, or skill-intensive goods, rather than having to attain mastery over the total production process. Firms initially performing the least-skilled tasks may learn through interaction with more advanced firms in the chain and thus can move to higher-value production activities.

India provides an example of this process. During the 1990s, India's software firms tended to be in the lower to middle end of the software development chain, specializing in contract programming, coding, and testing. By the early 2000s, its firms engaged in business and technology consulting, systems integration, product engineering, and other more skill-intensive activities as the firms learned through interaction with more skilled firms.

Although global supply chains yield economic efficiencies, they can be subject to global shocks. For example, if a country undergoes an economic downturn, or experiences internal conflict or natural disasters, other countries in the supply chain be adversely affected. During the Great Recession of 2007–2009, the U.S. demand for Chinese electronics declined, thus causing a decrease in the Chinese demand for electronics parts and components from other Asian suppliers. Another example is the 2011 earthquake and tsunami that hit Japan and disrupted supply chains of Toyota and Honda who manufactured autos at factories in the United States.

Advantages and Disadvantages of Outsourcing

Proponents of outsourcing maintain that it can create a win-win situation for the global economy. Obviously, outsourcing benefits a recipient country such as India. For example, some of India's people work for a subsidiary of Southwestern Airlines of the United States and make telephone reservations for Southwestern's travelers. Moreover, incomes increase for Indian vendors supplying goods and services to the subsidiary, and the Indian government receives additional tax revenue. The United States also benefits from outsourcing in several ways:

- *Reduced costs and increased competitiveness for Southwestern, which hires low-wage workers in India to make airline reservations.* In the United States, many offshore jobs are viewed as relatively undesirable or of low prestige; whereas in India, they are often considered attractive. Thus, Indian workers may have higher motivation and out-produce their U.S. counterparts. The higher productivity of Indian workers leads to falling unit costs for Southwestern.
- *New exports.* As business expands, Southwestern's Indian subsidiary may purchase additional goods from the United States, such as computers and telecommunications equipment. These purchases result in increased earnings for U.S. companies such as AT&T and additional jobs for American workers.
- *Repatriated earnings.* Southwestern's Indian subsidiary returns its earnings to the parent company; these earnings are plowed back into the U.S. economy. Many offshore providers are, in fact, U.S. companies that repatriate earnings.

Simply put, proponents of outsourcing contend that if U.S. companies cannot locate work abroad they will become less competitive in the global economy as their competitors reduce costs by outsourcing. This process will weaken the U.S. economy and threaten more American jobs. Proponents also note that job losses tend to be temporary and that the creation of new industries and new products in the United States will result in more lucrative jobs for Americans. As long as the U.S. workforce retains its high level of skills and remains flexible as companies position themselves to improve their productivity, high-value jobs will not disappear in the United States.

Of course, what is good for the economy as a whole may not be good for a particular individual. The benefits of outsourcing to the United States do not eliminate the burden on Americans who lose their jobs or find lower-wage jobs because of foreign outsourcing. American labor unions often lobby Congress to prevent outsourcing, and several U.S. states have considered legislation to severely restrict their governments from contracting with companies that move jobs to low-wage developing countries.[14]

Outsourcing and the U.S. Automobile Industry

Developments in the U.S. automobile industry over the past century illustrate the underlying forces behind outsourcing. In the early 1900s, it took only 700 parts for workers at Ford Motor Company to produce a Model T. With this relatively small number of parts, Ford blended the gains of large-scale mass production with the gains of a high degree of specialization within a single plant. Workers were highly specialized and usually performed one single task along an automated assembly line, while the plant was vertically integrated and manufactured the vehicle starting from raw materials.

As consumers became wealthier and insisted on more luxurious vehicles, competitors to Ford emerged. Ford was forced to develop a family of models, each fitted with comfortable seats, radios, and numerous devices to improve safety and performance. As cars became more sophisticated, Ford could no longer produce them efficiently within a single plant. As the number of tasks outgrew the number of operations that could be efficiently conducted within a plant, Ford began to outsource production. The firm has attempted to keep strategically important tasks and production in-house while noncore tasks are purchased from external suppliers. As time has passed, increasing numbers of parts and services have come to be considered noncore, and Ford has farmed out production to a growing number of external suppliers, many of which are outside the United States. Today, about 70 percent of a typical Ford vehicle comes from parts, components and services purchased from external suppliers. Clearly, without the development toward increased specialization and outsourcing, today's cars would be either closer to Model T technology in quality or they would be beyond the budgets of ordinary people. By the 2000s, service industries, such as information technology and bill processing, were undergoing similar developments as the automobile industry had in the past.[15]

The iPhone Economy and Global Supply Chains

Apple Inc. is a multinational company that produces consumer electronics, computer software, and commercial servers. Headquartered in Cupertino, CA, the company was founded by Steve Jobs and Steve Wozniak in 1976. Although Apple used to produce its goods in America, today most are produced abroad. Virtually all iPhones, iPads, iMacs and other Apple products are made in Asia, Europe, and elsewhere. Apple employs 40,000 workers in the United States but has 700,000 workers in China; Apple licenses the production of its devices to Foxconn Technology Group that is headquartered in Taiwan and is the world's largest maker of consumer electronics products. What would it take to make iPhones in the United States?

In its early days, Apple usually did not look outside the United States for manufacturing sites. For example, for several years after Apple began producing the Macintosh in 1983, the company boasted that the Mac was a computer "Made in America." However, this began to change at the turn of the century when Apple switched to foreign manufacturing.

---

[14]Jagdish Bhagwati, et. al., "The Muddles Over Outsourcing," *Journal of Economic Perspectives*, Fall 2004, pp. 93–114. See also McKinsey Global Institute, *Offshoring: Is It a Win-Win Game?* (Washington, DC: McKinsey Global Institute, 2003).

[15]World Trade Organization, *World Trade Report 2005* (Geneva, Switzerland), pp. 268–274.

Asia's attractiveness was partly due to its less expensive, semiskilled workers. That was not the main motivation for Apple because the cost of labor is negligible compared with the expense of purchasing parts and running supply chains that combine components and services from hundreds of companies. Apple maintains that the vast scale of overseas factories as well as the flexibility, perseverance, and skills of foreign workers have become so superior to their American counterparts that manufacturing in the United States is no longer a realistic option for most Apple products.

For example, Apple used a Chinese factory to revamp the production of the iPhone just weeks before it was introduced to the market. Apple had redesigned the iPhone's screen at the last minute, necessitating an assembly line overhaul. New screens began arriving at the plant around midnight. To implement a speedy changeover, the plant foreman woke up the workers sleeping in the company's crowded dormitories and the overhaul began. Within four days, the plant overhaul was complete and began producing 10,000 iPhones a day with a new, unscratchable glass screen. Workers at this plant toil up to 12 hours a day, six days a week. Apple's executives noted that the plant's speed and flexibility are superb and there is no American plant that can rival it. However, critics maintain that in China, human costs are built into the iPhone and other Apple products. They note that Apple's desire to increase product quality and decrease production costs has resulted in the firm and its suppliers often ignoring safety conditions for workers, disposal of hazardous waste, employment of underage workers, excessive overtime, and the like. Bleak working conditions have also been documented at Chinese factories manufacturing products for Hewlett-Packard, Dell, IBM, Sony, and others.

Yet some aspects of the iPhone are American. The product's software, for example, and its innovative marketing characteristics were mostly developed in the United States. Also, Apple has built a data center in North Carolina and key semiconductors inside the iPhone are made in Austin, Texas factory by Samsung, of South Korea. However, those facilities do not provide many jobs for Americans. Apple's North Carolina data center employs only 100 full-time workers and the Samsung plant employs about 2,400 workers. Simply put, if you expand production from one million phones to 25 million phones, you don't need many additional programmers.

In defending its strategy of production outsourcing, Apple notes that there are not enough American workers with the skills the company needs or U.S. factories with sufficient speed and flexibility. According to Apple, a crucial challenge in setting up plants in the United States is finding a technical work force. In particular, Apple and other technology companies say they need engineers with more than high school training, but not necessarily a bachelor's degree. Americans at that skill level are hard to find. Simply put, Apple's outsourcing is not merely motivated by low wages in China.[16]

Outsourcing Backfires for Boeing 787 Dreamliner

Although outsourcing may have contributed to greater efficiencies in auto production, it created problems for Boeing in the production of jetliners. In 2007, the first wings for Boeing's new $150 million jetliner, the 787 Dreamliner, landed in Seattle, Washington, ready-made in Japan. Three Japanese firms were awarded 35 percent of the design and manufacturing work for the 787, with Boeing performing final assembly in only three-day's time. Other nations, such as Italy, China, and Australia, were also involved in

---

[16]Charles Duhigg and Keith Bradsher, "How the U.S. Lost Out on iPhone Work," *The New York Times*, January 21, 2012; "In China, Human Costs Are Built Into an iPad," *The New York Times*, January 25, 2012 at http://www.nytimes.com.; Rich Karlgaard, "In Defense of Apple's China Plants," *The Wall Street Journal*, February 2, 2012, p. A-13; Greg Linden, Kenneth Kraemer, and Jason Dedrick, "Innovation and Job Creation in a Global Economy: The Case of Apple's iPod," *Journal of International Commerce and Economics*, 2011.

TABLE 2.7

Producing the Boeing 787: Examples of How Boeing Outsources Its Work

Country	Part/Activity
Japan	Wing, mid-fuselage section, fixed trailing edge, wing box
China	Rudder, vertical fin, fairing panels
South Korea	Wing tip, tail cone
Australia	Inboard flap, movable trailing edge
Canada	Engine pylon fairing, main landing gear door
Italy	Horizontal stabilizer
United Kingdom	Main landing gear, nose landing gear

Source: "Boeing 787: Parts From Around the World Will Be Swiftly Integrated," *The Seattle Times*, September 11, 2005, "Boeing Shares Work, But Guards Its Secrets," *The Seattle Times*, May 15, 2007, and "Outsourcing at Crux of Boeing Strike," *The Wall Street Journal*, September 8, 2008.

supplying sections of the 787, as seen in Table 2.7. Boeing maintained that by having contractors across the world build large sections of its airplanes, the firm could decrease the time required to build its jets by more than 50 percent and reduce the plane's development cost from $10 billion to $6 billion. Simply put, Boeing has manufactured just 35 percent of the plane before assembling the final aircraft at its plant outside Seattle; 65 percent of the plane's manufacturing comes from abroad.

To decrease costs, Boeing required foreign suppliers to absorb some of the costs of developing the plane. In return for receiving contracts to make sections of the 787, foreign suppliers invested billions of dollars, drawing from whatever subsidies were available. For example, Japan's government provided loans of up to $2 billion to the three Japanese suppliers of Boeing, and Italy provided regional infrastructure for its supplier company. This spreading of risk allowed Boeing to decrease its developmental costs and thus be a more effective competitor against Airbus.

The need to find engineering talent and technical capacity was another motive behind Boeing's globalization strategy. According to Boeing executives, the complexity of designing and producing the 787 requires that people's talents and capabilities are brought together from all over the world. Also, sharing work with foreigners helps Boeing maintain close relationships with its customers. For example, Japan has spent more money buying Boeing jetliners than any other country: Boeing shares its work with the Japanese, and the firm in turn secures a virtual monopoly in jetliner sales to Japan.

But the strategy backfired when Boeing's suppliers fell behind in getting their jobs done, which resulted in the 787's production being more than four years behind schedule. The suppliers' problems ranged from language barriers to snarls that erupted when some contractors themselves outsourced chunks of work. Boeing was forced to turn to its own union workforce to piece together the first few airplanes after their sections arrived at the firm's factory in Seattle, with thousands of missing parts. That action resulted in anger and anxiety among union workers who maintained that if Boeing had let them build the 787 in the first place, they would have achieved the production goal. Boeing workers also feared that the firm would eventually attempt to allow foreign contractors to go one step further and install their components directly in the 787. Although Boeing officials insisted that they had no intentions to do this, they refused to give union workers assurances in writing.

By giving up control of its supply chain, Boeing had lost the ability to oversee each step of production. Problems often were not discovered until parts came together at Boeing's Seattle plant. Fixes were not easy and cultures among suppliers often clashed.

Boeing officials lamented that it seemed like the Italians only worked three days a week (they were always on vacation) while the Japanese worked six days a week. Also, there were apprehensions among Boeing workers that they were giving up their trade secrets to the Japanese and Chinese and that they would soon be their competition.

Outsourcing was intended to save money, but in Boeing's case it backfired. The 787 came in at several billion dollars over budget and over three years behind schedule before it made first flight in late 2011. The plane's Lithium-ion batteries overheated that caused additional downtime to correct. Boeing officials admitted that they outsourced work to people who were not up to the task, the result being poorly made components, problems with electrical systems and environmental controls, and missed deadlines that disrupted the production schedule for the entire plane. Simply put, Boeing spent a lot more money in trying to recover than it would have spent if it kept many of the key technologies closer to Boeing.[17]

Reshoring Production to the United States

For several decades, many American firms with high labor costs found that they could realize huge savings by sending work to countries where wages were much lower. However, by 2013 producers were increasingly rethinking their offshoring strategies. Prominent firms such as Caterpillar, Ford Motor Company, Google, Apple, and General Electric were bringing some of their production back to the United States. Why?

The most important reason was that wages in China and India were increasing by 10–20 percent a year while manufacturing pay in the United States and Europe remained sluggish. Therefore, the wage gap was narrowing. True, other countries such as Vietnam and Bangladesh are competing to replace China as low-wage havens. However, they lack China's scale, efficiency, and supply chains.

America's companies were also realizing the downside of distance. The cost of shipping goods around the world by ocean freight was increasing sharply, and goods often spent weeks in transit. Rising shipping, rail, and road costs are especially harmful for companies that produce goods with relatively low value, such as consumer goods and appliances. Also, locating production far away from customers in large, new markets makes it difficult to customize products and respond quickly to changing local demand. Companies are increasingly factoring in the risk that natural disasters or geopolitical shocks could disrupt supply chains.

Therefore, Emerson, an electrical equipment maker, has moved factories from Asia to the United States to be closer to its customers. Lenovo, a Chinese technology company, has started making personal computers in North Carolina in order to customize them for American customers. IKEA, a Swedish firm that makes furniture and other products for the home, has opened a factory in the United States in order to reduce delivery costs. Desa, a power tools firm, has returned production from China to the United States because savings on transport and raw materials offset higher labor costs. Also, consider the following examples of reshoring.[18]

- In 2014, Whirlpool Corp. moved part of its washing machine production from its plant in Monterrey, Mexico, to a plant in Clyde, Ohio; the company's largest washing machine factory. Although wages for production workers in Clyde averaged $18 to $19 an hour, about five times higher than in Monterrey, the firm maintained that the shift would decrease costs overall. Why? The Clyde plant is more automated and

---

[17]Steve Denning, "What Went Wrong At Boeing?", *Forbes*, January 21, 2013.

[18]"Here, There and Everywhere: Outsourcing and Offshoring," *The Economist*, January 19, 2013; James Hagerty, "Whirlpool Jobs Return to U.S." *The Wall Street Journal*, December 20, 2013, p. B-4.; James Hagerty, "America's Toilet Turnaround," *The Wall Street Journal*, September 25, 2013, pp. B-1 and B-8.

electricity costs are much lower than in Monterrey. Also, Whirlpool could save on transportation because the washing machines would not have to be shipped across a border before going into the company's American distribution network. Whirlpool also announced that it would increase production of washing machines for Mexico's market at the Monterrey plant and would not need to reduce its Mexican workforce. Similar to other companies, Whirlpool is trying to produce goods closer to where it sells them, thus decreasing the time required to respond to changes in demand.

- After decades of moving production overseas, by 2014 American producers of toilets were ramping up production in the United States. Among these companies were Kohler Co., American Standard Brands, and Mansfield Plumbing Co. The reasons for reshoring included the desire to get products to American customers faster, reduce shipping costs, respond quickly to changes in consumer preferences, and offer a "Made in U.S.A." label that the companies believe is increasingly popular.

However, the magnitude of the reshoring movement should not be overstated. Most of the companies involved have been bringing back only some of their production destined for the American market. Much of the production that they offshored during the past few decades remains overseas. At the writing of this text, the extent that reshoring will continue for the United States was unclear.

SUMMARY

1. To the mercantilists, stocks of precious metals represented the wealth of a nation. The mercantilists contended that the government should adopt trade controls to limit imports and promote exports. One nation could gain from trade only at the expense of its trading partners because the stock of world wealth was fixed at a given moment in time and because not all nations could simultaneously have a favorable trade balance.

2. Smith challenged the mercantilist views on trade by arguing that, with free trade, international specialization of factor inputs could increase world output, which could be shared by trading nations. All nations could simultaneously enjoy gains from trade. Smith maintained that each nation would find it advantageous to specialize in the production of those goods in which it had an absolute advantage.

3. Ricardo argued that mutually gainful trade is possible even if one nation has an absolute disadvantage in the production of both commodities compared with the other nation. The less productive nation should specialize in the production and export of the commodity in which it has a comparative advantage.

4. Comparative costs can be illustrated with the production possibilities schedule. This schedule indicates the maximum amount of any two products

an economy can produce, assuming that all resources are used in their most efficient manner. The slope of the production possibilities schedule measures the MRT that indicates the amount of one product that must be sacrificed per unit increase of another product.

5. Under constant-cost conditions, the production possibilities schedule is a straight line. Domestic relative prices are determined exclusively by a nation's supply conditions. Complete specialization of a country in the production of a single commodity may occur in the case of constant-costs.

6. Because Ricardian trade theory relied solely on supply analysis, it was not able to determine actual terms of trade. This limitation was addressed by Mill in his theory of reciprocal demand. This theory asserts that within the limits to the terms of trade, the actual terms of trade are determined by the intensity of each country's demand for the other country's product.

7. The comparative advantage accruing to manufacturers of a particular product in a particular country can vanish over time when productivity growth falls behind that of foreign competitors. Lost comparative advantages in foreign markets reduce the sales and profits of domestic companies as well as the jobs and wages of domestic workers.

8. In the real world, nations tend to experience increasing-cost conditions. Thus, production possibilities schedules are drawn bowed outward. Relative product prices in each country are determined by both supply and demand factors. Complete specialization in production is improbable in the case of increasing costs.

9. According to the comparative-advantage principle, competition forces high-cost producers to exit from the industry. In practice, the restructuring of an industry can take a long time because high-cost producers often cling to capacity by nursing along antiquated plants. Exit barriers refer to various cost conditions that make lengthy exit a rational response for high-cost producers.

10. The first empirical test of Ricardo's theory of comparative advantage was made by MacDougall. Comparing the export patterns of the United States and the United Kingdom, MacDougall found that wage rates and labor productivity were important determinants of international trade patterns. A more recent test of the Ricardian model conducted by Golub, also supports Ricardo.

KEY CONCEPTS AND TERMS

Autarky (p. 36)
Basis for trade (p. 29)
Commodity terms of trade (p. 42)
Complete specialization (p. 40)
Constant opportunity costs (p. 36)
Consumption gains (p. 38)
Dynamic gains from international trade (p. 43)
Exit barriers (p. 55)
Free trade (p. 30)
Gains from international trade (p. 29)

Importance of being unimportant (p. 42)
Increasing opportunity costs (p. 46)
Labor theory of value (p. 30)
Marginal rate of transformation (MRT) (p. 36)
Mercantilists (p. 29)
No-trade boundary (p. 41)
Outer limits for the equilibrium terms of trade (p. 40)
Outsourcing (p. 58)
Partial specialization (p. 50)
Price-specie-flow doctrine (p. 30)

Principle of absolute advantage (p. 31)
Principle of comparative advantage (p. 32)
Production gains (p. 37)
Production possibilities schedule (p. 35)
Region of mutually beneficial trade (p. 41)
Terms of trade (p. 38)
Theory of reciprocal demand (p. 41)
Trade triangle (p. 40)
Trading possibilities line (p. 39)

STUDY QUESTIONS

1. Identify the basic questions with which modern trade theory is concerned.

2. How did Smith's views on international trade differ from those of the mercantilists?

3. Develop an arithmetic example that illustrates how a nation could have an absolute disadvantage in the production of two goods and still have a comparative advantage in the production of one of them.

4. Both Smith and Ricardo contended that the pattern of world trade is determined solely by supply conditions. Explain.

5. How does the comparative-cost concept relate to a nation's production possibilities schedule? Illustrate how differently shaped production possibilities schedules give rise to different opportunity costs.

6. What is meant by constant opportunity costs and increasing opportunity costs? Under what conditions will a country experience constant or increasing costs?

7. Why is it that the pre-trade production points have a bearing on comparative costs under increasing-cost conditions but not under conditions of constant-costs?

8. What factors underlie whether specialization in production will be partial or complete on an international basis?

9. The gains from specialization and trade are discussed in terms of *production gains* and *consumption gains*. What do these terms mean?

10. What is meant by the term *trade triangle*?

11. With a given level of world resources, international trade may bring about an increase in total world output. Explain.

12. The maximum amount of steel or aluminum that Canada and France can produce if they use all the factors of production at their disposal with the best technology available to them is shown (hypothetically) in Table 2.8.

TABLE 2.8

Steel and Aluminum Production

	Canada	France
Steel (tons)	500	1200
Aluminum (tons)	1500	800

Assume that production occurs under constant-cost conditions. On graph paper, draw the production possibilities schedules for Canada and France; locate aluminum on the horizontal axis and steel on the vertical axis of each country's graph. In the absence of trade, assume that Canada produces and consumes 600 tons of aluminum and 300 tons of steel and that France produces and consumes 400 tons of aluminum and 600 tons of steel. Denote these autarky points on each nation's production possibilities schedule.

a. Determine the MRT of steel into aluminum for each nation. According to the principle of comparative advantage, should the two nations specialize? If so, which product should each country produce? Will the extent of specialization be complete or partial? Denote each nation's specialization point on its production possibilities schedule. Compared to the output of steel and aluminum that occurs in the absence of trade, does specialization yield increases in output? If so, by how much?

b. Within what limits will the terms of trade lie if specialization and trade occur? Suppose Canada and France agree to a terms of trade ratio of 1:1 (1 ton of steel = 1 ton of aluminum). Draw the terms of trade line in the diagram of each nation. Assuming 500 tons of steel are traded for 500 tons of aluminum, are Canadian consumers better off as the result of trade? If so, by how much? How about French consumers?

c. Describe the trade triangles for Canada and France.

13. The hypothetical figures in Table 2.9 give five alternate combinations of steel and autos that Japan and South Korea can produce if they fully use all factors of production at their disposal with the best technology available to them. On graph paper, sketch the production possibilities schedules of Japan and South Korea. Locate steel on the vertical axis and autos on the horizontal axis of each nation's graph.

TABLE 2.9

Steel and Auto Production

JAPAN		SOUTH KOREA	
Steel (tons)	Autos	Steel (tons)	Autos
520	0	1200	0
500	600	900	400
350	1100	600	650
200	1300	200	800
0	1430	0	810

a. The production possibilities schedules of the two countries appear bowed out, from the origin. Why?

b. In autarky, Japan's production and consumption points along its production possibilities schedule are assumed to be 500 tons of steel and 600 autos. Draw a line tangent to Japan's autarky point and from it calculate Japan's MRT of steel into autos. In autarky, South Korea's production and consumption points along its production possibilities schedule are assumed to be 200 tons of steel and 800 autos. Draw a line tangent to South Korea's autarky point and from it calculate South Korea's MRT of steel into autos.

c. Based on the MRT of each nation, should the two nations specialize according to the principle of comparative advantage? If so, in which product should each nation specialize?

d. The process of specialization in the production of steel and autos continues in Japan and South Korea until their relative product prices, or MRTs, become equal. With specialization, suppose the MRTs of the two nations converge at MRT = 1. Starting at Japan's autarky point, slide along its production possibilities schedule until the slope of the tangent line equals 1. This becomes Japan's production point under partial specialization. How many tons of steel and how many autos will Japan produce at this point? In

© Cengage Learning®

like manner, determine South Korea's production point under partial specialization. How many tons of steel and how many autos will South Korea produce? For the two countries, do their combined production of steel and autos with partial specialization exceed their output in the absence of specialization? If so, by how much?

e. With the relative product prices in each nation now in equilibrium at 1 ton of steel equal to 1 auto (MRT = 1), suppose 500 autos are exchanged at this terms of trade.

(1) Determine the point along the terms of trade line at which Japan will locate after trade occurs. What are Japan's consumption gains from trade?

(2) Determine the point along the terms of trade line at which South Korea will locate after trade occurs. What are South Korea's consumption gains from trade?

14. Table 2.10 gives hypothetical export price indexes and import price indexes (1990 = 100) for Japan, Canada, and Ireland. Compute the commodity terms of trade for each country for the period 1990–

2006. Which country's terms of trade improved, worsened, or showed no change?

TABLE 2.10

Export Price and Import Price Indexes

Country	EXPORT PRICE INDEX		IMPORT PRICE INDEX	
	1990	**2006**	**1990**	**2006**
Japan	100	150	100	140
Canada	100	175	100	175
Ireland	100	167	100	190

© Cengage Learning®

15. Why is it that the gains from trade could not be determined precisely under the Ricardian trade model?

16. What is meant by the theory of reciprocal demand? How does it provide a meaningful explanation of the international terms of trade?

17. How does the commodity terms of trade concept attempt to measure the direction of trade gains?

EXPLORING FURTHER

For a presentation of *Comparative Advantage in Money Terms*, go to *Exploring Further 2.1* that can be found at **www.cengage.com/economics/Carbaugh**.

For a presentation of indifference curves that show the role of each country's tastes and preferences in determining the autarky points and how gains from trade are distributed, go to *Exploring Further 2.2* that can be found at **www.cengage.com/economics/Carbaugh**.

For a presentation of *Offer Curves and the Equilibrium Terms of Trade*, go to *Exploring Further 2.3* that can be found at **www.cengage.com/economics/Carbaugh**.

Sources of Comparative Advantage

In Chapter 2, we learned how the principle of comparative advantage applies to the trade patterns of countries. The United States, for example, has a comparative advantage in, and exports considerable amounts of chemicals, semiconductors, computers, generating equipment, jet aircraft, agricultural products, and the like. It has comparative disadvantages in, and depends on other countries for cocoa, coffee, tea, raw silk, spices, tin, and natural rubber. Imported products also compete with U.S. products in many domestic markets: Japanese automobiles and televisions, Swiss cheese, and Austrian snow skis are some examples. Even the American pastime of baseball relies greatly on imported baseballs and gloves.

What determines a country's comparative advantage? There is no single answer to this question. Sometimes comparative advantage is determined by natural resources or climate, abundance of cheap labor, accumulated skills and capital, and government assistance granted to a particular industry. Some sources of comparative advantage are long lasting, such as huge oil deposits in Saudi Arabia; others can evolve over time like worker skills, education, and technology.

In this chapter, we consider the major sources of comparative advantage: differences in technology, resource endowments, and consumer demand, and the existence of government policies, economies of scale in production, and external economies. We will also consider the impact of transportation costs on trade patterns.

FACTOR ENDOWMENTS AS A SOURCE OF COMPARATIVE ADVANTAGE

When Ricardo formulated the principle of comparative advantage he did not explain what ultimately determines comparative advantage. He simply took it for granted that relative labor productivity, labor costs and product prices differed in the two countries before trade. Moreover, Ricardo's assumption of labor as the only factor of production ruled out an explanation of how trade affects the distribution of income among various factors of production within a nation and why certain groups favor free trade while other groups oppose it. As we will see, trade theory suggests that some people will suffer losses from free trade.

In the 1920s and 1930s, Swedish economists Eli Heckscher and Bertil Ohlin formulated a theory addressing two questions left largely unexplained by Ricardo: What determines comparative advantage and what effect does international trade have on the earnings of various factors of production in trading nations? Because Heckscher and Ohlin maintained that factor (resource) endowments determine a nation's comparative advantage, their theory became known as the **factor-endowment theory**. It is also known as the **Heckscher–Ohlin theory**.[1] Ohlin was awarded the 1977 Nobel prize in economics for his contribution to the theory of international trade.

The Factor-Endowments Theory

The factor-endowment theory asserts that the immediate basis for trade is the difference between pre-trade relative product prices of trading nations. These prices depend on the production possibilities curves and tastes and preferences (demand conditions) in the trading countries. Because production possibilities curves depend on technology and resource endowments, the ultimate determinants of comparative advantage are technology, resource endowments, and demand. The factor-endowment theory assumes that technology and demand are approximately the same between countries; it emphasizes the role of relative differences in resource endowments as the ultimate determinant of comparative advantage.[2] Note that it is the resource–endowment ratio, rather than the absolute amount of each resource available, that determines comparative advantage.

According to the factor-endowment theory, a nation will export the product that uses a large amount of the relatively abundant resource, and it will import the product that in production uses the relatively scarce resource. Therefore, the factor-endowment theory predicts that India, with its relative abundance of labor, will export shoes and shirts while the United States, with its relative abundance of capital, will export machines and chemicals.

What does it mean to be relatively abundant in a resource? Table 3.1 illustrates hypothetical resource endowments in the United States and China that are used in the production of aircraft and textiles. The U.S. **capital/labor ratio** equals 0.5 (100 machines/200 workers = 0.5) that means there is 0.5 machines per worker. In China, the capital/labor ratio is 0.02 (20 machines/1,000 workers = 0.02) that means there is 0.02 machines per worker. Since the U.S. capital/labor ratio exceeds China's capital/labor ratio, we call the United States the relatively capital abundant country and China the relatively capital-scarce country. Conversely, China is called the relatively labor abundant country and the United States the relatively labor scarce country.

---

[1] Eli Heckscher's explanation of the factor-endowment theory is outlined in his article "The Effects of Foreign Trade on the Distribution of Income," *Economisk Tidskrift*, 21 (1919), pp. 497–512. Bertil Ohlin's account is summarized in his *Interregional and International Trade* (Cambridge, MA: Harvard University Press, 1933). See also Edward Leamer, *The Heckscher–Ohlin Model in Theory and Practice*, Princeton Studies in International Finance, No. 77, February 1995.

[2] The factor-endowment theory also assumes that the production of goods is conducted under perfect competition, suggesting that individual firms exert no significant control over product price; that each product is produced under identical production conditions in the two countries; that if a producer increases the use of both resources by a given proportion, output will increase by the same proportion; that resources are free to move within a country, so that the price of each resource is the same in the two industries within each country; that resources are not free to move between countries, so that pre-trade payments to each resource can differ internationally; and that there are no transportation costs nor barriers to trade.

TABLE 3.1

Producing Aircraft and Textiles: Factor Endowments in the United States and China

Resource	United States	China
Capital	100 machines	20 machines
Labor	200 workers	1,000 workers

© Cengage Learning®

How does the relative abundance of a resource determine comparative advantage according to the factor-endowment theory? When a resource is relatively abundant, its relative cost is less than in countries where it is relatively scarce. Therefore, before the two countries trade, their comparative advantages are that capital is relatively cheap in the United States and labor is relatively cheap in China. So, the United States has a lower relative price in aircraft, that use more capital and less labor. China's relative price is lower in textiles that use more labor and less capital. The effect of resource endowments on comparative advantage can be summarized as follows:

Differences in relative resource endowments → Differences in relative resource prices → Differences in relative product prices → Pattern of comparative advantage

The predictions of the factor-endowment theory can be applied to the data in Table 3.2 that illustrates capital/labor ratios for selected countries in 2011. To permit useful international comparisons, total capital stocks per worker are shown in 2005 U.S. dollar prices to reflect the actual purchasing power of the dollar in each country. We see that the United States had less capital per worker than some other industrial countries, but more capital per worker than the developing countries. According to the factor-endowment theory, we can conclude that the United States has a comparative advantage in capital-intensive products in relation to developing countries, but not with all industrial countries.

TABLE 3.2

Total Capital Stock per Worker of Selected Countries in 2011*

Industrial Country		Developing Country	
Japan	$297,565	South Korea	$233,959
United States	292,658	Mexico	85,597
Germany	251,468	Colombia	67,292
Australia	250,949	Brazil	64,082
Canada	198,930	China	57,703
Sweden	190,793	Philippines	34,913
Russia	107,182	Vietnam	24,721

*In 2005 U.S. dollar prices.

Source: From Robert Feenstra, Robert Inklaar, and Marcel Timmer, University of Groningen, Groningen Growth and Development Centre, *Penn World Table*, Version 8.0, 2013, available at www.rug.nl/research/ggdc/data/penn-world-table.

Visualizing the Factor-Endowment Theory

Figure 3.1 provides a graphical illustration of the factor-endowment theory. Figure 3.1 shows the production possibilities curves of the United States, assumed to be the relatively capital abundant country, and China, assumed to be the relatively labor abundant country. The figure also assumes that aircraft are relatively capital intensive in their production process and textiles are relatively labor intensive in their production process.

Because the United States is the relatively capital abundant country and aircraft are the relatively capital-intensive good, the United States has a greater capability in producing aircraft than China. Thus, the production possibilities curve of the United States is skewed (biased) toward aircraft, as shown in Figure 3.1. Similarly, because China is the relatively labor abundant country and textiles are a relatively labor intensive good, China has a greater capability in producing textiles than does the United States. China's production possibilities curve is skewed toward textiles.

Suppose that in autarky, both countries have the same demand for textiles and aircraft that results in both countries producing and consuming at point A in Figure 3.1(a).[3] At this point, the absolute slope of the line tangent to the U.S. production possibilities curve is smaller (U.S. MRT = 0.33) than that of the absolute slope of the line tangent to China's production possibilities curve (China's MRT = 4.0). Thus, the United States has a lower relative price for aircraft than China. This finding means that the United States has a comparative advantage in aircraft while China has a comparative advantage in textiles.

FIGURE 3.1

The Factor-Endowment Theory

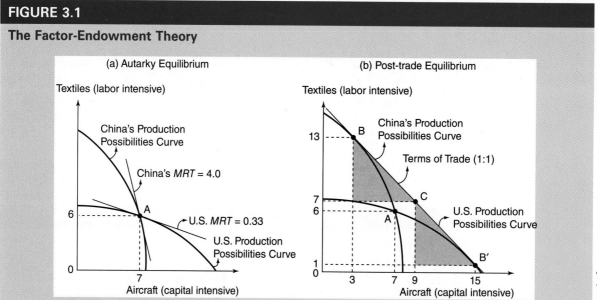

A country exports the good whose production is intensive in its relatively abundant factor. It imports the good whose production is intensive in its relatively scarce factor.

© Cengage Learning®

---

[3]Note that the factor-endowment theory does not require that tastes and preferences be identical for the United States and China. It only requires that they be approximately the same. This approximation means that community indifference curves have about the same shape and position in all countries, as discussed in *Exploring Further 2.2* in Chapter 2. For simplicity, Figure 3.1 assumes exact equality of tastes and preferences.

Although Figure 3.1(*a*) helps us visualize the pattern of comparative advantage, it does not identify the ultimate cause of comparative advantage. In our trading example, capital is relatively cheap in the relatively capital abundant country (the United States) and labor is relatively cheap in the relatively labor abundant country (China). It is because of this difference in relative resource prices that the United States has a comparative advantage in the relatively capital-intensive good (aircraft) and China has a comparative advantage in the relatively labor intensive good (textiles). The factor endowment theory asserts that the difference in relative resource abundance is the cause of the pre-trade differences in the relative product prices between the two countries.

Most of the analysis of the gains from trade in Chapter 2 applies to the factor-endowment model seen in Figure 3.1(*b*). With trade, each country continues to specialize in the production of the product of its comparative advantage until its product price equalizes with that of the other country. Specialization continues until the United States reaches point *B'* and China reaches point *B*, the points where each country's production possibilities curve is tangent to the common relative price line that is assumed to have an absolute slope of 1.0. This relative price line becomes the equilibrium terms of trade. Let's assume that with trade both nations prefer a post-trade consumption combination of aircraft and textiles given by point *C*. To achieve this point, the United States exports six aircraft for six units of textiles and China exports six units of textiles for six aircraft. Because point *C* is beyond the autarky consumption point *A*, each country realizes gains from trade.

The factor-endowment model explains well why labor abundant countries such as China would export labor intensive products such as textiles and toys and capital abundant countries such as the United States would export aircraft and machinery. However, it does not adequately explain two-way trade that widely exists: many countries export steel and automobiles, but they also import them. Also, the factor-endowment theory does not satisfactorily explain why wealthy countries such as the United States and Europe that have similar endowments of labor and capital, trade more intensively with those with dissimilar endowments. You will learn about additional trade theories as you read this chapter.

Applying the Factor-Endowment Theory to U.S.–China Trade

The essence of the factor-endowment theory is seen in trade between the United States and China. In the United States, human capital (skills), scientific talent, and engineering talent are relatively abundant, but unskilled labor is relatively scarce. Conversely, China is relatively rich in unskilled labor while relatively scarce in scientific and engineering talent. Thus, the factor-endowment theory predicts that the United States will export to China goods embodying relatively large amounts of skilled labor and technology, such as aircraft, software, pharmaceuticals, and high-tech components of electrical machinery and equipment; China will export to the United States goods for which a relatively large amount of unskilled labor is used, such as apparel, footwear, toys, and the final assembly of electronic machinery and equipment.

Table 3.3 lists the top U.S. merchandise exports to China and the top Chinese merchandise exports to the United States in 2012. The pattern of U.S.–China trade appears to fit quite well to the predictions of the factor-endowment theory. Most of the U.S. exports to China were concentrated in higher skilled industries such as computers, chemicals, and transportation equipment including aircraft. Conversely, Chinese exports to the United States tended to fall into the lower skilled industries such as electronics, toys, sporting equipment, and apparel. These trade data provide only a rough overview of U.S.–Chinese trade patterns and do not prove the validity of the factor-endowment theory.

TABLE 3.3

U.S.–China Merchandise Trade: 2012 (billions of dollars)

U.S. EXPORTS TO CHINA			U.S. IMPORTS FROM CHINA		
Product	Value	Percent	Product	Value	Percent
Agricultural products	20.7	18.7	Electronics	158.4	37.2
Computers and electronics	13.9	12.6	Toys, sporting equipment	36.6	8.6
Transportation equipment	15.7	14.2	Apparel	32.1	7.5
Chemicals	12.9	11.7	Electrical equipment	30.5	7.2
Machinery	9.9	8.9	Leather products	24.6	5.8
All others	37.4	33.9	All others	143.4	33.7
Total	110.5	100.0	Total	425.6	100.0

Source: From U.S. Department of Commerce, International Trade Administration, available at http://www.ita.doc.gov. Scroll down to TradeStats Express (http://tse.export.gov/) and to *National Trade Data.* See also Foreign Trade Division, U.S. Census Bureau.

Chinese Manufacturers Beset By Rising Wages and a Rising *Yuan*

For several decades, a vast pool of inexpensive labor fostered China's manufacturing boom. China's workers have toiled for a small fraction of the cost of their American or European competitors. However, as China's economy has expanded, its workers have become harder to find and keep, especially on the coasts where China's exporting factories are clustered. China's one-child policy has resulted in the number of young adults shrinking, resulting in labor scarcity. Moreover, although the country's inland villages contain millions of potential workers for its coastal factories, China's land policies and household registration system discourage migration to the cities. Villagers risk losing family plots if they do not tend them. They cannot enroll their children in city schools or benefit from other government services until they have been officially declared as permanent urban residents that can take years. The supply of factory workers is not infinite, even in China.

With fewer workers heading to China's manufacturing zones, the result is upward pressure on wages. Unrest has increased in China as workers have demonstrated for higher wages: strikes, stoppages, and suicides have afflicted companies such as Honda that have factories on China's coast. Higher wages at home and low wage competition from countries such as Vietnam are making it more difficult for China to maintain rapid export growth. Many economists maintain that the high growth phase will soon run out. Increasingly, China will have to rely on technology, infrastructure, and education as sources of growth.

Although higher wages will improve the lives of urban workers, they will make it more difficult for Chinese exporters of low end merchandise like toys and apparel to continue to compete on price. Exporters will have to increase productivity to make up for higher wages and begin producing higher end products that are less sensitive to price increases. If wages increase in China, its workers would have more money to spend, some that will be spent on imported goods. This spending will result in increasing pressure on trade, a main drive of China's economic growth.

Consider Lever Style Inc., a Chinese manufacturer of blouses and shirts. In 2013, the firm began moving apparel production to Vietnam where wages were less than half those in China; the firm expected that Vietnam would be producing about 40 percent of its clothes within a few years. Lever Style's management considered the relocation as a matter of survival. After a decade of almost 20 percent annual wage increases in China, Lever Style said that it was increasingly difficult to make money in China. As production shifts to Vietnam, Lever Style said it could offer its customers discounts up to 10 percent per garment. That is attractive to American retailers, whose profit margins tend to average one percent to two percent. Although the move is intended to allow Lever Style's prices to be held in check, competition for labor in places like Vietnam and Cambodia is pushing up wages in those countries as well.[4]

Another factor contributing to China's export woes is the strengthening (appreciating) *yuan*. As discussed in Chapter 15, the United States has long maintained that the yuan has been kept artificially low to boost China's exports, and that the yuan is undervalued. However, from 2011 to 2014 (at the writing of this textbook), the yuan's exchange value was appreciating against the dollar that made China's goods more expensive overseas and decreased profits in local currency terms. Therefore, some low end manufacturers were abandoning China for cheaper locations abroad.

Higher wages and a stronger yuan alone are not sufficient to cause firms to leave China. The country has the world's best supply chains of parts and components for industries and its infrastructure works well. Moreover, China has become a huge market in its own right. Therefore, China will likely remain an attractive site for many manufacturers.

TRADE CONFLICTS GLOBALIZATION DRIVES CHANGES FOR U.S. AUTOMAKERS

The history of the U.S. automobile industry can be divided into distinct eras: the emergence of Ford Motor Company as a dominant producer in the early 1900s; the shift of dominance to General Motors in the 1920s; and the rise of foreign competition since the 1970s.

Foreign producers have become effective rivals of the Big Three (GM, Ford, and Chrysler) which used to be insulated from competitive pressures on their costs and product quality. The result has been a steady decrease in the Big Three's share of the U.S. automobile market from more than 70 percent in 1999 to about 45 percent in 2011. For decades, the competitive threat of foreign companies was greatest in the small car segment of the U.S. market. Now, the Big Three also face stiff competition on the lucrative turf of pickup trucks, minivans, and sport utility vehicles.

Several factors detracted from the cost competitiveness of the Big Three during the first decade of the 2000s. First, the Big Three were saddled with large pension obligations and health care costs for their, negotiated by the United Auto Workers (UAW) and the Big Three when times were better for these firms. These benefit costs were much higher than for American workers of nonunionized Toyota and Honda, with their younger workforces and fewer retirees. Relatively high wages represented another cost disadvantage of the Big Three. In 2008, for example, wages for Big

Three production workers averaged about 33 percent more than for American production workers at Toyota and Honda. Industry analysts estimate that labor cost accounts for about 10 percent of the cost of manufacturing an automobile. Moreover, Toyota and Honda have been widely viewed as the most efficient producers of automobiles in the world.

As global competition intensified and the U.S. economy fell into the Great Recession of 2007–2009, the Big Three's sales, market share, and profitability deteriorated. In 2009, GM and Chrysler declared bankruptcy. Therefore, the UAW agreed to a series of concessions to preserve the jobs of their members. They accepted higher premiums and copayments for health care and they set up a second tier wage for entry level workers at about half the wage for current workers. UAW workers also agreed to suspend bonuses and cost of living increases. These adjustments brought the pay of Big Three production workers closer to that of their Japanese competitors. However, auto workers in the United States are paid much higher wages and benefits than auto workers in China, India, and South America.

As competition in the U.S. auto market has become truly international, it is highly unlikely that the Big Three will ever regain the dominance that on allowed them to dictate which vehicles Americans bought and at what prices. Toyota and Honda will likely remain as major threats to their financial stability.

iStockphoto.com/photosoup

---

[4]Deborah Kan, *China Inc. Moves Offshore*, Reuters Video Gallery, July 20, 2011, at www.reuters.com/video/; Kathy Chu, "China Manufacturers Survive by Moving to Asian Neighbors," *The Wall Street Journal*, May 1, 2013 and "China Grapples With Labor Shortage as Workers Shun Factories," *The Wall Street Journal*, May 1, 2013.

Factor-Price Equalization

In Chapter 2, we learned that international trade tends to equalize product prices among trading partners. Can the same be said for resource prices?[5]

To answer this question, consider Figure 3.2. The figure continues our example of comparative advantage in aircraft and textiles by illustrating the process of **factor-price equalization**. Recall that the Chinese demand for inexpensive American aircraft results

---

FIGURE 3.2

The Factor-Price Equalization Theory

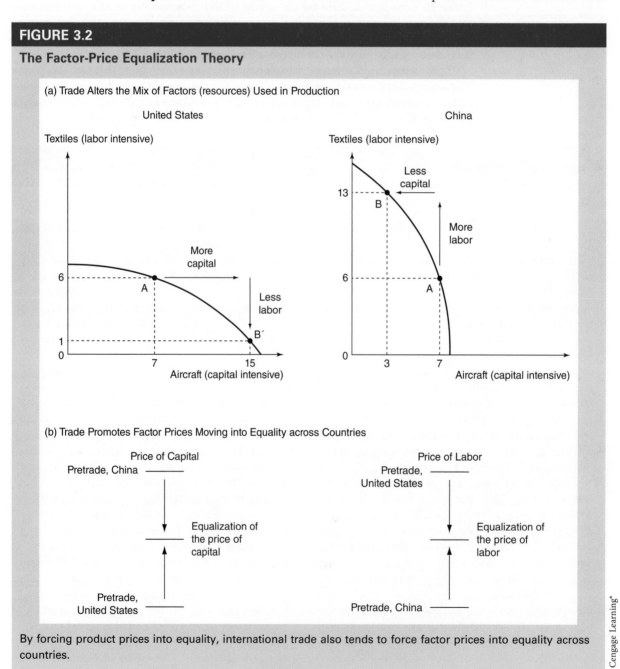

By forcing product prices into equality, international trade also tends to force factor prices into equality across countries.

© Cengage Learning®

---

[5]See Paul A. Samuelson, "International Trade and Equalization of Factor Prices," *Economic Journal*, June 1948, pp. 163–184, and "International Factor-Price Equalization Once Again," *Economic Journal*, June 1949, pp. 181–197.

in an increased American demand for its abundant resource, capital; the price of capital thus rises in the United States. As China produces fewer aircraft, its demand for capital decreases, and the price of capital falls. The effect of trade is to equalize the price of capital in the two nations. Similarly, the American demand for cheap Chinese textiles leads to an increased demand for labor in China, its abundant resource; the price of labor rises in China. With the United States producing fewer textiles, its demand for labor decreases and the price of labor falls. With trade, the price of labor tends to equalize in the two trading partners. We conclude that by redirecting demand away from the scarce resource and toward the abundant resource in each nation, trade leads to factor-price equalization. In each nation, the cheap resource becomes relatively more expensive, and the expensive resource becomes relatively less expensive until price equalization occurs.

Indian computer engineers provide an example of factor-price equalization. Without immigration restrictions, the computer engineers could migrate to the United States where wage rates are much higher, thus increasing the relative supply of computer engineering skills and lessening the upward pressure on computer engineering wages in the United States. Although such migration has occurred it has been limited by immigration restrictions. What was the market's response to the restrictions? Computer engineering skills that could no longer be supplied through migration now arrive through trade in services. Computer engineering services occur in India and are transmitted via the Internet to business clients in the United States and other countries. In this manner, trade serves as a substitute for immigration.

The forces of globalization have begun to even things out between the United States and India. As more U.S. tech companies poured into India in the first decade of the 2000s, they soaked up the pool of high end computer engineers who were making about 25 percent of what their counterparts earned in the United States. The result was increasing competition for the most skilled Indian computer engineers and a narrowing U.S.–India gap in their compensation. By 2007, India's Software and Service Association estimated wage inflation in its industry at 10 to 15 percent a year, while some tech executives said it was closer to 50 percent. In the United States, wage inflation in the software sector was less than three percent. For experienced, top level Indian engineers, salaries increased to between $60,000 and $100,000 a year, pressing against salaries earned by computer engineers in the United States. Wage equalization was occurring between India and the United States. Taking into account the time difference with India, some Silicon Valley firms concluded that they were not saving any money by locating there anymore and began to bring jobs home to American workers.

Although the tendency toward the equalization of resource prices may sound plausible, in the real world, we do not see full factor-price equalization. Table 3.4 shows 2011 indexes of hourly compensation for nine countries Wages differed by a factor of about ten from workers in the highest wage country (Norway) to workers in the lowest wage country (Mexico). There are several reasons why differences in resource prices exist.

Most income inequality across countries results from uneven ownership of human capital. The factor-endowment model assumes that all labor is identical. However, labor across countries differs in terms of human capital that includes education, training, skill, and the like. We do not expect a computer engineer in the United States with a Ph.D. and 25 years' experience to be paid the same wage as a college graduate taking his/her first job as a computer engineer in Peru.

Also, the factor-endowment model assumes that all countries use the same technology for producing a particular good. When a new and better technology is developed, it tends to replace older technologies. This process can take a long time, especially between

TABLE 3.4

Indexes of Hourly Compensation for Manufacturing Workers in 2011 (U.S. = 100)

Norway	181
Germany	133
Austria	121
Netherlands	119
Canada	103
Japan	101
South Korea	53
Brazil	33
Mexico	18

Source: From U.S. Department of Labor, Bureau of Labor Statistics, available at Web site http://www.bls.gov. Scroll to International Labor Comparisons and to Indexes of Hourly Compensation in U.S. Dollars (U.S. = 100).

advanced and developing countries. Returns paid to resource owners across countries will not equalize when two countries produce the same good using different technologies. Machinery workers using superior production technologies in Germany tend to be paid more than workers using inferior production technologies in Algeria.

Transportation costs and trade barriers can prevent product prices from equalizing. Such market imperfections reduce the volume of trade, limiting the extent that product prices and resource prices can become equal.

Resource prices may not fully equalize across nations can be explained in part by the assumptions underlying the factor-endowment theory are not completely borne out in the real world.

Who Gains and Loses from Trade? The Stolper–Samuelson Theorem

Recall that in Ricardo's theory, a country as a whole benefits from comparative advantage. Also, Ricardo's assumption of labor as the only factor of production rules out an explanation of how trade affects the distribution of income among various factors of production within a nation, and why certain groups favor free trade whereas other groups oppose it. In contrast, the factor-endowment theory provides a more comprehensive way to analyze the gains and losses from trade. The theory does this by providing predictions of how trade affects the income of groups representing different factors of production such as workers and owners of capital.

The effects of trade on the distribution of income are summarized in the **Stolper–Samuelson theorem**, an extension of the theory of factor-price equalization.[6] According to this theorem, the export of a product that embodies large amounts of a relatively cheap, abundant resource makes this resource more scarce in the domestic market. The increased demand for the abundant resource results in an increase in its price and an increase in its income. At the same time, the income of the resource used intensively in the import-competing product (the initially scarce resource) decreases as its demand falls. The increase in the income to each country's abundant resource comes at the expense of the scarce resource's income. The Stolper–Samuelson theorem states that an

---

[6]Stolper, W. F. and P. A. Samuelson, "Protection and Real Wages." *Review of Economic Studies*, Vol. 9, pp. 58–73, 1941.

increase in the price of a product increases the income earned by resources that are used intensively in its production. Conversely, a decrease in the price of a product reduces the income of the resources that it uses intensively.

Note that the Stolper–Samuelson theorem does not state that all the resources used in the export industries are better off, or that all the resources used in the import-competing industries are harmed. Rather, the abundant resource that fosters comparative advantage realizes an increase in income and the scarce resource realizes a decrease in its income regardless of industry. Trade theory concludes that some people will suffer losses from free trade, even in the long-term.

Although the Stolper–Samuelson theorem provides some insights regarding the income distribution effects of trade, it tells only part of the story. An extension of the Stolper–Samuelson theorem is the **magnification effect** that suggests the change in the price of a resource is greater than the change in the price of the good that uses the resource intensively in its production process. Suppose that as the United States starts trading, the price of aircraft increases by six percent and the price of textiles decreases by three percent. According to the magnification effect, the price of capital must increase by more than six percent, and the price of labor must decrease by more than two percent. If the price of capital increases by eight percent, owners of capital are better off because their ability to consume aircraft and textiles (that is, their real income) is increased. However, workers, because their ability to consume the two goods is decreased (their real income falls), are worse off. In the United States, owners of capital gain from free trade while workers lose.

The Stolper–Samuelson theorem has important policy implications. The theorem suggests that even though free trade may provide overall gains for a country, there are winners and losers. Given this conclusion, it is not surprising that owners of abundant resources tend to favor free trade, while owners of scarce factors tend to favor trade restrictions. The U.S. economy has an abundance of skilled labor, so its comparative advantage is in producing skill-intensive goods. The factor-endowment model suggests that the United States will tend to export goods requiring relatively large amounts of skilled labor and import goods requiring large amounts of unskilled labor. International trade in effect increases the supply of unskilled labor to the U.S. economy, lowering the wages of unskilled American workers compared to those of skilled workers. Skilled workers—who are already at the upper end of the income distribution—find their incomes increasing as exports expand, while unskilled workers are forced into accepting even lower wages in order to compete with imports. According to the factor-endowment theory, then, international trade can aggravate income inequality, at least in a country such as the United States where skilled labor is abundant. This is a reason why unskilled workers in the United States often support trade restrictions.

Is International Trade a Substitute for Migration?

Immigrants provide important contributions to the U.S. economy. They help the economy grow by increasing the size of the labor force, they assume jobs at the lower end of the skill distribution where few native born Americans are available to work, and they take jobs that contribute to the United States being a leader in technological innovation. In spite of these advantages, critics maintain that immigrants take jobs away from Americans, suppress domestic wages, and consume sizable amounts of public services. They contend that legal barriers are needed to lessen the flow of immigrants into the United States. If the policy goal is to reduce immigration, could international trade be used to achieve this result rather than adopting legal barriers? The factor-endowment model of Heckscher and Ohlin addresses this question.

According to the factor-endowment theory, international trade can provide a substitute for the movement of resources from one country to another in its effects on resource prices. The endowments of resources among the countries of the world are not equal. A possible market effect would be movements of capital and labor from countries where they are abundant and inexpensive to countries where they are scarce and more costly, thus decreasing the price differences.

The factor-endowment theory also supports the idea that such international movements in resources are not essential, because the international trade in products can achieve the same result. Countries that have abundant capital can specialize in capital-intensive products and export them to countries where capital is scarce. In a sense, capital is embodied in products and redistributed through international trade. The same conclusion pertains to land, labor, and other resources.

A key effect of an international movement of a resource is to change the scarcity or abundance of that resource and alter its price; that is, to increase the price of the abundant resource by making it more scarce compared to other resources. When Polish workers migrate to France, wage rates tend to increase in Poland because labor becomes somewhat more scarce there; also, wage rates in France tend to decrease (or at least increase more slowly than they would otherwise) because the scarcity of labor declines. The same outcome occurs when the French purchase Polish products that are manufactured by labor intensive methods: Polish export industries demand more workers, and Polish wages tend to increase. In this manner, international trade can serve as a substitute for international movements of resources through its effect on resource prices.[7]

An example of international trade as a substitute for labor migration is the North American Free Trade Agreement of 1995. Signed by Canada, Mexico, and the United States, the agreement eliminated trade restrictions among the three nations. At that time, former President Bill Clinton noted that NAFTA would result in an even more rapid closing of the gap between the wage rates of Mexico and the United States. As the benefits of economic growth spread in Mexico to working people, they will have more income to buy American products and there will be less illegal immigration because more Mexicans will be able to support their children by staying home. While NAFTA may have helped lessen the flow of migrants from Mexico to the United States, other factors continued to encourage migration—high birth rates in Mexico, the collapse of the peso that resulted in recession, and the loss of jobs to other countries, especially China, where average wages are less than half of Mexico's. Although international trade and economic growth would lessen the flow of Mexicans to the United States, achieving this result would take years, perhaps decades.

International trade and labor migration are not necessarily substitutes: they may be complements, especially over the short and medium terms. As trade expands and an economy attempts to compete with imports, some of its workers may become unemployed. The uprooting of these workers may force some of them to seek employment abroad where job prospects are better. In this manner, increased trade can result in an increase in migration flows. During the first decade of the 2000s, Mexico lost thousands of jobs to China, whose average wages were half of Mexico's and whose exports to other countries were increasing. This loss provided additional incentive for Mexican workers to migrate to the United States to find jobs. The topic of immigration is further discussed in Chapter 9.

---

[7]Robert Mundell, "International Trade and Factor Mobility," *American Economic Review*, June 1957.

Specific Factors: Trade and the Distribution of Income in the Short Run

A key assumption of the factor-endowment model and its Stolper–Samuelson theorem is that resources such as labor and capital can move effortlessly among industries within a country while they are completely immobile among countries. For example, Japanese workers are assumed to be able to shift back and forth between automobile and rice production in Japan, although they cannot move to China to produce these products.

Although such factor mobility among industries may occur in the long-term, many factors are immobile in the short-term. Physical capital (such as factories and machinery) is generally used for specific purposes; a machine designed for computer production cannot suddenly be used to manufacture jet aircraft. Similarly, workers often acquire certain skills suited to specific occupations and cannot immediately be assigned to other occupations. These types of factors are known in trade theory as specific factors. Specific factors are those that cannot move easily from one industry to another. Thus, the **specific-factors theory** analyzes the income distribution effects of trade in the short-term when resources are immobile among industries. This is in contrast to the factor-endowment theory and its Stolper–Samuelson theorem that apply to the long-term mobility of resources in response to differences in returns.

To understand the effects of specific factors and trade, consider steel production in the United States. Suppose that capital is specific to producing steel, labor is mobile between the steel industry and other industries, and capital is not a substitute for labor in producing steel. Also suppose that the United States has a comparative disadvantage in steel. With trade, output decreases in the import-competing steel industry. As the relative price of steel decreases, labor moves out of the steel industry to take employment in export industries having comparative advantage. This movement causes the fixed stock of capital to become less productive for U.S. steel companies. As output per machine declines, the returns to capital invested in the steel industry decrease. At the same time, as output in export industries increases, labor moves to these industries and begins working. Hence, output per machine increases in the export industries, and the return to capital increases. The specific-factors theory concludes that resources specific to import-competing industries tend to lose as a result of trade, while resources specific to export industries tend to gain as a result of trade. This analysis helps explain why U.S. steel companies since the 1960s have lobbied for import restrictions to protect their specific factors that suffer from foreign competition.

The specific-factors theory helps explain Japan's rice policy. Japan permits only small quantities of rice to be imported, even though rice production in Japan is more costly than in other nations such as the United States. It is widely recognized that Japan's overall welfare would rise if free imports of rice were permitted. However, free trade would harm Japanese farmers. Although rice farmers displaced by imports might find jobs in other sectors of Japan's economy, they would find changing employment to be time consuming and costly. Moreover, as rice prices decrease with free trade, so would the value of Japanese farming land. It is no surprise that Japanese farmers and landowners strongly object to free trade in rice; their unified political opposition has influenced the Japanese government more than the interests of Japanese consumers. *Exploring Further 3.1* provides a more detailed presentation of the specific-factors theory; it can be found at www.cengage.com/economics/Carbaugh.

Does Trade Make the Poor Even Poorer?

Before leaving the factor-endowment theory, consider this question: Is your income pulled down by workers in Mexico or China? That question has underlined many

Americans' fears about their economic future. They worry that the growth of trade with low wage developing nations could reduce the demand for low skilled workers in the United States and cause unemployment and wage decreases for U.S. workers.

The wage gap between skilled and unskilled workers has widened in the United States during the past 40 years. Over the same period, imports increased as a percentage of gross domestic product. These facts raise two questions: Is trade harming unskilled workers? If it is, then is this an argument for an increase in trade barriers?

Economists agree that some combination of trade, technology, education, immigration, and union weakness has held down wages for unskilled American workers; but apportioning the blame is tough, partly because income inequality is so pervasive. Economists have attempted to disentangle the relative contributions of trade and other influences on the wage discrepancy between skilled workers and unskilled workers. Their approaches share the analytical framework shown by Figure 3.3. This framework views the wages of skilled workers "relative" to those of unskilled workers as the outcome of the interaction between supply and demand in the labor market.

The vertical axis of Figure 3.3 shows the wage ratio that equals the wage of skilled workers divided by the wage of unskilled workers. The figure's horizontal axis shows the labor ratio, that equals the quantity of skilled workers available divided by the quantity of unskilled workers. Initially we assume that the supply curve of skilled workers relative to unskilled workers is fixed and is denoted by S_0. The demand curve for skilled workers relative to unskilled workers is denoted by D_0. The equilibrium wage ratio is 2.0, found at the intersection of the supply and demand curves, and suggests that the wages of skilled workers are twice as much as the wages of unskilled workers.

FIGURE 3.3

Inequality of Wages between Skilled and Unskilled Workers

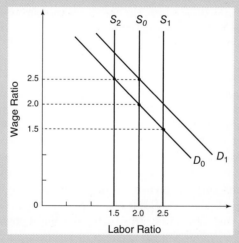

By increasing the demand for skilled relative to unskilled workers, expanding trade or technological improvements result in greater inequality of wages between skilled and unskilled workers. Also, immigration of unskilled workers intensifies wage inequality by decreasing the supply of skilled workers relative to unskilled workers. However, expanding opportunities for college education results in an increase in the supply of skilled relative to unskilled workers, thus reducing wage inequality. In the figure, the wage ration equals wage of skilled workers/ wage of unskilled workers. The labor ratio equals the quantity of skilled workers/quantity of unskilled workers.

In the figure, a shift in either the supply curve or demand curve of skilled workers available relative to unskilled workers will induce a change in the equilibrium wage ratio. Let us consider resources that can affect wage inequality in the United States.

- *International trade and technological change.* Trade liberalization and falling transportation and communication costs result in an increase in the demand curve of skilled workers relative to unskilled workers, say, to D_1 in the figure. Assuming a constant supply curve, the equilibrium wage ratio rises to 2.5, suggesting that the wages of skilled workers are 2.5 times as much as the wages of unskilled workers. Similarly, skill biased technological improvements lead to an increase in the demand for skilled workers relative to unskilled workers, thus promoting higher degrees of wage inequality.
- *Immigration.* Immigration of unskilled workers results in a decrease in the supply of skilled workers relative to unskilled workers. Assuming that the demand curve is constant, as the supply curve shifts from S_0 to S_2, the equilibrium wage ratio rises to 2.5, thus intensifying wage inequality.
- *Education and training.* As the availability of education and training increases, so does the ratio of skilled workers to unskilled workers, as seen by the increase in the supply curve from S_0 to S_1. If the demand curve remains constant, then the equilibrium wage ratio will fall from 2.0 to 1.5. Additional opportunities for education and training thus serve to reduce the wage inequality between skilled and unskilled workers.

We have seen how trade and immigration can promote wage inequality. However, economists have found that their effects on the wage distribution have been small. In fact, the vast majority of wage inequality is because of domestic sources, especially technology. One often cited study by William Cline, estimated that during the past three decades technological change has been about four times more powerful in widening wage inequality in the United States than trade, and that trade accounted for only 7.0 percentage points of all the unequalizing forces at work during that period. His conclusions are reinforced by the research of Robert Lawrence that concludes rising wage inequality during the first decade of the 2000s more closely corresponds to asset-market performance and technological and institutional innovations than to international trade in goods and services. The minor importance of trade implies that any policy that focuses narrowly on trade to deal with wage inequality is likely to be ineffective[8]

Economists generally agree that trade has been relatively unimportant in widening wage inequality. Also, trade's impact on wage inequality is overwhelmed not just by technology but also by education and training. Indeed, the shifts in labor demand away from less educated workers are the most important factors behind the eroding wages of the less educated. Such shifts appear to be the result of economy wide technological and organizational changes in how work is performed.

IS THE FACTOR-ENDOWMENT THEORY A GOOD PREDICTOR OF TRADE PATTERNS?

Following the development of the factor-endowment theory, little empirical evidence was brought to bear about its validity. All that came forth were intuitive examples such as labor abundant India exporting textiles or shoes; capital abundant Germany exporting

---

[8]William Cline, *Trade and Income Distribution*, Institute for International Economics, Washington, DC, 1997, p. 264 and Robert Lawrence, *Blue Collar Blues: Is Trade to Blame for Rising U.S. Income Inequality?* Institute for International Economics, Washington DC, 2008, pp. 73–74.

machinery and automobiles; or land abundant Australia exporting wheat and meat. However, some economists demanded stronger evidence concerning the validity of the factor-endowment theory.

The first attempt to investigate the factor-endowment theory empirically was undertaken by Wassily Leontief in 1954.[9] It had been widely recognized that in the United States capital was relatively abundant and labor was relatively scarce. According to the factor-endowment theory, the United States will export capital-intensive goods and its import-competing goods will be labor intensive. Leontief tested this proposition by analyzing the capital/labor ratios for some 200 export industries and import-competing industries in the United States, based on trade data for 1947. Leontief found that the capital/labor ratio for U.S. export industries was lower (about $14,000 per worker year) than that of its import-competing industries (about $18,000 per worker year). Leontief concluded that exports were *less* capital-intensive than import-competing goods. These findings that contradicted the predictions of the factor-endowment theory, became known as the **Leontief paradox**. To strengthen his conclusion, Leontief repeated his investigation in 1956 only to again find that U.S. import-competing goods were more capital intensive than U.S. exports. Leontief's discovery was that America's comparative advantage was something other than capital-intensive goods.

The doubt cast by Leontief on the factor-endowment theory sparked many empirical studies. These tests have been mixed. They conclude that the factor-endowment theory is relatively successful in explaining trade between industrialized and developing countries. The industrialized countries export capital-intensive (and temperate-climate land-intensive) products to developing countries, and import labor and tropical land-intensive goods from them. However, a large amount of international trade is not between industrialized and developing countries, but among industrialized countries with similar resource endowments. This suggests that the determinants of trade are more complex than those illustrated in the basic factor-endowment theory. Factors such as technology, economies of scale, demand conditions, imperfect competition, and a time dimension to comparative advantage must also be considered. In the following sections, we will examine these factors.

SKILL AS A SOURCE OF COMPARATIVE ADVANTAGE

One resolution of the Leontief paradox depends on the definition of capital. The exports of the United States are not intensive in capital such as tools and factories. Instead, they are skill-intensive, meaning that they are intensive in "human capital." U.S. exporting industries use a significantly higher proportion of highly educated workers to other workers as compared to U.S. import-competing industries. Boeing represents one of America's largest exporting companies. Boeing employs large numbers of mechanical and computer engineers having graduate degrees relative to the number of manual workers. Conversely, Americans import lots of shoes and textiles that are often manufactured by workers with little formal education.

In general, countries endowed with highly-educated workers have their exports concentrated in skill-intensive goods, while countries with less educated workers export goods that require little skilled labor. Figure 3.4 provides an example of this tendency. It compares the goods the United States imports from Germany, where the average adult

---

[9]Wassily W. Leontief, "Domestic Production and Foreign Trade: The American Capital Position Reexamined," *Proceedings of the American Philosophical Society* 97, September 1953.

FIGURE 3.4

Education, Skill Intensity, and U.S. Import Shares, *1998*

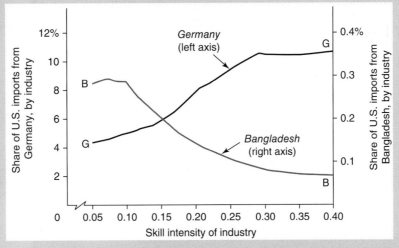

The figure suggests that countries that are abundant in skilled labor capture larger shares of U.S. imports in industries that intensively use those factors. Conversely, countries that are abundant in unskilled labor capture larger shares of U.S. imports in industries that intensively use those factors.

Adapted from John Romalis, "Factor Proportions and the Structure of Commodity Trade," American Economic Review, Vol. 94, No. 1, 2004, pp. 67–97.

has in excess of ten years of formal education, with the goods the United States imports from Bangladesh, where the average adult has only 2.5 years of formal education. In each country, industries are ranked according to their skill intensity: increasing skill intensity is shown by a rightward movement along the horizontal axis of the figure. The figure shows that Germany captures large shares of U.S. imports of skill-intensive goods, and much smaller shares for goods that sparingly require skilled labor. This is seen by the schedule representing Germany (GG) to be upward sloping: as a German industry becomes more skill intensive, its share of exports to the United States increases. Conversely, Bangladesh exhibits the opposite trade pattern with its exports to the United States concentrated in goods that require little skilled labor. Given the downward slope of Bangladesh's schedule (BB), as a Bangladesh industry becomes less skill intensive, its share of exports to the United States increases. The figure concludes that countries capture larger shares of the world trade of goods that more intensively use their abundant factors.

ECONOMIES OF SCALE AND COMPARATIVE ADVANTAGE

For some goods, economies of scale may be a source of comparative advantage. **Economies of scale** (increasing returns to scale) exist when expansion of the scale of production capacity of a firm or industry causes total production costs to increase less proportionately than output. Therefore, long-run average costs of production decrease. Economies of scale are classified as internal economies and external economies.[10]

[10]Paul Krugman, "New Theories of Trade Among Industrial Countries," *American Economic Review*, 73, No. 2, May 1983, pp. 343–347, and Elhanan Helpman, "The Structure of Foreign Trade," *Journal of Economic Perspectives*, 13, No. 2, Spring 1999, pp. 121–144.

Internal Economies of Scale

Internal economies of scale arise within a firm itself and are built into the shape of its long-run average cost curve. For an automobile producer, the first auto is expensive to produce, but each subsequent auto costs much less than the one before because the large setup costs can be spread across all units. Companies such as Toyota reduce unit costs because of labor specialization, managerial specialization, efficient capital, and other factors. As the firm expands its output by increasing the size of its plant, it slides downward along its long-run average cost curve because of internal economies of scale.

Figure 3.5 illustrates the effect of economies of scale on trade. Assume that a U.S. auto firm and a Mexican auto firm are each able to sell 100,000 vehicles in their respective countries. Also assume that identical cost conditions result in the same long-run average cost curve for the two firms, *AC*. Note that scale economies result in decreasing unit costs over the first 275,000 autos produced.

Initially, there is no basis for trade, because each firm realizes a production cost of $10,000 per auto. Suppose that rising income in the United States results in demand for 200,000 autos, while the Mexican auto demand remains constant. The larger demand allows the U.S. firm to produce more output and take advantage of economies of scale. The firm's cost curve slides downward until its cost equals $8,000 per auto. Compared to the Mexican firm, the U.S. firm can produce autos at a lower cost. With free trade, the United States will now export autos to Mexico.

Internal economies of scale provide additional cost incentives for *specialization* in production. Instead of manufacturing only a few units of each product that domestic

FIGURE 3.5

Economies of Scale as a Basis for Trade

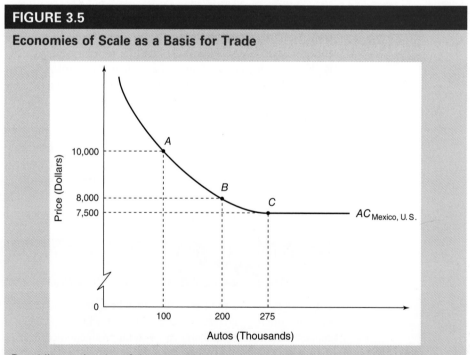

By adding to the size of the domestic market, international trade permits longer production runs by domestic firms, which can lead to greater efficiency and reductions in unit costs.

consumers desire to purchase, a country specializes in the manufacture of large amounts of a limited number of goods and trades for the remaining goods. Specialization in a few products allows a manufacturer to benefit from longer production runs that lead to decreasing average costs.

A key aspect of increasing–returns trade theory is the **home market effect**: countries will specialize in products that have a large domestic demand. Why? By locating close to its largest market, an industry can minimize the cost of shipping its products to its customers while still taking advantage of economies of scale. Auto companies will locate in Germany rather than France if it is clear that Germans are likely to buy more cars. That way the company can produce low-cost cars and not have to pay much to ship them to its largest market.

But the home market effect also has a disturbing implication. If industries tend to locate near their largest markets, what happens to small market areas? Other things equal, they're likely to become unindustrialized as factories and industries move to take advantage of scale economies and low transportation costs. Hence, trade could lead to small countries and rural areas becoming peripheral to the economic core; the backwater suppliers of commodities. As Canadian critics have phrased it, "With free trade, Canadians would become hewers of wood and drawers of water." However, other things are not strictly equal: comparative-advantage effects exist alongside the influence of increasing returns so the end result of open trade is not a foregone conclusion.

External Economies of Scale

The previous section considered how internal economies of scale that are *within* the control of a firm, can be a source of comparative advantage. Economies of scale can also rise *outside* a firm, but within an industry. For example, when an industry's scope of operations expands because of the creation of a better transportation system, the result is a decrease in cost for a company operating within that industry.

External economies of scale exist when the *firm's* average costs decrease as the *industry's* output increases. This cost reduction could be caused by a decrease in the prices of the resources employed by the firm or in the amount of resources per unit of output. This effect is shown by a downward shift of the firm's long run average cost curve. External economies of scale can occur in a number of situations:

- The rising concentration of an industry's firms in a particular geographic area attracts larger pools of a specialized type of worker needed by the industry, thus reducing the cost of hiring for a firm.
- New knowledge about production technology spreads among firms in the area through direct contacts among firms or as workers transfer from firm to firm. Rather than having to pay a consultant, a firm may be able to pick up useful technical knowledge from its workers mixing with workers of other firms.
- If a country has an expanding industry it will be a source of economic growth, and through this, the government can collect additional tax revenues. Recognizing this, the government can invest in better research and development facilities at local universities so that several businesses in that area can benefit.
- Access to specialized inputs increases with the clustering of component suppliers close to the center of manufacturing. Many auto component suppliers locate in the Detroit–Windsor area where General Motors, Ford, and Chrysler produce automobiles. With the increase in the number of suppliers come increased competition and a lower price of components for an auto company.

External economies of scale help explain why New York has a comparative advantage in financial services, California's Silicon Valley has a comparative advantage in semiconductors, and Hollywood has a comparative advantage in movies.

External economies of scale have resulted in Dalton, Georgia becoming the carpet manufacturing capital of the world. The location of the carpet industry in Dalton can be traced back to a wedding gift given in 1895 by a teenage girl, Catherine Whitener, to her brother and his bride. The gift was an unusual tufted bedspread. Copying a quilt pattern, Catherine sewed thick cotton yarns with a running stitch into unbleached muslin, clipped the ends of the yarn so they would fluff out, and washed the spread in hot water to hold the yarns by shrinking the fabric. Interest grew in Catherine's bedspreads, and in 1900, she made the first sale of a spread for $2.50. Demand became so great for the spreads that by the 1930s, local women had haulers take the stamped sheeting and yarns to front porch workers. Often entire families worked to hand tuft the spreads for $0.10 to $0.25 per spread. Nearly 10,000 local men, women, and children were involved in the industry. When mechanized carpet making was developed after World War II, Dalton became the center of the new industry because specialized tufting skills were required and the city had a ready pool of workers with those skills, thus reducing hiring costs.

Dalton is now home to more than 170 carpet plants, 100 carpet outlet stores, and more than 30,000 people employed by these firms. Supporting the carpet industry are local yarn manufacturers, machinery suppliers, dye plants, printing shops, and maintenance firms. The local workforce has acquired specialized skills for operating carpet making equipment. Because firms that are located outside of Dalton cannot use the suppliers or the skilled workers available to factories in Dalton, they tend to have higher production costs. Although there is no particular reason why Dalton became the carpet making capital of the world, external economies of scale provided the area with a comparative advantage in carpet making once firms established there.

OVERLAPPING DEMANDS AS A BASIS FOR TRADE

The home market effect has implications for another theory of trade, the **theory of overlapping demands**. This theory was formulated by Staffan Linder, a Swedish economist in the 1960s.[11] According to Linder, the factor-endowment theory has considerable explanatory power for trade in primary products (natural resources) and agricultural goods. It does not explain trade in *manufactured goods* because the main force influencing the manufactured-good trade is domestic *demand conditions*. Because much of international trade involves manufactured goods, demand conditions play an important role in explaining overall trade patterns.

Linder states that firms within a country are generally motivated to manufacture goods for which there is a large domestic market. This market determines the set of goods that these firms will have to sell when they begin to export. The foreign markets with greatest export potential will be found in nations with consumer demand similar to those of domestic consumers. A nation's exports are thus an extension of the production for the domestic market.

Going further, Linder contends that consumer demand is conditioned strongly by their income levels. A country's average or *per capita income* will yield a particular

---

[11]Staffan B. Linder, *An Essay on Trade and Transformation* (New York: Wiley, 1961), Chapter 3.

TRADE CONFLICTS   DOES A "FLAT WORLD" MAKE RICARDO WRONG?

The possibility that the United States could lose from free trade is at the heart of some recent critiques of globalization. One critique contends that the world has tended to become "flat" as comparative advantages have dwindled or dried up. Proponents of this view note that as countries such as China and India undergo economic development and become more similar to the United States, a level playing field emerges. The flattening of the world is largely due to countries becoming interconnected as the result of the Internet, wireless technology, search engines and other innovations. Consequently, capitalism has spread like wildfire to China, India, and other countries where factory workers, engineers and software programmers are paid a fraction of what their American counterparts are paid. As China and India develop and become more similar to the United States, the United States could become worse off with trade.

However, not all economists agree with this view. They see several problems with this critique. First, the general view of globalization is that it is a phenomenon marked by increased international economic interdependence. However, the above critique is of a situation in which development in China and India lead to less trade, not more. If China and the United States have differences that allow for gains from trade (for example, differences in technologies and productive capabilities), then removing those differences may decrease the amount of trade and thus decrease the gains from that trade. The worst case scenario in this situation would be a complete elimination of trade. This is the opposite of the typical concern that globalization involves an overly rapid pace of international economic interdependence.

The second problem with the critique is that it ignores the ways in which modern trade differs from Ricardo's simple model. The advanced nations of the world have substantially similar technology and factors of production, and seemingly similar products such as automobiles and electronics are produced in many countries, with substantial trade back and forth. This is at odds with the simplest prediction of the Ricardian model, under which trade should disappear once each country is able to make similar products at comparable prices. Instead, the world has observed substantially increased trade since the end of World War II. This increase reflects the fact that there are gains to *intra-industry trade*, in which broadly similar products are traded in both directions between nations; for example, the United States both imports and exports computer components. Intra-industry trade reflects the advantages garnered by consumers and firms from the increased varieties of similar products made available by trade, as well as the increased competition and higher productivity spurred by trade. Given the historical experience that trade flows have continued to increase between advanced economies even as production technologies have become more similar, one would expect the potential for mutually advantageous trade to remain even if China and India were to develop so rapidly as to have similar technologies and prices as the United States.

Finally, it is argued that the world is not flat at all. While India and China may have very large labor forces, only a small fraction of Indians are prepared to compete with Americans in industries like information technology, while China's authoritarian regime is not compatible with the personal computer. The real problem is that comparative advantage can change very rapidly in a dynamic economy. Boeing might win today, Airbus tomorrow, and then Boeing may be back in play again.

Source: Thomas Friedman, *The World Is Flat*, Farrar, (New York: Straus and Girous, 2005), Jagdish Bhagwati, *In Defense of Globalization*, (New York: Oxford University Press, 2004, Martin Wolf, *Why Globalization Works*, (New Haven, CT: Yale University Press, 2004): and *Economic Report of the President*, 2005, pp. 174–175.

pattern of demand. Nations with high per capita incomes will demand high quality manufactured goods (luxuries), while nations with low per capita incomes will demand lower quality goods (necessities).

The Linder hypothesis explains which nations will most likely trade with each other. Nations with similar per capita incomes will have overlapping demand structures and will likely consume similar types of manufactured goods. Wealthy (industrial) nations are more likely to trade with other wealthy nations, and poor (developing) nations are more likely to trade with other poor nations.

Linder does not rule out all trade in manufactured goods between wealthy and poor nations. Because of unequal income distribution within nations, there will always be some overlapping of demand structures; some people in poor nations are wealthy, and some people in wealthy nations are poor. However, the potential for trade in manufactured goods is small when the extent of demand overlap is small.

Linder's theory is in rough accord with the facts. A high proportion of international trade in manufactured goods takes place among the relatively high income (industrial) nations: Japan, Canada, the United States, and the European nations. Much of this trade involves the exchange of similar products: each nation exports products that are much like the products it imports. However, Linder's theory is not borne out by developing country trade. The bulk of lower income, developing countries tend to have more trade with high income countries than with other lower income countries.

INTRA-INDUSTRY TRADE

The trade models considered so far have dealt with **inter-industry trade**—the exchange between nations of products of different industries. Examples include computers and aircraft traded for textiles and shoes, or finished manufactured items traded for primary materials. Inter-industry trade involves the exchange of goods with *different* factor requirements. Nations having large supplies of skilled labor tend to export sophisticated manufactured products, while nations with large supplies of natural resources export resource–intensive goods. Much of inter-industry trade is between nations having vastly different resource endowments (such as developing countries and industrial countries) and can be explained by the principle of comparative advantage (the Heckscher–Ohlin model).

Inter-industry trade is based on **inter-industry specialization**: each nation specializes in a particular industry (say, steel) in which it enjoys a comparative advantage. As resources shift to the industry with a comparative advantage, certain other industries having comparative disadvantages (say, electronics) contract. Resources move geographically to the industry where comparative costs are lowest. As a result of specialization, a nation experiences a growing *dissimilarity* between the products that it exports and the products it imports.

Although some inter-industry specialization occurs, this generally has not been the type of specialization that industrialized nations have undertaken in the post-World War II era. Rather than emphasizing entire industries, industrial countries have adopted a narrower form of specialization. They have practiced **intra-industry specialization**, focusing on the production of particular products or groups of products within a given industry (for example, subcompact autos rather than full size sedans). With intra-industry specialization, the opening up of trade does not generally result in the elimination or wholesale contraction of entire industries within a nation; however, the range of products produced and sold by each nation changes.

Advanced industrial nations have increasingly emphasized **intra-industry trade**—two-way trade in a similar commodity. Computers manufactured by IBM are sold abroad, while the United States imports computers produced by Hitachi of Japan. Table 3.5 provides examples of intra-industry trade for the United States. As the table indicates, the United States is involved in two-way trade in many goods such as airplanes and computers.

TABLE 3.5

Intra-Industry Trade Examples: Selected U.S. Exports and Imports, 2012 (in millions of dollars)

Category	Exports	Imports
Crude oil	2,504	312,799
Steel	19,787	19,458
Chemicals (inorganic)	35,537	24,763
Civilian aircraft	94,366	10,289
Toys, games, sporting goods	10,450	33,466
Televisions	5,054	33,466
Computers	16,942	65,759
Telecommunications equipment	38,551	52,796

Source: From U.S. Census Bureau, *U.S. International Trade in Goods and Services: FT 900*, 2013. See also U.S. Census Bureau, *Statistical Abstract of the U.S.*

The existence of intra-industry trade appears to be *incompatible* with the models of comparative advantage previously discussed. In the Ricardian and Heckscher–Ohlin models, a country does not simultaneously export and import the same product. California is a major importer of French wines as well as a large exporter of its own wines; the Netherlands imports Lowenbrau beer while exporting Heineken. Intra-industry trade involves flows of goods with *similar* factor requirements. Nations that are net exporters of manufactured goods embodying sophisticated technology also purchase such goods from other nations. Most of intra-industry trade is conducted among industrial countries, especially those in Western Europe, whose resource endowments are similar. The firms that produce these goods tend to be oligopolies, with a few large firms constituting each industry.

Intra-industry trade includes trade in homogeneous goods as well as in differentiated products. For *homogeneous goods*, the reasons for intra-industry trade are easy to grasp. A nation may export and import the same product because of *transportation costs*. Canada and the United States, for example, share a border whose length is several thousand miles. To minimize transportation costs (and thus total costs), a buyer in Albany, New York may import cement from a firm in Montreal, Quebec while a manufacturer in Seattle, Washington sells cement to a buyer in Vancouver, British Columbia. Such trade can be explained by the fact that it is less expensive to transport cement from Montreal to Albany than to ship cement from Seattle to Albany.

Another reason for intra-industry trade in homogeneous goods is *seasonal*. The seasons in the Southern Hemisphere are opposite those in the Northern Hemisphere. Brazil may export seasonal items (such as agricultural products) to the United States at one time of the year and import them from the United States at another time during the same year. Differentiation in time also affects electricity suppliers. Because of heavy fixed costs in electricity production, utilities attempt to keep plants operating close to full capacity, meaning that it may be less costly to export electricity at off-peak times when domestic demand is inadequate to ensure full-capacity utilization and import electricity at peak times.

Although some intra-industry trade occurs in homogeneous products, available evidence suggests that most intra-industry trade occurs in *differentiated products*. Within manufacturing, the levels of intra-industry trade appear to be especially high in machinery, chemicals, and transportation equipment. A significant share of the output of modern economies consists of differentiated products within the same broad product group. Within the automobile industry, a Ford is not identical to a Honda, a Toyota, or a Chevrolet. Two-way trade flows can occur in differentiated products within the same broad product group.

For industrial countries, intra-industry trade in differentiated manufactured goods often occurs when manufacturers in each country produce for the "majority" consumer demand within their country while ignoring "minority" consumer demand. This unmet need is fulfilled by imported products. Most Japanese consumers prefer Toyotas to General Motors vehicles; yet some Japanese consumers purchase vehicles from General Motors, while Toyotas are exported to the United States. Intra-industry trade increases the range of choices available to consumers in each country, as well as the degree of competition among manufacturers of the same class of product in each country.

Intra-industry trade in differentiated products can also be explained by overlapping demand segments in trading nations. When U.S. manufacturers look overseas for markets in which to sell, they often find them in countries having market segments that are similar; for example, luxury automobiles sold to high-income buyers. Nations with similar income levels can be expected to have similar tastes, and thus sizable overlapping market segments as envisioned by Linder's theory of overlapping demand; they are expected to engage heavily in intra-industry trade.

Besides marketing factors, economies of scale associated with differentiated products also explain intra-industry trade. A nation may enjoy a cost advantage over its foreign competitor by specializing in a few varieties and styles of a product (for example, subcompact autos with a standard transmission and optional equipment) while its foreign competitor enjoys a cost advantage by specializing in other variants of the same product (subcompact autos with automatic transmission, air conditioning, DVD player, and other optional equipment). Such specialization permits longer production runs, economies of scale, and decreasing unit costs. Each nation exports its particular type of auto to the other nation, resulting in two-way auto trade. In contrast to inter-industry trade that is explained by the principle of comparative advantage, intra-industry trade can be explained by *product differentiation and economies of scale*.

With intra-industry specialization, fewer adjustment problems are likely to occur than with inter-industry specialization, because intra-industry specialization requires a shift of resources within an industry instead of between industries. Inter-industry specialization results in a transfer of resources from import-competing to export-expanding sectors of the economy. Adjustment difficulties can occur when resources, notably labor, are occupationally and geographically immobile in the short-term; massive structural unemployment may result. In contrast, intra-industry specialization often occurs without requiring workers to exit from a particular region or industry (as when workers are shifted from the production of large-size automobiles to subcompacts); the probability of structural unemployment is lessened.

TECHNOLOGY AS A SOURCE OF COMPARATIVE ADVANTAGE: THE PRODUCT CYCLE THEORY

The explanations of international trade presented so far are similar in that they presuppose a *given* and unchanging state of technology that is the process firms use to turn inputs into goods and services. The basis for trade was ultimately attributed to such factors as differing labor productivities, factor endowments, and national demand structures. In a dynamic world, technological changes occur in different nations at different rates of speed. Technological innovations commonly result in new methods of producing existing commodities, production of new commodities, or commodity improvements. These factors can affect comparative advantage and the pattern of trade.

Japanese automobile companies such as Toyota and Honda have succeeded by greatly improving the processes for designing and manufacturing automobiles. This improvement allowed Japan to become the world's largest exporter of automobiles, selling large numbers to Americans and people in other countries. Japan's comparative advantage in automobiles has been supported by the superior production techniques developed by that country's manufacturers that allowed them to produce more vehicles with a given amount of capital and labor than their European or American counterparts. Therefore, Japan's comparative advantage in automobiles is caused by differences in technology; the techniques in production.

Although differences in technology are an important source of comparative advantage at a particular point in time, technological advantage is often transitory. A country may lose its comparative advantage as its technological advantage disappears. Recognition of the importance of such dynamic changes has given rise to another explanation of international trade: the **product life cycle theory**. This theory focuses on the role of technological innovation as a key determinant of the trade patterns in manufactured products.[12]

According to this theory, many manufactured goods such as electronic products and office machinery undergo a predictable *trade cycle*. During this cycle, the home country initially is an exporter, then loses its competitive advantage to its trading partners and eventually may become an importer of the commodity. The stages that many manufactured goods go through comprise the following:

1. Manufactured good is introduced to home market.
2. Domestic industry shows export strength.
3. Foreign production begins.
4. Domestic industry loses competitive advantage.
5. Import competition begins.

The introduction stage of the trade cycle begins when an innovator establishes a technological breakthrough in the production of a manufactured good. At the start, the relatively small local market for the product and technological uncertainties imply that mass production is not feasible. The manufacturer will most likely operate close to the local market to gain quick feedback on the quality and overall appeal of the product. Production occurs on a small scale using high skilled workers. The high price of the new product will also offer high returns to the specialized capital stock needed to produce the new product.

During the trade cycle's next stage, the domestic manufacturer begins to export its product to foreign markets having similar tastes and income levels. The local manufacturer finds that during this stage of growth and expansion, its market becomes large enough to expand production operations and sort out inefficient production techniques. The home country manufacturer is therefore able to supply increasing amounts to the world markets.

As the product matures and its price falls, the capability for standardized production results in the possibility that more efficient production can occur by using low-wage labor and mass production. At this stage in the product's life, it is most likely that production will move toward economies that have resource endowments relatively plentiful in low-wage labor, such as China or Malaysia. The domestic industry enters its mature stage as innovating businesses establish branches abroad and the outsourcing of jobs occurs.

---

[12]See Raymond Vernon, "International Investment and International Trade in the Product Life Cycle," *Quarterly Journal of Economics*, 80, 1966, pp. 190–207.

Although an innovating nation's monopoly position may be prolonged by legal patents, it will most likely break down over time because in the long-term, knowledge tends to be a free good. The benefits an innovating nation achieves from its technological gap are short lived, because import competition from foreign producers begins. Once the innovative technology becomes fairly commonplace, foreign producers begin to imitate the production process. The innovating nation gradually loses its comparative advantage and its export cycle enters a declining phase.

The trade cycle is complete when the production process becomes so standardized that it can be easily used by other nations. The technological breakthrough therefore no longer benefits only the innovating nation. In fact, the innovating nation may itself become a net importer of the product as its monopoly position is eliminated by foreign competition.

The product life cycle theory has implications for innovating countries such as the United States. The gains from trade for the United States are significantly determined by the dynamic balance between its rate of technological innovation and the rate of its technological diffusion to other countries. Unless the United States can generate a pace of innovation to match the pace of diffusion, its share of the gains from trade will decrease. Also, it can be argued that the advance of globalization has accelerated the rate of technological diffusion. What this advance suggests is that preserving or increasing the economy's gains from trade in the face of globalization will require acceleration in the pace of innovation in goods and service–producing activities.

The product life cycle theory also provides lessons for a firm desiring to maintain its competitiveness: to prevent rivals from catching up, it must continually innovate so as to become more efficient. Toyota Motor Corporation is generally regarded as the auto industry's leader in production efficiency. To maintain this position, the firm has continually overhauled its operations and work practices. In 2008, Toyota was working to decrease the number of components it uses in a typical vehicle by half and develop faster and more flexible plants to assemble these simplified cars. This simplification would allow workers to churn out nearly a dozen different cars on the same production line at a speed of one every 50 seconds, compared to Toyota's fastest plant that produces a vehicle every 56 seconds. The cut would increase the output per worker and reduce costs by about $1,000 per vehicle. By pushing out the efficiency target, Toyota was attempting to prevent the latter stages of the product cycle from occurring.

Radios, Pocket Calculators, and the International Product Cycle

The experience of U.S. and Japanese radio manufacturers illustrates the product life cycle model. Following World War II, the radio was a well-established product. U.S. manufacturers dominated the international market for radios because vacuum tubes were initially developed in the United States. As production technologies spread, Japan used cheaper labor and captured a large share of the world radio market. The transistor was then developed by U.S. companies. For a number of years, U.S. radio manufacturers were able to compete with the Japanese, who continued to use outdated technologies. Again, the Japanese imitated the U.S. technologies and were able to sell radios at more competitive prices.

Pocket calculators provide another illustration of a product that has moved through the stages of the international product cycle. This product was invented in 1961 by engineers at Sunlock Comptometer, Inc. and was marketed soon after at a price of approximately $1,000. Sunlock's pocket calculator was more accurate than slide rules (widely used by high school and college students at that time) and more portable than large mechanical calculators and computers that performed many of the same functions.

By 1970, several U.S. and Japanese companies had entered the market with competing pocket calculators; these firms included Texas Instruments, Hewlett-Packard, and Casio (of Japan). The increased competition forced the price down to about $400. As the 1970s progressed, additional companies entered the market. Several began to assemble their pocket calculators in foreign countries, such as Singapore and Taiwan, to take advantage of lower labor costs. These calculators were then shipped to the United States. Steadily improving technologies resulted in product improvements and falling prices; by the mid-1970s, pocket calculators sold routinely for $10 to $20, sometimes even less. It appears that pocket calculators had reached the standardized product stage of the product cycle by the late 1970s, with product technology available throughout the industry, price competition (and thus costs) of major significance, and product differentiation widely adopted. In a period of less than two decades, the international product cycle for pocket calculators was complete.

Japan Fades in the Electronics Industry

The essence of the product cycle theory can also be seen in the Japanese electronics industry.[13] In the late 1980s, Japan seemed prepared to dominate the world's electronics market. The Japanese had seemingly formulated a superior business model where active government intervention in export oriented industries, along with protection of Japanese firms from foreign competition, led to high growth rates and trade surpluses. Japan's achievements in electronics were notable as Sharp, Panasonic, Sony, and other Japanese firms flooded the world market with their cameras, television sets, video cassette recorders (VCRs), and the like.

The Japanese electronics industry weakened during the first decade of the 2000s, with exports declining and losses increasing. Japanese executives blamed their problems on the appreciation of the yen's exchange value that made their products more expensive and less attractive to foreign buyers. A strong yen could not assume all of the burden for Japan's problems. According to analysts, the main source of the problem was Japanese firms' ignorance of two basic principles. First, as countries mature, their sources of comparative advantage change. Although abundant skilled labor, inexpensive capital, and price may initially be critical determinants of competitiveness, as time passes, innovation in products and production processes becomes more significant. Second, competitiveness is not just about what products to offer to the market, but also about what products not to offer.

Ignoring these principles, Japanese firms attempted to compete with upstart electronics firms like Samsung (South Korea) on the basis of inexpensive capital and manufacturing efficiency rather than product innovation. The Japanese kept producing products that were formerly profitable, such as semiconductors and consumer audio-video products that eventually lost market share to newly invented products from abroad. Also, when Japanese firms failed, their solution was mergers. Their rationale was that combining several losing firms into one would turn them into a winner as the result of economies of large scale production. However, the merger of Japanese electronics firms could not keep pace with the rapidly changing world of digital electronics. Firms such as Intel and Texas Instruments abandoned standardized products, where price is key to competitiveness, and invented more sophisticated and profitable products, thus leapfrogging the Japanese.

---

[13]Richard Katz, "What's Killing Japanese Electronics?" *The Wall Street Journal*, March 22, 2012, at http://online.wsj.com/; Michael Porter, "The Five Competitive Forces That Shape Strategy", *Harvard Business Review*, January 2008, pp. 79–93; Ian King, "Micron Biggest Winner as Elpida Bankruptcy Sidelines Rival," *Bloomberg News*, February 27, 2012 at http://www.bloomberg.com/.

Today almost four-fifths of Japan's electronics output consists of parts and components that often go into other firm's products, such as Apples' iPad. However, most of the profit goes to Apple that invents new and popular products rather than the firms that produce their parts. Whether its smartphones or personal computers, Japanese firms are no longer the market leaders.

DYNAMIC COMPARATIVE ADVANTAGE: INDUSTRIAL POLICY

David Ricardo's theory of comparative advantage has influenced international trade theory and policy for almost 200 years. It implies that nations are better off by promoting free trade and allowing competitive markets to determine what should be produced and how.

Ricardian theory emphasizes specialization and reallocation of existing resources found domestically. It is essentially a static theory that does not allow for a dynamic change in industries' comparative advantage or disadvantage over the course of several decades. The theory overlooks the fact that additional resources can be made available to the trading nation because they can be created or imported.

The remarkable postwar economic growth of the East Asian countries appears to be based on a modification of the static concept of comparative advantage. The Japanese were among the first to recognize that comparative advantage in a particular industry can be created through the mobilization of skilled labor, technology, and capital. They also realized that, in addition to the business sector, government can establish policies to promote opportunities for change through time. Such a process is known as **dynamic comparative advantage**. When government is actively involved in creating comparative advantage, the term **industrial policy** applies.

In its simplest form, industrial policy is a strategy to revitalize, improve, and develop an industry. Proponents maintain that government should enact policies that encourage the development of emerging, "sunrise" industries (such as high-technology). This strategy requires that resources be directed to industries in which productivity is highest, linkages to the rest of the economy are strong (as with semiconductors), and future competitiveness is important. Presumably, the domestic economy will enjoy a higher average level of productivity and will be more competitive in world markets as a result of such policies.

A variety of government policies can be used to foster the development and revitalization of industries; examples are antitrust immunity, tax incentives, R&D subsidies, loan guarantees, low-interest-rate loans, and trade protection. Creating comparative advantage requires government to identify the "winners" and encourage resources to move into industries with the highest growth prospects.

To better understand the significance of dynamic comparative advantage, we might think of it in terms of the classic example of Ricardo's theory of comparative advantage. His example showed that, in the eighteenth century, Portugal and England would each have gained by specializing respectively in the production of wine and cloth, even though Portugal might produce both cloth and wine more cheaply than England. According to static comparative advantage theory, both nations would be better off by specializing in the product in which they had an existing comparative advantage.

However, by adhering to this prescription, Portugal would sacrifice long-run growth for short-run gains. If Portugal adopted a dynamic theory of comparative advantage instead, it would specialize in the growth industry of that time (cloth). The Portuguese government (or Portuguese textile manufacturers) would initiate policies to foster the development of its cloth industry. This strategy would require Portugal to think in terms of acquiring or creating strength in a "sunrise" sector instead of simply accepting the existing supply of resources and using that endowment as productively as possible.

Countries have used industrial policies to develop or revitalize basic industries, including steel, autos, chemicals, transportation, and other important manufactures. Each of these industrial policies differs in character and approach; common to all is an active role for government in the economy. Usually, industrial policy is a strategy developed collectively by government, business, and labor through some sort of tripartite consultation process.

Advocates of industrial policy typically cite Japan as a nation that has been highly successful in penetrating foreign markets and achieving rapid economic growth. Following World War II, the Japanese were the high-cost producers in many basic industries (such as steel). In this situation, a static notion of comparative advantage would require the Japanese to look to areas of lesser disadvantage that were more labor intensive (such as textiles). Such a strategy would have forced Japan into low-productivity industries that would eventually compete with other East Asian nations having abundant labor and modest living standards.

Instead, the Japanese invested in basic industries (steel, autos, and later electronics, including computers) that required intensive employment of capital and labor. From a short-run, static perspective, Japan appeared to pick the wrong industries. From a long-run perspective, those were the industries in which technological progress was rapid, labor productivity rose quickly, and unit costs decreased with the expansion of output. They were also industries that one would expect rapid growth in demand as national income increased.

These industries combined the potential to expand rapidly, thus adding new capacity, with the opportunity to use the latest technology and promote a strategy of cost reduction founded on increasing productivity. Japan, placed in a position similar to that of Portugal in Ricardo's famous example, refused to specialize in "wine" and chose "cloth" instead. Within three decades, Japan became the world's premier low-cost producer of many of the products that it initially started in a high-cost position.

Critics of industrial policy contend that the causal factor in Japanese industrial success is unclear. They admit that some of the Japanese government's targeted industries—such as semiconductors, steel, shipbuilding, and machine tools—are probably more competitive than they would have been in the absence of government assistance. They assert that Japan also targeted some losers, such as petrochemicals and aluminum, and that the returns on investment were disappointing and capacity had to be reduced. Moreover, several successful Japanese industries did not receive government assistance—motorcycles, bicycles, paper, glass, and cement.

Industrial-policy critics contend that if all trading nations took the route of using a combination of trade restrictions on imports and subsidies on exports, a "beggar-thy-neighbor" process of trade-inhibiting protectionism would result. They also point out that the implementation of industrial policies can result in pork barrel politics, in which politically powerful industries receive government assistance. It is argued that in a free market, profit maximizing businesses have the incentive to develop new resources and technologies that change a country's comparative advantage. This incentive raises the question of whether the government does a better job than the private sector in creating comparative advantage.

WTO RULES THAT ILLEGAL GOVERNMENT SUBSIDIES SUPPORT BOEING AND AIRBUS

An example of industrial policy is the government subsidies that apply to the commercial jetliner industry as seen in Boeing and Airbus. The world's manufacturers of commercial jetliners operate in an oligopolistic market that has been dominated by

Boeing of the United States and the Airbus Company of Europe, although competition is emerging from producers in Canada, Brazil, China, and other countries. During the 1970s, Airbus sold less than 5.0 percent of the world's jetliners; today, it accounts for about half of the world market.

The United States has repeatedly complained that Airbus receives unfair subsidies from European governments. American officials argue that these subsidies place their company at a competitive disadvantage. Airbus allegedly receives loans for the development of new aircraft; these loans are made at below market interest rates and can amount to 70 to 90 percent of an aircraft's development cost. Rather than repaying the loans according to a prescribed timetable as typically would occur in a competitive market, Airbus can repay them after it delivers an aircraft. Airbus can avoid repaying the loans in full if sales of its aircraft fall short. Although Airbus says that has never occurred, Boeing contends that Airbus has an advantage by lowering its commercial risk, making it easier to obtain financing. The United States maintains that these subsidies allow Airbus to set unrealistically low prices, offer concessions and attractive financing terms to airlines, and write off development costs.

Airbus has defended its subsidies on the grounds that they prevent the United States from holding a worldwide monopoly in commercial jetliners. In the absence of Airbus, European airlines would have to rely exclusively on Boeing as a supplier. Fears of dependence and the loss of autonomy in an area on the cutting edge of technology motivate European governments to subsidize Airbus.

Airbus also argues that Boeing benefits from government assistance. Rather than receiving direct subsidies like Airbus, Boeing receives indirect subsidies. Governmental organizations support aeronautics and propulsion research that is shared with Boeing. Support for commercial jetliner innovation also comes from military sponsored research and military procurement. Research financed by the armed services yields indirect but important technological spillovers to the commercial jetliner industry, most notably in aircraft engines and aircraft design. Boeing subcontracts part of the production of its jetliners to nations such as Japan and China whose producers receive substantial governmental subsidies. The state of Washington provides tax breaks to Boeing who has substantial production facilities in the state. According to Airbus, these subsidies enhance Boeing's competitiveness.

As a result of the subsidy conflict between Boeing and Airbus, the United States and Europe in 1992 negotiated an agreement to curb subsidies for the two manufacturers. The principal element of the accord was a 33 percent cap on the amount of government subsidies that these manufacturers could receive for product development. In addition, the indirect subsidies were limited to 4.0 percent of a firm's commercial jetliner revenue.

Although the subsidy agreement helped calm trade tensions between the United States and Europe, by the first decade of the 2000s the subsidy dispute was heating up again. The United States criticized the European Union for granting subsidies to Airbus and called for the European Union to renegotiate the 1992 subsidy deal. In 2005, Boeing and Airbus filed suits at the World Trade Organization (WTO) that contended that each company was receiving illegal subsidies from the governments of Europe and the United States.

During 2010–2011, the WTO ruled that both Boeing and Airbus received illegal subsidies from their governments. The WTO determined that Airbus received about $20 billion in illegal aid and that about $2.7 in illegal aid was granted to Boeing. In response to these rulings, Boeing stated that it was prepared to accept compliance and thus not receive illegal aid. However, Airbus resisted abandoning aid from the governments of Europe.

At the writing of this text in 2014, the subsidy dispute continued. Both Boeing and Airbus accused each other of not complying with the WTO's rulings concerning the illegality of their subsidies. It remains to be seen how compliance with the rulings will be resolved.

TRADE CONFLICTS   DO LABOR UNIONS STIFLE COMPETITIVENESS?

For more than a century, labor unions have attempted to improve wages, benefits, and working conditions for their members. In the United States, unions represented about one-third of all workers in the 1950s. By 2011, unions represented only about 12 percent of the American labor force–8 percent of the labor force in the private sector and 36 percent of public sector workers. Many private sector union members belong to industrial unions, such as the United Auto Workers (UAW), which represents workers at American auto firms, tractor and earth moving equipment firms such as Caterpillar and John Deere, and Boeing in the aerospace industry.

During the 1950s and 1960s, organized labor in the United States was generally receptive to free trade, an era when U.S. producers were strong in international markets. However, labor union leaders began to express their concerns about free trade in the 1970s as their members encountered increased competition from producers in Japan and Western Europe. Since that time, American union leaders have generally opposed efforts to liberalize trade.

Some analysts note that unions can have adverse effects on firms' competitiveness when they set wages and benefits above those of a competitive market. Unions can also impose restrictive work rules that decrease productivity and stifle innovation. Also, union emphasis on seniority over merit in promotion and pay can hinder the incentive for worker effort. Moreover, strikes can lessen a firm's ability to maintain market share.

An influential study by Hirsch concluded that unions tend to result in compensation rising faster than productivity, diminishing profits while also lessening the ability of firms to remain price competitive. This has caused unionized companies to lose market share to nonunionized firms in domestic and international markets: classic examples of this tendency include American auto and steel companies. Hirsch found that unions will typically raise labor costs to a firm by 15 to 20 percent, while delivering a negligible increase in productivity. Thus, the profits of unionized firms tend to be 10 to 20 percent lower than similar nonunion firms. Also, the typical unionized firm has 6 percent lower capital investment than an equivalent nonunion firm, and a 15 percent lower share of spending on research and development. However, Hirsch found that the evidence does not show a higher failure rate among unionized firms.

However, other analysts contend that unions can increase the sense of worker loyalty to the firm and decrease worker turnover, thus increasing worker productivity and reducing costs to the firm for hiring and training. They also note that unions are a major force for greater social equality, and it is virtually impossible to have decent health care, pensions and other worker benefits without a strong labor movement. Moreover, they note that the United States, which has a far lower rate of unionization than many other advanced countries, has consistently maintained huge trade deficits. If low rates of unionization determine trade competitiveness, shouldn't the United States be close to the top?

Source: Daniel Griswold, "Unions, Protectionism, and U.S. Competitiveness," *Cato Journal*, Vol. 30, No. 1, Winter 2010, pp. 181–196. See also Barry Hirsch, "Sluggish Institutions in a Dynamic World: Can Unions and Industrial Competition Coexist?" *Journal of Economic Perspectives*, 2008, Vol. 22, No. 1 and Richard Freeman and James Medoff, *What Do Unions Do?* New York, Basic Books, 1984.

iStockphoto.com/photosoup

GOVERNMENT REGULATORY POLICIES AND COMPARATIVE ADVANTAGE

Besides providing subsidies to enhance competitiveness, governments impose regulations on business to pursue goals such as workplace safety, product safety, and a clean environment. In the United States, these regulations are imposed by the Occupational Safety and Health Administration, the Consumer Product Safety Commission, and the Environmental Protection Agency. Although government regulations may improve the wellbeing of the public, they can result in higher costs for domestic firms. According to the American Iron and Steel Institute, U.S. steel producers today are technologically advanced, low-cost, environmentally responsible, and customer focused. Yet they continue to face regulatory burdens from the U.S. government that impair their competitiveness and trade prospects.

Strict government regulations applied to the production of goods and services tend to increase costs and erode an industry's competitiveness. This is relevant for both export and import competing firms. Even if government regulations are justified on social welfare grounds, the adverse impact on trade competitiveness and the associated job loss have long been a cause for policy concern. Let us examine how governmental regulations on business can affect comparative advantage.

Figure 3.6 illustrates the trade effects of pollution regulations imposed on the production process. Assume a world of two steel producers, South Korea and the United States. The supply and demand schedules of South Korea and those of the United States are indicated by $S_{S.K.0}$ and $D_{S.K.0}$, and by $S_{U.S.0}$ and $D_{U.S.0}$. In the absence of trade, South Korean producers sell 5 tons of steel at $400 per ton, while 12 tons of steel are sold in the United States at $600 per ton. South Korea thus enjoys a comparative advantage in steel production.

With free trade, South Korea moves toward greater specialization in steel production, and the United States produces less steel. Under increasing-cost conditions, South Korea's costs and prices rise, while prices and costs fall in the United States. The basis for further growth of trade is eliminated when prices in the two countries are equal at $500 per ton. At this price, South Korea produces 7 tons, consumes 3 tons, and exports 4 tons, and the United States produces 10 tons, consumes 14 tons, and imports 4 tons.

Suppose that the production of steel results in discharges into U.S. waterways, leading the Environmental Protection Agency to impose pollution regulations on domestic steel producers. Meeting these regulations adds to production costs, resulting in the U.S. supply schedule of steel shifting to $S_{U.S.1}$. The environmental regulations thus provide

FIGURE 3.6

Trade Effects of Governmental Regulations

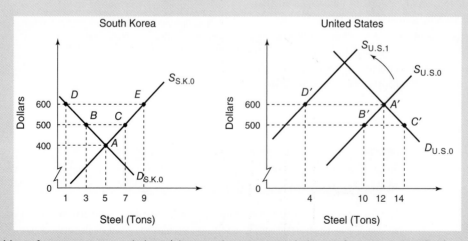

The imposition of government regulations (clean environment, workplace safety, product safety) on U.S. steel companies leads to higher costs and a decrease in market supply. This imposition detracts from the competitiveness of U.S. steel companies and reduces their share of the U.S. steel market.

an additional cost advantage for South Korean steel companies. As South Korean companies expand steel production, say, to 9 tons, higher production costs result in a rise in price to $600. At this price, South Korean consumers demand only 1 ton. The excess supply of 8 tons is earmarked for sale to the United States. As for the United States, 12 tons of steel are demanded at the price of $600, as determined by South Korea. Given supply schedule $S_{U.S.1}$, U.S. firms now produce only 4 tons of steel at the $600 price. The excess demand, 8 tons, is met by imports from South Korea. For U.S. steel companies, the costs imposed by pollution regulations lead to further comparative disadvantage and a smaller share of the U.S. market.

Environmental regulation thus results in a policy trade-off for the United States. By adding to the costs of domestic steel companies, environmental regulations make the United States more dependent on foreign-produced steel. However, regulations provide American households with cleaner water and air, and thus a higher quality of life. Also, the competitiveness of other American industries, such as forestry products, may benefit from cleaner air and water. These effects must be considered when forming an optimal environmental regulatory policy. The same principle applies to the regulation of workplace safety by the Occupational Safety and Health Administration and the regulation of product safety by the Consumer Product Safety Commission.

TRANSPORTATION COSTS AND COMPARATIVE ADVANTAGE

Besides embodying production costs, the principle of comparative advantage includes the costs of moving goods from one nation to another. **Transportation costs** refer to the costs of moving goods, including freight charges, packing and handling expenses, and insurance premiums. These costs are an obstacle to trade and impede the realization of gains from trade liberalization. Differences across countries in transport costs are a source of comparative advantage and affect the volume and composition of trade.

Trade Effects

The trade effects of transportation costs can be illustrated with a conventional supply and demand model based on increasing-cost conditions. Figure 3.7(a) illustrates the supply and demand curves of autos for the United States and Canada. Reflecting the assumption that the United States has the comparative advantage in auto production, the U.S. and Canadian equilibrium locations are at points E and F, respectively. In the absence of trade, the U.S. auto price, $4,000, is lower than that of Canada, $8,000.

When trade is allowed, the United States will move toward greater specialization in auto production, whereas Canada will produce fewer autos. Under increasing-cost conditions, the U.S. cost and price levels rise and Canada's price falls. The basis for further growth of trade is eliminated when the two countries' prices are equal, at $6,000. At this price, the United States produces 6 autos, consumes 2 autos, and exports 4 autos; Canada produces 2 autos, consumes 6 autos, and imports 4 autos. Therefore, $6,000 becomes the equilibrium price for both countries because the excess auto supply of the United States just matches the excess auto demand in Canada.

The introduction of transportation costs into the analysis modifies the conclusions of this example. Suppose the per-unit cost of transporting an auto from the United States to Canada is $2,000, as shown in Figure 3.7(b). The United States would find it advantageous to produce autos and export them to Canada until its relative price advantage is eliminated. But when transportation costs are included in the analysis, the U.S. export

FIGURE 3.7

Free Trade Under Increasing-Cost Conditions

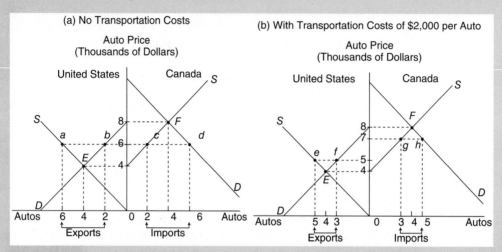

In the absence of transportation costs, free trade results in the equalization of prices of traded goods, as well as resource prices, in the trading nations. With the introduction of transportation costs, the low-cost exporting nation produces less, consumes more, and exports less; the high-cost importing nation produces more, consumes less, and imports less. The degree of specialization in production between the two nations decreases as do the gains from trade.

© Cengage Learning®

price reflects domestic production costs *plus* the cost of transporting autos to Canada. The basis for trade thus ceases to exist when the U.S. auto price plus the transportation cost rises to equal Canada's auto price. This equalization occurs when the U.S. auto price rises to $5,000 and Canada's auto price falls to $7,000, the difference between them being the $2,000 per-unit transportation cost. Instead of a single price ruling in both countries, there will be two domestic auto prices, differing by the cost of transportation.

Compared with free trade in the absence of transportation costs, when transportation costs are included the high-cost importing country will produce more, consume less, and import less. The low-cost exporting country will produce less, consume more, and export less. Transportation costs, therefore, tend to reduce the volume of trade, the degree of specialization in production among the nations concerned, and thus the gains from trade.

The inclusion of transportation costs in the analysis modifies our trade model conclusions. A product will be traded internationally as long as the pre-trade price differential between the trading partners is greater than the cost of transporting the product between them. When trade is in equilibrium, the price of the traded product in the exporting nation is less than the price in the importing country by the amount of the transportation cost.

Transportation costs also have implications for the factor-price equalization theory presented earlier in this chapter. Recall that this theory suggests that free trade tends to equalize product prices and factor prices so that all workers earn the same wage rate and all units of capital earn the same interest income in both nations. Free trade permits factor-price equalization to occur because factor inputs that cannot move to another country are implicitly being shipped in the form of products. However, looking at the real world we see U.S. autoworkers earning more than South Korean autoworkers. One possible reason for this differential is transportation costs. By making low-cost South Korean autos more expensive for U.S. consumers, transportation costs reduce the volume of autos shipped from South Korea to the United States. This reduced trade volume stops the process of commodity- and factor-price equalization before it is complete. In other words, the prices of U.S. autos and the wages of U.S. autoworkers do not fall to the levels of those in South Korea. Transportation costs thus provide some relief to high-cost domestic workers who are producing goods subject to import competition.

The cost of shipping a product from one point to another is determined by a number of factors, including distance, weight, size, value, and the volume of trade between the two points in question. Since the 1960s, the cost of international transportation has decreased significantly relative to the value of U.S. imports. From 1965 to the first decade of the 2000s, transportation costs as a percentage of the value of all U.S. imports decreased from ten percent to less than four percent. This decline in the relative cost of international transportation has made imports more competitive in U.S. markets and contributed to a higher volume of trade for the United States. Falling transportation costs have been due largely to technological improvements, including the development of large dry-bulk containers, large-scale tankers, containerization, and wide-bodied jets. Moreover, technological advances in telecommunications have reduced the economic distances among nations.[14]

Falling Transportation Costs Foster Trade

If merchants everywhere appear to be selling imports, there is a reason. International trade has been growing at a rapid pace. What underlies the expansion of international commerce? The worldwide decrease in trade barriers, such as tariffs and quotas, is certainly one reason. The economic opening of nations that have traditionally been minor players, such as Mexico and China, is another. But one factor behind the trade boom has largely been unnoticed: the declining costs of getting goods to the market.

Today, transportation costs are a less severe obstacle than they used to be. One reason is that the global economy has become much less transport intensive than it once was. In the early 1900s, for example, manufacturing and agriculture were the two most important industries in most nations. International trade thus emphasized raw materials, such as iron ore and wheat, or processed goods such as steel. These sorts of goods are heavy and bulky, resulting in a relatively high-cost of transporting them compared with the value of the goods themselves. As a result, transportation costs had much to do with the volume of trade. Over time, however, world output has shifted into goods whose value is unrelated to their size and weight. Finished manufactured goods, not raw commodities, dominate the flow of trade. Therefore, less transportation is required for every dollar's worth of exports or imports.

Productivity improvements for transporting goods have also resulted in falling transportation costs. In the early 1900s, the physical process of importing or exporting was difficult. Imagine a British textile firm desiring to sell its product in the United States. First, at the firm's loading dock, workers would have lifted bolts of fabric into the back of a truck. The truck would head to a port and unload its cargo, bolt by bolt, into a dockside

---

[14]Jean-Paul Rodrigue, *Transportation, Globalization and International Trade*, 2013, New York, Routledge; Alberto Behar and Anthony Venables, "Transportation Costs and International Trade," *Handbook of Transport Economics*, Ed. Andre de Palma and others, Edward Elgar, Northampton MA, 2010; David Hummels, "Transportation Costs and International Trade in the Second Era of Globalization," *Journal of Economic Perspectives*, Vol. 21, No. 3, Summer 2007, pp. 131–154.

warehouse. As a vessel prepared to set sail, dockworkers would remove the bolts from the warehouse and hoist them into the hold, where other dockworkers would stow them in place. When the cargo reached the United States, the process would be reversed. Indeed, this sort of shipment was a complicated task, requiring much effort and expense. With the passage of time came technological improvements such as modern ocean liners, standard containers for shipping goods, computerized loading ports, and freight companies such as United Parcel Service and Federal Express that specialize in using a combination of aircraft and trucks to deliver freight quickly. These and other factors have resulted in falling transportation costs and increased trade among nations.

Recent decades have witnessed a growth in world trade that was supported by decreases in transportation costs and trade barriers. However, when oil prices surged in 2008 and 2011, rising transport costs became an increasing challenge to world trade. For example, economists estimated that transportation costs were the equivalent of a 10–11 percent tariff on goods coming into U.S. ports when the price of a barrel of oil rose to $145 per barrel in 2008. This is compared with the equivalent of only three percent when oil was selling for $20 a barrel in 2000.

Rising shipping costs suggest that trade should be both dampened and diverted as markets look for shorter, and thus, less costly transportation routes. As transportation cost rise, markets tend to substitute goods that are from closer locations rather than from locations half way around the world carrying hugely inflated shipping costs. For example, Emerson Electric Co., a St. Louis based manufacturer of appliance motors and other electrical equipment, shifted some of its production from Asia to Mexico and the United States in 2008, in part to offset increasing transportation costs by being closer to customers in North America.

SUMMARY

1. The immediate basis for trade stems from relative product price differences among nations. Because relative prices are determined by supply and demand conditions, such factors as resource endowments, technology, and national income are ultimate determinants of the basis for trade.

2. The factor-endowment theory suggests that differences in relative factor endowments among nations underlie the basis for trade. The theory asserts that a nation will export that product in the production of which a relatively large amount of its abundant and cheap resource is used. Conversely, it will import commodities in the production of which a relatively scarce and expensive resource is used. The theory also states that with trade, the relative differences in resource prices between nations tend to be eliminated.

3. According to the Stolper–Samuelson theorem, increases in income occur for the abundant resource

that is used to determine comparative advantage. Conversely, the scarce factor realizes a decrease in income.

4. The specific-factors theory analyzes the income distribution effects of trade in the short run when resources are immobile among industries. It concludes that resources specific to export industries tend to gain as a result of trade.

5. Contrary to the predictions of the factor endowment model, the empirical tests of Wassily Leontief demonstrated that for the U.S. exports are labor intensive and import competing goods are capital intensive. His findings became known as the Leontief paradox.

6. By widening the size of the domestic market, international trade permits firms to take advantage of longer production runs and increasing efficiencies (such as mass production). Such economies of scale

can be translated into lower product prices, which improve a firm's competitiveness.

7. Staffan Linder offers two explanations for world trade patterns. Trade in primary products and agricultural goods conforms well to the factor-endowment theory. But trade in manufactured goods is best explained by overlapping demand structures among nations. For manufactured goods, the basis for trade is stronger when the structure of demand in the two nations is more similar—that is, when the nations' per capita incomes are similar.

8. Besides inter-industry trade, the exchange of goods among nations includes intra-industry trade—two-way trade in a similar product. Intra-industry trade occurs in homogeneous goods as well as in differentiated products.

9. One dynamic theory of international trade is the product life cycle theory. This theory views a variety of manufactured goods as going through a trade cycle, during which a nation initially is an exporter, then loses its export markets, and finally becomes an importer of the product. Empirical studies have demonstrated that trade cycles do exist for manufactured goods at some times.

10. Dynamic comparative advantage refers to the creation of comparative advantage through the mobilization of skilled labor, technology, and capital; it can be initiated by either the private or public sector. When government attempts to create comparative advantage, the term *industrial policy* applies. Industrial policy seeks to encourage the development of emerging, sunrise industries through such measures as tax incentives and R&D subsidies.

11. Business regulations can affect the competitive position of industries. These regulations often result in cost increasing compliance measures, such as the installation of pollution control equipment, which can detract from the competitiveness of domestic industries.

12. International trade includes the flow of services between countries as well as the exchange of manufactured goods. As with trade in manufactured goods, the principle of comparative advantage applies to trade in services.

13. Transportation costs tend to reduce the volume of international trade by increasing the prices of traded goods. A product will be traded only if the cost of transporting it between nations is less than the pre-trade difference between their relative commodity prices.

KEY CONCEPTS AND TERMS

Capital/labor ratio (p. 70)
Dynamic comparative advantage (p. 96)
Economies of scale (p. 85)
External economies of scale (p. 87)
Factor-endowment theory (p. 70)
Factor-price equalization (p. 76)
Heckscher–Ohlin theory (p. 70)

Home market effect (p. 87)
Industrial policy (p. 96)
internal economies of scale (p. 86)
Inter-industry specialization (p. 90)
Inter-industry trade (p. 90)
Intra-industry specialization (p. 90)
Intra-industry trade (p. 90)
Leontief paradox (p. 84)

Magnification effect (p. 79)
Product life cycle theory (p. 93)
Specific-factors theory (p. 81)
Stolper–Samuelson theorem (p. 78)
Theory of overlapping demands (p. 88)
Transportation costs (p. 101)

STUDY QUESTIONS

1. What are the effects of transportation costs on international trade patterns?
2. Explain how the international movement of products and of factor inputs promotes an equalization of the factor prices among nations.

3. How does the factor-endowment theory differ from Ricardian theory in explaining international trade patterns?
4. The factor-endowment theory demonstrates how trade affects the distribution of income within trading partners. Explain.

5. How does the Leontief paradox challenge the overall applicability of the factor-endowment model?

6. According to Staffan Linder, there are two explanations for international trade patterns—one for manufactures and another for primary (agricultural) goods. Explain.

7. Do recent world trade statistics support or refute the notion of a product life cycle for manufactured goods?

8. How can economies of scale affect world trade patterns?

9. Distinguish between intra-industry trade and inter-industry trade. What are some major determinants of intra-industry trade?

10. What is meant by the term *industrial policy*? How do governments attempt to create comparative advantage in sunrise sectors of the economy? What are some problems encountered when attempting to implement industrial policy?

11. How can governmental regulatory policies affect an industry's international competitiveness?

12. International trade in services is determined by what factors?

13. Table 3.6 illustrates the supply and demand schedules for calculators in Sweden and Norway. On graph paper, draw the supply and demand schedules of each country.

   a. In the absence of trade, what are the equilibrium price and quantity of calculators produced in Sweden and Norway? Which country has the comparative advantage in calculators?

   b. Assume there are no transportation costs. With trade, what price brings about balance in exports and imports? How many calculators are traded at this price? How many calculators are produced and consumed in each country with trade?

   c. Suppose the cost of transporting each calculator from Sweden to Norway is $5. With trade, what is the impact of the transportation cost on the price of calculators in Sweden and Norway? How many calculators will each country produce, consume, and trade?

   d. In general, what can be concluded about the impact of transportation costs on the price of the traded product in each trading nation? The extent of specialization? The volume of trade?

TABLE 3.6

Supply and Demand Schedules for Calculators

	SWEDEN			NORWAY	
Price	Quantity supplied	Quantity demanded	Price	Quantity supplied	Quantity demanded
$ 0	0	1200	$0	–	1800
5	200	1000	5	–	1600
10	400	800	10	–	1400
15	600	600	15	0	1200
20	800	400	20	200	1000
25	1000	200	25	400	800
30	1200	0	30	600	600
35	1400	–	35	800	400
40	1600	–	40	1000	200
45	1800	–	45	1200	0

© Cengage Learning®

EXPLORING FURTHER

For a more detailed presentation of the specific-factors theory, go to *Exploring Further 3.1* which can be found at **www.cengage.com/economics/Carbaugh.**

Tariffs

According to the free-trade argument, open markets based on comparative advantage and specialization result in the most efficient use of world resources. Not only do free trade and specialization enhance world welfare, but they can also benefit each participating nation. Every nation can overcome the limitations of its own productive capacity to consume a combination of goods that exceeds the best it can produce in isolation.

However, free-trade policies often meet resistance among those companies and workers who face losses in income and jobs because of import competition. Policymakers are thus torn between the appeal of greater global efficiency in the long run made possible by free trade and the needs of the voting public whose main desire is to preserve short run interests such as employment and income. The benefits of free trade may take years to achieve and are spread over wide segments of society, whereas the costs of free trade are immediate and fall on specific groups such as workers in an import-competing industry.

When forming an international trade policy, a government must decide where to locate along the following spectrum:

← Protectionism

Autarky   ------------------------   Free Trade
(closed market)   Trade liberalization→   (open market)

As a government protects its producers from foreign competition, it encourages its economy to move closer to a state of isolationism, or autarky. Nations like Cuba and North Korea have traditionally been highly closed economies and therefore are closer to autarky. Conversely, if a government does not regulate the exchange of goods and services between nations, it moves to a free-trade policy. Countries such as Hong Kong (now part of the People's Republic of China) and Singapore are largely free-trade countries. The remaining countries of the world lie somewhere between these extremes. Rather than considering which of these two extremes a government should pursue, policy discussions generally consider where along this spectrum a country should locate—that is, "how much" trade liberalization or protectionism to pursue.

This chapter considers barriers to trade. In particular, it focuses on the role that tariffs play in the global trading system.

THE TARIFF CONCEPT

A **tariff** is simply a tax levied on a product when it crosses national boundaries. The most widespread tariff is the *import tariff* that is a tax levied on an imported product. This tax is collected before the shipment can be unloaded at a domestic port; the collected money is called a customs duty. A less common tariff is an *export tariff* that is a tax imposed on an exported product. Export tariffs have often been used by developing nations. Cocoa exports have been taxed by Ghana, and oil exports have been taxed by the Organization of Petroleum Exporting Countries (OPEC) in order to raise revenue or promote scarcity in global markets and hence increase the world price.

Did you know that the United States cannot levy export tariffs? When the U.S. Constitution was written, southern cotton producing states feared that northern textile manufacturing states would pressure the federal government into levying export tariffs to depress the price of cotton. An export duty would lead to decreased exports and a fall in the price of cotton within the United States. As the result of negotiations, the Constitution was worded to prevent export taxes: "No tax or duty shall be laid on articles exported from any state."

Tariffs may be imposed for protection or revenue purposes. A **protective tariff** is designed to reduce the amount of imports entering a country, thus insulating import-competing producers from foreign competition. This tariff allows an increase in the output of import-competing producers that would not have been possible without protection. A **revenue tariff** is imposed for the purpose of generating tax revenues and may be placed on either exports or imports.

Over time, tariff revenues have decreased as a source of government revenue for advanced nations, including the United States. In 1900, tariff revenues constituted more than 41 percent of U.S. government receipts; in 2010, the figure stood at about 1.0 percent. However, many developing nations currently rely on tariffs as a sizable source of government revenue. Table 4.1 shows the percentage of government revenue that several selected nations derive from tariffs.

TABLE 4.1

Taxes on International Trade as a Percentage of Government Revenues, 2011: Selected Countries

Developing Countries	Percentage	Advanced Countries	Percentage
Bahamas	43.3	New Zealand	2.8
Ethiopia	29.7	Australia	1.8
Liberia	28.5	Japan	1.6
Bangladesh	26.5	United States	1.3
Grenada	25.6	Switzerland	1.0
Russian Federation	25.6	Norway	0.2
Philippines	19.5	Ireland	0.1
India	14.3	World average	3.9

Source: From *World Bank Data* at http://data.worldbank.org. See also International Monetary Fund, *Government Finance Statistics, Yearbook*, Washington, DC.

Some tariffs vary according to the time of entry into the United States, as occurs with agricultural goods such as grapes, grapefruit, and cauliflower. This tariff reflects the harvest season for these products. When these products are out of season in the United States, the tariff is low. Higher tariffs are imposed when U.S. production in these goods increases during harvest season.

Not all goods that enter the United States are subject to tariffs. In 2013, only about 30 percent of U.S. imports were dutiable (subject to import duties) while 70 percent of imports were free of tariffs.[1] That U.S. imports are duty free is mainly because of free-trade agreements that the United States reaches with other countries (North American Free Trade Agreement) and trade preferences that the United States gives to imports from developing countries (Generalized System of Preferences program). Also, a sizable portion of most favored nation (MFN) tariffs are duty free. These topics are discussed in Chapters 6, 7, and 8 of this textbook.

TYPES OF TARIFFS

Tariffs can be specific, *ad valorem*, or compound. A **specific tariff** is expressed in terms of a fixed amount of money per physical unit of the imported product. A U.S. importer of a German computer may be required to pay a duty to the U.S. government of $100 per computer, regardless of the computer's price. Therefore, if 100 computers are imported, the tariff revenue of the government equals $10,000 inequality. In the figure, the wage ration equals wage of skilled workers/wage of unskilled workers. The labor ration equals the quantity of skilled workers/quantity of unskilled workers. ($100 × 100 = $10,000).

An **ad valorem (of value) tariff**, much like a sales tax, is expressed as a fixed percentage of the value of the imported product. Suppose that an ad valorem duty of 2.5 percent is levied on imported automobiles. If $100,000 worth of autos are imported, the government collects $2,500 in tariff revenue ($100,000 × 2.5% = $2,500). This $2,500 is collected whether 5, $20,000 Toyotas are imported or 10 $10,000 Nissans. Most of the tariffs levied by the U.S. government are ad valorem tariffs.

A **compound tariff** is a combination of specific and ad valorem tariffs. A U.S. importer of a television might be required to pay a duty of $20 plus 5 percent of the value of the television. Table 4.2 lists U.S. tariffs on certain items.

What are the relative merits of specific, ad valorem, and compound tariffs?

Specific Tariff

As a fixed monetary duty per unit of the imported product, a specific tariff is relatively easy to apply and administer, particularly to standardized commodities and staple products where the value of the dutiable goods cannot be easily observed. A main disadvantage of a specific tariff is that the degree of protection it affords domestic producers varies *inversely* with changes in import prices. A specific tariff of $1,000 on autos will discourage imports priced at $20,000 per auto to a greater degree than those priced at $25,000. During times of rising import prices, a given specific tariff loses some of its protective effect. The result is to encourage domestic producers to produce less expensive goods, for which the degree of protection against imports is higher. On the other hand, a specific tariff has the advantage of providing domestic producers more protection during

---

[1]The effective tariff is a measure that applies to a single nation. In a world of floating exchange rates, if all nominal or effective tariff rates rose, the effect would be offset by a change in the exchange rate.

TABLE 4.2

Selected U.S. Tariffs

Product	Duty Rate
Brooms	$0.32 each
Fishing reels	$0.24 each
Wrist watches (without jewels)	$0.29 each
Ball bearings	2.4% ad valorem
Electrical motors	6.7% ad valorem
Bicycles	5.5% ad valorem
Wool blankets	$0.18/kg + 6% ad valorem
Electricity meters	$0.16 each + 1.5% ad valorem
Auto transmission shafts	$0.25 each + 3.9% ad valorem

Source: From U.S. International Trade Commission, *Tariff Schedules of the United States*, Washington, DC, Government Printing Office, 2013, available at http://www.usitc.gov/tata/index.htm.

a business recession, when cheaper products are purchased. Specific tariffs thus cushion domestic producers progressively against foreign competitors who cut their prices.

Ad Valorem Tariff

Ad valorem tariffs usually lend themselves more satisfactorily to manufactured goods because they can be applied to products with a wide range of grade variations. As a percentage applied to a product's value, an ad valorem tariff can distinguish among small differentials in product quality to the extent that they are reflected in product price. Under a system of ad valorem tariffs, a person importing a $20,000 Honda would have to pay a higher duty than a person importing a $19,900 Toyota. Under a system of specific tariffs, the duty would be the same.

Another advantage of an ad valorem tariff is that it tends to maintain a constant degree of protection for domestic producers during periods of changing prices. If the tariff rate is a 20 percent ad valorem and the imported product price is $200, the duty is $40. If the product's price increases to $300, the duty collected rises to $60; if the product price falls to $100, the duty drops to $20. An ad valorem tariff yields revenues proportionate to values, maintaining a constant degree of relative protection at all price levels. An ad valorem tariff is similar to a proportional tax in that the real proportional tax burden or protection does not change as the tax base changes. In recent decades, in response to global inflation and the rising importance of world trade in manufactured products, ad valorem duties have been used more often than specific duties.

The determination of duties under the ad valorem principle at first appears to be simple, but in practice it has suffered from administrative complexities. The main problem has been trying to determine the value of an imported product, a process referred to as **customs valuation**. Import prices are estimated by customs appraisers who may disagree on product values. Moreover, import prices tend to fluctuate over time, making the valuation process rather difficult.

Another customs-valuation problem stems from variations in the methods used to determine a commodity's value. For example, the United States has traditionally used **free-on-board (FOB) valuation**, whereby the tariff is applied to a product's value as it leaves the exporting country. But European countries have traditionally used a **cost-insurance-freight (CIF) valuation**, whereby ad valorem tariffs are levied as a

TABLE 4.3

Average Import Tariff Rates* for Selected Countries, 2012 (in percentages)

Advanced Country	Average Tariff Rate
Bahamas	18.9
South Korea	8.7
Brazil	7.9
China	4.1
United States	1.6
Japan	1.3
Germany	1.1
Canada	0.9
World average	3.0

*Tariff rate, applied simple mean, all products.

Source: From *World Bank Data* at http://data.worldbank.org.

percentage of the imported commodity's total value as it arrives at its final destination. The CIF price thus includes transportation costs, such as insurance and freight.

Compound Tariff

Compound duties are often applied to manufactured products embodying raw materials that are subject to tariffs. In this case, the specific portion of the duty neutralizes the cost disadvantage of domestic manufactures that results from tariff protection granted to domestic suppliers of raw materials, and the ad valorem portion of the duty grants protection to the finished–goods industry. In the United States there is a compound duty on woven fabrics ($0.485 cents per kilogram plus 38 percent). The specific portion of the duty ($0.485 cents) compensates U.S. fabric manufacturers for the tariff protection granted to U.S. cotton producers, while the ad valorem portion of the duty (38 percent) provides protection for their own woven fabrics.

How high are import tariffs around the world? Table 4.3 provides examples of tariffs of selected advanced and developing countries.

EFFECTIVE RATE OF PROTECTION

In our previous discussion of tariffs, we assumed that a given product is produced entirely in one country. For example, a desktop computer produced by Dell (a U.S. firm) could be the output that results from using only American labor and components. However, this ignores the possibility that Dell imports some parts used in producing desktops, such as memory chips, hard-disk drives, and microprocessors.

When some inputs used in producing finished desktops are imported, the amount of protection given to Dell depends not only on the tariff rate applied to desktops, but also on whether there are tariffs on inputs used to produce them. The main point is that when Dell imports some of the inputs required to produce desktops, the tariff rate on desktops may not accurately indicate the protection being provided to Dell.

TRADE CONFLICTS TRADE PROTECTIONISM INTENSIFIES AS GLOBAL ECONOMY FALLS INTO THE GREAT RECESSION

Global economic downturns can be a catalyst for trade protectionism. As economies shrink, nations have incentive to protect their struggling producers by establishing barriers against imported goods. Consider the Great Recession of 2007–2009.

As the global economy fell into recession, there occurred a decrease in the demand for goods and services and thus a decline in international trade. Exports declined by 30 percent or more for countries as diverse as Indonesia, France, South Africa, and the Philippines. Increasingly, firms and workers worried about the harm that was inflicted on them by their foreign competitors who were seeking customers throughout the globe. China was the country targeted by the most governments for protectionist measures.

Although leaders of the Group of 20 large economies unanimously pledged not to resort to protectionism in 2008 and 2009, virtually all of them slipped at least a little bit. Russia increased tariffs on imported automobiles, India raised tariffs on steel imports, and Argentina established new obstacles to imported auto parts and shoes. Also, in 2009 the United States imposed tariffs of between 25 percent and 35 percent on imports of tires from China for the next three years. This policy essentially priced out of the market 17 percent of all tires sold in the United States and forced up the market price for consumers.

During the Great Depression of the 1930s, countries raised import tariffs to protect producers damaged by foreign competition. The United States increased import tariffs on some 20,000 goods that provoked widespread retaliation from its trading partners. Such tariff increases contributed to the volume of world trade shrinking by a quarter. A lesson from this era is that once trade barriers are increased, they can severely damage global supply chains. It can take years of negotiation to dismantle trade barriers and years before global supply chains can be restored. In spite of this lesson, governments have continued to adopt protectionist policies as their economies slide into recession.

In analyzing tariffs, economists distinguish between the nominal tariff rate and the effective tariff rate. The **nominal tariff rate** is the rate that is published in the country's tariff schedule. This rate applies to the value of a *finished product* that is imported into a country. The **effective tariff rate** takes into account not only the nominal tariff rate on a finished product, but also any tariff rate applied to *imported inputs* that are used in producing the finished product.[1]

If a finished desktop enters the United States at a zero tariff rate, while imported components used in desktop production are taxed, then Dell is taxed instead of protected. A nominal tariff on a desktop protects the production of Dell, while a tariff on imported components taxes Dell by increasing its costs. The effective tariff rate recognizes these two effects.

The effective tariff rate refers to the level of protection being provided to Dell by a nominal tariff on desktops and the tariff on inputs used in desktop production. Specifically, it measures the percentage increase in domestic production activities (value added) per unit of output made possible by tariffs on both the finished desktop and on imported inputs. A given tariff on a finished desktop will have a greater protective effect if it is combined with a low tariff on imported inputs than if the tariff on imported inputs is high.

To illustrate this principle, assume Dell adds value by assembling computer components that are produced abroad. Suppose the imported components can enter the United States on a duty free basis (zero tariff). Suppose also that 20 percent of a desktop's final value can be attributed to domestic assembly activities (value added). The remaining 80 percent reflects the value of the imported components. Let the cost of the desktop's components be the same for both Dell and its foreign competitor, say, Sony Inc. of Japan. Assume that Sony can produce and sell a desktop for $500.

Suppose the United States imposes a nominal tariff of ten percent on desktops, so that the domestic import price rises from $500 to $550 per unit, as seen in Table 4.4. Does this mean that Dell realizes an effective rate of protection equal to 10 percent? Certainly not! The imported components enter the country duty free (at a nominal tariff rate less than that on the finished desktop), so the effective rate of protection is 50 percent. Compared with what would exist under free trade, Dell can incur 50 percent more production activities and still be competitive.

Table 4.4 shows the figures in detail. Referring to Table 4.4(a), under free trade (zero tariff), a Sony desktop could be imported for $500. To meet this price, Dell would have to hold its assembly costs to $100. Referring to Table 4.4(b), under the protective umbrella of the tariff, Dell can incur up to $150 of assembly costs and still meet the $550 price of imported desktops. The result is that Dell's assembly costs could rise to a level of 50 percent above what would exist under free-trade conditions: $(\$150 - \$100)/\$100 = 0.5$.

In general, the effective tariff rate is given by the following formula:

$$e = \frac{(n - ab)}{(1 - a)}$$

where

e = The effective rate of protection
n = The nominal tariff rate on the final product
a = The ratio of the value of the imported input to the value of the finished product
b = The nominal tariff rate on the imported input

When the values from the desktop example are plugged into this formula, we obtain the following:

$$e = \frac{0.1 - 0.8\,(0)}{1 - 0.8} = 0.5 \text{ or } 50 \text{ percent}$$

The nominal tariff rate of ten percent levied on the finished desktop thus allows a 50 percent increase in domestic production activities—five times the nominal rate.

TABLE 4.4

The Effective Rate of Protection

(a) Free Trade: No Tariff on Imported Sony Desktops

SONY'S DESKTOP	COST	DELL'S DESKTOP	COST
Component parts	$400	Imported component parts	400
Assembly activity (value added)	100	Assembly activity (value added)	100
Import price	$500	Domestic price	$500

(b) 10 Percent Tariff on Imported Sony Desktops

SONY'S DESKTOP	COST	DELL'S DESKTOP	COST
Component parts	$400	Imported component parts	$400
Assembly activity (value added)	100	Assembly activity (value added)	150
Nominal tariff	50	Domestic price	$550
Import price	$550		

TABLE 4.5

China's Nominal and Effective Tariff Rates in Forestry Products, 2001

Product	Nominal Rate (%)	Effective Rate (%)
Mouldings	9.4	26.6
Furniture	11.0	21.8
Veneers	4.0	9.4
Plywood	8.4	11.7
Fiberboard	7.5	9.2
Particleboard	9.6	10.6

Source: From Manatu Aorere, *Tariff Escalation in the Forestry Sector*, New Zealand Ministry of Foreign Affairs and Trade, Wellington, New Zealand, August 2002.

However, a tariff on imported desktop components reduces the level of effective protection for Dell. This reduction means that in the above formula, the higher the value of *b*, the lower the effective–protection rate for any given nominal tariff on the finished desktop. Suppose that imported desktop components are subject to a tariff rate of 5.0 percent. The effective rate of protection would equal 30 percent:

$$e = \frac{0.1 - 0.8\,(0.05)}{1 - 0.8} = 0.3 \text{ or } 30 \text{ percent}$$

This is less than the 50 percent effective rate of protection that occurs when there is no tariff on imported components.

From these examples we can draw several conclusions. When the tariff on the finished product exceeds the tariff on the imported input, the effective rate of protection exceeds the nominal tariff. If the tariff on the finished product is less than the tariff on the imported input, the effective rate of protection is less than the nominal tariff and may even be negative. Such a situation might occur if the home government desired to protect domestic suppliers of raw materials more than domestic manufacturers.[2] Because national governments generally admit raw materials and other inputs either duty free or at a lower rate than finished goods, effective tariff rates are usually higher than nominal rates. Table 4.5 provides examples of nominal and effective tariff rates for China in 2001.

TARIFF ESCALATION

When analyzing the tariff structures of nations, we often see that processed goods face higher import tariffs than those levied on basic raw materials. Logs may be imported tariff-free while processed goods such as plywood, veneers, and furniture face higher import tariffs. The purpose of this tariff strategy is to protect, say, the domestic plywood industry by enabling it to import logs (used to produce plywood) tariff free or at low

---

[2]Besides depending on the tariff rates on finished desktops and components used to produce them, the effective rate of protection depends on the ratio of the value of the imported input to the value of the finished product. The degree of effective protection for Dell increases as the value added by Dell declines (the ratio of the value of the imported input to the value of the final product increases). That is, the higher the value of *a* in the formula, the greater the effective protection rate for any given nominal tariff rate on desktops.

TABLE 4.6

Tariff Escalations in Advanced and Developing Countries, 2008

Country	AGRICULTURE PRODUCTS		INDUSTRIAL PRODUCTS	
	Primary Products	Processed Products	Primary Products	Processed Products
Bangladesh	17.5	23.0	9.1	15.4
Uganda	17.5	20.3	4.2	11.7
Argentina	5.7	11.5	2.9	9.5
Brazil	6.5	12.1	4.2	10.7
Russia	6.9	9.2	5.3	9.5
United States	1.0	2.8	1.3	2.8
Japan	4.5	10.9	0.5	1.9
World	12.0	15.1	5.6	7.7

Source. From *World Bank Data* at http://data.worldbank.org.

rates while maintaining higher tariffs on imported plywood that competes against domestic plywood.

This policy is referred to as **tariff escalation**: although raw materials are often imported at zero or low tariff rates, the nominal and effective protection increases at each stage of production. As seen in Table 4.6, tariffs often rise significantly with the level of processing in many countries. This is especially true for agricultural products.

The tariff structures of the industrialized nations may indeed discourage the growth of processing, hampering diversification into higher value–added exports for the less developed nations. The industrialized nations' low tariffs on primary commodities encourage the developing nations to expand operations in these sectors, while the high protective rates levied on manufactured goods pose a significant entry barrier for any developing nation wishing to compete in this area. From the point of view of less developed nations, it may be in their best interest to discourage disproportionate tariff reductions on raw materials. The effect of these tariff reductions is to magnify the discrepancy between the nominal and effective tariffs of the industrialized nations, worsening the potential competitive position of the less developed nations in the manufacturing and processing sectors.

OUTSOURCING AND OFFSHORE ASSEMBLY PROVISION

Outsourcing is a key aspect of the global economy. Electronic components made in the United States are shipped to another country with low labor costs such as Singapore, for assembly into television sets. The assembled sets are then returned to the United States for further processing or packaging and distribution. This type of production sharing has evolved into an important competitive strategy for producers who locate each stage of production in the country where it can be at least cost.

The Tariff Act of 1930 created an **offshore assembly provision (OAP)** that provides favorable treatment to products assembled abroad from U.S. made components. Under OAP, when U.S. made components are sent abroad and assembled there to become a finished good, the cost of the U.S. components is not included in the dutiable value of the imported assembled good into which it has been incorporated. American import duties thus apply only to the *value added in the foreign assembly process*, provided that the U.S. manufactured components are used in assembly operations. Manufactured goods entering the United States under OAP have included motor vehicles, office machines, television sets, aluminum cans, semiconductors, and the like. These products have represented about 8–10 percent of total U.S. imports in recent years.

The OAP pertains to both American and foreign companies. A U.S. computer company could produce components in the United States, send them to Taiwan for assembly, and ship finished computers back to the United States under favorable OAP. Alternatively, a Japanese photocopier firm desiring to export to the United States could purchase U.S made components, assemble them in Japan and ship finished photocopiers to the United States under favorable OAP. One of the effects of OAP is to reduce the effective rate of protection of foreign assembly activity and shift demand from domestic to foreign assembly, as explained below.

Suppose that ABC Electronics Co. is located in the United States and manufactures televisions sets worth $300 each. Included in a set are components worth $200 that are produced by the firm in the United States. To reduce labor costs, consider the firm sends these components to its subsidiary in South Korea where relatively low-wage Korean workers assemble the components, resulting in finished television sets. Assume that Korean assembly is valued at $100 per set. After being assembled in South Korea, the finished sets are imported into the United States for sale to American consumers. What will the tariff duty be on these sets?

In the absence of the OAP, the full value of each set, $300, is subject to the tariff. If the tariff rate on such televisions is 10 percent, a duty of $30 would be paid on each set entering the United States, and the price to the U.S. consumer would be $330.[3] Under OAP, however, the 10 percent tariff rate is levied on the value of the imported set *minus* the value of the U.S. components used in manufacturing the set. When the set enters the United States, its dutiable value is thus $300 − $200 = $100, and the duty is $0.1 \times \$100 = \$10$. The price to the U.S. consumer after the tariff has been levied is $300 + $10 = $310. With the OAP system, the effective tariff rate is only 3.3 percent ($10/$300) instead of the 10 percent shown in the tariff schedule.

Therefore, the effect of the OAP is to reduce the effective rate of protection of the South Korean assembly activity and to shift demand from American to Korean assemblers. Opponents of the OAP emphasize that the OAP makes imported television sets more price competitive in the U.S. market. They also stress the associated displacement of American assembly workers and the accompanying negative effects on the U.S. balance of trade. However, this "tariff break" is available only if U.S. made components are used to manufacture television sets. This suggests a simultaneous shift of demand from foreign to American made components. Defenders of the OAP emphasize the associated positive effects on the production and exporting of American components. Indeed, the OAP has been a controversial provision in U.S. tariff policy.

DODGING IMPORT TARIFFS: TARIFF AVOIDANCE AND TARIFF EVASION

When a country imposes a tariff on imports, there are economic incentives to dodge it. One way of escaping a tariff is to engage in **tariff avoidance**, the legal utilization of the tariff system to one's own advantage in order to reduce the amount of tariff that is payable by means that are within the law. By contrast, **tariff evasion** occurs when individuals or firms evade tariffs by illegal means such as smuggling imported goods into a country. Let us consider each of these methods.

---

[3]This example assumes that the United States is a "small" country, as discussed later in this chapter.

Ford Strips Its Wagons to Avoid High Tariff

Several times a month, Ford Motor Company ships its Transit Connect five-passenger wagons from its factory in Turkey to Baltimore, Maryland. Once the passenger wagons arrive in Baltimore, the majority of them are driven to a warehouse where workers listening to rock music rip out the rear windows, seats, and seat belts. Why?

Ford's behavior is part of its efforts to cope with a lengthy trade conflict. In the 1960s, Europe imposed high tariffs on imported chickens, primarily intended to discourage American sales to West Germany. President Lyndon Johnson retaliated with a 25 percent tariff on imports of foreign made trucks and commercial vans (motor vehicles for the transport of goods). This tariff exists today and applies to trucks and commercial vans even if they are produced by an American company in a foreign country. However, the U.S. tariff on imports of vehicles in the category of "wagons" and "cars" (motor vehicles for the transport of persons) face a much lower 2.5 percent tariff.

Realizing that a 25 percent tariff would significantly add to the price of its cargo vans sold in the United States, and thus detract from their competitiveness, in 2009 Ford embarked on a program to avoid this tariff. Here's how it works. Ford ships the Transit Connects wagons to the United States that face a 2.5 percent tariff. Once the wagons reach a processing facility in Baltimore, they are transformed into cargo vans. The rear windows are removed and replaced by a sheet of metal, and the rear seats and seat belts are removed and a new floorboard is screwed into place. Although the vehicles start as five-passenger wagons, Ford converts them into two-seat cargo vans. The fabric is shredded, the steel parts are broken down, and everything is sent along with the glass to be recycled. According to U.S. customs officials, this practice complies with the letter of the law.

Transforming wagons into cargo vans costs Ford hundreds of dollars per vehicle, but the process saves the company thousands in terms of tariff duties. On a $25,000 passenger wagon a 2.5 percent tariff would result in a duty of only $625 ($25,000 × 0.025 = $625). This compares to a duty of $6,250 that would result from a 25 percent tariff imposed on a cargo van ($25,000 × 0.25 = $6,250). The avoidance of the higher tariff on cargo vans would save Ford $5,625 on each vehicle ($6,250 − $625 = $5,625) minus the cost of transforming the passenger wagon into a cargo van. Smart, huh?

Ford's transformation process is only one way to avoid tariffs. Other auto makers have avoided U.S. tariffs using different techniques. Toyota Motor Corp., Nissan Motor Co., and Honda Motor Co. took the straightforward route and built plants in the United States, instead of exporting vehicles from Japan to the United States that are subject to import tariffs.[4]

Smuggled Steel Evades U.S. Tariffs

Each year, about 38 million tons of steel with a value of about $12 billion are imported by the United States. About half of this steel is subject to tariffs that range from pennies to hundreds of dollars a ton. The amount of the tariff depends on the type of steel product (there are about 1,000) and on the country of origin (there are about 100). These tariffs are applied to the selling price of the steel in the United States. American customs inspectors scrutinize the shipments that enter the United States to make sure that tariffs are properly assessed. However, monitoring shipments is difficult given the limited staff of the customs service. Therefore, the risk of being caught for smuggling and the odds of penalties being levied are modest, while the potential for illegal profit is high.

[4]Drawn from "To Outfox the Chicken Tax, Ford Strips Its Own Vans," *The Wall Street Journal*, September 23, 2009, p. A-1.

Ivan Dubrinski smuggled 20,000 tons of steel into the United States in the first decade of the 2000s. It was easy. All he did was modify the shipping documents on a product called "reinforcing steel bar" to make it appear that it was part of a shipment of another type of steel called "flat-rolled." This deception saved him about $38,000 in import duties. Multiply this tariff evasion episode many times over and you have avoided millions of dollars in duties. The smuggling of steel concerns the U.S. government that loses tariff revenue and also the U.S. steel industry, that maintains it cannot afford to compete with products made cheaper by tariff evasion.

Although larger U.S. importers of steel generally pay correct duties, it is the smaller, often fly-by-night importers that are more likely to try to slip illegal steel into the country. These traders use one of three methods to evade tariffs. One method is to falsely reclassify steel that would be subject to a tariff as a duty free product. Another is to detach markings that the steel came from a country subject to tariffs and make it appear to have come from one that is exempt. A third method involves altering the chemical composition of a steel product enough so that it can be labeled duty free.

TRADE CONFLICTS GAINS FROM ELIMINATING IMPORT TARIFFS

What would be the effects if the United States unilaterally removed tariffs and other restraints on imported products? On the positive side, tariff elimination lowers the price of the affected imports and may lower the price of the competing U.S. good, resulting in economic gains to the U.S. consumer. Lower import prices also decrease the production costs of firms that buy less costly intermediate inputs, such as steel. On the negative side, the lower price to import-competing producers, as a result of eliminating the tariff, results in profit reductions; work-ers become displaced from the domestic industry that loses protection; and the U.S. government loses tax revenue as the result of eliminating the tariff.

In 2011 the U.S. International Trade Commission estimated the annual economic welfare gains from eliminating significant import restraints from their existing levels. The result would have been equivalent to a welfare gain of about $2.6 billion to the U.S. economy. The largest welfare gain would come from liberalizing trade ethanol, textiles and apparel, and dairy products, as seen in Table 4.7.

TABLE 4.7

Economic Welfare Gains from Liberalization of Significant Import Restraints*, 2015 (millions of dollars)

Import-Competing Industry	Annual change in Economic Welfare
Ethanol	1,513
Textiles and apparel	514
Dairy	223
Footwear and leather products	215
Tobacco	63
Tuna	16
Costume jewelry	12

*Import tariffs, tariff-rate quotas, and import quotas.

Source: From U.S. International Trade Commission, *The Economic Effects of Significant U.S. Import Restraints*, Washington, DC, Government Printing Office, 2011.

Although customs inspectors attempt to scrutinize imports, once the steel gets by them they can do little about it. They cannot confiscate the smuggled steel because it is often already sold and in use. Meanwhile, the people buying the steel get a nice price break and the American steel companies that compete against smuggled steel, find their sales and profits declining.[5]

POSTPONING IMPORT TARIFFS

Besides allowing the avoidance of tariffs, U.S. tariff law allows the postponement of tariffs. Let us see how a bonded warehouse and a foreign-trade zone can facilitate the postponing of tariffs.

Bonded Warehouse

According to U.S. tariff law, dutiable imports can be brought into the United States and temporarily left in a **bonded warehouse**, duty free. Importers can apply for authorization from the U.S. Customs Service to have a bonded warehouse on their own premises or they can use the services of a public warehouse that has received such authorization. Owners of storage facilities must be bonded to ensure that they will satisfy all customs duty obligations. This condition means that the bonding company guarantees payment of customs duties in the event that the importing company is unable to do so.

Imported goods can be stored, repacked, or further processed in the bonded warehouse for up to five years. Domestically produced goods are not allowed to enter a bonded warehouse. If warehoused at the initial time of entry, no customs duties are owed. When the time arrives to withdraw the imported goods from the warehouse, duties must be paid on the value of the goods at the time of withdrawal rather than at the time of entry into the bonded warehouse. If the goods are withdrawn for exportation, payment of duty is not required.

While the goods are in the warehouse, the owner may subject them to various processes necessary to prepare them for sale in the market. Such processes might include the repacking and mixing of tea, the bottling of wines, and the roasting of coffee. However, imported components cannot be assembled into final products in a bonded warehouse, nor can the manufacturing of products take place.

A main advantage of a bonded warehouse entry is that no duties are collected until the goods are withdrawn for domestic consumption. The importer has the luxury of controlling the money for the duty until it is paid upon withdrawal of the goods from the bonded warehouse. If the importer cannot find a domestic buyer for its goods or if the goods cannot be sold at a good price domestically, the importer has the advantage of selling merchandise for exportation that cancels the obligation to pay duties. Also, paying duties when goods first arrive in the country can be expensive, and using a bonded warehouse allows importers time to access funds from the sale of the goods to pay the duties rather than having to pay duties in advance.

Foreign-Trade Zone

Similar to a bonded warehouse, a **foreign-trade zone** (FTZ) is an area within the United States where business can operate without the responsibility of paying customs duties on imported products or materials for as long as they remain within this area and do not enter the U.S. marketplace. Customs duties are due only when goods are transferred

---

[5]Drawn from "Steel Smugglers Pull Wool over the Eyes of Customs Agents to Enter U.S. Market," *The Wall Street Journal*, November 1, 2001, pp. A-1 and A-14.

from the FTZ for U.S. consumption. If the goods never enter the U.S. marketplace, then no duties are paid on those items.

What distinguishes an FTZ from a bonded warehouse? With an FTZ, once merchandise has moved in to it, you can do just about anything to the merchandise. You can re-package goods, repair or destroy damaged ones, assemble component parts into finished products, and export either the parts or finished products. The manufacturing of goods is also allowed in FTZs. Therefore, importers who use FTZs can conduct a broader range of business activities than can occur in bonded warehouses that permit only the storage of imported goods and limited repackaging and processing activities.

Many FTZs are situated at U.S. seaports, such as the Port of Seattle, but some are located at inland distribution points. There are currently more than 230 FTZs throughout the United States. Among the businesses that enjoy FTZ status are Exxon, Caterpillar, General Electric, and International Business Machines (IBM).

The FTZ program encourages U.S. based business operations by removing certain disincentives associated with manufacturing in the United States. The duty on a product manufactured abroad and imported into the United States is paid at the rate of the finished product rather than that of the individual parts, materials, or components of the product. A U.S. based company would find itself at a disadvantage relative to its foreign competitor if it had to pay a higher rate on parts, materials, or components imported for use in the manufacturing process (this is known as "inverted tariffs"). The FTZ program corrects this imbalance by treating a product manufactured in a FTZ, for purposes of tariff assessment, as if it were produced abroad.

Suppose an FTZ user imports a motor that carries a 5.0 percent duty rate, and uses it in the manufacture of a lawn mower that is free of duty. When the lawn mower leaves the FTZ and enters the U.S. marketplace, the duty rate on the motor drops from the 5.0 percent rate to the free lawn mower rate. By participating in the FTZ program, the lawn mower manufacturer has eliminated the duty on this component, and thus decreased the component cost by 5.0 percent.

An FTZ can also help a firm eliminate import duties on product waste and scrap. Suppose a U.S. chemical company imports raw material that carries a 10 percent duty to produce a particular chemical that also carries a 10 percent duty. Part of the production process involves bringing the imported raw material to high temperatures. During this process, 20 percent of the raw material is lost as heat. If the chemical company imports $1 million of raw material per year, it will pay $100,000 ($1 million $\times$ 0.1 = $100,000) in duty as the raw material enters the United States. However, by participating in the FTZ program, it does not pay duty on the raw material until it leaves the zone and enters the U.S. marketplace. Because 20 percent of the raw material is lost as heat during the manufacturing process, the raw material is now worth only $800,000. Assuming that all the finished chemical is sold in the United States, the 10 percent customs duty totals only $80,000. This is a savings of $20,000. While it may appear that the FTZ program benefits only the U.S. chemical company, it is important to remember that its competitors who make the same product abroad already have the benefit of not having to pay on the waste loss in the production of their chemical.

FTZ's Benefit Motor Vehicle Importers

Toyota Motor Co. is an example of a company that benefits from the U.S. FTZ program. Toyota has vehicle processing centers located within FTZ sites in the United States. Before imported Toyotas are shipped to American dealers, the processing centers clean them, install accessories such as radios and CD players, and so on. A primary benefit of the processing center's being located within a FTZ site is customs duty deferral—the postponement of the payment of duties until the vehicle has been processed and shipped to the dealer.

For parts imported into the United States, Toyota also has parts distribution centers that are located within FTZ sites. Because of extended warranties, Toyota must maintain a large inventory of parts within the United States for a lengthy period of time that makes the FTZ program attractive from the perspective of duty deferral. Also, a large number of parts may become obsolete and have to be destroyed. By obtaining FTZ designation on its parts distribution center, Toyota can avoid the payment of customs duties on those parts that become obsolete and are destroyed.

Another benefit to Toyota of a FTZ is the potential reduction in the dutiable value of the imported vehicle according to the inverted duty principle, as discussed above. Suppose that a CD player that is imported from Japan is installed at a Toyota processing center within a FTZ site. In 2011 the duty on the imported CD player was 4.4 percent and the duty on a final Toyota automobile was 2.5 percent. Toyota has the ability to reduce the duty on the cost of the CD player by 1.9 percent ($4.4\% - 2.5\% = 1.9\%$) by having the CD player installed at its processing center within the FTZ site.

TARIFF EFFECTS: AN OVERVIEW

Before we make a detailed investigation of tariffs, let us consider an introductory overview of their effects.

Tariffs are taxes on imports. They make the item more expensive for consumers, thus reducing demand. Suppose there is a U.S. company and a foreign company supplying computers. The price of the U.S. made computer is $1,000 and the price of foreign-made computer is $750. The U.S. computer company is not able to stay competitive in this situation.

Suppose that the United States imposes an import tariff of $300 per computer. The tariff increases the price of imported computers above the foreign price by the amount of the tariff; $300. American suppliers of computers who compete with suppliers of imported computers can now sell their computers for the foreign price plus the amount of the tariff, $1,050 ($750 + $300 = $1,050). As the price of computers increases, both imported and domestic consumption decreases. At the same time, the higher price has encouraged American suppliers to expand output. Imports are reduced as domestic consumption decreases and domestic production increases. Notice that a tariff need not push the price of the imported computer above the price of its domestic counterpart for the American computer industry to prosper. The tariff should be just high enough to reduce the price differential between the imported computer and the American made computer.

If no tariff is imposed, as under free trade, Americans would have saved money by buying the cheaper foreign computer. The U.S. computer industry would either have to become more efficient in order to compete with the less expensive imported product or face extinction.

Although the tariff benefits producers in the U.S. computer industry, it imposes costs to the U.S. economy:

- Computer buyers will have to pay more for their protected U.S. made computers than they would have for the imported computers under free trade.
- Jobs will be lost at retail and shipping companies that import foreign made computers.
- The extra cost of the computers gets passed on to whatever products and services that use these computers in the production process.

These costs will have to be weighed against the number of jobs the tariff would save to get a true picture of the impact of the tariff.

Now that we have an overview of the effects of a tariff, let us consider tariffs in a more detailed manner. We will examine the effects of tariffs for a small importing country and a large importing country. Let us begin by reviewing the concepts of consumer surplus and produce surplus as discussed in the next section of this text.

TARIFF WELFARE EFFECTS: CONSUMER SURPLUS AND PRODUCER SURPLUS

To analyze the effect of trade policies on national welfare, it is useful to separate the effects on consumers from those on producers. For each group, a measure of welfare is needed; these measures are known as consumer surplus and producer surplus.

Consumer surplus refers to the difference between the amount that buyers would be willing and able to pay for a good and the actual amount they do pay. To illustrate, assume that the price of a Pepsi is $0.50. Being especially thirsty, assume you would be willing to pay up to $0.75 for a Pepsi. Your consumer surplus on this purchase is $0.25 ($0.75 − $0.50 = $0.25). For all Pepsis bought, consumer surplus is merely the sum of the surplus for each unit.

Consumer surplus can also be depicted graphically. Let us first remember that the height of the market demand curve indicates the maximum price that buyers are willing and able to pay for each successive unit of the good, and in a competitive market, buyers pay a single price (the equilibrium price) for all units purchased. Referring now to Figure 4.1(a), consider the market price of gasoline is $2 per gallon. If buyers purchase four gallons at this price, they spend $8, represented by area *ACED*. For those four

FIGURE 4.1

Consumer Surplus and Producer Surplus

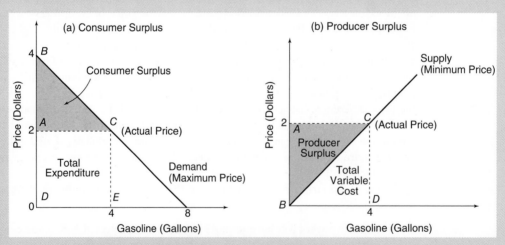

Consumer surplus is the difference between the maximum amount buyers are willing to pay for a given quantity of a good and the amount actually paid. Graphically, consumer surplus is represented by the area under the demand curve and above the good's market price. Producer surplus is the revenue producers receive over and above the minimum necessary for production. Graphically, producer surplus is represented by the area above the supply curve and below the good's market price.

gallons, buyers would be willing and able to spend $12, as shown by area *ABCED*. The difference between what buyers actually spend and the amount they are willing and able to spend is consumer surplus; in this case, it equals $4 and is denoted by area *ABC*.

The size of the consumer surplus is affected by the market price. A decrease in the market price will lead to an increase in the quantity purchased and a larger consumer surplus. Conversely, a higher market price will reduce the amount purchased and shrink the consumer surplus.

Let us now consider the other side of the market; producers. **Producer surplus** is the revenue producers receive over and above the minimum amount required to induce them to supply a good. This minimum amount has to cover the producer's total variable costs. Recall that total variable cost equals the sum of the marginal cost of producing each successive unit of output.

In Figure 4.1(*b*), the producer surplus is represented by the area above the supply curve of gasoline and below the good's market price. Recall that the height of the market supply curve indicates the lowest price that producers are willing to supply gasoline; this minimum price increases with the level of output because of rising marginal costs. Suppose that the market price of gasoline is $2 per gallon, and four gallons are supplied. Producers receive revenues totaling $8, represented by area *ACDB*. The minimum revenue they must receive to produce four gallons equals the total variable cost that equals $4 and is depicted by area *BCD*. Producer surplus is the difference, $4 ($8 − $4 = $4), and is depicted by *area ABC*.

If the market price of gasoline rises, more gasoline will be supplied and the producer surplus will rise. It is equally true that if the market price of gasoline falls, the producer surplus will fall. In the following sections, we will use the concepts of consumer surplus and producer surplus to analyze the effects of import tariffs on a nation's welfare.

TARIFF WELFARE EFFECTS: SMALL NATION MODEL

To measure the effects of a tariff on a nation's welfare, consider the case of a nation whose imports constitute a small portion of the world market supply. This **small nation** would be a *price taker*, facing a constant world price level for its import commodity. This is not a rare case; many nations are not important enough to influence the terms at which they trade.

In Figure 4.2, a small nation before trade produces autos at market equilibrium point *E*, as determined by the intersection of its domestic supply and demand schedules. At the equilibrium price of $9,500, the quantity supplied is 50 autos, and the quantity demanded is 50 autos. Now suppose that the economy is opened to foreign-trade and that the world auto price is $8,000. Because the world market will supply an unlimited number of autos at the price of $8,000, the world supply schedule would appear as a horizontal (perfectly elastic) line. Line S_{d+w} shows the supply of autos available to small nation consumers from domestic and foreign sources combined. This overall supply schedule is the one that would prevail in free trade.

Free-trade equilibrium is located at point *F* in the figure. Here the number of autos demanded is 80, whereas the number produced domestically is 20. The import of 60 autos fulfills the excess domestic auto demand. Compared with the situation before trade occurred, free trade results in a fall in the domestic auto price from $9,500 to $8,000. Consumers are better off because they can import more autos at a lower price. However, domestic producers now sell fewer autos at a lower price than they did before trade.

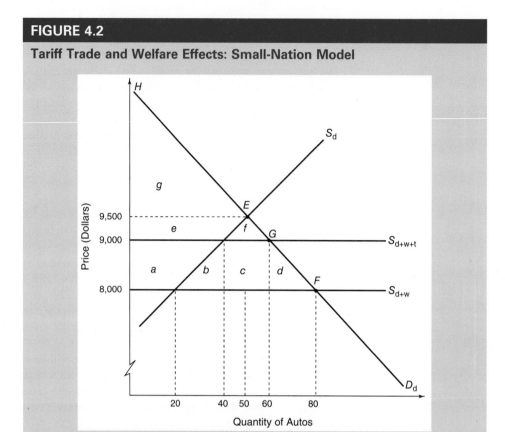

FIGURE 4.2

Tariff Trade and Welfare Effects: Small-Nation Model

For a small nation, a tariff placed on an imported product is shifted totally to the domestic consumer via a higher product price. Consumer surplus falls as a result of the price increase. The small nation's welfare decreases by an amount equal to the protective effect and consumption effect, the so-called deadweight losses due to a tariff.

Under free trade, the domestic auto industry is being damaged by foreign competition. Industry sales and revenues are falling and workers are losing their jobs. Suppose management and labor unites and convinces the government to levy a protective tariff on auto imports. Assume the small nation imposes a tariff of $1,000 on auto imports. Because this small nation is not important enough to influence world market conditions, the world supply price of autos remains constant, unaffected by the tariff. This lack of price change means that the small nation's terms of trade remains unchanged. The introduction of the tariff *raises the home price of imports by the full amount of the duty, and the increase falls entirely on the domestic consumer.* The overall supply shifts upward by the amount of the tariff, from S_{d+w} to S_{d+w+t}.

The protective tariff results in a new equilibrium quantity at point G, where the domestic auto price is $9,000. Domestic production increases by 20 units, whereas domestic consumption falls by 20 units. Imports decrease from their pre-tariff level of 60 units to 20 units. This reduction can be attributed to falling domestic consumption and rising domestic production. The effects of the tariff are to impede imports and protect domestic producers. But what are the tariff's effects on the *nation's welfare*?

Figure 4.2 shows that before the tariff was levied, *consumer surplus* equaled areas $a + b + c + d + e + f + g$. With the tariff, consumer surplus falls to areas $e + f + g$, an overall loss in consumer surplus equal to areas $a + b + c + d$. This change affects the nation's welfare in a number of ways. The welfare effects of a tariff include a revenue effect, redistribution effect, protective effect, and consumption effect. As might be expected, the tariff provides the government with additional tax revenue and benefits domestic auto producers; however, at the same time it wastes resources and harms the domestic consumer.

The tariff's **revenue effect** represents the government's collections of duty. Found by multiplying the number of imports (20 autos) times the tariff ($1,000), government revenue equals area c, or $20,000. This revenue represents the portion of the loss in consumer surplus in monetary terms that is transferred to the government. For the nation as a whole, the revenue effect does *not* result in an overall welfare loss; the consumer surplus is merely shifted from the private to the public sector.

The **redistributive effect** is the transfer of the consumer surplus in monetary terms, to the domestic producers of the import-competing product. This is represented by area a, that equals $30,000. Under the tariff, domestic home consumers will buy from domestic firms 40 autos at a price of $9,000, for a total expenditure of $360,000. At the free trade price of $8,000, the same 40 autos would have yielded $320,000. The imposition of the tariff thus results in home producers' receiving additional revenues totaling areas $a + b$, or $40,000 (the difference between $360,000 and $320,000). However, as the tariff encourages domestic production to rise from 20 to 40 units, producers must pay part of the increased revenue as higher costs of producing the increased output, depicted by area b, or $10,000. The remaining revenue, $30,000, area a, is a net gain in producer income. The redistributive effect is a transfer of income from consumers to producers. Like the revenue effect, it does *not* result in an overall loss of welfare for the economy.

Area b, totaling $10,000, is referred to as the **protective effect** of the tariff. This effect illustrates the loss to the domestic economy resulting from wasted resources used to produce additional autos at increasing unit costs. As the tariff induced domestic output expands, resources that are less adaptable to auto production are eventually used, increasing unit production costs. This increase means that resources are used less efficiently than they would have been with free trade, in which case autos would have been purchased from low-cost foreign producers. A tariff's protective effect thus arises because less efficient domestic production is substituted for more efficient foreign production. Referring to Figure 4.2, as domestic output increases from 20 to 40 units, the domestic cost of producing autos rises, as shown by supply schedule S_d. The same increase in autos could have been obtained at a unit cost of $8,000 before the tariff was levied. Area b, that depicts the protective effect, represents a loss to the economy equal to $10,000. Notice that the calculation of the protection effect simply involves the calculation of the area of triangle b. Recall from geometry that the area of a triangle equals (base × height)/2. The height of triangle b equals the increase in price due to the tariff ($1,000); the triangle's base (20 autos) equals the increase in domestic auto production due to the tariff. The protection effect is thus $(20 \times \$1,000)/2 = \$10,000$.

Most of the consumer surplus lost because of the tariff has been accounted for: c went to the government as revenue; a was transferred to home producers as income; and b was lost by the economy because of inefficient domestic production. The **consumption effect**, represented by area d, that equals $10,000 is the residual not accounted for elsewhere. The residual arises from the decrease in consumption resulting from the tariff's artificially increasing the price of autos from $8,000 to $9,000. A loss of welfare occurs because of the increased price and lower consumption. Notice that the calculation of the consumption effect involves the calculation of the area of triangle d. The height of the triangle ($1,000) equals the price increase in autos because of the tariff; the base (20 autos) equals the reduction in domestic consumption based on the tariff. The consumption effect is thus $(20 \times \$1,000)/2 = \$10,000$.

Like the protective effect, the consumption effect represents a real cost to society, not a transfer to other sectors of the economy. Together, these two effects equal the **deadweight loss** of the tariff (areas $b + d$ in the figure).

As long as it is assumed that a nation accounts for a negligible portion of international trade, its levying an import tariff necessarily lowers its national welfare. This is because there is no favorable welfare effect resulting from the tariff that would offset the deadweight loss of the consumer surplus. If a nation could impose a tariff that would improve its terms of trade to its trading partners, it would enjoy a larger share of the gains from trade. This would tend to increase its national welfare, offsetting the deadweight loss of consumer surplus. Because it is so insignificant relative to the world market, a small nation is unable to influence the terms of trade. Levying an import tariff *reduces* a small nation's welfare.

TARIFF WELFARE EFFECTS: LARGE NATION MODEL

The support for free trade by economists may appear so pronounced that one might conclude that a tariff could never be beneficial. This is not necessarily true. A tariff may increase national welfare when it is imposed by an importing nation that is large enough so that changes in the quantity of its imports, by means of tariff policy, influence the world price of the product. This **large nation** status applies to the United States that is a large importer of autos, steel, oil, and consumer electronics and to other economic giants such as Japan and the European Union.

If the United States imposes a tariff on automobile imports, prices increase for American consumers. The result is a decrease in the quantity demanded, that may be significant enough to force Japanese firms to reduce the prices of their exports. Because Japanese firms can produce and export smaller amounts at a lower marginal cost, they are likely to prefer to reduce their price to the United States to limit the decrease in their sales. The tariff's effect is thus shared between U.S. consumers who pay a higher price than under free trade for each auto imported, and Japanese firms who realize a lower price than under free trade for each auto exported. The difference between these two prices is the tariff duty. The welfare of the United States rises when it can shift some of the tariff to Japanese firms via export price reductions. The *terms of trade* improves for the United States at the expense of Japan.

What are the economic effects of an import tariff for a large country? Referring to Figure 4.3, line S_d represents the domestic supply schedule and line D_d depicts the home demand schedule. Autarky equilibrium occurs at point E. With free trade, the importing nation faces a total supply schedule of S_{d+w}. This schedule shows the number of autos that both domestic and foreign producers together offer domestic consumers. The total supply schedule is upward sloping rather than horizontal because the foreign supply price is not a fixed constant. The price depends on the quantity purchased by an importing country who is a large buyer of the product. With free trade, our country achieves market equilibrium at point F. The price of autos falls to $8,000, domestic consumption rises to 110 units, and domestic production falls to 30 units. Auto imports totaling 80 units satisfy the excess domestic demand.

Suppose that the importing nation imposes a specific tariff of $1,000 on imported autos. By increasing the selling cost, the tariff results in a shift in the total supply schedule from S_{d+w} to S_{d+w+t}. Market equilibrium shifts from point F to point G while the product price rises from $8,000 to $8,800. The tariff levying nation's consumer surplus falls by an amount equal to areas $a + b + c + d$. Area a, totaling $32,000, represents the

FIGURE 4.3

Tariff Trade and Welfare Effects: Large-Nation Model

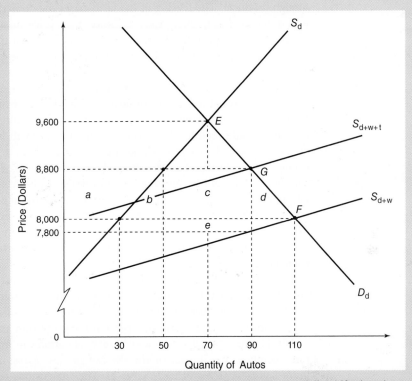

For a large nation, a tariff on an imported product may be partially shifted to the domestic consumer via a higher product price and partially absorbed by the foreign exporter via a lower export price. The extent by which a tariff is absorbed by the foreign exporter constitutes a welfare gain for the home country. This gain offsets some (all) of the deadweight welfare losses due to the tariff's consumption and protective effects.

© Cengage Learning®

redistributive effect; this amount is transferred from domestic consumers to domestic producers. Areas $d + b$ depict the tariff's deadweight loss, the deterioration in national welfare because of reduced consumption (*consumption effect* = $8,000) and an inefficient use of resources (*protective effect* = $8,000).

As in the small nation example, a tariff's *revenue effect* equals the import tariff multiplied by the quantity of autos imported. This effect yields areas $c + e$, or $40,000. Notice that the tariff revenue accruing to the government now comes from foreign producers as well as domestic consumers. This result differs from the small nation case in which the supply schedule is horizontal and the tariff's burden falls entirely on domestic consumers.

The tariff of $1,000 is added to the free trade import price of $8,000. Although the price in the protected market will exceed the foreign supply price by the amount of the duty, it will *not* exceed the free trade foreign supply price by this amount. Compared with the free trade foreign supply price of $8,000, the domestic consumers pay only an additional $800 per imported auto. This is the portion of the tariff shifted to the consumer. At the same time, the foreign supply price of autos falls by $200. This means that foreign producers earn smaller revenues, $7,800, for each auto exported. Because foreign production takes place under increasing-cost conditions, the reduction of imports from abroad triggers a decline in foreign production and unit costs decline. The reduction in the foreign supply price of $200 represents that portion of the tariff borne by the foreign producer. The levying of the tariff raises the domestic price of the import by only part of the duty as foreign producers lower their prices in an attempt to maintain sales in the tariff levying nation. The importing nation finds that its terms of trade has improved if the price it pays for auto imports decreases while the price it charges for its exports remains the same.

Thus, the *revenue effect* of an import tariff in the large nation includes two components. The first is the amount of tariff revenue shifted from domestic consumers to the tariff levying government; in Figure 4.3, this amount equals the level of imports (40 units) multiplied by the portion of the import tariff borne by domestic consumers ($800). Area *c* depicts the **domestic revenue effect**, t equals $32,000. The second element is the tariff revenue extracted from foreign producers in the form of a lower supply price. Found by multiplying auto imports (40 units) by the portion of the tariff falling on foreign producers ($200), the **terms-of-trade effect** is shown as area *e*, that equals $8,000. Note that the terms-of-trade effect represents a redistribution of income from the foreign nation to the tariff levying nation because of the new terms of trade. The tariff's revenue effect thus includes the domestic revenue effect and the terms-of-trade effect.

A nation that is a major importer of a product is in a favorable trade situation. It can use its tariff policy to improve the terms at which it trades and therefore its national welfare. But remember that the negative welfare effect of a tariff is the deadweight loss of the consumer surplus that results from the protection and consumption effects. Referring to Figure 4.3, to decide if a tariff levying nation can improve its national welfare, we must compare the impact of the deadweight loss (areas $b + d$) with the benefits of a more favorable terms of trade (area *e*). The conclusions regarding the welfare effects of a tariff are as follows:

1. If *e* is greater than $(b + d)$ national welfare is increased.
2. If *e* equals $(b + d)$ national welfare remains constant.
3. If *e* is less than $(b + d)$ national welfare is diminished.

In the preceding example, the domestic economy's welfare would decline by an amount equal to $8,000. This is because the deadweight welfare losses totaling $16,000 more than offset the $8,000 gain in welfare attributable to the terms-of-trade effect.

The Optimum Tariff and Retaliation

We have seen that a large nation can improve its terms of trade by imposing a tariff on imports. However, a tariff causes the volume of imports to decrease, that lessens the nation's welfare by reducing its consumption of low-cost imports. There is a gain because of improved terms of trade and a loss due to reduced import volume.

Referring to Figure 4.4, a nation optimizes its economic welfare by imposing a tariff rate at which the positive difference between the gain of improving terms of trade (area *e*) and the loss in economic efficiency from the protective effect (area *b*) and the consumption effect (area *d*) is at a maximum. The **optimum tariff** refers to such a tariff rate. It makes sense that the lower the foreign elasticity of supply, the more the large country can get its trading partners to accept lower prices for the large country's imports.

A likely candidate for a nation imposing an optimum tariff would be the United States; it is a large importer compared with world demand of autos, electronics, and other

FIGURE 4.4

How an Import Tariff Burdens Domestic Exporters

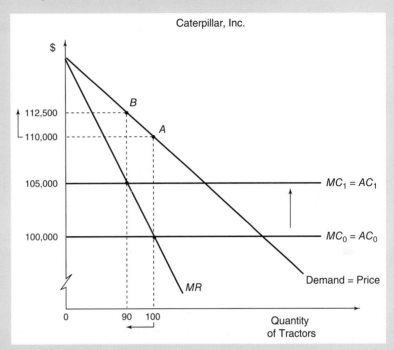

A tariff placed on imported steel increases the costs of a steel-using manufacturer. This increase leads to a higher price charged by the manufacturer and a loss of international competitiveness.

products. An optimum tariff is only beneficial to the importing nation. Because any benefit accruing to the importing nation through a lower import price implies a loss to the foreign exporting nation, imposing an optimum tariff is a **beggar-thy-neighbor** policy that could invite retaliation. After all, if the United States were to impose an optimal tariff of 25 percent on its imports, why should Japan and the European Union not levy tariffs of 40 or 50 percent on their imports? When all countries impose optimal tariffs, it is likely that everyone's economic welfare will decrease as the volume of trade declines. The possibility of foreign retaliation may be a sufficient deterrent for any nation considering whether to impose higher tariffs.

A classic case of a tariff induced trade war was the implementation of the Smoot–Hawley Tariff Act by the U.S. government in 1930. This tariff was initially intended to provide relief to U.S. farmers. Senators and members of Congress from industrial states used the technique of vote trading to obtain increased tariffs on manufactured goods. The result was a policy that increased tariffs on more than a thousand products with an average nominal duty on protected goods of 53 percent! Viewing the Smoot–Hawley tariff as an attempt to force unemployment on its workers, 12 nations promptly increased their duties against the United States. American farm exports fell to one-third of their former level, and between 1930 and 1933 total U.S. exports fell by almost 60 percent. Although the Great Depression accounted for much of that decline, the adverse psychological impact of the Smoot–Hawley tariff on business activity cannot be ignored.

EXAMPLES OF U.S. TARIFFS

Let us now consider two examples of tariffs that have been imposed to protect American producers from foreign competition.

Obama's Tariffs on Chinese Tires

President Barack Obama's import tariffs on tires provide an example of protectionism intended to aid a domestic industry. As a condition for China's entering the World Trade Organization in 2001, it agreed that other nations could clamp down on surges of imports from China without having to prove unfair trade practices. This special safeguard lasted until 2013. The surge became real when China increased its shipments of tires for automobiles and light trucks to the United States by almost 300 percent during 2004–2008 to $1.8 billion. Four American tire plants were closed and about 4,500 tire production jobs were lost during that period according to the United Steelworkers (USW) union.

In response to a complaint by the USW, Obama imposed a tariff in 2009 in addition to the existing tariff, for a three-year period on imports of tires from China. The tariff was applied to low price tires, roughly $50 to $60 apiece, that constitute the bulk of the tires China exports to the United States. The amount of the additional tariff was set at 35 percent in the first year, 30 percent in the second year, and 25 percent in the third year. The move would cut off about 17 percent of all tires sold in the United States. Obama justified his tariff policy by stating that he was simply enforcing the rule the Chinese had accepted. Critics maintained that Obama was pandering to blue collar workers and union leaders who were needed to support his legislative agenda regarding health care and other issues.

The tariff signaled Obama's desire to keep his word announced during his presidential campaign about protecting American jobs, many of which have moved to China and left employment holes in American manufacturing industries. The USW hailed the decision by declaring that it was the right thing to do for beleaguered American tire workers. Officials of China's government stated that Obama's decision sent the wrong signal to the world: not only was it a grave act of trade protectionism, but it violated rules of the World Trade Organization and contradicted open market commitments that the U.S. government made at the G20 financial summit in 2009.

According to the Obama administration, the tariffs would significantly reduce tire imports from China and boost U.S. industry sales and prices, resulting in increased profitability. This profitability would result in the preservation of jobs and the creation of new ones, as well as encourage investment. Also, the tariff would have little or no impact on the U.S. production of automobiles and light trucks because tires account for a very small share of the total cost of those products. Moreover, tires account for a relatively small share of the annual cost of owning and operating an automobile or light truck.

Critics contended that the story was more complicated. They noted that the USW petition for the tariff increase was not supported by American tire companies because they had already abandoned making low-cost tires in the United States: Tire company officials declared that it was not profitable to produce inexpensive tires in domestic plants in view of competition from foreign companies. Most American tire companies, such as Goodyear Tire and Rubber Co. and Cooper Tire and Rubber Co., manufacture low-cost tires in China that they sell in the United States. Any other American tire manufacturer that wanted to get involved in the low end business would have to revamp factory lines to produce such tires, a costly and complicated practice that would require considerable time. Critics also noted that if Chinese tire exports to the United States were blocked by the tariff, low wage manufacturers in other countries would replace them. However, it would take many months for producers in places like Brazil and

Indonesia to pick up the slack. In the meantime, shortages of low end tires would likely appear in the U.S. market resulting in prices increasing by an estimated 20 to 30 percent. Therefore, it was not clear that the Obama tariffs would actually lead to more jobs for the American tire worker or be good for the nation as a whole, according to the critics.

The imposition of the tire tariffs provided mixed evidence of their effects. The biggest beneficiaries of the tariffs were probably tire producers in Indonesia, South Korea, and Thailand, that replaced supply from China during the 3-year period of the tariffs.

Should Footwear Tariffs Be Given the Boot?

In 2013 shoppers were busy hunting for bargains at shoe departments of Target, Walmart and other discount stores. They encountered a wide assortment of shoes for children and adults. What they may have not realized was that most of the shoes sold at stores in the United States are produced abroad and are subject to substantial import tariffs. Why impose high tariffs on footwear?

American footwear tariffs began in the 1930s. At that time, there was a large shoe industry in the United States that produced mostly rubber and canvas footwear. Tariffs protected these producers from less expensive imports. Although many U.S. tariffs have been greatly decreased or eliminated since the 1930s, footwear tariffs have remained mostly unchanged. Although the U.S. footwear has benefitted from tariff protection, it is now virtually extinct; almost 99 percent of all footwear sold in America is currently imported. Nevertheless footwear tariff rates have continued and are high as 67.5 percent. Why does the U.S. government impose high tariffs on footwear when there is virtually no American industry to protect?

Critics contend that footwear tariffs are a hidden tax on a household necessity, increasing costs for consumers Also, they note that discount store sneakers are subject to a 48 percent tariff, while leather dress shoes are taxed at only 8.5 percent. Therefore, a Wall Street executive pays a lower tariff rate on his Italian leather loafers while low income households pay more than five times this tariff rate for their shoes. Footwear tariffs are regressive and thus burden people at the lower end of the income ladder more than the wealthy.

In 2013 the Affordable Footwear Act was introduced to Congress. This legislation attempts to abolish the most severe of these footwear tariffs—the sizable tariffs on lower to moderately priced footwear no longer produced in America. The passage of this legislation would result in the removal of tariffs on about one-third of all footwear imports. The goal is to ultimately reduce the price of shoes, a product that everyone buys, especially lower income households. The legislation ensures that protections continue for the few remaining U.S. footwear producers.

Critics of the Affordable Footwear Act consider high shoe tariffs as essential in shielding U.S. footwear producers from foreign competition. New Balance Inc. operates factories employing about 1,400 people in the United States. The company maintains that a reduction in footwear tariffs could harm its workers. Yet proponents of the Affordable Footwear Act contend that U.S. footwear companies generally produce specialty and high value shoes, not the types of inexpensive shoes that are subject to the tariff cut provisions of the Affordable Footwear Act. At the writing of this text, it remains to be seen whether the Affordable Footwear Act will be passed by the U.S. government.[6]

---

[6]H.R. 1708: *Affordable Footwear Act of 2013*, 113th Congress, 2013–2015; "Shoe Importers Push to Cut Long-Standing Tariff," *Los Angeles Times*, July 1, 2012; Eric Martin, "New Balance Wants Its Tariffs, Nike Doesn't," *Bloomberg Businessweek*, May 3, 2012; "Footwear Business Hopes to Stomp Out Higher Outdoor Shoe Tariffs," CBS/Denver, November 29, 2012; Edward Gresser and Bryan Riley, "Give Shoe Taxes the Boot," *Progressive Economy*, The Heritage Foundation, April 24, 2012; "A Shoe Tariff with a Big Footprint," *The Wall Street Journal*, November 22, 2012.

TRADE CONFLICTS   COULD A HIGHER TARIFF PUT A DENT IN THE FEDERAL DEBT?

The debt of the U.S. government is of much concern to policymakers and citizens alike. Solutions range from raising income taxes to cutting spending on national defense and entitlements. In an old U.S. customs house in New York City, there is a sign that says that at one time the U.S. government paid for all of its debt from a war by imposing tariffs on imported goods. Could a higher import tariff of, say, 20 percent currently be used to pay for Medicare and noticeably reduce the federal debt?

It is true that tariffs originally accounted for the bulk of federal government revenue—in 1795, about 95 percent of federal receipts came from tariff revenue. However, the importance of tariffs declined as tariffs were reduced and the income tax, enacted in 1913, came to be the major source of federal revenue. Today, tariffs are present on about 30 percent of goods imported by the United States and they generate only about $25 billion of revenue per year, amounting to 1.2 percent of federal revenue. Also,

the average U.S. tariff rate is about 2 percent of the price of an imported good.

So should the government raise tariffs to 20 percent, a tenfold increase of the current rate? Multiply the $25 billion of annual revenue that the federal government collects from tariffs by 10 and you would get an additional $250 billion of revenue each year, assuming that imports do not decrease if they go up in price by 20 percent, a dubious assumption. But let's not deal with that assumption. Because right now the U.S. government is borrowing over a trillion dollars a year to cover its deficit. Uh.... Eliminating that much debt would require a gigantic tariff, again assuming no decrease in import purchases. That could invite retaliatory tariffs imposed by our trading partners. Raising tariffs are not a good option for getting the United States out of debt.

Source: Paul Solman, "Could a Higher Import Tariff Pay for Medicare and Get the U.S. Out of Debt?" The Business Desk, January 5, 2012.

HOW A TARIFF BURDENS EXPORTERS

The benefits and costs of protecting domestic producers from foreign competition as discussed earlier in this chapter are based on the direct effects of an import tariff. Import-competing producers and workers can benefit from tariffs through increases in output, profits, jobs, and compensation. A tariff imposes costs on domestic consumers in the form of higher prices for protected products and reductions in the consumer surplus. There is also a net welfare loss for the economy because not all of the loss in the consumer surplus is transferred as gains to domestic producers and the government (the protective effect and consumption effects).

A tariff carries additional burdens. In protecting import-competing producers, a tariff leads indirectly to a reduction in domestic exports. The net result of protectionism is to move the economy toward greater self sufficiency, with lower imports and exports. For domestic workers, the protection of jobs in import-competing industries comes at the expense of jobs in other sectors of the economy, including exports. Although a tariff is intended to help domestic producers, the economy wide implications of a tariff are adverse for the export sector. The welfare losses because of restrictions in output and employment in the economy's export industry may offset the welfare gains enjoyed by import-competing producers.

Because a tariff is a tax on imports, the burden of a tariff falls initially on importers who must pay duties to the domestic government. However, importers generally try to shift increased costs to buyers through price increases. The resulting higher prices of imports injure domestic exporters in at least three ways.

First, exporters often purchase imported inputs subject to tariffs that *increase the cost of inputs*. Because exporters tend to sell in competitive markets where they have little ability to dictate the prices they receive, they generally cannot pass on a tariff induced increase in cost to their buyers. Higher export costs thus lead to higher prices and reduced overseas sales.

Consider the hypothetical case of Caterpillar Inc., a U.S. exporter of tractors. In Figure 4.4, suppose the firm realizes constant long run costs, suggesting that marginal cost equals average cost at each level of output. Let the production cost of a tractor equal $100,000, denoted by $MC_0 = AC_0$. Caterpillar Inc. maximizes profits by producing 100 tractors, the point at which marginal revenue equals marginal cost, and selling them at a price of $110,000 per unit. The firm's revenue thus totals $11 million ($100 \times \$110,000$) while its costs total $10 million ($100 \times \$100,000$); the firm realizes profits of $1 million. Suppose now that the U.S. government levies a tariff on steel imports while foreign nations allow steel to be imported duty free. If the production of tractors uses imported steel, and competitively priced domestic steel is not available, the tariff leads to an increase in Caterpillar's costs to $105,000 per tractor, as denoted by $MC_1 = AC_1$. Again the firm maximizes profits by operating where marginal revenue equals marginal cost. However, Caterpillar must charge a higher price, $112,500; the firm's sales decrease to 90 tractors and profits decrease to $675,000 [($112,500 − $105,000) \times 90 = \$675,000$]. The import tariff applied to steel represents a tax on Caterpillar that reduces its international competitiveness. Protecting domestic steel producers from import competition can thus lessen the export competitiveness of domestic steel using producers.

Tariffs also *raise the cost of living* by increasing the price of imports. Workers have the incentive to demand correspondingly higher wages, resulting in higher production costs. Tariffs lead to expanding output for import-competing producers that bid for workers, causing wages to rise. As these higher wages pass through the economy, export producers ultimately face higher wages and production costs that lessen their competitive position in international markets.

In addition, import tariffs have *international repercussions* that lead to reductions in domestic exports. Tariffs cause the quantity of imports to decrease that decreases other nations' export revenues and ability to import. The decline in foreign export revenues results in a smaller demand for a nation's exports and leads to falling output and employment in its export industries.

If domestic export producers are damaged by import tariffs, why don't they protest such policies more vigorously? One problem is that tariff induced increases in costs for export producers are subtle and invisible. Many exporters may not be aware of their existence. Also, the tariff–induced cost increases may be of such magnitude that some potential export producers are incapable of developing and have no tangible basis for political resistance.

U.S. steel using companies provide an example of exporters opposing tariffs on imported steel. Their officials contend that restrictions on steel imports are harmful to U.S. steel using industries that employ about 13 million workers compared to less than 200,000 workers employed by American steel producers. In the global economy, U.S. steel users must compete with efficient foreign manufacturers of all types of consumer and industrial installations, machines, and conveyances—everything from automobiles and earth moving equipment to nuts and bolts. Forcing U.S. manufacturers to pay considerably more for steel inputs than their foreign competitors would deal U.S. manufacturers a triple blow: increase raw material costs; threaten access to steel products not manufactured in the United States; and increase competition from abroad for the products they make. It would simply send our business offshore, devastating U.S. steel using companies; most of them small businesses.[7]

TARIFFS AND THE POOR

Empirical studies often maintain that the welfare costs of tariffs can be high. Tariffs also affect the distribution of income within a society. A legitimate concern of government officials is whether the welfare costs of tariffs are shared uniformly by all people in a country, or whether some income groups absorb a disproportionate share of the costs.

Several studies have considered the income distribution effects of import tariffs. They conclude that tariffs tend to be inequitable because they impose the most severe costs on *low income families*. Tariffs, for example, are often applied to products at the lower end of the price and quality range. Basic products such as shoes and clothing are subject to tariffs and these items constitute a large share of the budgets of low income families. Tariffs can be likened to sales taxes on the products protected, and as typically occurs with sales taxes, their effects are *regressive*. U.S. tariff policy is tough on the poor: young single mothers purchasing cheap clothes and shoes at Walmart often pay tariff rates five to ten times higher than rich families pay when purchasing at elite stores such as Nordstrom.[8] International trade agreements have eliminated most U.S. tariffs on high technology products like airplanes, semiconductors, computers, medical equipment, and medicines. The agreements have also reduced rates to generally less than 5.0 percent on mid range manufactured products like autos, TV sets, pianos, felt-tip pens, and many luxury consumer goods. Moreover, tariffs on natural resources such as oil, metal ores, and farm products like chocolate and coffee that are not grown in the United States are generally close to zero. However, inexpensive clothes, luggage, shoes, watches, and silverware have been excluded from most tariff reforms and tariffs remain relatively high. Clothing tariffs, for example, are usually in the 10 to 32 percent range.

Tariffs vary from one product to the next. They are much higher on cheap goods than luxuries. This disparity occurs because elite firms such as Ralph Lauren, Coach, or Oakley, that sell brand name and image, find small price advantages relatively unimportant. Because they have not lobbied the U.S. government for high tariffs, rates on luxury goods such as silk lingerie, silver-handled cutlery, leaded glass beer mugs, and snakeskin handbags are low. Producers of cheap water glasses, stainless steel cutlery, nylon lingerie, and plastic purses benefit by adding a few percentage points to their competitors' prices. On the cheapest goods, tariffs are even higher than the overall averages for consumer goods suggest, as seen in Table 4.8. U.S. tariffs are highest on goods that are the most important to the poor. The U.S. tariff system is not unique in being toughest on the poor. The tariffs of most U.S. trade partners operate in a similar fashion.

Besides bearing down hard on the poor, U.S. tariff policy affects different countries in different ways. Tariff policy especially burdens countries that specialize in the cheapest goods, noticeably poor countries in Asia and the Middle East. Average tariffs on European exports to the United States—mainly autos, computers, power equipment, and

---

[7]U.S. Senate Finance Committee, *Testimony of John Jenson*, February 13, 2002.

[8]Edward Gresser, "Toughest on the Poor: America's Flawed Tariff System," *Foreign Affairs*, November–December, 2002, pp. 19–23 and Susan Hickok, "The Consumer Cost of U.S. Trade Restraints," Federal Reserve Bank of New York, *Quarterly Review,* Summer 1985, pp. 10–11.

TABLE 4.8

U.S. Tariffs are High on Cheap Goods, Low on Luxuries

Product	Tariff Rate (percent)
Women's Underwear	
Man-made fiber	16.2
Cotton	11.3
Silk	2.4
Men's knitted shirts	
Synthetic fiber	32.5
Cotton	20.0
Silk	1.9
Handbags	
Plastic-sided	16.8
Leather, under $20	10.0
Reptile leather	5.3

Source: From U.S. International Trade Commission, *Tariff Schedules of the United States*, Washington, DC, Government Printing Office, 2008, available at http://www.usitc.gov/.

chemicals—today barely exceed one percent. Developing countries such as Malaysia that specialize in information technology goods face tariff rates just as low. So do oil exporters such as Saudi Arabia and Nigeria. Asian countries like Cambodia and Bangladesh are hit hardest by U.S. tariffs; their cheap consumer goods often face tariff rates of 15 percent or more, some ten times the world average.

ARGUMENTS FOR TRADE RESTRICTIONS

The **free-trade argument** is, in principle, persuasive. It states that if each nation produces what it does best and permits trade, over the long run all will enjoy lower prices and higher levels of output, income, and consumption than could be achieved in isolation. In a dynamic world, comparative advantage is constantly changing due to shifts in technologies, input productivities, and wages, as well as demand. A free market compels adjustment to take place. Either the efficiency of an industry must improve or else resources will flow from low productivity uses to those with high productivity. Tariffs and other trade barriers are viewed as tools that prevent the economy from undergoing adjustment, resulting in economic stagnation.

Although the free-trade argument tends to dominate in the classroom, virtually all nations have imposed restrictions on the international flow of goods, services, and capital. Often, proponents of protectionism say that free trade is fine in theory, but it does not apply in the real world. Modern trade theory assumes perfectly competitive markets whose characteristics do not reflect real world market conditions. Moreover, even though protectionists may concede that economic losses occur with tariffs and other restrictions, they often argue that noneconomic benefits such as national security more than offset the economic losses. In seeking protection from imports, domestic industries and labor unions attempt to secure their economic welfare. Over the years, many arguments have been advanced to pressure the president and Congress to enact restrictive measures.

Job Protection

The issue of jobs has been a dominant factor in motivating government officials to levy trade restrictions on imported goods. During periods of economic recession, workers are especially eager to point out that cheap foreign goods undercut domestic production, resulting in a loss of domestic jobs to foreign labor. Alleged job losses to foreign competition historically have been a major force behind the desire of most U.S. labor leaders to reject free-trade policies.

This view has a serious omission: it fails to acknowledge the dual nature of international trade. Changes in a nation's imports of goods and services are closely related to changes in its exports. Nations export goods because they desire to import products from other nations. When the United States imports goods from abroad, foreigners gain purchasing power that will eventually be spent on U.S. goods, services, or financial assets. American. export industries then enjoy gains in sales and employment, whereas the opposite occurs with U.S. import-competing producers. Rather than promoting overall unemployment, imports tend to generate job opportunities in some industries as part of the process by which they decrease employment in other industries. The job gains because of open trade policies tend to be less visible to the public than the readily observable job losses stemming from foreign competition. The more conspicuous losses have led many U.S. business and labor leaders to combine forces in their opposition to free trade.

Trade restraints raise employment in the protected industry (such as steel) by increasing the price (or reducing the supply) of competing import goods. Industries that are primary suppliers of inputs to the protected industry also gain jobs. However, industries that purchase the protected product (such as auto manufacturers) face higher costs. These costs are then passed on to the consumer through higher prices, resulting in decreased sales. Employment falls in these related industries.

Economists at the Federal Reserve Bank of Dallas have examined the effects on U.S. employment of trade restrictions on textiles and apparel, steel, and automobiles. They conclude that trade protection has little or no positive effect on the level of employment in the long run. Trade restraints tend to provide job gains for only a few industries while they result in job losses spread across many industries.[9]

A striking fact about efforts to preserve jobs is that each job often ends up costing domestic consumers more than the worker's salary! In 1986, the annual consumer cost of protecting each job preserved in the specialty steel industry in the United States was reported to be $1 million a year; this was far above the salary a production employee in that industry receives. The fact that costs to consumers for each production job saved are so high supports the argument that an alternative approach should be used to help workers, and that workers departing from an industry facing foreign competition should be liberally compensated (subsidized) for moving to new industries or taking early retirement.[10]

Protection against Cheap Foreign Labor

One of the most common arguments used to justify the protectionist umbrella of trade restrictions is that tariffs are needed to defend domestic jobs against cheap foreign labor. As indicated in Table 4.9, production workers in Germany and the United States have

---

[9]Linda Hunter, "U.S. Trade Protection: Effects on the Industrial and Regional Composition of Employment," Federal Reserve Bank of Dallas, *Economic Review*, January 1990, pp. 1–13.

[10]Other examples of the annual cost of import restrictions per job saved to the American consumer include: bolts and nuts, $550,000; motorcycles, $150,000; mushrooms, $117,000; automobiles, $105,000; and footwear, $55,000. See Gary Hufbauer, et. al. *Trade Protection in the United States: 31 Case Studies*, Washington, DC: Institute for International Economics, 1986.

TABLE 4.9

Hourly Compensation Costs in U.S. Dollars for Production Workers in Manufacturing, 2011

Country	Hourly Compensation (dollars per hour)
Denmark	51.67
Germany	47.38
Canada	36.56
United States	35.53
New Zealand	23.38
South Korea	18.91
Taiwan	9.34
Mexico	6.48
Philippines	2.01

Source: From U.S. Department of Labor, Bureau of Labor Statistics, *International Comparisons of Hourly Compensation Costs in Manufacturing, 2012*, available at http://www.bls.gov.

been paid much higher wages in terms of the U.S. dollar, than workers in countries such as the Philippines and Mexico. It could be argued that low wages abroad make it difficult for U.S. producers to compete with producers using cheap foreign labor and that unless U.S. producers are protected from imports, domestic output and employment levels will decrease.

When Maytag moved its production of clothes washers and dryers from Iowa to Mexico, cheap labor was the main reason. The same consideration resulted in Levi Strauss and Co., the famous American jeans manufacturer, to relocate from the United States to Mexico and China.

Indeed, it is widely believed that competition from goods produced in low wage countries is unfair and harmful to American workers. Moreover, it is thought that companies that produce goods in foreign countries to take advantage of cheap labor should not be allowed to dictate the wages paid to American workers. A solution: Impose a tariff or tax on goods brought into the United States equal to the wage differential between foreign and U.S. workers in the same industry. That way, competition would be confined to who makes the best product, not who works for the least amount of money. If Calvin Klein wants to manufacture sweatshirts in Pakistan, his firm would be charged a tariff or tax equal to the difference between the earnings of a Pakistani worker and a U.S. apparel worker.

Although this viewpoint may have widespread appeal, it fails to recognize the links among efficiency, wages, and production costs. Even if domestic wages are higher than those abroad, if domestic labor is more productive than foreign labor, domestic labor costs may still be competitive. Total labor costs reflect not only the wage rate but also the output per labor hour. If the productive superiority of domestic labor more than offsets the higher domestic wage rate, the home nation's labor costs will actually be less than they are abroad. Low wages in developing countries are often offset by higher productivity in the United States.

Table 4.10 shows labor productivity (output per worker), wages, and unit labor costs in manufacturing, relative to the United States, for several nations during 2006–2009. We see that wages in these nations were only fractions of U.S. wages; however, labor productivity levels in these nations were also fractions of U.S. labor productivity. Even if wages

TABLE 4.10

Productivity, Wages, and Unit Labor Costs, Relative to the United States: Total Manufacturing, (United States = 1.0)

Country	Labor Productivity Relative to United States	Wages Relative to United States*	Unit Labor Cost Relative to United States	
Hong Kong (2008)	0.21	0.44	2.09	
Maritius (2007)	0.06	0.12	2.00	
South Africa (2008)	0.14	0.27	1.93	
European Union (2009)	0.46	0.84	1.83	
United Kingdom (2009)	0.50	0.84	1.68	U.S. More Competitive
Singapore (2008)	0.40	0.61	1.53	U.S. Less Competitive
Japan (2008)	0.67	0.72	1.07	
Mexico (2009)	0.18	0.17	0.94	
South Korea (2006)	0.71	0.61	0.86	
Poland (2006)	0.26	0.20	0.77	
China (2008)	0.12	0.08	0.67	

*At market exchange rate.

Source: The author wishes to thank Professor Steven Golub of Swarthmore College, who provided data for this table. Refer to his *CESifo Working Paper* at the Center for Economic Studies, University of Munich, Munich, Germany, 2011. See also Janet Ceglowski and Stephen Golub, "Are China's Labor Costs Still Low?" This paper was prepared for the CESifo conference on *China and the Global Economy Post Crisis*, held in Venice, Italy, July 18–19, 2011.

in a foreign country are lower than in the United States, the country would have higher unit labor costs if its labor productivity is sufficiently lower than U.S. labor productivity. This was the case for countries such as Hong Kong, South Africa, Japan, and the United Kingdom where the unit labor cost ratio (unit labor cost ratio = wage ratio / labor productivity ratio) was greater than 1.0. These nations' unit labor costs exceeded those of the United States because the productivity gap of their workers exceeded the wage gap. Low wages by themselves do not guarantee low production costs. If they did, countries such as Botswana and Malaysia would dominate world trade.

Another limitation of the cheap foreign labor argument is that low wage nations tend to have a competitive advantage only in the production of goods requiring greater labor and little of the other factor inputs—that is, only when the wage bill is the largest component of the total costs of production. It is true that a high wage nation may have a relative cost disadvantage compared with its low-wage trading partner in the production of labor intensive commodities. But this does not mean that foreign producers can undersell the home country across the board in all lines of production, causing the overall domestic standard of living to decline. Foreign nations should use the revenues from their export sales to purchase the products in which the home country has a competitive advantage—products requiring a large share of the factors of production that are abundant domestically.

Recall that the factor-endowment theory suggests that as economies become interdependent through trade, resource payments tend to become equal in different nations given competitive markets. A nation with expensive labor will tend to import products embodying large amounts of labor. As imports rise and domestic output falls, the resulting decrease in demand for domestic labor will cause domestic wages to fall to the foreign level.

Fairness in Trade: A Level Playing Field

Fairness in trade is another reason given for protectionism. Business firms and workers often argue that foreign governments play by a different set of rules than the home government, giving foreign firms unfair competitive advantages. Domestic producers contend that import restrictions should be enacted to offset these foreign advantages, thus creating a **level playing field** on which all producers can compete on equal terms.

American companies often allege that foreign firms are not subject to the same government regulations regarding pollution control and worker safety; this is especially true in many developing nations (such as Mexico and South Korea) where environmental laws and enforcement have been lax. Moreover, foreign firms may not pay as much in corporate taxes and may not have to comply with employment regulations such as affirmative action, minimum wages, and overtime pay. Also, foreign governments may erect high trade barriers that effectively close their markets to imports or they may subsidize their producers so as to enhance their competitiveness in world markets.

These fair trade arguments are often voiced by organized lobbies that are losing sales to foreign competitors. They may sound appealing to the voters because they are couched in terms of fair play and equal treatment. However, there are several arguments against levying restrictions on imports from nations that have high trade restrictions or that place lower regulatory burdens on their producers.

First, trade benefits the domestic economy even if foreign nations impose trade restrictions. Although foreign restrictions that lessen our exports may decrease our welfare, retaliating by levying our own import barriers—that protect inefficient domestic producers—decreases our welfare even more.

Second, the argument does not recognize the potential impact on global trade. If each nation were to increase trade restrictions whenever foreign restrictions were higher than domestic restrictions, a worldwide escalation in restrictions would occur; this would lead to a lower volume of trade, falling levels of production and employment, and a decline in welfare. There may be a case for threatening to levy trade restrictions unless foreign nations reduce their restrictions; but if negotiations fail and domestic restrictions are employed, the result is undesirable. Other countries' trade practices are seldom an adequate justification for domestic trade restrictions.

Maintenance of the Domestic Standard of Living

Advocates of trade barriers often contend that tariffs are useful in maintaining a high level of income and employment for the home nation. It is argued that by reducing the level of imports, tariffs encourage home spending that stimulates domestic economic activity. As a result, the home nation's level of employment and income will be enhanced.

Although this argument appears appealing on the surface, it merits several qualifications. All nations together cannot levy tariffs to bolster domestic living standards. This is because tariffs result in a redistribution of the gains from trade among nations. To the degree that one nation imposes a tariff that improves its income and employment it does so at the expense of its trading partners' living standard. Nations adversely affected by trade barriers are likely to impose retaliatory tariffs, resulting in a lower level of welfare for all nations. It is little wonder that tariff restrictions designed to enhance a nation's standard of living at the expense of its trading partner are referred to as *beggar-thy-neighbor* policies.

Equalization of Production Costs

Proponents of a **scientific tariff** seek to eliminate what they consider to be unfair competition from abroad. Owing to such factors as lower wage costs, tax concessions, or government subsidies, foreign sellers may enjoy cost advantages over domestic firms. To offset any such advantage, tariffs equivalent to the cost differential should be imposed. Such provisions were actually part of the U.S. Tariff Acts of 1922 and 1930.

In practice, the scientific tariff suffers from a number of problems. Because costs differ from business to business within a given industry, how can costs actually be compared? Suppose that all U.S. steelmakers were extended protection from all foreign steelmakers. This protection would require the costs of the most efficient foreign producer to be set equal to the highest costs of the least efficient U.S. company. Given today's cost conditions, prices would certainly rise in the United States. This rise would benefit the more efficient U.S. companies that would enjoy economic profits, but the U.S. consumer would be subsidizing inefficient production. Because the scientific tariff approximates a prohibitive tariff, it completely contradicts the notion of comparative advantage and wipes out the basis for trade and gains from trade.

Infant-Industry Argument

One of the more commonly accepted cases for tariff protection is the **infant-industry argument**. This argument does not deny the validity of the case for free trade. However, it contends that for free trade to be meaningful, trading nations should temporarily shield their newly developing industries from foreign competition. Otherwise, mature foreign businesses that are at the time more efficient can drive the young domestic businesses out of the market. Only after the young companies have had time to become efficient producers should the tariff barriers be lifted and free trade take place.

Although there is some truth in the infant-industry argument, it must be qualified in several respects. First, once a protective tariff is imposed, it is difficult to remove, even after industrial maturity has been achieved. Special interest groups can often convince policy makers that further protection is justified. Second, it is difficult to determine which industries will be capable of realizing comparative-advantage potential and thus merit protection. Third, the infant-industry argument generally is not valid for mature, industrialized nations such as the United States, Germany, and Japan. Fourth, there may be other ways of insulating a developing industry from cutthroat competition. Rather than adopt a protective tariff, the government could grant a subsidy to the industry. A subsidy has the advantage of not distorting domestic consumption and relative prices; its drawback is that instead of generating revenue, as an import tariff does, a subsidy spends revenue.

Noneconomic Arguments

Noneconomic considerations also enter into the arguments for protectionism. One such consideration is *national security*. The national security argument contends that a country may be put in jeopardy in the event of an international crisis or war if it is heavily dependent on foreign suppliers. Even though domestic producers are not as efficient, tariff protection should be granted to ensure their continued existence. A good application of this argument involves the major oil importing nations that saw several Arab nations impose oil boycotts on the West to win support for the Arab position against Israel during the 1973 Middle East conflict. However, the problem is stipulating what constitutes an essential industry. If the term is defined broadly, many industries may be able to win import protection, and then argument loses its meaning.

The national security argument for protectionism also has implications for foreign investments such as foreign acquisitions of American companies and assets. Although the United States has traditionally welcomed foreign investment, it provides authority to the president to suspend or prohibit any foreign acquisition, merger, or takeover of a U.S. corporation determined to threaten the national security of the United States. Examples of actions generally considered harmful to the security of the United States include the denial of critical technology or key products to the U.S. government or U.S. industry, moving critical technology or key products offshore that are important for national defense or homeland security, and shutting down or sabotaging a critical facility in the United States. Therefore, the U.S. government reviews foreign investment transactions beyond the defense industrial base, including energy and natural resources, technology, telecommunications, transportation, and manufacturing. Such reviews have become more stringent since the September 11, 2001 terrorist attack against the United States.[11]

Another noneconomic argument is based on *cultural* and *sociological* considerations. New England may desire to preserve small scale fishing; West Virginia may argue for tariffs on hand blown glassware on the grounds that these skills enrich the fabric of life; certain products such as narcotics may be considered socially undesirable and restrictions or prohibitions may be placed on their importation. These arguments constitute legitimate reasons and cannot be ignored. All the economist can do is point out the economic consequences and costs of protection and identify alternative ways of accomplishing the same objective.

In Canada, many nationalists maintain that Canadian culture is too fragile to survive without government protection. The big threat: U.S. cultural imperialism. To keep the Yanks in check, Canada has long maintained some restrictions on sales of U.S. publications and textbooks. By the 1990s, the envelope of Canada's cultural protectionism was expanding. The most blatant example was a 1994 law that levied an 80 percent tax on Canadian ads in Canadian editions of U.S. magazines—in effect, an effort to kill off the U.S. intruders. Without protections for the Canadian media, the cultural nationalists feared that U.S. magazines such as *Sports Illustrated, Time*, and *Business Week* could soon deprive Canadians of the ability to read about themselves in *Maclean's* and *Canadian Business*. Although U.S. protests of the tax ultimately led to its abolishment, the Canadian government continued to examine other methods of preserving the culture of its people.

Most of the arguments justifying tariffs are based on the assumption that the national welfare, as well as the individual's welfare, will be enhanced. The strategic importance of tariffs for the welfare of import-competing producers is one of the main reasons that reciprocal tariff liberalization has been so gradual. It is no wonder that import-competing producers make such strong and politically effective arguments that increased foreign competition will undermine the welfare of the nation as a whole as well as their own. Although a liberalization of tariff barriers may be detrimental to a particular group, we must be careful to differentiate between the individual's welfare and the national welfare. If tariff reductions result in greater welfare gains from trade and if the adversely affected party can be compensated for the loss it has faced, the overall national welfare will increase. However, proving that the gains more than offset the losses in practice is difficult.

---

[11]Edward Graham and David Marchick, *U.S. National Security and Foreign Direct Investment*, Washington, DC: Institute for International Economics, 2006.

TRADE CONFLICTS   PETITION OF THE CANDLE MAKERS

Free trade advocate Frederic Bastiat presented the French Chamber of Deputies with a devastating satire of protectionists' arguments in 1845. His petition asked that a law be passed requiring people to shut all windows, doors, and so forth so that the candle industry would be protected from the "unfair" competition of the sun. He argued that this would be a great benefit to the candle industry, creating many new jobs and enriching suppliers. Consider the following excerpts from his satire:

We are subjected to the intolerable competition of a foreign rival, who enjoys, it would seem, such superior facilities for the production of light, that he is flooding the domestic market with it at an incredibly low price. From the moment he appears, our sales cease, all consumers turn to him, and a branch of French industry whose ramifications are innumerable is at once reduced to complete stagnation. This rival is no other than the sun.

We ask you to be so good as to pass a law requiring the closing of all windows, dormers, skylights, shutters, curtains, and blinds--in short, all openings, holes, chinks,

and fissures through which the light of the sun is wont to enter houses, to the detriment of our industries.

By shutting out as much as possible all access to natural light, you create the necessity for artificial light. Is there in France an industry which will not, through some connection with this important object, be benefited by it? If more tallow be consumed, there will arise a necessity for an increase of cattle and sheep. If more oil be consumed, it will cause an increase in the cultivation of the olive tree. Navigation will profit as thousands of vessels would be employed in the whale fisheries. There is, in short, no market which would not be greatly developed by the granting of our petitions.

Although it is undoubtedly true that the French candle industry would benefit from a lack of sunlight, consumers would obviously not be happy about being forced to pay for light that they could get for free were there no government intervention.

Source: Frederic Bastiat, *Economic Sophisms*, edited and translated by Arthur Goddard, New York, D. Van Nostrand, 1964.

THE POLITICAL ECONOMY OF PROTECTIONISM

Recent history indicates that increasing dependence on international trade yields uneven impacts across domestic sectors. The United States has enjoyed comparative advantages in such products as agricultural commodities, industrial machinery, chemicals, and scientific instruments. However, some of its industries have lost their comparative advantage and suffered from international trade—among them are apparel and textiles, motor vehicles, electronic goods, basic iron and steel, and footwear. Formulating international trade policy in this environment is difficult. Free trade can yield substantial benefits for the overall economy through increased productivity and lower prices, but specific groups may benefit if government provides them some relief from import competition. Government officials must consider these opposing interests when setting the course for international trade policy.

Considerable attention has been devoted to what motivates government officials when formulating trade policy. As voters, we do not have the opportunity to go to the polls and vote for a trade bill. Instead, formation of trade policy rests in the hands of elected officials and their appointees. It is generally assumed that elected officials form policies to maximize votes and thus remain in office. The result is a bias in the political system that favors protectionism.

The **protection-biased sector** of the economy generally consists of import-competing producers, labor unions representing workers in that industry, and suppliers to the producers in the industry. Seekers of protectionism are often established firms in an aging industry that have lost their comparative advantage. High costs may be due to lack of modern technology, inefficient management procedures, outmoded work rules, or high payments to domestic workers. The **free-trade-biased sector** generally comprises exporting companies, their workers, and their suppliers. It also consists of consumers, including wholesalers and retail merchants of imported goods.

Government officials understand that they will likely lose the political support of, say, the United Auto Workers (UAW) if they vote against increases in tariffs on auto imports. They also understand that their vote on this trade issue will not be the key factor underlying the political support provided by many other citizens. Their support can be retained by appealing to them on other issues while voting to increase the tariff on auto imports to maintain UAW support.

The United States protection policy is thus dominated by special interest groups that represent producers. Consumers generally are not organized and their losses due to protectionism are widely dispersed, whereas the gains from protection are concentrated among well organized producers and labor unions in the affected sectors. Those harmed by a protectionist policy absorb individually a small and difficult to identify cost. Many consumers, though they will pay a higher price for the protected product, do not associate the higher price with the protectionist policy and are unlikely to be concerned about trade policy. However, special interest groups are highly concerned about protecting their industries against import competition. They provide support for government officials who share their views and lobby against the election of those who do not. Clearly, government officials seeking reelection will be sensitive to the special interest groups representing producers.

The political bias favoring domestic producers is seen in the tariff escalation effect, discussed earlier in this chapter. Recall that the tariff structures of industrial nations often result in lower import tariffs on intermediate goods and higher tariffs on finished goods. U.S. imports of cotton yarn have traditionally faced low tariffs, while higher tariffs have been applied to cotton fabric imports. The higher tariff on cotton fabrics appears to be the result of the ineffective lobbying efforts of diffused consumers, who lose to organized U.S. fabric producers lobbying for protectionism. But for cotton yarn, the protectionist outcome is less clear. Purchasers of cotton yarn are U.S. manufacturers who want low tariffs on imported inputs. These companies form trade associations and can pressure Congress for low tariffs as effectively as U.S. cotton suppliers, who lobby for high tariffs. Protection applied to imported intermediate goods such as cotton yarn is then less likely.

Not only does the interest of the domestic producer tend to outweigh that of the domestic consumer in trade policy deliberations, but import-competing producers also tend to exert stronger influence on legislators than do export producers. A problem faced by export producers is that their gains from international trade are often in addition to their prosperity in the domestic market; producers that are efficient enough to sell overseas are often safe from foreign competition in the domestic market. Most deliberations on trade policy emphasize protecting imports and the indirect damage done by import barriers to export producers tends to be spread over many export industries. But import-competing producers can gather evidence of immediate damage caused by foreign competition, including falling levels of sales, profits, and employment. Legislators tend to be influenced by the more clearly identified arguments of import-competing producers and see that a greater number of votes are at stake among their constituents than among the constituents of the export producers.

A Supply and Demand View of Protectionism

The political economy of import protection can be analyzed in terms of supply and demand. Protectionism is supplied by the domestic government, while domestic companies and workers are the source of demand. The supply of protection depends on (1) the costs to society, (2) the political importance of import-competing producers, (3) adjustment costs, and (4) public sympathy.

Enlightened government officials realize that although protectionism provides benefits to domestic producers, society as a whole pays the *costs*. These costs include the losses of consumer surplus because of higher prices and the resulting deadweight losses as import volume is reduced, lost economies of scale as opportunities for further trade are foregone, and the loss of incentive for technological development provided by import competition. The higher the costs of protection to society the less likely it is that government officials will shield an industry from import competition.

The supply of protectionism is also influenced by the *political importance* of the import-competing industry. An industry that enjoys strong representation in the legislature is in a favorable position to win import protection. It is more difficult for politicians to disagree with 1 million autoworkers than with 20,000 copper workers. The national security argument for protection is a variant on the consideration of the political importance of an industry. The U.S. coal and oil industries were successful in obtaining a national security clause in U.S. trade law permitting protection if imports threaten to impair domestic security.

The supply of protection also tends to increase when domestic firms and workers face large costs of adjusting to rising import competition (for example, unemployment or wage concessions). This protection is seen as a method of delaying the full burden of *adjustment*.

Finally, as *public sympathy* for a group of domestic businesses or workers increases (if workers are paid low wages and have few alternative work skills) a greater amount of protection against foreign-produced goods tends to be supplied.

On the demand side, factors that underlie the domestic industry's demand for protectionism are (1) comparative disadvantage, (2) import penetration, (3) concentration, and (4) export dependence.

The demand for protection rises as the domestic industry's *comparative disadvantage* intensifies. This is seen in the U.S. steel industry that has vigorously pursued protection against low-cost Japanese and South Korean steel manufacturers in recent decades.

Higher levels of *import penetration* that suggests increased competitive pressures for domestic producers also trigger increased demands for protection. A significant change in the nature of support for protectionism occurred in the late 1960s when the AFL-CIO abandoned its long held belief in the desirability of open markets and supported protectionism. This shift in the union's position was due primarily to the rapid rise in import penetration ratios that occurred during the 1960s in such industries as electrical consumer goods and footwear.

Another factor that may affect the demand for protection is *concentration* of domestic production. The U.S. auto industry, for example, is dominated by the Big Three. Support for import protection can be financed by these firms without fear that a large share of the benefits of protectionism will accrue to nonparticipating firms. Conversely, an industry that comprises many small producers (meat packing) realizes that a substantial share of the gains from protectionism may accrue to producers who do not contribute their fair share to the costs of winning protectionist legislation. The demand for protection tends to be stronger the more concentrated the domestic industry.

Finally, the demand for protection may be influenced by the degree of *export dependence*. One would expect that companies whose foreign sales constitute a substantial portion of total sales (Boeing) would not be greatly concerned about import protection. Their main fear is that the imposition of domestic trade barriers might invite retaliation overseas that would ruin their export markets. *In Exploring Further 4.1,* located at www.cengage.com/economics/Carbaugh, we introduce offer curves in the analysis of tariffs.

SUMMARY

1. Even though the free-trade argument has strong theoretical justifications, trade restrictions are widespread throughout the world. Trade barriers consist of tariff restrictions and nontariff trade barriers.

2. There are several types of tariffs. A specific tariff represents a fixed amount of money per unit of the imported commodity. An ad valorem tariff is stated as a fixed percentage of the value of an imported commodity. A compound tariff combines a specific tariff with an ad valorem tariff.

3. Concerning ad valorem tariffs, several procedures exist for the valuation of imports. The free-on-board (FOB) measure indicates a commodity's price as it leaves the exporting nation. The cost-insurance-freight (CIF) measure shows the product's value as it arrives at the port of entry.

4. The effective tariff rate tends to differ from the nominal tariff rate when the domestic import-competing industry uses imported resources whose tariffs differ from those on the final commodity. Developing nations have traditionally argued that many advanced nations escalate the tariff structures on industrial commodities to yield an effective rate of protection several times the nominal rate.

5. American trade laws mitigate the effects of import duties by allowing U.S. importers to postpone and prorate over time their duty obligations by means of bonded warehouses and foreign-trade zones.

6. The welfare effects of a tariff can be measured by its protective effect, consumption effect, redistributive effect, revenue effect, and terms-of-trade effect.

7. If a nation is small compared with the rest of the world, its welfare necessarily falls by the total amount of the protective effect plus the consumption effect if it levies a tariff on imports. If the importing nation is large relative to the world, the imposition of an import tariff may improve its international terms of trade by an amount that more than offsets the welfare losses associated with the consumption effect and the protective effect.

8. Because a tariff is a tax on imports, the burden of a tariff falls initially on importers, who must pay duties to the domestic government. However, importers generally try to shift increased costs to buyers through price increases. Domestic exporters, who purchase imported inputs subject to tariffs, thus face higher costs and a reduction in competitiveness.

9. Although tariffs may improve one nation's economic position, any gains generally come at the expense of other nations. Should tariff retaliations occur, the volume of international trade decreases, and world welfare suffers. Tariff liberalization is intended to promote freer markets so

that the world can benefit from expanded trade volumes and the international specialization of inputs.

10. Tariffs are sometimes justified on the grounds that they protect domestic employment and wages, help create a level playing field for international trade, equate the cost of imported products with the cost of domestic import-competing products, allow domestic industries to be insulated temporarily from foreign competition until they can grow and develop, or protect industries necessary for national security.

KEY CONCEPTS AND TERMS

Ad valorem tariff (p. 109)
Beggar-thy-neighbor
  policy (p. 129)
Bonded warehouse (p. 119)
Compound tariff (p. 109)
Consumer surplus (p. 122)
Consumption effect (p. 125)
Cost-insurance-freight (CIF)
  valuation (p. 110)
Customs valuation (p. 110)
Deadweight loss (p. 126)
Domestic revenue effect (p. 128)
Effective tariff rate (p. 112)
Foreign-trade zone (FTZ) (p. 119)

Free-on-board (FOB)
  valuation (p. 110)
Free-trade argument (p. 135)
Free-trade-biased sector (p. 143)
Infant-industry
  argument (p. 140)
Large nation (p. 126)
Level playing field (p. 139)
Nominal tariff rate (p. 112)
Offshore-assembly provision
  (OAP) (p. 115)
Optimum tariff (p. 128)
Outsourcing (p. 115)
Producer surplus (p. 123)

Protection-biased sector (p. 143)
Protective effect (p. 125)
Protective tariff (p. 108)
Redistributive effect (p. 125)
Revenue effect (p. 125)
Revenue tariff (p. 108)
Scientific tariff (p. 140)
Small nation (p. 123)
Specific tariff (p. 109)
Tariff (p. 108)
Tariff avoidance (p. 116)
Tariff escalation (p. 115)
Tariff evasion (p. 116)
Terms-of-trade effect (p. 128)

STUDY QUESTIONS

1. Describe a specific tariff, an ad valorem tariff, and a compound tariff. What are the advantages and disadvantages of each?

2. What methods do customs appraisers use to determine the values of commodity imports?

3. Under what conditions does a nominal tariff applied to an import product overstate or understate the actual, or effective, protection afforded by the nominal tariff?

4. Less developed nations sometimes argue that the industrialized nations' tariff structures discourage the less developed nations from undergoing industrialization. Explain.

5. Distinguish between consumer surplus and producer surplus. How do these concepts relate to a country's economic welfare?

6. When a nation imposes a tariff on the importation of a commodity, economic inefficiencies develop that detract from the national welfare. Explain.

7. What factors influence the size of the revenue, protective, consumption, and redistributive effects of a tariff?

8. A nation that imposes tariffs on imported goods may find its welfare improving should the tariff result in a favorable shift in the terms of trade. Explain.

9. Which of the arguments for tariffs do you feel are most relevant in today's world?

10. Although tariffs may improve the welfare of a single nation, the world's welfare may decline. Under what conditions would this be true?

11. What impact does the imposition of a tariff normally have on a nation's terms of trade and volume of trade?

12. Suppose that the production of $1 million worth of steel in Canada requires $100,000 worth of taconite. Canada's nominal tariff rates for importing these goods are 20 percent for steel and 10 percent

for taconite. Given this information, calculate the effective rate of protection for Canada's steel industry.

13. Would a tariff imposed on U.S. oil imports promote energy development and conservation for the United States?

14. What is meant by the terms *bonded warehouse* and *foreign-trade zone*? How does each of these help importers mitigate the effects of domestic import duties?

15. Assume the nation of Australia is "small" and thus unable to influence world price. Its demand and supply schedules for TV sets are shown in Table 4.11. Using graph paper, plot the demand and supply schedules on the same graph.

TABLE 4.11

Demand and Supply: TV Sets (Australia)

Price of TVS	Quantity Demanded	Quantity Supplied
$500	0	50
400	10	40
300	20	30
200	30	20
100	40	10
0	50	0

© Cengage Learning®

a. Determine Australia's market equilibrium for TV sets.
   (1) What are the equilibrium price and quantity?
   (2) Calculate the value of Australian consumer surplus and producer surplus.

b. Under free-trade conditions, suppose Australia imports TV sets at a price of $100 each. Determine the free-trade equilibrium, and illustrate graphically.
   (1) How many TV sets will be produced, consumed, and imported?
   (2) Calculate the dollar value of Australian consumer surplus and producer surplus.

c. To protect its producers from foreign competition, suppose the Australian government levies a specific tariff of $100 on imported TV sets.
   (1) Determine and show graphically the effects of the tariff on the price of TV sets in Australia, the quantity of TV sets supplied by Australian producers, the quantity of TV

sets demanded by Australian consumers, and the volume of trade.
   (2) Calculate the reduction in Australian consumer surplus due to the tariff induced increase in the price of TV sets.
   (3) Calculate the value of the tariff's consumption, protective, redistributive, and revenue effects.
   (4) What is the amount of deadweight welfare loss imposed on the Australian economy by the tariff?

16. Assume that the United States, as a steel importing nation, is large enough so that changes in the quantity of its imports influence the world price of steel. The U.S. supply and demand schedules for steel are illustrated in Table 4.12, along with the overall amount of steel supplied to U.S. consumers by domestic and foreign producers.

TABLE 4.12

Supply and Demand: Tons of Steel (United States)

Price/Ton	Quantity Supplied (Domestic)	Quantity Supplied (Domestic + Imports)	Quantity Demanded
$100	0	0	15
200	0	4	14
300	1	8	13
400	2	12	12
500	3	16	11
600	4	20	10
700	5	24	9

© Cengage Learning®

Using graph paper, plot the supply and demand schedules on the same graph.

a. With free trade, the equilibrium price of steel is $ _____ per ton. At this price, _____ tons are purchased by U.S. buyers, _____ tons are supplied by U.S. producers, and _____ tons are imported.

b. To protect its producers from foreign competition, suppose the U.S. government levies a specific tariff of $250 per ton on steel imports.
   (1) Show graphically the effect of the tariff on the overall supply schedule of steel.
   (2) With the tariff, the domestic price of steel rises to $ _____ per ton. At this price, U.S. buyers purchase _____ tons, U.S. producers

supply _____ tons, and _____ tons are imported.

(3) Calculate the reduction in U.S. consumer surplus due to the tariff-induced price of steel, as well as the consumption, protective, redistribution, and domestic revenue effects. The deadweight welfare loss of the tariff equals $_____.

(4) By reducing the volume of imports with the tariff, the United States forces the price of imported steel down to $_____. The U.S. terms of trade (improves/worsens), that leads to (an increase/a decrease) in U.S. welfare. Calculate the terms-of-trade effect.

(5) What impact does the tariff have on the overall welfare of the United States?

EXPLORING FURTHER

For a presentation of Offer Curves in the Analysis of Tariffs, go to *Exploring Further 4.1* that can be found at **www.cengage.com/economics/Carbaugh.**

Nontariff Trade Barriers

This chapter considers policies other than tariffs that restrict international trade. Referred to as **nontariff trade barriers (NTBs)**, such measures have been on the rise since the 1960s and have become the most widely discussed topics at recent rounds of international trade negotiations. Although tariffs have come down in recent decades, NTBs have multiplied. This is not surprising. After all, the political forces that give rise to high tariffs do not disappear once tariffs are brought down. Instead, they tend to seek protection through other channels.

NTBs encompass a variety of measures. Some have unimportant trade consequences; labeling and packaging requirements can restrict trade but generally only marginally. Other NTBs have significantly affected trade patterns; examples include absolute import quotas, tariff-rate quotas, voluntary export restraints, subsidies, and domestic content requirements.

ABSOLUTE IMPORT QUOTA

The best known nontariff barrier is the import quota that limits the total quantity of goods that may enter a country within a given time period. There are two types of import quotas; absolute quota and tariff-rate quota. Both place restrictions on imported goods and are enforced by the department of U.S. Customs and Border Protection at ports of entry throughout the United States.

An **absolute quota** is a physical restriction on the quantity of goods that can be imported during a specific time period, normally a year; the quota generally limits imports to a level below what would occur under free-trade conditions. An absolute quota might state that no more than 1 million kilograms of cheese or 20 million kilograms of wheat can be imported during some specific time period. Imports in excess of a specified quota may be held for the opening of the next quota period by placing them in a bonded warehouse or a foreign trade zone, or they may be exported or destroyed under supervision of the government's customs department. To administer the quota, the government allocates **import licenses** to importers, permitting them to import the product only up to a prescribed limit regardless of market demand.

One way to limit imports is through a **global quota**. This technique permits a specified number of goods to be imported each year, but it does not specify from where the product is shipped or who is permitted to import. When the specified amount has been imported (the quota is filled), additional imports of the product are prevented for the remainder of the year.

However, the global quota becomes unwieldy because of the rush of both domestic importers and foreign exporters to get their goods shipped into the country before the quota is filled. Those who import early in the year get their goods; those who import late in the year may not. Global quotas are plagued by accusations of favoritism against merchants fortunate enough to be the first to capture a large portion of the business.

To avoid the problems of a global quota system, import quotas have usually been allocated to specific countries; this type of quota is known as a **selective quota**. A country might impose a global quota of 30 million apples per year, of which 14 million must come from the United States, 10 million from Mexico, and 6 million from Canada. Customs officials in the importing nation monitor the quantity of a particular good that enters the country from each source; once the quota for that source has been filled, no more goods are permitted to be imported.

Another feature of quotas is that their use may lead to a domestic monopoly of production and higher prices. Because a domestic firm realizes that foreign producers cannot surpass their quotas, it may raise its prices. Tariffs do not necessarily lead to monopoly power because no limit is established on the amount of goods that can be imported into the nation.

Following World War II, absolute quotas were a popular form of protectionism as countries sought to strictly limit the quantity of imports. However, as the world moved towards trade liberalization in the 1960s and 1970s, absolute quotas were removed from international trade in manufactured goods. By the 1990s, absolute quotas were phased out of trade in agricultural goods and replaced by tariff-rate quotas. As we will learn, not only is a tariff-rate quota is a less restrictive trade barrier than an absolute quota, but it is easier to negotiate reductions in tariff rates than increases in absolute quotas during World Trade Organization rounds of trade liberalization.

Trade and Welfare Effects

Like a tariff, an absolute quota affects an economy's welfare. Figure 5.1 represents the case of cheese, involving U.S. trade with the European Union (EU). Suppose the United States is a "small" country in terms of the world cheese market. Assume that $S_{U.S.}$ and $D_{U.S.}$ denote the supply and demand schedules for cheese in the United States. The S_{EU} represents the supply schedule of the EU. Under free trade, the price of EU cheese and U.S. cheese equals $2.50 per pound. At this price, U.S. firms produce 1 pound, U.S. consumers purchase 8 pounds, and imports from the EU total 7 pounds.

Suppose the United States limits its cheese imports to a fixed quantity of 3 pounds by imposing an import quota. Above the free trade price, the total U.S. supply of cheese now equals U.S. production plus the quota. In Figure 5.1, this is illustrated by a shift in the supply curve from $S_{U.S.}$ to $S_{U.S.+Q}$. The reduction in imports from 7 pounds to 3 pounds raises the equilibrium price to $5.00; this leads to an increase in the quantity supplied by U.S. firms from 1 pound to 3 pounds and a decrease in the U.S. quantity demanded from 8 pounds to 6 pounds.

FIGURE 5.1

Import Quota: Trade and Welfare Effects

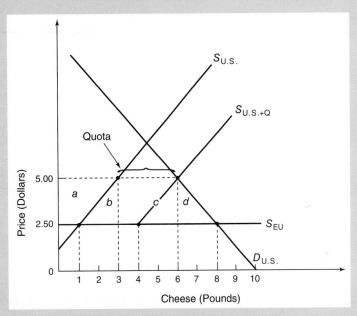

By restricting available supplies of an imported product, a quota leads to higher import prices. This price umbrella allows domestic producers of the import-competing good to raise prices. The result is a decrease in the consumer surplus. Of this amount, the welfare loss to the importing nation consists of the protective effect, the consumption effect, and that portion of the revenue effect that is captured by the foreign exporter.

Absolute quotas can be analyzed in terms of the same welfare effects identified for tariffs in the preceding chapter. Because the quota in our example results in a price increase to $5.00 per pound, the U.S. consumer surplus falls by an amount equal to area $a + b + c + d$ ($17.50). Area a ($5.00) represents the *redistributive effect*, area b ($2.50) represents the *protective effect*, and area d ($2.50) represents the *consumption effect*. The *deadweight loss* of welfare to the economy resulting from the quota is depicted by the protective effect plus the consumption effect.

But what about the quota's *revenue effect*, denoted by area c ($7.50)? This amount arises from the fact that U.S. consumers must pay an additional $2.50 for each of the 3 pounds of cheese imported under the quota, as a result of the quota induced scarcity of cheese. The revenue effect represents a "windfall profit," also known as a "quota rent." The quota rent accrues to whoever has the right to bring imports into the country and sell these goods in the protected market. Where does this windfall profit go?

To determine the distribution of the quota's revenue effect, it is useful to think of a series of exchanges as seen in the following example. Suppose that European exporting companies sell cheese to grocery stores (importing companies) in the United States, that sell it to U.S. consumers:[1]

---

[1] This example assumes that European exporting companies purchase cheese from European producers who operate in a competitive market. Because each producer is too small to affect the market price, it cannot capture any windfall profit arising under an import quota.

European exporting → U.S. grocery stores → U.S. consumers
companies (importing companies)

The distribution of the quota's revenue effect will be determined by the prices that prevail in the exchanges between these groups. Who obtains this windfall profit will depend on the competitive relation between the exporting and importing companies concerned.

One outcome occurs when European exporting companies are able to collude and in effect become a monopoly seller. If grocers in the United States behave as competitive buyers, they will bid against one another to buy European cheese. The delivered price of cheese will be driven up from $2.50 to $5.00 per pound. European exporting companies thus capture the windfall profit of the quota. The windfall profit captured by European exporters becomes a welfare loss for the U.S. economy, in addition to the deadweight losses resulting from the protective and consumption effects.

Instead, suppose that U.S. grocers organize as a single importing company (for example, Safeway grocery stores) and become a monopoly buyer. Also assume that European exporting companies operate as competitive sellers. Now, U.S. importing companies can purchase cheese at the prevailing world price of $2.50 per pound and resell it to U.S. consumers at a price of $5.00 per pound. In this case, the quota's revenue effect accrues to the importing companies. Because these companies are American, this accrual does not represent a welfare loss for the U.S. economy.

Alternatively, the U.S. government may collect the quota's revenue effect from the importing companies. Suppose the government sells import licenses to U.S. grocers. By charging for permission to import, the government receives some or all of the quota's windfall profit. If import licenses are auctioned off to the highest bidder in a competitive market, the government will capture all of the windfall profit that would have accrued to importing companies under the quota. Because the quota's revenue effect accrues to the U.S. government, this accrual does not represent a welfare loss for the U.S. economy (assuming that the government returns the revenue to the economy). This point will be discussed further in the next section of this text.

Allocating Quota Licenses

Because an import quota restricts the quantity of imports, usually below the free trade quantity, not all domestic importers can obtain the same number of imports that they could under free trade. Governments thus allocate the limited supply of imports among domestic importers.

In oil and dairy products, at one time the U.S. government issued import licenses on the basis of their historical share of the import market. This method discriminated against importers seeking to import goods for the first time. In other cases, the U.S. government has allocated import quotas on a *pro rata* basis, whereby U.S. importers receive a fraction of their demand equal to the ratio of the import quota to the total quantity demanded collectively by U.S. importers.

Another method of allocating licenses among domestic importers is to auction import licenses to the highest bidder in a competitive market. This technique has been used in Australia and New Zealand. Consider a hypothetical quota on U.S. imports of textiles. The quota pushes the price of textiles in the United States above the world price, making the United States an unusually profitable market. Windfall profits can be captured by U.S. importers (for example, Sears and Wal-Mart) if they buy textiles at the lower world price and sell them to U.S. buyers at the higher price made possible because of the quota. Given these windfall profits, U.S. importers would likely be willing to pay for the rights to import textiles. By auctioning import licenses to the highest bidder in a competitive market, the government could capture the windfall profits (the revenue effect shown as area c in Figure 5.1). Competition among importers to obtain the licenses would drive up the auction price to a level at which no windfall profits would remain, thus transferring the entire revenue effect to the government. The auctioning of import licenses would turn a quota into something akin to a tariff that generates tax revenue for the government.

Quotas versus Tariffs

Previous analysis suggests that the revenue effect of absolute quotas differs from that of import tariffs. These two commercial policies can also differ in the impact they have on the volume of trade. The following example illustrates how, during periods of growing demand, an absolute quota restricts the volume of imports by a greater amount than does an equivalent import tariff.

Figure 5.2 represents a hypothetical trade situation for the United States in autos. The U.S. supply and demand schedules for autos are given by $S_{U.S.0}$ and $D_{U.S.0}$, and S_{J0} represents the Japanese auto supply schedule. Suppose the U.S. government has the option of levying a tariff or a quota on auto imports to protect U.S. companies from foreign competition.

In Figure 5.2(a), a tariff of $1,000 raises the price of Japanese autos from $6,000 to $7,000; auto imports would fall from 7 million units to 3 million units. In Figure 5.2(b), an import quota of 3 million units would put the United States in a trade position identical to that which occurs under the tariff: the quota induced scarcity of autos results in a rise

---

FIGURE 5.2

Trade Effects of Tariffs Versus Quotas

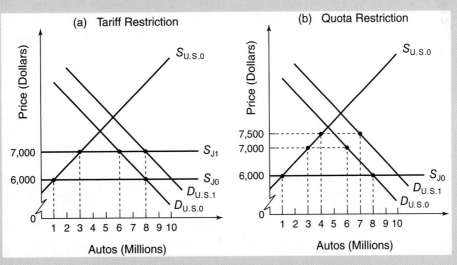

In a growing market, an import tariff is a less restrictive trade barrier than an equivalent import quota. With an import tariff, the adjustment that occurs in response to an increase in domestic demand is an increase in the amount of the product that is imported. With an import quota, an increase in demand induces an increase in product price. The price increase leads to a rise in production and a fall in consumption of the import-competing good, while the level of imports remains constant.

© Cengage Learning®

in the price from $6,000 to $7,000. So far, it appears that the tariff and the quota are equivalent with respect to their restrictive impact on the volume of trade.

Now suppose the U.S. demand for autos rises from $D_{U.S.0}$ to $D_{U.S.1}$. Figure 5.2(a) shows that, despite the increased demand, the price of auto imports remains at $7,000. This is because the U.S. price cannot differ from the Japanese price by an amount exceeding the tariff duty. Auto imports rise from 3 million units to 3 million units. Under an import tariff, then, domestic adjustment takes the form of an increase in the quantity of autos imported rather than a rise in auto prices.

In Figure 5.2(b), an identical increase in demand induces a rise in domestic auto prices. Under the quota, there is no limit on the extent to which the U.S. price can rise above the Japanese price. Given an increase in domestic auto prices, U.S. companies are able to expand production. The domestic price will rise until the increased production plus the fixed level of imports are commensurate with the domestic demand. Figure 5.2(b) shows that an increase in demand from $D_{U.S.0}$ to $D_{U.S.1}$ forces auto prices up from $7,000 to $7,500. At the new price, domestic production equals 4 million units, and domestic consumption equals 7 million units. Imports total 3 million units, the same amount as under the quota before the increase in domestic demand. Adjustment thus occurs in domestic *prices* rather than in the quantity of autos imported.

During periods of growing demand, an absolute quota is a more restrictive trade barrier than an equivalent import tariff. Under a quota, the government arbitrarily limits the quantity of imports. Under a tariff, the domestic price can rise above the world price only by the amount of the tariff; domestic consumers can still buy unlimited quantities of the import if they are willing and able to pay that amount. Even if the domestic industry's comparative disadvantage grows more severe, the quota prohibits consumers from switching to the imported good. Thus, a quota assures the domestic industry a ceiling on imports regardless of changing market conditions.[2]

A quota is a more restrictive barrier to imports than a tariff. A tariff increases the domestic price, but it cannot limit the number of goods that can be imported into a country. Importers who are successful enough to be able to pay the tariff duty still get the product. Also, a tariff may be offset by the price reductions of a foreign producer that can cut costs or slash profit margins. Tariffs allow for some degree of competition. However, by imposing an absolute limit on the imported good, a quota is more restrictive than a tariff and suppresses competition. The degree of protection provided by a tariff is determined by the market mechanism, but a quota forecloses the market mechanism. Finally, tariffs generate revenue for the government. This is revenue that would be lost to the government under a quota unless it charged a license fee on importers. As a result, member countries of the World Trade Organization agreed to eliminate absolute quotas and replace them with tariff-rate quotas and eventually tariffs.

TARIFF-RATE QUOTA: A TWO-TIER TARIFF

Another type of import quota is the **tariff-rate quota**. The U.S. government has imposed this restriction on imports such as steel, brooms, cattle, fish, sugar, milk, and other agricultural products.

---

[2]You might test your understanding of the approach used here by working out the details of two other hypothetical situations: (a) a reduction in the domestic supply of autos caused by rising production costs and (b) a reduction in domestic demand due to economic recession.

A tariff-rate quota displays both tariff-like and quota-like characteristics. This device allows a specified number of goods to be imported at a lower tariff rate (the *within-quota rate*), whereas any imports above this level face a higher tariff rate (the *over-quota rate*). Therefore, there is no absolute limitation on the amount of the product that may be imported during the quota period. In practice, the over-quota tariff rate is often set high enough to prohibit the importation of the product into the domestic market.

A tariff-rate quota has two components: a quota that defines the maximum volume of imports and charges the within-quota tariff; and an over-quota tariff. A tariff-rate quota is a *two-tier tariff*. Tariff-rate quotas are applied for each trade year and if not filled during a particular year, the market access under the quota is lost. Table 5.1 provides examples of tariff-rate quotas applied to U.S. imports.

The tariff-rate quota appears to differ little from the absolute quota discussed earlier in this chapter. The distinction is that under an absolute quota it is legally impossible to import more than a specified amount. In principle, under a tariff-rate quota, imports can exceed this specified amount, but a higher, over-quota tariff is applied on the excess. In practice, however, many over-quota tariff are prohibitively high and effectively exclude imports in excess of the quota.

Concerning the administration of tariff-rate quotas, **license on demand allocation** is the most common technique of enforcement for the quotas. Under this system, licenses are required to import at the within-quota tariff as enforced by the department of U.S. Customs and Border Protection. Before the quota period begins, potential importers are invited to apply for import licenses. If the demand for licenses is less than the quota, the system operates like a first come, first serve system. Usually, if demand exceeds the quota, the import volume requested is reduced proportionally among all applicants. Other techniques for allocating quota licenses are historical market share and auctions.

When the World Trade Organization (WTO) was established in 1995 (see Chapter 6), member countries changed their systems of import protection for those agricultural products helped by government farm programs. The WTO requires members to convert to tariffs all NTBs (absolute quotas, variable levies, discretionary licensing, outright import bans, etc.) applicable to imports from other members. In other words, it put all nontariff barriers on a common standard—tariff—that any exporter could readily measure and understand. Members are allowed to adopt tariff-rate quotas as a transitional instrument during this conversion period. At the writing of this text, the duration of this conversion period had not been defined. Tariff-rate quotas will likely be around for some time to come. The welfare effects of a tariff-rate quota are discussed in *Exploring Further 5.1*, available at www.cengage.com/economics/Carbaugh.

TABLE 5.1

Examples of U.S. Tariff-Rate Quotas

Product	Within-Quota Tariff Rate	Import-Quota Threshold	Over-Quota Tariff Rate
Peanuts	$0.935/kg	30,393 tons	187.9% ad valorem
Beef	$0.44/kg	634,621 tons	31.1% ad valorem
Milk	$0.32/L	5.7 million L	$0.885/L
Blue cheese	$0.10/kg	2.6 million kg	$2.60/kg
Cotton	$04.4/kg	2.1 million kg	$0.36/kg

Source: From U.S. International Trade Commission, *Harmonized Tariff Schedule of the United States*, (Washington, DC, U.S. Government Printing Office, 2013.

Tariff-Rate Quota Bittersweet for Sugar Consumers

The U.S. sugar industry provides an example of the effects of a tariff-rate quota. Traditionally, U.S. sugar growers have received government subsidies in the form of a guaranteed minimum price for sugar. However, this artificially high price can attract lower priced imported sugar, driving down the price. To prevent this outcome, the U.S. government intervenes in the market a second time by implementing tariff-rate quotas that discourage imported sugar from entering the domestic market.

Tariff-rate quotas for raw cane sugar are allocated on a country-by-country basis among 41 countries in total, while those for refined sugar are allocated in a global first come, first served basis. For sugar entering the U.S. market within the tariff rate-quota, a lower tariff is applied. For sugar imports in excess of the tariff-rate quota, a much higher tariff rate is established that virtually prohibits these imports. In this manner, the tariff-rate quota approximates the trade volume limit of an absolute quota that was discussed earlier in this chapter. However, the U.S. government has the option of establishing higher tariff-rate quota amounts whenever it believes that the domestic supply of sugar may be inadequate to meet domestic demand.

The effect of the tariff-rate quota is to restrict the supply of foreign sugar from entering the United States, thus causing the price of sugar in the domestic market to increase substantially. The U.S. price of sugar has often been almost twice the world market price because of the tariff-rate quota. The world price of sugar averaged $.26 per pound in 2013 compared with $.43 in the United States. That resulted in higher costs for American food companies and led to higher prices at the grocery store. Therefore, some manufacturers of candies, chocolates, and breakfast cereal, that use substantial amounts of sugar, relocated to Canada and Mexico where sugar prices are much lower. Hershey Foods closed plants in Colorado, California, and Pennsylvania and relocated them to Canada; Brach's moved its Chicago candy production to Mexico. To add to the controversy, analysts estimate that almost half of the sugar program benefits go to only 1 percent of sugar growers. Is protecting a small group of rich sugar barons justified?

The sugar tariff-rate quota is a classic example of concentrated benefits and dispersed costs. The quota provides enormous revenues for a small number of American sugar growers and refiners. However, the costs of providing these benefits are spread across the U.S. economy, specifically to American families as consumers and sugar-using producers such as soft drink companies. The U.S. government's trade policy for sugar is "bittersweet" for American consumers.[3]

EXPORT QUOTAS

Besides implementing import quotas, countries have used **export quotas** to restrain trade. When doing so, they typically negotiate a market sharing pact known as a voluntary export restraint agreement, also known as an orderly marketing agreement. The agreement's main purpose is to moderate the intensity of international competition, allowing less efficient domestic producers to participate in markets that would otherwise have been lost to foreign producers that sell a superior product at a lower price. Japan may impose quotas on its steel exports to Europe, or Taiwan may agree to cutbacks on

[3]Bryan Riley, *Abolish the Costly Sugar Program to Lower Sugar Prices*, The Heritage Foundation, December 5, 2012; U.S. International Trade Commission, *The Economic Effects of Significant U.S. Import Restraints*, Washington, DC, 2011; Mark Groombridge, *America's Bittersweet Sugar Policy*, Cato Institute, Washington, DC, December 4, 2001.

textile exports to the United States. The export quotas are voluntary in the sense that they are an alternative to more stringent trade restraints that might be imposed by an importing nation. Although voluntary export quotas governed trade in television sets, steel, textiles, autos, and ships during the 1980s, recent international trade agreements have prevented further use of this trade restriction.

Voluntary export quotas tend to have identical economic effects to equivalent import quotas, except being implemented by the exporting nation. The revenue effect of an export quota is captured by the foreign exporting company or its government. The welfare effects of an export quota are further examined in *Exploring Further 5.2*, available at www.cengage.com/economics/Carbaugh.

An analysis of the major U.S. voluntary export restraint agreements of the 1980s (automobiles, steel, and textiles and apparel) concluded that about 67 percent of the costs to American consumers of these restraints was captured by foreign exporters as profit.[4] From the viewpoint of the U.S. economy as a whole, voluntary export restraints tend to be more costly than tariffs. Let us consider a voluntary export restraint agreement from the 1980s.

Japanese Auto Restraints Put Brakes on U.S. Motorists

In 1981, as domestic auto sales fell, protectionist sentiment gained momentum in the U.S. Congress, and legislation was introduced calling for import quotas. This momentum was a major factor in the Reagan administration's desire to negotiate a voluntary restraint pact with the Japanese. Japan's acceptance of this agreement was apparently based on its view that voluntary limits on its auto shipments would derail any protectionist momentum in Congress for more stringent measures.

The restraint program called for self-imposed export quotas on Japanese auto shipments to the United States for three years, beginning in 1981. First-year shipments were to be held to 1.68 million units, 7.7 percent below the 1.82 million units exported in 1980. The quotas were extended annually with some upward adjustment in the volume numbers, until 1984.

The purpose of the export agreement was to help U.S. automakers by diverting U.S. customers from Japanese to U.S. showrooms. As domestic sales increased, so would jobs for American autoworkers. It was assumed that Japan's export quota would assist the U.S. auto industry as it went through a transition period of reallocating production toward smaller, more fuel-efficient autos and adjusting production to become more cost competitive.

Not all Japanese auto manufacturers were equally affected by the export quota. By requiring Japanese auto companies to form an export cartel against the U.S. consumer, the quota allowed the large, established firms (Toyota, Nissan, and Honda) to increase prices on autos sold in the United States. To derive more revenues from a limited number of autos, Japanese firms shipped autos to the United States with fancier trim, bigger engines and more amenities such as air conditioners and deluxe stereos as standard equipment. Product enrichment also helped the Japanese broaden their hold on the U.S. market and enhance the image of their autos. As a result, the large Japanese manufacturers earned record profits in the United States. However, the export quota was unpopular with smaller Japanese automakers, such as Suzuki and Isuzu who felt that the quota allocation favored large producers over small producers.

The biggest loser was the U.S. consumer who had to pay an extra $660 for each Japanese auto purchased and an extra $1,300 for each American made auto in 1984.

[4]David Tarr, *A General Equilibrium Analysis of the Welfare and Employment Effects of U.S. Quotas in Textiles, Autos, and Steel*, Washington, DC, Federal Trade Commission, 1989.

From 1981 to 1984, U.S. consumers paid an additional $15.7 billion to purchase autos because of the quota. Although the quota saved some 44,000 jobs for American autoworkers, the consumer cost per job saved was estimated to be more than $100,000.[5]

By 1985, Toyota, Honda, and Nissan had established manufacturing plants in the United States. This result had been sought by the United Auto Workers (UAW) and the U.S. auto companies. Their view was that taking such action, the Japanese would have to hire American workers and would also face the same competitive manufacturing conditions as U.S. auto companies. Things did not turn out the way that the American auto interests anticipated. When manufacturing in the U.S. market, the Japanese companies adjusted their production and developed new vehicles specifically designed for this market. Although their exports did decrease, vehicles produced at the Japanese transplant factories more than filled the market gap so that the U.S. producers' share of the market declined. Moreover, the UAW was unsuccessful in organizing workers at most transplant factories and therefore the Japanese were able to continue to keep labor costs down.

DOMESTIC CONTENT REQUIREMENTS

Today, many products such as autos and aircraft embody worldwide production. Domestic manufacturers of these products purchase resources or perform assembly functions outside the home country—a practice known as outsourcing or production sharing. General Motors obtains engines from its subsidiaries in Mexico, Chrysler purchases ball joints from Japanese producers, and Ford acquires cylinder heads from European companies. Firms have used outsourcing to take advantage of lower production costs overseas, including lower–wage rates. Domestic workers often challenge this practice, maintaining that outsourcing means that cheap foreign labor takes away their jobs and imposes downward pressure on the wages of those workers who are able to keep their jobs. Countries that have used domestic content requirements include Argentina, Mexico, Brazil, Uruguay, China, and others.[6]

To limit the practice of outsourcing, organized labor has lobbied for the use of **domestic content requirements**. These requirements stipulate the minimum percentage of a product's total value that must be produced domestically if the product is to qualify for zero tariff rates. The effect of content requirements is to pressure both domestic and foreign firms that sell products in the home country to use domestic inputs (workers) in the production of those products. The demand for domestic inputs thus increases, contributing to higher input prices. Manufacturers generally lobby against domestic content requirements because they prevent manufacturers from obtaining inputs at the lowest cost, thereby contributing to higher product prices and loss of competitiveness.

Worldwide, local content requirements have received the most attention in the automobile industry. Developing countries have often used content requirements to foster domestic automobile production, as shown in Table 5.2.

[5]U.S. International Trade Commission, *A Review of Recent Developments in the U.S. Automobile Industry Including an Assessment of the Japanese Voluntary Restraint Agreements*, Washington, DC, Government Printing Office, 1985.

[6]See U.S. Department of Commerce, International Trade Administration, Office of Automotive Affairs, *Compilation of Foreign Motor Vehicle Import Requirements* at http://trade.gov.

Figure 5.3 illustrates possible welfare effects of an Australian content requirement on automobiles. Assume that D_A denotes the Australian demand schedule for Toyota automobiles while S_J depicts the supply price of Toyotas exported to Australia; $24,000. With free trade, Australia imports 500 Toyotas. Japanese resource owners involved in manufacturing this vehicle realize incomes totaling $12 million, denoted by area $c + d$.

TABLE 5.2

Normal Value and the Margin of Dumping: Delicious Apples, Regular Storage, 1987–1988*

U.S. FOB per Packed Box (42 pounds)	Normal Value (in dollars)
Growing and harvesting costs	5.50
Packing, marketing, and storing costs	5.49
Total costs	10.99
Profit (8% margin)	0.88
Total normal value	11.87
Margin of Dumping	**Percentage**
Range	0–63.44
Weighted-average margin	32.53

*The weighted-average dumping margin for controlled atmosphere storage apples was 23.86%.

Source: From *Statement of Reasons: Final Determination of Dumping Respecting Delicious Apples Originating in or Exported from the United States of America*, Revenue Canada, Customs and Excise Division, December 1988.

FIGURE 5.3

Welfare Effects of a Domestic Content Requirement

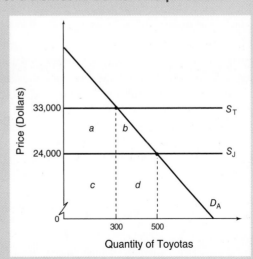

A domestic content requirement leads to rising production costs and prices to the extent that manufacturers are "forced" to locate production facilities in a high-cost nation. Although the content requirement helps preserve domestic jobs, it imposes welfare losses on domestic consumers.

© Cengage Learning®

Suppose the Australian government imposes a domestic content requirement on autos. This policy causes Toyota to establish a factory in Australia to produce vehicles replacing the Toyotas previously imported by Australia. Assume that the transplant factory combines Japanese management with Australian resources (labor and materials) in vehicle production. Also assume that high Australian resource prices (wages) cause the transplant's supply price to be $33,000, denoted by S_T. Under the content requirement, Australian consumers demand 300 vehicles. Because production has shifted from Japan to Australia, Japanese resource owners lose $12 million in income. Australian resource owners gain $9.9 million in income (area $a + c$) minus the income paid to Japanese managers and the return to Toyota's capital investment (factory) in Australia.

However, the income gains of Australian resource owners inflict costs on Australian consumers. Because the content requirement causes the price of Toyotas to increase by $9,000, the Australian consumer surplus decreases by area $a + b$ ($3.6 million). Of this amount, area b ($900,000) is a deadweight welfare loss for Australia. Area a ($2.7 million) is the consumer cost of employing higher priced Australian resources instead of lower priced Japanese resources; this amount represents a redistribution of welfare from Australian consumers to Australian resource owners. Similar to other import restrictions, content requirements lead to the subsidizing by domestic consumers of the domestic producer.

TRADE CONFLICTS   HOW "FOREIGN" IS YOUR CAR?

Did you know that U.S. buyers of cars and light trucks can learn how American or foreign their new vehicle is? On cars and trucks weighing 8,500 pounds or less, the law requires content labels telling buyers where the parts of the vehicle were made. Content is measured by the dollar value of components, not the labor cost of assembling vehicles.

The percentages of North American (U.S. and Canadian) and foreign parts must be listed as an average for each car line. Manufacturers are free to design the label, that can be included on the price sticker or fuel economy sticker or can be separate. Table 5.3 provides examples of the North American content of vehicles sold in the United States for the 2013 model year.

TABLE 5.3

North American Content of Automobiles Sold in the United States, 2013 Model Year

Vehicle	Assembly	North American Parts Content
Toyota Avion	Georgetown, Kentucky	85%
Chevrolet Express	Wentzville, Missouri	82
Toyota Sienna	Princeton, Indiana	80
Honda Accord	Marysville, Ohio	80
Honda Cross Tour	East Elizabeth, Ohio	80
Ford Expedition	Louisville, Kentucky	80
Chrysler 200	Sterling Heights, Michigan	79
Jeep Liberty	Toledo, Ohio	76
Chevy Traverse	Lansing, Michigan	76

Source: Collected by author at car dealer lots.

SUBSIDIES

National governments sometimes grant **subsidies** to their producers to help improve their market position. By providing domestic firms a cost advantage, a subsidy allows them to market their products at prices lower than warranted by their actual cost or profit considerations. Governmental subsidies assume a variety of forms, including outright cash disbursements, tax concessions, insurance arrangements, and loans at below-market interest rates.

For purposes of our discussion, two types of subsidies can be distinguished: a **domestic production subsidy** that is granted to producers of import-competing goods; and an **export subsidy** that goes to producers of goods that are to be sold overseas. In both cases, the government adds an amount to the price the purchaser pays rather than subtracting from it. The net price actually received by the producer equals the price paid by the purchaser plus the subsidy. The subsidized producer is thus able to supply a greater quantity at this price. Let us use Figure 5.4 to analyze the effects of these two types of subsidies.

Domestic Production Subsidy

If a country decides that the public welfare necessitates the maintenance of a semiconductor industry or aircraft industry, would it not be better just to subsidize it directly,

FIGURE 5.4

Trade and Welfare Effects of Subsidies

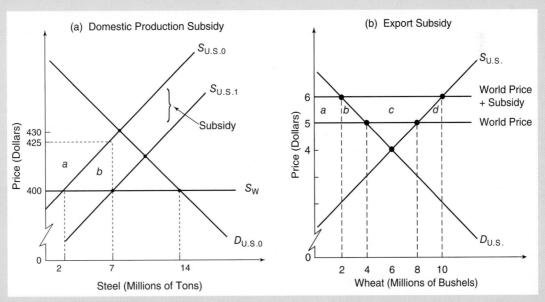

A government subsidy granted to import-competing producers leads to increased domestic production and reduced imports. The subsidy revenue accruing to the producer is absorbed by producer surplus and high-cost production (protective effect). A subsidy granted to exporters allows them to sell their products abroad at prices below their costs. However, it entails a deadweight welfare loss to the home country in the form of the protective effect and the consumption effect.

rather than preventing imports of a product? The purpose of a domestic production subsidy is to encourage the output and thus vitality of import-competing producers.

Figure 5.4(*a*) illustrates the trade and welfare effects of a production subsidy granted to import-competing producers. Assume that the initial supply and demand schedules for steel in the United States are depicted by curves $S_{U.S.0}$ and $D_{U.S.0}$, so that the market equilibrium price is $430 per ton. Assume also, because the United States is a small buyer of steel, changes in its purchases do not affect the world price of $400 per ton. Given a free trade price of $400 per ton, the United States consumes 14 million tons of steel, produces 2 million tons, and imports 12 million tons.

To partially insulate domestic producers from foreign competition, suppose the U.S. government grants them a production subsidy of $25 per ton of steel. The cost advantage made possible by the subsidy results in a shift in the U.S. supply schedule from $S_{U.S.0}$ to $S_{U.S.1}$. Domestic production expands from 2 to 7 million tons, and imports fall from 12 to 7 million tons. These changes represent the subsidy's trade effect.

The subsidy also affects the national welfare of the United States. According to Figure 5.4(*a*), the subsidy permits U.S. output to rise to 7 million tons. At this output, the net price to the steelmaker is $425—the sum of the price paid by the consumer ($400) plus the subsidy ($25). To the U.S. government, the total cost of protecting its steelmakers equals the amount of the subsidy ($25) times the amount of output to which it is applied (7 million tons), or $175 million.

Where does this subsidy revenue go? Part of it is redistributed to the more efficient U.S. producers in the form of a *producer surplus*. This amount is denoted by area *a* ($112.5 million) in the figure. There is also a *protective effect*, whereby more costly domestic output is allowed to be sold in the market as a result of the subsidy. This effect is denoted by area *b* ($62.5 million) in the figure. To the United States as a whole, the protective effect represents a deadweight loss of welfare.

To encourage production by its import-competing producers, a government might levy tariffs or quotas on imports. Tariffs and quotas involve larger sacrifices in national welfare than occur under an equivalent subsidy. Unlike subsidies, tariffs and quotas distort choices for domestic consumers (resulting in a decrease in the domestic demand for imports) in addition to permitting less efficient home production to occur. The result is the familiar consumption effect of protection, whereby a deadweight loss of the consumer surplus is borne by the home nation. This welfare loss is absent in the subsidy case. A subsidy tends to yield the same result for domestic producers as does an equivalent tariff or quota, but at a *lower* cost in terms of the nation's welfare.

However, subsidies are not free goods because they must be financed by someone. The direct cost of the subsidy is a burden that must be financed out of tax revenues paid by the public. Moreover, when a subsidy is given to an industry it is often in return for accepting government conditions on key matters (such as wage and salary levels). Therefore, a subsidy may not be as superior to other types of commercial policies as this analysis suggests.

Export Subsidy

Rather than granting a production subsidy to import-competing producers, a government could pay a subsidy on exports only. The most common product groups where export subsidies are applied are agricultural and dairy products.

Figure 5.4(*b*) shows the effects of an export subsidy. Assume that the supply and demand curves of the United States for wheat are shown by curves $S_{U.S.}$ and $D_{U.S.}$, so the autarky equilibrium price is $4 per bushel. Assume also that because the United States is a relatively small producer of wheat, changes in its output do not affect the world price. At the world price of $5 per bushel, the United States produces eight million bushels, purchases four million bushels, and thus exports four million bushels.

Suppose that the U.S. government makes a payment of $1 on each bushel of wheat exported in order to encourage export sales. The subsidy allows U.S. exporting firms to receive revenue of $6 per bushel that is equal to the world price ($5) plus the subsidy ($1). Although the subsidy is not available on domestic sales, these firms are willing to sell to domestic consumers only at the higher price of $6 per bushel. This is because the firms would not sell wheat in the United States for a price less than $6 per bushel; they could always earn that amount on sales to the rest of the world. As the price rises from $5 to $6 per bushel, the quantity purchased in the United States falls from four million bushels to two million bushels, the quantity supplied rises from eight million bushels to ten million bushels, and the quantity of exports increases from four million bushels to eight million bushels.

The welfare effects of the export subsidy on the U.S. economy can be analyzed in terms of the consumer and producer surpluses. The export subsidy results in a decrease in the consumer surplus of area $a + b$ in the figure ($3 million) and an increase in the producer surplus of area $a + b + c$ ($9 million). The taxpayer cost of the export subsidy equals the per unit subsidy ($1) times the quantity of wheat exported (8 million bushels), resulting in area $b + c + d$ ($8 million). Thus, U.S. wheat producers gain at the expense of the U.S. consumer and taxpayer.

The export subsidy entails a deadweight loss of welfare to the U.S. economy. This consists of area d ($1 million), that is a deadweight loss because of the increasing domestic cost of producing additional wheat, and area b ($1 million) that is lost consumer surplus because the price has increased.

In this example, we assumed that the exporting country is a relatively small country. In the real world, the exporting country may be a relatively large producer in the world market, and will realize a decrease in its terms of trade when it imposes a subsidy on exports. Why would this occur? In order to export more product firms would have to reduce the price. A decrease in the price of the exported good would worsen the exporting country's terms of trade.

The Export Enhancement Program provides an example of the use of export subsidies by the United States. Established in 1985, this program attempts to offset the adverse effects on U.S. agricultural exports because of unfair trade practices or subsidies by competing exporters; particularly the EU. This program allows U.S. exporters to sell their products in targeted markets at prices below their costs by providing cash bonuses. It has played a major role in the export of many agricultural products such as wheat, barley, poultry, and dairy products.

DUMPING

The case for protecting import-competing producers from foreign competition is bolstered by the antidumping argument. **Dumping** is recognized as a form of international price discrimination. Dumping occurs when foreign buyers are charged lower prices than domestic buyers for an identical product, after allowing for transportation costs and tariff duties. Selling in foreign markets at a price below the cost of production is also considered dumping.

Forms of Dumping

Commercial dumping is generally viewed as sporadic, predatory, or persistent in nature. Each type is practiced under different circumstances.

Sporadic dumping (distress dumping) occurs when a firm disposes of excess inventories on foreign markets by selling abroad at lower prices than at home. This form of dumping may be the result of misfortune or poor planning by foreign producers. Unforeseen changes in supply and demand conditions can result in excess inventories and thus in dumping. Although sporadic dumping may be beneficial to importing consumers, it can be quite disruptive to import-competing producers who face falling sales and short-run losses. Temporary tariff duties can be levied to protect home producers, but because sporadic dumping has minor effects on international trade, governments are reluctant to grant tariff protection under these circumstances.

Predatory dumping occurs when a producer temporarily reduces the prices charged abroad to drive foreign competitors out of business. When the producer succeeds in acquiring a monopoly position, prices are then raised commensurate with its market power. The new price level must be sufficiently high to offset any losses that occurred during the period of cutthroat pricing. The firm would presumably be confident in its ability to prevent the entry of potential competitors long enough for it to enjoy economic profits. To be successful, predatory dumping has to be practiced on a massive basis to provide consumers with sufficient opportunity for bargain shopping. Home governments are generally concerned about predatory pricing for monopolizing purposes and may retaliate with antidumping duties that eliminate the price differential. Although predatory dumping is a theoretical possibility, economists have not found empirical evidence that supports its existence. With the prospect of a long and costly period of predation and the likelihood of a limited ability to deter subsequent entry by new rivals, the chances of actually earning full monopoly profits seems remote.

Persistent dumping, as its name suggests, goes on indefinitely. In an effort to maximize economic profits, a producer may consistently sell abroad at lower prices than at home. The rationale underlying persistent dumping is explained in the next section.

International Price Discrimination

Consider the case of a domestic seller that enjoys market power as a result of barriers that restrict competition at home. Suppose this firm sells in foreign markets that are highly competitive. This scenario means that the domestic consumer response to a change in price is less than that abroad; the home demand is less elastic than the foreign demand. A profit maximizing firm would benefit from international price discrimination, charging a *higher* price at home, where competition is weak and demand is less elastic, and a *lower* price for the same product in foreign markets to meet competition. The practice of identifying separate groups of buyers of a product and charging different prices to these groups results in increased revenues and profits for the firm as compared to what would occur in the absence of price discrimination.

Figure 5.5 illustrates the demand and cost conditions of South Korean Steel Inc. (SKS), who sells steel to buyers in South Korea (less elastic market) and in Canada (more elastic market); the total steel market consists of these two submarkets. Let D_{SK} be the South Korean steel demand and D_C be the Canadian demand, with the corresponding marginal revenue schedules represented by MR_{SK} and MR_C, respectively. The D_{SK+C} denotes the market demand schedule, found by adding horizontally the demand schedules of the two submarkets; similarly, MR_{SK+C} represents the market marginal revenue schedule. The marginal cost and average total cost schedules of SKS are denoted respectively by MC and ATC.

FIGURE 5.5

International Price Discrimination

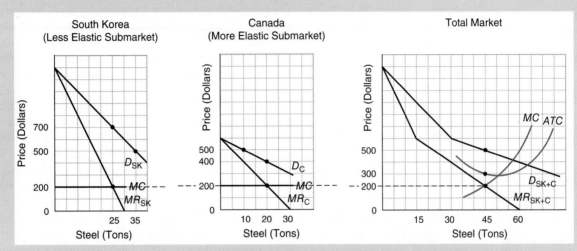

A price–discriminating firm maximizes profits by equating marginal revenue, in each submarket, with marginal cost. The firm will charge a higher price in the less elastic demand (less competitive) market and a lower price in the more elastic demand (more competitive) market. Successful dumping leads to additional revenue and profits for the firm compared to what would be realized in the absence of dumping.

South Korean Steel maximizes total profits by producing and selling 45 tons of steel, at which marginal revenue equals marginal cost. At this output level, ATC = $300 per ton, and total cost equals $13,500 ($300 × 45 tons). The firm faces the problem of how to distribute the total output of 45 tons and set price in the two submarkets in which it sells. Should the firm sell steel to South Korean and Canadian buyers at a uniform (single) price, or should the firm practice discriminating pricing?

As a *non-discriminating* seller, SKS sells 45 tons of steel to South Korean and Canadian buyers at the single price of $500 per ton, the maximum price permitted by demand schedule D_{SK+C} at the MR = MC output level. To see how many tons of steel are sold in each submarket, construct a horizontal line in Figure 5.5 at the price of $500. The optimal output in each submarket occurs where the horizontal line intersects the demand schedules of the two nations. Thus, SKS sells 35 tons of steel to South Korean buyers at $500 per ton and receives revenues totaling $17,500. The firm sells 10 tons of steel to Canadian buyers at $500 per ton and realizes revenue of $5,000. Sales revenues in both submarkets combined equal $22,500. With a total cost of $13,500, SKS realizes a profit of $9,000.

Although SKS realizes a profit as a non-discriminating seller, its profits are not optimal. By engaging in price discrimination, the firm can increase its total revenues without increasing its costs, and thus increase its profits. The firm accomplishes this by charging *higher* prices to South Korean buyers, who have less elastic demand schedules, and *lower* prices to Canadian buyers, who have more elastic demand schedules.

As a price–discriminating seller, SKS again faces the problem of how to distribute the total output of 45 tons of steel, and set price in the two submarkets in which it sells. To accomplish this, the firm follows the familiar MR = MC principle, whereby the marginal revenue of each submarket equals the marginal cost at the profit maximizing output. This principle can be shown in Figure 5.5 by first constructing a horizontal line from

$200, the point where $MC = MR_{SK+C}$. The optimal output and price in each submarket is then found where this horizontal line intersects the MR schedules of the submarkets. SKS sells 25 tons of steel to South Korean buyers at a price of $700 per ton and receives revenues totaling $17,500. The firm sells 20 tons of steel to Canadian buyers at a price of $400 per ton and collects revenues of $8,000. The combined revenues of the two submarkets equal $25,500, a sum $3,000 greater than in the absence of price discrimination. With a total cost of $13,500, the firm realizes a profit of $12,000, compared to $9,000 under a single pricing policy. As a price–discriminating seller, SKS thus enjoys a higher revenue and profit.

Notice that the firm took advantage of its ability to price discriminate, charging different prices in the two submarkets: $700 per ton to South Korean steel buyers and $400 per ton to Canadian buyers. For international price discrimination to be successful, certain conditions must hold. First, to ensure that at any price the demand schedules in the two submarkets have different demand elasticities, the submarkets' demand conditions must differ. Domestic buyers, for example, may have income levels or tastes and preferences that differ from those of the buyers abroad. Second, the firm must be able to separate the two submarkets, preventing any significant resale of commodities from the lower priced to the higher priced market. This is because any resale by consumers will tend to neutralize the effect of differential prices and narrow the discriminatory price structure to the point at which it approaches a single price to all consumers. Because of high transportation costs and governmental trade restrictions, markets are often easier to separate internationally than nationally.

ANTIDUMPING REGULATIONS

Despite the benefits that dumping may offer to importing consumers, governments have often levied penalty duties against commodities they believe are being dumped into their markets from abroad. U.S. antidumping law is designed to prevent price discrimination and below cost sales that injures U.S. industries. Under U.S. law, an **antidumping duty** is levied when the U.S. Department of Commerce determines a class or kind of foreign merchandise is being sold at *less than fair value* (LTFV) and the U.S. International Trade Commission (ITC) determines that LTFV imports are causing or threatening material injury (such as unemployment and lost sales and profits) to a U.S. industry. Such antidumping duties are imposed in addition to the normal tariff in order to neutralize the effects of price discrimination or below cost sales.

The **margin of dumping** is calculated as the amount that the foreign market value exceeds the U.S. price. Foreign market value is defined in one of two ways. According to the **priced-based definition**, dumping occurs whenever a foreign company sells a product in the U.S. market at a price below that for which the same product sells in the home market. When a home nation price of the good is not available (if the good is produced only for export and is not sold domestically) an effort is made to determine the price of the good in a third market.

In cases where the price-based definition cannot be applied, a **cost-based definition** of foreign market value is permitted. Under this approach, the Commerce Department "constructs" a foreign market value equal to the sum of (1) the cost of manufacturing the merchandise, (2) general expenses, (3) profit on home market sales, and (4) the cost of packaging the merchandise for shipment to the United States. The amount for general expenses must equal at least 10 percent of the cost of manufacturing, and the amount for profit must equal at least 8.0 percent of the manufacturing cost plus general expenses.

TRADE CONFLICTS SWIMMING UPSTREAM: THE CASE OF VIETNAMESE CATFISH

In 2003, the U.S. government was strongly criticized for assaulting catfish imports from Vietnam. According to Senator John McCain and other critics, this policy was an example of how wealthy countries preach the gospel of free trade when it comes to finding markets for their manufactured goods, but become highly protectionist when their farmers face competition. Let us consider this trade dispute.

After pursuing pro capitalistic reforms, Vietnam became one of globalization's success stories in the 1990s. The nation transformed itself from being a rice importer to the world's second largest rice exporter and also an exporter of coffee. Vietnam's rural poverty rate declined from 70 to 30 percent. The normalization of communication between the governments of Vietnam and the United States resulted in American trade missions intended on increasing free enterprise in Vietnam.

On one of these trade missions, delegates saw much promise in Vietnamese catfish, with the country's Mekong Delta and cheap labor providing a competitive advantage. Within several years, some half-million Vietnamese were earning income from the catfish trade. Vietnam captured 20 percent of the frozen catfish fillet market in the United States, forcing down prices. To the alarm of catfish farmers in Mississippi, the hub of the U.S. catfish industry, even local restaurants were serving Vietnamese catfish.

Before long, Vietnamese farmers faced a nasty trade war waged by Mississippi's catfish farmers involving product labeling and antidumping tariffs. Although these farmers are usually not large agribusinesses, they were strong enough to persuade the U.S. government to close the catfish market to the Vietnamese farmers whose enterprise it had originally encouraged.

The government declared that out of 2,000 types of catfish, only the American born family could be called "catfish." So the Vietnamese could market their fish in America only by using Vietnamese words such as "tra" and "basa." Mississippi catfish farmers issued warnings of a "slippery catfish wannabe," saying such fish were "probably not even sporting real whiskers" and "floating around in Third World rivers nibbling on who knows what." This disinformation campaign resulted in decreased sales of Vietnamese catfish in the United States.

Not satisfied with its labeling success, the Mississippi catfish farmers initiated an antidumping case against Vietnamese catfish. In this case, the U.S. Department of Commerce did not have strong evidence that the imported fish were being sold in America more cheaply than in Vietnam, or below their cost of production. Rather than leaving Mississippi catfish farmers to the forces of international competition, the department declared Vietnam a "nonmarket" economy. This designation implied that Vietnamese farmers must not be covering all the costs they would in a market economy such as the United States, and thus were dumping catfish into the American market. Tariffs ranging from 37 to 64 percent were imposed by the department on Vietnamese catfish. The U.S. International Trade Commission made the tariffs permanent by stating that the American catfish industry was injured by unfair competition due to dumping by Vietnam. According to critics, this nonmarket designation should not have been used because the U.S. government was encouraging Vietnam to become a market economy.

Source: "Harvesting Poverty: The Great Catfish War," *The New York Times*, July 22, 2003, p. 18 and The World Bank, *Global Economic Prospects*, 2004, Washington, DC, p. 85.

Antidumping cases begin with a complaint filed concurrently with the Commerce Department and the International Trade Commission. The complaint comes from within an import-competing industry (from a firm or labor union) and consists of evidence of the existence of dumping and data that demonstrate material injury or threat of injury.

The Commerce Department first makes a preliminary determination as to whether or not dumping has occurred, including an estimate of the size of the dumping margin. If the preliminary investigation finds evidence of dumping, U.S. importers must immediately pay a special tariff (equal to the estimated dumping margin) on all imports of the product in question. The Commerce Department then makes its final determination as to whether or not dumping has taken place, as well as the size of the dumping margin. If the Commerce Department rules that dumping did not occur, special tariffs previously collected are rebated to U.S. importers. Otherwise, the International Trade Commission determines whether or not material injury has occurred as the result of the dumping.

If the International Trade Commission rules that import-competing firms were not injured by the dumping, the special tariffs are rebated to U.S. importers. If both the International Trade Commission and the Commerce Department rule in favor of the dumping petition, a permanent tariff is imposed that equals the size of the dumping margin calculated by the Commerce Department in its final investigation.

In recent years, the average antidumping duty imposed by the United States has been about 45 percent, with some duties exceeding 100 percent. The impact of these duties on trade has been substantial, with targeted imports typically falling 50 to 70 percent over the first three years of protection. Let us consider some cases involving dumping.

Whirlpool Agitates for Antidumping Tariffs on Clothes Washers

Whirlpool Corporation is the world's leading producer of major home appliances with 68,000 employees and 66 manufacturing and technology research centers throughout the world. The firm markets clothes washers and dryers, refrigerators, and other appliances under brand names such as Whirlpool, Maytag, and KitchenAid in almost every country around the world.

The origins of Whirlpool date back to 1908 when Lou Upton invested his savings in a venture to produce household equipment. When that company did not pan out, Upton was offered the opportunity to select something of value from the failed venture as compensation for his investment. He selected the patents on a hand washing machine that he thought might be electrified. With his patents and innovation vision, Upton joined his uncle and brother to producer motor driven wringer washers. With the passage of time, Whirlpool prospered and become the world's leading producer of major home appliances.

By the early 2000s, Whirlpool faced intense competition from foreign appliance producers in countries such as South Korea and Mexico. Increasingly, Whirlpool contended that these producers were selling their government subsidized appliances in the United States at prices "substantially less than fair value" as defined by U.S. trade law. The result was lost market share for Whirlpool, decreases in its appliance production, and job losses for its workers.

In 2011 Whirlpool filed anti-dumping and anti-subsidy petitions against clothes washer makers Samsung and LG. The petitions asked the U.S. Department of Commerce and the U.S. International Trade Commission to investigate washers produced in South Korea and Mexico and then sold in the United States at prices below fair value. In 2013, the Commerce Department and International Trade Commission ruled that Samsung and LG practiced unlawful pricing for clothes washers originating from South Korea and Mexico, and that Whirlpool was materially damaged by these trade practices. Per the ruling, the U.S. customs officials imposed anti-dumping and anti-subsidy import tariffs ranging from 11 percent to 151 percent for various Samsung and LG products.

In reaction to the ruling, Whirlpool declared that it would restore a level competitive playing field that enables Whirlpool and other U.S. appliance producers to continue investing in America to produce the high quality products that consumers deserve.

However, Samsung and LG indicated that they were disappointed in the decision and the move will ultimately reduce choice in washers for some American.[7]

Canadians Press Washington Apple Producers for Level Playing Field

Not only have foreign producers dumped products in the United States, but U.S. firms have sometimes dumped goods abroad.

In 1989, the Canadian government ruled that U.S. Delicious apples, primarily those grown in Washington, had been dumped on the Canadian market, causing injury to 4,500 commercial apple growers. As a result of the ruling, a 42-pound box of Washington apples could not be sold in Canada for less than $11.87 (in USD), the "normal value" (analogous to the U.S. concept of "fair value") established by the Canadian government for regular storage apples. Canadian importers purchasing U.S. apples at below normal value had to pay an antidumping duty to the Canadian government so that the total purchase price equaled the established value. The antidumping order was for the five years from1989 to 1994.

The Canadian apple growers' complaint alleged that extensive tree planting in the United States during the late 1970s and early 1980s resulted in excess apple production. In 1987 and 1988, Washington growers experienced a record harvest and inventories that exceeded storage capacities. The growers dramatically cut prices in order to market their crop, leading to a collapse of the North American price of Delicious apples.

When Washington apple growers failed to provide timely information, the Canadian government estimated the normal value of a box of U.S. apples using the best information available. As seen in Table 5.2, the normal value for a box of apples in the crop year 1987–1988 was $11.87 (USD). During this period, the U.S. export price to Canada was about $9 (USD) a box. Based on a comparison of the export price and the normal value of apples, the weighted average dumping margin was determined to be 32.53 percent.

The Canadian government determined that the influx of low priced Washington apples into the Canadian market displaced Canadian apples and resulted in losses to Canadian apple growers of $1 to $6.40 (Canadian $) per box during the 1987–1988 growing season. The Canadian government ruled that the dumped apples injured Canadian growers and imposed antidumping duties on Washington apples.

IS ANTIDUMPING LAW UNFAIR?

Supporters of antidumping laws maintain that they are needed to create a "level playing field" for domestic producers that face unfair import competition. Antidumping laws ensure a level playing field by offsetting artificial sources of competitive advantage. By making up the difference between the dumped price and fair market value, an antidumping duty puts the domestic producer back on an equal footing. Critics note that although protected industries may gain from antidumping duties, consumers of the protected good and the wider economy typically lose more, as discussed in Chapter 4. It is not surprising that antidumping law is subject to criticism, as discussed below.

---

[7]"Whirlpool Wins, Rivals to Face Big Import Duty," *The Blade*, January 24, 2013; "Whirlpool Wins Decision in Anti-Dumping Case, *Crain's Detroit Business*, January 24, 2013; "Whirlpool Files Anti-Dumping Petitions Against Samsung and LG, *Daily News*, January 2, 2012; U.S. Department of Commerce, *U.S. Department of Commerce Anti-dumping Ruling Supports U.S. Manufacturers*, July 20, 2012.

Should Average Variable Cost Be the Yardstick for Defining Dumping?

Under current rules, dumping can occur when a foreign producer sells goods in the United States at less than fair value. Fair value is equated with average total cost plus an eight percent allowance for profit. However, many economists argue that fair value should be based on *average variable cost* rather than average total cost, especially when the domestic economy realizes a temporary downturn in demand.

Consider the case of a radio producer under the following assumptions: (1) The producer's physical capacity is 150 units of output over the given time period. (2) The domestic market's demand for radios is price-inelastic, whereas foreign demand is price-elastic. Refer to Table 5.4. Suppose the producer charges a uniform price (no dumping) of $300 per unit to both domestic and foreign consumers. With domestic demand inelastic, domestic sales total 100 units. But with elastic demand conditions abroad, suppose the producer cannot market any radios at the prevailing price. Sales revenues would equal $30,000, with variable costs plus fixed costs totaling $30,000. Without dumping, the firm would find itself with an excess capacity of 50 radios. Moreover, the firm would just break even on its domestic market operations.

Suppose this producer decides to dump radios abroad at lower prices than at home. As long as all variable costs are covered, any price that contributes to fixed costs will permit larger profits (smaller losses) than those realized with idle plant capacity at hand. According to Table 5.5, by charging $300 to home consumers, the firm can sell 100 units. Suppose that by charging a price of $250 per unit, the firm is able to sell an additional 50 units abroad. The total sales revenue of $42,500 would not only cover variable costs plus fixed costs, but would permit a profit of $2,500.

TABLE 5.4

Dumping and Excess Capacity

	No Dumping	Dumping
Home sales	100 units @ $300	100 units @ $300
Export sales	0 units @ $300	50 units @ $250
Sales revenue	$30,000	$42,500
Less variable costs of $200 per unit	−20,000	−30,000
	$10,000	$12,500
Less total fixed costs of $10,000	−10,000	−10,000
Profit	$0	$2,500

© Cengage Learning®

TABLE 5.5

Venezuela Supply of and Demand for Television Sets

Price per TV set	Quantity Demanded	Quantity Supplied
$100	900	0
200	700	200
300	500	400
400	300	600
500	100	800

© Cengage Learning®

With dumping, the firm is able to increase profits even though it is selling abroad at a price less than the average total cost (average total cost = $40,000/150 = $267). Firms facing excess production capacity may thus have the incentive to stimulate sales by cutting prices charged to foreigners—perhaps to levels that just cover average variable cost. Of course, domestic prices must be sufficiently high to keep the firm operating profitably over the relevant time period.

Many economists argue that antidumping laws, that use average total cost as a yardstick to determine fair value, is unfair. They note that economic theory suggests under competitive conditions, firms price their goods at average variable costs that are below average total costs. Therefore, the antidumping laws punish firms that are simply behaving in a manner typical of competitive markets. Moreover, the law is unfair because U.S. firms selling at home are not subject to the same rules. Indeed, it is quite possible for a foreign firm that is selling at a loss both at home and in the United States to be found guilty of dumping, when U.S. firms are also taking losses and selling in the domestic market at exactly the same price.

Should Antidumping Law Reflect Currency Fluctuations?

Another criticism of antidumping law is that it does not account for currency fluctuations. Consider the price-based definition of dumping: selling at lower prices in a foreign market. Because foreign producers often must set their prices for foreign customers in terms of a foreign currency, fluctuations in exchange rates can cause them to "dump" according to the legal definition. Suppose the Japanese yen appreciates against the U.S. dollar; that means that it takes fewer yen to buy a dollar. But if Japanese steel exporters are meeting competition in the United States and setting their prices in dollars, the appreciation of the yen will cause the price of their exports in terms of the yen to decrease, making it appear that they are dumping in the United States. Under the U.S. antidumping law, American firms are not required to meet the standard imposed on foreign firms selling in the United States. Does the antidumping law redress unfairness—or create it?

Are Antidumping Duties Overused?

Until the 1990s, antidumping actions were a protectionist device used almost exclusively by a few rich countries: the United States, Canada, Australia, and Europe. Since then, there has been an increase in the number of antidumping cases brought by many developing nations such as Mexico, India, and Turkey. Rising use by other nations has meant that the United States itself has become a more frequent target of antidumping measures.

The widening use of antidumping duties is not surprising given the sizable degree of trade liberalization that has occurred across the world economy. However, the proliferation of antidumping duties is generally viewed by economists as a disturbing trend, a form of backdoor protectionism that runs counter to the post-World War II trend of reducing barriers to trade. Although antidumping actions are legal under the rules of the World Trade Organization, there is concern of a vicious cycle where antidumping duties by one country invite retaliatory duties by other countries.

For U.S. producers, it has become much easier to obtain relief from import competition in the form of antidumping duties. One reason is that the scope for initiating an antidumping action has been widened from preventing predatory pricing to any form of international price discrimination. More aggressive standards for assessing the role of imports in harming domestic industries have also contributed to greater use of antidumping duties.

Critics of U.S. antidumping policy maintain that the U.S. Department of Commerce almost always finds that dumping has occurred, although positive findings of material injury by the U.S. International Trade Commission are less frequent. Critics also note that in many cases where imports were determined to be dumped under existing rules, they would not have been questioned as posing an anticompetitive threat under the same countries' antitrust laws. In other words, the behavior of the importers, if undertaken by a domestic firm, would not have been questioned as anticompetitive or otherwise generally harmful.

OTHER NONTARIFF TRADE BARRIERS

Other NTBs consist of governmental codes of conduct applied to imports. Even though such provisions are often well disguised, they remain important sources of commercial policy. Let's consider three such barriers: government procurement policies, social regulations, and sea transport and freight regulations.

Government Procurement Policies

Because government agencies are large buyers of goods and services, they are attractive customers for foreign suppliers. If governments purchased goods and services only from the lowest cost suppliers, the pattern of trade would not differ significantly from that which occurs in a competitive market. However, most governments favor domestic suppliers over foreign ones in the procurement of materials and products. This is evidenced by the ratio of imports to total purchases in the public sector is much smaller than in the private sector.

Governments often extend preferences to domestic suppliers in the form of **buy–national policies**. The U.S. government, through explicit laws, openly discriminates against foreign suppliers in its purchasing decisions. Although most other governments do not have formally legislated preferences for domestic suppliers, they often discriminate against foreign suppliers through hidden administrative rules and practices. Such governments utilize closed bidding systems that restrict the number of companies allowed to bid on sales, or they may publicize government contracts in such a way as to make it difficult for foreign suppliers to make a bid.

To stimulate domestic employment during the Great Depression, in 1933 the U.S. government passed the Buy–American Act. This act requires federal agencies to purchase materials and products from U.S. suppliers if their prices are not "unreasonably" higher than those of foreign competitors. A product, to qualify as domestic, must have at least a 50 percent domestic component content and must be manufactured in the United States. As it stands today, U.S. suppliers of civilian agencies are given a six percent preference margin. This margin means that a U.S. supplier receives the government contract as long as the U.S. low bid is no more than six percent higher than the competing foreign bid. This preference margin rises to 12 percent if the low domestic bidder is situated in a labor surplus area and to 50 percent if the purchase is made by the Department of Defense. These preferences are waived when it is determined that the U.S.-produced good is not available in sufficient quantities or is not of satisfactory quality.

By discriminating against low-cost foreign suppliers in favor of domestic suppliers, buy–national policies are a barrier to free trade. Domestic suppliers are given the leeway to use less efficient production methods and to pay resource prices higher than those permitted under free trade. This leeway yields a higher cost for government projects and deadweight welfare losses for the nation in the form of the protective and consumption effects.

The Buy–American restrictions of the U.S. government have been liberalized with the adoption of the Tokyo Round of Multilateral Trade Negotiations in 1979. However, the pact does not apply to the purchase of materials and products by state and local government agencies. More than 30 states currently have Buy–American laws, ranging from explicit prohibitions on purchases of foreign products to loose policy guidelines favoring U.S. products.

For example, during 2001–2004 the California Transit Authority rebuilt portions of the earthquake damaged San Francisco–Oakland Bay Bridge. However, the project cost about $4 billion, three times more than the agency originally expected. One reason was California's Buy–American rules that required that foreign steel could be used on the bridge only if its cost was at least 25 percent less than domestic steel. In this case, the difference was only 23 percent, so the state had to purchase domestic steel. That difference added $400 million to the price tag. Although this requirement benefitted domestic steel producers, it was difficult to see how it helped California taxpayers.[8]

TRADE CONFLICTS U.S. FISCAL STIMULUS AND BUY AMERICAN LEGISLATION

As the U.S. government moved toward enacting its $787 billion fiscal stimulus legislation during the recession of 2007–2009, debate emerged over whether government funded projects should use only U.S. made materials. According to proponents of Buy–American legislation, not one dollar of stimulus expenditures should be spent on foreign goods; instead, taxpayers' dollars should be used to buy U.S. made goods and thus support the jobs of Americans.

The initial fiscal stimulus bill sponsored by the House of Representatives stipulated that none of the funds made available by the bill could be used for infrastructure projects unless all of the iron and steel used in a project are produced in the United States. The Senate version went even further, mandating that all manufactured goods used in construction projects come from U.S. producers. This legislation was strongly favored by U.S. labor unions and companies such as U.S. Steel Corp.

Although President Barack Obama supported Buy–American legislation during his presidential campaign in 2008, his enthusiasm weakened by 2009. The initial foreign reaction to possible Buy–American legislation was outrage. The European Union warned that passage of the legislation would result in the United States violating past trade agreements and intensifying the possibility of a trade war that could plunge the world into depression. Also, U.S. exporting companies such as Caterpillar argued that foreign retaliation would greatly reduce their sales abroad: Caterpillar noted that in 2009, 60 percent of its revenue was from foreign sales.

In response to these concerns, Obama came out against Buy–American provisions that signaled blatant protectionism. He wound up signing a fiscal stimulus bill that included a watered down version of the Buy–American provisions contained in the House and Senate stimulus bills. For example, federal agencies can waive Buy–American preferences if they inflate the cost of a construction project by more than 25 percent or are deemed to be against the public interest. City and state (municipal) governments in the United States are not obligated to honor the trade agreements of the federal government: They have been able to enact Buy-American preferences that exclude firms in Canada, Mexico, and other countries from bidding on municipal construction contracts for schools, water treatment plants, and the like.

iStockphoto.com/photosoup

---

[8]"Steep Cost Overruns, Delays Plague Efforts to Rebuild Bay Bridge," *Los Angeles Times*, May 29, 2004.

Social Regulations

Since the 1950s, nations have assumed an increasing role in regulating the quality of life for society. **Social regulation** attempts to correct a variety of undesirable side effects in an economy that relate to health, safety, and the environment—effects that markets, left to themselves, often ignore. Social regulation applies to a particular issue, such as environmental quality, and affects the behavior of firms in many industries such as automobiles, steel, and chemicals.

CAFÉ Standards

Although social regulations may advance health, safety, and environmental goals, they can also serve as barriers to international trade. Consider the case of fuel economy standards imposed by the U.S. government on automobile manufacturers.

Originally enacted in 1975, **corporate average fuel economy standards (CAFÉ)** represent the foundation of U.S. energy conservation policy. Applying to all passenger vehicles sold in the United States, the standards are based on the average fuel efficiency of all vehicles sold by all manufacturers. As of 2011, the CAFÉ requirement for passenger cars was 30.2 miles per gallon for passenger cars and 24.1 miles per gallon for light trucks. Manufacturers whose average fuel economy falls below this standard are subject to fines.

During the 1980s, CAFÉ requirements were used not only to promote fuel conservation but also to protect the jobs of U.S. autoworkers. The easiest way for U.S. car manufacturers to improve the average fuel efficiency of their fleets would have been to import smaller, more fuel efficient vehicles from their subsidiaries in Asia and Europe. However, this would have decreased employment in an already depressed industry. The U.S. government thus enacted *separate but identical* standards for domestic and imported passenger cars. General Motors, Ford, and Chrysler, that manufactured vehicles in the United States and also sold imported cars, would be required to fulfill CAFÉ targets for *both* categories of vehicles. Thus, U.S. firms could not fulfill CAFÉ standards by averaging the fuel economy of their imports with their less fuel efficient, domestically produced vehicles. By calculating domestic and imported fleets separately, the U.S. government attempted to force domestic firms not only to manufacture more efficient vehicles but also to produce them in the United States! In short, government regulations sometimes place effective import barriers on foreign commodities, whether they are intended to do so or not, which aggravates foreign competitors.

Europe Has a Cow over Hormone-Treated U.S. Beef

The EU's ban on hormone-treated meat is another case where social regulations can lead to a beef. Growth promoting hormones are used widely by livestock producers to speed up growth rates and produce leaner livestock more in line with consumer preferences for diets with reduced fat and cholesterol. However, critics of hormones maintain that they can cause cancer for consumers of meat.

In 1989, the EU enacted its ban on the production and importation of beef derived from animals treated with growth promoting hormones. The EU justified the ban as necessary to protect the health and safety of consumers.

The ban was immediately challenged by U.S. producers who used the hormones in about 90 percent of their beef production. According to the United States, there was no scientific basis for the ban that restricted beef imports on the basis of health concerns. Instead, the ban was merely an attempt to protect the relatively high-cost European beef industry from foreign competition. American producers noted that when the ban was imposed, European producers had accumulated large, costly-to-store beef surpluses that resulted in enormous political pressure to limit imports of beef. According to the

United States, the EU's emphasis on health concerns was thus a smokescreen for protecting an industry with comparative disadvantage.

The trade dispute eventually went to the WTO (see Chapter 6), that ruled the EU's ban on hormone treated beef was illegal and resulted in lost annual U.S. exports of beef to the EU in the amount of $117 million. Nonetheless, the EU, citing consumer preference, refused to lift its ban. The WTO authorized the United States to impose tariffs high enough to prohibit $117 million of European exports to the United States. The United States exercised its right and slapped 100-percent tariffs on a list of European products that included tomatoes, Roquefort cheese, prepared mustard, goose liver, citrus fruit, pasta, hams, and other products. The U.S. hit list focused on products from Denmark, France, Germany, and Italy—the biggest supporters of the EU's ban on hormone treated beef.

By effectively doubling the prices of the targeted products, the 100-percent tariffs pressured the Europeans to liberalize their imports of American beef products. In 2009, the EU and the United States agreed that the EU would keep its ban on hormone treated beef but that the United States would gradually lift its import duties in exchange for a steep increase in the EU's duty free import quotas on beef that is not treated with growth promoting hormones. By 2012, the United States lifted its import duties on all targeted European goods, thus ending the trade dispute. Although EU farmers had feared a surge in imports of U.S. beef, this failed to materialize.

Sea Transport and Freight Regulations

During the 1990s, U.S. shipping companies serving Japanese ports complained of a highly restrictive system of port services. They contended that Japan's association of stevedore companies (companies that unload cargo from ships) used a system of prior consultations to control competition, allocate harbor work among themselves, and frustrate the implementation of any cost cutting by shipping companies.

In particular, shipping companies contended that they were forced to negotiate with the Japanese stevedore company association on everything from arrival times to choice of stevedores and warehouses. Because port services were controlled by the stevedore company association, foreign carriers could not negotiate with individual stevedore companies about prices and schedules. Moreover, U.S. carriers maintained that the Japanese government approved these restrictive practices by refusing to license new entrants into the port service business and supporting the requirement that foreign carriers negotiate with Japan's stevedore company association.

A midnight trip to Tokyo Bay illustrates the frustration of U.S. shipping companies. The lights are dimmed and the wharf is quiet, even though the Sealand Commerce has just docked. At 1:00 A.M., lights turn on, cranes swing alive, and trucks appear to unload the ship's containers that carry paper plates, computers, and pet food from the United States. However, at 4:00 A.M., the lights shut off and the work ceases. Longshoremen don't return until 8:30 A.M. and take three more hours off later in the day. They unloaded only 169 of 488 containers that they must handle before the ship sails for Oakland. At that rate, the job takes until past noon; but at least it isn't Sunday when docks close altogether.

When the Sealand Commerce reaches Oakland, however, U.S. dockworkers unload and load 24 hours a day, taking 30 percent less time for about half the price. To enter Tokyo Bay, the ship had to clear every detail of its visit with Japan's stevedore company association; to enter the U.S. port the ship will merely notify port authorities and the Coast Guard. According to U.S. exporters, this unequal treatment on waterfronts is a trade barrier because it makes U.S. exports more expensive in Japan.

In 1997, the United States and Japan found themselves on the brink of a trade war after the U.S. government decided to direct its Coast Guard and customs service to bar Japanese-flagged ships from unloading at U.S. ports. The U.S. government demanded that foreign shipping companies be allowed to negotiate directly with Japanese stevedore companies to unload their ships, thus giving carriers a way around the restrictive practices of Japan's stevedore company association. After consultation between the two governments, an agreement was reached to liberalize port services in Japan. As a result, the United States rescinded its ban against Japanese ships.

SUMMARY

1. With the decline in import tariffs in the past two decades, nontariff trade barriers (NTBs) have gained in importance as a measure of protection. NTBs include such practices as (a) import quotas, (b) orderly marketing agreements, (c) domestic content requirements, (d) subsidies, (e) antidumping regulations, (f) discriminatory government procurement practices, (g) social regulations, and (h) sea transport and freight restrictions.

2. An import quota is a government imposed limit on the quantity of a product that can be imported. Quotas are imposed on a global (worldwide) basis or a selective (individual country) basis. Although quotas have many of the same economic effects as tariffs, they tend to be more restrictive. A quota's revenue effect generally accrues to domestic importers or foreign exporters, depending on the degree of market power they possess. If government desired to capture the revenue effect, it could auction import quota licenses to the highest bidder in a competitive market.

3. A tariff-rate quota is a two-tier tariff placed on an imported product. It permits a limited number of goods to be imported at a lower tariff rate, whereas any imports beyond this limit face a higher tariff. Of the revenue generated by a tariff-rate quota, some accrues to the domestic government as tariff revenue and the remainder is captured by producers as windfall profits.

4. Because an export quota is administered by the government of the exporting nation (supply-side restriction), its revenue effect tends to be captured by sellers from the exporting nation. For the importing nation, the quota's revenue effect is a welfare loss in addition to the protective and consumption effects.

5. Domestic content requirements try to limit the practice of foreign sourcing and encourage the development of domestic industry. They typically stipulate the minimum percentage of a product's value that must be produced in the home country for that product to be sold tariff free. Domestic content protection tends to impose welfare losses on the domestic economy in the form of higher production costs and higher priced goods.

6. Government subsidies are sometimes granted as a form of protection to domestic exporters and import-competing producers. They may take the form of direct cash bounties, tax concessions, credit extended at low interest rates, or special insurance arrangements. Direct production subsidies for import-competing producers tend to involve a smaller loss in economic welfare than do equivalent tariffs and quotas. The imposition of export subsidies results in a terms-of-trade effect and an export revenue effect.

7. International dumping occurs when a firm sells its product abroad at a price that is less than average total cost or less than that charged to domestic buyers of the same product. Dumping can be sporadic, predatory, or persistent in nature. Idle productive capacity may be the reason behind dumping. Governments often impose stiff penalties against foreign commodities that are believed to be dumped in the home economy.

8. Government rules and regulations in areas such as safety and technical standards and marketing requirements can have a significant impact on world trade patterns.

KEY CONCEPTS AND TERMS

Absolute quota (p. 149)
Antidumping duty (p. 166)
Buy–national policies (p. 172)
Corporate average fuel economy
  standards (CAFÉ) (p. 174)
Cost-based definition of
  dumping (p. 166)
Domestic content
  requirements (p. 158)
Domestic production
  subsidy (p. 161)

Dumping (p. 163)
Export quotas (p. 156)
Export subsidy (p. 161)
Global quota (p. 150)
Import license (p. 150)
License on demand
  allocation (p. 155)
Margin of dumping
  (p. 166)
Nontariff trade barriers
  (NTBs) (p. 149)

Persistent dumping
  (p. 164)
Predatory dumping
  (p. 164)
Price-based definition of
  dumping (p. 166)
Selective quota (p. 150)
Social regulation (p. 174)
Sporadic dumping (p. 164)
Subsidies (p. 161)
Tariff-rate quota (p. 154)

STUDY QUESTIONS

1. In the past two decades, NTBs have gained in importance as protectionist devices. What are the major NTBs?

2. How does the revenue effect of an import quota differ from that of a tariff?

3. What are the major forms of subsidies that governments grant to domestic producers?

4. What is meant by voluntary export restraints and how do they differ from other protective barriers?

5. Should U.S. antidumping laws be stated in terms of average total production costs or average variable costs?

6. Which is a more restrictive trade barrier—an import tariff or an equivalent import quota?

7. Differentiate among sporadic, persistent, and predatory dumping.

8. A subsidy may provide import-competing producers the same degree of protection as tariffs or quotas but at a lower cost in terms of national welfare. Explain.

9. Rather than generating tax revenue as do tariffs, subsidies require tax revenue. Therefore, they are not an effective protective device for the home economy. Do you agree?

10. In 1980, the U.S. auto industry proposed that import quotas be imposed on foreign-produced cars sold in the United States. What would be the likely benefits and costs of such a policy?

11. Why did the U.S. government in 1982 provide import quotas as an aid to domestic sugar producers?

12. Which tends to result in a greater welfare loss for the home economy: (a) an import quota levied by the home government or (b) a voluntary export quota imposed by the foreign government?

13. What would be the likely effects of export restraints imposed by Japan on its auto shipments to the United States?

14. Why might U.S. steel using firms lobby against the imposition of quotas on foreign steel sold in the United States?

15. Concerning international dumping, distinguish between the price- and cost-based definitions of foreign market value.

16. Table 5.5 illustrates the demand and supply schedules for television sets in Venezuela, a "small" nation that is unable to affect world prices. On graph paper, sketch Venezuela's demand and supply schedules of television sets.

a. Suppose Venezuela imports TV sets at a price of $150 each. Under free trade, how many sets does Venezuela produce, consume, and import? Determine Venezuela's consumer surplus and producer surplus.

b. Assume that Venezuela imposes a quota that limits imports to 300 TV sets. Determine the quota induced price increase and the resulting decrease in consumer surplus. Calculate the quota's redistributive, consumption, protective, and revenue effects. Assuming that Venezuelan import companies organize as buyers and bargain favorably with competitive foreign exporters, what is the overall welfare loss to Venezuela as a result of the quota? Suppose that foreign exporters organize as a monopoly seller. What is the overall welfare loss to Venezuela as a result of the quota?

c. Suppose that, instead of a quota, Venezuela grants its import-competing producers a subsidy of $100 per TV set. In your diagram, draw the subsidy-adjusted supply schedule for Venezuelan producers. Does the subsidy result in a rise in the price of TV sets above the free trade level? Determine Venezuela's production, consumption, and imports of TV sets under the subsidy. What is the total cost of the subsidy to the Venezuelan government? Of this amount, how much is transferred to Venezuelan producers in the form of producer surplus, and how much is absorbed by higher production costs due to inefficient domestic production? Determine the overall welfare loss to Venezuela under the subsidy.

17. This question applies to the welfare effects of an export quota that is examined in *Exploring Further 5.2*, available at www.cengage.com/economics/Carbaugh. Table 5.6 illustrates the demand and supply schedules for computers in Ecuador, a "small" nation that is unable to affect world prices. On graph paper, sketch Ecuador's demand and supply schedules of computers.

a. Assume that Hong Kong and Taiwan can supply computers to Ecuador at a per unit price of $300 and $500, respectively. With free trade, how many computers does Ecuador import? From which nation does it import?

b. Suppose Ecuador and Hong Kong negotiate a voluntary export agreement in which Hong Kong imposes on its exporters a quota that limits shipments to Ecuador to 40 computers. Assume Taiwan does not take advantage of the situation by exporting computers to Ecuador. Determine the quota induced price increase and the reduction in consumer surplus for Ecuador. Determine the quota's redistributive,

TABLE 5.6

Computer Supply and Demand: Ecuador

Price of Computer	Quantity Demanded	Quantity Supplied
$0	100	—
200	90	0
400	80	10
600	70	20
800	60	30
1000	50	40
1200	40	50
1400	30	60
1600	20	70
1800	10	80
2000	0	90

© Cengage Learning®

protective, consumption, and revenue effects. Because the export quota is administered by Hong Kong, its exporters will capture the quota's revenue effect. Determine the overall welfare loss to Ecuador as a result of the quota.

c. Again assume that Hong Kong imposes an export quota on its producers that restricts shipments to Ecuador to 40 computers, but now suppose that Taiwan, a non-restrained exporter, ships an additional 20 computers to Ecuador. Ecuador thus imports 60 computers. Determine the overall welfare loss to Ecuador as a result of the quota.

d. In general, when increases in non-restrained supply offset part of the cutback in shipments that occur under an export quota, will the overall welfare loss for the importing country be greater or smaller than that which occurs in the absence of non-restrained supply? Determine the amount in the example of Ecuador.

18. Figure 5.6 illustrates the practice of international dumping by British Toys, Inc. (BTI). Figure 5.6(*a*) shows the domestic demand and marginal revenue schedules faced by BTI in the United Kingdom (UK), and Figure 5.6(*b*) shows the demand and marginal revenue schedules faced by BTI in Canada. Figure 5.6(*c*) shows the combined demand and marginal revenue schedules for the two markets, as well as BTI's average total cost and marginal cost schedules.

FIGURE 5.6

International Dumping Schedules

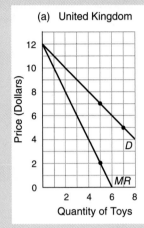

(a) United Kingdom

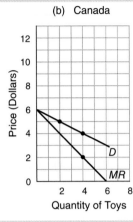

(b) Canada

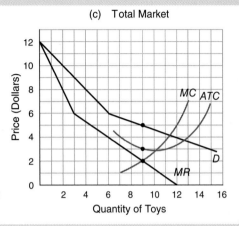

(c) Total Market

© Cengage Learning®

a. In the absence of international dumping, BTI would charge a uniform price to U.K. and Canadian customers (ignoring transportation costs). Determine the firm's profit maximizing output and price, as well as total profit. How much profit accrues to BTI on its U.K. sales and on its Canadian sales?

b. Suppose now that BTI engages in international dumping. Determine the price that BTI charges its U.K. buyers and the profits that accrue on U.K. sales. Also determine the price that BTI charges its Canadian buyers and the profits that accrue on Canadian sales. Does the practice of international dumping yield higher profits than the uniform pricing strategy and if so, by how much?

19. Why is a tariff-rate quota viewed as a compromise between the interests of the domestic consumer and those of the domestic producer? How does the revenue effect of a tariff-rate quota differ from that of an import tariff?

Trade Regulations and Industrial Policies

P revious chapters have examined the benefits and costs of tariff and nontariff trade barriers. This chapter discusses the major trade policies of the United States. It also considers the role of the World Trade Organization in the global trading system, the industrial policies implemented by nations to enhance the competitiveness of their producers, and the nature and effects of international economic sanctions used to pursue foreign policy objectives.

U.S. TARIFF POLICIES BEFORE 1930

As Table 6.1 makes clear U.S. tariff history has been marked by fluctuations. The dominant motive behind the early tariff laws of the United States was to provide the government with an important source of tax revenue. This *revenue* objective was the main reason Congress passed the first tariff law in 1789. This law allowed only the federal government to levy uniform tariffs, ranging from 5 to 15 percent, so the former system of separate state tariff rates disappeared. Tariffs were the largest source of federal revenue during this era, accounting for over 90 percent of federal revenue during the 1790s. As the economy diversified and developed alternative sources of tax revenue, such as the income tax and payroll tax, justification for the revenue argument was weakened. The tariffs collected by the federal government today are only about one percent of total federal revenues; a negligible amount.

As the revenue argument weakened, the *protective* argument for tariffs developed strength. In 1791, Alexander Hamilton presented to Congress his famous "Report on Manufacturers," which proposed the young industries of the United States be granted import protection until they could grow and prosper—the *infant-industry* argument. Although Hamilton's writings did not initially have a legislative impact, by the 1820s protectionist sentiments in the United States were well established, especially in the Northern states where manufacturing industries were being developed. However, intense political opposition to higher tariffs came from Southerners who had almost no manufacturing industry and imported many products with high tariffs. Southerners

TABLE 6.1

U.S. Tariff History: Average Tariff Rates

Tariff Laws and Dates	Average Tariff Rate* (%)
McKinley Law, 1890	48.4
Wilson Law, 1894	41.3
Dingley Law, 1897	46.5
Payne–Aldrich Law, 1909	40.8
Underwood Law, 1913	27.0
Fordney–McCumber Law, 1922	38.5
Smoot–Hawley Law, 1930	53.0
1930–1949	33.9
1950–1969	11.9
1970–1989	6.4
1990–1999	5.2
2000–2009	3.5
2013	3.5

*Simple average.

Source: From U.S. Department of Commerce, *Statistical Abstract of the United States*, various issues and World Trade Organization, *World Tariff Profiles*, 2012.

claimed that they would have to pay more for manufactured imports while getting less for the cotton they sold abroad.

The surging protectionist movement reached its high point in 1828 with the passage of the so-called Tariff of Abominations. This measure increased duties to an average level of 45 percent, the highest in the years prior to the Civil War, and provoked the South that wanted low duties for its imported manufactured goods. The South's opposition to this tariff led to the passage of the Compromise Tariff of 1833, that provided for a downsizing of the tariff protection afforded U.S. manufacturers. During the 1840s and 1850s, the U.S. government found that it faced an excess of tax receipts over expenditures. Therefore, the government passed the Walker tariffs that cut duties to an average level of 23 percent in order to eliminate the budget surplus. Further tariff cuts took place in 1857, bringing the average tariff levels to their lowest point since 1816, at around 16 percent.

During the Civil War era, tariffs were again raised with the passage of the Morill Tariffs of 1861, 1862, and 1864. These measures were primarily intended as a means of paying for the Civil War. By 1870, protection climbed back to the heights of the 1840s; this time the tariff levels would not be reduced. During the latter part of the 1800s, U.S. policy makers were impressed by the arguments of American labor and business leaders who complained that *cheap foreign labor* was causing goods to flow into the United States. The enactment of the McKinley and Dingley Tariffs largely rested upon this argument. By 1897, tariffs on protected imports averaged 46 percent.

Although the Payne–Aldrich Tariff of 1909 marked the turning point against rising protectionism, it was the enactment of the Underwood Tariff of 1913 that reduced duties to 27 percent on average. Trade liberalization might have remained on a more permanent basis had it not been for the outbreak of World War I. Protectionist pressures built up during the war years and maintained momentum after the war's conclusion.

During the early 1920s, the *scientific tariff* concept was influential and in 1922 the Fordney–McCumber Tariff contained, among other provisions, one that allowed the president to increase tariff levels if foreign production costs were below those of the United States. Average tariff rates climbed to 38 percent under the Fordney–McCumber law.[1]

SMOOT–HAWLEY ACT

The high point of U.S. protectionism occurred with the passage of the **Smoot–Hawley Act** in 1930, under which U.S. average tariffs were raised to 53 percent on protected imports. As the Smoot–Hawley bill moved through the U.S. Congress, formal protests from foreign nations flooded Washington, eventually adding up to a document of 200 pages. Nevertheless, both the House of Representatives and the Senate approved the bill. Although about a thousand U.S. economists beseeched President Herbert Hoover to veto the legislation, he did not do so and the tariff was signed into law on June 17, 1930. Simply put, the Smoot–Hawley Act tried to divert national demand away from imports and toward domestically produced goods.

The legislation provoked retaliation by 25 trading partners of the United States. Spain implemented the Wais Tariff in reaction to U.S. tariffs on cork, oranges, and grapes. Switzerland boycotted U.S. exports to protest new tariffs on watches and shoes. Canada increased its tariffs threefold in reaction to U.S. tariffs on timber, logs, and many food products. Italy retaliated against tariffs on olive oil and hats with tariffs on U.S. automobiles. Mexico, Cuba, Australia, and New Zealand also participated in the tariff wars. Other beggar-thy-neighbor policies, such as foreign-exchange controls and currency depreciations, were also implemented. The effort by several nations to run a trade surplus by reducing imports led to a breakdown of the international trading system. Within two years after the Smoot–Hawley Act, U.S. exports decreased by nearly two-thirds. Figure 6.1 shows the decline of world trade as the global economy fell into the Great Depression.

How did President Hoover fall into such a protectionist trap? The president felt compelled to honor the 1928 Republican platform calling for tariffs to aid the weakened farm economy. The stock market crash of 1929 and the imminent Great Depression further led to a crisis atmosphere. Republicans had been sympathetic to protectionism for decades. Now they viewed import tariffs as a method of fulfilling demands that government should initiate positive steps to combat domestic unemployment.

President Hoover felt bound to tradition and to the platform of the Republican Party. Henry Ford spent an evening with Hoover requesting a presidential veto of what he referred to as "economic stupidity." Other auto executives sided with Ford. Tariff legislation had never before been vetoed by a president and Hoover was not about to set a precedent. Hoover remarked that "with returning normal conditions, our foreign trade will continue to expand."

---

[1]Throughout the 1800s the United States levied high tariffs on imported goods, the infant-industry argument being an important motive. The second half of the 1800s was also a period of rapid economic growth for the country. According to protectionists, these tariffs provided the foundation for a growing economy. However, free traders note that such conclusions are unwarranted because this era was also a time of massive immigration to the United States, which fostered economic growth. See T. Norman Van Cott and Cecil Bohanon, "Tariffs, Immigration, and Economic Insulation," *The Independent Review*, Spring 2005, pp. 529–542.

FIGURE 6.1

Smoot–Hawley Protectionism and World Trade, 1929–1933 (millions of dollars)

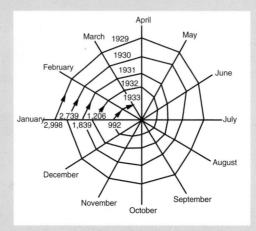

The figure shows the pattern of world trade from 1929 to 1933. Following the Smoot–Hawley Tariff Act of 1930, that raised U.S. tariffs to an average level of 53 percent, other nations retaliated by increasing their own import restrictions, and the volume of world trade decreased as the global economy fell into the Great Depression.

Source: Data taken from League of Nations, *Monthly Bulletin of Statistics*, February, 1934. See also Charles Kindleberger, *The World in Depression* (Berkeley, CA: University of California Press, 1973), p. 170.

By 1932, U.S. trade with other nations had collapsed. Presidential challenger Franklin Roosevelt denounced the trade legislation as ruinous. Hoover responded that Roosevelt would have U.S. workers compete with peasant labor overseas. Following Hoover's defeat in the presidential election of 1932, the Democrats dismantled the Smoot–Hawley legislation. But they used caution, relying on reciprocal trade agreements instead of across-the-board tariff concessions by the United States. Sam Rayburn, the speaker of the House of Representatives, insisted that any party member who wanted to be a member of the House Ways and Means Committee had to support trade reciprocity instead of protectionism. The Smoot–Hawley approach was discredited and the United States pursued trade liberalization via reciprocal trade agreements.

RECIPROCAL TRADE AGREEMENTS ACT

The combined impact on U.S. exports of the Great Depression and the foreign retaliatory tariffs imposed in reaction to the Smoot–Hawley Act resulted in a reversal of U.S. trade policy. In 1934, Congress passed the **Reciprocal Trade Agreements Act** that changed U.S. trade policies by transferring authority from the Congress that generally favored domestic import-competing producers, to the president, who tended to consider the national interest when forming trade policy. This changed tipped the balance of power in favor of lower tariffs and set the stage for a wave of trade liberalization. Specifically aimed at tariff reduction, the act contained two features: negotiating authority and generalized reductions.

Under this law, the president was given the unprecedented authority to negotiate *bilateral* tariff reduction agreements with foreign governments (for example, between the United States and Sweden). Without congressional approval, the president could lower tariffs by up to 50 percent of the existing level. Enactment of any tariff reductions was dependent on the willingness of other nations to reciprocally lower their tariffs on U.S. goods. From 1934 to 1947, the United States entered into 32 bilateral tariff agreements, and over this period the average level of tariffs on protected products fell to about half of the 1934 levels.

The Reciprocal Trade Agreements Act also provided generalized tariff reductions through the **most favored nation** (MFN) clause. This clause means that countries cannot normally discriminate between their trading partners: Grant one country a lower tariff rate for one of its products and you must do the same for all other countries. In general, MFN means that every time a country reduces a trade barrier or opens up a market, it must do so for the same goods or services from all of its trading partners whether rich or poor. In 1998, the U.S. government replaced the term most favored nation with **normal trade relations**.

Although the Reciprocal Trade Agreements Act tipped the political balance of power in favor of lower tariffs, its piecemeal, bilateral approach limited the trade liberalization efforts of the United States. The United States recognized that a more comprehensive approach was needed to liberalize trade on a multilateral basis.

GENERAL AGREEMENT ON TARIFFS AND TRADE

Partly in response to trade disruptions during the Great Depression, the United States and some of its allies sought to impose order on trade flows after World War II. The first major postwar step toward liberalization of trade on a multilateral basis was the **General Agreement on Tariffs and Trade** (GATT) signed in 1947. GATT was crafted as an agreement among contracting parties, the member nations, to decrease trade barriers and place all nations on an equal footing in trading relations. GATT was never intended to become an organization; instead, it was a set of agreements among countries around the world to reduce trade barriers and establish broad rules for commercial policy.

In 1995, GATT was transformed into the **World Trade Organization (WTO)**. The WTO embodies the main provisions of GATT, but its role was expanded to include a mechanism intended to improve GATT's process for resolving trade disputes among member nations. Let us first discuss the major principles of the original GATT system.

Trade without Discrimination

According to GATT, a member country should not discriminate between its trading partners. The two pillars of the nondiscrimination principle were the MFN principle (normal trade relations) and the national treatment principle.

According to the MFN principle, if a member of GATT granted another member a lower tariff rate for one of its products, it had to do the same for all other GATT members. The MFN thus meant "favor one, favor all." Some exceptions are allowed. Countries can establish a free-trade agreement that applies only to goods traded within the group, thus discriminating against goods from nonmembers, or they can provide developing countries special access (low tariffs) to their markets. A country might also increase trade barriers against goods that are deemed to be traded unfairly from certain countries.

Granting MFN status or imposing differential tariffs has been used as an instrument of foreign policy. A nation may punish unfriendly nations with high import tariffs on their goods and reward friendly nations with low tariffs. The United States has granted MFN status to most of the nations with which it trades. As of 2014, the United States did not grant normal trade relation status to Cuba and North Korea. U.S. tariffs on imports from these countries are often three or four (or more) times as high as those on comparable imports from nations receiving MFN status, as seen in Table 6.2. The United States has granted temporary MFN to several other countries such as Vietnam and Russia.

The second aspect of trade without discrimination involved the national treatment principle. Under this principle, GATT members had to treat imported and domestically produced goods equally, once the foreign goods have entered the market. Therefore, domestic regulations and internal taxes could not be biased against foreign products. Tariffs could apply to foreign products when they entered a country as imports.

The Canadian periodicals industry illustrates the use of discriminatory taxes that have violated the national treatment principle. A long standing policy of the Canadian government has been to protect its magazine industry as a medium of Canadian ideas and interests and a tool for the promotion of Canadian culture. In the 1990s, the Canadian government levied a steep tax on U.S. magazines such as *Sports Illustrated* that were sold to Canadians. The intent of the tax was to make it unprofitable for U.S. firms to publish special edition periodicals aimed at the Canadian market, thereby protecting the advertising revenues of Canadian publications. These taxes were found to violate the national treatment rules established in GATT because they discriminated against foreign magazines.

Promoting Freer Trade

Another goal of GATT was to promote freer trade through its role in the settlement of trade disputes. Historically, trade disputes consisted of matters strictly between the disputants; no third party was available to whom they might appeal for a favorable remedy.

TABLE 6.2

U.S. Tariffs on Imports from Nations Granted, and Not Granted, Normal Trade Relation Status: Selected Examples

	TARIFF (PERCENT)	
Product	With Normal Trade Relation Status	Without Normal Trade Relation Status
Hams	$0.12/kg	$0.72/kg
Sour cream	$0.32/liter	$0.15/liter
Butter	$0.123/liter	$0.309/liter
Fish	3% ad valorem	25% ad valorem
Saws	4% ad valorem	30% ad valorem
Cauliflower	10% ad valorem	50% ad valorem
Coffee	10% ad valorem	20% ad valorem
Woven fabrics	15.7% ad valorem	81% ad valorem
Babies' shirts	20.2% ad valorem	90% ad valorem
Gold necklaces	5% ad valorem	80% ad valorem

Source: From U.S. International Trade Commission, *Harmonized Tariff Schedule of the United States*, Washington, DC: Government Printing Office, various issues.

As a result, conflicts often remained unresolved for years. When they were settled, the stronger country generally won at the expense of the weaker country. GATT improved the dispute resolution process by formulating complaint procedures and providing a conciliation panel that a victimized country could express its grievance. GATT's dispute settlement process did not include the authority to enforce the conciliation panel's recommendations—a weakness that inspired the formation of the WTO.

GATT also obligated its members to use tariffs rather than quotas to protect their domestic industry. GATT's presumption was that quotas were inherently more trade distorting than tariffs because they allowed the user to discriminate between suppliers, were not predictable and transparent to the exporter, and imposed a maximum ceiling on imports. Here, too, exceptions were made to GATT's prohibition of quotas. Member nations could use quotas to safeguard their balance-of-payments, promote economic development, and allow the operation of domestic agricultural support programs. Voluntary export restraint agreements, that used quotas, also fell outside the quota restrictions of GATT because the agreements were voluntary.

Predictability: Through Binding and Transparency

Sometimes promising not to increase a trade barrier can be as important as reducing one because the promise provides businesses a clearer view of their future opportunities. Under GATT, when countries agreed to open their markets for goods or services, they would "bind" their commitments. These bindings amounted to ceilings on import tariff rates. For developed countries, the bound rates have generally been the rates actually charged. Most developing countries have bound the rates somewhat higher than the actual rates charged, so the bound rates serve as a ceiling. A country could change its bindings but only after negotiating with its trading partners; that meant compensating them for a loss of trade. The result of this was a much higher degree of market security for traders and investors.

Also, the GATT system tried to improve predictability and stability by making countries' trade rules as clear and public (transparent) as possible. Countries were required to disclose their trade policies and practices publically within the country or by notifying the GATT secretariat.

Multilateral Trade Negotiations

Prior to GATT, trade agreements involved bilateral negotiation between, say, the United States and a single foreign country. With the advent of GATT, trade negotiations were conducted on a multilateral basis that involved all GATT members participating in the negotiations. With the passage of time, GATT evolved to include almost all the main trading nations, although some were nonmembers. Therefore, "multilateral" was used to describe the GATT system instead of "global" or "world." To promote freer trade, GATT sponsored a series of negotiations, to reduce tariffs and nontariff trade barriers as summarized in Table 6.3.

The first round of GATT negotiations completed in 1947, achieved tariff reductions averaging 21 percent. However, tariff reductions were much smaller in the GATT rounds of the late 1940s and 1950s. During this period, protectionist pressures intensified in the United States as the war-damaged industries of Japan and Europe were reconstructed: the negotiation process was slow and tedious and nations often were unwilling to consider tariff cuts on many goods.

During the period 1964–1967, GATT members participated in the **Kennedy Round** of trade negotiations, named after U.S. President John F. Kennedy who issued an

TABLE 6.3

GATT Negotiating Rounds

Negotiating Round and Coverage	Years	Number of Participants	Tariff Cut Achieved (percent)
Addressed Tariffs			
Geneva	1947	23	21
Annecy	1949	13	2
Torquay	1951	38	3
Geneva	1956	26	4
Dillon Round	1960–1961	26	2
Kennedy Round	1964–1967	62	35
Addressed Tariff and Nontariff Barriers			
Tokyo Round	1973–79	99	33
Uruguay Round	1986–93	125	34
Doha Round	2002–	149	—

© Cengage Learning®

initiative calling for the negotiations. A multilateral meeting of GATT participants occurred at which the form of negotiations shifted from a product-by-product format to an across-the-board format. Tariffs were negotiated on broad categories of goods and a given rate reduction applied to the entire group a more streamlined approach. The Kennedy Round cut tariffs on manufactured goods by an average of 35 percent to an average *ad valorem* level of 10.3 percent.

The GATT rounds from the 1940s to the 1960s focused almost entirely on tariff reduction. As average tariff rates in industrial nations decreased during the postwar period, the importance of nontariff barriers increased. In response to these changes, negotiators shifted emphasis to the issue of nontariff distortions in international trade.

At the **Tokyo Round** of 1973–1979, signatory nations agreed to tariff cuts that took the across-the-board form initiated in the Kennedy Round. The average tariff on manufactured goods of the nine major industrial countries was cut from 7.0 percent to 4.7 percent, a 39 percent decrease. Tariff reductions on finished products were deeper than those on raw materials, thus tending to decrease the extent of tariff escalation. After the Tokyo Round, tariffs were so low that they were not a significant barrier to trade in industrial countries. A second accomplishment of the Tokyo Round was the agreement to remove or lessen many nontariff barriers. Codes of conduct were established in six areas: customs valuation, import licensing, government procurement, technical barriers to trade (such as product standards), antidumping procedures, and countervailing duties.

In spite of the trade liberalization efforts of the Tokyo Round, during the 1980s, world leaders felt that the GATT system was weakening. Members of GATT had increasingly used bilateral arrangements such as voluntary export restraints and other trade-distorting actions like subsidies that stemmed from protectionist domestic policies. World leaders also felt that GATT needed to encompass additional areas, such as trade in intellectual property, services, and agriculture. They also wanted GATT to give increasing attention to the developing countries that felt bypassed by previous GATT rounds of trade negotiations.

These concerns led to the **Uruguay Round** from 1986–1993. The Uruguay Round achieved across-the-board tariff cuts for industrial countries averaging 40 percent. Tariffs were eliminated entirely in several sectors, including steel, medical equipment, construction equipment, pharmaceuticals, and paper. Many nations agreed for the first time to bind, or cap, a significant portion of their tariffs, giving up the possibility of future rate increases above the bound levels. Progress was also made by the Uruguay Round in decreasing or eliminating nontariff barriers. The government procurement code opened a wider range of markets for signatory nations. The Uruguay Round made extensive efforts to eliminate quotas on agricultural products and required nations to rely instead on tariffs. In the apparel and textile sector, various bilateral quotas were phased out by 2005. The safeguards agreement prohibited the use of voluntary export restraints.

In 1999, members of the WTO (see next section) kicked off a new round of trade negotiations in Seattle, Washington for the 2000s. The participants established an agenda that included trade in agriculture, intellectual property rights, labor and environmental matters, and help for less developed nations. Believing that they had been taken to the cleaners in previous trade negotiations, developing nations were determined not to allow that to occur again. Disagreements among developing nations and industrial nations were a major factor that resulted in a breakdown of the meetings. The meeting became known as "The Battle in Seattle" because of the rioting and disruption that took place in the streets during the meeting.

Although trade liberalization proponents were discouraged by the collapse of the Seattle meeting, they continued to press for another round of trade talks. The result was the **Doha Round** that was launched in Doha, Qatar in 2002. The rhetoric of the Doha Round was elaborate: it would decrease trade distorting subsidies on farm goods; slash manufacturing tariffs by developing countries; cut tariffs on textiles and apparel products that poor countries especially cared about; free up trade in services; and negotiate global rules in four new areas—competition, investment, government procurement, and trade facilitation.

In spite of its ambitious aims, the Doha Round has shown little progress. The Doha Round immediately encountered difficulties as developing countries refused to accept the central bargain: large reductions in their industrial tariffs in exchange for greater access to the agricultural markets of the rich nations. Talks faltered in 2003 and finally collapsed in 2008. Skeptics have noted that if the Doha talks were not successful, it may be time to reconsider the size of these huge multilateral rounds and perhaps resort to bilateral trade agreements among a relatively small number of countries as the next best alternative. At the writing of this text, multilateral trade agreements were increasingly giving away to regional ones.

WORLD TRADE ORGANIZATION

On January 1, 1995, the day that the Uruguay Round took effect, GATT was transformed into the WTO. This transformation turned GATT from a trade accord into a membership organization responsible for governing the conduct of trade relations among its members. The GATT obligations remain at the core of the WTO. However, the WTO agreement requires that its members adhere not only to GATT rules, but also to the broad range of trade pacts that have been negotiated under GATT auspices in recent decades. This undertaking ends the free ride of many GATT members (especially developing countries) that benefited from, but refused to join in, new agreements negotiated in GATT since the 1970s. Today the WTO consists of 159 nations accounting for over 97 percent of world trade.

TRADE CONFLICTS AVOIDING TRADE BARRIERS DURING THE GREAT RECESSION

Global economic downturns are often a catalyst for trade protectionism. As economies shrink, nations have incentives to protect their struggling industries by establishing barriers against imported goods. During the Great Depression of the 1930s, the United States increased import tariffs on some 20,000 goods that was followed by other countries raising their trade barriers (including tariffs, import quotas, and exchange controls) against the United States. This contributed to a collapse in world trade and a deepening of the global economic slump. However, during the Great Recession of 2007–2009 there was much less resorting to trade barriers than during the Great Depression. Why?

Today, economic historians recognize that the severe protectionism of the 1930s was not simply motivated by the desire for relief from foreign competition. Instead, it was also the result of government officials' reluctance to abandon the gold standard and allow their currencies to depreciate. As discussed in Chapter 15, under the gold standard a country tied the value of its currency to a particular amount of gold. This meant that the exchange rate between any two currencies on gold was also fixed that provided businesses certainty about the terms on which international trade would be conducted. Therefore, maintaining the fixed exchange rates of the gold standard was a goal that many governments clung to during the Great Depression.

Many governments were unable to use monetary and fiscal policy to stimulate weak economies; monetary policy was constrained by the gold standard and fiscal policy by the balanced budget doctrine that government spending should be reduced in conjunction with falling tax revenues. Because exchange rate depreciation, monetary policy, and fiscal policy were ruled out as economic adjustment mechanisms, policymakers turned instead to higher trade barriers as a means of restricting imports and bolstering a weak economy. During the 1930s, governments had relatively few policy instruments other than protectionism, for dealing with economic downturns; thus the widespread use of protectionism. In contrast, countries that went off the gold standard and allowed their currencies to depreciate did not have to resort to protectionism.

However, by 2007–2009 governments had expanded their arsenal of economic adjustment mechanisms. Many countries had flexible exchange rates that meant currency depreciation helped reduce trade deficits. Expansionary fiscal and monetary policies were widely used to stimulate weak economies during the Great Recession, although it is debatable about their success. Countries are much more integrated into the global economy than in the 1930s and it is widely understood that trade disruptions caused by protectionism would be much more costly. What's more, the composition of the labor force has greatly changed from agriculture and manufacturing to services. This means that fewer workers are directly affected by international trade and the constituency for protectionist policies is smaller than in the past. Finally, countries have signed agreements and are members of institutions such as the World Trade Organization and the North American Free Trade Agreement that are intended to promote free trade.

Of course, trade protectionism around the globe increased during the Great Recession. However, the protectionist response to this recession was relatively muted.

Source: Douglas Irwin, Trade Policy Disaster: Lessons From the 1930s, *The MIT Press*, Cambridge, MA, 2012; Douglas Irwin, *Peddling Protectionism: Smooth–Hawley and the Great Depression*, Princeton University Press, 2011; Barry Eichengreen and Douglas Irwin, "The Slide to Protectionism in the Great Depression," *The Journal of Economic History*, Vol. 70, No. 4, December 2010, pp. 871–897.

How different is the WTO from the old GATT? The WTO is a full-fledged international organization, headquartered in Geneva, Switzerland; the old GATT was basically a provisional treaty serviced by an ad hoc secretariat. The WTO has a far wider scope than the old GATT, bringing into the multilateral trading system for the first time, trade in services, intellectual property, and investment. The WTO also administers a unified package of agreements to which all members are committed; in contrast, the GATT framework included many side agreements (for example, antidumping measures and subsidies) whose membership was limited to a few nations. Moreover, the WTO reverses policies of protection in certain "sensitive" areas (agriculture and textiles) that were more or less tolerated in the old GATT. The WTO is not a government; individual nations remain free to set their own appropriate levels of environment, labor, health, and safety protections.

Through various councils and committees, the WTO administers the many agreements contained in the Uruguay Round plus agreements on government procurement and civil aircraft. It oversees the implementation of the tariff cuts and reduction of nontariff measures agreed to in the negotiations. The WTO is also a watchdog of international trade, regularly examining the trade regimes of individual members. In its various bodies, members flag proposed or draft measures by others that can cause trade conflicts. Members are also required to update various trade measures and statistics that are maintained by the WTO in a large database.

Under the WTO, when members open their markets through the removal of barriers to trade, they "bind" their commitments. Therefore, when they reduce their tariffs through negotiations, they commit to bind the tariff reduction at a fixed level negotiated with their trading partners beyond which tariffs may not be increased. The binding of tariffs in the WTO provides a stable and predictable basis for trade, a fundamental principle underlying the operation of the institution. A provision is made for the renegotiation of bound tariffs. This provision means that a country can increase a tariff if it receives the approval of other countries that generally requires providing compensation by decreasing other tariffs. Currently, virtually all tariff rates in developed countries are bound, as are about 75 percent of the rates in developing countries.

Settling Trade Disputes

A major objective of the WTO is to strengthen the GATT mechanism for settling trade disputes. The old GATT dispute mechanism suffered from long delays, the ability of accused parties to block decisions of GATT panels that went against them, and inadequate enforcement. The dispute settlement mechanism of the WTO addresses each of these weaknesses. It guarantees the formation of a dispute panel once a case is brought and sets time limits for each stage of the process. The decision of the panel may be taken to a newly created appellate body, but the accused party can no longer block the final decision. The dispute settlement issue was especially important to the United States because this nation was the most frequent user of the GATT dispute mechanism.

The first case settled by the WTO involved a dispute between the United States and several other countries. In 1994, the U.S. government adopted a regulation imposing certain conditions on the quality of the gasoline sold in the United States. The aim of this resolution, established by the Environmental Protection Agency (EPA) under the Clean Air Act, was to improve air quality by reducing pollution caused by gasoline emissions. The regulation set different pollution standards for domestic and imported gasoline. It was challenged before the WTO by Venezuela and later by Brazil.

According to Venezuelan officials, there was a violation of the WTO's principle of national treatment that suggests once imported gasoline is on the U.S. market it cannot receive treatment less favorable than domestically produced gasoline. Venezuela argued that its gasoline was being submitted to controls and standards much more rigorous than those imposed on gasoline produced in the United States.

The United States argued that this discrimination was justified under WTO rules. The United States maintained that clean air is an exhaustible resource and that it was justified under WTO rules to preserve it. It also claimed that its pollution regulations were necessary to protect human health that is also allowed by the WTO. The major condition is that these provisions should not be protectionism in disguise.

Venezuela refuted that argument. Venezuela was in no way questioning the right of the United States to impose high environmental standards. However, it said that if the United States wanted clean gasoline then it should have submitted both the domestic and imported gasoline to the same high standards.

The new regulations put in place by the United States had an important impact for Venezuela and for its gasoline producers. Venezuela maintained that producing the gasoline according to the EPA's double standard was much more expensive than if Venezuela had followed the same specifications as American producers. Moreover, the U.S. market was critically important for Venezuela because two-thirds of Venezuela's gasoline exports were sold to the United States.

When Venezuela realized that the discriminatory aspects of the American gasoline regime would not be modified by the United States, it brought the case to the WTO. Brazil also complained about the discriminatory aspect of U.S. regulation. The two complaints were heard by a WTO panel that ruled in 1996 the United States unjustly discriminated against imported gasoline. When the United States appealed this ruling, a WTO appellate board confirmed the findings of the panel. The United States agreed to cease its discriminatory actions against imported gasoline by revising its environmental laws. Venezuela and Brazil were satisfied by the action of the United States.

Does the WTO Reduce National Sovereignty?

Do WTO rules or dispute settlements reduce the sovereignty of the United States or other countries? The United States benefits from WTO dispute settlement by having a set of rules that it can hold other countries accountable for their trade actions. At the same time, the U.S. government was careful to structure the WTO dispute settlement rules to preserve the rights of Americans. Nevertheless, critics on both the left and right such as Ralph Nader and Patrick Buchanan, contend that by participating in the WTO the United States has seriously undermined its sovereignty.

Proponents note that the findings of a WTO dispute settlement panel cannot force the United States to change its laws. Only the United States determines exactly how it will respond to the recommendations of a WTO panel, if at all. If a U.S. measure is found to be in violation of a WTO provision, the United States may on its own decide to change the law; compensate a foreign country by lowering its trade barriers of equivalent amount in another sector; or do nothing and possibly undergo retaliation by the affected country in the form of increased barriers to U.S. exports of an equivalent amount. America retains full sovereignty in its decision of whether or not to implement a panel recommendation. WTO agreements do not preclude the United States from establishing and maintaining its own laws or limit the ability of the United States to set its environmental, labor, health, and safety standards at the level it considers appropriate. The WTO does not allow a nation to use trade restrictions to enforce its own environmental, labor, health, and safety standards when they have selective and discriminatory effects against foreign producers.

Economists generally agree that the real issue raised by the WTO is not whether it decreases national sovereignty, but whether the specific obligations it imposes on a nation are greater or less than the benefits the nation receives from applying the same requirements to others (along with itself). According to this standard, the benefits of the United States of joining the WTO greatly exceed the costs. By granting the United States the status of normal trade relations with all 153 members, the agreement improves U.S. access to foreign markets. Moreover, it reduces the ability of other nations to impose restrictions to limit access to their markets. If the United States withdrew from the WTO it would lose the ability to use the WTO mechanism to induce other nations to decrease their own trade barriers and would harm U.S. exporting firms and their workers. Economists generally contend that the WTO puts some constraints on the decision making of the private and public sectors, but the costs of these constraints are outweighed by the economic benefits that citizens derive from freer trade.

Should Retaliatory Tariffs Be Used for WTO Enforcement?

Critics contend that the WTO's dispute settlement system based on tariff retaliation places smaller countries without much market power, at a disadvantage. Suppose that Ecuador, a small country, receives WTO authorization to retaliate against unfair trade practices of the United States, a large country. With competitive conditions, if Ecuador applies a higher tariff to imports from the United States, its national welfare will decrease as explained in Chapter 4. Therefore, Ecuador may be reluctant to impose a retaliatory tariff even though it has the approval of the WTO.

For countries large enough to affect prices in world markets, the issue is less clear. This is because a retaliatory tariff may improve a large country's terms of trade, thus enhancing its national welfare. If the United States raises a tariff barrier, it reduces the demand for the product on world markets. The decreased demand makes imports less expensive for the United States so to pay for these imports, the United States can export less. The terms of trade (ratio of export prices to import prices) improves for the United States. This improvement offsets at least some of the welfare reductions that take place through less efficiency because of increasing the tariff.

Although a small country could decide to impose retaliatory tariffs to teach a larger trading partner a lesson, it will find such behavior relatively more costly to initiate than its larger trading partner because it cannot obtain favorable movements in its terms of trade. Therefore, the limited market power of small countries makes them less likely to induce compliance to WTO rulings through retaliation. The problems smaller nations face in retaliating are the opposite of the special benefits they gain in obtaining WTO tariff concessions without being required to make reciprocal concessions.

Some maintain that the WTO's current dispute settlement system should be modified. For example, free traders object to retaliatory tariffs on the grounds that the WTO's purpose is to reduce trade barriers. Instead, they propose that offending countries should be assessed monetary fines. A system of fines has the advantage of avoiding additional trade protection and not placing smaller countries at a disadvantage. This system encounters the problem of deciding how to place a monetary value on violations. Fines might be difficult to collect because the offending country's government would have to initiate specific budgetary authorization. The notion of accepting an obligation to allow foreigners to levy monetary fines on a nation such as the United States would likely be criticized as taxation without representation and the WTO would be attacked as undermining national sovereignty.

American export subsidies provide an example of retaliatory tariffs authorized by the WTO. From 1984 to 2004, the U.S. tax code provided a tax benefit that enabled American exporters to exempt between 15 to 30 percent of their export income from U.S. taxes. In 1998, the European Union (EU) lodged a complaint with the WTO arguing that the U.S. tax benefit was an export subsidy in violation of WTO agreements. This complaint led to the WTO's ruling in 2003 that the tax benefit was illegal and the EU could immediately impose $4 billion in punitive duties on U.S. exports to Europe. Although the EU gave the U.S. government time to eliminate its export subsidy program, inertia resulted in continuation of the program. Europe began implementing retaliatory tariffs in 2004. A 5.0 percent penalty tariff was levied on U.S. exports such as jewelry, refrigerators, toys, and paper. The penalty climbed by one percentage point for each month U.S. lawmakers failed to bring U.S. tax laws in line with the WTO ruling. This tariff marked the first time that the United States came under WTO penalties for failure to adhere to its rulings. Although some in Congress resisted surrendering to the WTO on anything, the pressure provided by the tariffs convinced Congress to repeal the export subsidies.

Does the WTO Harm the Environment?

In recent years, the debate has intensified on the links between trade and the environment and the role that the WTO should play in promoting environment friendly trade. A central concern of those who have raised the profile of this issue in the WTO is that there are circumstances where trade and the pursuit of trade liberalization may have harmful environmental effects. Indeed, these concerns were voiced when thousands of environmentalists descended on the WTO summit in Seattle in 1999. They protested the WTO's influence on everything from marine destruction to global warming. Let us consider the opposing views on the links between trade and the environment.[2]

Harming the Environment

Two main arguments are made as to how trade liberalization may harm the environment. First, trade liberalization leads to a "race to the bottom" in environmental standards. If some countries have low environmental standards, industry is likely to shift production of environmentally intensive or highly polluting products to such pollution havens. Trade liberalization can make the shift of smokestack industries across borders to pollution havens even more attractive. If these industries then create pollution with globally adverse effects, trade liberalization can, indirectly, promote environmental degradation. Worse, trade induced competitive pressure may force countries to lower their environmental standards encouraging trade in products creating global pollution.

Why would developing nations adopt less stringent environmental policies than industrial nations? Poorer nations may place a higher priority on the benefits of production (more jobs and income) relative to the benefits of environmental quality than wealthy nations. Developing nations may have greater environmental capacities to reduce pollutants by natural processes (such as Latin America's rain forest capacity to reduce carbon dioxide in the air) than do industrial nations that suffer from the effects of past pollution. Developing nations can tolerate higher levels of emissions without increasing pollution levels. The introduction of a polluting industry into a sparsely populated developing nation will likely have less impact on the capacity of the environment to reduce pollution by natural processes than it would have in a densely populated industrial nation.

A second concern of environmentalists about the role of trade relates to social preferences. Some practices may simply be unacceptable for certain people or societies so they oppose trade in products that encourage such practices. These practices can include killing dolphins in the process of catching tuna and using leg-hold traps for catching animals for their furs. During the 1990s, relations between environmentalists and the WTO clashed when the WTO ruled against a U.S. ban on the imports of shrimp from countries using nets that trap turtles after complaints by India, Malaysia, Pakistan, and Thailand. The United States was found guilty of violating world trade law when it banned imports of Mexican tuna caught in ways that drown dolphins. Indeed, critics maintained that the free-trade policies of the WTO contradicted the goal of environmental quality.

---

[2]World Trade Organization, *Annual Report*, Geneva, Switzerland, 1998, pp. 54–55 and "Greens Target WTO's Plan for Lumber," *The Wall Street Journal*, November 24, 1999, pp. A2 and A4.

To most economists, any measure that liberalizes trade enhances productivity and growth, puts downward pressure on inflation by increasing competition and creates jobs. In Japan, tariffs are so high on imported finished wood products that U.S. firms don't have much of a market there. High local prices limit domestic demand in Japan. If tariffs were abolished, demand for lumber products from the United States could surge creating additional logging jobs in the United States and additional import related jobs in Japan.

But environmentalists view the tariff elimination differently. Their main concern is that a nontariff market that would result in lower prices would stimulate so much demand that logging would intensify in the world's remaining ancient forests, that they say serve as habitat for complex ecosystems that would otherwise not survive intact in forests that have been cut into fragments. Such old forests still exist across much of Alaska, Canada, and Russia's Siberian region. Environmentalists note that in Pennsylvania, New York, and other states in the Northeast, the forests have been so chopped up that many large predators have been driven from the land leaving virtually no check on the deer population. Deer are in a state of overpopulation.

Trade liberalization proponents play down the adverse impacts, arguing that reduced tariffs would boost world economies by decreasing the cost of housing, paper, and other products made from wood, while actually helping forest conditions. Timber officials in the United States say they could go into a country like Indonesia and persuade local firms to adopt more conservation minded techniques.

Improving the Environment

On the other hand, it is argued that trade liberalization may improve the quality of the environment rather than promote degradation. First, trade stimulates economic growth and growing prosperity is one of the key factors in societies' demand for a cleaner environment. As people get richer they want a cleaner environment—and they acquire the means to pay for it. Granted, trade can increase the cost of the wrong environmental policies. If farmers freely pollute rivers, higher agricultural exports will increase pollution. The solution to this is not to shut off exports: it is to impose tougher environmental laws that make polluters pay.

Second, trade and growth can encourage the development and dissemination of environment friendly production techniques as the demand for cleaner products grows and trade increases the size of markets. International companies may also contribute to a cleaner environment by using the most modern and environmentally clean technology in all their operations. This is less costly than using differentiated technology based on the location of production and helps companies to maintain a good reputation.

Although there is no dispute that in theory intensified competition could give rise to pollution havens, the empirical evidence suggests that it has not happened on a significant scale. The main reason is that the costs imposed by environmental regulation are small relative to other cost considerations, so this factor is unlikely to be at the basis of relocation decisions. The U.S. Census Bureau finds that even the most polluting industries spend no more than two percent of their revenues on abating pollution. Other factors such as labor costs, transportation costs, and the adequacy of infrastructure are much more costly. For all the talk of a race to the bottom, there is no evidence of a competitive lowering of environmental standards.

WTO Rules against China's Hoarding of Rare Earth Metals

China's trade policy on rare earth metals (industrial raw materials) provides an example of the WTO's involvement of trade and the environment. In 2011, the WTO ruled that

China had no legal right to impose export restrictions on nine rare earth metals, such as zinc and manganese, which are crucial to the production of high technology goods from fiber optic cables to smart phones, electric cars, computer monitors, and weapons. China had been using export tariffs and export quotas to reduce overseas sales of these essential resources. China is a "large country" in rare earth metals accounting for almost 97 percent of the world's output.

Why would a country restrict the export of raw materials and decrease the world supply? By restricting export sales, the supply of raw materials in the domestic market will increase, reducing the price faced by domestic buyers. By limiting the export of a good and decreasing world supply, the world price of the export good may be driven upward, improving the exporting country's terms of trade. The exporting country may want to conserve a scarce resource. Export limitations on raw materials would increase the domestic manufacturers' access to raw materials needed in production and also hold down the cost of these inputs giving them a competitive advantage in global markets.

Figure 6.2 illustrates the effects of Chinese export tariffs applied to zinc, a rare earth metal. Assume that China produces a large share of total world output of zinc. In the figure, S_C denotes China's domestic supply curve, D_C its domestic demand curve, and D_{C+W} the total world demand curve for zinc. The distance between D_C and D_{C+W} at each price represents the rest of the world's demand for zinc. Equilibrium is reached where supply curve S_C intersects demand curve D_{C+Wt}. At this point, China would produce 9 million pounds, of which 4 million pounds are sold domestically and 5 million pounds are exported. A price of $1.05 would apply to both domestic sales and exports.

Now assume China imposes a tax of $0.30 on each pound of zinc that is exported. A tax on foreign buyers decreases the amount they are willing to pay Chinese sellers, so the demand curve shifts downward, from D_{C+W} to $D_{C+W\ (Tax)}$. Equilibrium occurs where the new demand curve intersects the supply curve at a quantity of 7 million

FIGURE 6.2

China's Export Restrictions on Raw Materials

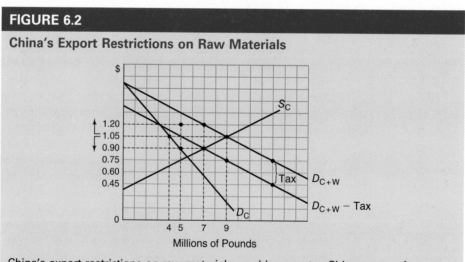

China's export restrictions on raw materials would guarantee Chinese manufacturers access to the raw materials needed in processing, as well as holding down the cost of these inputs to Chinese manufacturers. Also, the export restrictions would drive up the prices of raw materials used by foreign manufacturers that compete against the Chinese, placing them at a competitive disadvantage.

pounds, with 5 million pounds sold in China and 2 million pounds exported abroad. Foreign consumers pay $1.20 per pound; this includes the lower price of $0.90 going to Chinese producers and $0.30 going to the Chinese government as tax revenue. However, Chinese consumers pay only $0.90 per pound because the export tax does not apply to them. China's export tax on zinc results in a combination of a lower domestic price and a higher world price. An alternative scheme for restricting exports is the implementation of an export quota that can yield the same effects on prices and volume.

Concerning the environment, China does not impose stringent regulations on mining rare earths like many other countries do. In China, the waste from rare earth mining is pumped into artificial ponds with earthen dams where the seepage and waste has caused health related issues. The lack of stringent environmental regulations gives China's producers a cost advantage compared to their foreign competitors.

In defending its trade policy, China contended that its export restrictions are essential to protect its environment and scarce resources. WTO rules allow export controls for environmental reasons as long as such measures are made effective in conjunction with restrictions on domestic production or consumption. Such restrictions cannot be used to discriminate against users and refiners of materials in other nations.

The United States and other complainants in the natural resource case maintained that China's export restrictions were a discriminatory protectionist policy. The effect of these restrictions was to reduce the supply of key resources abroad and drive up world prices higher than China's domestic prices. This disadvantaged foreign producers that used these resources as inputs and that competed against the Chinese. Steps to limit sales of raw materials abroad were seen as a bid by China to attract more manufacturing to its shores. The WTO ruling was a setback to China's policy of hoarding rare earth metals. In response to the ruling, China said that it would make modifications to its export controls to avoid penalties.

By 2014, China's attempt to control the market for rare earth metals was dwindling. New supplies for many minerals were appearing as uncertainty over China's reliability and a period of higher prices stimulated investment in new mining projects elsewhere, such as Greenland and Russia. China's share of global production fell to about 80 percent, down from 95 percent in 2010. At the writing of this textbook, it remains to be seen how these modifications will play out.

Future of the World Trade Organization

The failure of the Doha Round to achieve a successful multilateral trade agreement has led some observers to question whether the WTO's principle of nondiscriminatory trade applies in today's world. Although much trade between major economies is still conducted on a nondiscriminatory basis (most favored nation principle) there is also a "spaghetti bowl" of regional and bilateral trade deals. In recent years, multilateral trade pacts have been increasingly giving way to regional ones and the structure of world trade has evolved towards a more fragmented system.

A major barrier to multilateral trade deals is the evolving balance of world economic power. Brazil, Russia, India, and China (the BRICs) visualize themselves as countries still poor enough to need protection for their industries while the rich should reduce their own trade barriers, especially to agriculture. The rich countries generally consider the BRICs as major economic competitors whose state capitalism is not compatible with a free and open world economy.

Also, trade liberalization now proceeds along two different tracks. One, favored by the United States, attempts to enforce environmental and labor protection, harmonize health, safety, and technical standards, and address the protection of intellectual property. The other track, desired by China, emphasizes decreasing tariffs outside sensitive sectors. It is difficult to achieve a multilateral trade agreement when the views of negotiating countries greatly differ.

Perhaps the WTO is a victim of its own success. Thanks to previous rounds of tariff reductions, further liberalization offers progressively less economic benefit. Countries may have less incentive to pursue trade liberalization according to the WTO approach. The decline of the WTO's concept of multilateralism may not greatly affect large countries that can negotiate regional agreements to their own advantage. Small countries without much bargaining power may be disadvantaged.[3]

TRADE PROMOTION AUTHORITY (FAST TRACK AUTHORITY)

If international trade agreements were subject to congressional amendments, achieving such pacts would be arduous, if not hopeless. The provisions that had been negotiated by the president would soon be modified by a deluge of congressional amendments that would quickly meet the disapproval of the trading partner(s) that accepted the original terms.

To prevent this scenario, the mechanism of **trade promotion authority** (also known as **fast track authority**) was devised in 1974. Under this provision, the president must formally notify Congress of his/her intent to enter trade negotiations with another country. This notification starts a clock in which Congress has 60 legislative days to permit or deny "fast track" authority. If fast track authority is approved, the president has a limited time period to complete the trade negotiations; extensions of this time period are permissible with congressional approval. Once the negotiations are completed, their outcome is subject only to a straight up-or-down vote (without amendment) in both houses of Congress within 90 legislative days of submission. In return, the president agrees to consult actively with Congress and the private sector throughout the negotiation of the trade agreement.

Fast track authority was instrumental in negotiating and implementing major trade agreements such as the Uruguay Round Agreements Act of 1994 and the North American Free Trade Agreement of 1993. Most analysts contend that the implementation of future trade agreements will require fast track authority for the president. Efforts to renew fast track authority have faced stiff opposition, largely due to congressional concerns about delegating too much discretionary authority to the president and disagreements over the goals of U.S. trade negotiations. In particular, labor unions and environmentalists have sought to ensure that trade agreements will address their concerns. They believe that high labor and environmental standards in the United States put American producers at a competitive disadvantage and that increased trade with countries with lax standards may lead to pressure to lower U.S. standards. If other countries are to trade with the United States, shouldn't they have similar labor and environmental standards?

Supporters of fast track authority have generally argued that, although labor and environmental standards are important, they do not belong in a trade agreement. Instead, these issues should be negotiated through secondary agreements that accompany a trade agreement. Labor leaders and environmentalists contend that past secondary agreements have lacked enforcement provisions and have done little to improve the quality of life abroad.

---

[3]Greg Ip, "The Gated Globe," *The Economist*, October 12, 2013, pp. 3–20.

SAFEGUARDS (THE ESCAPE CLAUSE): EMERGENCY PROTECTION FROM IMPORTS

In addition to the WTO's addressing of unfair trade practices, the United States itself has adopted a series of **trade remedy laws** designed to produce a fair trading environment for all parties engaging in international trade. These laws include the escape clause, countervailing duties, antidumping duties, and unfair trading practices. Table 6.4 summarizes the provisions of the U.S. trade remedy laws that are discussed in the following sections.

The **escape clause** provides temporary **safeguards** (relief) to U.S. firms and workers who are substantially injured from surges in imports that are fairly traded. To offset surging imports, the escape clause allows the president to terminate or make modifications in trade concessions granted foreign nations and to levy trade restrictions. The most common form of relief is tariff increases, followed by tariff-rate quotas and trade adjustment assistance. Import relief can be enacted for an initial period of four years and extended for another four years. The temporary nature of safeguards is to give the domestic industry time to adjust to import competition. It is common for safeguards to decline during the period in which they are imposed so as to gradually wean the domestic industry from protectionism.

An escape clause action is initiated by a petition from an American industry to the USITC, that investigates and recommends a response to the president. To receive relief, the industry must demonstrate that it has been substantially injured by foreign competition. The industry must also prepare a statement that shows how safeguards will help it adjust to import competition. An affirmative decision by the USITC is reported to the president who determines what remedy is in the national interest.

Most recipients of safeguard relief come from manufacturing, such as footwear, steel, fishing tackle and rods, and clothespins. Agricultural products are the second largest category, including asparagus, mushrooms, shrimp, honey, and cut flowers. Table 6.5 provides examples of safeguard relief granted to U.S. industries.

TABLE 6.4

Trade Remedy Law Provisions

Statute	Focus	Criteria for Action	Response
Fair trade (escape clause)	Increasing imports	Increasing imports are substantial cause of injury	Duties, quotas, tariff-rate quotas, orderly marketing arrangements, adjustment assistance
Subsidized imports (countervailing duty)	Manufacturing production, or export subsidies	Material injury or threat of material injury	Duties
Dumped imports (antidumping duty)	Imports sold below cost of production or below foreign market price	Material injury or threat of material injury	Duties
Unfair trade (Section 301)	Foreign practices violating a trade agreement or injurious to U.S. trade	Unjustifiable, unreasonable, or discriminatory practices, burdensome to U.S. commerce	All appropriate and feasible action

© Cengage Learning®

TABLE 6.5	

Safeguard Relief Granted under the Escape Clause: Selected Examples

Product	Type of Relief
Porcelain-on-steel cooking ware	Additional duties imposed for four years of $0.20, $0.20, $0.15, and $0.10 per pound in the first, second, third, and fourth years, respectively
Prepared or preserved mushrooms 15%,	Additional duties imposed for three years of 20%, and 10% ad valorem in the first, second, and third years, respectively
High-carbon ferrochromium	Temporary duty increase
Color TV receivers	Orderly marketing agreements with Taiwan and Korea
Footwear	Orderly marketing agreements with Taiwan and Korea

Source: From *Annual Report of the President of the United States on the Trade Agreements Program*, Washington, DC: Government Printing Office, various issues.

Although safeguard relief was invoked often during the 1970s, in recent decades it has been rarely used. This is partly because safeguard relief has proven to be a difficult way to win protection against imports because presidential action is required for it to be granted, and presidents have often been reluctant to grant such relief. Instead, safeguard relief has been overshadowed by antidumping duties, whose implementation does not require presidential action and whose injury standards are not as stringent.

One argument for safeguard provisions is that they are a political necessity for the formation of agreements to liberalize trade. Without the assurance of a safety net to protect domestic producers from surging imports, trade liberalization agreements would be impossible to achieve. Another argument for safeguards is a more practical political argument. Governments appease domestic producers that maintain strong lobbying power, even at the detriment of foreign producers of like products, simply because the domestic producers are voting constituents. It is argued that a better solution to the pressure on domestic producers is to impose these temporary measures from time to time to reduce strain on the industry rather than to take any permanent action that might dismantle liberal trade policies in general. The problem with this justification is that there are usually other possible ways to reduce this pressure that do not involve restrictions on imports to the disadvantage of foreign producers, such as government aid and tax relief.

U.S. Safeguards Limit Surging Imports of Textiles from China

Surging textile exports from China to the United States provide an example of how safeguards can be used to stabilize a market. Producers of textiles and apparel have benefitted from some of the most substantial and long lasting trade protection granted by the U.S. government in recent times. In 1974, the United States and Europe negotiated a system of rules to restrict competition from developing exporting countries employing low-cost labor. Known as the **Multifiber Arrangement (MFA)**, quotas were negotiated each year on a country-by-country basis, assigning the quantities of specific textile and apparel items that could be exported from developing countries to the industrial countries. Although the MFA was initially intended as a short-term measure to give industrialized countries time to adjust to the rigors of global competition; because of extensions, it lasted until 2005.

The MFA helped create textile and apparel industries in some countries were these sectors would likely not have emerged on their own, simply because these countries were granted rights to export. Impoverished countries such as Bangladesh, Cambodia, and Costa Rica grew to rely on garment exports as a means of providing jobs and income for their people. Without the MFA, many developing countries that benefitted from the quotas might have lost out in a more competitive environment.

When the MFA came to an end in 2005, importers were allowed to buy textile products in any volume from any country. This affected the geographic distribution of industrial production in favor of China, the world's lowest cost and largest supplier of textile products. China was poised to become the main beneficiary of trade liberalization under the removal of the quota.

The superior competitive position of China resulted in its textile and apparel exports surging to the markets of Europe and the United States in 2005. To soften the shock wave, the Chinese government took voluntary measures including strengthening self-discipline among its textile exporters, curbing investment in the sector and encouraging big textile companies to invest abroad. The government also added an export tax to reduce the competitiveness of 148 textile and apparel products in foreign markets. Nevertheless, Chinese exports continued to flow rapidly to the markets of the United States and Europe.

Alarmed that Chinese garments might overwhelm domestic producers, the U.S. government imposed safeguard quotas that restricted the rise in imports to 7.5 percent on Chinese trousers, shirts, and underwear. In November 2005, the safeguard quotas were replaced by a textile agreement with China that imposed annual limits on 34 categories of clothing running through 2008. Economists estimated that the restrictions would drive up clothing prices between $3 billion and $6 billion annually; an amount that would translate into $10 to $20 higher bills for the average U.S. family.

COUNTERVAILING DUTIES: PROTECTION AGAINST FOREIGN EXPORT SUBSIDIES

As consumers, we tend to appreciate the low prices of foreign subsidized steel. Foreign export subsidies are resented by import-competing producers who must charge higher prices because they do not receive such subsidies. From their point of view, the export subsidies give foreign producers an unfair competitive advantage.

As viewed by the WTO, export subsidies constitute unfair competition. Importing countries can retaliate by levying a **countervailing duty**. The size of the duty is limited to the amount of the foreign export subsidy. Its purpose is to increase the price of the imported good to its fair market value.

Upon receipt of a petition from a U.S. industry or firm, the U.S. Department of Commerce will conduct a preliminary investigation as to whether or not an export subsidy was given to a foreign producer. If the preliminary investigation finds a reasonable indication of an export subsidy, U.S. importers must immediately pay a special tariff (equal to the estimated subsidy margin) on all imports of the product in question. The Commerce Department then conducts a final investigation to determine whether an export subsidy was in fact granted, as well as the amount of the subsidy. If it determines that there was no export subsidy, the special tariff is rebated to the U.S. importers. Otherwise, the case is investigated by the U.S. International Trade Commission, that determines if the import-competing industry suffered material injury as a result of the subsidy.[4] If both the Commerce Department and the International Trade Commission rule in favor of the

---

[4]For those nations that are signatories to the WTO Subsidy Code, the International Trade Commission must determine that their export subsidies have injured U.S. producers before countervailing duties are imposed. The export subsidies of nonsignatory nations are subject to countervailing duties immediately following the Commerce Department's determination of their occurrence; the International Trade Commission does not have to make an injury determination.

subsidy petition, a permanent countervailing duty is imposed that equals the size of the subsidy margin calculated by the Commerce Department in its final investigation. Once the foreign nation stops subsidizing exports of that product, the countervailing duty is removed.

Lumber Duties Hammer Home Buyers

Let us consider a countervailing duty involving the U.S. lumber industry. Since the 1980s, the United States and Canada have quarreled over softwood lumber. The stakes are enormous: Canadian firms export billions of dollars' worth of lumber annually to U.S. customers.

The lumber dispute has followed a repetitive pattern. U.S. lumber producers accuse their Canadian rivals of receiving government subsidies. In particular, they allege that the Canadians pay unfairly low tree cutting fees to harvest timber from lands owned by the Canadian government. In the United States, lumber producers pay higher fees for the right to cut trees in government forests. Canadian regulations permit provincial governments to reduce their tree cutting fees when lumber prices decline to keep Canadian sawmills profitable. To U.S. producers, this amounts to an unfair subsidy granted to their Canadian competitors.

In 1996, the Coalition for Fair Lumber Imports, a group of U.S. sawmill companies, won a countervailing duty petition with the U.S. government charging that domestic lumber companies were hurt by subsidized exports from Canada. The complaint led to the imposition of a tariff-rate quota to protect U.S. producers. According to the trade restraint, up to 14.7 billion board feet of Canadian lumber exports from Canada to the United States could enter duty free. The next 0.65 billion board feet of exports was subject to a tariff of $50 per thousand board feet. The Canadian government also agreed to raise the tree cutting fees it charged provincial producers. The result was that Canadian lumber exports to the United States fell about 14 percent.

The U.S. lumber industry maintained that this tariff-rate quota created a level playing field in which American and Canadian producers could fairly compete. However, critics argued that the trade restriction failed to take into account the interests of American lumber users in the lumber dealing, homebuilding, and home furnishing industries. It also overlooked the interests of American buyers of new homes and home furnishings according to the critics. They noted that the trade restrictions increased the price of lumber from 20 to 35 percent; thus, the cost of the average new home increased from $800 to $1,300.[5]

U.S. and Canadian lumber producers have continued to wrestle over the issue of lumber subsidies since the 1990s. It remains to be seen how this issue will be resolved.

ANTIDUMPING DUTIES: PROTECTION AGAINST FOREIGN DUMPING

In recent years, relatively few American firms have chosen to go through the cumbersome process of obtaining relief though countervailing duties. Instead, they have found another way to obtain protection against imports: they have found it much easier to accuse foreign firms of dumping in the U.S. market and convince the U.S. government to impose antidumping duties on these goods. From the perspective of American firms trying to obtain protection from imports, antidumping is where the action is.

---

[5]Brink Lindsey, Mark Groombridge, and Prakash Loungani, *Nailing the Homeowner: The Economic Impact of Trade Protection of the Softwood Lumber Industry*, CATO Institute, July 6, 2000 pp. 5–8.

TRADE CONFLICTS WOULD A CARBON TARIFF HELP SOLVE THE CLIMATE PROBLEM?

Many scientists consider carbon dioxide to be a contributor to global warming. This colorless, odorless gas is released into the environment whenever oil, coal, and other fossil fuels are burned. Among the policies to reduce the consumption of fossil fuels are annual limits placed the number of tons of a pollutant that a firm can emit into the atmosphere and a tax placed on each ton of pollutant that a firm emits. These policies especially raise the cost of pollution for carbon dioxide intensive industries such as steel, aluminum, chemicals, paper, and cement.

The issue of economic competitiveness has been a sticking point in global negotiations to reduce emissions. If the United States independently raises the penalty for carbon dioxide emissions by imposing emission caps or taxes, its producers will be at a competitive disadvantage because the cost of regulating carbon dioxide will be embodied in the overall price of goods—increasing costs relative to goods produced in countries with little or no carbon dioxide regulations. Instead of paying these higher costs, U.S. firms might relocate to countries with lower pollution enforcement standards, thus costing Americans jobs while failing to decrease global emissions.

One way to protect American firms would be to place a "carbon tariff" on goods that are imported from nations that have less strict regulations to limit their carbon dioxide emissions. Presumably, the tariff would be higher on imports from polluting nations such as China than on imports from energy efficient Brazil. Proponents of carbon tariffs maintain that by increasing the price of imported goods, a tariff would protect domestic industries from the competitive disadvantage they incur when adhering to pollution regulations. They also contend that a carbon tariff provides an incentive for other countries to enact pollution regulations.

There are several arguments against imposing a carbon tariff. First, this sort of tariff would be hard to implement because of lack of knowledge about the carbon dioxide content of imports. Customs officials would have to know precisely how much steel is in each automobile and where and how every bit of that steel is produced; a difficult task. An automobile from Indonesia made of steel imported from energy efficient Germany should presumably be taxed at a different rate than the same Indonesian model made of steel from energy inefficient China. This would be tough.

Another argument against enacting carbon tariffs is that they might result in a trade war with damaging effects for domestic industry: they target developing countries whose cooperation is essential for global climate policy. The legitimacy of carbon tariffs under the rules of the World Trade Organization is uncertain. The principle of free trade as promoted by the WTO, suggests that countries should make goods that embody their comparative advantage. Imposing a carbon tariff to discourage carbon intensive producers works against the principle of comparative advantage for countries such as China and India that would likely challenge it at the WTO. Carbon tariffs might be found to be illegal by the WTO, depending on how they are implemented.

Indeed, there are many practical and political complexities of implementing carbon tariffs. It remains to be seen if they will become a major part of global climate policy.

Source: "Can Trade Restrictions Be Justified on Environmental Grounds?" *The Economist*, February 23, 2013; David Drake, *Carbon Tariffs*, Working Paper 12–29, Harvard Business School, October 19, 2011; Tim Wilson and Caitlin Brown, *Costly, Ineffectual and Protectionist Carbon Tariffs*, Melbourne, Australia: Institute of Public Affairs, 2010; Olive Heffernan, *Would a Carbon Tariff Even Work?* Nature Publishing Group: Macmillan Publishers Limited, January 2010.

The objective of U.S. antidumping policy is to offset two unfair trading practices by foreign nations: export sales in the United States at prices below the average total cost of production, and price discrimination in which foreign firms sell in the United States at a price less than that charged in the exporter's home market. Both practices can inflict economic hardship on U.S. import-competing producers; by reducing the price of the foreign export in the U.S. market, they encourage U.S. consumers to buy a smaller quantity of the domestically produced good.

Antidumping investigations are initiated upon a written request by the import-competing industry that includes evidence of (1) dumping; (2) material injury, such as lost sales, profits, or jobs; and (3) a link between the dumped imports and the alleged injury. Antidumping investigations commonly involve requests that foreign exporters and domestic importers fill out detailed questionnaires. Parties that elect not to complete questionnaires can be put at a disadvantage with respect to case decisions; findings are made on the best information available, that may simply be information supplied by the domestic industry in support of the dumping allegation. The number of antidumping cases dwarfs those of other trade remedies. The Commerce Department determines if dumping did occur and the International Trade Commission determines if the domestic industry was harmed because of dumping.

If these agencies determine that dumping is occurring and is causing material injury to the domestic industry, then the U.S. response is to impose an antidumping duty (tariff) on dumped imports equal to the margin of dumping. The effect of the duty is to offset the extent to which the dumped goods' prices fall below average total cost, or below the price at which they are sold in the exporter's home market. Antidumping duties are generally large, often in the neighborhood of 60 percent. According to the International Trade Commission, imports subject to antidumping duties of over 50 percent tend to increase by 33 percent in price and decrease by 73 percent in volume as compared to the year prior to the petition for antidumping duties.[6]

An antidumping case can be terminated prior to conclusion of the investigation if the exporter of the product to the United States agrees to cease dumping, stop exporting the product to the United States, increase the price to eliminate the dumping, or negotiate some other agreement that will decrease the quantity of imports. Indeed, the mere threat of an antidumping investigation may induce foreign companies to increase their export prices and thus to stop any dumping they were practicing.

Are antidumping laws good for a nation? Economists tend to be dubious of antidumping duties because they increase the price of imported goods and decrease consumer welfare. According to economic analysis, low prices are a problem in need of remedy only if they tend to result in higher prices in the long run. Economists generally consider antidumping duties appropriate only when they combat predatory pricing designed to monopolize a market by knocking competitors out of business. The consensus among economists is that antidumping laws have virtually nothing to do with addressing predatory pricing, so their existence is without economic justification.

Supporters of antidumping laws admit that they are not intended to combat predatory pricing or to enhance consumer welfare in the economists' definition of the term. However, they justify antidumping laws, not on the criterion of efficiency, but on the criterion of fairness. Even though dumping may benefit consumers in the short run, they contend that it is unfair for domestic producers to have to compete with unfairly traded goods.

Remedies against Dumped and Subsidized Imports

Recall that the direct effect of dumping and subsidizing imports is to lower import prices, an effect that provides benefits and costs for the importing country. There are benefits to consumers if imports are finished goods and to consuming industries that use imports as intermediate inputs into their own production (*downstream* industry). Conversely, there are costs to the import-competing industry, its workers, and other domestic industries selling intermediate inputs to production of the import-competing industry (*upstream* industry). Dumping at prices below fair market value and subsidizing exports are considered unfair trade practices under international trade law; they can be

---

[6]U.S. International Trade Commission, *The Economic Effects of Antidumping and Countervailing Duty Orders and Suspension Agreements*, Washington, DC: International Trade Commission, June 1995.

neutralized by the imposition of antidumping or countervailing duties on dumped or subsidized imports.

Figure 6.3 illustrates the effects of unfair trade practices on Canada, a nation too small to influence the foreign price of steel; for simplicity, the figure assumes that Canada's steel, iron ore, and auto companies operate in competitive markets. In Figure 6.3(a), S_C and D_C represent the Canadian supply and demand for steel. Suppose that South Korea, that has a comparative advantage in steel, supplies steel to Canada at the fair trade price of $600 per ton. At this price, Canadian production equals 200 tons, consumption equals 300 tons, and imports equal 100 tons.

Now suppose that as a result of South Korean dumping and subsidizing practices, Canada imports steel at $500 per ton; the margin of dumping and subsidization would equal $100 ($600 − $500 = $100). The unfair trade practice reduces Canadian production from 200 tons to 100 tons, increases Canadian consumption from 300 tons to 400 tons, and increases Canadian imports from 100 tons to 300 tons. Falling prices and quantities, in turn, lead to falling investment and employment in the Canadian steel industry. Although the producer surplus of Canadian steelmakers decreases by area a due to unfair trade, Canadian buyers find their consumer surplus rising by area $a + b + c + d$. The Canadian steel market as a whole benefits from unfair trade because the gains to its consumers exceed the losses to its producers by area $b + c + d$!

Unfair trade also affects Canada's upstream and downstream industries. If the Canadian iron-ore industry (upstream) supplies mainly to Canadian steelmakers, the demand for Canadian iron ore will decrease as their customers' output falls based on competition from cheaper imported steel. As illustrated in Figure 6.3(b), without unfair trade the quantity of iron ore demanded by Canadian steelmakers is Q_0 tons at a price of P_0 per ton.

FIGURE 6.3

Effects of Dumped and Subsidized Imports and Their Remedies

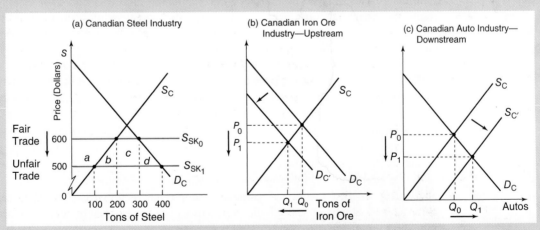

Dumped or subsidized imports provide benefits to consumers if imports are finished goods and to consuming producers that use the imports as intermediate inputs into their own production; they inflict costs on the import-competing domestic producers, their workers, and other domestic producers selling intermediate inputs to the import-competing producers. An antidumping or countervailing duty inflicts costs on consumers if imports are finished goods and on consuming producers that use the imports as intermediate inputs into their own production; benefits are provided to import-competing domestic producers, their workers, and other domestic producers selling intermediate inputs to the protected industry.

Because of unfair trade in the steel industry, the demand for iron ore decreases from D_C to D_C; production falls as do revenues and employment in this industry. In autos (downstream), production will increase as manufacturing costs decrease because of the availability of cheaper imported steel. As illustrated in Figure 6.3(c), Canadian auto production increases from Q_0 units to Q_1 units as the supply curve shifts downward from S_C to $S_{C'}$, with accompanying positive effects on revenues and employment; the decrease in production costs also improves the Canadian auto industry's competitiveness in international markets.

Suppose that unfair trade in steel results in the imposition by the Canadian government of an antidumping duty or countervailing duty on imported steel equal to the margin of dumping or subsidization ($100). The effect of an exact offsetting duty in the steel industry is a regaining of the initial prices and quantities in Canada's steel, iron ore, and auto industries, as seen in Figure 6.3. The duty raises the import price of unfairly traded steel in Canada, leading to increased steel production by Canadian steelmakers; this results in increased demand and higher prices for Canadian iron ore, but also implies increased production costs, higher prices, and lower sales for Canadian automakers. With the import duty, the decrease in the consumer surplus more than offsets the increase in the producer surplus in the Canadian steel market.

The U.S. International Trade Commission estimated the economic effects of antidumping duties and countervailing duties for U.S. petitioning industries and their upstream suppliers and downstream consumers for the year 1991. The study concluded that these duties typically benefited successful petitioning industries by raising prices and improving output and employment. However, the costs to the rest of the economy were far greater. The study estimated that the U.S. economy would have experienced a net welfare gain of $1.59 billion in the year 1991 had U.S. antidumping duties and countervailing duties *not* been in effect. In other words, these duties imposed costs on consumers, downstream industries, and the economy as a whole at least $1.59 billion greater than the benefits enjoyed by the successful petitioning industries and their employees.[7] Remember that the purpose of antidumping and countervailing duty laws is not to protect consumers but rather to discourage unfairly traded imports that cause harm to competing domestic industries and workers.

U.S. Steel Companies Lose an Unfair Trade Case and Still Win

For years, the U.S. steel industry has dominated at the complaint department of the U.S. International Trade Commission. The steel industry has swamped the USITC with numerous petitions alleging that foreign steel has been subsidized or dumped into the U.S. market. However, the steel industry has not always been successful in its petitions against cheap imports; it has lost more cases than it has won.

To the steel industry, winning isn't everything. Just filing and arguing its cases is part of its competitive strategy. Steel companies know that they can use the trade laws to influence the supply of steel in the marketplace and thus limit foreign competition. Whenever the market gets weak, for whatever reason, they can file an unfair trade case.

Here's how the strategy works. The market gets soft, and the steel companies file trade cases alleging foreign subsidization or dumping, and then imports from the target companies decrease. The case proceeds for a year or so, allowing domestic steelmakers to increase market share and raise prices. Even if the USITC rules against the case, the market has time to recover.

[7]U.S. International Trade Commission, *The Economic Effects of Antidumping and Countervailing Duty Orders and Suspension Agreements*, Washington, DC: International Trade Commission, June 1995.

Once a case is filed, it takes months to proceed through a four-stage legal process, and time benefits domestic steelmakers. American steelmakers usually win the first round, in which the industry has to show the USITC a "reasonable indication" of harm from imports. Armed with that finding, the U.S. Department of Commerce can set preliminary duties on the imports. Importers must post a financial bond to cover those duties. Then, the Commerce Department determines the final duties, based on the extent of foreign subsidization or dumping, and the case goes back to the USITC for a final determination of injury. If the U.S. companies lose, the duty is never collected, and the bond is lifted. However, if they win, the importer may be liable for the full amount.

During this process, U.S. importers have the right to continue importing. They might continue to import if they feel strongly that the U.S. steelmakers will lose the case. However, the USITC is a political body, with some of the presidentially appointed commissioners being free traders and others tending to be more protectionist. Because U.S. importers realize that they run a big risk if they are wrong, the response is usually to stop importing when a case is filed.

Just by filing unfair trade cases, the U.S. steel industry may win. Whatever it spends on legal fees, it may recoup many times over in extra revenue. That's the great thing about filing: even if you lose, you still win.

SECTION 301: PROTECTION AGAINST UNFAIR TRADING PRACTICES

Section 301 of the Trade Act of 1974 gives the U.S. trade representative (USTR) the authority, subject to the approval of the president, and the means to respond to unfair trading practices by foreign nations. Included among these unfair practices are foreign trade restrictions that hinder U.S. exports and foreign subsidies that hinder U.S. exports to third-country markets. The USTR responds when they determine that such practices result in "unreasonable" or "discriminatory" burdens on U.S. exporters. The legislation was primarily a congressional response to dissatisfaction with GATT's ineffectiveness in resolving trade disputes.

Section 301 investigations are usually initiated on the basis of petitions by adversely affected U.S. companies and labor unions; they can also be initiated by the president. If after investigation it is determined that a foreign nation is engaging in unfair trading practices, the USTR is empowered to (1) impose tariffs or other import restrictions on products and services and (2) deny the foreign country the benefits of trade agreement concessions.

Although the ultimate sanction available to the United States is retaliatory import restrictions, the purpose of Section 301 is to obtain the successful resolution of conflicts. In a large majority of cases, Section 301 has been used to convince foreign nations to modify or eliminate what the United States has considered to be unfair trading practices; only in a small minority of cases has the United States retaliated against foreign producers by means of tariffs or quotas. Foreign nations have often likened Section 301 to a "crowbar" approach to resolve trade disputes that invites retaliatory trade restrictions. At least two reasons have been advanced for the limitations of this approach to opening foreign markets to U.S. exports: (1) Nationalism unites the people of a foreign nation against U.S. threats of trade restrictions; and (2) The foreign nation reorients its economy toward trading partners other than the United States.

An example of a Section 301 case is the banana dispute between the United States and Europe. In 1993, the EU implemented a single EU wide regime on banana imports. The regime gave preferential entry to bananas from the EU's former colonies, including parts of the Caribbean, Africa, and Asia. It also restricted entry from other countries, including several in Latin America where U.S. companies predominate. According to the United States, the EU's banana regime resulted in unfair treatment for American companies. United States trade officials maintained that Chiquita Brands International and Dole Food Co., that handle and distribute bananas from Latin American nations, lost half of their business because of the EU's banana regime. As a result, the United States and several Latin American countries brought this issue to the WTO and successfully argued their case. The WTO ruled that the EU's banana regime discriminated against U.S. and Latin American distribution companies and banana exports from Latin American countries. After a prolonged struggle, Europe modified its behavior and the tariff was lifted.

PROTECTION OF INTELLECTUAL PROPERTY RIGHTS

In the 1800s, Charles Dickens criticized U.S. publishers for printing unauthorized versions of his works without paying him one penny. U.S. copyright protection did not apply to foreign (British) authors, so Dickens's popular fiction could be pirated without punishment. In recent years, it is U.S. companies whose profit expectations have been frustrated. Publishers in South Korea run off copies of bootlegged U.S. textbooks without providing royalty payments. American research laboratories find themselves in legal tangles with Japanese electronics manufacturers concerning patent infringement.

Certain industries and products are well known targets of pirates, counterfeiters, and other infringers of **intellectual property rights (IPRs)**. Counterfeiting is common in industries such as automobile parts, jewelry, sporting goods, and watches. Piracy of audio and videotapes, computer software, and printed materials is widespread throughout the world. Industries in which product life cycles are shorter than the time necessary to obtain and enforce a patent are also subject to thievery; examples are photographic equipment and telecommunications. Table 6.6 provides examples of IPR violations in China.

Intellectual property is an invention, idea, product, or process that has been registered with the government and awards the inventor (or author) exclusive rights to use the invention for a given time period. Governments use several techniques to protect

TABLE 6.6

Examples of Intellectual Property Right Violations in China

Affected Firm	Violation in China
Epson	Copying machines and ink cartridges are counterfeited.
Microsoft	Counterfeiting of Windows and Windows NT, with packaging virtually indistinguishable from the real product and sold in authorized outlets.
Yamaha	5 of every 6 JYM150-A motorcycles and ZY125 scooters bearing Yamaha's name are fake in China. Some state owned factories manufacture copies four months following the introduction of a new model.
Gillette	Up to one-fourth of its Parker pens, Duracell batteries, and Gillette razors sold in China are pirated.
Anheuser-Busch	Some 640 million bottles of fake Budweiser beer are sold annually in China.
Bestfoods	Bogus versions of Knorr bouillon and Skippy Peanut Butter lead to tens of millions of dollars in forgone sales each year.

Source: From U.S. Trade Representative, *National Trade Estimate Report on Foreign Trade Barriers*, various issues, available at http://www.ustr.gov.

intellectual property. *Copyrights* are awarded to protect works of original authorship (music compositions and textbooks); most nations issue copyright protection for the remainder of the author's life plus 50 years. *Trademarks* are awarded to manufacturers and provide exclusive rights to a distinguishing name or symbol (Coca-Cola). *Patents* secure to an inventor for a term, usually 15 years or more, the exclusive right to make, use, or sell the invention.

In spite of efforts to protect IPRs, competing firms sometimes infringe on the rights of others by making a cheaper imitation of the original product. In 1986, the courts ruled that Kodak had infringed on Polaroid's patents for instant cameras and awarded Polaroid more than $900 million in damages. Another infringement would occur if a company manufactured an instant camera similar to Polaroid's and labeled and marketed it as a Polaroid camera; this is an example of a counterfeit product.

The lack of effective international procedures for protecting IPRs becomes a problem when the expense of copying an innovation (including the cost of penalties if caught) is less than the cost of purchasing or leasing the technology. Suppose that Warner–Lambert Drug Co. develops a product that cures the common cold, called "Cold-Free," and the firm plans to export it to Taiwan. If Cold-Free is not protected by a patent in Taiwan, either because Taiwan does not recognize IPRs or Warner–Lambert has not filed for protection, cheaper copies of Cold-Free could legally be developed and marketed. If Warner–Lambert's trademark is not protected, counterfeit cold remedies that are indistinguishable from Cold-Free could be legally sold in Taiwan. These copies would result in reduced sales and profits for Warner–Lambert. If "Cold-Free" is a trademark that consumers strongly associate with Warner–Lambert, a counterfeit product of noticeably inferior quality could adversely affect Warner–Lambert's reputation and detract from the sales of both Cold-Free and other Warner–Lambert products.

Although most nations have regulations protecting IPRs, many problems have been associated with trade in products affected by IPRs. One problem is differing IPR regulations across nations. The United States uses a first-to-invent rule when determining patent eligibility, whereas most other nations employ a first-to-file rule. Another problem is lack of enforcement of international IPR agreements. These problems stem largely from differing incentives to protect intellectual property, especially between nations that are innovating, technological exporters and those that are aren't technological importers. Developing nations lacking in research and development and patent innovation, sometimes pirate foreign technology and use it to produce goods at costs lower than could be achieved in the innovating nation. Poorer developing nations often find it difficult to pay the higher prices that would prevail if innovated products (such as medical supplies) were provided patent protection. They have little incentive to provide patent protection to the products they need.

As long as the cost of pirating technology, including the probability and costs of being caught, is less than the profits captured by the firm doing the pirating, technology pirating tends to continue. However, pirating reduces the rate of profitability earned by firms in the innovating nations that in turn deters them from investing in research and development. Over time, this lack of investment leads to fewer products and welfare losses for the people of both nations.

The United States has faced many obstacles in trying to protect its intellectual property. Dozens of nations lack adequate legal structures to protect the patents of foreign firms. Others have consciously excluded certain products (such as chemicals) from protection to support their industries. Even in developed countries where legal safeguards exist, the fast pace of technological innovation often outruns the protection provided by the legal system.

TRADE CONFLICTS THE GLOBALIZATION OF IDEAS AND INTELLECTUAL PROPERTY RIGHTS

Like goods and services, ideas flow across national borders. From the United States to India, people trade ideas and everyone benefits from it. The global flow of ideas is apparent in the smart phones, MP3 players, computers, e-readers and other technologies that fill our lives.

An idea is a set of instructions to produce a new good, increase quality, or reduce costs. Because an idea can be used by different producers simultaneously, it is not scarce in the same way that a good or service is scarce. An architect using the Pythagorean theorem to calculate the length of a triangle's side does not prevent anyone else from using this concept at the same time. Once the cost of creating a new set of instructions has been incurred, the instructions can be used over again at no additional cost. Ideas become more valuable as the number of uses increases. This means that the value of the Pythagorean theorem increases with the number of buildings under design and construction. If there are many architects in different parts of the world designing buildings, there are efficiency gains from sharing this idea that drive economic growth.

This does not imply that an idea should be used by everyone for free. To protect ideas from imitators, nations have developed intellectual property rights in the form of patents, trademarks, and copyrights. Patents protect investors from imitators making, using, and selling in countries where the patent is granted.

Although measuring the flow of ideas is difficult, patent filings provide some evidence on the production of ideas. What we learn from this data is that global idea production has traditionally been dominated by the United States, Germany, and Japan, as shown in Table 6.7. However, idea production has recently surged in the developing economies such as China and South Korea.

TABLE 6.7

Patent Filings by Selected Countries in 2012

Country	Number of Patent Filings
United States	51,625
Japan	43,660
Germany	18,764
China	18,617
South Korea	11,848
France	7,851
Switzerland	4,190
Netherlands	4,071

Source: From World Intellectual Property Organization, *The International Patent System: Monthly Statistics Report*, September 2013 at www.wipo.int/ipstats/en.

Economists have found that capital goods imports have accounted for 20 to 30 percent of the growth in U.S. output per hour between 1967 and 2008. Such gains arise because it is possible to develop and produce ideas in separate locations. Today, a computer can be designed in the United States, produced in Taiwan and imported back to the United States for consumption. Lower transportation costs and the creation, reallocation, and integration of global production facilities have made it possible to move the physical production of an idea where labor costs are low. U.S. capital and labor can therefore be reallocated to more productive uses. This includes the high tech manufacture of aerospace and biotech products, health care equipment, and computer electronics, for which the key drivers of production are ideas.

Source: Anthony Landry, "The Globalization of Ideas," *Economic Letter*, November 2010, Federal Reserve Bank of Dallas. See also Michele Cavallo and Anthony Landry, "The Quantitative Role of Capital Goods Imports in U.S. Growth," *American Economic Review*, Vol. 100, No. 2, 2010, pp. 78–82.

iStockphoto.com/photosoup

Microsoft Scorns China's Piracy of Software

China's rapid economic transformation has presented both opportunities and challenges to many U.S. businesses. Although firms such as Boeing and General Electric have realized success in the China market, U.S. firms have reported losses associated with IPR infringement in China, including losses in sales, profits, license and royalty fees, as well as damage to brand names and product reputation. Analysts have estimated that U.S.

firms' reported losses from IPR infringement in China amounted to about $48 billion in 2009, as seen in Table 6.8.

Consider the case of Microsoft Corp., the maker of computer software. Microsoft is among the firms whose sales have suffered because of Chinese piracy. In 2011, Microsoft's revenue in China was only about 5 percent of what it received in the United States, even though personal computer sales in the two countries were about the same. In China, illegal copies of Microsoft's Office and Windows programs were sold on street corners for $2 to $3 each, a fraction of their retail price, despite attempts by the company to discourage illegal counterfeiting. Also, Microsoft's software revenue per personal computer sold in China was only about a sixth of the amount it earned in India. Microsoft's total revenue in China, with a population 1.3 billion, was less than what it received in the Netherlands in 2011, a country of fewer than 17 million.

Microsoft has rejected the argument widespread in China, that many Chinese consumers use pirated software because authentic versions are too expensive. Although Microsoft recognizes that not everyone in China can afford a personal computer, the firm maintains that if you can afford a PC, you can afford the software that accompanies it. Despite having frustrations about piracy, Microsoft has continued to invest in China that will soon be the world's largest PC market.

The company has historically attempted a cooperative strategy with Chinese officials, reaching deals to require Chinese PC makers to ship their products with legitimate copies of Office and Windows from their factories. China's government has admitted counterfeiting problems but contends that it is making efforts to improve the situation. The Chinese government has ordered all state institutions to buy authentic software. Nevertheless, analysts have estimated that about 78 percent of the PC software installed in China in 2011 was pirated. Indeed, China's counterfeit and piracy market is the biggest

TABLE 6.8

Reported Losses* from Intellectual Property Right Infringement in China on U.S. Businesses, 2009

Losses by Sector	$ Billion
Information and other services	26.7
High-tech and heavy manufacturing	18.5
Chemical manufacturing	2.0
Consumer goods manufacturing	0.8
Transportation manufacturing	0.2
	48.2
Losses by Type of Intellectual Property Right Infringement	
Copyright infringement	23.7
Trademark infringement	6.1
Patent infringement	1.3
Misappropriation of trade secrets	1.1
Other	16.0
	48.2

*In response to a U.S. International Trade Commission survey.

Source: U.S. International Trade Commission, *China: Effects of Intellectual Property Infringement and Indigenous Innovation Policies on the U.S. Economy,* May 2011.

in the world and copyright infringement in the country has long been a sticking point in U.S.–Chinese relations.

TRADE ADJUSTMENT ASSISTANCE

According to the free-trade argument, in a dynamic economy in which trade proceeds according to the comparative-advantage principle, resources flow from uses with lower productivity to those with higher productivity. Consumers gain by having a wider variety of goods to choose from at lower prices. It is also true that as countries adopt freer trade policies, both winners and losers emerge. Some firms and industries will become more efficient and grow as they expand into overseas markets whereas others will contract, merge, or perhaps even fail when faced with increased competition. While this adjustment process may be healthy for a dynamic economy, it can be a harsh reality for firms and workers in import-competing industries.

One way to balance the gains of freer trade that are realized broadly throughout the economy with the costs that tend to be more concentrated, is to address the needs of firms and workers that have been adversely affected. Many industrial nations have done this by enacting programs for giving **trade adjustment assistance** to those who incur hardships because of trade liberalization. The underlying rationale comes from the notion that if society in general enjoys welfare gains from the increased efficiency stemming from trade liberalization, some sort of compensation should be provided for those who are injured by import competition. As long as freer trade generates significant gains to the nation, the winners can compensate the losers and still enjoy some of the gains from freer trade.

The U.S. trade adjustment assistance program assists domestic workers displaced by foreign trade and increased imports. The program provides benefits such as extended income support beyond normal unemployment insurance benefits, services such as job training, and allowances for job search and relocation. To businesses and communities, the program offers technical aid in moving into new lines of production, market research assistance, and low interest loans. The major beneficiaries of the program have been workers and firms in the apparel and textile industry, followed by the oil and gas, electronics, and metal and machinery industries. Traditionally, trade displaced workers are older and less educated than typical workers and have worked only in one industry. They take longer to find another job and when they find one, are more likely to see their wages decrease. In 2009, the program was expanded to include service, not just manufacturing workers.

INDUSTRIAL POLICIES OF THE UNITED STATES

Besides enacting regulations intended to produce a fair trading environment for all parties engaging in international business, the United States has implemented *industrial policies* to enhance the competitiveness of domestic producers. As discussed in Chapter 3, such policies involve government channeling of resources into specific, targeted industries that it views as important for future economic growth. Among the methods used to channel resources are tax incentives, loan guarantees, and low interest loans.

What has been the U.S. approach to industrial policy? The U.S. government has attempted to provide a favorable climate for business given the social, environmental, and safety constraints imposed by modern society. Rather than formulating a coordinated industrial policy to affect particular industries, the U.S. government has generally emphasized macroeconomic policies (fiscal and monetary policies) aimed at objectives as economic stability, growth, and the broad allocation of the gross domestic product.

However, there is no doubt that the U.S. government uses a number of measures to shape the structure of the economy that would be called "industrial policies" in other nations. The most notable of these measures is agricultural policy. In agriculture, a farmer who initiates a major innovation can be imitated by many other farmers who capture the benefits without sharing the risks. To rectify this problem, the U.S. government is involved in research in agricultural techniques and in the dissemination of this information to farmers through its agricultural extension service, as well as the fostering of large scale projects such as irrigation facilities. The U.S. government has also provided support for the shipping, aerospace, shipbuilding, energy, and defense industries, primarily on the grounds of national security.

Another element of U.S. industrial policy is export promotion. The U.S. government furnishes exporters with marketing information and technical assistance, in addition to trade missions that help expose new exporters to foreign customers. The government also promotes exports by sponsoring exhibits of U.S. goods at international trade fairs and establishing overseas trade centers that enable U.S. businesses to exhibit and sell machinery and equipment. The United States also encourages exports by allowing its manufacturers to form export trade associations to facilitate the marketing of U.S. products abroad.

The United States provides export subsidies to its producers to promote international sales. The U.S. **Export-Import Bank (Eximbank)** is the official export credit agency of the U.S. government. Founded in 1934, its purpose is to provide cheap credit for foreign customers who purchase American made products. Such credit is provided through a variety of loan, loan guarantee, and insurance programs. These programs are available to any American export firm regardless of size. The Eximbank does not compete with private sector lenders, but rather provides financing for transactions that would otherwise not occur because commercial lenders are either unable or unwilling to accept the risks inherent in the deal. Table 6.9 provides examples of direct loans and loan guarantees made by Eximbank. Major beneficiaries of Eximbank credit have included aircraft, telecommunications, power generating equipment, and energy developments. Firms such

TABLE 6.9

Examples of Loans Provided by Eximbank of the United States

Foreign Borrower/U.S. Exporter	Purpose
Banco Santander Noroeste of Brazil/General Electric	Locomotives
Government of Bulgaria/Westinghouse	Instruments
Air China/Boeing	Aircraft
Government of Croatia/Bechtel International	Highway construction
Government of Ghana/Wanan International	Electrical equipment
Government of Indonesia/IBM	Computer hardware
Japan Airlines/Boeing	Aircraft
Fevisa Industrial of Mexico/Pennsylvania Crusher Inc.	Glass manufacturing equipment
Delta Communications of Mexico/Motorola	Communications equipment

Source: From Export-Import Bank of the United States, *Annual Report*, various issues, http://www.exim.gov.

as Boeing, General Electric, Caterpillar, and Westinghouse have enjoyed substantial benefits from these programs as well as many small and medium size firms. Because of the fees and interest it charges borrowers, the Eximbank is self sustaining.

Proponents of the Eximbank contend that American companies that use its financing compete in a global marketplace in which foreign companies and their governments systematically use export credit financing. A Chinese locomotive company can offer government export financing to international buyers that makes their trains less expensive in foreign markets such as India. When an American company such as General Electric is competing for that locomotive sale, it ought to be able to provide comparable financing for its locomotives. Such policies ensure a level playing field for American companies in a competitive global marketplace.

In offering cheap credit in financing exports, Eximbank has sometimes been criticized because some of its funds are borrowed from the U.S. Treasury. Critics question whether U.S. tax revenues should subsidize exports to foreign countries at interest rates lower than could be obtained from private institutions. To this extent, it is true that tax funds distort trade and redistribute income toward exporters.

Officially supported lending for U.S. exports is also provided by the **Commodity Credit Corporation (CCC)**, a government owned corporation administered by the U.S. Department of Agriculture. The CCC makes available export credit financing for eligible agricultural commodities. The interest rates charged by the CCC are usually slightly below the prevailing rates charged by private financial institutions. We will next consider two cases of industrial policy.

U.S. Airlines and Boeing Spar over Export-Import Bank Credit

In 2010, major airlines in the United States joined to oppose billions of dollars in subsidies for jetliners bought by their foreign rivals from Boeing Co. What they opposed was the export-financing practices of the U.S. Eximbank that provides cheap credit to foreign countries and companies that purchase American made products. Such credit is extended to foreign customers at below-market interest rates that do not qualify for loans from commercial lenders. In 2010, about 35 percent of Boeing's sales was supported by credit provided by the U.S. Eximbank.

Carriers such as Delta Airlines and Southwest Airlines contended that because they are American companies, they cannot receive these export subsidies that can greatly increase an airline's access to funding and cut its cost of borrowing while their foreign rivals can benefit from such subsidies. Delta maintained that its interest rate on jetliner purchases from Boeing was 4.5 percentage points higher than the rate paid by carriers in the United Arab Emirates. These international rivals obtained longer term financing and were able to finance a higher percentage of the purchase price than Delta. Delta maintained that giving foreign rivals access to cheap financing puts it at a cost disadvantage and floods the world airline market with uneconomic capacity.

Export subsidies are large because bankers generally dislike lending directly to airlines other than a handful of those with strong credit ratings. Rather than assuming the risk of default when making loans to airlines, bankers want the loans to be guaranteed by the government. Some bankers who are willing to accept more risk and thus charge higher interest rates on loans have maintained that the practices of the U.S. Eximbank squeeze them out of the market.

The dispute amounted to a conflict over which contributes more to the U.S. economy—airlines or plane manufacturers, and how the government can support them without distorting markets. According to Delta, the U.S. government must realize that export credit does more than help Boeing; it also has negative consequences for the American airline industry. Boeing criticized Delta's position by noting that curtailing export credit would jeopardize U.S. aerospace competitiveness as governments in Canada, Brazil, and Europe have ramped up access to export credit.

For the U.S. economy as a whole, the subsidy conflict revealed a tradeoff. Economic gains accrued to Boeing in the form of increased sales, profits, more jobs, and higher earnings for its workers. Increased jetliner exports by Boeing also strengthened the U.S. balance of trade. The cost disadvantage placed on American airlines by the export subsidy led to decreasing sales and profits, losses in jobs and earnings for their workers, and a weakening of the U.S. trade balance as American airlines lost market share to foreign airlines. It remains to be seen how this conflict will be resolved.[8]

U.S. Solar Industry Dims as China's Industrial Policy Lights Up

Solar energy has been harnessed by humans since ancient times using a range of ever evolving technologies. Although there is no denying solar energy's promise and potential, debate remains about how the industry should develop. Should the market be relied on to determine winners and losers or should industrial policy carry out the task, whereby governments subsidize their producers to enhance their competitiveness?

The bankruptcy of three American solar power companies in 2011 left China's industry with a dominant sales position; about two-thirds of the market. Another major producer of solar energy, Germany, was also retrenching in that year. Although some American, Japanese, and European solar companies had a technological edge over their Chinese rivals, they maintained that they could not beat the Chinese when it came to cost. They noted that the Chinese government has been particularly effective in developing an industrial policy that provides Chinese manufacturers with a number of advantages in the global solar industry, including access to lower cost capital, subsidized electricity rates, free access to land, and much a shortened permitting process for factories. China's solar energy producers have realized huge economies of scale that result in decreasing production cost and increased competitiveness. China is not alone in using industrial policy to promote clean energy. The EU and the United States provide governmental support for solar energy, including tax credits for buyers and low interest rate loans and loan guarantees for solar companies.

At the heart of the solar industry's problems in 2011 were sharply decreasing prices for solar panels and their components—wafers, cells, polysilicon, and the modules themselves. The reason was obvious: there were simply too many manufacturers trying to sell their products. The glut of manufacturers was because of factors including efforts by the U.S. government to promote clean technology, venture capitalists pouring into the sector, investors purchasing stock issues of solar companies during an upswing in oil prices, and an increased sense of urgency for climate change. European governments offered substantial subsidies for solar installation, stimulating demand in the market. The abundant production of solar panels resulted in cutthroat price competition. In 2010, solar panels sold for $1.60 per watt, on average. By 2011, the going price was between $.90 per watt and $1.05 per watt. Despite the buyers' market, customers were not purchasing solar panels fast enough to match the increase in supply. The result was the bankruptcy of numerous producers.

---

[8]"Carriers Oppose Plane Subsidies," *Wall Street Journal*, October 7, 2010, p. B-3 and "U.S., European Airlines to Seek Curbs on Aircraft Subsidies," *Bloomberg*, October 6, 2010 at http://www.bloomberg.com/news.

The bankruptcy of Solyndra Inc. in 2011, a California company making solar panels, received much publicity. In 2010, President Barack Obama visited Solyndra and touted it as a leading company in a growing industry. The company found that it could not compete with cheaper Chinese manufactured solar panels, so it defaulted on its government guaranteed loan of $535 million. This resulted in attacks by critics of Obama who tried to make the failed solar panel company both a symbol of the failure of industrial policy in solar energy and a club with which to beat alternative renewable energy of all kinds.

INDUSTRIAL POLICIES OF JAPAN

Although the United States has generally not used explicit industrial policies to support specific industries, such policies have been used elsewhere. Consider the case of Japan.

Japan has become a technological leader in the post–World War II era. During the 1950s, Japan's exports consisted primarily of textiles and other low tech products. By the 1960s and 1970s, its exports emphasized capital-intensive products such as autos, steel, and ships. By the 1980s and 1990s, Japan had become a major world competitor in high tech goods such as optical fibers and semiconductors.

Advocates of industrial policy assert that government assistance for emerging industries has helped transform the Japanese economy from low tech to heavy industry to high tech. They claim that protection from imports, R&D subsidies and the like fostered the development of Japanese industry. Clearly, the Japanese government provided assistance to shipbuilding and steel during the 1950s, to autos and machine tools during the 1960s, and to high tech industries beginning in the early 1970s. Since the mid-1970s, the government's industrial policy has been more modest and subtle.

To implement its industrial policies in manufacturing, the Japanese government has created the **Ministry of Economy, Trade and Industry** (METI). This ministry attempts to facilitate the shifting of resources into high tech industries by targeting specific industries for support. With the assistance of consultants from leading corporations, trade unions, banks, and universities, METI forms a consensus on the best policies to pursue. The next step of industrial policy is to increase domestic R&D, investment, and production. Targeted industries have received support in the form of trade protection, allocations of foreign exchange, R&D subsidies, loans at below market interest rates, loans that must be repaid if a firm becomes profitable, favorable tax treatment, and joint government–industry research projects intended to develop promising technologies.

Without government support, it is improbable that Japanese semiconductor, telecommunications equipment, fiber optics, and machine tool industries would be as competitive as they are. Not all Japanese industrial policies have been successful, however, as seen in the cases of computers, aluminum, and petrochemicals. Even industries in which Japan is competitive in world markets such as shipbuilding and steel have witnessed prolonged periods of excess capacity. Some of Japan's biggest success stories (TVs, stereos, and VCRs) were not the industries' most heavily targeted by the Japanese government. Although Japan has the most visible industrial policy of the industrialized nations, the importance of that policy to Japan's success should not be exaggerated.[9]

[9]R. Beason and D. Weinstein, "Growth, Economies of Scale, and Targeting in Japan: 1955–1990," Review of economics and Statistics, May 1996.

STRATEGIC TRADE POLICY

Beginning in the 1980s, a new argument for industrial policy gained prominence. The theory behind **strategic trade policy** is that government can assist domestic companies in capturing economic profits from foreign competitors.[10] Such assistance entails government support for certain "strategic" industries (such as high technology) that are important to future domestic economic growth and provide widespread benefits (externalities) to society.

The essential notion underlying strategic trade policy is *imperfect competition.* Many industries participating in trade, the argument goes, are dominated by a small number of large companies—large enough for each company to significantly influence market price. Such market power gives these companies the potential to attain long run economic profits. According to the strategic trade policy argument, government policy can alter the terms of competition to favor domestic companies over foreign companies and shift economic profits in imperfectly competitive markets from foreign to domestic companies.

A standard example is the aircraft industry.[11] With the high fixed costs of introducing a new aircraft and a significant learning curve in production that leads to decreasing unit production costs, this industry can support only a small number of manufacturers. The aircraft industry is also an industry that typically is closely associated with national prestige.

Assume that two competing manufacturers, Boeing (representing the United States) and Airbus (a consortium owned jointly by four European governments) are considering whether to construct a new aircraft. If *either* firm manufactures the aircraft by itself, it will attain *profits* of $100 million. If *both* firms manufacture the aircraft, they will each suffer a *loss* of $5 million.

Now assume the European governments decide to subsidize Airbus production in the amount of $10 million. Even if both companies manufacture the new aircraft, Airbus is now certain of making a $5 million profit. The point is this: Boeing will *cancel* its new aircraft project. The European subsidy ensures not only that Airbus will manufacture the new aircraft but also that Boeing will suffer a loss if it joins in. The result is that Airbus achieves a profit of $110 million and can easily repay its subsidy to the European governments. If we assume that the two manufacturers produce entirely for export, the subsidy of $10 million results in a transfer of $100 million in profits from the United States to Europe. Figure 6.4 summarizes these results. The welfare effects of strategic trade policy are discussed in *Exploring Further 6.1* that can be found at www.cengage .com/economics/Carbaugh.

Consider another example. Suppose the electronics industry has just two companies, one in Japan and one in the United States. In this industry, learning by doing reduces unit production costs indefinitely with the expansion of output. Assume the Japanese government considers its electronics industry to be "strategic" and imposes trade barriers

[10]The argument for strategic trade policy was first presented in J. Brander and B. Spencer, "International R&D Rivalry and Industrial Strategy," *Review of Economic Studies* 50 (1983), pp. 707–722. See also P. Krugman, ed., *Strategic Trade Policy and the New International Economics* (Cambridge, MA, MIT Press, 1986) and P. Krugman, "Is Free Trade Passe?" *Economic Perspectives,* Fall 1987, pp. 131–144.

[11]Paul Krugman, "Is Free Trade Passe?" *Economic Perspectives,* Fall 1987, pp. 131–144 and R. Baldwin and P. Krugman, "Industrial Policy and International Competition in Wide-Bodied Jet Aircraft," in R. Baldwin, ed., *Trade Policy Issues and Empirical Analysis* (Chicago: University of Chicago Press, 1988), pp. 45–77.

FIGURE 6.4

Effects of a European Subsidy Granted to Airbus

Hypothetical Payoff Matrix: Millions of Dollars

Without Subsidy

		Airbus	
		Produces	Does Not Produce
Boeing	Produces	Airbus −5 Boeing −5	Airbus 0 Boeing 100
	Does Not Produce	Airbus 100 Boeing 0	Airbus 0 Boeing 0

With European Subsidy

		Airbus	
		Produces	Does Not Produce
Boeing	Produces	Airbus −5 Boeing −5	Airbus 0 Boeing 100
	Does Not Produce	Airbus 110 Boeing 0	Airbus 0 Boeing 0

According to the theory of strategic trade policy, government subsidies can assist domestic firms in capturing economic profits from foreign competitors.

Source: Paul Krugman, "Is Free Trade Passe?" *Economic Perspectives*, Fall 1987, pp. 131–144.

that close its domestic market to the U.S. competitor; consider that the United States keeps its electronics market open. The Japanese manufacturer can expand its output and reduce its unit cost. Over a period of time, this competitive advantage permits it to drive the U.S. manufacturer out of business. The profits the U.S. company had extracted from U.S. buyers are transferred to the Japanese.

Advocates of strategic trade policy recognize that the classical argument for free trade considered externalities at length. The difference, they maintain, is that the classical theory was based on *perfect competition* and does not appreciate the most likely source of the externality, whereas modern theories based on imperfect competition does. The externality in question is the ability of companies to capture the fruits of expensive innovation. Classical theory based on perfect competition neglected this factor because large fixed costs are involved in innovation and research and development, and such costs ensure the number of competitors in an industry will be small.

The strategic trade policy concept has been criticized on several grounds. From a political perspective, special interest groups may dictate who will receive government support. Also, if a worldwide cycle of activist trade policy retaliation and counter retaliation were to occur, all nations would be worse off. Governments lack the information to intervene intelligently in the marketplace. In the Boeing–Airbus example, the activist government must know how much profit would be achieved as a result of proceeding with the new aircraft, both with and without foreign competition. Minor miscalculations could result in an intervention that makes the home economy worse off instead of better. Finally, the mere existence of imperfect competition does not guarantee that there is a strategic opportunity to be pursued, even by an omniscient government. There must also be a continuing source of economic profits with no potential competition to erase them. But *continuing* economic profits are probably less common than governments think.

The case of the European subsidization of aircraft during the 1970s provides an example of the benefits and costs encountered when applying the strategic trade policy concept. During the 1970s, Airbus received a government subsidy of $1.5 billion. The subsidy was intended to help Airbus offset the 20 percent cost disadvantage it faced on the production of its A300 aircraft compared to that of its main competitor, the Boeing 767.

Did the subsidy help the European nations involved in the Airbus consortium? Evidence suggests it did not. Airbus itself lost money on its A300 plane and continued to face cost disadvantages relative to Boeing. European airlines and passengers did benefit because the subsidy kept Airbus prices lower; however, the amount of Airbus's losses roughly matched this gain. Because the costs of the subsidy had to be financed by higher taxes, Europe was probably worse off with the subsidy. The United States also lost, because Boeing's profits were smaller and not fully offset by lower prices accruing to U.S. aircraft users; but the European subsidy did not drive Boeing out of the market. The only obvious gainers were other nations, whose airlines and passengers enjoyed benefits from lower Airbus prices at no cost to themselves.

ECONOMIC SANCTIONS

Instead of promoting trade, governments may *restrict* trade for domestic and foreign policy objectives. **Economic sanctions** are government mandated limitations placed on customary trade or financial relations among nations. They have been used to protect the domestic economy, reduce nuclear proliferation, set compensation for property expropriated by foreign governments, combat international terrorism, preserve national security, and protect human rights. The nation initiating the economic sanctions, the *imposing nation*, hopes to impair the economic capabilities of the *target nation* to such an extent that the target nation will succumb to its objectives.

The imposing nation can levy several types of economic sanctions. *Trade sanctions* involve boycotts on imposing-nation exports. The United States has used its role as a major producer of grain, military hardware, and high technology goods as a lever to win overseas compliance with its foreign policy objectives. Trade sanctions may also include quotas on imposing-nation imports from the target nation. *Financial sanctions* can entail limitations on official lending or aid. During the late 1970s, the U.S. policy of freezing the financial assets of Iran was seen as a factor in the freeing of the U.S. hostages. Table 6.10 provides examples of economic sanctions levied by the United States for foreign policy objectives.

TABLE 6.10

Selected Economic Sanctions of the United States

Year	Target Country	Objectives
2014	Russia	Discourage Annexation of Crimea
2010	Iran	Discourage nuclear proliferation
1998	Pakistan and India	Discourage nuclear proliferation
1993	Haiti	Improve human rights
1992	Serbia	Terminate civil war in Bosnia–Herzegovina
1990	Iraq	Terminate Iraq's military takeover of Kuwait
1985	South Africa	Improve human rights
1981	Soviet Union	Terminate martial law in Poland
1979	Iran	Release U.S. hostages; settle expropriation claims
1961	Cuba	Improve national security

© Cengage Learning®

FIGURE 6.5

Effects of Economic Sanctions

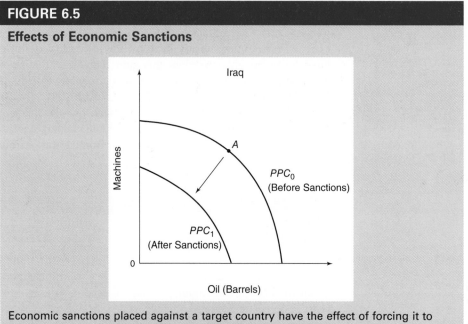

Economic sanctions placed against a target country have the effect of forcing it to operate inside its production possibilities curve. Economic sanctions can also result in an inward shift in the target nation's production possibilities curve.

© Cengage Learning®

Figure 6.5 can be used to illustrate the goal of economic sanctions levied against a target country, say, Iraq. The figure shows the hypothetical production possibilities curve of Iraq for machines and oil. Prior to the imposition of sanctions, suppose that Iraq is able to operate at maximum efficiency as shown by point *A* along production possibilities curve PPC_0. Under the sanctions program, a refusal of the imposing nations to purchase Iraqi oil leads to idle wells, refineries, and workers in Iraq. Unused production capacity forces Iraq to move inside PPC_0. If imposing nations also impose export sanctions on productive inputs, and curtail equipment sales to Iraq, the output potential of Iraq would decrease. This is shown by an inward shift of Iraq's production possibilities curve to PPC_1. Economic inefficiencies and reduced production possibilities caused by economic sanctions are intended to inflict hardship on the people and government of Iraq. Over time, sanctions may cause a reduced growth rate for Iraq. Even if short run welfare losses from sanctions are not large, they can appear in inefficiencies in the usage of labor and capital, deteriorating domestic expectations and reductions in savings, investment, and employment. Sanctions do reduce Iraq's output potential.

Factors Influencing the Success of Sanctions

The historical record of economic sanctions provides some insight into the factors that govern their effectiveness. Among the most important determinants of the success of economic sanctions are: (1) the number of nations imposing sanctions, (2) the degree to which the target nation has economic and political ties to the imposing nation(s), (3) the extent of political opposition in the target nation, and (4) cultural factors in the target nation.

Although unilateral sanctions may have some success in achieving intended results, it helps if sanctions are imposed by a large number of nations. Multilateral sanctions generally result in greater economic pressure on the target nation than do unilateral measures. Multilateral measures also increase the probability of success by demonstrating that more than one nation disagrees with the target nation's behavior and enhances the political legitimacy of the effort. International ostracism can have a significant psychological impact on the people of a target nation. Failure to generate strong multilateral cooperation can result in sanctions' becoming counterproductive; disputes among the imposing nations over sanctions can be interpreted by the target nation as a sign of disarray and weakness.

Sanctions tend to be more effective if the target nation had substantial economic and political relationships with the imposing nation(s) before the sanctions are imposed. Then the potential costs to the target nation are high if it does not comply with the wishes of the imposing nation(s). Western sanctions against South Africa during the 1980s helped convince the government to reform its apartheid system, in part because South Africa conducted four-fifths of its trade with six Western industrial nations and obtained almost all of its capital from the West.

Strength of political opposition within the target nation also affects the success of sanctions. When the target government faces substantial domestic opposition, economic sanctions can lead powerful business interests (such as companies with international ties) to pressure the government to conform to the imposing nation's wishes. Selected, moderate sanctions with the threat of more severe measures to follow, inflict economic hardship on domestic residents while providing an incentive for them to lobby for compliance to forestall more severe sanctions; the political advantage of levying graduated sanctions may outweigh the disadvantage of giving the target nation time to adjust its economy. If harsh, comprehensive sanctions are imposed immediately, domestic business interests have little incentive to pressure the target government to modify its policy; the economic damage has already been done.

When the people of the target nation have strong cultural ties to the imposing nation(s), they are likely to identify with the imposing nation's objectives that enhances the effectiveness of sanctions. South African whites have generally thought of themselves as part of the Western community. When economic sanctions were imposed on South Africa in the 1980s because of its apartheid practices, many liberal whites felt isolated and morally ostracized by the Western world; this encouraged them to lobby the South African government for political reforms.

Economic Sanctions and Weapons of Mass Destruction: North Korea and Iran

For decades the United States and the United Nations have imposed economic sanctions against countries that have been implicated in the use of terrorism and the development of chemical, biological, and nuclear weapons. Are economic sanctions useful in discouraging this behavior? Let us consider the cases of Iran and North Korea.

Since 1950 when North Korea invaded South Korea, the United States and the United Nations have imposed numerous sanctions against North Korea. The use of sanctions has been justified on the grounds that North Korea is a threat to global security through its sponsorship of terrorism and its proliferation of weapons of mass destruction such as nuclear bombs and missiles.

Among the sanctions that have been used against North Korea are bans on trade and the entry of North Korean ships and people into other countries. The United

States has applied financial sanctions to banks that conduct business with North Korea. Once a bank is targeted, it is effectively terminated from the U.S. financial system. The bank cannot clear U.S. dollars and it cannot have transactions with other U.S. banks and financial institutions.

In 2005, the United States blacklisted a bank in Macao, called Banco Delta Asia, that provided illicit financial services to the government of North Korea: it helped the North Koreans feed counterfeit US $100 bills into circulation, laundered money from drug deals, and financed cigarette smuggling. Because this bank was a main conduit for North Korea to the international financial system, the sanctions had a chilling effect on North Korean trade and finance. Nevertheless, the sanctions were unable to halt North Korea from testing a nuclear weapon.

One reason why sanctions have not been able to pressure North Korea into changing its behavior is because North Korea's trade and financial relations with the rest of the world are limited. These limited relations restrict the scope of sanctions and their leverage on North Korea. Another problem is that China and South Korea, the main economic lifelines of North Korea, have refrained from implementing substantial sanctions against their neighbor for fear of possible turmoil in the region. To date, it appears that the government of North Korea considers nuclear weapons as vital to its political survival. It will be difficult for sanctions to fulfill their goal of stopping North Korea from developing nuclear weapons.

The case of Iran also demonstrates the limitations of sanctions as a deterrent to the development of nuclear weapons. Since 1987, the United States has implemented numerous sanctions against Iran, such as trade and financial sanctions. These sanctions were intensified in 2006 when Iran openly pursued the development of a nuclear reactor. Iran insisted that it was merely fostering nuclear energy, but other countries have been suspicious that this technology can be shifted to the development of nuclear bombs. In 2011, the United States implemented sanctions targeting Iran's central bank and oil exports. A year later, the United States blacklisted Iran's shipping, shipbuilding and energy sectors. The result was a sharp drop in the value of Iran's currency, the *rial,* an increase in the rate of inflation to over 50 percent, a dramatic decline in Iran's gross domestic product, and an unemployment rate of 20 percent. Iran's oil exports that fund nearly half of Iran's government spending, fell by about half, from 2.5 million barrels a day to about 1.25 million barrels. The drop was driven by an EU embargo and U.S. pressure on Iranian oil customers.

Proponents of sanctions have maintained that Iran's economy is vulnerable to outside economic pressure. Iran relies on foreign capital and investment to develop its untapped oil fields and fledgling nuclear energy sector. Iran's sizeable role in oil production makes it difficult for oil dependent countries such as the United States to impose severe sanctions against Iran. As U.S. trade with Iran has decreased in the past two decades, Iran's trade with the rest of the world has increased, reducing the leverage that the United States has against Iran. Iran continues to export oil to China, India, South Korea, and Japan, the main sources of its oil revenues.

With the pressure of the sanctions mounting, in 2013 the government of Iran indicated that it was ready to resolve the nation's nuclear standoff with the West. This resulted in an interim agreement between Iran and the West: some of the sanctions against Iran were eased in exchange for Iran promising to temporarily curb part of its nuclear program. The hope was that the interim agreement would eventually lead to a permanent nuclear agreement. At the writing of this text, it remains to be seen how negotiations will play out.

SUMMARY

1. United States trade policies have reflected the motivation of many groups, including government officials, labor leaders, and business management.

2. United States tariff history has been marked by ups and downs. Many of the traditional arguments for tariffs (revenue, jobs) have been incorporated into U.S. tariff legislation.

3. The Smoot–Hawley Act of 1930 raised U.S. tariffs to an all time high, with disastrous results. Passage of the Reciprocal Trade Act of 1934 resulted in generalized tariff reductions by the United States as well as the enactment of most favored nation provisions.

4. The purposes of the General Agreement on Tariffs and Trade were to decrease trade barriers and place all nations on an equal footing in trading relations. In 1995, GATT was transformed into the World Trade Organization that embodies the main provisions of GATT and provides a mechanism intended to improve the process of resolving trade disputes among member nations. The Tokyo Round and Uruguay Round of multilateral trade negotiations went beyond tariff reductions to liberalize various nontariff trade barriers.

5. Trade remedy laws can help protect domestic firms from stiff foreign competition. These laws include the escape clause, provisions for antidumping and countervailing duties, and Section 301 of the 1974 Trade Act, that addresses unfair trading practices of foreign nations.

6. The escape clause provides temporary protection to U.S. producers who desire relief from foreign imports that are fairly traded.

7. Countervailing duties are intended to offset any unfair competitive advantage that foreign producers might gain over domestic producers because of foreign subsidies.

8. Economic theory suggests that if a nation is a net importer of a product subsidized or dumped by foreigners, the nation as a whole gains from the foreign subsidy or dumping. This is because the gains to domestic consumers of the subsidized or dumped good more than offset the losses to domestic producers of the import-competing goods.

9. U.S. antidumping duties are intended to neutralize two unfair trading practices: export sales in the United States at prices below average total cost, and international price discrimination in which foreign firms sell in the United States at a price lower than that charged in the exporter's home market.

10. Section 301 of the Trade Act of 1974 allows the U.S. government to levy trade restrictions against nations that are practicing unfair competition, if trade disagreements cannot be successfully resolved.

11. Intellectual property includes copyrights, trademarks, and patents. Foreign counterfeiting of intellectual property has been a significant problem for many industrial nations.

12. Because foreign competition may displace import-competing producers, the United States and other nations have initiated programs of trade adjustment assistance involving government aid to adversely affected businesses, workers, and communities.

13. The United States has been reluctant to formulate an explicit industrial policy in which government picks winners and losers among products and firms. Instead, the U.S. government has generally taken a less activist approach in providing assistance to domestic producers (such as the Export-Import Bank and export trade associations).

14. According to the strategic trade policy concept, government can assist firms in capturing economic profits from foreign competitors. The strategic trade policy concept applies to firms in imperfectly competitive markets.

15. Economic sanctions consist of trade and financial restraints imposed on foreign nations. They have been used to preserve national security, protect human rights, and combat international terrorism.

KEY CONCEPTS AND TERMS

Commodity Credit Corporation
(CCC) (p. 214)
Countervailing duty (p. 201)
Doha Round (p. 189)
Economic sanctions (p. 219)
Escape clause (p. 199)
Export-Import Bank (p. 213)
Fast track authority (p. 198)
General Agreement on Tariffs and
Trade (GATT) (p. 185)
Intellectual property rights
(IPRs) (p. 208)

Kennedy Round (p. 187)
Ministry of Economy, Trade and
Industry (METI) (p. 216)
Most favored nation (MFN)
clause (p. 185)
Multifiber Arrangement
(MFA) (p. 200)
Normal trade relations (p. 185)
Reciprocal Trade Agreements
Act (p. 184)
Safeguards (p. 199)
Section 301 (p. 207)

Smoot–Hawley Act (p. 183)
Strategic trade policy (p. 217)
Tokyo Round (p. 188)
Trade adjustment
assistance (p. 212)
Trade promotion authority (p. 198)
Trade remedy laws (p. 199)
Uruguay Round (p. 189)
World Trade Organization
(WTO) (p. 185)

STUDY QUESTIONS

1. To what extent have the traditional arguments that justify protectionist barriers actually been incorporated into U.S. trade legislation?
2. At what stage in U.S. trade history did protectionism reach its high point?
3. What is meant by the most favored nation clause, and how does it relate to the tariff policies of the United States?
4. GATT and its successor, the WTO, have established a set of rules for the commercial conduct of trading nations. Explain.
5. What are trade remedy laws? How do they attempt to protect U.S. firms from unfairly (fairly) traded goods?
6. What is intellectual property? Why has intellectual property become a major issue in recent rounds of international trade negotiations?
7. How does the trade adjustment assistance program attempt to help domestic firms and workers who are displaced as a result of import competition?
8. Under the Tokyo Round of trade negotiations, what were the major policies adopted concerning nontariff trade barriers? What about the Uruguay Round?
9. Describe the industrial policies adopted by the U.S. government. How have these policies differed from those adopted by Japan?
10. If the United States is a net importer of a product that is being subsidized or dumped by Japan, not only do U.S. consumers gain, but they also gain more than U.S. producers lose from the Japanese subsidies or dumping. Explain why this is true.
11. What is the purpose of strategic trade policy?
12. What is the purpose of economic sanctions? What problems do they pose for the nation initiating the sanctions? When are sanctions most successful in achieving their goals?
13. Assume that the nation of Spain is "small" and unable to influence the Brazilian (world) price of steel. Spain's supply and demand schedules are illustrated in Table 6.11. Assume that Brazil's price is $400 per ton of steel. Using graph paper, plot the

TABLE 6.11

Steel Supply and Demand for Spain

Price	Quantity (million tons) Supplied	Quantity (million tons) Demanded
$ 0	0	12
200	2	10
400	4	8
600	6	6
800	8	4
1000	10	2
1200	12	0

© Cengage Learning®

demand and supply schedules of Spain and Brazil on the same graph.

a. With free trade, how many tons of steel will be produced, purchased, and imported by Spain? Calculate the dollar value of Spanish producer and consumer surpluses.

b. Suppose the Brazilian government grants its steel firms a production subsidy of $200 per ton. Plot Brazil's subsidy adjusted supply schedule on your graph.

(1) What is the new market price of steel? At this price, how much steel will Spain produce, purchase, and import?

(2) The subsidy helps/hurts Spanish firms because their producer surplus rises/falls by $ _____; Spanish steel users realize a rise/fall in the consumer surplus of $ _____. The Spanish economy as a whole benefits/suffers from the subsidy by an amount totaling $ _____.

EXPLORING FURTHER

For a discussion of the welfare effects of strategic trade policy, go to *Exploring Further 6.1* which can be found at **www.cengage.com/economics/carbaugh.**

Trade Policies for the Developing Nations

It is a commonly accepted practice to array all nations according to real income and then draw a dividing line between the advanced and developing ones. Included in the category of **advanced nations** are those of North America and Western Europe, plus Australia, New Zealand, and Japan. Most nations of the world are classified as developing, or less developed, nations. The **developing nations** are most of those in Africa, Asia, Latin America, and the Middle East. Table 7.1 provides economic and social indicators for selected nations. In general, advanced nations are characterized by relatively high levels of gross domestic product per capita, longer life expectancies, and higher levels of adult literacy. Most of the world's population live in the poorer developing countries.

Although international trade can provide benefits to domestic producers and consumers, some economists maintain that the current international trading system hinders economic development in the developing nations. They believe that conventional international trade theory based on the principle of comparative advantage is irrelevant for these nations. This chapter examines the reasons some economists provide to explain their misgivings about the international trading system. The chapter also considers policies aimed at improving the economic conditions of the developing nations.

DEVELOPING-NATION TRADE CHARACTERISTICS

If we examine the characteristics of developing-nation trade, we find that developing nations are highly dependent on advanced nations. A majority of developing nation exports goes to the advanced nations, and most developing nation imports originate in advanced nations. Trade among developing nations is relatively minor, although it has increased in recent years.

Another characteristic is the composition of developing nations' exports, with its emphasis on **primary products** (agricultural goods, raw materials, and fuels). Of the

TABLE 7.1

Basic Economic and Social Indicators for Selected Nations, 2011

	Gross National Income per Capita*	Life Expectancy (years)	Adult Literacy (percent)
Switzerland	$52,530	83	99
United States	50,120	79	99
Japan	34,890	83	99
Chile	19,820	79	97
Mexico	15,770	77	93
Algeria	7,550	71	73
Indonesia	4,440	70	92
Guinea	940	56	30
Burundi	540	53	67

*Converted into international dollars using purchasing-power-parity rates. An international dollar has the same purchasing power as a U.S. dollar has in the United States.

Source: From The World Bank at http://www.worldbank.org/data.

manufactured goods that are exported by developing nations, many (such as textiles) are labor intensive and include only modest amounts of technology in their production.

In the past three decades, the dominance of primary products in developing-nation trade has lessened. Many developing nations have been able to increase their exports of manufactured goods and services relative to primary products: these nations include China, India, Mexico, South Korea, Hong Kong, Bangladesh, Sri Lanka, Turkey, Morocco, Indonesia, Vietnam, and so on. Nations that have integrated into the world's industrial markets have realized significant poverty reduction.

How have developing nations been able to move into exports of manufactured products? Investments in both people and factories have played a role. The average educational levels and capital stock per worker have risen sharply throughout the developing world. Also, improvements in transport and communications, in conjunction with developing nation reforms, allowed the production chain to be broken into components, with developing nations playing a key role in global production sharing. Also, the liberalization of trade barriers in developing nations after the mid-1980s increased their competitiveness. This increase was especially true for manufactured goods and processed primary products. Developing nations are gaining ground in higher technology exports. Nevertheless, they have been frustrated about modest success in exporting these goods to advanced nations.

Many developing nations with a total population of around 2 billion people still have not integrated strongly into the global industrial economy; many of these nations are in Africa and the former Soviet Union. Their exports usually consist of a narrow range of primary products. These nations have often been handicapped by poor infrastructure, inadequate education, rampant corruption, and high trade barriers. Also, transport costs to advanced nation markets are often higher than the tariffs on their goods, so that transport costs are even more of a barrier to integration than the trade policies of rich nations. For these developing nations, incomes have been falling and poverty has been rising in the past 20 years. It is important for them to diversify exports by breaking into global markets for manufactured goods and services where possible. Why are some countries so much poorer than others?

TENSIONS BETWEEN DEVELOPING NATIONS AND ADVANCED NATIONS

In spite of the trade frustrations of developing nations, most scholars and policymakers today agree that the best strategy for a poor country is to develop to take advantage of international trade. In the past two decades, many developing nations saw the wisdom of this strategy and opened their markets to international trade and foreign investment. Ironically, in spite of scholars' support for this change, the advanced world has sometimes maintained its own barriers to imports from these developing nations. Why is this so?

Think of the world economy as a ladder. On the bottom rungs are developing nations that produce mainly textiles and other low tech goods. Toward the top are the United States, Japan, and the other advanced nations that manufacture sophisticated software, electronics, and pharmaceuticals. Up and down the middle rungs are all the other nations, producing everything from memory chips, to autos, to steel. From this perspective, economic development is simple: Everyone attempts to climb to the next rung. This process works well if the topmost nations can create new industries and products, adding another rung to the ladder: older industries can move overseas while new jobs are generated at home. But if innovation stalls at the highest rung, then Americans must compete with lower wage workers in developing nations.

A predicament faced by developing nations is that in order to make progress, they must displace producers of the least advanced goods that are still being produced in the advanced nations. If Zambia is going to produce textiles and apparel, it will compete against American and European producers of these goods. As producers in advanced nations suffer from import competition, they tend to seek trade protection in order to avoid it. However, this protection denies critical market access to developing nations, thwarting their attempts to grow. Thus, there is a bias against their catching up to the advanced nations.

Those who are protected in advanced nations from competition with developing nations tend to include those who are already near the bottom of the advanced nations' income distributions. Many of these people work in labor-intensive industries and have limited skills and low wages. Income redistribution programs ought to aid, not hinder, these people. To some extent, advanced nations face a tradeoff between helping their own poor and helping the world's poor. Critics note that the world as a whole needs to treat all poor as its own and those international institutions ought to ensure fairness to all who are in poverty. The World Trade Organization (WTO) is responsible for preventing advanced nations' trade policies from tilting too far in favor of their own people and against the rest of the world. This is why recent WTO meetings have been filled with tensions between poor and rich nations.

Providing developing nations with greater access to the markets of advanced nations will not solve all the developing nations' problems. They face structural weaknesses in their economies that are compounded by nonexistent or inadequate institutions and policies in the fields of law and order, sustainable macroeconomic management, and public services.

TRADE PROBLEMS OF THE DEVELOPING NATIONS

The theory of comparative advantage maintains that all nations can enjoy the benefits of free trade if they specialize in production of those goods in which they have a comparative advantage and exchange some of them for goods produced by other nations. Policy makers in the United States and many other advanced nations maintain that the market oriented structure of the international trading system furnishes a setting in which the benefits of comparative advantage can be realized. They claim that the existing international trading system has provided widespread benefits and that the trading interests of all nations are best served by pragmatic, incremental changes in the existing system. Advanced nations also maintain that to achieve trading success, they must administer their own domestic and international economic policies.

On the basis of their trading experience with advanced nations, some developing nations have become dubious of the *distribution* of trade benefits between themselves and advanced nations. They have argued that the protectionist trading policies of advanced nations hinder the industrialization of many developing nations. Accordingly, developing nations have sought a new international trading order with improved access to the markets of advanced nations. Among the problems that have plagued developing nations have been unstable export markets, worsening terms of trade, and limited access to the markets of advanced nations.

Unstable Export Markets

One characteristic of some developing nations is that their exports are concentrated in only one or a few primary products. This situation is shown in Table 7.2 that illustrates the dependence of selected developing nations on a single primary product. A poor harvest or a decrease in market demand for that product can significantly reduce export revenues and seriously disrupt domestic income and employment levels.

Economists maintain that a key factor underlying the instability of primary-product prices and producer revenues is the low price elasticity of the demand and supply schedules for products such as tin, copper, and coffee.[1] Recall that the price elasticity of

---

TABLE 7.2

Developing Nation Dependence on Primary Products, 2012

Nation	Major Export product	Major Export Product as a Percentage of Total Exports
Nigeria	Oil	95
Saudi Arabia	Oil	90
Venezuela	Oil	82
Benin	Cotton	81
Burundi	Coffee	80
Malawi	Tobacco	70
Zambia	Copper	62
Ethiopia	Coffee	60

Source: From The World Bank Group, *Data and Statistics: Country at a Glance Tables*, available at http://www.worldbank.org/data. See also Central Intelligence Agency, *World Factbook*, available at www.cia.gov.

---

[1]For most commodities, price elasticities of demand and supply are estimated to be in the range of 0.2–0.5, suggesting that a 1-percent change in price results in only a 0.2-percent change in quantity. A classic empirical study of this topic comes from Jerre Behman, "International Commodity Agreements: An Evaluation of the UNCTAD Integrated Commodity Program," in William Cline, ed., *Policy Alternatives for a New International Economic Order* (New York: Praeger, 1979), pp. 118–121.

demand (supply) refers to the percentage change in quantity demanded (supplied) resulting from a one percent change in price. To the extent that demand and supply schedules are relatively *inelastic*, suggesting that the percentage change in price exceeds the percentage change in quantity, a small shift in either schedule can induce a large change in price and revenues.

Figure 7.1 illustrates the supply and demand schedules for coffee, pertaining to the market as a whole. Assume that these schedules are highly inelastic. The market is in equilibrium at point A, where the market supply schedule S_0 intersects the market demand schedule D_0. The revenues of coffee producers total $22.5 million, determined by multiplying the equilibrium price ($4.50) times the quantity of pounds sold (5 million).

Referring to Figure 7.1(*a*), suppose that decreasing foreign incomes cause the market demand curve for coffee to decrease to D_1. With the supply of coffee being inelastic, the decrease in demand causes a substantial decline in market price, from $4.50 to $2.00 per pound. The revenue of coffee producers falls to $8 million. Part of this decrease represents a fall in producer profit. We conclude that coffee prices and earnings can be highly volatile when market supply is inelastic.

Not only do changes in demand induce wide fluctuations in price when supply is inelastic, but changes in supply induce wide fluctuations in price when demand is inelastic. The latter situation is illustrated in Figure 7.1(*b*). Suppose that favorable growing conditions cause a rightward shift in the market supply curve of coffee to S_1. The result is a substantial drop in price from $4.50 to $2 per pound and producer revenues fall to $14 million ($2 \times 7$ million pounds = $14 million). We see that prices and revenues can be volatile when demand conditions are inelastic.

FIGURE 7.1

Export Price Instability for a Developing Nation

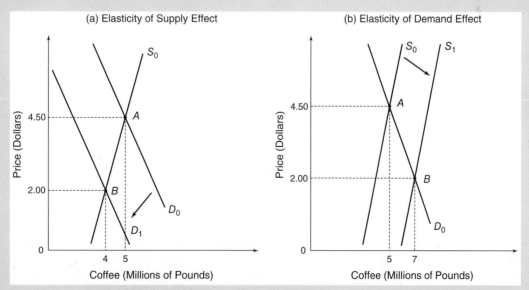

When the supply of a commodity is highly price inelastic, decreases (or increases) in demand will generate wide variations in price. When the demand for a commodity is highly price inelastic, increases (or decreases) in supply will generate wide variations in price.

Falling Commodity Prices Threaten Growth of Exporting Nations

During the first decade of the 2000s, increasing commodity prices and favorable growing conditions benefitted producers and governments in many developing nations. Higher prices resulted in rising profits and increasing tax revenues that were used by governments to pay off some of their debts and spend more on social programs. In Latin America, stronger commodity markets contributed to economic growth that averaged 5 percent per year during 2003–2008 as compared to 3.5 percent per year during the previous three decades.

However, that upward cycle took a sharp hit when many advanced economies plunged into recession in 2008 and 2009. As these economies shrank, so did their demand for commodities. Lower demand resulted in a dramatic tumbling in the prices of copper, tin, iron ore, soybeans, oil and the like. As export revenues declined, commodity producing nations such as Peru and Bolivia had to put on the shelf natural resource investments such as iron ore extraction.

Brazil paid a steep price for relying on primary products, such as soybeans and iron ore, for 40 percent of its exports. The price of soybeans decreased from $600 per ton to $365 per ton during 2008–2009. As Brazil's export prices declined, so did its once sizable trade surplus. Brazil's corporations such as mining giant Cia.Vale do Rio Doce, had to cut back production and lay off workers. Also, the region's big gas and oil producers, including Bolivia, Ecuador, and Venezuela, were hit hard by the global economic downturn.

The economies of many developing nations are tied to primary products and a majority of their exports go to advanced nations. When advanced nations encounter economic downturns, they can be quickly transmitted to their developing country trading partners as seen in the global economic downturn of 2008–2009.

Worsening Terms of Trade

How the gains from international trade are distributed among trading partners has been controversial, especially among developing nations whose exports are concentrated in primary products. These nations generally maintain that the benefits of international trade accrue disproportionately to the advanced nations.

Developing nations complain that their commodity terms of trade has deteriorated in the past century or so, suggesting that the prices of their exports relative to their imports have fallen. Worsening terms of trade have been used to justify the refusal of many developing nations to participate in trade liberalization negotiations. It also has underlain developing nations' demands for preferential treatment in trade relations with advanced nations.

Observers maintain that the monopoly power of manufacturers in the advanced nations results in higher prices. Gains in productivity accrue to manufacturers in the form of higher earnings rather than price reductions. Observers further contend that the export prices of primary products of developing nations are determined in competitive markets. These prices fluctuate downward as well as upward. Gains in productivity are shared with foreign consumers in the form of lower prices. Developing nations maintain that market forces cause the prices they pay for imports to rise faster than the prices commanded by their exports, resulting in a deterioration in their commodity terms of trade. As income rises, people tend to spend more on manufactured goods than primary goods, thus contributing to a worsening in the developing nations' terms of trade.

The developing nations' assertion of worsening commodity terms of trade was supported by a United Nations (UN) study in 1949.[2] The study concluded that from

---

[2]United Nations Commission for Latin America, *The Economic Development of Latin America and Its Principal Problems*, 1950.

the period 1876–1880 to 1946–1947, the prices of primary products compared with those of manufactured goods fell by 32 percent. Because of inadequacies in data and the problems of constructing price indexes, the UN study was hardly conclusive. Other studies led to opposite conclusions about terms of trade movements.

In 2004, economists at the United Nations found that between 1961 and 2001, the average prices of agricultural commodities sold by developing nations fell by almost 70 percent relative to the price of manufactured goods purchased from developed nations. Such terms of trade declines were especially harmful for the poorest nations of Sub-Saharan Africa. Also, the World Bank estimated that between 1970 and 1997 declining terms of trade cost non-oil exporting nations in Africa the equivalent of 119 percent of their combined annual gross domestic product in lost revenues. In theory, a decline in the terms of trade could be counteracted by increases in the quantity produced and exported so as to maintain or increase the value of export earnings. In practice, export quantities did not grow sufficiently in the nations of Africa to cover the loss.[3]

Regarding other developing nations—such as China, India, and Russia—and other developing world oil exporters, the declining terms of trade argument appears to hold less well in recent years. Many of these nations have been able to realize economies of scale in the production of certain other primary products such as corn or cotton, and have diversified their economies away from exclusive reliance on raw material exports.

It is difficult to conclude whether the developing nations as a whole have experienced a deterioration or an improvement in their terms of trade. Conclusions about terms of trade movements become clouded by the choice of the base year used in comparisons, the problem of making allowances for changes in technology and productivity as well as for new products and product qualities, and the methods used to value exports and imports and to weight the commodities used in the index.

Limited Market Access

In the past two decades, developing nations as a whole have improved their penetration of world markets. Global protectionism has been a hindrance to their market access. This is especially true for agriculture and labor-intensive manufactured products such as clothing and textiles. These products are important to the world's poor because they represent more than half of low income nations' exports and about 70 percent of least developed nations' export revenues.

Tariffs imposed by the advanced nations on imports from developing nations tend to be higher than those they levy on other advanced nations. The differences in tariff averages reflect in part the presence of major trading blocs such as the European Union (EU) and the North American Free Trade Agreement (NAFTA), that have abolished tariffs for advanced nation trade partners. Also, because developing nations did not actively participate in multilateral trade liberalization agreements prior to the 1990s, their products tended to be omitted from the sharp reductions in tariffs made in those rounds. Average tariff rates in rich nations are low, but they maintain barriers in exactly the areas where developing nations have comparative advantage: agriculture and labor-intensive manufactured goods.

Developing nations also are plagued by tariff escalation, as discussed in Chapter 4. In advanced nations, tariffs escalate steeply, especially on agricultural products. Tariff

---

[3]Food and Agriculture Organization (FAO) of the United Nations, *The State of Agricultural Commodity Markets*, Rome, Italy, 2004, pp. 8–12. See also Kevin Watkins and Penny Fowler, *Rigged Rules and Double Standards: Trade, Globalization and the Fight Against Poverty*, Oxfam Publishing, Oxford, England, 2002, Chapter 6.

escalation has the potential of decreasing demand for processed imports from developing nations, restricting their diversification into higher value added exports. Though less prevalent, tariff escalation also affects imports of industrial products, especially at the semi-processed stage. Examples of such products, in which many developing nations have a comparative advantage, include textiles and clothing, leather and leather products, wood, paper, furniture, metals, and rubber products.

Moreover, protectionist barriers have caused developing country producers of textiles and clothing to forego sizable export earnings. For decades, advanced nations imposed quotas on imports of these products. Although the Uruguay Round Agreement on Textiles and Clothing resulted in the abolishment of the quotas in 2005, market access in textiles and clothing will remain restricted because tariff barriers are high.

Antidumping and countervailing duties have become popular substitutes for traditional trade barriers that are gradually being reduced in the course of regional and multilateral trade liberalization. Developing nations have argued that advanced nations such as the United States have limited access to their markets through aggressive use of antidumping and countervailing duties. Such policies have resulted in significant reductions in export volumes and market shares, according to the developing nations.

Indeed, poor nations have leaned on the United States and Europe to reduce trade barriers. Rich nations note that poor nations need to reduce their own tariffs that are often higher than those of their rich counterparts, as seen in Table 7.3. Tariff escalation is also widely practiced by developing nations; their average tariff for fully processed agricultural and manufactured products is higher than on unprocessed products. Although trade among developing nations is a much smaller share of total trade, average tariffs in manufactured goods are about three times higher for trade among developing nations than for exports to advanced nations. Critics note that developing nations are part of their own problem and they should liberalize trade.

TABLE 7.3

Tariffs of Selected Developing Nations and Advanced Nations, All Products, 2012

Country	Average Applied Tariff Rate*
Bahamas	35.9%
Maldives	20.5
Zimbabwe	19.5
Brazil	13.7
India	13.0
South Korea	12.1
Russian Federation	9.5
European Union	5.1
Japan	4.4
Canada	3.7
United States	3.5

*Average applied tariff rates are duties that are actually charged on imports. These can be below the bound rates which are commitments to increase a rate of duty beyond an agreed level. Once a rate of duty is bound, it may not be raised without compensating the affected parties.

Source: From the World Trade Organization, *World Tariff Profiles*, 2012.

However, this argument does not sit well with many poor nations. They contend that quickly reducing tariffs could throw their already fragile economies into an even worse state. Just as is the case in rich nations that reduce tariffs, some workers will inevitably lose jobs as businesses switch to the lowest cost centers. Unlike the United States and European nations, poor nations do not have a social safety net and reeducation programs to cushion the blow. The message that the developing world receives is that it should do some market liberalization of its own. Nevertheless, it is paradoxical for advanced nations to want developing nations to lift their trade barriers, yet advanced nations like the United States and Canada benefitted from significant trade barriers during their developing stages.

Agricultural Export Subsidies of Advanced Nations

Global protectionism in agriculture is another problem for developing nations. In addition to using tariffs to protect their farmers from import-competing products, advanced nations support their farmers with sizable subsidies. Subsidies are often rationalized on the noneconomic benefits of agriculture such as food security and maintenance of rural communities. By encouraging the production of agricultural commodities, subsidies discourage agricultural imports, thus displacing developing country shipments to advanced country markets. Also, the unwanted surpluses of agricultural commodities that result from government support are often dumped onto world markets with the aid of export subsidies. This dumping depresses prices for many agricultural commodities and reduces the revenues of developing nations.

Rice farmers in West Africa complain that U.S. and European export subsidies depress world prices and make it difficult for them to compete. In 2007, an average ton of U.S. rough rice cost $240 to sow, tend, and harvest. By the time that rice left a U.S. port for export, U.S. subsidies reduced the price to foreign buyers to $205. The production cost in West Africa was $230 a ton. West African farmers could not compete in their own market. As rice farmers have gone bankrupt in West Africa, they have often attempted to journey illegally to Europe to find jobs. Thousands have died as they crossed the Mediterranean at more dangerous spots to avoid detection by European patrols.

The complaints of West Africa's cotton farmers have mirrored those of its rice farmers. They note that U.S. exports of cotton have been aided by sizable subsidies. West African farmers feel that life is unfair when they must compete against American farmers as well as the U.S. government.

American food aid policies tend to intensify this controversy. It is true that U.S. food donated to the developing world has saved millions of lives made destitute by the failure of their farms. Growers in developing nations complain that the U.S. government purchases surplus grain from American farmers and sends it halfway around the world, instead of first purchasing what foreigners grow. By law, the United States is bound to send homegrown food for assistance, instead of spending cash on foreign produce in all but the most exceptional cases. This policy supports American farmers, processors, and shippers, as well as the world's hungry. The complaints of West African farmers do not get much sympathy in the United States where farmers oppose the U.S. government's spending of taxpayer money to purchase foreign crops.

Many developing nations are net importers of agricultural products and therefore benefit from these subsidies. Because these subsidies decrease the prices of the products that they purchase on global markets, many developing nations would suffer by their elimination.

Bangladesh's Sweatshop Reputation

Another problem facing developing countries is sweatshop factories. A sweatshop is a factory that has poor and unsafe working conditions, unreasonable hours, unfair wages, child labor, and a lack of benefits for workers. Consider the case of the Bangladesh clothing industry.

Bangladesh provides the world's clothing industry something unique: millions of workers who quickly churn out huge amounts of well made jeans, T-shirts, and underwear for the lowest wages in the world. Not only has the clothing industry served as a major source of economic growth for Bangladesh, but it is second only to China as the largest exporter of clothing sold by retailers such as Walmart, Sears, Gap, and J.C. Penny.

During 1974–2005, world trade in clothing was governed by the MultiFiber Arrangement (MFA) that imposed quotas on the amount developing countries could export to developed countries. Developing countries have a competitive advantage in clothing production because it is labor intensive and has low labor costs. When the MFA expired in 2005, Bangladesh was expected to suffer the most since it would likely face more competition, particularly from China. This was not the case. It turns out that even in the face of other economic giants; Bangladesh's labor was relatively cheap. Orders for Bangladesh's clothes kept coming even after the MFA expired.

Strong demand for clothes resulted in the number of clothing factories in Bangladesh increasing to about 5,500 in 2013, up 30 percent since 2005. This rapid growth strained the country's electrical, power, and gas systems. It also resulted in a shortage of land in Bangladesh that caused many factories to build up, rather than out. Although many multi-story factories were safely constructed, some were not: Additional floors were sometimes hastily added without reference to fire and safety codes. As a result, working conditions in Bangladesh's clothing industry became suspect as the race to add manufacturing capacity set the stage for a series of horrific accidents—several deadly clothing factory fires and the collapse of an eight-story building that killed more than 1,100 workers in 2013.

Critics maintained that European and American tastes for cheap clothes fueled the Bangladesh clothing boom and ultimately horrific accidents for its workers. They noted that as labor costs in China, the world's low-cost factor floor, have increased rapidly, clothing producers have switched to lower cost alternatives like Vietnam, Cambodia, and Bangladesh, where the entry level wage for garment workers is less than $40 a month—about a fourth of a worker's wages in China. The result is factories striving to meet the growing demands of retailers by ignoring the rights of workers and cutting corners on safety. When the inevitable disasters result, the retailers throw up their hands and distance themselves from what was happening in these factories.

The tragedies of Bangladesh's workers raised the pressure on Western retailers to not only pay compensation to victims, but to also improve fire and building safety in the country for the long run. Collecting compensation for victims after disasters is difficult, especially because of the many layers between brands and the workers that produce their clothing. It is common for retailers to distance themselves from workers through a complex system of production orders placed with multinational middlemen that are then subcontracted to factories that can be three or four steps removed from the retailers.

Following the building collapse in Bangladesh, several of the world's largest European apparel companies agreed to finance fire safety and building improvements in the factories they use in Bangladesh. Walmart publically blacklisted about 250 Bangladesh factories that it considered to be unsafe. Several other major retailers, such as Sears, still considered some of those same factories safe and received shipments of sweaters and other clothing from them. The contrast illustrates how differing standards and approaches can complicate efforts to determine which factories in Bangladesh are safe, even as calls for change grow louder.[4]

[4]"Major Retailers Join Bangladesh Safety Plan," *The New York Times*, May 13, 2013; "Apparel Makers Promise Bangladesh Factory Safety," *Dow Jones Business News*, May 13, 2013; "Jonathan Lahey and Anne D'Innocenzio, "Bangladesh Increasingly Risky for Clothing Makers," *The Boston Globe*, May 13, 2013; "Before Dhaka Collapse, Some Firms Fled Risk," *The Wall Street Journal*, May 8, 2013; "Global Standards for Garment Industry Under Scrutiny After Bangladesh Disaster," *PBS News Hour*, April 26, 2013.

STABILIZING PRIMARY-PRODUCT PRICES

Although developing nations have shown some improvement in exports of manufactured goods, agriculture and natural resource products remain a main source of employment. As we have learned, the export prices and revenues for these products can be quite volatile.

In an attempt to stabilize export prices and revenues of primary products, developing nations have attempted to form **international commodity agreements (ICAs)**. These agreements are between leading producing and consuming nations of commodities such as coffee, rubber and cocoa about matters such as stabilizing prices, assuring adequate supplies to consumers, and promoting the economic development of producers. To promote stability in commodity markets, ICAs have relied on production and export controls, buffer stocks, and multilateral contracts. We should note that these measures have generally had only limited (if any) success in improving the economic conditions of developing nations, and that other methods of helping these nations are needed.

Production and Export Controls

If an ICA accounts for a large share of total world output (or exports) of a commodity, its members may agree on **production and export controls** to stabilize export revenues. Production and export controls affect the price of commodities by influencing the world supply of the commodity. The total quantity of production or exports allowed under a commodity agreement is based on the *target price* that is agreed to by member nations. If it is thought that the price of tin will decrease below the target price in the future, producing nations will be assigned a lower production level or export quota. By making tin more scarce, its price will remain at the target level. Conversely, if it is anticipated that the price of tin will increase above the target price in the future, producing nations will be allowed to increase their levels of production and exports.

An obstacle in attempting to impose limits on production and exports is the distribution of the limits among producing nations. If a decline in the total quantity of coffee exports is needed to offset a falling price, how would that decline be allocated among individual producers? Small producers may be hesitant to decrease their levels of output when prices are declining. Another problem is the appearance of new producers of coffee that may be drawn into the market by artificially high prices. Producing nations just embarking on the production or export of coffee would likely be reluctant to reduce their levels of production or exports at that time. Producers have the incentive to cheat on output restrictions and enforcement is difficult.

Buffer Stocks

Another technique for limiting commodity price swings is the **buffer stock**, in which a producers' association (or international agency) is prepared to buy and sell a commodity in large amounts. The buffer stock consists of supplies of a commodity financed and held by the producers' association. The buffer stock manager *buys* from the market when supplies are abundant and prices are falling below acceptable levels, and *sells* from the buffer stock when supplies are tight and prices are high.

Figure 7.2 illustrates the hypothetical price stabilization efforts of the International Tin Agreement. Assume that the association sets a price range with a floor of $3.27 per pound and a ceiling of $4.02 per pound to guide the stabilization operations of the buffer stock manager. Starting at equilibrium point A in Figure 7.2(*a*), suppose the buffer stock

---

FIGURE 7.2

Buffer Stock: Price Ceiling and Price Support

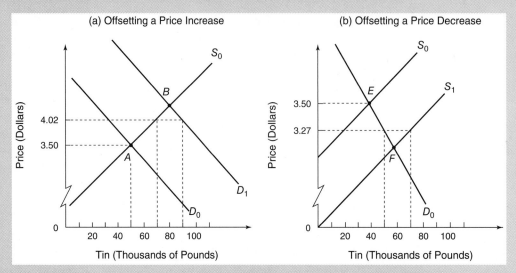

(a) Offsetting a Price Increase

(b) Offsetting a Price Decrease

During periods of rising tin demand, the buffer-stock manager sells tin to prevent the price from rising above the ceiling level. However, prolonged defense of the ceiling price may result in depletion of the tin stockpile that undermines the effectiveness of this price stabilization tool and lending to an upward revision of the ceiling price. During periods of abundant tin supplies, the manager purchases tin to prevent the price from falling below the floor level. Again, prolonged defense of the price floor may exhaust the funds to purchase excess supplies of tin at the floor price and may lead to a downward revision of the floor price.

---

manager sees the demand for tin rising from D_0 to D_1. To defend the ceiling price of $4.02, the manager must be prepared to sell 20,000 pounds of tin to offset the excess demand for tin at the ceiling price. Conversely, starting at equilibrium point E in Figure 7.3(b), suppose the supply of tin rises from S_0 to S_1. To defend the floor price of $3.27, the buffer stock manager must purchase the 20,000-pound excess supply that exists at that price.

Proponents of buffer stocks contend that the scheme offers the primary producing nations several advantages. A well run buffer stock can promote economic efficiency because primary producers can plan investment and expansion if they know that prices will not gyrate. It is also argued that soaring commodity prices invariably ratchet industrial prices upward, whereas commodity price decreases exert no comparable downward pressure. By stabilizing commodity prices, buffer stocks can moderate the price inflation of the advanced nations. Buffer stocks in this context are viewed as a means of providing primary producers more stability than is allowed by the free market.

Setting up and administering a buffer stock program is not without costs and problems. The basic difficulty in stabilizing prices with buffer stocks is agreeing on a target price that reflects long-term market trends. If the target price is set too low, the buffer stocks will become depleted as the stock manager sells the commodity on the open market in an attempt to hold market prices in line with the target price. If the target price is set too high, the stock manager must purchase large quantities of the commodity in an effort to support market prices. The costs of holding the stocks tend to be high because they include transportation expenses, insurance, and labor costs. In their choice of price targets, buffer stock officials have often made poor decisions. Rather than conduct massive stabilization operations, buffer stock officials will periodically revise target prices should they fall out of line with long-term price trends.

Multilateral Contracts

Multilateral contracts are another method of stabilizing commodity prices. Such contracts generally stipulate a *minimum price* at which importers will purchase guaranteed quantities from the producing nations and a *maximum price* at which producing nations will sell guaranteed amounts to the importers. Such purchases and sales are designed to hold prices within a target range. Trading under a multilateral contract has often occurred among several exporting and importing nations, as in the case of the International Sugar Agreement and the International Wheat Agreement.

One possible advantage of the multilateral contract as a price stabilization device is that, in comparison with buffer stocks or export controls, it results in less distortion of the market mechanism and the allocation of resources. This result is because the typical multilateral contract does not involve output restraints and thus does not check the development of more efficient low-cost producers. If target prices are not set near the long-term equilibrium price, however, discrepancies will occur between supply and demand. Excess demand would indicate a ceiling too low, whereas excess supply would suggest a floor too high. Multilateral contracts also tend to furnish only limited market stability given the relative ease of withdrawal and entry by participating members.

Does the Fair Trade Movement Help Poor Coffee Farmers?

We have seen that low commodity prices are troublesome for producers in developing nations. Can consumers of commodities be of assistance to producers? Consider the case of coffee produced in Nicaragua.

Nicaraguan coffee farmer Santiago Rivera has traveled far beyond his mountain home to publicize what is known as the fair trade coffee movement. Have you heard of fair trade coffee? You soon may. Started in Europe in the early 1990s, the objective of the fair trade coffee movement is to increase the income of poor farmers in developing nations by implementing a system where the farmers can sell their beans directly to roasters and retailers, bypassing the traditional practice of selling to middlemen in their own nations.

This arrangement permits farmers, who farm mainly in the mountainous regions of Latin America and other tropical regions where high flavor, high priced beans sold to gourmet stores are grown, to earn as much as $1.26 per pound for their beans, compared with the $0.40 per pound they were getting from middlemen.

Under the fair trade system, farmers organize in cooperatives of as many as 2,500 members that set prices and arrange for export directly to brokerage firms and other distributors. Middlemen—known as "coyotes" in Nicaragua—previously handled this role. So far, 500,000 of the developing world's 4 million coffee farmers have joined the fair trade movement. The movement has led to incidents of violence in some places in Latin America, mostly involving the middlemen who are being bypassed.

The fair trade coffee movement is the latest example of how social activists are using free market economics to foster social change. Organizers of the movement say they have signed up eight gourmet roasters and about 120 stores, including big chains like Safeway, Inc. Fair trade coffee carries a logo identifying it as such.

Fair trade achieved great success in Europe, where fair trade coffee sells in 35,000 stores and has sales of $250 million a year. In some nations like the Netherlands and Switzerland, fair trade coffee accounts for as much as five percent of total coffee sales. Based on those achievements, organizers in Europe are expanding their fair trade efforts to include other commodity items, including sugar, tea, chocolate, and bananas. Fair-trade activists admit that selling Americans on the idea of buying coffee with a social theme will be more challenging than it was in Europe. Americans, they note, tend to be less aware of social problems in the developing world than Europeans. The fair trade movement has yet to get the support of major U.S. coffee houses such as Maxwell and Folgers. Nevertheless, organizers are trying to nudge Seattle's two coffee giants, Starbuck's Coffee Co. and the Seattle Coffee Co., into agreeing to purchase some of the fair trade coffee. However, critics question the extent to which "fair traded" coffee actually helps. They note that the biggest winners are not the farmers, but rather the retailers that sometimes charge huge markups on fair traded coffee while promoting themselves as corporate citizens. They can get away with it because consumers generally are given little or no information about how much of a product's price goes to farmers.

THE OPEC OIL CARTEL

Although many developing nations have not seen significant improvements in their economies in recent decades, some have realized notable gains: once such group is those developing nations endowed with oil reserves. Instead of just forming agreements to stabilize prices and revenues, oil exporting nations have formed cartels intended to increase price and thus realize "monopoly" profits. The most successful cartel in recent history is the Organization of Petroleum Exporting Countries.

The **Organization of Petroleum Exporting Countries (OPEC)** is a group of nations that sells petroleum on the world market. The OPEC nations attempt to support prices higher than would exist under more competitive conditions to maximize member-nation profits. After operating in obscurity throughout the 1960s, OPEC was able to capture control of petroleum pricing in 1973 and 1974, when the price of oil rose from approximately $3 to $12 per barrel. Triggered by the Iranian revolution in 1979, oil prices doubled from early 1979 to early 1980. By 1981, the price of oil averaged almost $36 per barrel. The market power of OPEC stemmed from a strong and inelastic demand for oil combined with its control of about half of world oil production and two-thirds of world oil reserves. Largely because of world recession and falling demand, oil prices fell to $11 per barrel in 1986, only to rebound thereafter.

Prior to OPEC, oil producing nations behaved like individual competitive sellers. Each nation by itself was so unimportant relative to the overall market that changes in its export levels did not significantly affect international prices over a sustained period of time. By agreeing to restrict competition among themselves via production quotas, the oil exporting nations found that they could exercise considerable control over world oil prices, as seen in the price hikes of the 1970s.

Maximizing Cartel Profits

A **cartel** attempts to support prices higher than they would be under more competitive conditions, thus increasing the profits of its members. Let us consider some of the difficulties encountered by a cartel in its quest for increased profits.

Assume that there are ten suppliers of oil of equal size, in the world oil market and that oil is a standardized product. As a result of previous price wars, each supplier charges a price equal to minimum average cost. Suppliers are afraid to raise their price because they fear that the others will not do so and all of their sales will be lost.

Rather than engage in cutthroat price competition, suppose these suppliers decide to collude and form a cartel. How will a cartel go about maximizing the collective profits of its members? The answer is by behaving like a profit maximizing monopolist: restrict output and drive up price.

Figure 7.3 illustrates the demand and cost conditions of the 10 oil suppliers as a group. Figure 7.3(a) and the group's average supplier. Figure 7.3(b). Before the cartel is organized, the market price of oil under competition is $20 per barrel. Because each supplier is able to achieve a price that just covers its minimum average cost, economic profit equals zero. Each supplier in the market produces 150 barrels per day. Total industry output equals 1,500 barrels per day ($150 \times 10 = 1500$).

Suppose the oil suppliers form a cartel in which the main objective is to maximize the collective profits of its members. To accomplish this objective, the cartel must first establish the profit maximizing level of output; this output is where marginal revenue equals marginal cost. The cartel then divides the cartel output among its members by setting up production quotas for each supplier.

In Figure 7.3(a), the cartel will maximize group profits by restricting output from 1,500 barrels per day to 1,000 barrels per day. This means that each member of the cartel must decrease its output from 150 barrels to 100 barrels per day, as shown in Figure 7.3(b). This production quota results in a rise in the market price of a barrel of oil from $20 to $30. Each member realizes a profit of $8 per barrel ($30 − $22 = $8) and a total profit of $800 on the 100 barrels of oil produced (area a).

The next step is to ensure that no cartel member sells more than its quota. This is a difficult task, because each supplier has the incentive to sell more than its assigned quota

FIGURE 7.3

Maximizing OPEC Profits

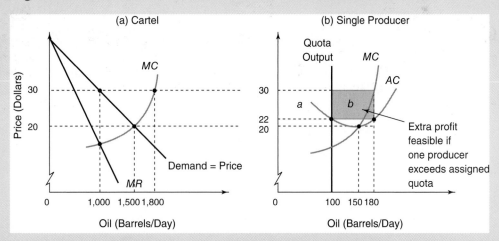

As a cartel, OPEC can increase the price of oil from $20 to $30 per barrel by assigning production quotas to its members. The quotas decrease output from 1,500 to 1,000 barrels per day and permit producers that were pricing oil at average cost to realize a profit. Each producer has the incentive to increase output beyond its assigned quota, to the point at which the OPEC price equals marginal cost. But if all producers increase output in this manner, there will be a surplus of oil at the cartel price, forcing the price of oil back to $20 per barrel.

at the cartel price. But if all cartel members sell more than their quotas, the cartel price will fall toward the competitive level and profits will vanish. Cartels thus attempt to establish penalties for sellers that cheat on their assigned quotas.

In Figure 7.3(*b*), each cartel member realizes economic profits of $800 by selling at the assigned quota of 100 barrels per day. However, an *individual* supplier knows that it can increase its profits if it sells more than this amount at the cartel price. Each individual supplier has the incentive to increase output to the level at which the cartel price, $30, equals the supplier's marginal cost; this occurs at 180 barrels per day. At this output level, the supplier would realize economic profits of $1,440, represented by area $a + b$. By cheating on its agreed upon production quota, the supplier is able to realize an increase in profits of $640 ($1,440 − $800 = $640), denoted by area *b*. Note that this increase in profits occurs if the price of oil does not decrease as the supplier expands output; that is, if the supplier's extra output is a negligible portion of the industry supply.

A single supplier may be able to get away with producing more than its quota without significantly decreasing the market price of oil. But if each member of the cartel increases its output to 180 barrels per day to earn more profits, total output will be 1,800 barrels ($180 \times 10 = 1,800$). To maintain the price at $30, however, industry output must be held to only 1,000 barrels per day. The excess output of 800 barrels puts downward pressure on price that causes economic profits to decline. If economic profits fall back to zero (the competitive level), the cartel will likely break up. Besides the problem of cheating, several other obstacles arise in forming a cartel:

Number of Sellers   Generally speaking, the larger the number of sellers, the more difficult it is to form a cartel. Coordination of price and output policies among three sellers that dominate the market is more easily achieved than when there are ten sellers each having ten percent of the market.

Cost and Demand Differences   When cartel members' costs and product demands differ, it is more difficult to agree on price. Such differences result in a dissimilar profit maximizing price for each member, so there is no single price that can be agreed upon by all members.

Potential Competition   The potential increased profits under a cartel may attract new competitors. Their entry into the market triggers an increase in product supply that leads to falling prices and profits. A successful cartel thus depends on its ability to block the market entry of new competitors.

Economic Downturn   Economic downturn is generally problematic for cartels. As market sales dwindle in a weakening economy, profits fall. Cartel members may conclude that they can escape serious decreases in profits by reducing prices, in expectation of gaining sales at the expense of other cartel members.

Substitute Goods   The price making ability of a cartel is weakened when buyers can substitute other goods (coal and natural gas) for the good that it produces (oil).

OPEC as a Cartel

OPEC has generally disavowed the term *cartel*. However, its organization is composed of a secretariat, conference of ministers, board of governors, and an economic commission. OPEC has repeatedly attempted to formulate plans for systematic production control among its members as a way of firming up oil prices. However, OPEC hardly controls prices. The group currently controls less than 40 percent of world supply, an insufficient amount to establish an effective cartel. OPEC's production agreements have not always lived up to expectations because too many member nations have violated the agreements by producing more than their assigned quotas. Since 1983, when production quotas were first assigned to members, OPEC's actual production levels have almost always been greater than its target levels, meaning that countries have been selling more oil than their authorized amounts. OPEC does not have any club with which to enforce its edicts.

The exception is Saudi Arabia, owner of the world's largest reserves and lowest production costs. The Saudis spend immense capital to maintain more production capacity than they use, allowing them to influence, or threaten to influence prices over the short run.

To offset the market power of OPEC, the United States and other importing nations might initiate policies to increase the supply and/or decrease demand. Achieving these measures involves difficult choices for Americans, such as the following:

- *Raising the fuel economy standards mandated by the federal government.* Analysts estimated that if the gas mileage of new cars had increased by only one mile per gallon each year since 1987, and the mileage of light trucks by a half-mile per gallon, the United States would be saving 1.3 million barrels of oil each day. Increasing fuel economy standards would meet resistance from auto producers who would see their production costs increasing because of this policy.
- *Increasing the federal excise tax on gasoline.* Although the resulting hike in the price of gasoline would provide an incentive for consumers to conserve, this would conflict with the preference of Americans for low priced gasoline. Rising gasoline prices would especially harm low income consumers with the least ability to pay.
- *Allowing oil companies to drill on federal land designated as wilderness in Alaska, where there is a good chance that oil might be found.* Perhaps, but what happens when the wilderness is destroyed, never to return? Who pays for that?
- *Diversifying imports.* Although it could be expensive, the United States might forge closer ties with oil producers outside the Middle East to diminish dependence on this unstable region. This would require the United States to work even more closely with unsavory regimes in nations like Angola, Indonesia, and Vietnam. OPEC oil is cheap to extract from the ground. While it costs deepwater drillers like ExxonMobil or Conoco $6 to $8 to produce a barrel in the Gulf of Mexico or the North Sea, the Saudis and Kuwaitis spend a fraction of that—$1 a barrel or less. This cost advantage enhances OPEC's market power.
- *Developing alternate sources of energy such as biofuels and wind power.* Perhaps. But these tend to require governmental subsidies financed by taxpayers.

In spite of the difficulty of achieving the above measures, change has come about. The rise of OPEC in the 1970s inspired the United States and other countries to produce more energy, including oil. Today we see modern wind and solar industries, nuclear power and coal as sources of electric power, the development of new technologies to produce natural gas, and so on. In particular, U.S. crude oil production has dramatically risen as hydraulic fracturing and other technologies have unlocked large resources of oil previously trapped in shale rock in North Dakota and Texas. Shale deposits in other areas, such as Pennsylvania, are yielding mostly natural gas. World oil production is about 50 percent greater than the early 1970s, as oil production has expanded in the Gulf of Mexico, Canada, and other countries. As a result, OPEC no longer calls the shots in the world oil market as it did years ago.

TRADE CONFLICTS DOES FOREIGN DIRECT INVESTMENT HINDER OR HELP ECONOMIC DEVELOPMENT?

One of the requirements for economic development in a low income economy is an increase in the nation's stock of capital. A developing nation may increase the amount of capital in the domestic economy by encouraging foreign direct investment. Foreign direct investment occurs when foreign firms either locate production plants in the domestic economy or acquire a substantial ownership position in a domestic firm. This topic will be discussed further in Chapter 9.

Many developing economies have attempted to restrict foreign direct investment because of nationalist sentiment and concerns about foreign economic and political influence. One reason for this sentiment is that many developing nations have operated as colonies of more developed economies. This colonial experience has often resulted in a legacy of concern that foreign direct investment may serve as a modern form of economic colonialism that foreign companies might exploit the resources of the host nation.

In recent years, restrictions on foreign direct investment in many developing economies have been substantially reduced as a result of international treaties, external pressure from the IMF or World Bank, or unilateral actions by governments that have come to believe that foreign direct investment will encourage economic growth in the host nation. This has resulted in a rather dramatic expansion in the level of foreign direct investment in some developing economies.

Foreign direct investment may encourage economic growth in the short run by increasing aggregate demand in the host economy. In the long run, the increase in the stock of capital raises the productivity of labor, leads to higher incomes, and further increases aggregate demand. However, another long run impact comes through the transfer of technological knowledge from advanced to developing economies. Many economists argue that this transfer of technology may be the primary benefit of foreign direct investment.

It is often argued that it is necessary to restrict foreign direct investment in a given industry for national security purposes. This reasoning serves as a justification for prohibitions on investment in defense industries and in other industries that are deemed essential for national security. Most governments would be concerned if their weapons were produced by companies owned by firms in nations that might serve as future enemies.

Environmentalists are concerned that the growth of foreign direct investment in developing economies may lead to a deterioration in the global environment since investment is expanding more rapidly in nations that have relatively lax environmental standards. The absence of restrictive environmental standards is one of the reasons for the relatively high rate of return on capital investment in less developed economies. Technology transfer from the developed economies may also result in the adoption of more efficient and environmentally sound production techniques than would have been adopted in the absence of foreign investment.

Source: John Kane, *Does Foreign Direct Investment Hinder or Help Economic Development?* South-Western Policy Debate, 2004.

AIDING THE DEVELOPING NATIONS

We have learned that the oil exporting nations are a special group of developing nations that have realized substantial wealth in recent decades. Most developing nations are not in this favorable situation. Dissatisfied with their economic performance and convinced that many of their problems are because of the shortcomings of the existing international trading system, developing nations have pressed collective demands on the advanced nations for institutions and policies that improve the climate for economic development. Among the institutions and policies that have been created to support developing nations are the World Bank, the International Monetary Fund, and the generalized system of preferences.

The World Bank

During the 1940s, two international institutions were established to ease the transition from wartime to a peacetime environment and help prevent a recurrence of the turbulent economic conditions of the Great Depression era. The World Bank and the International Monetary Fund were established at the United Nations Monetary and Financial Conference held at Bretton Woods, New Hampshire in July 1944. Developing nations view these institutions as sources of funds to promote economic development and financial stability.

The **World Bank** is an international organization that provides loans to developing nations aimed toward poverty reduction and economic development. It lends money to member governments and their agencies and to private firms in the member nations. The World Bank is not a "bank" in the common sense. It is one of the UN's specialized agencies made up of 188 member nations. These nations are jointly responsible for how the institution is financed and how its money is spent.

The "World Bank Group" is the name that has come to be used for five closely associated institutions. The International Bank for Reconstruction and Development and the International Development Association provide low-cost loans and grants to developing nations. The International Finance Corporation provides equity, long-term loans, loan guarantees, and advisory services to developing nations that would otherwise have limited access to capital. The Multilateral Investment Guarantee Agency encourages foreign investment in developing nations by providing guarantees to foreign investors against losses caused by war, civil disturbance, and the like. In addition, the International Center for Settlement of Investment Disputes encourages foreign investment by providing international facilities for conciliation and arbitration of investment disputes, thus helping foster an atmosphere of mutual confidence between developing nations and foreign investors.

The World Bank provides both loans and grants to developing members that cannot obtain money from other sources at reasonable terms. These funds are for specific development projects such as hospitals, schools, highways, and dams. The World Bank is involved in projects as diverse as raising AIDS awareness in Guinea, supporting education of girls in Bangladesh, improving health care delivery in Mexico, and helping India rebuild after a devastating earthquake. The World Bank provides low interest rate loans, and in some cases interest free loans to developing nations that have little or no capacity to borrow on market terms.

In recent years, the World Bank has financed debt refinancing activities of some of the heavily indebted developing nations. The bank encourages private investment in developing nations, as shown in Table 7.4. It receives its funds from contributions of wealthy developed nations. Some 10,000 development professionals from nearly every country in the world work in the World Bank's Washington, DC, headquarters or in its 109 country offices. They provide many technical assistance services for members.

When attempting to help developing nations fight malaria and build dams and schools, the World Bank must also deal with the problem of fraud and corruption: Corrupt government officials and contractors sometimes divert development dollars into their pockets rather than allowing them to benefit the masses of the poor. Because money is fungible, it is difficult for the World Bank to trace the disbursed funds to identify the source of corruption. Thus, poor nations lose huge amounts of funds from the World Bank because of the misuse of money, yet their taxpayers still have to repay the World Bank. According to critics, between 5 and 25 percent of the funds the World Bank has lent since 1946 have been misused. This misuse has resulted in millions of

TABLE 7.4

World Bank Lending by Sector, 2011 (Millions of dollars)

Developing Nation Sector	$ millions
Agriculture, Fishing, and Forestry	2,128
Education	1,733
Energy and Mining	5,807
Finance	897
Health and Social Services	6,707
Industry and Trade	2,167
Information and Communication	640
Law and Justice	9,673
Transportation	8,638
Water, Sanitation, and Flood Protection	4,617
	43,007

Source: From the World Bank, "World Bank Lending by Theme and Sector," *Annual Report 2012*, available at http://www.worldbank.org/.

poverty stricken people losing opportunities to improve their health, education, and economic condition. For two decades, the World Bank has poured money into poor nations clearly unable to repay. It remains to be seen if the World Bank can adopt safeguards that would ensure the funds entrusted to it are used productively for their intended purpose.

As globalization transforms the world economy, the World Bank's role is diminishing. There are new competitors that channel funds to developing nations. Sovereign wealth funds from Singapore to Abu Dhabi are searching for profit in remote places. Nations such as China, Brazil, India, and Russia are funding infrastructure and industry for even the poorest nations, to lock in access to raw materials and export markets.

International Monetary Fund

Another source of aid to developing nations (as well as advanced nations) is the **International Monetary Fund (IMF)** that is headquartered in Washington, DC. Consisting of 188 nations, the IMF can be thought of as a bank for the central banks of member nations. Over a given time period, some nations will face balance-of-payments surpluses, and others will face deficits. A nation with a deficit initially draws on its stock of foreign currencies, such as the dollar, that are accepted in payment by other nations. The deficit nation will sometimes have insufficient amounts of currency. That is when other nations, via the IMF, can provide assistance. By making available currencies to the IMF, the surplus nations channel funds to nations with temporary deficits. Over the long run, deficits must be corrected and the IMF attempts to ensure that this adjustment will be as prompt and orderly as possible.

IMF funds come from two major sources: quotas and loans. Quotas (or subscriptions), that are pooled funds of member nations, generate most IMF funds. The size of a member's quota depends on its economic and financial importance in the world; nations with larger economic importance have larger quotas. The quotas are increased periodically as a means of boosting the IMF's resources. The IMF also obtains funds through loans from member nations. The IMF has lines of credit with major advanced nations as well as with Saudi Arabia.

All IMF loans are subject to some degree of *conditionality*. This attachment means that to obtain a loan, a deficit nation must agree to implement economic and financial policies as stipulated by the IMF. These policies are intended to correct the member's balance-of-payments deficit and promote noninflationary economic growth. The conditionality attachment to IMF lending has often met strong resistance from deficit nations. The IMF has sometimes demanded that deficit nations undergo austerity programs including severe reductions in public spending, private consumption, and imports in order to live within their means.

Critics of the IMF note that its bailouts may contribute to the so called *moral hazard* problem, whereby nations realize the benefits of their decisions when things go well but are protected when things go poorly. If nations do not suffer the costs of bad decisions, won't they be encouraged to make other bad decisions in the future? A second area of concern is the contractionary effect of the IMF's restrictive monetary and fiscal policy conditions. Won't such conditions cause business and bank failures, induce a deeper recession, and limit government spending to help the poor? Many analysts feel the answer is yes.

Generalized System of Preferences

Given inadequate access to markets of advanced nations, developing nations have pressed them to reduce their tariff walls. To help developing nations strengthen their international competitiveness and expand their industrial base, many advanced nations have extended nonreciprocal tariff preferences to exports of developing nations. Under this **generalized system of preferences (GSP)**, major advanced nations temporarily reduce tariffs on designated manufactured imports from developing nations below the levels applied to imports from other advanced nations. The GSP is not a uniform system because it consists of many individual schemes that differ in the types of products covered and the extent of tariff reduction. The GSP attempts to promote economic development in developing nations through increased trade rather than foreign aid.

Trade preferences granted by advanced nations are voluntary. They are not WTO obligations. Donor nations determine eligibility criteria, product coverage, the size of preference margins, and the duration of the preference. In practice, advanced country governments rarely grant deep preferences in sectors where developing nations have a large export potential. Thus, developing nations often obtain only limited preferences in sectors where they have a comparative advantage. The main reason for limited preferences is that in some sectors there is strong domestic opposition to liberalization in advanced nations.

Since its origin in 1976, the U.S. GSP program has extended duty free treatment to about 3,000 items. Criteria for eligibility include not aiding international terrorists and complying with international environmental, labor, and intellectual property laws. The U.S. program grants complete tariff free and quota free access to eligible products from eligible nations. Beneficiaries of the U.S. program include 130 developing nations and their dependent territories. Like the GSP programs of other advanced nations, the U.S. program excludes certain import sensitive products from preferential tariff treatment. Textiles and apparel, footwear, and some agricultural products are not eligible for the GSP. Also, a country's GSP eligibility for a given product may be removed if annual exports of that product reach $100 million or if there is significant damage to domestic industry. From time to time, as GSP participants have grown wealthier, they have been "graduated" out of the program. Among the alumni are Hong Kong, Singapore, Malaysia, Taiwan, and Singapore.

Although the GSP program provides preferential access to advanced nations' markets, several factors erode its effectiveness in reducing trade barriers faced by poor nations.

First, preferences mainly apply to products that already face relatively low tariffs. Second, tariff preferences can also be eroded by nontariff measures, such as anti-dumping duties and safeguards. Products and nations have been removed from GSP eligibility because of lobbying by domestic interest groups in importing nations. Preferences do little to assist the majority of the world's poor. Most of those living on less than $1 per day live in nations like India and Pakistan that receive limited preferences in products in which they have a comparative advantage. As a result, developing nations have been frustrated about limited access to the markets of advanced nations.

Does Aid Promote Growth of Developing Nations?

Does aid promote growth of the developing nations? Debates about the effectiveness of aid go back decades. Critics maintain that aid has fostered government bureaucracies, prolonged bad governments, favored the wealthy in poor nations, or just been squandered. They note widespread poverty in South Asia and Africa despite four decades of aid, and point out nations that have received sizable aid have had miserable records—such as Haiti, the Democratic Republic of the Congo, Somalia, and Papua New Guinea. In their view, aid programs should be substantially altered, drastically cut, or eliminated altogether.

Proponents counter that these contentions, while partially true, are overstated. They indicate that although aid has sometimes been ineffective, it has enhanced poverty reduction and growth in some nations and prevented worse performance in others. Many of the shortcomings of aid have more to do with donors than beneficiaries, especially since much aid is doled out to political allies instead of promoting development. They cite a number of successful nations that have received significant aid such as South Korea, Indonesia, Botswana, Mozambique, and Tanzania. In the 40 years since aid became widespread, they note that poverty indicators have declined in many nations and health and education indicators have increased faster than during any other 40-year period in human history.

Researchers at the Center for Global Development in Washington, DC have attempted to resolve this debate by distinguishing between types of aid granted to developing nations. Aid for the development of infrastructure—such as transportation systems, communications, energy generation, and banking services—is considered to have relatively strong effects on economic growth, and is designated as *growth oriented aid*. However, aid for disaster and humanitarian relief, food supply, water sanitation, and the like tend to have less immediate effects on economic growth. Each $1 in growth oriented aid over a four year period was found to yield $1.64 in increased income in the average recipient country, amounting to an annual rate of return of about 13 percent. The researchers concluded that there is a positive, causal relation between growth oriented aid and growth on average, although not in every country. Aid flows aimed at growth have produced results.[5]

How to Bring Developing Nations in from the Cold

Nobel Prize winning economist Joseph Stiglitz has been an outspoken critic of the World Bank and the International Monetary Fund since resigning from his position as chief economist at the World Bank in 1999. These organizations generally view trade liberalization and market economies as sources of economic growth. Stiglitz contends that

---

[5]Steven Radelet, Michael Clemens, and Rikhil Bhavnani, "Aid and Growth," *Finance and Development*, September 2005, pp. 16–20.

developing nations that have opened themselves to trade, deregulated their financial markets, and abruptly privatized national enterprise have too often experienced more economic and social disruption than growth. Pressing these nations to liberalize their economies may result in failure. Let us consider excerpts from a speech that Stiglitz gave on this topic.[6]

I am delighted that Mr. Michael Moore, the Director General of the World Trade Organization, has called on members to provide more help to developing nations. I want to reinforce Mr. Moore's call. I will argue that basic notions of equity and a sense of fair play require that the next round of trade negotiations be more balanced— that is, more reflective of the interests and concerns of the developing world—than has been the case in earlier rounds.

The stakes are high. There is a growing gap between the developed and the less developed nations. The international community is doing too little to narrow this gap. Even as the ability of developing nations to use aid effectively has increased, the level of development assistance has diminished, with aid per capita to the developing world falling by nearly a third in the 1990s. Too often, the cuts in aid budgets have been accompanied by the slogan of "Trade, not aid," together with exhortations for the developing world to participate fully in the global marketplace. Developing nations have been lectured about how government subsidies and protectionism distort prices and impede growth. But all too often there is a hollow ring to these exhortations. As developing nations do take steps to open their economies and expand their exports, in too many sectors they find themselves confronting significant trade barriers—leaving them, in effect, with neither aid nor trade. They quickly run up against dumping duties, when no economist would say they are really engaged in dumping, or they face protected or restricted markets in their areas of natural comparative advantage, like agriculture or textiles.

In these circumstances, it is not surprising that critics of liberalization within the developing world quickly raise cries of hypocrisy. Developing nations often face great pressure to liberalize quickly. When they raise concerns about job loss, they receive the doctrinaire reply that markets create jobs, and that the resources released from the protected sector can be redeployed productively elsewhere. But all too often, the jobs do not appear quickly enough for those who have been displaced; and all too often, the displaced workers have no resources to buffer themselves, nor is there a public safety net to catch them as they fall.

What are developing nations to make of the rhetoric in favor of rapid liberalization, when rich nations—nations with full employment and strong safety nets—argue that they need to impose protective measures to help those adversely affected by trade? Or when rich nations play down the political pressures within developing nations—insisting that they must "face up to the hard choices"—but at the same time excuse their own trade barriers and agricultural subsidies by citing "political pressures"?

Let me be clear: there is no doubt in my mind that trade liberalization will be of benefit to the developing nations, and to the world more generally. But trade liberalization must be balanced, and it must reflect the concerns of the developing world. It must be balanced in agenda, process, and outcomes. It must take in not only those sectors in which developed nations have a comparative advantage, like financial services, but also those in which developing nations have a special interest, like agriculture and construction services. Trade liberalization must take into account the marked disadvantage that developing nations have in participating meaningfully in negotiations.

---

[6]Excerpts from Joseph Stiglitz, "Two Principles for the Next Round, or, How to Bring Developing Countries in from the Cold," The World Bank, Washington, DC, September 21, 1999. See also Joseph Stiglitz, *Globalization and Its Discontents*, (New York: W. W. Norton, 2002).

Moreover, we must recognize the differences in circumstances between developed and developing nations. We know that developing nations face greater volatility, that opening to trade in fact contributes to that volatility, that developing nations have weak or non-existent safety nets, and that high unemployment is a persistent problem in many if not most developing nations. Simply put, the developed and less developed nations play on a playing field that is not level.

Standard economic analysis argues that trade liberalization, even unilateral opening of markets, benefits a country. In this view, job loss in one sector will be offset by job creation in another, and the new jobs will be higher-productivity than the old. It is this movement from low- to high-productivity jobs that represents the gain from the national perspective, and explains why, in principle, everyone can be made better off as a result of trade liberalization. This economic logic requires markets to be working well, however, and in many nations, underdevelopment is an inherent reflection of poorly functioning markets. Thus, new jobs are not created, or not created automatically. Moving workers from a low-productivity sector to unemployment does not increase output. A variety of factors contribute to the failure of jobs to be created, from government regulations, to rigidities in labor markets, to lack of access of capital.

Concerning future rounds of trade negotiations, adherence to the principles of fairness and comprehensiveness could hold open the promise of a more liberal and more equitable trading regime. While participants in previous rounds have often paid lip service to these principles, they have been honored mostly in the breach. Future adherence to these principles is absolutely essential for the success of the next round, and in particular if the developing nations are to become full partners in the process of trade liberalization.

ECONOMIC GROWTH STRATEGIES: IMPORT SUBSTITUTION VERSUS EXPORT LED GROWTH

Besides seeking economic assistance from advanced nations, developing nations have pursued two competing strategies for industrialization: an inward looking strategy (import substitution) in which industries are established largely to supply the domestic market, and foreign trade is assigned negligible importance; and an outward looking strategy (export led growth) of encouraging the development of industries in which the country enjoys comparative advantage, with heavy reliance on foreign nations as purchasers of the increased production of exportable goods.

Import Substitution

During the 1950s and 1960s, the industrialization strategy of **import substitution** became popular in developing nations such as Argentina, Brazil, and Mexico; some nations still use it today. Import substitution involves extensive use of trade barriers to protect domestic industries from import competition. The strategy is inward oriented in that trade and industrial incentives favor production for the domestic market over the export market. If fertilizer imports occur, import substitution calls for establishment of a domestic fertilizer industry to produce replacements for fertilizer imports. In the extreme, import substitution policies could lead to complete self sufficiency.

The rationale for import substitution arises from the developing nations' perspective on trade. Many developing nations feel that they cannot export manufactured goods because they cannot compete with established firms of the advanced nations, especially in view of the high trade barriers maintained by advanced nations. Given the need for economic growth and development, developing nations have no choice but to manufacture for themselves some of the goods they now import. The use of trade restrictions block imports and the domestic market is reserved for domestic manufacturers. This rationale is often combined with the infant-industry argument: protecting start up industries will allow them to grow to a size where they can compete with the industries of advanced nations.

In one respect, import substitution appears logical: If a good is demanded and imported, why not produce it domestically? The economist's answer is that it may be more costly to produce it domestically and cheaper to import it; comparative advantage should decide which goods are imported and which are exported.

Encouraging economic development via import substitution has several advantages as follows:

- The risks of establishing a home industry to replace imports are low because the home market for the manufactured good already exists.
- It is easier for a developing nation to protect its manufacturers against foreign competitors than to force advanced nations to reduce their trade restrictions on products exported by developing nations.
- To avoid the import tariff walls of the developing country, foreigners have an incentive to locate manufacturing plants in the country, providing jobs for local workers.

In contrast to these advantages, there are several disadvantages as follows:

- Because trade restrictions shelter domestic industries from international competition, they have no incentive to increase their efficiency.
- Given the small size of the domestic market in many developing nations, manufacturers cannot take advantage of economies of scale and thus have high unit costs.
- Because the resources employed in the protected industry would otherwise have been employed elsewhere; protection of import-competing producers automatically discriminates against all other industries, including potential exporting ones.
- Once investment is sunk in activities that were profitable only because of tariffs and quotas, any attempt to remove those restrictions is generally strongly resisted.
- Import substitution also breeds corruption. The more protected the economy, the greater the gains to be had from illicit activity such as smuggling.

During the 1970s, criticisms of import substitution industrialization became increasingly common. Empirical studies appeared to suggest that developing countries that adopted freer trade policies tended to grow faster than those that adopted protectionist policies. Therefore, many developing countries removed quotas and decreased tariffs by the mid 1980s.

Import Substitution Laws Backfire on Brazil

Although import substitution laws have been used by developing nations in their industrialization efforts, they sometimes backfire. Let us consider the example of Brazil.

In 1991, Enrico Misasi was the president of the Brazilian unit of Italian computer maker Olivetti Inc., but he did not have an Olivetti computer. The computer on his desk was instead manufactured by two Brazilian firms; it cost three times more than an Olivetti and its quality was inferior. Rather than manufacturing computers in Brazil, Olivetti, Inc. was permitted to manufacture only typewriters and calculators.

This anomaly was the result of import substitution policies practiced by Brazil until 1991. From the 1970s until 1991, importing a foreign personal computer—or a microchip, a fax, or dozens of other electronic goods—was prohibited. Not only were electronic imports prohibited, but foreign firms willing to invest in Brazilian manufacturing plants were also banned. Joint ventures were deterred by a law that kept foreign partners from owning more than 30 percent of a local business. These restrictions were intended to foster a homegrown electronics industry. Instead, even the law's proponents came to admit that the Brazilian electronics industry was uncompetitive and technologically outdated.

The costs of the import ban were clearly apparent by the early 1990s. Almost no Brazilian automobiles were equipped with electronic fuel injection or antiskid brake systems, both widespread throughout the world. Products such as Apple's Macintosh computer were not permitted to be sold in Brazil. Brazil chose to allow Texas Instruments to shut down its Brazilian semiconductor plant, resulting in a loss of 250 jobs, rather than permit Texas Instruments to invest $133 million to modernize its product line. By adhering to its import substitution policy, Brazil wound up a largely computer unfriendly nation: By 1991, only 12 percent of small- and medium-sized Brazilian companies were at least partially computerized, and only 0.5 percent of Brazil's classrooms were equipped with computers. Many Brazilian companies postponed modernization because computers available overseas were not manufactured in Brazil and could not be imported. Some Brazilian companies resorted to smuggling computers and other electrical equipment; those companies that adhered to the rules wound up with outdated and overpriced equipment.

Realizing that the import substitution policy had backfired on its computer industry, in 1991 the Brazilian government scrapped a cornerstone of its nationalistic approach by lifting the electronics import ban—though continuing to protect domestic industry with high import duties. The government also permitted foreign joint venture partners to raise their ownership shares from 30 to 49 percent and to transfer technology into the Brazilian economy.

Export Led Growth

Another development strategy is **export led growth**, or **export oriented policy**. This strategy is outward oriented because it links the domestic economy to the world economy. Instead of pursuing growth through the protection of domestic industries suffering comparative disadvantage, the strategy involves promoting growth through the export of manufactured goods. Trade controls are either nonexistent or low, in the sense that any disincentives to export resulting from import barriers are counterbalanced by export subsidies. Industrialization is viewed as a natural outcome of development instead of being an objective pursued at the expense of the economy's efficiency. By the mid-1980s, many developing nations were abandoning their import substitution strategies and shifting their emphasis to export led growth.

Export oriented policies have a three advantages: They encourage industries in which developing nations are likely to have a comparative advantage, such as labor-intensive manufactured goods; by providing a larger market in which to sell, they allow domestic manufacturers greater scope for exploiting economies of scale; by maintaining low restrictions on imported goods, they impose a competitive discipline on domestic firms that forces them to increase efficiency.

Economists at the World Bank have investigated the relation between openness to international trade and economic growth for developing nations. They divided a sample of 72 nations into "globalizers" and "nonglobalizers." The globalizers are defined as the 24 nations that achieved the largest increases in their ratio of trade to gross domestic product from 1975 to 1995. During the 1960s and 1970s, the nonglobalizers experienced somewhat faster growth of real income per capita on average than the globalizers. However, during the 1980s, globalizers experienced much higher growth rates; real income per capita grew an average of 3.5 percent a year in these nations, compared with

0.8 percent for the nonglobalizers. These findings support the concept that the economic performance of nations implementing export led growth policies has been superior to that of nations using import substitution policies.[7]

Is Economic Growth Good for the Poor?

Although the evidence strongly suggests that trade is good for growth, is growth good for poor workers in developing nations? Critics argue that growth tends to be bad for the poor if the growth in question has been promoted by trade or foreign investment. Investment inflows, they say, make economies less stable, exposing workers to the risk of financial crisis and to the attentions of advanced nation banks. Moreover, they contend that growth driven by trade provides Western multinational corporations a dominant role in third-world development. That is bad, because Western multinationals are not interested in development at all, only in making larger profits by ensuring that the poor stay poor. The proof of this, say critics, lies in the evidence that economic inequality increases even as developing nations, and advanced nations, increase their national income, and in the multinationals' use of sweatshops when producing goods. So if workers' welfare is your primary concern, the fact that trade promotes growth, even if true, misses the point.

There is strong evidence that growth aids the poor. Developing nations that have achieved continuing growth, as in East Asia, have made significant progress in decreasing poverty. The nations where widespread poverty persists, or is worsening, are those where growth is weakest, notably in Africa. Although economic policy can affect the extent of poverty, in the long run growth is much more important.

There is intense debate over the extent to which the poor benefit from economic growth. Critics argue that the potential benefits of economic growth for the poor are undermined or even offset entirely by sharp increases in inequality that accompany growth. On the other hand, proponents contend that liberal economic policies such as open markets and monetary and fiscal stability raise the incomes of the poor and everyone else in society proportionately.

Suppose it were true that income inequality is increasing between the advanced and developing nations. Would this be a terrible indictment of globalization? Perhaps not. It would be disturbing if inequality throughout the world were increasing because incomes of the poorest were decreasing in absolute terms, instead of in relative terms. However, this is rare. Even in Africa that is behaving poorly in relative terms, incomes have been increasing and broader indicators of development have been improving. Perhaps it is too little, but something is better than nothing.

Can All Developing Nations Achieve Export Led Growth?

Although exporting can promote growth for developing economies, it depends on the willingness and ability of advanced nations to go on absorbing large amounts of goods from developing nations. Pessimists argue that this process involves a fallacy of composition. If all developing nations tried to export simultaneously, the price of their exports would be driven down on world markets. Moreover, advanced nations may become apprehensive of foreign competition, especially during eras of high unemployment, and impose tariffs to reduce competition from imports. Will liberalizing trade be self defeating if too many developing nations try to export simultaneously?

---

[7]David Dollar and Aart Kraay, *Trade, Growth, and Poverty*, World Bank Development Research Group, 2001.

Although developing nations as a group are enormous in terms of geography and population, in economic terms they are small. Taken together, the exports of all the world's poor and middle income nations equal only five percent of world output. This is an amount approximately equivalent to the national output of the United Kingdom. Even if growth in the global demand for imports were somehow capped, a concerted export drive by those parts of the developing world not already engaged in the effort would put no great strain on the global trading system.

Pessimists also tend to underestimate the scope for intra-industry specialization in trade, that gives developing nations a further set of new trade opportunities. The same goes for new trade among developing nations, as opposed to trade with the advanced nations. Often, as developing nations grow, they move away from labor-intensive manufactures to more sophisticated kinds of production. This movement makes room in the markets they previously served for goods from nations that are not yet so advanced. In the 1970s, Japan withdrew from labor-intensive manufacturing, making way for exports from South Korea, Taiwan, and Singapore. In the 1980s and 1990s, South Korea, Taiwan, and Singapore did the same, as China began moving into those markets. As developing nations grow through exporting, their own demand for imports rises.

EAST ASIAN ECONOMIES

In spite of the sluggish economic performance of many developing nations, some have realized sustained economic growth, as shown in Table 7.5. One group of successful developing nations has come from East Asia, such as China and Indonesia. What accounts for their success?

The East Asian nations are highly diverse in natural resources, populations, cultures, and economic policies. They have in common several characteristics underlying their economic success: (1) high rates of investment and (2) high and increasing endowments of human capital because of universal primary and secondary education.

To foster competitiveness, East Asian governments have invested in their people and provided a favorable competitive climate for private enterprise. They have also kept their economies open to international trade. The East Asian economies have actively sought foreign technology, such as licenses, capital goods imports, and foreign training.

TABLE 7.5

East Asian Economies' Growth Rates of GDP per Capita, 2003–2012

Nation	Average Annual Growth Rate of GDP Per Capita
China	9.9%
Indonesia	4.3
Hong Kong, China	3.9
Thailand	3.9
Singapore	3.6
South Korea	3.3
Philippines	3.3
Malaysia	3.2

Source: World Bank, World Data Bank, *World Development Indicators*, available at http://www.data.worldbank.org. See also Central Intelligence Agency, *World Fact Book*, available at www.cia.gov.

The East Asian economies have generally discouraged the organization of trade unions—whether by deliberate suppression (South Korea and Taiwan), by government paternalism (Singapore), or by a laissez-faire policy (Hong Kong). The outcome has been the prevention of minimum wage legislation and the maintenance of free and competitive labor markets.

In the post-World War II era, trade policies in the East Asian economies (except Hong Kong) began with a period of import substitution. To develop their consumer goods industries, these nations levied high tariffs and quantitative restrictions on imported goods. They also subsidized some manufacturing industries such as textiles. Although these policies initially led to increased domestic production, as time passed they inflicted costs on the East Asian economies. Because import substitution policies encouraged the importing of capital and intermediate goods and discouraged the exporting of manufactured goods, they led to large trade deficits for the East Asian economies. To obtain the foreign exchange necessary to finance these deficits, the East Asian economies shifted to a strategy of outward orientation and export promotion.

Export push strategies were enacted in the East Asian economies by the late 1950s and 1960s. Singapore and Hong Kong set up trade regimes that were close to free trade. Japan, South Korea, and Taiwan initiated policies to promote exports while protecting domestic producers from import competition. Indonesia, Malaysia, and Thailand adopted a variety of policies to encourage exports while gradually reducing import restrictions. These measures contributed to an increase in the East Asian economies' share of world exports, with manufactured exports accounting for most of this growth.

The success of the East Asian economies has created problems, however. The industrialize-at-all-costs emphasis has left many of the East Asian economies with major pollution problems. Whopping trade surpluses have triggered a growing wave of protectionist sentiment overseas, especially in the United States that sees the East Asian economies depending heavily on the U.S. market for future export growth.

Flying Geese Pattern of Growth

It is widely recognized that East Asian economies have followed a **flying geese pattern of economic growth** in which nations gradually move up in technological development by following in the pattern of nations ahead of them in the development process. Taiwan and Malaysia take over leadership in apparel and textiles from Japan as Japan moves into the higher technology sectors of automotive, electronic, and other capital goods. A decade or so later, Taiwan and Malaysia are able to upgrade to automotive and electronics products, while the apparel and textile industries move to Thailand, Vietnam, and Indonesia.

To some degree, the flying geese pattern is a result of market forces: Labor abundant nations will become globally competitive in labor-intensive industries, such as footwear, and will graduate to more capital or skill-intensive industries as savings and education deepen the availability of capital and skilled workers. However, as the East Asian economies have demonstrated, more than just markets are necessary for flying geese development. Even basic labor-intensive products, such as electronics assembly, are increasingly determined by multinational enterprises and technologies created in advanced nations.

For East Asian economies, a strong export platform has underlain their flying geese pattern of development. East Asian governments have utilized several versions of an export platform, such as bonded warehouses, free trade zones, joint ventures, and strategic alliances with multinational enterprises. Governments supported these mechanisms with economic policies that aided the incentives for labor-intensive exports.[8]

---

[8]Terutomo Ozawa, *Institutions, Industrial Upgrading, and Economic Performance in Japan: The Flying-Geese Theory of Catch-Up Growth*, Cheltenham, U.K., Edward Elgar, 2005.

TRADE CONFLICTS IS STATE CAPITALISM WINNING?

From the 1980s to 2008, the discussion of the pros and cons of state directed capitalism versus free market capitalism appeared to be resolved. The robust performance of the U.S. economy, under laid by deregulation, globalization, and free trade in conjunction with the breakup of the Soviet Union and China's embracing capitalism affirmed the limitations of state run economies. Free market capitalism was generally viewed to work better.

However, the Great Recession of 2008–2009 reopened the discussion about the role of government in the economy. The severity of this economic downturn exposed the shortcomings of the advanced economies and resulted in many observers wondering whether the market capitalism model had crumbled. In the United States, Democrats wanted an activist government to create jobs and foster new industries, like wind power, to help America compete in the global economy. At the same time, Republicans wanted a smaller government to promote economic revitalization.

Government aid for economic development has tended to involve less controversy for developing countries. Countries such as Brazil, Malaysia, China, and Russia have favored "state capitalism" that integrates the powers of the state with the powers of capitalism. Under this system, governments create state owned businesses to manage the development of factors of production that they deem to be of critical importance to the state and to create large numbers of jobs. Examples of state owned businesses include communications firms in China, oil firms in Malaysia, and natural gas firms in Russia. Governments influence bank lending policies, own essential sectors of the economy, and freely steer the economy through bureaucratic decision making. Although state capitalism is a type of capitalism, it is one in which government behaves as the major economic player. The ability of state capitalistic nations like China, to achieve robust economic growth during the Great Recession, has caused observers to ponder if this economic system can achieve better economic results than the freer market model of the United States.

The importance of state capitalism is notable. In China, the government is the largest shareholder of the country's largest businesses. Also, state companies' account for about 80 percent of the value of the stock market in China, 6 percent in Russia, and 40 percent in Brazil. The 13 largest oil firms that control three-fourths of the world's oil reserves, are all government backed. So is Russia's Gazprom, the world's largest extractor of natural gas.

Although state capitalism is an alternative to market capitalism, it has its limitations. State giants utilize capital and talent that might have been used better by private companies. Also, although state firms have sometimes succeeded in imitating others, partly because they can use the government's influence to obtain access to technology, they often have been less successful in promoting new technological innovations. Finally, state capitalism operates well only when run by competent government officials that sometimes does not occur. This economic system can result in inequality, favoritism, and discontent, as seen in Egypt and Russia.

So who is on the right side, state capitalism or free market capitalism? History shows that every economic miracle eventually loses its luster as youthful exuberance gives way to economic maturity. As countries progress from agriculture and crafts to manufacturing and then to a service and knowledge economy, what rises comes down and levels out. During this evolution, the countryside empties out and no longer provides a seemingly infinite supply of cheap labor. Also, as fixed investment increases, its marginal return decreases, and each additional unit of capital fosters less output than the preceding one. This is one of the oldest principles in economics—the law of diminishing returns. The future success of state capitalism, as a model for economic development, remains an open question.

Source: Josef Joffe, "China's Coming Economic Slowdown," *Wall Street Journal*, October 26, 2013; James McGregor, *No Ancient Wisdom, No Followers: The Challenges of Chinese Authoritarian Capitalism*, Prospectus Press, Westport, CT, 2012; "State Capitalism," *The Economist*, January 21, 2012; Michael Schuman, "State Capitalism Versus the Free Market," *Time Business*, September 30, 2011 at http://business.time.com; and Ian Bremmer, "State Capitalism Comes of Age," *Foreign Affairs*, May–June 2009.

CHINA'S GREAT LEAP FORWARD

China is another East Asian country that has had remarkable economic success in recent years. Let us see why.

In the early 1970s, the People's Republic of China was an insignificant participant in the world market for goods and financial services. By 2005, China had grown to be the world's second largest economy, with a national output over half that of the United States and 60 percent larger than Japan's. What caused this transformation?

Modern China began in 1949, when a revolutionary communist movement captured control of the nation. Soon after the communist takeover, China instituted a Soviet model of central planning and import substitution with emphasis on rapid economic growth, particularly industrial growth. The state took over urban manufacturing, collectivized agriculture, eliminated household farming, and established compulsory production quotas. By discouraging the ability of markets to function, China's government stifled economic growth and left many of its people poor.

By the1970s, China could see its once poor neighbors—Japan, Singapore, Taiwan, and South Korea—enjoying extraordinary growth and prosperity. This led to China's marketizing its economy through small, step-by-step changes to minimize economic disruption and political opposition. In agriculture and industry, reforms were made to increase the role of the producing unit, to increase individual incentives, and to reduce the role of state planners. Many goods were sold for market-determined—not state-controlled—prices. Greater competition was allowed both between new firms and between new firms and state firms. Moreover, China opened its economy to foreign investment and joint ventures. The Chinese government's monopoly over foreign trade was also disbanded; in its place, economic zones were established in which firms could keep foreign exchange earnings and hire and fire workers. China has broken with the path of import substitution, where import barriers are established for the development of domestic industry. China is now remarkably open to international trade and imports play a large role in the Chinese economy.

Although China has dismantled much of its centrally planned economy, political freedoms have lagged behind. Recall the Chinese government's use of military force to end a pro-democracy demonstration in Beijing's Tiananmen Square in 1989 that led to loss of life and demonstrated the Communist Party's determination to maintain its political power. Under Communist Party rule there is no freedom of speech, making independent voices all but inaudible. China's evolution toward capitalism has thus consisted of expanded use of market forces under a communist political system. Today, China describes itself as a *socialist market economy.*

Concerning international trade, China has followed a pattern consistent with the principle of comparative advantage as explained by the factor-endowment theory discussed in Chapter 3. China's exports have emphasized the intensive use of labor, its abundant resource. Therefore, China has become a center of low wage manufacturing and exports sporting goods, toys, electronics, footwear, garments, textiles, and other goods. On the import side, China is a growing market for machinery, transportation equipment, and other capital goods that require higher levels of technologies than China can produce domestically. Most of China's economic expansion since 1978 has been driven by rapid growth in exports that embody labor as the main input and investments in infrastructure.

Challenges for China's Economy

In spite of China's leap forward, it still faces many obstacles if it is to surpass middle level income status and become a rich nation. Let us briefly consider some challenges for the Chinese economy.[9]

Privatization of Industry   No country in the modern world has attained continuing economic growth without significant reliance on private enterprise and decentralized private markets. China's economy still has an abundance of state owned enterprises with excessive employment and low productivity. Although their significance has decreased over time, they still account for about half of nonagricultural output. An example is the state controlled banking sector that makes loans to other large, inefficient, and unprofitable state companies. China's economy is also plagued with a vast array of price controls, restrictions on domestic labor migration, and other impediments to economic reforms necessary for sustained economic development. If China desires to continue to grow rapidly, it will have to decrease the presence of the state owned enterprises and substantially enlarge the private sector in telecommunications, finance, and many other fields.

Rising Labor Costs   A dwindling supply of inexpensive labor provides another challenge for China. China's one-child policy has resulted in youth becoming in short supply and the remainder of the population is aging. Thus China's workforce will start shrinking in a few year's time. Also, migration restrictions hinder workers from moving from farms to coastal cities where factories are located. As wages increase in China as the supply of workers diminishes, then the prices of its exports will rise, absent a proportional increase in labor productivity. The higher prices of exports from China should decrease the incentive of foreign consumers to purchase low end goods from China like textiles and toys. China will have emphasized other sources of growth than an endless supply of cheap labor.

China still has cheap labor in its interior, away from its developed coastal cities. Although moving manufacturing operations inland means lower wages, it also means higher transportation costs on China's crowded highways and railroads. Also, locating factories in China's hinterland places them in a better position to service China's growing domestic consumer market rather than exporting to consumers in the United States and elsewhere.

Faced with increasing wages within China, some companies are shifting production elsewhere to hold costs down. Yue Yuen Industrial Ltd., the world's largest shoe maker, has moved some of its manufacturing of low-cost shoes from China to countries such as Cambodia and Bangladesh. As factories relocate to other countries, local wages will increase faster than they did in China because their labor becomes scarcer. Also, because no other country can duplicate the massive scale of China, logistics will become an increasing portion of costs as companies must divide their manufacturing over several countries. This will make things more costly which means that the West will have to adopt new consumption trends.

Development of Infrastructure   The development of infrastructure remains a major objective of the Chinese government that has long recognized a modern economy operates on reliable telecommunications, rails and roads, and electricity. China's goal is to raise the country's infrastructure to the level of infrastructure of middle income countries while using increasingly efficient transportation systems to link the country together. This will require China to make large additional investments in airports, expressways,

---

[9]"China's Next Chapter," *McKinsey Quarterly, Number 3,* 2013.

port facilities, and rail track. To a large extent, funding for these projects will come from the Chinese government that supplies more than 90 percent of infrastructure financing.

One aspect of China's infrastructure policy concerns long distance trucking that accounts for about three-fourths of domestic freight shipments by volume. However, the trucking industry is fragmented and inefficient, especially in the country's interior regions where manufacturing and consumption are expanding substantially as companies move inland for cheaper labor and land. Although China is building roads in its interior regions at a rapid pace, the task is difficult given formidable terrain. Also, many new highways become congested almost as soon as they are constructed, and long transportation delays are commonplace.

Reliance on Investment Spending   Another challenge for China concerns the over reliance on investment and the under reliance on consumption. Chinese officials know that a rebalancing is needed because the substantial increases in investment that have fueled China's robust economic growth for the past three decades are not sustainable. Also, China's consumers cannot provide additional demand unless wealth is redistributed toward them. Household consumption accounts for only about 38 percent of China's gross domestic product, while it accounts for about 70 percent of the U.S. gross domestic product. Stated differently, consumers are not picking up the Chinese economy's slack as they must if they are to fuel economic growth now that the country's investment oriented model is reaching its limits.

As the Chinese officials acknowledge, the main objective of economic policy adjustment is to shift the country from a production (investment) oriented economy to one emphasizing household consumption. The government might increase the dividend payouts of state owned enterprises in order to increase the incomes and consumption of Chinese households. However, increasing the income of households at the expense of state owned enterprises is politically challenging, as powerful vested interest groups resist change. A rebalancing will significantly decrease the growth of aggregate spending on heavy manufacturing, construction, and other sectors that have historically benefitted from China's huge increase in investment. At the writing of this text, it remains to be seen the extent to which the Chinese government can rebalance its economy.

Environmental Future   Anyone who has traveled to China recently has likely experienced serious air pollution in its major cities. The air quality index in Beijing frequently exceeds a 500 threshold, while any rating above 300 means the air is unsafe to breathe. This means that children in Beijing inhale the equivalent of two packs of cigarettes a day just by breathing. Although manufacturing industries and Beijing's 5 million cars contribute to the city's crippling air pollution, most experts mainly blame the coal-burning electrical plants that power China's economic growth. China now burns almost half of the world's coal, roughly equal to the amount used by all other countries of the world combined, and Beijing is surrounded by a vast array of coal-burning power plants.

With its surging economy, China has depleted its own natural resources and is now draining resources from other countries as well. China's insatiable demand for wood has already deforested much of the country, resulting in land erosion and flooding. By 2020, according to forecasts, 25 percent of China's arable land will be gone and the country's water needs, waste water, and sulfur dioxide emissions will rise dramatically.

Although Chinese officials are aware of the problem, their response has been inadequate largely because the demands of continuing economic growth supersede environmental considerations. In the future, China will need to seize the opportunity to make its industries more environmentally sound and economic growth more sustainable.

Status in Global Finance As the world's largest saver, China has a major role to play in global financial markets. However, as a traditionally closed economy, China cannot open its doors overnight. To become a leading nation in global finance, China's domestic financial markets must deepen and further develop, and returns earned by households, corporations, and the government must increase if the country is to attract and deploy capital more effectively. The barriers that prevent individuals and companies from investing more freely outside of China's borders and the barriers that prevent foreign investors from investing within China will have to decline. China will have to build additional trust of global investors. Continued reform in China, coupled with its vast domestic savings and outsized role in world trade, could make the country an influential supplier of capital in the years ahead.

Convertibility of the Yuan As China's economic and financial influence increase, so will the use of its currency, the *yuan*, also called the *renminbi*. China wishes to make the yuan an international currency that might rival the U.S. dollar and the euro in global markets. Achieving this result will require China to develop deep and liquid capital markets for yuan-denominated financial assets, such as corporate bonds. Also, the yuan needs to become an international medium of exchange for financing transactions. This means that the yuan needs to be fully convertible, whereby an individual or business firm can convert it into foreign currencies for any reason and at any foreign exchange dealer or bank. Indeed, China's pursuit financial globalization will require time and patience.

China's Export Boom Comes at a Cost: How to Make Factories Play Fair

Although China has become a major exporter of manufactured goods it has come at a cost. As retailers such as Walmart and The Home Depot place pressure on Chinese suppliers to produce cheap goods at the lowest possible costs, concerns about product safety, the quality of the environment, and labor protections are brushed aside.

In 2007, Chinese firms were challenged by consumer advocates on the grounds that they were producing unsafe toys, cribs, electronic products, and the like. Mattel, the world's largest toymaker, issued three separate recalls for toys manufactured in China that contained hazardous lead paint and dangerous magnets; Disney recalled thousands of Baby Einstein blocks; smaller companies recalled everything from children's jewelry, key chains and notebooks to water bottles and flashlights. The biggest disappointment to children was the double recall of Thomas the Tank Engine toys when it was discovered that they contained unsafe levels of lead in the paint that can cause brain damage to children. Moreover, the Floating Eyeballs toy was recalled after it was found to be filled with kerosene. Critics maintained that these examples are part of a larger pattern. The U.S. economy has gone global and has outsourced more production to nations like China. At the same time, the U.S. government has cut back import regulation and inspection. As a result, American consumers are exposed to increasing numbers of products that are neither produced in the United States nor subject to American safety standards.

Protecting labor is another problem for China. U.S. retailers such as Eddie Bauer and Target continually demand lower prices from their Chinese suppliers, allowing American consumers to enjoy inexpensive clothes and sneakers. Price pressure creates a powerful incentive for Chinese firms to cheat on labor standards that American companies promote as a badge of responsible capitalism. These standards generally incorporate the official minimum wage of China that is set by local or provincial governments and ranges from $45 to $101 a month. U.S. companies typically say they adhere to the government mandated workweek of 40 to 44 hours, beyond which higher overtime pay is required. The pressure to cut costs has resulted in many Chinese factories ignoring these standards. By falsifying payrolls and time sheets, they have been able to underpay their workers and force them to work excessive hours at factories that often have health and safety problems. Conceding that the current system of auditing Chinese suppliers is failing to stop labor abuses, U.S. retailers are searching for ways to improve China's labor protections. It remains to be seen if these efforts will be successful.

Promoting a safe environment is another problem for China. In the last two decades since U.S. firms began turning to Chinese factories to churn out cheap T-shirts and jeans, China's air, land, and water have paid a heavy price. Environmental activists and the Chinese government note the role that U.S. multinational companies play in China's growing pollution problems by demanding ever lower prices for Chinese products. One way China's factories have historically kept costs down is by dumping waste water directly into rivers. Treating contaminated water costs more than $0.13 a metric ton, so large factories can save hundreds of thousands of dollars a year by sending waste water directly into rivers in violation of China's water pollution laws. The result is that prices in the United States are artificially low because Americans are not paying the costs of pollution. American companies that use Chinese products are subject to much criticism for not taking a hard enough line against polluting suppliers in China.

INDIA: BREAKING OUT OF THE THIRD WORLD

India is another example of an economy that has rapidly improved its economic performance following the adoption of freer trade policies. The economy of India is diverse, encompassing agriculture, handicrafts, manufacturing, and a multitude of services. Although two-thirds of the Indian workforce still earn their livelihood directly or indirectly through agriculture, services are a growing sector of India's economy. The advent of the digital age and the large number of young and educated Indians fluent in English are transforming India as an important destination for global outsourcing of customer services and technical support.

India and China have traveled different paths of development. China has followed the traditional development route of nations like Japan and South Korea, becoming a center for low wage manufacturing of goods. Realizing that it could not go head to head with China in manufacturing, India concluded that it had a better chance in exporting services. Consistent with the Heckscher–Ohlin theory, India's abundant factor has been the relatively well educated, English-speaking labor that provides a low-cost gateway to global services such as data processing operations, call centers, and the like. Although economic growth rates give China's goods-dominated strategy the superior track record so far, India's approach may pay off better over the long run. A look at per capita incomes around the world indicates that the wealth of nations eventually depends more in services than industry.

After gaining independence from Britain in 1947, India began practicing socialism and adopted an import substitution model to run its economy. Both of these resulted from India's fear of imperialism of any kind following its independence. Therefore, India's government initiated protectionist trade barriers and bans on foreign investment to restrict competition, strict regulations over private business and financial markets, a large public sector, and central planning. This resulted in India becoming isolated from the mainstream world from the 1950s to1980s. During this period, India's economy achieved only a modest rate of growth and poverty was widespread. Increasingly, people in India recognized that public sector policy had failed India.

By 1991, policy makers in India realized that their system of state controls and import substitution was strangling the economy and that reforms were needed. The result was a clear switch toward an outward oriented, market based economy. The requirement that government must approve industrial investment expenditures was terminated, quotas on imports were abolished, export subsidies were eliminated, and import tariffs were slashed from an average of 87 percent in 1990 to 33 percent in 1994. Also, Indian companies were allowed to borrow on international markets and the *rupee* was devalued. These reforms helped transform India from an agrarian, underdeveloped, and closed economy into a more open and progressive one that encourages foreign investment and draws more wealth from industry and services. The result has been a dramatic increase in economic growth and falling poverty rates.

India's outsourcing business illustrates how foreign investment and trade have benefitted the nation. The lifting of restrictions on foreign investment resulted in firms such as General Electric and British Airways moving information technology (IT) and other back office operations to India in the 1990s. The success of these companies showed the world that India was a viable destination for outsourcing, and additional companies set up operations in the nation. These multinationals trained thousands of Indian workers, many of whom transferred their skills to other emerging Indian firms. Indian workers benefitted from the thousands of jobs that were created and the rising incomes that resulted from foreign investment.

India's auto industry is another example of the benefits of trade and investment liberalization. Before the 1980s, prohibitions on foreign investment and high import tariffs shielded India's state owned automakers from global competition. These firms used obsolete technology to produce just two models and sold them at high prices. By the 1990s, tariffs were slashed on auto imports and bans on foreign investment were largely phased out. The result was an increase in autos imported into India and also the entry of foreign automakers that established assembly plants in the nation. As competition increased, labor productivity increased more than threefold for Indian auto workers who benefitted from higher wages. Also, auto prices declined, unleashing a surge in consumer demand, a rise in auto sales, and the creation of thousands of auto worker jobs. Today, India's auto industry produces 13 times more cars than it did in the early 1980s, and India exports vehicles to other nations. None of this would have been possible had India's automakers remained isolated from the world.

However, the dynamic growth of India's outsourcing and automobile industries stands in contrast to most of its economy, where restrictions on trade and foreign investment stifle competition and foster the survival of inefficient firms. Food retailing illustrates how Indian industry gets along when foreign investment is prohibited. As of 2007, labor productivity in this industry was only five percent of the U.S. level. Much of this discrepancy is because almost all of India's food retailers are street markets and mom-and-pop counter stores rather than modern supermarkets. Moreover, productivity averages just 20 percent of the U.S. level in Indian supermarkets as a result of their small scale and inefficient merchandising and marketing methods. In other developing nations, such as China and Mexico, global retailers such as Walmart have intensified competition that has increased productivity. However, these retailers have been prohibited from investing in India.

In spite of India's economic gains, the nation cannot afford to rest on its laurels; more than 250 million Indians still live below the official poverty line. Sustaining robust economic growth will require the nation to focus on improving its infrastructure such as roads, electric power generation, rail freight, and ports. India's recent infrastructure investments have not kept pace with economic developments. In contrast, China has invested heavily to build a world class infrastructure that can attract foreign investment and promote economic growth.

India is expected to become the world's most populous nation by 2030. This rate of population growth provides India the major advantage of an almost limitless labor supply and consumer demand. Nevertheless, it also illustrates the necessity of investing in education and health care and creating adequate opportunities for employment.

Most economists contend that India needs to systematically deregulate sectors such as retailing, the news media, and banking that have remained crippled by archaic policies. It also need to eliminate preferences for small scale, inefficient producers and repeal legislation blocking layoffs in medium and large sized firms. With deregulation and the opening of markets, vital foreign investments of capital and skills could flow more readily into India, making its industry more effective and the economy more robust. To ensure that India's economic growth reaches the whole nation, the government needs to reform its agriculture industry in order to generate jobs in rural areas.

India has made great progress, but further efforts will be needed to sustain its economic growth. With a rapidly rising population, India faces the challenge of creating millions of jobs to keep its people out of poverty. It remains to be seen whether India's government, private sector, and society at large will demonstrate the political will needed to work together and make this occur.

BRAZIL TAKES OFF

In 2001, economists at Goldman Sachs lumped Brazil with China, India, and Russia as economies that would come to dominate the world, there was considerable suspicion about Brazil. By 2011that suspicion appeared unfounded: Brazil's economy had grown to become the largest in Latin America and was the world's seventh largest economy.

Economic growth in Brazil has not always been on the upswing. During the 1930s–1960s, Brazil favored the industrialization policy of import substitution, as previously discussed in this chapter. This policy emphasized state directed economic development and it focused on the domestic market to the detriment of exports. A huge bureaucratic apparatus emerged, with the employment of import restrictions and controls over Brazil's exchange rate. Favoritism and corruption became widespread throughout the economy, policymakers turned a blind eye to inflation, and economic growth was sluggish. The government gradually came to realize that market liberalization and increased globalization were necessary if Brazil was to prosper.

In the 1990s, Brazil established a set of policies aimed at promoting economic growth. Inflation was tamed and spendthrift local and federal governments were required by law to rein in their debts. Brazil's central bank was granted autonomy from the government and charged with maintaining low inflation and ensuring that banks refrain from engaging in risky financial policies. Also, the economy was opened to international trade and foreign investment and many state industries were privatized. These and other policies set the stage for Brazil to become a rapidly growing economy in the early 2000s.

With a population of more than 190 million and abundant natural resources, Brazil currently produces tens of millions of tons of steel and cement and millions of refrigerators and television sets. It is also involved in high technology industries such as computers and aircraft. Proven mineral resources are extensive throughout Brazil, such as oil, natural gas, and manganese that generate export earnings. Also, Brazil vies with Australia as the world's largest exporter of iron ore, much of it to China. Brazil is abundant in arable land that has resulted in its becoming a major producer of agricultural products. Brazil's economy currently has two great strengths. It has a population of working age that is growing and an abundance of natural resources.

In some respects, Brazil outclasses other rapidly growing developing countries. Unlike China, it is a democracy. Unlike India, it has no insurgents, no ethnic and religious conflicts, nor hostile neighbors. Unlike Russia, it exports more than oil and military goods, and it treats foreign investors with respect.

In the future, Brazil needs to make transitions if it is to move up the ladder of economic development, including the need to save and invest more in roads, railways, and other types of infrastructures. It also needs to improve its climate for business development.

SUMMARY

1. Developing nations tend to be characterized by relatively low levels of gross domestic product per capita, shorter life expectancies, and lower levels of adult literacy. Many developing nations believe that the current international trading system, based on the principle of comparative advantage, is irrelevant for them.

2. Among the alleged problems facing the developing nations are (a) unstable export markets, (b) worsening terms of trade, and (c) limited market access.

3. Among the institutions and policies that have been created to support developing nations are the World Bank, the International Monetary Fund, and a generalized system of preferences.

4. International commodity agreements have been formed to stabilize the prices and revenues of producers of primary products. The methods used to attain this stability are buffer stocks, export controls, and multilateral contracts. In practice, these methods have yielded modest success.

5. The OPEC oil cartel was established in 1960 in reaction to the control that the major international oil companies exercised over the posted price of oil. OPEC has used production quotas to support prices and earnings above what could be achieved in more competitive conditions.

6. Besides seeking financial assistance from advanced nations, developing nations have promoted internal industrialization through policies of import

substitution and export promotion. Nations emphasizing export promotion have tended to realize higher rates of economic growth than nations emphasizing import substitution policies.

7. The East Asian economies have realized remarkable economic growth in recent decades. The foundation of such growth has included high rates of investment, the increasing endowments of an educated workforce, and the use of export promotion policies.

8. By the 1990s, China had become a high performing Asian economy. Although China has dismantled much of its centrally planned economy and permitted free enterprise to replace it, political freedoms have not increased. Today, China describes itself as a socialist market economy. Being heavily endowed with labor, China specializes in many labor-intensive products. In 2001, China became a member of the WTO.

9. India is another example of an economy that has rapidly improved its economic performance following the adoption of freer trade policies. After becoming independent from Britain in 1947, India began practicing socialism and adopted an import substitution policy to run its economy. By 1991, the policymakers of India realized that their system of state controls and import substitution was not working. Therefore, India adopted a more open economy that encourages foreign investment, and economic growth accelerated.

KEY CONCEPTS AND TERMS

Advanced nations (p. 227)

Buffer stock (p. 237)

Cartel (p. 240)

Developing
    nations (p. 227)

Export controls (p. 237)

Export led growth (p. 252)

Export oriented
    policy (p. 252)

Flying geese pattern of economic
    growth (p. 255)

Generalized system of preferences
    (GSP) (p. 247)

Import substitution (p. 250)

International commodity
    agreements (ICAs) (p. 237)

International Monetary Fund
    (IMF) (p. 246)

Multilateral contract (p. 239)

Organization of Petroleum
    Exporting Countries
    (OPEC) (p. 240)

Primary
    products (p. 227)

Production and export
    controls (p. 237)

World Bank (p. 245)

STUDY QUESTIONS

1. What are the major reasons for the skepticism of many developing nations regarding the comparative-advantage principle and free trade?

2. Stabilizing commodity prices has been a major objective of many primary product nations. What are the major methods used to achieve price stabilization?

3. What are some examples of international commodity agreements? Why have many of them broken down over time?

4. Why are the developing nations concerned with commodity price stabilization?

5. The average person probably had never heard of the Organization of Petroleum Exporting Countries until 1973 or 1974 when oil prices skyrocketed. In fact, OPEC was founded in 1960. Why did OPEC not achieve worldwide prominence until the 1970s? What factors contributed to OPEC's problems in the 1980s?

6. Why is cheating a typical problem for cartels?

7. The generalized system of preferences is intended to help developing nations gain access to world markets. Explain.

8. How are import substitution and export promotion policies used to aid in the industrialization of developing nations?

9. Describe the strategy that East Asia used from the 1970s to the 1990s to achieve high rates of economic growth. Can the Asian miracle continue in the new millennium?

10. How has China achieved the status of a high-performing Asian economy? Why has China's normal trade relation status been a source of controversy in the United States? What are the likely effects of China's entry into the WTO?

11. What led India in the 1990s to abandon its system of import substitution, and what growth strategy did India adopt?

Regional Trading Arrangements

Since World War II, advanced nations have significantly lowered their trade restrictions. This trade liberalization has stemmed from two approaches. The first is a reciprocal reduction of trade barriers on a nondiscriminatory basis. Under the General Agreement on Tariffs and Trade (GATT) and its successor, the World Trade Organization (WTO), member nations acknowledge that tariff reductions agreed on by any two nations would be extended to all other members. Such an international approach encourages a gradual relaxation of tariffs throughout the world.

A second approach to trade liberalization occurs when a small group of nations, typically on a regional basis, form a **regional trading arrangement**. Under this system, member nations agree to impose lower barriers to trade within the group than to trade with nonmember nations. Each member nation continues to determine its domestic policies, but the trade policy of each includes preferential treatment for group members. Regional trading arrangements (free trade areas and customs unions) have been an exception to the principle of nondiscrimination embodied in the World Trade Organization. This chapter investigates the operation and effects of two regional trading arrangements, the European Union and the North American Free Trade Agreement.

REGIONAL INTEGRATION VERSUS MULTILATERALISM

Recall that a major purpose of the WTO is to promote trade liberalization through worldwide agreements. However, getting a large number of countries to agree on reforms can be extremely difficult. By the early 2000s, the WTO was stumbling in its attempt to achieve a global trade agreement, and countries increasingly looked to narrow, regional agreements as an alternative. The number of regional trading agreements has risen from around 70 in 1990 to more than 300 today and they cover more than half of international trade. Are regional trading agreements building blocks or stumbling blocks to a multilateral trading system?[1]

---

[1]World Trade Organization, "The WTO and Preferential Trade Agreements: From Co-existence to Coherence," *World Trade Report*, 2011.

Trade liberalization under a regional trading arrangement is different from the multilateral liberalization embodied in the WTO. Under regional trading arrangements, nations reduce trade barriers only for a small group of partner nations, thus discriminating against the rest of the world. Under the WTO, trade liberalization by any one nation is extended to all WTO members, 159 nations, on a nondiscriminatory basis.

Although regional trading blocs can complement the multilateral trading system, by their very nature they are discriminatory and are a departure from the principle of normal trading relations, a cornerstone of the WTO system. Some analysts note regional trading blocs that decrease the discretion of member nations to pursue trade liberalization with outsiders are likely to become stumbling blocks to multilateralism. If Malaysia has already succeeded in finding a market in the United States, it would have only a limited interest in a free trade pact with the United States. But its less successful rival, Argentina, would be eager to sign a regional free-trade agreement and thus capture Malaysia's share of the U.S. market: not by making a better or cheaper product, but by obtaining special treatment under U.S. trade law. Once Argentina obtains its special privilege, what incentive would it have to go to WTO meetings and sign a multilateral free-trade agreement that would eliminate those special privileges?

Two other factors suggest that the members of a regional trading arrangement may not be greatly interested in worldwide liberalization. First, trade bloc members may not realize additional economies of scale from global trade liberalization that often provides only modest openings to foreign markets. Regional trade blocs that often provide more extensive trade liberalization may allow domestic firms sufficient production runs to exhaust scale economies. Second, trade bloc members may want to invest their time and energy in establishing strong regional linkages rather than investing them in global negotiations.

On the other hand, when structured according to principles of openness and inclusiveness, regional blocs can be building blocks rather than stumbling blocks to global free trade and investment. Regional blocs can foster global market openings in several ways. First, regional agreements may achieve deeper economic interdependence among members than do multilateral accords, because of the greater commonality of interests and the simpler negotiating processes. Second, a self reinforcing process is set in place by the establishment of a regional free trade area: as the market encompassed by a free trade area enlarges, it becomes increasingly attractive for nonmembers to join to receive the same trade preferences as member nations. Third, regional liberalization encourages the partial adjustment of workers out of import-competing industries in which the nation's comparative disadvantage is strong and into exporting industries in which its comparative advantage is strong. As adjustment proceeds, the portion of the labor force that benefits from liberalized trade rises and the portion that loses falls; this process promotes political support for trade liberalization in a self reinforcing process. For all of these reasons, when regional agreements are formed according to principles of openness, they may overlap and expand, promoting global free trade from the bottom up.

Let us next consider the various types of regional trading blocs and their economic effects.

TYPES OF REGIONAL TRADING ARRANGEMENTS

Since the mid-1950s, the term **economic integration** has become part of the vocabulary of economists. Economic integration is a process of eliminating restrictions on international trade, payments, and factor mobility. Economic integration results in the uniting of two or more national economies in a regional trading arrangement. Before proceeding, let us distinguish the types of regional trading arrangements.

A **free trade area** is an association of trading nations in which members agree to remove all tariff and nontariff barriers among themselves. Each member maintains its own set of trade restrictions against outsiders. An example of this stage of integration is the North American Free Trade Agreement (NAFTA) that consists of Canada, Mexico, and the United States. Beyond NAFTA, the United States has free-trade agreements with many other countries.[2] Like a free trade association, a **customs union** is an agreement among two or more trading partners to remove all tariff and nontariff trade barriers between themselves. In addition, each member nation imposes identical trade restrictions against nonparticipants. The effect of the common external trade policy is to permit free trade within the customs union, whereas all trade restrictions imposed against outsiders are equalized. A well known example is **Benelux** (Belgium, the Netherlands, and Luxembourg), that was formed in 1948.

A **common market** is a group of trading nations that permits (1) the free movement of goods and services among member nations, (2) the initiation of common external trade restrictions against nonmembers, and (3) the free movement of factors of production across national borders within the economic bloc. The common market thus represents a more complete stage of integration than a free trade area or a customs union. The **European Union (EU)**[3] achieved the status of a common market in 1992.

Beyond these stages, economic integration could evolve to the stage of **economic union**, in which national, social, taxation, and fiscal policies are harmonized and administered by a supranational institution. Belgium and Luxembourg formed an economic union during the 1920s. The task of creating an economic union is much more ambitious than achieving the other forms of integration. This is because a free trade area, customs union, or common market results primarily from the abolition of existing trade barriers; an economic union requires an agreement to transfer economic sovereignty to a supranational authority. The ultimate degree of economic union would be the unification of national monetary policies and the acceptance of a common currency administered by a supranational monetary authority. The economic union would thus include the dimension of a **monetary union**.

The United States serves as an example of a monetary union. Fifty states are linked together in a complete monetary union with a common currency, implying completely fixed exchange rates among the 50 states. The Federal Reserve serves as the single central bank for the nation; it issues currency and conducts the nation's monetary policy. Trade is free among the states, and both labor and capital move freely in pursuit of maximum returns. The federal government conducts the nation's fiscal policy and deals in matters concerning retirement and health programs, national defense, international affairs, and the like. Other programs, such as police protection and education, are conducted by state and local governments so that states can keep their identity within the union.

---

[2]Other U.S. free-trade agreement partner countries include Australia, Bahrain, Chile, Costa Rica, Dominican Republic, El Salvador, Guatemala, Honduras, Nicaragua, Israel, Jordan, Morocco, Oman, Peru, South Korea, Colombia, and Panama.

[3]Founded in 1957, the European Community was a collective name for three organizations: the European Economic Community, the European Coal and Steel Community, and the European Atomic Energy Commission. In 1994, the European Community was replaced by the European Union following ratification of the Maastricht Treaty by the 12 member countries of the European Community. For simplicity, the name European Union is used throughout this chapter in discussing events that occurred before and after 1994.

IMPETUS FOR REGIONALISM

Regional trading arrangements are pursued for a variety of reasons. A motivation of virtually every regional trading arrangement has been the prospect of enhanced economic growth. An expanded regional market can allow economies of large scale production, foster specialization, enhance learning-by-doing, and attract foreign investment. Regional initiatives can also foster a variety of noneconomic objectives such as managing immigration flows and promoting regional security. Regionalism may enhance and solidify domestic economic reforms. East European nations have viewed their regional initiatives with the European Union as a means of locking in their domestic policy shifts toward privatization and market oriented reform.

Smaller nations may seek safe haven trading arrangements with larger nations when future access to the larger nations' markets appears uncertain. This kind of access was an apparent motivation for the formation of NAFTA. In North America, Mexico was motivated to join NAFTA partially by fear of changes in U.S. trade policy toward a more managed or strategic trade orientation. Canada's pursuit of a free-trade agreement was significantly motivated by a desire to discipline the use of countervailing and antidumping duties by the United States.

As new regional trading arrangements are formed or existing ones are expanded or deepened, the opportunity cost of remaining outside an arrangement increases. Nonmember exporters could realize costly decreases in market share if their sales are diverted to companies of the member nations. This prospect may be sufficient to tip the political balance in favor of becoming a member of a regional trading arrangement, as exporting interests of a nonmember nation outweigh its import-competing interests. The negotiations between the United States and Mexico to form a free trade area appear to have strongly influenced Canada's decision to join NAFTA, and not be left behind in the movement toward free trade in North America.

EFFECTS OF A REGIONAL TRADING ARRANGEMENT

What are the possible welfare implications of *regional trading arrangements*? We can delineate the theoretical benefits and costs of such devices from two perspectives. First are the **static effects of economic integration** on productive efficiency and consumer welfare. Second are the **dynamic effects of economic integration** that relate to member nations' long run rates of growth. Because a small change in the growth rate can lead to a substantial cumulative effect on national output, the dynamic effects of trade policy changes can yield substantially larger magnitudes than those based on static models. Combined, these static and dynamic effects determine the overall welfare gains or losses associated with the formation of a regional trading arrangement.

Static Effects

The static welfare effects of lowering tariff barriers among members of a trade bloc are illustrated in the following example. Assume a world composed of three countries: Luxembourg, Germany, and the United States. Consider Luxembourg and Germany decide to form a customs union, and the United States is a nonmember. The decision to form a customs union requires that Luxembourg and Germany abolish all tariff restrictions between themselves while maintaining a common tariff policy against the United States.

FIGURE 8.1

Static Welfare Effects of a Customs Union

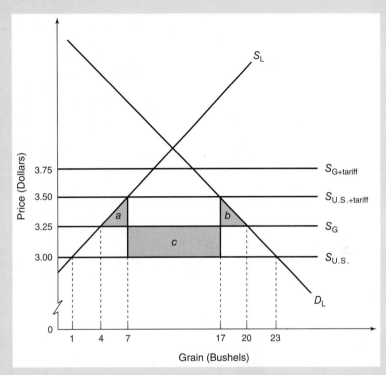

The formation of a customs union leads to a welfare increasing trade creation effect and a welfare decreasing trade diversion effect. The overall effect of the customs union on the welfare of its members, as well as on the world as a whole, depends on the relative strength of these two opposing forces.

Referring to Figure 8.1, assume the supply and demand schedules of Luxembourg to be S_L and D_L. Assume also that Luxembourg is small relative to Germany and the United States. This assumption means Luxembourg cannot influence foreign prices so that foreign supply schedules of grain are perfectly elastic. Let Germany's supply price be $3.25 per bushel and that of the United States, $3 per bushel. The United States is assumed to be the more efficient supplier.

Before the formation of the customs union, Luxembourg finds that under conditions of free trade, it purchases all of its import requirements from the United States. Germany does not participate in the market because its supply price exceeds that of the United States. In free-trade equilibrium, Luxembourg's consumption equals 23 bushels, production equals 1 bushel, and imports equal 22 bushels. If Luxembourg levies a tariff equal to $0.50 cents on each bushel imported from the United States (or Germany), then imports will fall from 22 bushels to 10 bushels.

Suppose as part of a trade liberalization agreement, Luxembourg and Germany form a customs union. Luxembourg's import tariff against Germany is dropped, but it is still maintained on imports from the nonmember United States. By removing the tariff, Germany now becomes the low price supplier. Luxembourg purchases all of its imports, totaling 16 bushels, from Germany at $3.25 per bushel while importing nothing from the United States.

The movement toward freer trade under a customs union affects world welfare in two opposing ways: a welfare increasing **trade creation effect** and a welfare reducing **trade diversion effect**. The overall consequence of a customs union on the welfare of its members, as well as on the world as a whole, depends on the relative strengths of these two opposing forces.

Trade creation occurs when a domestic production of one customs union member is replaced by another member's lower cost imports. The welfare of the member countries is increased by trade creation because it leads to increased production specialization according to the principle of comparative advantage. The trade creation effect consists of a *consumption effect* and a *production effect*.

Before the formation of the customs union and under its own tariff umbrella, Luxembourg imports from the United States at a price of $3.50 per bushel. Luxembourg's entry into the customs union results in its dropping all tariffs against Germany. Facing a lower import price of $3.25, Luxembourg increases its consumption of grain by three bushels. The welfare gain associated with this increase in consumption equals triangle *b* in Figure 8.1.

The formation of the customs union also yields a production effect resulting in a more efficient use of world resources. Eliminating the tariff barrier against Germany means that Luxembourg's producers must now compete against lower cost, more efficient German producers. Inefficient domestic producers drop out of the market, resulting in a decline in home output of three bushels. The reduction in the cost of obtaining this output equals triangle *a* in the figure. This triangle represents the favorable production effect. The overall trade creation effect is given by the sum of triangles $a + b$.

Although a customs union may add to world welfare by way of trade creation, its trade diversion effect generally implies a welfare loss. Trade diversion occurs when imports from a low-cost supplier outside the union are replaced by purchases from a higher cost supplier within the union. This diversion suggests that world production is reorganized less efficiently. In Figure 8.1, the total volume of trade increases under the customs union, part of this trade (ten bushels) has been diverted from a low-cost supplier, the United States, to a high-cost supplier, Germany. The increase in the cost of obtaining these ten bushels of imported grain equals area *c*. This is the welfare loss to Luxembourg, as well as to the world as a whole. Our static analysis concludes that the formation of a customs union will increase the welfare of its members, as well as the rest of the world, if the positive trade creation effect more than offsets the negative trade diversion effect. Referring to the figure, this occurs if $a + b$ is greater than *c*.

This analysis illustrates that the success of a customs union depends on the factors contributing to trade creation and diversion. Several factors that bear on the relative size of these effects can be identified. One factor is the kinds of nations that tend to benefit from a customs union. Nations whose pre-union economies are quite competitive are likely to benefit from trade creation because the formation of the union offers greater opportunity for specialization in production. Also, the larger the size and the greater the number of nations in the union, the greater the gains are likely to be, because there is a greater possibility that the world's low-cost producers will be union members. In the extreme case in which the union consists of the entire world, there exists only trade creation, not trade diversion. In addition, the scope for trade diversion is smaller when the customs union's common external tariff is lower rather than higher. Because a lower tariff allows greater trade to take place with nonmember nations, there will be less replacement of cheaper imports from nonmember nations by relatively high-cost imports from partner nations.

Dynamic Effects

Not all welfare consequences of a regional trading arrangement are static in nature. There may also be dynamic gains that influence member nation growth rates over the long run. These dynamic gains stem from the creation of larger markets by the movement to freer trade under customs unions. The benefits associated with a customs union's dynamic gains may more than offset any unfavorable static effects. Dynamic gains include *economies of scale, greater competition*, and a *stimulus of investment*.

Perhaps the most noticeable result of a customs union is market enlargement. Being able to penetrate freely into domestic markets of other member nations, producers can take advantage of economies of scale that would not have occurred in smaller markets limited by trade restrictions. Larger markets may permit efficiencies attributable to greater specialization of workers and machinery, the use of the most efficient equipment, and the more complete use of by products. Evidence suggests that significant economies of scale have been achieved by the EU in such products as steel, automobiles, footwear, and copper refining.

The European refrigerator industry provides an example of the dynamic effects of integration. Prior to the formation of the EU, each of the major European nations that produced refrigerators (Germany, Italy, and France) supported a small number of manufacturers that produced primarily for the domestic market. These manufacturers had production runs of fewer than 100,000 units per year, a level too low to permit the adoption of automated equipment. Short production runs translated into a high per unit cost. The EU's formation resulted in the opening of European markets and paved the way for the adoption of large scale production methods, including automated press lines and spot welding. By the late 1960s, the typical Italian refrigerator plant manufactured 850,000 refrigerators annually. This volume was more than sufficient to meet the minimum efficient scale of operation, estimated to be 800,000 units per year. The late 1960s also saw German and French manufacturers averaging 570,000 units and 290,000 units per year, respectively.[4]

Broader markets may also promote greater competition among producers within a customs union. It is often felt that trade restrictions promote monopoly power, whereby a small number of companies dominate a domestic market. Such companies may prefer to lead a quiet life, forming agreements not to compete on the basis of price. With the movement to more open markets under a customs union, the potential for successful collusion is lessened as the number of competitors expands. With freer trade, domestic producers must compete or face the possibility of financial bankruptcy. To survive in expanded and more competitive markets, producers must cut waste, keep prices down, improve quality, and raise productivity. Competitive pressure can also be an effective check against the use of monopoly power and in general a benefit to the nation's consumers.

In addition, trade can accelerate the pace of technical advance and boost the level of productivity. By increasing the expected rate of return to successful innovation and spreading research and development costs more widely, trade can propel a higher pace of investment spending in the latest technologies. Greater international trade can also enhance the exchange of technical knowledge among countries as human and physical capital move more freely. These inducements tend to increase an economy's rate of growth, causing, not just a one-time boost to economic welfare, but a persistent increase in income that grows steadily larger as time passes.

---

[4]Nicholas Owen, *Economies of Scale, Competitiveness, and Trade Patterns Within the European Community* (New York: Oxford University Press, 1983), pp. 119–139.

TRADE CONFLICTS IS THE U.S.–SOUTH KOREA FREE-TRADE AGREEMENT GOOD FOR AMERICANS?

After a four year drought in forming free trade partnerships, in 2011 the U.S. government approved agreements with South Korea, Panama, and Columbia. President Barack Obama was eager to approve the deals, because he believed they would help to create jobs in a weak U.S. economy. Most unions were skeptical. They feared that U.S. companies would just ship more jobs overseas now that they could take advantage of lower labor costs in those nations. Let us consider the U.S.–South Korea trade agreement.

Why could free trade with South Korea benefit the United States? South Korea has a large market, the fourth largest economy in Asia. The free-trade agreement would result in American exports becoming more attractive to about 50 million consumers.

How about jobs going overseas? Indeed, exports are only part of the story. Imports would also increase. This could cost Americans jobs in two ways: some Korean goods would be relatively less expensive than those produced in the United States, and some U.S. companies might ship jobs overseas.

Some American jobs will be lost because of the trade agreement. However, the key issue is whether the jobs created will exceed the number lost. This depends in part on which industries benefit and which suffer. According to industry analysts, dairy, fruit, pork, beef, poultry products, plastics, chemicals, and financial services would benefit. Prior to the trade agreement, South Korea had a 24 percent tariff on cherries and a 45 percent tariff on apples that significantly reduced U.S. fruit exports to South Korea. It is no wonder why U.S. farmers celebrated the approval of the free-trade agreement. Steel, textiles, semiconductors, and machine parts were expected to suffer as South Korean competition intensified under free trade.

Proponents of free trade note it is a normal characteristic of trade that some industries win while others lose. Trade creates incentives for nations to specialize in the products of their comparative advantage. Goods and services that one nation can produce at a lower cost are sold to another. Even if this does cost some short run jobs, it should place the United States in a more favorable long run position by revising its emphasis on the industries where it can best compete in the world market. With U.S. households buying less expensive South Korean goods because of free trade, they will have more money to spend on other goods, some of which will be produced by Americans.

What about those Americans who lose their jobs? To win Congressional approval of the trade agreement, Obama agreed to renew the Trade Adjustment Assistance Program, as discussed in Chapter 6 of this text. This provides workers who are laid off because of free trade pacts temporary income support and job retraining. Even though some jobs will be lost, those workers may find themselves in a better position to compete in more sustainable occupations.

In spite of this optimism, union officials generally lobbied against the U.S.–South Korea free-trade agreement. They argued that it will accelerate the race to the bottom by encouraging U.S. corporations to locate production in countries that have the lowest labor costs.

THE EUROPEAN UNION

In the years immediately after World War II, Western European countries suffered balance-of-payments deficits in response to reconstruction efforts. To shield their firms and workers from external competitive pressures, they initiated an elaborate network of tariff and exchange restrictions, quantitative controls, and state trading. However, in the 1950s these trade barriers were generally viewed as counterproductive. Therefore, Western Europe began to dismantle its trade barriers in response to successful tariff negotiations under the auspices of GATT. The hope was that by binding European nations together economically and financially, it would not be in their interest to go to war.

It was against this background of trade liberalization that the European Union, then known as the European Community, was created by the Treaty of Rome in 1957. The EU initially consisted of six nations: Belgium, France, Italy, Luxembourg, the Netherlands, and West Germany. By 1973, the United Kingdom, Ireland, and Denmark had joined the trade bloc. Greece joined the trade bloc in1981, followed by Spain and Portugal in 1987. In 1995, Austria, Finland, and Sweden were admitted into the EU. In 2004, ten other Central and Eastern European countries joined the EU: Cyprus, the Czech Republic, Estonia, Hungary, Latvia, Lithuania, Malta, Poland, Slovakia, and Slovenia. In 2007, Bulgaria and Romania joined the EU, and in 2013 Croatia also joined, bringing the membership to 28 countries. The EU views this enlargement process as an opportunity to promote stability in Europe and further the integration of the continent by peaceful means.

Pursuing Economic Integration

According to the Treaty of Rome, the EU agreed in principle to follow the path of economic integration and eventually become an economic union. In pursuing this goal, EU members first dismantled tariffs and established a free trade area in 1968. This liberalization of trade was accompanied by a fivefold increase in the value of industrial trade—higher than world trade in general. The success of the free trade area inspired the EU to continue its process of economic integration. In 1970, the EU became a fully fledged customs union when it adopted a common external tariff system for its members.

Economists have analyzed the economic impact of the EU on its members. Their studies have generally found that trade creation has exceeded trade diversion by 2 to 15 percent. In addition, analysts note that the EU has realized dynamic benefits from integration in the form of additional competition and investment and also economies of scale. For instance, it has been determined that many firms in small nations such as the Netherlands and Belgium, realized economies of scale by producing both for the domestic market and for export.[5]

After forming a customs union, the EU made little progress toward becoming a common market until 1985. The hostile economic climate (recession and inflation) of the 1970s led EU members to shield their citizens from external forces rather than dismantle trade and investment restrictions. By the 1980s, EU members were increasingly frustrated with barriers that hindered transactions within the bloc. European officials also feared that the EU's competitiveness was lagging behind that of Japan and the United States.

In 1985, the EU announced a detailed program for becoming a common market. This program resulted in the elimination of remaining nontariff trade barriers to intra-EU transactions by 1992. Examples of these barriers included border controls and customs red tape, divergent standards and technical regulations, conflicting business laws, and protectionist procurement policies of governments. The elimination of these barriers resulted in the formation of a European common market and turned the trade bloc into the second largest economy in the world, almost as large as the U.S. economy.

While the EU was becoming a common market, its heads of government agreed to pursue much deeper levels of integration. Their goal was to begin a process of replacing their central banks with a European Central Bank and replacing their national currencies with a single European currency. The **Maastricht Treaty** signed in 1991 set 2002 as the date this process would be complete. In 2002, a **European Monetary Union (EMU)** emerged with a single currency, known as the **euro**.

---

[5]Richard Harmsen and Michael Leidy, "Regional Trading Arrangements," in International Monetary Fund, World Economic and Financial Surveys, *International Trade Policies: The Uruguay Round and Beyond, Volume II*, 1994, p. 99.

When the Maastricht Treaty was signed, economic conditions in the various EU members differed substantially. The treaty specified that to be considered ready for monetary union, a country's economic performance would have to be similar to the performance of other members. Countries cannot, of course, pursue different rates of money growth, have different rates of economic growth, and different rates of inflation while having currencies that don't move up or down relative to each other. The first thing the Europeans had to do was align their economic and monetary policies.

This effort, called convergence, has led to a high degree of uniformity in terms of price inflation, money supply growth, and other key economic factors. The specific **convergence criteria** as mandated by the Maastricht Treaty follows:

- **Price stability.** Inflation in each prospective member is supposed to be no more than 1.5 percent above the average of the inflation rates in the three countries with the lowest inflation rates
- **Low long-term interest rates.** Long-term interest rates are to be no more than 2 percent above the average interest rate in those countries
- **Stable exchange rates.** The exchange rate is supposed to have been kept within the target bands of the monetary union with no devaluations for at least two years prior to joining the monetary union
- **Sound public finances.** One fiscal criterion is that the budget deficit in a prospective member should be at most 3 percent of GDP; the other is that the outstanding amount of government debt should be no more than 60 percent of a year's GDP.

The euro is the official currency of 18 of the 28 member states of the European Union. These states, known collectively as the eurozone, are Austria, Belgium, Cyprus, Estonia, Finland, France, Germany, Greece, Ireland, Italy, Latvia, Luxembourg, Malta, the Netherlands, Portugal, Slovakia, Slovenia, and Spain. Notably, the United Kingdom, Denmark, and Sweden have thus far decided not to convert to the euro. The euro is also used in another six European countries and is consequently used daily by some 330 million Europeans. Over 175 million people worldwide use currencies that are pegged to the euro, including more than 150 million people in Africa. The euro is the second largest reserve currency and the second most traded currency in the world after the U.S. dollar.

An important motivation for the EMU is the momentum it provides for political union, a long standing goal of many European policymakers. France and Germany initiated the EMU. Monetary union was viewed as an important way to anchor Germany securely in Europe. Moreover, the EMU provided France with a larger role in determining monetary policy for Europe that they would achieve with a common central bank. Prior to the EMU, Europe's monetary policy was mainly determined by the German Bundesbank.

Agricultural Policy

Besides providing free trade in industrial goods among its members, the EU has abolished restrictions on agricultural products traded internally. A **common agricultural policy** has replaced the agricultural stabilization policies of individual member nations that differed widely before the formation of the EU. A substantial element of the common agricultural policy has been the support of prices received by farmers for their produce. Schemes involving deficiency payments, output controls, and direct income payments have been used for this purpose. In addition, the common agricultural policy has supported EU farm prices through a system of **variable levies** that applies tariffs to agricultural imports entering the EU. Exports of any surplus quantities of EU produce have been assured through the adoption of **export subsidies**.

One problem confronting the EU's price support programs is that agricultural effi-ciencies differ among EU members. Consider the case of grains. German farmers, being high-cost producers, have sought high support prices to maintain their existence. The more efficient French farmers do not need as high a level of support prices as the Ger-mans do to keep them in operation. Nevertheless, French farmers have found it in their interest to lobby for high price supports. In recent years, high price supports have been applied to products such as beef, grains, and butter. The common agricultural policy has encouraged inefficient farm production by EU farmers and has restricted food imports from more efficient nonmember producers. Such trade diversion has been a welfare decreasing effect on the EU.

Variable Levies   Figure 8.2 illustrates the operation of a system of variable levies. Assume that S_{EU_0} and D_{EU_0} represent the EU's supply and demand schedules for wheat and the world price of wheat equals $3.50 per bushel. Also assume the EU wishes to guarantee its high-cost farmers a price of $4.50 per bushel. This price cannot be sustained as long as imported wheat is allowed to enter the EU at the free market price of $3.50 per bushel. Suppose the EU, to validate the support price, initiates a var-iable levy. Given an import levy of $1 per bushel, EU farmers are permitted to produce 5 million bushels of wheat as opposed to the 3 million bushels that would be produced under free trade. At the same time, EU imports total 2 million bushels instead of 6 million bushels.

Assume that, owing to increased productivity overseas, the world price of wheat falls to $2.50 per bushel. Under a variable levy system, the levy is determined daily and equals

FIGURE 8.2

Variable Levies

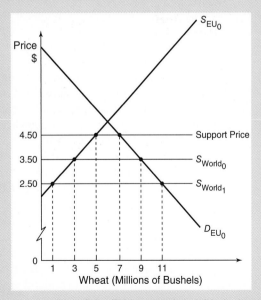

The common agricultural policy of the EU has used variable levies to protect EU farmers from low-cost foreign competition. During periods of falling world prices, the sliding scale nature of the variable levy results in automatic increases in the EU's import tariff.

© Cengage Learning®

the difference between the lowest price on the world market and the support price. The sliding scale nature of the variable levy results in the EU's increasing its import tariff to $2 per bushel. The support price of wheat is sustained at $4.50 and EU production and imports remain unchanged. EU farmers are insulated from the consequences of variations in foreign supply. Should EU wheat production decrease, the import levy can be reduced to encourage imports. Then EU consumers are protected against rising wheat prices.

The variable import levy tends to be more restrictive than a fixed tariff. It discourages foreign producers from absorbing part of the tariff and cutting prices to maintain export sales. Cutting prices only triggers higher variable levies. For the same reason, variable levies discourage foreign producers from subsidizing their exports in order to penetrate domestic markets

The completion of the Uruguay Round of trade negotiations in 1994 brought rules to bear on the use of variable levies. It required that all nontariff barriers, including variable levies, be converted to equivalent tariffs. The method of conversion used by the EU essentially maintained the variable levy system except for one difference. The actual tariff applied on agricultural imports can vary like the previous variable levy, depending on world prices. Now there is an upper limit applied to how high the tariff can rise.

Export Subsidies   The EU has also used a system of export subsidies to ensure that any surplus agricultural output will be sold overseas. The high price supports of the common agricultural policy have given EU farmers the incentive to increase production, often in surplus quantities. But the world price of agricultural commodities has generally been below the EU price. The EU pays its producers export subsidies so they can sell surplus produce abroad at the low price but still receive the higher, international support price. By encouraging exports, the government will reduce the domestic supply and eliminate the need for the government to purchase the excess.

The EU's policy of assuring a high level of income for its farmers has been costly. High support prices for products including milk, butter, cheese, and meat have led to high internal production and low consumption. The result has often been huge surpluses that must be purchased by the EU to defend the support price. To reduce these costs, the EU has sold surplus produce in world markets at prices well below the cost of acquisition. These subsidized sales have met with resistance from farmers in other countries. This is especially true for farmers in poor developing countries who argue that they are handicapped when they face imports whose prices are depressed because of export subsidies or when they face greater competition in their export markets for the same reason.

Virtually every industrial country subsidizes its agricultural products. As seen in Table 8.1, government programs accounted for 24 percent of the value of agricultural products in the EU in 2009. This amount is even higher in certain countries such as Switzerland and Japan, but it is much lower in others, including the United States, Australia, and New Zealand. Countries with relatively low agricultural subsidies have criticized the high subsidy countries as being too protectionist.

For a discussion of government procurement policy and the European Union, go to *Exploring Further 8.1* that can be found at www.cengage.com/economics/Carbaugh.

Is the European Union Really a Common Market?

For decades, members of the EU have tried to build a common market with uniform policies on product regulation, trade, and movement of factors of production. But are the policies of these countries really that common?

TABLE 8.1	
Government Support for Agriculture, 2010	
Country	**Producer-Subsidy Equivalents* as a Percent of Farm Prices**
Norway	61
Switzerland	54
Japan	50
Iceland	45
South Korea	45
European Union	20
Canada	18
Mexico	12
United States	7
Australia	2
New Zealand	1

*The producer subsidy equivalent represents the total assistance to farmers in the form of market price support, direct payments, and transfers that indirectly benefit farmers.

Source: From Organization of Economic Cooperation and Development (OECD), *Agricultural Policy Monitoring and Evaluation,* 2011. See also World Trade Organization, *Annual Report,* various issues.

Consider the case of Kellogg Co., the American producer of breakfast cereals. For years Kellogg has petitioned members of the EU to let it market identical vitamin fortified cereals throughout Europe. The firm's requests have run into numerous roadblocks. Government regulators in Denmark do not want vitamins added dreading that cereal consumers who already take multivitamins might surpass recommended daily doses that could jeopardize health. The Netherlands' regulators don't think that either folic acid or vitamin D is beneficial, so they don't want them included. However, Finland prefers more vitamin D than other nations to help Finns compensate for lack of sun. Kellogg has to produce four different varieties of cornflakes and other cereals at its plants in the United Kingdom.

The original concept of the EU was a common market based on uniform regulations. By producing for a single market throughout Europe, firms could attain production runs large enough to realize substantial economies of scale. Instead, persistent national differences have burdened firms with extra costs that stifle plant expansion and job creation.

This lack of consistency extends well beyond the domain of breakfast cereals. Caterpillar Inc. sells tractors throughout Europe. In Germany, its vehicles must include a louder backup horn and lights that are installed in different locations. The yield signs and license plate holders on the backs of tractors and other earth moving vehicles must differ, sometimes by just centimeters, from nation to nation. Officials at Caterpillar contend that there is no sound justification for such regulatory discrepancies. Discrepancies only make it hard to mass produce in an efficient manner.

Persistent regulatory differences between markets have adversely affected business expansion plans throughout Europe. Ikea Group, the Swedish furniture retailer, must pay for studies to prove that its entry into markets will not displace local businesses. According to Ikea, each study costs approximately $25,000 and takes about a year before a decision is made. Moreover, only 33 to 50 percent of Ikea's petitions result in approval.

Although members of the EU have advanced to higher levels of economic unification in the past 50 years, regulatory differences remain that have created barriers to trade and investment that stifle economic growth. These barriers have resulted in numerous legal battles between producers and national regulators, as well as between the European Commission and individual governments. Europe's common market remains uncommon.[6]

ECONOMIC COSTS AND BENEFITS OF A COMMON CURRENCY: THE EUROPEAN MONETARY UNION

As we learned, the formation of the EMU (also known as the eurozone) in 1999 resulted in the creation of a single currency (the euro) and a European Central Bank. Switching to a new currency is extremely difficult. Just imagine the task if each of the 50 U.S. states had its own currency and central bank, then had to agree with the other 49 states on a single currency and a single financial system. That's exactly what the Europeans have done.

The European Central Bank is located in Frankfurt, Germany, and is responsible for the monetary policy and exchange rate policies of the EMU. The European Central Bank alone controls the supply of euros, sets the short-term euro interest rate, and maintains permanently fixed exchange rates for the member countries. With a common central bank, the central bank of each participating nation performs operations similar to those of the 12 regional Federal Reserve Banks in the United States.

For Americans, the benefits of a common currency are easy to understand. Americans know they can walk into a McDonald's or Burger King anywhere in the United States and purchase hamburgers with dollar bills in their purses and wallets. The same was not true in European countries prior to the formation of the EMU. Because each was a distinct nation with its own currency, a French person could not buy something at a German store without first exchanging his French francs for German marks. This exchange would be like someone from St. Louis having to exchange her Missouri currency for Illinois currency each time she visits Chicago. To make matters worse, because marks and francs floated against each other within a range, the number of marks the French traveler receives today would probably differ from the number he would have received yesterday or tomorrow. On top of exchange rate uncertainty, the traveler also had to pay a fee to exchange the currency, making a trip across the border a costly proposition indeed. Although the costs to individuals can be limited because of the small quantities of money involved, firms can incur much larger costs. By replacing the various European currencies with a single currency, the euro, the EMU can avoid such costs. The euro helps lower the costs of goods and services, facilitates a comparison of prices within the EU, and promotes more uniform prices.

Optimum Currency Area

Much analysis of the benefits and costs of a common currency is based on the theory of optimum currency areas.[7] An **optimum currency area** is a region in which it is

---

[6]"Corn Flakes Clash Shows the Glitches in European Union," *The Wall Street Journal*, November 1, 2005, p. A-1.

[7]The theory of "optimum currency areas" was first analyzed by Robert Mundell, who won the 1999 Nobel Prize in Economics. See Robert Mundell, "A Theory of Optimum Currency Areas," *American Economic Review*, Vol. 51, September 1961, pp. 717–725.

TABLE 8.2	
Advantages and Disadvantages of Adopting a Common Currency	
Advantages	**Disadvantages**
The risks associated with exchange fluctuations are eliminated within a common currency area.	Absence of individual domestic monetary policy to counter macroeconomic shocks.
Costs of currency conversion are lessened.	Inability of an individual country to use inflation to reduce public debt in real terms.
The economies are insulated from monetary disturbances and speculation.	The transition from individual currencies to a single currency could lead to speculative attacks.
Political pressures for trade protection are reduced.	

© Cengage Learning®

economically preferable to have a single official currency rather than multiple official currencies. The United States can be considered an optimal currency area. It is inconceivable that the current volume of commerce among the 50 states would occur as efficiently in a monetary environment of 50 different currencies. Table 8.2 highlights some of the advantages and disadvantages of forming a common currency area.

According to the theory of optimum currency areas, there are gains to be had from sharing a currency across countries' boundaries. These gains include more uniform prices, lower transaction costs, and greater certainty for investors, and enhanced competition. A single monetary policy run by an independent central bank should promote price stability.

However, a single policy can also entail costs, especially if interest rate changes affect different economies in different ways. The broader benefits of a single currency must be compared against the loss of two policy instruments: an independent monetary policy and the option of changing the exchange rate. Losing these is particularly acute if a country or region is likely to suffer from economic disturbances (recession) that affects it differently from the rest of the single currency area, because it will no longer be able to respond by adopting a more expansionary monetary policy or adjusting its currency.

Optimum currency theory considers various reactions to economic shocks. The first is the mobility of labor: workers in the affected country must be able and willing to move freely to other countries. The second is the flexibility of prices and wages: the country must be able to adjust these in response to a disturbance. The third is some automatic mechanism for transferring fiscal resources to the affected country.

The theory of optimal currency areas concludes that for a currency area to have the best chance of success, countries involved should have similar business cycles and economic structures. The single monetary policy should affect all the participating countries in the same manner. There should be no legal, cultural, or linguistic barriers to labor mobility across borders, there should be wage flexibility, and there should be some system of stabilizing transfers.

Eurozone's Problems and Challenges

Although the EMU has resulted in some economic efficiencies for its members, it has also suffered from several problems. Recall that to be included in the EMU, countries

TRADE CONFLICTS EUROPEAN MONETARY "DISUNION"

A main goal of the European Monetary Union is to promote economic and political unification throughout Europe. Two world wars fought in Europe, plus the Depression of the 1930s that was fueled by protectionist trade policies, made a compelling case to dismantle the political and economic borders of post-World War II Europe. The United States encouraged closer economic ties to promote European reconstruction in view of expanding Soviet communism. Supporters maintained that monetary union would foster European peace and also restore European geopolitical power, with a currency on par with the U.S. dollar.

As Europe proceeded toward the euro and monetary union concerns about the lack of fiscal union to support it were swept aside. Some economists predicted that a monetary union without a political mechanism to supervise fiscal policy (reign in budget deficits) would eventually make the monetary union impossible to maintain. They also contended that a uniform monetary policy geared to the low inflation of Germany (the largest member) might result in an interest rate that was too low for smaller, high inflation countries like Greece, leading to trade deficits fueled by easy credit. These economists were often ridiculed by the European media for their alarmist views.

When the euro zone was being formed, the government of Germany insisted that Italy, as the fourth-largest European economy, be a founding member even though it did not fulfill the condition of sound government finances. Once debt ridden Italy was included, there was no argument for excluding high spending countries such as Greece, Ireland, and Portugal that became members of the euro zone. The euro zone consisted of the fiscally healthier countries such as Germany and the fiscally weak countries like Greece. As the global debt crisis emerged in 2008, it became increasingly apparent that the euro zone has a single currency, but the member countries are not identical.

Skeptics note that the euro was a bold venture that placed the cart before many horses. The basic problem is that the euro zone is not a single country. Initially eleven, and now seventeen, sovereign countries signed up for a currency union without first homogenizing their budget policies, tax systems, and bank regulations—that is, they did not form an economic union as discussed at the beginning of this chapter. They did so without creating a central government strong enough to enact cross border discipline fiscal or finance cross country transfers. Disunity within the euro zone mounted as some countries pursued sound fiscal policies while others pursued unsound policies. Fears have spread that the weak nations of the euro zone could default on their debt and might have to pull out of the euro zone.

To lessen such fears, the euro zone countries met in 2011 and pledged that each member would enact a constitutional rule to balance its budget and face penalties if its actual deficit exceeds 3 percent of its GDP. The fines could cost billions of euros. Critics maintain that there is no enforcement mechanism for this pledge and it could easily be violated and watered down to be completely ineffective. At the writing of this text, the determination of the euro zone members to achieve fiscal integrity remains unclear.

iStockphoto.com/photosoup

were supposed to fulfill certain economic criteria, such as small budget deficits, low inflation, and interest rates close to the eurozone's average. However, some countries (such as Greece) did not appear to fulfill these standards when they were accepted into the monetary union. These standards were sometimes ignored once countries became members of the monetary union. This put the eurozone on weak financial footing from its beginnings.

Another problem has been the integration of differing economies into a monetary union without a way to adjust these economies. During 1999–2013, productivity in the northern member nations (Germany) increased rapidly while productivity remained sluggish in the southern nations (Italy and Greece). This resulted in labor cost per unit of output in the north falling about 25 percent compared to the south. Normally, exchange rate adjustments would shrink this discrepancy. The exchange rates of the southern nations would depreciate relative to the currencies of the northern nations, increasing the competitiveness of the southern nations. However, within the eurozone there are no exchange rates to change since there is only one currency, the euro. Without an exchange rate as an adjustment mechanism, rebalancing economies would require southern workers to move freely to growing northern economies, prices rising in the north, wealthy northern nations subsidizing poorer southern nations, workers of poorer southern nations accepting unemployment to grind down wages, and so on. It is difficult to achieve these adjustments in practice, because political barriers abound throughout Europe.

Therefore, without the normal adjustment mechanisms to keep economic imbalances from destroying the eurozone, some analysts have pushed for the concept of fiscal union. This would result in the integration of the fiscal policies of the eurozone countries, including taxation and government spending programs. The idea would be to impose budget discipline on the laggard, deficit countries. Control over fiscal policy has been regarded essential to national sovereignty, and eurozone members have not been willing to give up their fiscal independence. The eurozone has a monetary union but it does not have a fiscal union.

Although fiscal policy remains the province of national governments of the eurozone, avoidance of excessive budget deficits is vital for the success of the monetary union. Because large budget deficits can lead to high interest rates and lower economic activity, budgetary restraint is desirable. Most countries have considerable difficulty in reducing budget deficits and debts to meet the convergence criteria of the EMU. Cutting government expenditures, especially on well established social programs, was (and is) politically difficult. In the face of aging populations in most countries, pressures on budgets may grow even stronger.

An important monetary policy challenge for the EMU is the ability of the European Central Bank to focus on price stability over the long-term. Some are concerned that over time, monetary policy may become too expansionary given the large number of countries voting on monetary policy, and the fact that strong anti inflationary actions are not well ingrained in countries like Greece, Portugal, Spain, Italy, and Cyprus.

The need for structural reform in European countries presents a challenge for EMU countries. Labor market flexibility is an important structural issue. Real (inflationary adjusted) wage flexibility in Europe is estimated to be half that of the United States. Labor mobility is quite low in Europe, not only between countries, but also within them. Incentives to work and acquire new skills are inadequate. Regulations that limit employers' ability to dismiss workers make them unwilling to hire and train new workers. Also, high taxes and generous unemployment benefits provided by European governments contribute to sluggish economies.

Analysts note that structural reforms are necessary for several reasons. First, they would lower the EU's persistently high structural unemployment rate. Second, firms would provide needed flexibility in adjusting to recessions, especially those that affected one or a few countries in the eurozone. If prices and wages were flexible downward, a decline in demand would be followed by lower prices, tending to raise demand. Increased labor mobility would be particularly useful in adjusting to recessions.

Will the Eurozone Survive?

As a result of the global financial crisis that began in 2007–2008, the EMU entered its first official recession. The severity of this downturn came close to breaking up the eurozone as financially weak members such as Greece, Portugal, Cyprus, and Spain teetered on the verge of bankruptcy. The response of the EMU to these problems has been slow.

Most observers contend that a long run solution to the EMU's economic problems will necessitate deeper political and fiscal integration as well as structural changes.

Greece provides an example of the eurozone's difficulties. The trouble began in 2008 when the government of Greece revealed that its budget deficit was more than three times as large as previously estimated; Greece's financial figures were fudged for years. With debt piling up, investors feared that Greece could not pay its debts. To shore up its financial position, the government of Greece resorted to budget cuts, a freeze on public sector wages, pension reforms, increased taxes, and efforts to rein in rampant tax evasion. The markets remained skeptical about the government's ability to deliver, partly because the austerity programs might crumble as social and political discontent increased. Finally, other euro zone countries, in conjunction with the International Monetary Fund, agreed on a package that gave Greece 110 billion euros in much needed loans.

At the writing of this text, the future of the euro zone was cloudy. Restoring Europe to financial health will take years because the troubled countries need to control their government deficits and improve their competitiveness. Creditor governments, especially Germany, maintain that the responsibility for this lengthy adjustment lies solely with borrowing countries such as Greece and Italy. Critics note that Germany's approach suffers from a fallacy of composition: it is not possible for everyone to save their way to prosperity—someone needs to be consuming. In Europe that should be countries like Germany and the Netherlands that were running current account surpluses. Yet the creditors were reluctant to accept that part of the solution.

NORTH AMERICAN FREE TRADE AGREEMENT

The success of Europe in forming the European Union inspired the United States to launch several regional free-trade agreements. During the 1980s, the United States entered into discussions for a free-trade agreement with Canada that became effective in 1989. This paved the way for Mexico, Canada, and the United States to form the **North American Free Trade Agreement (NAFTA)** that went into effect in 1994.

NAFTA's visionaries in the United States made a revolutionary gamble. Mexico's authoritarian political system, repressed economy, and resulting poverty were creating problems that could not be contained at the border in perpetuity; Mexican instability would eventually spill over the Rio Grande. The choice was easy— either help Mexico develop as part of an integrated North America, or watch the economic gap widen and the risks for the United States increase.

The establishment of NAFTA was expected to provide each member nation better access to the others' markets, technology, labor, and expertise. In many respects, there were remarkable fits between the nations: the United States would benefit from Mexico's pool of cheap and increasingly skilled labor, while Mexico would benefit from U.S. investment and expertise. Negotiating the free-trade agreement was difficult because it required meshing two large advanced industrial economies (United States and Canada) with that of a sizable developing nation (Mexico). The huge living standard gap between Mexico with its lower wage scale, and the United States and Canada was a politically sensitive issue. One of the main concerns about NAFTA was whether Canada and the United States as developed countries had much to gain from trade liberalization with Mexico. Table 8.3 highlights some of the likely gains and losses of integrating the Mexican and U.S. economies.

TABLE 8.3	
Winners and Losers in the United States under Free Trade with Mexico	
U.S. Winners	**U.S. Losers**
Higher skill, higher tech businesses and their workers benefit from free trade.	Labor intensive, lower wage, import-competing businesses lose from reduced tariffs on competing imports.
Labor-intensive businesses that relocate to Mexico benefit by reducing production costs.	Workers in import-competing businesses lose if their businesses close or relocate.
Domestic businesses that use imports as components in the production process, save on production costs.	
Consumers in the United States benefit from less expensive products because of increased competition with free trade.	

© Cengage Learning®

NAFTA's Benefits and Costs for Mexico and Canada

NAFTA's benefits to Mexico have been proportionately much greater than for the United States and Canada because these economies are many times larger than Mexico's. Eliminating trade barriers has led to increases in the production of goods and services for which Mexico has a comparative advantage. Mexico's gains have come at the expense of other low wage countries, such as Korea and Taiwan. Generally, Mexico has produced more goods that benefit from a low wage, low skilled workforce, such as tomatoes, avocados, fruits, vegetables, processed foods, sugar, tuna, and glass; labor-intensive manufactured exports such as appliances and economy automobiles have also increased. Rising investment spending in Mexico has helped increase wage incomes and employment, national output, and foreign exchange earnings; it also has facilitated the transfer of technology.

Although agriculture represents only four to five percent of Mexico's GDP, it supports about a quarter of the country's population. Most Mexican agricultural workers are subsistence farmers who plant grains and oilseeds in small plots that have supported them for generations. Mexican producers of rice, beef, pork, and poultry claim they have been devastated by U.S. competition in the Mexican market resulting from NAFTA. They claim they cannot compete against U.S. imports where easy credit, better transportation, better technology, and major subsidies give U.S. farmers an unfair advantage.

For Canada, initial concerns about NAFTA had less to do with the flight of low skilled manufacturing jobs, because trade with Mexico was much smaller than it was for the United States. Instead, the main concern was that closer integration with the U.S. economy would threaten Canada's social welfare model, either by causing certain practices and policies (such as universal health care or a generous minimum wage) to be considered as uncompetitive, or else by imposing downward pressure on the country's base of personal and corporate taxes, thus starving government programs of resources. Canada's social welfare model currently stands intact.

Canada's benefits from NAFTA have been mostly in the form of safeguards: maintenance of its status in international trade, no loss of its current free trade preferences in the U.S. market, and equal access to Mexico's market. Canada also desired to become part of any process that would eventually broaden market access to Central and South America. Although Canada hoped to benefit from trade with Mexico over time, most researchers have estimated that there have been relatively small gains because of the small amount of existing Canada Mexico trade.

Although it has succeeded in stimulating increased trade and foreign investment, NAFTA alone has not been enough to modernize Mexico or guarantee prosperity. This result has been a disappointment to many Mexicans. Trade and investment can do only so much. Since the beginnings of NAFTA, the government of Mexico has struggled to deal with the problems of corruption, poor education, red tape, crumbling infrastructure, lack of credit, and a tiny tax base. These factors greatly influence a country's economic development. For Mexico to become an economically advanced nation, it needs a better educational system, cheaper electricity, better roads, and investment incentives for generating growth—things that NAFTA cannot provide.

NAFTA's Benefits and Costs for the United States

NAFTA proponents maintain that the agreement has benefited the U.S. economy overall by expanding trade opportunities, reducing prices, increasing competition, and enhancing the ability of U.S. firms to attain economies of large scale production. The United States has produced more goods that benefit from large amounts of physical capital and a highly skilled workforce, including chemicals, plastics, cement, sophisticated electronics and communications gear, machine tools, and household appliances. American insurance companies have also benefited from fewer restrictions on foreign insurers operating in Mexico. American companies, particularly larger ones, have realized better access to cheaper labor and parts. The United States has benefited from a more reliable source of petroleum, less illegal Mexican immigration, and enhanced Mexican political stability as a result of the nation's increasing wealth. In spite of these benefits, the overall economic gains for the United States are estimated to be modest, because the U.S. economy is 25 times the size of the Mexican economy and many U.S.–Mexican trade barriers were dismantled prior to the implementation of NAFTA.

Economies of scale represent another benefit of NAFTA. A member of NAFTA can overcome the smallness of its domestic markets and realize economies of scale in production by exporting to other members. NAFTA has allowed U.S. manufacturing giants from General Motors to General Electric use economies of scale for their production lines. Prior to NAFTA, GM's assembly plants in Mexico assembled small volumes of many products that resulted in high costs and somewhat inferior quality. Now its plants in Mexico specialize in a few high volume products, resulting in low costs and higher quality. This result benefits both U.S. and Mexican consumers. For an analysis of the effects of economies of scale in manufacturing, go to *Exploring Further 8.2* that can be found at www.cengage.com/economics/Carbaugh.

Even ardent proponents of NAFTA acknowledge that it has inflicted pain on some segments of the U.S. economy. On the business side, the losers have been industries such as citrus growing and sugar that rely on trade barriers to limit imports of low priced Mexican goods. Other losers are unskilled workers, such as those in the apparel industry, whose jobs are most vulnerable to competition from low paid workers abroad.

American labor unions have been especially concerned that Mexico's low wage scale encourages U.S. companies to locate in Mexico, resulting in job losses in the United States. Cities such as Muskegon, Michigan that has thousands of workers cranking out such basic auto parts as piston rings are especially vulnerable to low wage Mexican competition. Indeed, the hourly manufacturing compensation for Mexican workers has been a small fraction of that paid to U.S. and Canadian workers.

According to NAFTA critics, there would be a "giant sucking sound" from U.S. companies moving to Mexico to capitalize on Mexico's cheap labor. After more than a decade, U.S. companies have not relocated to Mexico in the large numbers forecasted. International trade theory tells us why. As seen in Table 8.4, the productivity of the average American worker (gross domestic product per worker) was $104,503 in 2010 while the productivity of the average Mexican worker was $22,613. The U.S. worker was about 4.6 times as productive as the Mexican worker. Employers could pay U.S. workers 4.6 times as much as Mexican workers without any difference in cost

TABLE 8.4

Gross Domestic Product, Employment and Labor Productivity, 2012

Country	Gross Domestic Product (billions)	Employment (millions)*	Labor Productivity**
Australia	$1,542	11.5	$134,061
United States	16,245	142.5	114,045
Canada	1,821	17.5	104,021
Japan	5,960	62.7	95,121
United Kingdom	2,476	29.5	83,955
Germany	3,430	41.5	82,639
Mexico	1,117	48.1	23,231
China	8,221	746.9	11,007

*Employment = (1 − unemployment rate) × labor force.

**Labor productivity = GDP/number of persons employed. Due to rounding, numbers are not precise.

Source: Central Intelligence Agency, *World Fact Book*, http://www.cia.gov. See also World Bank Group, *Data and Statistics*, http://www.worldbank.org/data/ and International Monetary Fund, *International Financial Statistics*.

per unit of output. Also, companies operating in the United States benefit from a more stable legal and political system than exists in Mexico. The lower wages of Mexican workers have not motivated large numbers of U.S. companies to move to Mexico.

Another concern is Mexico's environmental regulations, criticized as being less stringent than those of the United States. American labor and environmental activists fear that polluting Mexican plants might cause plants in the United States that are cleaner but more expensive to operate, to close down. Environmentalists also fear that increased Mexican growth will bring increased air and water pollution. NAFTA advocates argue that a more prosperous Mexico might be more willing and able to enforce its environmental regulations; more economic openness is also associated with production closer to state-of-the-art technology that tends to be cleaner.

Proponents of NAFTA view it as an opportunity to create an enlarged productive base for the entire region through a new allocation of productive factors that would permit each nation to contribute to a larger pie. An increase in U.S. and Canadian trade with Mexico resulting from the reduction of trade barriers under NAFTA would partly displace U.S. and Canadian trade with other nations, including those in Central and South America, the Caribbean, and Asia. Some of this displacement would be expected to result in a loss of welfare associated with trade diversion—the shift from a lower cost supplier to a higher cost supplier. But because the displacement was expected to be small, it was projected to have a minor negative effect on the U.S. and Canadian economies.

To date, the effects of NAFTA on the U.S. economy have been relatively small. These effects have included increases in overall U.S. income and increases in U.S. trade with Mexico, but little impact on overall levels of unemployment, although with some displacement of workers from sector to sector. For particular industries or products with a greater exposure to intra-NAFTA trade, effects have generally been greater, including displacement effects on individual workers. Overall, studies have indicated that NAFTA has resulted in greater trade creation than trade diversion for the United States, thus improving its welfare.[8]

---

[8]See Daniel Lederman, William Maloney, and Luis Serven, *Lessons from NAFTA for Latin America and the Caribbean Countries: A Summary of Research Findings*, The World Bank, Washington, DC, December 2003 and Sidney Weintraub, ed., *NAFTA's Impact on North America: The First Decade*, Center for Strategic and International Studies, Washington, DC, 2004.

It is in politics, not economics, that NAFTA has had its biggest impact. The trade agreement has come to symbolize a close embrace between the United States and Mexico. Given the history of hostility between the two countries, this embrace is remarkable. U.S. officials realized that their chance of curbing the flow of illegal immigrants would be far greater if their southern neighbors wealthy instead of poor. The United States bought itself an ally with NAFTA. Besides NAFTA, there are other major Western hemisphere regional trade agreements as seen in Table 8.5.

U.S.–Mexico Trucking Dispute

Achieving an integrated North American market isn't as easy as it looks. Consider the conflict between free traders, who desire the efficiency of a deregulated trucking system, and social activists who express concerns about highway safety. Or is preservation of domestic jobs their real motive?

For decades, the safety of the North American trucking system has been of concern to Americans and Canadians. The United States and Canada have laws on their books limiting the number of consecutive hours a trucker can be on the road; truck drivers are tested for drug or alcohol use and trucks are inspected for safety requirements. In contrast, Mexico traditionally has maintained less stringent standards for its trucks and drivers. Mexico has no roadside inspection program or drug testing for drivers. It does not require logbooks or have weighing stations for trucks. It doesn't have a requirement for the labeling of hazardous or toxic cargo, or a system to verify drivers' licenses.

According to NAFTA, the United States, Mexico, and Canada agreed to open their roads to each other's cargo trucks. In 1995, on the day before NAFTA's cross border trucking provision was to begin, President Bill Clinton imposed restrictions on Mexican cargo trucks, citing trucking safety as his concern. Mexican trucks entering the United States were limited to a commercial zone within 25 miles of the Mexican border. Mexican goods transported into the United States beyond this commercial zone had to be loaded onto American trucks, a practice that pleased the U.S. Teamsters (truckers) union. In 2002, the U.S. government introduced 22 additional safety requirements that

TABLE 8.5		
Major Western Hemisphere Regional Trade Agreements		
Agreement	**Members**	**Year Effective**
Central American Free Trade Agreement (CAFTA)	Costs Rica, El Salvador, Guatemala, Honduras, Nicaragua, Dominican Republic, United States	2005
North American Free Trade Agreement (NAFTA)	Canada, Mexico, United States	1994
Southern Cone Common Market (MERCOSUR)	Argentina, Brazil, Paraguay, Uruguay	1991
Caribbean Community and Common Market	Antigua, Bahamas, Barbados, Barbuda, Belize, Dominica, Grenada, Guyana, Haiti, Jamaica, Montserrat, St. Kitts, Nevis, St. Lucia, St. Vincent, Surinam, Trinidad, and Tobago	1973
Andean Community	Bolivia, Colombia, Ecuador, Peru, Venezuela	1969
Central American Common Market	Costa Rica, El Salvador, Guatemala, Honduras, Nicaragua	1961

Mexican trucks would have to meet if they eventually received authority to travel throughout the United States. This measure went beyond the requirements that were applied to U.S. and Canadian trucks operating in the United States.

Feeling shut out of the U.S. transportation market, Mexico responded by protesting the trucking restrictions to a NAFTA arbitration panel that ruled that the United States was in violation of its NAFTA obligations. The result was an agreement in 2007 that established a pilot program that allowed a limited number of Mexican cargo trucks to travel throughout the United States under rigid safety regulations. After 18 months, the program proved that Mexican trucks and drivers were as safe as their U.S. and Canadian counterparts and that transportation cost savings provided benefits for American consumers. That was bad news for the Teamsters union and it placed political pressure on Congress to cancel the pilot program.

In 2009, the U.S. government terminated the pilot program, closing the southern border of the United States to Mexican cargo trucks. Mexico retaliated by releasing a list of 99 U.S. products that would face tariffs of 10 to 45 percent. Among the states hit hardest by Mexico's tariffs were California, Oregon, and Washington that exported a variety of agricultural products to Mexico. With the cost of imported American products higher, Mexicans substituted these products with goods from Latin America, Europe, and Canada. Clearly, American agricultural producers paid a dear price for the protectionism granted the Teamsters union. This led to American agriculture producers and their allies protesting these tariffs to President Barack Obama, demanding the trucking dispute be resolved.

In 2011, the governments of Mexico and the United States announced a deal to end the trucking conflict. Under the deal, Mexico agreed to end its tariffs applied to U.S. goods and in return, its trucks were allowed to travel throughout the United States. Stringent regulations were placed on Mexican trucks and drivers entering the United States. Mexican trucks have to carry recorders to ensure they do only cross border, not domestic runs, and track compliance with U.S. hours-of-service laws. These requirements are tougher than those established by NAFTA and somewhat tougher than those in force for American truckers. Analysts generally maintained that the number of Mexican trucks traveling deep into the United States would be modest in the first several years following the deal.

U.S.–Mexico Tomato Dispute

Another dispute between Mexico and the United States involves tomatoes.[9] The enactment of the NAFTA agreement in 1994 abolished American tariffs on Mexican products, including tomatoes. As competition intensified, American tomato growers accused Mexican growers of selling their tomatoes in the United States at prices less than fair value (dumping) and driving American growers out of business. The Americans petitioned for the levying of antidumping tariffs on Mexican tomatoes. The Mexican government contended that Mexican tomatoes were not sold in the United States at prices below fair value: Mexican grown tomatoes were more competitive due to superior technology, good weather, and lower labor costs. It would be unfair to punish Mexican growers for their competitiveness according to the Mexican government.

---

[9]Cathy Baylis and Jeffrey Perloff, *End Runs Around Trade Restrictions: The Case of the Mexican Tomato Suspension Agreements*, Giannini Foundation of Agricultural Economics, 2005; Richard Lopez, "Tomato Prices to Rise If U.S.–Mexico Trade Agreement Ends, Study Says," *Los Angeles Times*, January 24, 2013; Stephanie Strom, "United States and Mexico Reach Tomato Deal, Averting a Trade War," *The New York Times*, February 3. 2013.

To resolve this dispute, an agreement was reached in 1996 in which Mexico's largest growers placed a floor on the price of their tomatoes sold in the United States so they would not undercut American growers. The price floor was set at 17 cents per pound during summer months and 21 cents per pound during the winter. For the price floor to be effective, growers representing 85 percent of Mexico's tomato exports agreed to adhere to the minimum. In return, the United States agreed to refrain from enacting antidumping duties.

The minimum price agreement fulfilled the American growers' objective of preventing Mexican tomatoes from being exported to the United States at prices less than fair value. Analysts who studied the matter concluded that the agreement did not eliminate foreign competition for America's tomato growers. Why? When the price floor was in effect, Mexico exported more tomatoes to Canada while Canada and the rest of the world increased their tomato sales in the United States, thereby lessening the restrictive effect of the Mexican price floor.

During 2012–2013, American tomato growers lobbied for the termination of the price floor agreement, maintaining that they could not compete at the low prices set by the agreement. If the agreement would be abolished, they would be free to again petition the U.S. government to impose more restrictive antidumping tariffs that would result in Mexican tomatoes being sold in the United States at prices higher than those set by the price floor agreement.

In 2013 the United States and Mexico reached a new agreement on trade in tomatoes. The agreement increased the minimum sales price for Mexican tomatoes in the United States from 21 cents a pound to 31 cents for winter tomatoes, and for summer tomatoes from 17 cents per pound to 24.6 cents. The agreement increased the types of tomatoes covered by the pact to include all Mexican growers and exporters. Although the low-cost growers of Mexico were not pleased that the price floor was raised, they recognized the agreement restored stability to the American tomato market and therefore avoided a more costly trade war.

Is NAFTA an Optimum Currency Area?

The increasing convergence of the NAFTA countries has stimulated a debate on the issues of adopting a common currency and forming an American monetary union among Canada, Mexico, and the United States. Of central relevance to the economic suitability of such a monetary union is the concept of the optimum currency area, as discussed in this chapter.

According to the theory of optimum currency areas, the greater the linkages between countries, the more suitable it is for them to adopt a single official currency. One such linkage is the degree of economic integration among the three NAFTA members. As expected, trade within NAFTA is quite substantial. Canada and Mexico rank as the first and second, respectively, largest trading partners of the United States in terms of trade turnover (imports plus exports). Likewise, the United States is the largest trading partner of Canada and Mexico.

Another linkage is the similarity of economic structures among the three NAFTA members. Canada's advanced industrial economy resembles that of the United States. In the past decade, Canada's average real income per capita, inflation rate, and interest rate were very close to those of the United States. Mexico is a growing economy that is aspiring to maintain economic and financial stability with a much lower average real income per capita and significantly higher inflation and interest rates compared with those of Canada and the United States. The value of the peso relative to the U.S. dollar has been quite volatile, although the peso has been more stable against the Canadian dollar. Other problems endured by Mexico are high levels of external debt, balance-of-payments deficits, and weak financial markets.

Some analysts are skeptical of whether Mexico's adoption of the U.S. dollar as its official currency would be beneficial. If Mexico adopted the dollar, its central bank would be unable to use monetary policy to impact production and employment in the face of economic shocks that might further weaken its economy. However, adopting the dollar would offer Mexico several advantages, including the achievement of long-term credibility in Mexican financial markets, long-term monetary stability and reduced interest rates, and increased discipline and confidence as a result of reducing inflation to U.S. levels. Most observers feel that the case for Mexican participation in a North American optimum currency area is questionable on economic grounds. The Mexican government has shown interest in dollarizing its economy in an attempt to develop stronger political ties to the United States.

Canadians have generally expressed dissatisfaction concerning adoption of the U.S. dollar as their official currency. In particular, Canadians are concerned about the loss of national sovereignty that such a policy would entail. They also note that there is no added benefit of credibility to monetary and fiscal discipline, since Canada, like the United States, is already committed to achieving low inflation, low interest rates, and a low level of debt relative to gross domestic product. The case for Canadian participation in any North American currency area is less strong on political grounds than economically. At the writing of this text, the likelihood of a North American currency area in the near term appeared to be dim.

SUMMARY

1. Trade liberalization has assumed two main forms. One involves the reciprocal reduction of trade barriers on a nondiscriminatory basis, as seen in the operation of the World Trade Organization. The other approach involves the establishment by a group of nations of regional trading arrangements among themselves. The European Union and the North American Free Trade Agreement are examples of regional trading arrangements.

2. The term *economic integration* refers to the process of eliminating restrictions on international trade, payments, and factor input mobility. The stages of economic integration are (a) free trade area, (b) customs union, (c) common market, (d) economic union, and (e) monetary union.

3. The welfare implications of economic integration can be analyzed from two perspectives. First are the static welfare effects, resulting from trade creation and trade diversion. Second are the dynamic welfare effects that stem from greater competition, economies of scale, and the stimulus to investment spending that economic integration makes possible.

4. From a static perspective, the formation of a customs union yields net welfare gains if the consumption and production benefits of trade creation more than offset the loss in world efficiency owing to trade diversion.

5. Several factors influence the extent of trade creation and trade diversion: (a) the degree of competitiveness that member nation economies have prior to formation of the customs union, (b) the number and size of its members, and (c) the size of its external tariff against nonmembers.

6. The European Union was originally founded in 1957 by the Treaty of Rome. Today it consists of 27 members. By 1992, the EU had essentially reached the common market stage of integration. Empirical evidence suggests that the EU has realized welfare benefits in trade creation that have outweighed the losses from trade diversion. One of the stumbling blocks confronting the EU has been its common agricultural policy that has required large government subsidies to support European farmers. The Maastricht Treaty of 1991

called for the formation of a monetary union for eligible EU members that was initiated in 1999.

7. The formation of the European Monetary Union in 1999 resulted in the creation of a single currency (the euro) and a European Central Bank. With a common central bank, the central bank of each participating nation performs operations similar to those of the 12 regional Federal Reserve Banks in the United States.

8. Much of the analysis of the benefits and costs of Europe's common currency is based on the theory of optimum currency areas. According to this theory, the gains to be had from sharing a currency across countries' boundaries include more uniform prices, lower transactions costs, increased certainty for investors, and enhanced competition. These gains must be compared against the loss of an independent monetary policy and the option of changing the exchange rate.

9. In 1989, the United States and Canada successfully negotiated a free-trade agreement under which free trade between the two nations would be phased in over a 10-year period. This agreement was followed by negotiation of the North American Free Trade Agreement by the United States, Mexico, and Canada.

10. By the 1990s, nations of Eastern Europe and the former Soviet Union were making the transition from centrally planned economies to market economies. These transitions reflected the failure of central planning systems to provide either political freedom or a decent standard of living.

11. It is widely agreed that the transition of the economies of Eastern Europe and the former Soviet Union into healthy market economies will require major restructuring: (a) establishing sound fiscal and monetary policies; (b) removing price controls; (c) opening economies to competitive market forces; (d) establishing private property rights and a legal system to protect those rights; and (e) reducing government's involvement in the economy.

KEY CONCEPTS AND TERMS

Benelux (p. 269)

Common agricultural policy (p. 276)

Common market (p. 269)

Convergence criteria (p. 276)

Customs union (p. 269)

Dynamic effects of economic integration (p. 270)

Economic integration (p. 268)

Economic union (p. 269)

Euro (p. 275)

European Monetary Union (EMU) (p. 275)

European Union (EU) (p. 269)

Export subsidies (p. 276)

Free trade area (p. 269)

Maastricht Treaty (p. 275)

Monetary union (p. 269)

North American Free Trade Agreement (NAFTA) (p. 284)

Optimum currency area (p. 280)

Regional trading arrangement (p. 267)

Static effects of economic integration (p. 270)

Trade creation effect (p. 272)

Trade diversion effect (p. 272)

Variable levies (p. 276)

STUDY QUESTIONS

1. How can trade liberalization exist on a nondiscriminatory basis versus a discriminatory basis? What are some actual examples of each?

2. What is meant by the term *economic integration*? What are the various stages that economic integration can take?

3. How do the static welfare effects of trade creation and trade diversion relate to a nation's decision to form a customs union? Of what importance to this decision are the dynamic welfare effects?

4. Why has the so called common agricultural policy been a controversial issue for the European Union?

5. What are the welfare effects of trade creation and trade diversion for the European Union, as determined by empirical studies?

6. Table 8.6 depicts the supply and demand schedules of gloves for Portugal, a small nation that is unable to affect the world price. On graph paper, draw the supply and demand schedules of gloves for Portugal.

TABLE 8.6

Supply and Demand for Gloves: Portugal

Price ($)	Quantity Supplied	Quantity Demanded
0	0	18
1	2	16
2	4	14
3	6	12
4	8	10
5	10	8
6	12	6
7	14	4
8	16	2
9	18	0

© Cengage Learning®

a. Assume that Germany and France can supply gloves to Portugal at a price of $2 and $3, respectively. With free trade, which nation exports gloves to Portugal? How many gloves does Portugal produce, consume, and import?

b. Suppose Portugal levies a 100 percent nondiscriminatory tariff on its glove imports. Which nation exports gloves to Portugal? How many gloves will Portugal produce, consume, and import?

c. Suppose Portugal forms a customs union with France. Determine the trade creation effect and the trade diversion effect of the customs union. What is the customs union's overall effect on the welfare of Portugal?

d. Suppose instead that Portugal forms a customs union with Germany. Is this a trade diverting or trade creating customs union? By how much does the customs union increase or decrease the welfare of Portugal?

EXPLORING FURTHER

For a discussion of government procurement policy and the European Union, go to *Exploring Further 8.1* which can be found at **www.cengage.com/economics/Carbaugh**

For an analysis of the effects of economies of scale in manufacturing, go to *Exploring Further 8.2* which can be found at **www.cengage.com/economics/Carbaugh**.

International Factor Movements and Multinational Enterprises

C H A P T E R

9

Our attention so far has been on the international flow of goods and services. However, some of the most dramatic changes in the world economy have been due to the international flow of factors of production, comprising labor and capital. In the 1800s, European capital and labor (along with African and Asian labor) flowed to the United States and fostered its economic development. In the 1960s, the United States sent large amounts of investment capital to Canada and Western Europe; in the 1980s and 1990s, investment flowed from Japan to the United States. Today, workers from southern Europe find employment in northern European factories, while Mexican workers migrate to the United States. The tearing down of the Berlin Wall in 1990 triggered a massive exodus of workers from East Germany to West Germany.

The economic forces underlying the international movement in factors of production are virtually identical to those underlying the international flow of goods and services. Productive factors move when they are permitted to from nations where they are abundant (low productivity) to nations where they are scarce (high productivity). Productive factors flow in response to differences in returns (such as wages and yields on capital) as long as these are large enough to more than outweigh the cost of moving from one country to another.

This chapter considers the role of international capital flows (investment) as a substitute for trade in capital-intensive products. Special attention is given to the multinational enterprise that carries on the international reallocation of capital. The chapter also analyzes the international mobility of labor as a substitute for trade in labor-intensive products.

THE MULTINATIONAL ENTERPRISE

Although the term *enterprise* can be precisely defined, there is no universal agreement on the exact definition of a **multinational enterprise (MNE)**. A close look at some representative MNEs suggests that these businesses have a number of identifiable features. Operating in many host countries, MNEs often conduct research and development

(R&D) activities in addition to manufacturing, mining, extraction, and business/service operations. The MNE cuts across national borders and is often directed from a company planning center that is distant from the host country. Both stock ownership and company management are usually multinational in character. A typical MNE has a high ratio of foreign sales to total sales, often 25 percent or more. Regardless of the lack of agreement as to what constitutes an MNE, there is no doubt that the multinational phenomenon is massive. Table 9.1 provides a glimpse of some of the world's largest corporations.

Multinationals may diversify their operations along vertical, horizontal, and conglomerate lines within the host and source countries. **Vertical integration** often occurs when the parent MNE decides to establish foreign subsidiaries to produce intermediate goods or inputs that go into the production of a finished good. For industries such as oil refining and steel, such *backward integration* may include the extraction and processing of raw materials. Most manufacturers tend to extend operations backward only to the production of component parts. The major international oil companies represent a classic case of backward vertical integration on a worldwide basis. Oil production subsidiaries are located in areas such as the Middle East, whereas the refining and marketing operations occur in the industrial nations of the West. Multinationals may also practice *forward integration* in the direction of the final consumer market. Automobile manufacturers may establish foreign subsidiaries to market the finished goods of the parent company. In practice, most vertical foreign investment is backward. Multinationals often wish to integrate their operations vertically to benefit from economies of scale and international specialization.

Horizontal integration occurs when a parent company producing a commodity in the source country sets up a subsidiary to produce an identical product in the host country. These subsidiaries are independent units in productive capacity and are established to produce and market the parent company's product in overseas markets. Coca-Cola and Pepsi-Cola are bottled not only in the United States but also throughout much of the world. Multinationals sometimes locate production facilities overseas to avoid stiff foreign tariff barriers that would place their products at a competitive disadvantage. Parent companies also like to locate close to their customers because differences in national preferences may require special designs for their products.

TABLE 9.1

The World's Largest Corporations, 2013

Firm	Headquarters	Revenues ($ billions)
Royal Dutch Shell	Netherlands	481.7
Walmart Stores	United States	469.2
ExxonMobil	United States	449.9
Sinopec Group	China	428.2
China National Petroleum	China	408.6
BP	United Kingdom	388.3
State Grid	China	298.4
Toyota Motor	Japan	265.7
Volkswagen	Germany	247.6
Total	France	234.3

Source: From "The 2013 Global 500," *Fortune*, available at http://www.fortune.com.

TABLE 9.2

Direct Investment Position of the United States on a Historical Cost Basis, 2013*

Country	U.S. DIRECT INVESTMENT ABROAD		FOREIGN DIRECT INVESTMENT IN U.S.	
	Amount (billions of dollars)	Percentage	Amount (billions of dollars)	Percentage
Canada	351.8	7.9	225.3	8.5
Europe	2,477.0	55.6	1,876.2	70.8
Latin America	869.3	19.5	95.6	3.6
Africa	61.4	1.4	5.3	0.0
Middle East	42.8	1.0	20.6	1.0
Asia and Pacific	651.3	14.6	427.8	16.1
	4,453.3	100.0	2,650.8	100.0

*Historical cost valuation is based on the time the investment occurred, with no adjustment for price changes.

Source: From U.S. Department of Commerce, *U.S. Direct Investment Position Abroad and Foreign Direct Investment Position in the United States on a Historical-Cost Basis*. See also U.S. Department of Commerce, *Survey of Current Business* (Washington, DC: Government Printing Office).

Besides making horizontal and vertical foreign investments, MNEs may diversify into nonrelated markets in what is known as **conglomerate integration**. In the 1980s, U.S. oil companies stepped up their nonenergy acquisitions in response to anticipated declines of the future investment opportunities for oil and gas. ExxonMobil acquired a foreign copper mining subsidiary in Chile, and Tenneco bought a French company producing automotive exhaust systems.

To carry out their worldwide operations, MNEs rely on **foreign direct investment**—acquisition of a controlling interest in an overseas company or facility. Foreign direct investment typically occurs when (1) the parent company obtains sufficient common stock in a foreign company to assume voting control (the U.S. Department of Commerce defines a company as directly foreign owned when a "foreign person" holds a ten percent interest in the company); (2) the parent company acquires or constructs new plants and equipment overseas; (3) the parent company shifts funds abroad to finance an expansion of its foreign subsidiary; or (4) earnings of the parent company's foreign subsidiary are reinvested in plant expansion.

Table 9.2 summarizes the position of the United States with respect to foreign direct investment in 2013. Data are provided concerning U.S. direct investment abroad and foreign direct investment in the United States. In recent years, the majority of U.S. foreign direct investment has flowed to Europe, Latin America, and Canada, especially in the manufacturing sector. Most foreign direct investment in the United States has come from Europe, Canada, and Asia—areas that have invested heavily in U.S. manufacturing, petroleum, and wholesale trade facilities.

MOTIVES FOR FOREIGN DIRECT INVESTMENT

The case for opening markets to foreign direct investment is as compelling as it is for trade. More open economies enjoy higher rates of private investment that is a major determinant of economic growth and job creation. Foreign direct investment is actively courted by countries, because it generates spillovers such as improved management and better technology. As is true with firms that trade, firms and sectors where foreign direct investment is intense tend to have higher average labor productivity and pay higher wages. Outward investment allows firms to remain competitive and supports employment at home. Investment abroad stimulates exports of machinery and other capital goods.

New MNEs do not pop up haphazardly in foreign nations; they develop as a result of conscious planning by corporate managers. Both economic theory and empirical studies support the idea that foreign direct investment is conducted in anticipation of *future profits*. It is generally assumed that investment flows from regions of low anticipated profit to those of high anticipated profit after allowing for risk. Although expected profits may ultimately explain the process of foreign direct investment, corporate management may emphasize a variety of other factors when asked about their investment motives. These factors include market demand conditions, trade restrictions, investment regulations, labor costs, and transportation costs. All these factors have a bearing on cost and revenue conditions and hence on the level of profit.

Demand Factors

The quest for profits encourages MNEs to search for new markets and sources of demand. Some MNEs set up overseas subsidiaries to tap foreign markets that cannot be maintained adequately by export products. This set up sometimes occurs in response to dissatisfaction over distribution techniques abroad. Consequently, a business may set up a foreign marketing division and, later, build manufacturing facilities. This incentive may be particularly strong with the realization that local taste and design differences exist. A close familiarity with local conditions is of utmost importance to a successful marketing program.

The location of foreign manufacturing facilities may be influenced by the fact that some parent companies find their productive capacity already sufficient to meet domestic demands. If they wish to enjoy growth rates that exceed the expansion of domestic demand, they must either export or establish foreign production operations. General Motors (GM) has felt that the markets of such countries as the United Kingdom, France, and Brazil are strong enough to permit the survival of GM manufacturing subsidiaries. Boeing has centralized its manufacturing operations in the United States and exports abroad because an efficient production plant for jet planes is a large investment relative to the size of most foreign markets.

Market competition may also influence a firm's decision to set up foreign facilities. Corporate strategies may be defensive in nature if they are directed at preserving market shares from actual or potential competition. The most certain method of preventing foreign competition from becoming a strong force is to acquire foreign businesses. For the United States, the 1960s and early 1970s witnessed a tremendous surge in the acquisition of foreign businesses. Approximately half of the foreign subsidiaries operated by U.S. MNEs were originally acquired through the purchase of existing concerns during this era. GM exemplifies this practice, purchasing and setting up auto producers around the globe. General Motors has been successful in gaining control of many larger foreign model firms, including Monarch (GM Canada) and Opel (GM Germany). It did not acquire smaller model firms such as Toyota, Datsun, and Volkswagen; all of which have become significant competitors for GM.

Cost Factors

Multinationals often seek to increase profit levels through reductions in production costs. Such cost reducing foreign direct investments may take a number of forms. The pursuit of essential raw materials may underlie a company's intent to go multinational. This is particularly true of the extractive industries and certain agricultural commodities. United Fruit has established banana producing facilities in Honduras to take advantage of the natural trade advantages afforded by the weather and growing conditions. Similar types of natural trade advantages explain why Anaconda has set up mining operations in Bolivia and Shell produces and refines oil in Indonesia. Natural supply advantages such as resource endowments or climatic conditions may indeed influence a company's decision to invest abroad.

Production costs include factors other than material inputs, notably labor. *Labor costs* tend to differ among national economies. Multinationals may be able to hold costs down by locating part or all of their productive facilities abroad. Many U.S. electronics firms have had their products produced or at least assembled abroad to take advantage of cheap foreign labor. (The mere fact that the United States may pay higher wages than those prevailing abroad does not necessarily indicate higher costs. High wages may result from U.S. workers' being more productive than their foreign counterparts. Only when high U.S. wages are not offset by superior U.S. labor productivity will foreign labor become more attractive.)

Multinational location can also be affected by transportation costs, especially in industries where transportation costs are a high fraction of product value. When the cost of transporting raw materials used by an MNE is significantly higher than the cost of shipping its finished products to markets, the MNE will generally locate production facilities closer to its raw material sources than to its markets; lumber, basic chemicals, aluminum, and steel are among the products that fit this description. Conversely, when the cost of transporting finished products is significantly higher than the cost of transporting the raw materials that are used in their manufacture, MNEs locate production facilities close to their markets. Beverage manufacturers such as Coca-Cola and Pepsi-Cola, transport syrup concentrate to plants all over the world that add water to the syrup, bottle it, and sell it to consumers. When transportation costs are a minor fraction of product value, MNEs tend to locate where the availability and cost of labor and other inputs provide them the lowest manufacturing cost. Multinationals producing electronic components, garments, and shoes offer examples of this process.

Government policies may also lead to foreign direct investment. Some nations seeking to lure foreign manufacturers to set up employment generating facilities in their countries may grant subsidies such as preferential tax treatment or free factory buildings to MNEs. More commonly, direct investment may be a way of circumventing import tariff barriers. The high tariffs that Brazil levies on auto imports means foreign auto producers wishing to sell in the Brazilian market must locate production facilities in that country. Another example is the response of U.S. business to the formation of the European Union (EU) that imposed common external tariffs against outsiders while reducing trade barriers among member nations. American companies were induced to circumvent these barriers by setting up subsidiaries in the member nations. Japanese businesses that located additional auto assembly plants in the United States in the 1980s and 1990s defused mounting protectionist pressures.

SUPPLYING PRODUCTS TO FOREIGN BUYERS: WHETHER TO PRODUCE DOMESTICALLY OR ABROAD

Once a firm knows that foreign demand for its goods exists, it must ascertain the lowest cost method of supplying these goods abroad. Suppose Anheuser-Busch (A-B) of the United States wants to sell its Budweiser beer in Canada. Anheuser considers the following: (1) build a brewery in Wisconsin to produce Bud for sale to U.S. consumers in the Upper Midwest and also to Canadian consumers (direct exporting); (2) build a brewery in Canada to produce Bud and sell it to Canadian consumers (foreign direct investment); or (3) license the rights to a Canadian brewery to produce and market Bud in Canada. The method A-B chooses depends on the extent of economies of scale, transportation and distribution costs, and international trade barriers. These considerations are discussed in the following sections.

Direct Exporting versus Foreign Direct Investment/Licensing

Let us consider A-B's strategy of supplying Bud to Canadians via direct exporting as opposed to foreign direct investment or a licensing agreement. We will first analyze the influence of economies of scale on this strategy. One would expect economies of scale to encourage A-B to export Bud to Canada when the quantity of beer demanded in Canada is relatively small, and to encourage Canadian production via either a licensing agreement or foreign direct investment when a large quantity of beer is demanded.

To illustrate this principle, assume that average production cost curves are identical for A-B's potential brewery in Wisconsin, A-B's potential brewery in Canada, and a Canadian brewery that could be licensed to produce Bud. These cost curves are denoted by AC in Figure 9.1. As these breweries increase output, the average costs of producing a case of beer decrease up to a point, after which average costs no longer decrease but stabilize.

Suppose A-B estimates that U.S. consumers will demand 200 cases of Bud per year as shown in Figure 9.1. Producing this quantity at A-B's Wisconsin brewery allows the realization of sizable economies of scale that result in a production cost of $8 per case. Also assume that Canadians are estimated to demand a relatively small quantity of Bud, say 100 cases. Because the Wisconsin brewery already produces 200 cases for U.S.

FIGURE 9.1

The Choice between Direct Exporting and Foreign Direct Investment/Licensing

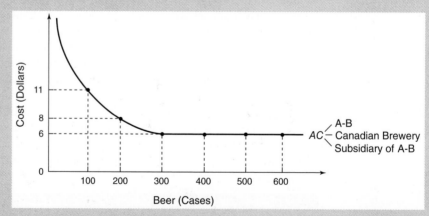

When the Canadian market's size is large enough to permit efficient production in Canada, a U.S. firm increases profits by establishing a Canadian production subsidiary or licensing the rights to a Canadian firm to produce and market its product in Canada. The U.S. firm increases profits by exporting its product to Canada when the Canadian market is too small to permit efficient production.

© Cengage Learning®

consumption, increasing output to meet the extra demand in Canada permits the brewery to slide down its average cost curve until it produces 300 cases at a cost of $6 per case.

The alternative to producing Bud in Wisconsin and exporting it to Canada is to produce it in Canada. Because Canadian consumers are estimated to demand only 100 cases of Bud, the size of the market is too small to allow economies of scale to be fully realized. A-B's potential brewery in Canada or the licensed Canadian brewer would produce Bud at a cost of $11 per case. The production cost saving for A-B of brewing Bud in Wisconsin and exporting it to Canada is $5 per case ($11 − $6 = $5). If the cost of transporting and distributing Bud to Canadians is less than this amount, A-B would maximize profits by exporting Bud to Canada.

If the quantity of Bud demanded in Canada exceeds 300 cases, it might be more profitable for A-B to use a licensing agreement or foreign direct investment. To illustrate this possibility, refer to Figure 9.1. Suppose that Canadians are estimated to demand 400 cases of Bud per year whereas the quantity of Bud demanded by U.S. consumers remains at 200 cases. With economies of scale exhausted at 300 cases, the larger Canadian demand does not permit A-B to produce Bud at a cost lower than $6 per case. By producing 400 cases, the licensed Canadian brewery or the Canadian subsidiary brewery of A-B could match the efficiency of A-B's Wisconsin brewery and each would realize a production cost of $6 per case. Given equal production costs, A-B minimizes total cost by avoiding the additional cost of transporting and distributing beer to Canadians. Thus, A-B increases profits by either licensing its beer technology to a Canadian brewer or investing in a brewing subsidiary in Canada.

Similar to transportation costs, trade restrictions can neutralize production cost advantages. If Canada has high import tariffs the production cost advantage of A-B's Wisconsin brewery may be offset, so that foreign direct investment or licensing is the only feasible way of penetrating the Canadian market.

Foreign Direct Investment versus Licensing

Once a firm chooses foreign production as a method of supplying goods abroad, it must decide whether it is more efficient to establish a foreign production subsidiary or license the technology to a foreign firm to produce its goods. In the United Kingdom there are Kentucky Fried Chicken establishments that are owned and run by local residents. The parent U.S. organization merely provides its name and operating procedures in return for royalty fees paid by the local establishments. Although licensing is widely used in practice, it presupposes that local firms are capable of adapting their operations to the production process or technology of the parent organization.

Figure 9.2 portrays the hypothetical cost conditions confronting A-B as it contemplates whether to license Bud production technology to a Canadian brewery or invest in a Canadian brewing subsidiary. Curve $AVC_{Subsidiary}$ represents the average variable cost (such as labor and materials) of A-B's brewing subsidiary, and AVC_{Canada} represents the average variable cost of a Canadian brewery. The establishment of a foreign brewing subsidiary also entails fixed costs denoted by curve $AFC_{Subsidiary}$. These include expenses of coordinating the subsidiary with the parent organization and the sunk costs of assessing the market potential of the foreign country. The total unit costs that A-B faces when establishing a foreign subsidiary are given by $ATC_{Subsidiary}$.

Comparing $ATC_{Subsidiary}$ with AVC_{Canada}, for a relatively small market of less than 400 cases of beer, the Canadian brewery has an absolute cost advantage. Licensing Bud production technology to a Canadian brewery in this case is more profitable for A-B. If the Canadian market for Bud exceeds 400 cases, A-B's brewing subsidiary has an absolute cost advantage; A-B increases profits by supplying beer to Canadians via foreign direct investment.

FIGURE 9.2

The Choice between Foreign Direct Investment and Licensing

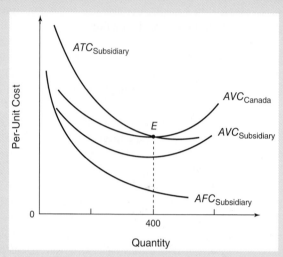

The decision to establish foreign operations through direct investment or licensing depends on (1) the extent to which capital is used in the production process, (2) the size of the foreign market, and (3) the amount of fixed cost a business must bear when establishing an overseas facility.

Several factors influence the output level at which A-B's brewing subsidiary begins to realize an absolute cost advantage compared to the Canadian brewery (400 cases in Figure 9.2). To the extent that production is capital intensive and A-B's brewing subsidiary can acquire capital at a lower cost than that paid by the Canadian brewery, the variable cost advantage of the subsidiary is greater. This neutralizes the influence of a fixed cost disadvantage for the subsidiary at a lower level of output. The amount of the brewing subsidiary's fixed costs also has a bearing on this minimum output level. Smaller fixed costs lower the subsidiary's average total costs, again resulting in a smaller output at which the subsidiary first begins to have an absolute cost advantage.

As noted, international business decisions are influenced by such factors as production costs, fixed costs of locating overseas, the relative importance of labor and capital in the production process, and the size of the foreign market. Another factor is the element of risk and uncertainty. When determining where to locate production operations, management is concerned with possibilities such as currency fluctuations and subsidiary expropriations.

COUNTRY RISK ANALYSIS

Although investing or lending abroad can be rewarding, these activities come with accompanying risks. The Russian government might expropriate the assets of foreign investors or make foreign loan repayments illegal. Thus, MNES and banks carry out a **country risk analysis** to help them decide whether to do business abroad.

TRADE CONFLICTS DO U.S. MULTINATIONALS EXPLOIT FOREIGN WORKERS?

Do U.S. multinational businesses exploit workers in developing countries? According to critics, maximizing profits is the only thing that matters to multinationals: They search the globe for the cheapest labor when deciding where to locate factories. The only gain from this behavior, critics argue, accrues to the owners of the businesses who have shifted operations from low-wage factories in industrialized countries to poverty wage factories in developing countries. According to critics, workers in developing countries are underpaid.

Indeed, multinationals are in business for profits. But this does not seem to be troublesome for many workers in developing countries who compete to work for them. People who go to work for a foreign owned business do so because they prefer it to the alternative, whatever that may be. In their own view, the new jobs make them better off.

Assume that the critics are right and that these workers are being exploited. One remedy would be to admonish multinationals for operating in developing countries. If multinationals stopped hiring workers in developing countries, the workers would, in their own estimation, become worse off. Another course is to entice multinationals to pay workers in developing countries wages that are as high as the wages paid to workers in industrial countries. This would discourage direct investment in developing countries. Why? Workers in developing countries are paid less than workers in industrial countries because they are generally less productive: They often work with less advanced machinery and the surrounding infrastructure is inadequate and that reduces productivity. These workers are attractive to multinationals, in spite of their lower productivity, because they are cheap. If you were to wipe out that offsetting advantage, you would make them unemployable. Bucking under pressure to extend U.S. or European pay scales to developing countries could mean shutting down local factories—hurting people, not helping them.

Productivity aside, should "responsible" multinationals pay their developing country employees more than other local workers? To hire workers, they may not have to provide a premium over local wages if they can offer other advantages, such as a modern factory in which to work rather than a sweatshop. By participating in the local labor market and adding to the total demand for labor, the multinationals would most likely be increasing wages for all workers, not just those they employ.

However, evidence suggests that multinationals do pay a wage premium that apparently reflects the desire to recruit relatively skilled workers. Economists at the Peterson Institute of International Economics estimate that during the 1990s, the wages paid by multinationals to poor country workers were about double the local manufacturing wage; wages paid by multinationals to workers in middle income countries were about 1.8 times the local manufacturing wage. Do U.S. multinationals underpay workers in developing countries? By U.S. standards, they do. But U.S. standards are irrelevant in developing countries: few workers are paid at U.S. levels in these countries. The key point is that by local standards, these workers typically fare quite well.

Source: From Edward Graham, *Fighting the Wrong Enemy* (Washington, DC: Institute for International Economics, 2000).

iStockphoto.com/photosoup

Individuals holding positions of responsibility with internationally oriented firms and banks engage in country risk analysis by evaluating the risk for each country in which they are considering doing business. Officers at Chase Manhattan Bank may establish limits on the amount of loans they are willing to make to clients in Turkey according to the risk of terrorism, as well as market factors. If Toyota fears runaway inflation and escalating labor costs in Mexico, it may refrain from establishing an auto assembly plant there.

Assessing the cost and benefits of doing business abroad entails analyses of political, financial, and economic risk. *Political risk* analysis is intended to assess the political stability of a country and includes criteria such as government stability, corruption, domestic conflict, religious tensions, and ethnic tensions. *Financial risk* analysis investigates a country's ability to finance its debt obligations and includes factors such as foreign debt as a percentage of gross domestic product (GDP), loan default, and exchange rate stability. *Economic risk* analysis determines a country's current economic strengths and weaknesses by looking at its rate of growth in GDP, per capita GDP, inflation rate, and the like. Analysts then calculate a composite country risk rating based on these three categories of risk. This composite rating provides an overall assessment of the risk of doing business in some country.

Country risk analysis is intended for a particular user. A company engaged in international tourism will be concerned about country risk as it applies to its attractiveness as a vacation destination. In this case, the composite risk rating of Venezuela may not be of much use. It is possible that Venezuela might be considered high risk in its composite rating, but not present a substantial risk to travelers because its composite risk is decreased by such factors as low financial or economic risk, a miserable investment climate, or other factors that do not threaten tourists. However, Israel might be judged as moderately risky overall due to a stable government and sound economic policies, but still present significant political risk to tourists because of religious and ethnic tensions. In these cases, a better understanding of risk can be ascertained by taking into account particular components of risk such as law and order or internal conflict, rather than the composite risk rating.

When conducting country risk analysis, MNEs and banks may obtain help from organizations that analyze risk. Political Risk Services publishes a monthly report called the *International Country Risk Guide*.[1] The guide provides individual ratings on more than 130 advanced and developing countries for political, financial, and economic risk, plus a composite rating. In calculating the composite risk rating, the political risk factors are given a weighting of 50 percent while the financial and economic risk factors each contribute 25 percent. Examples of composite ratings are provided in Table 9.3. In assessing a country's composite risk, a higher score indicates a lower risk and a lower score indicates a higher risk. Such information can be helpful to a firm as a predictive tool for international investments and financial transactions.

TABLE 9.3

Selected Country Risks Ranked by Composite Ratings, January 2013

Country	Composite Risk Rating (100 point maximum)	
Norway	90.8	Very Low Risk
Switzerland	89.0	
Canada	83.5	↑
South Korea	81.0	
United States	75.8	
China	75.0	
Ukraine	67.5	
Pakistan	55.8	
Zimbabwe	51.5	↓
Somalia	43.5	Very High Risk

Source: From Political Risk Services, *International Country Risk Guide*.

[1]There are other services that measure country risk, some of the more popular ones being *Euromoney*, Economist Intelligence Unit, Bank of America World Information Services, Business Environment Risk Intelligence, Institutional Investor, Standard and Poor's Rating Group, and Moody's Investor Services.

After a firm determines a country's risk rating, it must decide whether that risk is tolerable. If the risk is estimated to be too high, then the firm does not need to pursue the feasibility of the proposed project any further. If the risk rating of a country is in the acceptable range, any project related to that country deserves further consideration. In terms of the *International Country Risk Guide*'s ratings of country risk, the following categories are used to identify levels of risk: (1) low risk, 80–100 points; (2) moderate risk, 50–79 points; (3) high risk, 0–49 points. These broad categories must be tempered to fit the needs of particular MNEs and banks.

INTERNATIONAL TRADE THEORY AND MULTINATIONAL ENTERPRISE

Perhaps the main explanation of the development of MNEs lies in the strategies of corporate management. The reasons for engaging in international business can be outlined in terms of the comparative-advantage principle. Corporate managers see advantages they can exploit in the forms of access to factor inputs, new technologies and products, and managerial know-how. Organizations establish overseas subsidiaries largely because profit prospects are best enhanced by foreign production.

From a trade theory perspective, the MNE analysis is fundamentally in agreement with the predictions of the comparative-advantage principle. Both approaches contend that a given commodity will be produced in a low-cost country. The major difference between the MNE analysis and the conventional trade model is that the former stresses the international movement of factor inputs whereas the latter is based on the movement of merchandise among nations.

International trade theory suggests that the aggregate welfare of both the source and host countries is enhanced when MNEs make foreign direct investments for their own benefit. The presumption is that if businesses can earn a higher return on overseas investments than on those at home, resources are transferred from lower to higher productive uses and on balance, the world allocation of resources will improve. Analysis of MNEs is essentially the same as conventional trade theory that rests on the movement of products among nations.

Despite the basic agreement between conventional trade theory and the MNE analysis, there are some notable differences. The conventional model presupposes that goods are exchanged between independent organizations on international markets at competitively determined prices. But MNEs are generally vertically integrated companies whose subsidiaries manufacture intermediate goods as well as finished goods. In an MNE, sales become *intra-firm* when goods are transferred from subsidiary to subsidiary. Although such sales are part of international trade, their value may be determined by factors other than a competitive pricing system.

JAPANESE TRANSPLANTS IN THE U.S. AUTOMOBILE INDUSTRY

Since the 1980s, the growth of Japanese direct investment in the U.S. auto industry has been widely publicized. Japanese automakers have invested billions of dollars in U.S. based assembly facilities, known as **transplants**, as seen in Table 9.4. Establishing transplants in the United States provides a number of benefits to Japanese automakers, including opportunities to:

- Silence critics who insist that autos sold in the United States must be built there.
- Avoid the potential import barriers of the United States.

TABLE 9.4

Foreign Auto Plants in the United States

Plant Name/Parent Company	Location
Honda of America, Inc. (Honda)	Marysville, Ohio, Lincoln Alabama East Liberty, Ohio, Greensburg, Indiana
Toyota Motor Manufacturing, USA, Inc. (Toyota)	Georgetown, Kentucky, Huntsville, Alabama Princeton, Indiana, San Antonio, Texas Buffalo, West Virginia Blue Springs, Mississippi
Nissan Motor Manufacturing Corp. (Nissan)	Smyrna, Tennessee, Decherd, Tennessee Canton, Mississippi
Mazda Motor Manufacturing, USA, Inc. (Mazda)	Claycomo, Missouri
Volkswagen, USA, Inc. (Volkswagen)	Chattanooga, Tennessee

© 2015 Cengage Learning®

- Gain access to an expanding market at a time when the Japanese market is nearing saturation.
- Provide a hedge against fluctuations in the yen-dollar exchange rate.

Toyota has pledged to produce in North America at least two-thirds of the vehicles it sells in the region. It regards manufacturing more vehicles in the United States as a type of political insurance. By sprinkling manufacturing jobs across many states, Toyota has built a network of state and federal government officials friendly to the company.

The growth of Japanese investment in the U.S. auto industry has led to both praise and concern over the future of U.S. owned auto manufacturing and parts supplier industries. Proponents of foreign direct investment maintain that it fosters improvement in the overall competitive position of the domestic auto assembly and parts industries. They also argue that foreign investment generates jobs and provides consumers with a wider product choice at lower prices than would otherwise be available. However, the United Auto Workers (UAW) union maintains that this foreign investment results in job losses in the auto assembly and parts supplier industries.

One factor that influences the number of workers hired is a company's *job classifications* that stipulate the scope of work each employee performs. As the number of job classifications increases, the scope of work decreases, along with the flexibility of using available employees; this decrease can lead to falling worker productivity and rising production costs.

Japanese affiliated auto companies have traditionally used significantly fewer job classifications than traditional U.S. auto companies. Japanese transplants use work teams, and each team member is trained to do all the operations performed by the team. A typical Japanese affiliated assembly plant has three to four job classifications: one team leader, one production technician, and one or two maintenance technicians. Often, jobs are rotated among team members. In contrast, traditional U.S. auto plants have enacted more than 90 different job classifications, and employees generally perform only those operations specifically permitted for their classification. These trends have contributed to the superior labor productivity of Japanese transplants compared to the U.S. Big Three (GM, Ford, and Chrysler). Although powerful forces within the U.S. Big Three have resisted change, international competition has forced U.S. automakers to slowly dismantle U.S. management and production methods and remake them along Japanese lines.

For policy makers, the broader issue is whether the Japanese transplants have lived up to expectations. When the Japanese initiated investment in U.S. auto manufacturing facilities in the 1980s, many Americans viewed them as models for a revitalized U.S. auto industry and new customers for U.S. auto parts suppliers. Transplants were seen as a way of providing jobs for U.S. autoworkers whose jobs were dwindling as imports increased. When the transplant factories were announced, Americans anticipated that transplant production would be based primarily on American parts, material, and labor; transplant production would displace imports in the U.S. market while transferring new management techniques and technology to the United States.

Certainly, the transplant factories boosted the economies in the regions where they located. There is also no doubt that the transplants helped to transfer Japanese quality control, just-in-time delivery, and other production techniques to the United States. However, the original expectations of the transplants were only partially fulfilled. Skeptics contended that Japanese manufacturing operations were twice as likely to import parts for assembly in the United States as the average foreign company, and four times as likely to import parts as the average U.S. company. Extensive use of imported parts by Japanese transplants contributed to a U.S. automotive trade deficit with Japan and resulted in fewer jobs for U.S. autoworkers.

INTERNATIONAL JOINT VENTURES

Another area of MNE involvement is **international joint ventures**. A joint venture is a business organization established by two or more companies that combines their skills and assets. It may have a limited objective (research or production) and be short lived. It may also be multinational in character, involving cooperation among several domestic and foreign companies. Joint ventures differ from mergers in that they involve the creation of a *new* business firm, rather than the union of two existing companies.

There are three types of international joint ventures. The first is a joint venture formed by two businesses that conduct business in a third country. A U.S. oil firm and a UK oil firm may form a joint venture for oil exploration in the Middle East. Second is the formation of a joint venture with local private interests. Honeywell Information Systems of Japan was formed by Honeywell, Inc., of the United States and Mitsubishi Office Machinery Company of Japan to sell information system equipment to the Japanese. The third type of joint venture includes participation by local government. Bechtel of the United States, Messerschmitt–Boelkow–Bolhm of West Germany, and National Iranian Oil (representing the government of Iran) formed the Iran Oil Investment Company for oil extraction in Iran.

Several reasons have been advanced to justify the creation of joint ventures. Some functions such as R&D can involve costs too large for any one company to absorb by itself. Many of the world's largest copper deposits have been owned and mined jointly by the largest copper companies on the grounds that joint financing is required to raise enough capital. The exploitation of oil deposits is often done by a consortium of several oil companies. Exploratory drilling projects typically involve several companies united in a joint venture, and several refining companies traditionally own long distance crude oil pipelines. Oil refineries in foreign countries may be co-owned by several large U.S. and foreign oil companies.

Another factor that encourages the formation of international joint ventures is the restrictions some governments place on the foreign ownership of local businesses. Governments in developing nations often close their borders to foreign companies unless they are willing to take on local partners. Mexico, India, and Peru require that their own national companies represent a major interest in any foreign company conducting business within their borders. The foreign investor is forced to either accept local equity participation or forgo operation in the country. Such government policies are defended on the grounds that joint ventures result in the transfer of managerial techniques and know-how to the developing nation. Joint ventures may also prevent the possibility of excessive political influence on the part of foreign investors. Also, joint ventures help minimize dividend transfers abroad and thus strengthen the developing nation's balance-of-payments.

International joint ventures are also viewed as a means of forestalling protectionism against imports. Apparently motivated by the fear that rising protectionism might restrict their access to U.S. markets, Japanese manufacturers (Toyota Motor Enterprise) increasingly formed joint ventures with U.S. enterprises in the 1980s. Such ventures typically resulted in U.S. workers' assembling Japanese components, with the finished goods sold to U.S. consumers. Not only did this process permit Japanese production to enter the U.S. market, but it also blurred the distinction between U.S. and Japanese production. Just who is us? And who is them? The rationale for protecting domestic output and jobs from foreign competition is lessened.

There are disadvantages to forming an international joint venture. A joint venture is a cumbersome organization compared with a single organization. Control is divided, creating the problem of "two masters." Success or failure depends on how well companies can work together despite having different objectives, corporate cultures, and ways of doing things. The action of corporate chemistry is difficult to predict, but it is critical, because joint venture agreements usually provide both partners an ongoing role in management. When joint venture ownership is divided equally, as often occurs, deadlocks in decision making can take place. If balance is to be preserved between different economic interests, negotiation must establish a hierarchical command. Even when negotiated balance is achieved, it can be upset by changing corporate goals or personnel.

Welfare Effects

International joint ventures can yield both welfare increasing and welfare decreasing effects for the domestic economy. Joint ventures lead to *welfare gains* when (1) the newly established business adds to preexisting productive capacity and fosters additional competition, (2) the newly established business is able to enter new markets that neither parent could have entered individually, or (3) the business yields cost reductions that would have been unavailable if each parent performed the same function separately. The formation of a joint venture may also result in *welfare losses*. For instance, it may give rise to increased market power, suggesting greater ability to influence market output and price. This is especially likely to occur when the joint venture is formed in markets in which the parents conduct business. Under such circumstances, the parents, through their representatives in the joint venture, agree on prices and output in the very market that they themselves operate. Such coordination of activities limits competition, reinforces upward pressure on prices, and lowers the level of domestic welfare.

Let's consider an example that contrasts two situations: two competing companies sell autos in the domestic market; the two competitors form a joint venture that operates as a single seller (a monopoly) in the domestic market. We would expect to see a higher price and smaller quantity when the joint venture behaves as a monopoly. This result will always occur as long as the marginal cost curve for the joint venture is identical to the horizontal sum of the marginal cost curves of the individual competitors. The result of this *market power effect* is a deadweight welfare loss for the domestic economy—a reduction in consumer surplus that is not offset by a corresponding gain to producers. If the formation of the joint venture entails *productivity gains* that neither parent can realize prior to its formation, domestic welfare may increase. This is because a smaller amount of the domestic economy's resources is now required to produce any given output. Whether domestic welfare rises or falls because of the joint venture depends on the magnitudes of these two opposing forces.

Figure 9.3 illustrates the welfare effects of two parent companies' forming a joint venture in the market in which they operate. Assume that Sony Auto Company of Japan and American Auto Company of the United States are the only two firms producing autos for sale in the U.S. market. Assume each company realizes constant long run costs, suggesting that the average total cost equals marginal cost at each level of output. Let the cost schedules of each company prior to the formation of the joint venture be $MC_0 = ATC_0$, which equals \$10,000. Thus, $MC_0 = ATC_0$ becomes the long run market supply schedule for autos.

Assume that Sony Auto Company and American Auto Company initially operate as competitors, charging a price equal to marginal cost. In Figure 9.3, market equilibrium exists at point A, where 100 autos are sold at a price of \$10,000 per unit. Consumer surplus totals area $a + b + c$. Producer surplus does not exist, given the horizontal supply schedule of autos (recall that producer surplus equals the sum of the differences between the market price and each of the minimum prices indicated on the supply schedule for quantities between zero and the market output).

FIGURE 9.3

Welfare Effects of an International Joint Venture

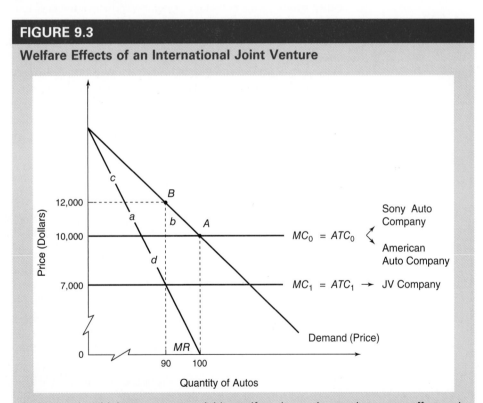

An international joint venture can yield a welfare decreasing market power effect and a welfare increasing cost reduction effect. The source of the cost reduction effect may be lower resource prices or improvements in technology and productivity. The joint venture leads to improvements in national welfare if its cost reduction effect is due to improvements in technology and productivity and if it more than offsets the market-power effect.

Now suppose that the two competitors announce the formation of a joint venture known as JV Company that manufactures autos for sale in the United States. The autos sold by JV replace the autos sold by the two parents in the United States.

Consider the formation of JV Company entails new production efficiencies that result in cost reductions. Let JV's new cost schedule, $MC_1 = ATC_1$, be located at $7,000. As a monopoly, JV maximizes profit by equating marginal revenue with marginal cost. Market equilibrium exists at point B, where 90 autos are sold at a price of $12,000 per unit. The price increase leads to a reduction in consumer surplus equal to area $a + b$. Of this amount, area a is transferred to JV as producer surplus. Area b represents the loss of consumer surplus that is *not* transferred to JV and becomes a deadweight welfare loss for the U.S. economy (the consumption effect).

Against this deadweight welfare loss lays the efficiency effect of JV Company: a decrease in unit costs from $10,000 to $7,000 per auto. JV can produce its profit maximizing output, 90 autos, at a cost reduction equal to area d as compared with the costs that would exist if the parent companies produced the same output. Area d represents additional producer surplus that is a welfare gain for the U.S. economy. Our analysis concludes that for the United States, the formation of JV Company is desirable if area d exceeds area b.

It has been assumed that JV Company achieves cost reductions that are unavailable to either parent as a stand-alone company. Whether the cost reductions benefit the overall U.S. economy depends on their source. If they result from *productivity* improvements (new work rules leading to higher output per worker), a welfare gain exists for the economy because fewer resources are required to produce a given number of autos and the excess can be shifted to other industries. However, the cost reductions stemming from JV Company's formation may be *monetary* in nature. Being a newly formed company, JV may be able to negotiate wage concessions from domestic workers that could not be achieved by the American Auto Company. Such a cost reduction represents a transfer of dollars from domestic workers to JV profits and does not constitute an overall welfare gain for the economy.

MULTINATIONAL ENTERPRISES AS A SOURCE OF CONFLICT

Advocates of MNEs often point out the benefits these enterprises can provide for the nations they affect, including both the source country where the parent organization is located and the host country where subsidiary firms are established. Benefits allegedly exist in the forms of additional levels of investment and capital, creation of new jobs, and the development of technologies and production processes. Critics contend that MNEs often create trade restraints, cause conflict with national economic and political objectives, and have adverse effects on a nation's balance-of-payments. These arguments perhaps explain why some nations frown on direct investment, while others welcome it. This section examines some of the more controversial issues involving multinationals. The frame of reference is the U.S. MNE, although the same issues apply no matter where the parent organization is based.

Employment

One of the most hotly debated issues surrounding the MNE is its effects on employment in both the host and source countries. Multinationals often contend that their foreign direct investment yields favorable benefits to the labor force of the recipient nation.

Setting up a new multinational automobile manufacturing plant in Canada creates more jobs for Canadian workers. But the MNE's effect on jobs varies from business to business. One source of controversy arises when the direct investment spending of foreign based MNEs is used to purchase already existing local businesses rather than to establish new ones. In this case, the investment spending may not result in additional production capacity and may not have noticeable effects on employment in the host country. Another problem arises when MNEs bring in foreign managers and other top executives to run the subsidiary in the host country. In U.S. oil companies located in Saudi Arabia, the Saudis are increasingly demanding their own people be employed in higher level positions.

As for the source country, the issues of runaway jobs and cheap foreign labor are of vital concern to home workers. Because labor unions are confined to individual countries, the multinational nature of these businesses permits them to escape much of the collective bargaining influence of domestic unions. It is also pointed out that MNEs can seek out those countries where labor has minimal market power.

The ultimate impact that MNEs have on employment in the host and source countries seems to depend in part on the time scale. In the short run, the source country will likely experience an employment decline when production is shifted overseas. Other industries in the source country may find foreign sales rising over time. This is because foreign labor consumes as well as produces and tends to purchase more as employment and income increase as a result of increased investment. Perhaps the main source of controversy stems from the fact that the MNEs are involved in rapid changes in technology and in the transmission of productive enterprise to host countries. Although such efforts may promote global welfare in the long run, the potential short run adjustment problems facing source country labor cannot be ignored.

Caterpillar Bulldozes Canadian Locomotive Workers

The ability of a company to reduce its labor cost tends to increase when the company has market alternatives in the hiring of workers. Consider the case of Caterpillar, Inc., headquartered in Peoria, Illinois. Caterpillar is a global producer of heavy machinery, diesel engines, construction and mining equipment, tractors, and the like.

In 2012, Caterpillar shut down a 62-year-old railroad locomotive plant in London, Ontario that employed about 450 workers. The Canadian Auto Workers (CAW) union that represented most of the workers described the closure as selfish behavior on the part of Caterpillar's management. Also, the CAW noted that upon announcing the closure of the plant, Caterpillar immediately publicized the opening of a new locomotive plant in Muncie, Indiana. At this plant, workers have the right but are not compelled to join a labor union. Caterpillar made it clear that it had no desire to negotiate with union representatives at the Muncie plant. Why?

By moving production to Muncie, where unemployment was high and nonunion workers were plentiful, Caterpillar could pay workers wages about half the Ontario level: Caterpillar offered jobs ranging from $12 to $18.50 per hour, in contrast to wages averaging $35 (U.S. dollars) at the Ontario plant. Considering the Ontario plant's labor costs to be noncompetitive, Caterpillar demanded from its workers a 50 percent cut in wages, but this was rejected by the CAW. After ten months of unsuccessful negotiations, Caterpillar announced that its wage dispute with the CAW could not be resolved. Caterpillar locked out its Canadian workers and shut down the locomotive factory. Besides moving to Muncie, Caterpillar increased its locomotive production in Mexico and Brazil where wages were lower than in Canada or the United States.

Caterpillar's strategy of closing a unionized plant differed from its chief competitor in locomotives; General Electric Co. In 2011, GE peacefully negotiated a four-year contract with its unionized workers that raised annual wages by about 2.25 percent. This resulted in GE's locomotive workers in Erie, PA earning $25–$36 an hour, about double that of Caterpillar's wages in Muncie. GE announced it would open another locomotive producing plant in Fort Worth, Texas, a state where union membership is low and wages would be less than the levels paid to its Erie workers.[2]

Technology Transfer

Besides promoting runaway jobs, multinationals can foster the transfer of technology (knowledge and skills applied to how goods are produced) to other nations. Such a process is known as **technology transfer**.

Technology has been likened to a contagious disease: it spreads further and more quickly if there are more personal contacts. Foreign trade is viewed as a channel through which people in different nations make contacts and people in one nation get to know about the products of other nations. Foreign direct investment is an even more effective method of technology transfer. When foreign firms with technological advantages establish local production subsidiaries, the personal contacts between these subsidiaries and local firms are more frequent and closer than when firms are located abroad.

International trade and foreign direct investment also facilitate technology transfer via the so called *demonstration effect*: as a firm shows how its products operate, this sends important information to other firms that such products exist and are usable. Technology transfer is also aided by the *competition effect*: when a foreign firm manufactures a superior product that is popular among consumers, other firms are threatened. To survive, they must innovate and improve the quality of their products.

Although technology transfer may increase the productivity and competitiveness of recipient nations, donor nations may react against it because it is detrimental to their economic base. Donor nations contend that the establishment of production operations abroad by MNEs decreases their export potential and leads to job losses for their workers. By sharing technical knowledge with foreign nations, a donor nation may eventually lose its international competitiveness, causing a decrease in its rate of economic growth.

Consider the case of the technology transfer to China in the mid-1990s. After decades of mutual hostility, the United States hoped that by the 1990s China would open itself to the outside world and engage in free trade so foreign nations could trade with China according to the principle of comparative advantage. Instead, China used its leverage as a large buyer of foreign products to pressure MNEs to localize production and transfer technology to China to help it become competitive. With MNEs willing to outbid each other to woo Chinese bureaucrats, China was in a favorable position to reap the benefits of technology transfer.

Microsoft Corporation, under the threat of having its software banned, co-developed a Chinese version of Windows 95 with a local partner and agreed to aid efforts to develop a Chinese software industry. Another example was General Motors. To beat Ford for the right to become a partner in manufacturing sedans in Shanghai, GM agreed to bring in dozens of joint ventures for auto parts and to design most of the car in China. It also agreed to establish five research institutes to teach Chinese engineers to turn

[2]James Hagerty, "Caterpillar Closes Plant in Canada After Lockout," *The Wall Street Journal*, February 4, 2012, p. B-1. See also, James Hagerty and Alistair MacDonald, "As Unions Lose Their Grip, Indiana Lures Manufacturing Jobs," *The Wall Street Journal*, March 18, 2012, pp. A-1 and A-12 and Shruti Date Sing, "Caterpillar Factory Closing Deal Ratified by CAW," *Bloomberg News*, February 23, 2012.

technological theory in fields such as power trains and fuel injection systems into commercial applications.

American multinationals argued that transferring technology to China was largely risk free because a competitive challenge from China was decades away. However, the acceleration of technology transfer in the mid-1990s became increasingly unpopular with U.S. labor unions that feared their members were losing jobs to lower paid Chinese workers. United States government officials also feared that the technology transfer was helping create a competitor of extreme proportions. Let us consider the case of General Electric's technology transfer to China.

General Electric's Trade-Off for Entry into the Chinese Market: Short-Term Sales for Long-Term Competition For decades, General Electric (GE) had an effective strategy for being competitive in the Chinese market for power generating equipment: sell the best equipment at the lowest price. By the first decade of the 2000s, the formula was altered. Besides offering high-quality gas-fired turbines at a competitive price, GE had to agree to share with the Chinese sophisticated technology for producing the turbines. To be considered for turbine contracts worth several billion dollars, GE, Mitsubishi, Siemens, and other competitors were obligated to form joint ventures with state owned Chinese power companies. General Electric was also required to transfer to its new partners the technology and advanced manufacturing specifications for its gas-fired turbine that GE had spent more than $500 million to develop. Officials from GE noted that the Chinese wanted to have complete access to its technology, while GE wanted to protect the technology in which it made a large financial investment.

The vast size of China's electricity market convinced GE executives that this market was worth pursuing in spite of the technology demands. The U.S. market for gas-fired turbines was weak because of past spending sprees to increase capacity by power companies and utilities. On the other hand, China was expected to spend more than $10 billion a year constructing electricity plants in the near future. General Electric officials thus faced the trade-off of short-term sales in China for long-term competition from Chinese manufacturers. In the end, GE won an order for 13 of its gas-fired turbines, and as part of the agreement also had to share technology with its Chinese partners.

Before the gas-fired turbine venture with GE, Chinese manufacturers had mastered only the technology required for making much less efficient steam powered turbines. That technology was obtained in part through previous joint ventures with firms such as Westinghouse Electric Co. The Chinese demanded the technology behind the more efficient gas-fired turbines.

General Electric officials noted that Chinese competition was not imminent in highly advanced products like gas-fired turbines. In the past, even after acquiring expertise from foreign corporations, Chinese firms lacked the skill necessary to fully exploit the technology and become competitive in world markets. By the time Chinese companies mastered the technology they initially obtained from GE, GE had developed more advanced technologies. Nonetheless, Chinese officials looked ahead to new rounds of power generating equipment bidding by GE and its competitors, when Chinese officials hoped to obtain even more lucrative technology sharing deals.[3]

Boeing Transfers Technology to China Boeing provides another example of technology transfer. Since the 1970s, Boeing Co. has maintained an enviable position in

---

[3]"China's Price for Market Entry: Give Us Your Technology, Too," *The Wall Street Journal*, February 26, 2004, pp. A-1 and A-6.

China. The firm sells jetliners to China and currently accounts for about half of the country's commercial aircraft. Analysts estimate that about 5,000 jetliners worth a total of $600 billion will be sold in China between 2013 and 2030. Is Boeing about to lose its lucrative position in China?

China is increasingly using its leverage as a large buyer of aircraft to pressure Boeing for the same type of concessions it commonly extracts from other foreign firms that conduct business there. China often requires them to acquire local partners and share proprietary technology in exchange for access to its fast-growing market.

To secure China's orders for its 787 Dreamliner, Boeing agreed not only to outsource an unprecedented amount of the jetliner's parts production to partners in China (and also in Europe and Japan), but to transfer to them unprecedented technological know-how. Prior to the 787, Boeing had kept almost all of the control of jetliner design and provided foreign suppliers precise engineering specifications for building parts, the only exception being jet engines that have traditionally been designed and produced by companies such as Rolls Royce, Pratt and Whitney, and General Electric. The 787 program deviated from this strategy. Boeing provided major suppliers a large portion of its production manual, "How to Build a Commercial Airplane," a guide that its engineers have been working on for the last five decades. This manual provided foreign suppliers considerable insight to the art of building a jetliner.

Commercial Aircraft Corporation of China (Comac), a government sponsored plane maker that plans to launch its first jetliner by 2016. It requires a lot of technology to build a jetliner, a technology China does not yet have and that's where Boeing enters the picture. In 2012, Chinese officials notified Boeing that it will have to fork over more intellectual property if it wants to keep selling planes in China. This resulted in Boeing and Comac forming a technology joint venture in which the companies will work together on biofuels and fuel efficiency technologies. American critics point out that this is the first step on the familiar path of technology transfer to a Chinese competitor. Although the joint venture is supposed to focus only on new technologies, there is no way to keep Comac researchers working along with Boeing engineers and gaining a lot more than that.

Comac is not just any competitor: it is backed by the Chinese government. Will the government pressure Chinese airlines to buy planes from Comac, at the expense of Boeing or Airbus? Will China have the continental clout to persuade other Asian carriers to buy from Comac? Like Asian automakers, Comac may someday compete globally, including in the United States. This would strike at the very heart of the existing Boeing–Airbus duopoly in control of most of the world's large commercial aviation market.[4]

National Sovereignty

Another controversial issue involving the conduct of MNEs is their effect on the economic and political policies of the host and source governments. Many nations fear that the presence of MNEs in a given country results in a loss of its national sovereignty. MNEs may resist government attempts to redistribute national income through taxation.

---

[4]Donald Barlett and James Steele, *The Betrayal of the American Dream*, Public Affairs/Persus Books Group, New York, 2012; Dennis Shea, *The Impact of International Technology Transfer on American Research and Development*, Committee on Science, Space, and Technology, Subcommittee on Investigations and Oversight, U.S. House of Representatives, December 5, 2012; The Boeing Company, *2011 Annual Report*, Chicago, Illinois; Dick Nolan, "Is Boeing's 787 Dreamliner a Triumph or a Folly?" *Harvard Business Review*, December 23, 2009.

By using accounting techniques that shift profits overseas, an MNE may be able to evade the taxes of a host country. An MNE could accomplish this evasion by raising prices on goods from its subsidiaries in nations with modest tax rates to reduce profits on its operations in a high tax nation where most of its business actually takes place.

The political influence of MNEs is also questioned by many, as illustrated by the case of Chile. For years, U.S. businesses had pursued direct investments in Chile, largely in copper mining. When Salvador Allende was in the process of winning the presidency, he was opposed by U.S. businesses fearing that their Chilean operations would be expropriated by the host government. International Telephone and Telegraph tried to prevent the election of Allende and attempted to promote civil disturbances that would lead to his fall from power. Another case of MNEs' meddling in host country affairs is that of United Brands (now Chiquita), who engaged in food product sales. In 1974, the company paid a $1.25 million bribe to the president of Honduras in return for an export tax reduction applied to bananas. When the payoff was revealed, the president was removed from office.

There are other areas of controversy. Suppose a Canadian subsidiary of a U.S. based MNE conducts trade with a country subject to U.S. trade embargoes. Should U.S. policymakers outlaw such activities? The Canadian subsidiary may be pressured by the parent organization to comply with U.S. foreign policy. During international crises, MNEs may move funds rapidly from one financial center to another to avoid losses (make profits) from changes in exchange rates. This conduct makes it difficult for national governments to stabilize their economies.

In a world where national economies are interdependent and factors of production are mobile, the possible loss of national sovereignty is often viewed as a necessary cost whenever direct investment results in foreign control of production facilities. Whether the welfare gains accruing from the international division of labor and specialization outweigh the potential diminution of national independence involves value judgments by policymakers and interested citizens.

Balance-of-Payments

The United States offers a good example of how an MNE can affect a nation's balance-of-payments. The *balance-of-payments* is an account of the value of goods and services, capital movements (including foreign direct investment), and other items that flow into or out of a country. Items that make a positive contribution to a nation's payments position include exports of goods and services and capital inflows (foreign investment entering the home country), whereas the opposite flows weaken the payments position. At first glance, we might conclude that when U.S. MNEs make foreign direct investments, these payments represent an outflow of capital from the United States and hence a negative factor on the U.S. payments position. Although this view may be true in the short run, it ignores the positive effects on trade flows and earnings that direct investment provides in the long run.

When a U.S. MNE sets up a subsidiary overseas it generally purchases U.S. capital equipment and materials needed to run the subsidiary. Once in operation, the subsidiary tends to purchase additional capital equipment and other material inputs from the United States. Both of these factors stimulate U.S. exports, strengthening its balance-of-payments position.

Another long run impact that U.S. foreign direct investment has on its balance-of-payments is the return inflow of income generated by overseas operations. Such income includes earnings of overseas affiliates, interest and dividends, and fees and royalties. These items generate inflows of revenues for the economy and strengthen the balance-of-payments position.

Transfer Pricing

Controversy also confronts MNEs in their use of **transfer pricing**, the pricing of goods within an MNE. Goods from the company's production division may be sold to its foreign marketing division, or inputs obtained by a parent company can come from a foreign subsidiary. The transfer price may be a purely arbitrary figure that means it may be unrelated to costs incurred or to operations carried out. The choice of the transfer prices affects the division of the total profit among the parts of the company and thus influences its overall tax burden.

Suppose that Dell Inc. produces computers in the United States and buys microchips from its own subsidiary in Malaysia. Also suppose that corporate taxes are 34 percent in the United States and 20 percent in Malaysia. Imagine that Dell tells its subsidiary to sell microchips to Dell at a grossly inflated price (the transfer price). Dell has a large business expense to deduct when determining its taxable income on its other profitable operations in the United States. To the extent that transfer pricing allows Dell to reduce its taxable income in the United States, the firm avoids being taxed at the rate of 34 percent. The increased income of Dell's Malaysian subsidiary that occurs because of the inflated transfer price is taxed at the lower rate of 20 percent. Dell can reduce its overall tax burden by reporting most of its income in Malaysia, the low-tax country, even though the income is earned in the United States, the high-tax country. The tax paid to the U.S. government decreases while the tax paid to the Malaysian government increases. In other words, one government's loss is the other government's gain. So one government is expected to want to legislate against unfair transfer pricing practices while the other government is expected to resist such legislation.

Both foreign governments and the U.S. government are interested in the part that transfer prices play in the realization of corporate profits. Abuses in pricing across national borders are illegal if they can be proved. According to U.S. Internal Revenue Service (IRS) regulations, enterprises dealing with their own subsidiaries are required to set prices "at arm's length" just as they would for unrelated customers that are not part of the same corporate structure. This process means that prices must relate to actual costs incurred and to operations actually carried out. Proving the prices that one subsidiary charges another are far from market prices is difficult.

INTERNATIONAL LABOR MOBILITY: MIGRATION

Historically the United States has been a favorite target for international **migration**. Because of its vast inflow of migrants, the United States has been described as the melting pot of the world. Table 9.5 indicates the volume of immigration to the United States from the 1820s to 2011. Western Europe was a major source of immigrants during this era, with Germany, Italy, and the United Kingdom among the largest contributors. In recent years, large numbers of Mexicans have migrated to the United States as well as people from Asia. Migrants have been motivated by better economic opportunities and noneconomic factors such as politics, war, and religion.

Although international labor movements can enhance the world economy's efficiency, they are often restricted by government controls. The United States, like most countries, limits immigration. Following waves of immigration at the turn of the century, the Immigration Act of 1924 was enacted. Besides restricting the overall flow of immigrants to the United States, the act implemented a quota that limited the number of immigrants from each foreign country. Because the quotas were based on the number of U.S. citizens who had previously emigrated from those countries, the allocation system favored emigrants

TRADE CONFLICTS   APPLE USES TAX LOOPHOLES TO DODGE TAXES

When Barack Obama became President, he declared it is time to slash tax breaks for U.S. firms that ship our jobs overseas and give those tax breaks to companies that create jobs in the United States. His goal was to create jobs for Americans, make the tax code fairer, and raise additional revenue for the federal government. Among the tax breaks that Obama had in mind are *foreign tax credits* and *tax deferrals*.

According to U.S. tax law, an MNE headquartered in the United States is permitted credits against its U.S. income tax liabilities in an amount equal to the income taxes it pays to foreign governments. Assuming that an Irish subsidiary earns $100,000 taxable income and Ireland's corporate income tax rate is 12.5 percent, the company would pay the Irish government $12,500. If that income were applied to the parent company in the United States, the tax owed to the U.S. government would be $35,000, given a corporate income tax rate of 35 percent. Under the tax credit system, the parent company would pay the U.S. government only $22,500 ($35,000 − $12,500 = $22,500). The rationale of the foreign tax credit is that MNEs headquartered in the United States should not be subject to double taxation.

United States based MNEs also enjoy a tax deferral advantage. Under U.S. tax laws, the parent company has the option of deferring U.S. taxes paid on the income of its foreign subsidiary as long as that income is retained overseas rather than repatriated to the United States. This system amounts to an interest free loan extended by the U.S. government to the parent for as long as the income is maintained abroad. Retained earnings of an overseas subsidiary can be reinvested abroad without being subject to U.S. taxes. Therefore, the tax deferral puts a U.S.-based MNE that has a subsidiary in China, on the same footing as a local company operating in China or on the same footing as a French based MNE that operates a subsidiary in China. When the income is repatriated to the United States, it is no longer being used by that subsidiary, so there is no longer any need for that tax leveling. The MNE gets taxed by the United States but with a foreign tax credit for the foreign tax that has previously been paid.

Apple Inc. provides an example of a global company that uses tax loopholes to cut taxes. Not only are Apple's iPhones, iPods, and other products high quality and popular throughout the world, but the firm's designers and engineers have a well-earned reputation for creativity. Apple performs most of its product design, software development, and other high-wage functions in the United States. The firm has typically reported only about 30 percent of its profits as being from the United States. Why? To reduce its taxes, Apple designs its business to locate as much profit as possible in those countries where taxes are low. At the same time, it allocates as many costs as possible to those high-tax countries, like the United States where deductions are especially valuable. A deduction is worth 35 cents on the dollar in the United States where the corporate tax rate is 35 percent; but deductions are worth only one third as much in Ireland, where the corporate tax rate is 12.5 percent. As of 2014, Apple had over $100 billion more than two-thirds of its total profits stashed away in offshore accounts and not subject to U.S. corporate income taxes. These profits would be subject to U.S. taxes only when they were brought home or repatriated.

Although Apple's tax avoidance practices were legal under the U.S. tax system, critics said that they were unfair and should be reformed. Reforming the tax system has become increasingly important because early tax principles of the 1900s that assume transactions begin and end in one country, do not match practices of the 2000s, in which the Internet and globalization have made it easy for a business transaction to involve several countries. Historically, the notion of conducting business in another country and concluding sales without having a permanent establishment or tax presence in that country was not physically possible. In the era of the Internet, it is possible for firms to attain global outreach and conduct business in several countries without creating a tax presence in those countries. International tax avoidance needs to be dealt with on a cooperative basis between nations, on principles that apply fairly to all countries.

Source: Gary Hufbauer and Martin Vieiro, *Corporate Taxation and U.S. MNCs: Ensuring a Competitive Economy*, Policy Brief, Washington, DC: Peterson Institute for International Economics, April 2013; McKinsey Global Institute, *Growth and Competitiveness in the United States: The Role of Its Multinational* Companies, Washington, DC 2010; Kimberly Clausing, "Multinational Firm Tax Avoidance and Tax Policy," *National Tax Journal*, Vol. 62, December 2009.

iStockphoto.com/photosoup

TABLE 9.5	
U.S. Immigration 1820–2011	
Period	**Number (thousands)**
1820–1840	743
1841–1860	4,311
1861–1880	5,127
1881–1900	8,934
1901–1920	14,531
1921–1940	4,636
1941–1960	3,551
1961–1980	7,815
1981–2000	16,433
2001–2011	11,563

Source: From U.S. Department of Homeland Security, Office of Immigration Statistics, *Yearbook of Immigration Statistics*, 2011, available at http://www.uscis.gov/graphics/shared/statistics/yearbook/. See also U.S. Department of Commerce, Bureau of the Census, *Statistical Abstracts of the United States*, Washington, DC: Government Printing Office, available at www.census.gov/.

from northern Europe relative to southern Europe. In the late 1960s, the quota formula was modified that led to increasing numbers of Asian immigrants to the United States.

The Effects of Migration

Figure 9.4 illustrates the economics of labor migration. Assume the world consists of two countries, the United States and Mexico that are initially in isolation. The horizontal axes denote the total quantity of labor in the United States and Mexico, and the vertical axes depict the wages paid to labor. For each country, the demand schedule for labor is designated by the value of the marginal product (VMP) of labor.[5] Also assume a fixed labor supply of seven workers in the United States, denoted by $S_{U.S._0}$, and seven workers in Mexico, denoted by S_{M_0}.

The equilibrium wage in each country is determined at the point of intersection of the supply and demand schedules for labor. In Figure 9.4(a), the U.S. equilibrium wage is \$9 and total labor income is \$63; this amount is represented by the area $a + b$. The remaining area under the labor demand schedule is area c that equals \$24.50; this value represents the share of the nation's income accruing to owners of capital.[6] In Figure 9.4(b)

---

[5]The VMP of labor refers to the amount of money producers receive from selling the quantity that was produced by the last worker hired; in other words, VMP = product price × the marginal product of labor. The VMP curve is the labor demand schedule. This curve follows from an application of the rule that a business hiring under competitive conditions finds it most profitable to hire labor up to the point at which the price of labor (wage rate) equals its VMP. The location of the VMP curve depends on the marginal productivity of labor and the price of the product that it produces. Under pure competition, price is constant. Therefore, it is because of diminishing marginal productivity that the labor demand schedule is downward sloping.

[6]How do we know that area c represents the income accruing to U.S. owners of capital? My analysis assumes two productive factors, labor and capital. The total income (value of output) that results from using a given quantity of labor with a fixed amount of capital equals the area under the VMP curve of labor for that particular quantity of labor. Labor's share of that area is calculated by multiplying the wage rate times the quantity of labor hired. The remaining area under the VMP curve is the income accruing to the owners of capital.

FIGURE 9.4

Effects of Labor Migration from Mexico to the United States

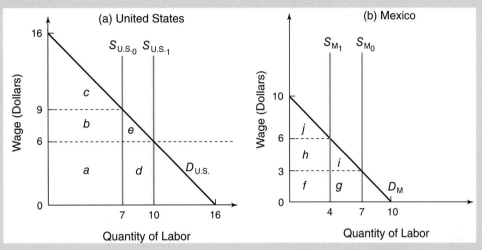

Prior to migration, the wage rate in the United States exceeds that of Mexico. Responding to the wage differential, Mexican workers immigrate to the United States; this leads to a reduction in the Mexican labor supply and an increase in the U.S. labor supply. Wage rates continue to rise in Mexico and fall in the United States until they eventually are equalized. The labor migration hurts native U.S. workers but helps U.S. owners of capital; the opposite occurs in Mexico. Because migrant workers flow from uses of lower productivity to higher productivity, world output expands.

© Cengage Learning®

the equilibrium wage for Mexico is $3; labor income totals $21 represented by area $f + g$; capital owners enjoy incomes equaling area $h + i + j$, or $24.50.

Suppose labor can move freely between Mexico and the United States and assume that migration is costless and occurs solely in response to wage differentials. Because U.S. wage rates are relatively high, there is an incentive for Mexican workers to migrate to the United States and compete in the U.S. labor market; this process will continue until the wage differential is eliminated. Imagine three workers migrate from Mexico to the United States. In the United States, the new labor supply schedule becomes $S_{U.S._1}$; the excess supply of labor at the $9 wage rate causes the wage rate to fall to $6. In Mexico, the labor emigration results in a new labor supply schedule at S_{M_1}; the excess demand for labor at wage rate $3 causes the wage rate to rise to $6. The effect of **labor mobility** is to equalize wage rates in two countries.[7]

Our next job is to assess how labor migration in response to wage differentials affects the world economy's efficiency. Does world output expand or contract with open migration? For the United States, migration increases the labor supply from $S_{U.S._0}$ to $S_{U.S._1}$. This increase leads to an expansion of output; the value of the additional output is denoted by area $d + e$ ($22.50). For Mexico, the decrease in labor supply from S_{M_0} to S_{M_1} results in a contraction in output; the value of the lost output is represented by

---

[7]Wage rate equalization assumes unrestricted labor mobility in which workers are concerned only about their incomes. It also assumes that migration is costless for labor. In reality, there are economic and psychological costs of migrating to another country. Such costs may result in only a small number of persons' finding the wage gains in the immigrating country high enough to compensate them for their migration costs. Thus, complete wage equalization may not occur.

area $g + i$ ($13.50). The result is a net gain of $9 in world output as a result of labor migration. This is because the VMP of labor in the United States exceeds that of Mexico throughout the relevant range. Workers are attracted to the United States by the higher wages. These higher wages signal to Mexican labor the higher value of worker productivity, attracting workers to those areas where they will be most efficient. As workers are used more productively, world output expands.

Migration also affects the *distribution of income*. As we will see, the gains in world income resulting from labor mobility are not distributed equally among all nations and factors of production. The United States as a whole benefits from immigration; its overall income gain is the sum of the losses by native U.S. workers, gains by Mexican immigrants now living in the United States, and gains by U.S. owners of capital. Mexico experiences overall income losses as a result of its labor emigration; however, workers remaining in Mexico gain relative to Mexican owners of capital. As previously suggested, the Mexican immigrants gain from their relocation to the United States.

For the United States, the gain in income as a result of immigration is denoted by area $d + e$ ($22.50) in Figure 9.4(a). Of this amount, Mexican immigrants capture area d ($18), while area e ($4.50) is the extra income accruing to U.S. owners of capital thanks to the availability of additional labor to use with the capital. Immigration forces wage rates down from $9 to $6. The earnings of the native U.S. workers fall by area b ($21); this amount is transferred to U.S. owners of capital.

As for Mexico, its labor emigration results in a decrease in income equal to $g + i$ ($13.50); this decrease represents a transfer from Mexico to the United States. The remaining workers in Mexico gain area h ($12) as a result of higher wages. However, Mexican capital owners lose because less labor is available for use with their capital.

Although immigration may lower wage rates for some native U.S. workers, it should also be noted that these lower wage rates benefit U.S. producers. Lower wage rates also result in lower equilibrium product prices, thereby benefiting consumers. From society's perspective, the gains from immigration to producers and consumers should be weighed against the losses to low-wage workers.

We can conclude that the effect of labor mobility is to increase overall world income and to redistribute income from labor to capital in the United States and from capital to labor in Mexico. Migration has an impact on the distribution of income similar to an increase in exports of labor-intensive goods from Mexico to the United States.

Immigration as an Issue

The preceding example makes it clear why domestic labor groups in capital abundant nations often prefer restrictions on immigration; open immigration tends to reduce their wages. When migrant workers are unskilled as is typically the case, the negative effect on wages mainly affects unskilled domestic workers. Conversely, domestic manufacturers will tend to favor unrestricted immigration as a source of cheap labor.

Another controversy about immigrants is whether they are a drain on government resources. Nations that provide generous welfare payments to the economically disadvantaged may fear they will induce an influx of nonproductive people who will not produce as did the immigrants of Figure 9.4, but enjoy welfare benefits at the expense of domestic residents and working immigrants. Fiscal relief may not be far away. The children of immigrants will soon enter the labor force and begin paying taxes, thus supporting not only their children's education, but also their parents' retirement. In a matter of two generations, most immigrant families tend to assimilate to the point that their fiscal burdens are indistinguishable from those of other natives. When it's all added up, most long run calculations show that immigrants make a net positive contribution to public coffers.

Developing nations have sometimes feared open immigration policies because they can result in a **brain drain**—emigration of highly educated and skilled people from developing nations to industrial nations, thus limiting the growth potential of the developing nations. The brain drain has been encouraged by national immigration laws, as in the United States and other industrial nations that permit the immigration of skilled persons while restricting that of unskilled workers.

In the previous labor migration example, we implicitly assumed that the Mexican workers' migration decision was more or less permanent. In practice, most labor migration is temporary, especially in the EU. A country such as France will allow the immigration of foreign workers on a temporary basis when needed; these workers are known as **guest workers**. During periods of business recession, France will refuse to issue work permits when foreign workers are no longer needed. Such a practice tends to insulate the French economy from labor shortages during business expansions and labor surpluses during business recessions. The labor adjustment problem is shifted to the labor emigrating countries.

Illegal migration is also a problem. In the United States this type of migration has become a political hot potato, with millions of illegal immigrants finding employment in the so-called underground economy, often below minimum wage. Some 3 to 15 million illegal immigrants are estimated to be in the United States; many of them from Mexico. For the United States and especially the western states, immigration of Mexican workers has provided a cheap supply of agricultural and low-skilled workers. For Mexico, it has been a major source of foreign exchange and a safety cushion against domestic unemployment. Illegal immigration also affects the distribution of income for U.S. natives because it tends to reduce the income of low-skilled U.S. workers. There is no consensus on the size of this impact.[8]

On the other hand, immigrants not only diversify an economy but may also contribute to economic growth. Because immigrants are often different from natives, the economy as a whole profits. In many instances, immigrants cause prices to fall that benefits all consumers, and enables the economy to domestically produce a wider variety of goods than natives could alone. If immigrants weren't different from natives, they would only augment the population and scale of the economy, but not have an effect on the overall growth rate of per capita income. Immigration best enhances economic growth when immigrants are highly skilled, more innovative and entrepreneurial, attract capital, and work in occupations where native born labor is scarce.

As we learned from Figure 9.4, immigrants increase the supply of labor in the economy. This results in a lower market wage for all workers *if all workers are the same*. But all workers are not the same. Some natives will compete with immigrants for positions because they possess similar skills; others will work alongside immigrants, complementing the immigrants' skills with their own. This skill distinction means that not all native workers will receive a lower wage. Those who compete with (are substitutes for) immigrants will receive a lower wage than they would without immigration, while those who complement immigrants will receive a higher wage. Most analyses of various countries have found that a ten percent increase in the immigrant share of the population reduces native wages by one percent at most. This finding suggests that most immigrants are not substituting for native labor—skilled or unskilled—but are, instead, complementing it.[9]

Advocates of increased immigration note that children do not begin working the minute they are born. Producing an adult worker requires substantial expenditures in the form of food, clothing, shelter, education, and other child rearing costs. These investments in human capital formation are quite substantial. Immigrant workers, unlike newborn children, are able to begin engaging in productive activities upon their arrival

---

[8]Pia Orrenius and Madeline Zavodny, "From Brawn to Brains: How Immigration Works for America," *Annual Report*, Federal Reserve Bank of Dallas, 2010, pp. 4–17.

[9]Friedberg, R. M. and J. Hunt, "The Impact of Immigrants on Host Country Wages, Employment and Growth," *Journal of Economic Perspectives* (Spring 1995), pp. 23–44.

in the country. The cost of much of their human capital formation was borne by the country from where they emigrated. Because most immigrants arrive at a stage in their life in which they are relatively productive, higher immigration rates generally result in an increase in the proportion of the population that is working. As the proportion of the population that is working rises, per capita income also rises.

Concern over the future of social security is also used to support relaxed immigration restrictions. Declining birthrates in the United States, combined with rising life spans, result in a steady increase in the ratio of retired to working individuals over the next few decades. An increase in the number of younger immigrants could help to alleviate this problem.

Does Canada's Immigration Policy Provide a Model for the United States?

Like the United States, Canada is a country where immigration is an important contributor to its society and culture. Having a sparse population and an abundance of unsettled land, Canada enacted a liberal immigration policy that is motivated by a desire for economic expansion. Today, the goal of the immigration system is to encourage youthful, bilingual, high-skill immigration in order to build human capital within Canada's aging labor force. Canada's immigration policy puts in place incentives to treat foreign workers not as foes but as friends whose labor and skills are essential to the economy.

Canada currently solicits immigrants from more than 200 countries of origin, with China, India, and the Philippines being the most important contributors. Immigration population growth is concentrated in or near large cities such as Montreal, Toronto, and Vancouver.

In Canada there are three categories of immigrants: closely related persons of Canadian residents living in Canada, skilled workers and business people who fit labor market needs, and people accepted as immigrants for humanitarian reasons or who are escaping persecution or unusual punishment in their homelands. To determine whom it should allow in, Canada uses a point system. You do not need a job or an employer, just skills. Applicants are awarded points for English or French language abilities, education, and job experience.

Canada's immigration program is run by both provincial governments and the federal government in Ottawa. Provinces can sponsor a limited number of worker based residencies each year, based on population. Each province can select whomever it wants for whatever reason. The federal government cannot question either the provinces criteria or their methods of recruitment; its role is limited to conducting a security, criminal, and health check on foreigners picked by the provinces. The federal government issues limited numbers of permanent residency for skilled workers each year as well as providing temporary worker admissions to Canada in industries including hospitality, food construction, manufacturing, and oil and natural gas extraction.

Why has Canada accepted immigrants with open arms? Because it must. Canadians realize the positive benefits of immigration including economic development and the creation of jobs for native born Canadians. This is because a large proportion of Canadian immigrants are highly skilled people who are net contributors to the economy. Also, with a sparse population and low birth rate, Canada needs immigrants for population growth and economic development.

About two thirds of Canada's permanent visas are granted for Canada's economic needs, including the filling of labor shortages; in contrast, about two-thirds of U.S. green cards are granted for family reunions. Canadians consider multiculturalism as a key ingredient of their national identity. They contend that people who are exposed to different viewpoints and cultures are more likely to cooperate with one another or reach a compromise when differences occur and become more productive by learning from others. Canadians generally see immigration as adding to the social fabric of the country. Finally, Canada has little reason to fear illegal immigration. Although Canada and the United States share a long border, millions of Americans do not wish to move

TRADE CONFLICTS DOES U.S. IMMIGRATION POLICY HARM DOMESTIC WORKERS?

Does U.S. immigration policy harm domestic workers? Some analysts maintain that the overall benefits from immigration are small, so it is doubtful these benefits play an important role in the policy debate. Others maintain that immigration has significant effects on the economy. They note that highly skilled immigrants help create jobs for domestic workers while less skilled workers fill jobs most Americans do not desire, such as cooking in restaurants, picking apples and cherries, and cleaning offices, adding to the economic vitality of the nation.

Most U.S. residents today are the descendants of immigrants who arrived in the United States during the past 150 years. Concerns about the effect of immigration on domestic workers, however, have resulted in the passage of several laws designed to restrict immigration. Unions in particular have argued for a more restrictive immigration policy on the grounds that immigration lowers the wage and employment levels for domestic residents.

No substantial restrictions were placed on immigration into the United States until the passage of the Quota Law of 1921. This law set quotas on the number of immigrants based on the country of origin. The Quota Law primarily restricted immigration from eastern and southern Europe. The Immigration and Nationality Act Amendments of 1965 eliminated the country specific quota system and instead established a limit on the maximum number of immigrants allowed into the United States. Under this act, preferential treatment is given to those who immigrate for the purpose of family reunification. Those possessing exceptional skills are also given priority. No limit is placed on the number of political refugees allowed to immigrate into the United States. Not all immigrants enter the country through legal channels. Individuals often enter on student or tourist visas and begin working in violation of their visa status. Other individuals enter the country illegally without a valid U.S. visa. The Immigration Reform and Control Act of 1986 addresses the issue of illegal immigration by imposing substantial fines on employers that hire illegal immigrants.

The Illegal Immigration Reform and Immigrant Responsibility Act of 1996 provided several new restrictions to immigration. Host families can only accept immigrants if the host family receive an income that is at least 125 percent of the poverty level. This act also requires the Immigration and Naturalization Service maintain stricter records of entry and exit by nonresident aliens.

to Canada. In other words, the United States serves as a buffer zone for unauthorized immigration that reduces Canadian anxiety about it.

Canada emphasizes open immigration policies that accept talented foreigners who have the skills the country needs and the desire to succeed. Canada has transformed itself into an immigrant country, with a foreign born population (20 percent) exceeding that of the United States (13 percent). Most Canadians feel that this infusion of talent has added to the economic vitality of Canada.

In 2013 Canada began to overhaul its immigration program that places greater emphasis on factors such as an applicant's job skills and fluency in French or English. The objective is to fix what the Canadian government sees as an increasing economic division between locals and many of the immigrants that Canada selected under the former system, whereby immigrants have fallen behind locals in terms of wages. The new system considers whether immigrants have employment arranged in Canada and if they have specific skills in demand such as data processing. Canada also considers adaptability that includes factors such as time spent previously in Canada. It remains to be seen how the revised system will play out.[10]

---

[10]Alistair MacDonald, "As Disparities Grow, Canada Tightens Its Immigration Rules," *Wall Street Journal*, August 31, 2013; A. E. Challinor, *Canada's Immigration Policy: A Focus on Human Capital*, Washington, DC: Migration Policy Institute, September 2011; Fareed Zakaria, "Global Lessons: The GPS Roadmap for Making Immigration Work," *CNN TV Special*, June 10, 2012; E. G. Austin, "Immigration: The United States v Canada," *The Economist*, May 20, 2011; Elisabeth Smick, *Canada's Immigration Policy*, Council on Foreign Relations, New York, July 6, 2006.

SUMMARY

1. Today the world economy is characterized by the international movement of factor inputs. The MNE plays a central part in this process.

2. There is no single agreed upon definition of what constitutes an MNE. Some of the most identifiable characteristics of multinationals are the following: (a) Stock ownership and management are multinational in character; (b) company headquarters may be far removed from the country where a particular activity occurs; and (c) foreign sales represent a high proportion of total sales.

3. Multinationals have diversified their operations along vertical, horizontal, and conglomerate lines.

4. Among the major factors that influence decisions to undertake foreign direct investment are (a) market demand, (b) trade restrictions, (c) investment regulations, and (d) labor productivity and costs.

5. In planning to set up overseas operations, a business must decide whether to construct (or purchase) plants abroad or extend licenses to foreign businesses to produce its goods.

6. The theory of MNE essentially agrees with the predictions of the comparative-advantage principle. However, conventional trade theory assumes that commodities are traded between independent, competitive businesses, whereas MNEs are often vertically integrated businesses, with substantial intra-firm sales. Thus, MNEs may use transfer pricing to maximize overall company profits rather than the profits of any single subsidiary.

7. In recent years, companies have increasingly linked with former rivals in a vast array of joint ventures. International joint ventures can yield welfare increasing effects as well as market power effects.

8. Some of the more controversial issues involving MNEs are (a) employment, (b) technology transfer, (c) national sovereignty, (d) balance-of-payments, and (e) taxation.

9. International labor migration occurs for economic and noneconomic reasons. Migration increases output and decreases wages in the country of immigration, as it decreases output and increases wages in the country of emigration. For the world as a whole, migration leads to net increases in output.

KEY CONCEPTS AND TERMS

Brain drain (p. 320)
Conglomerate integration (p. 297)
Country risk analysis (p. 302)
Foreign direct investment (p. 297)
Guest workers (p. 321)
Horizontal integration (p. 296)

International joint
  ventures (p. 307)
Labor mobility (p. 319)
Migration (p. 316)
Multinational enterprise
  (MNE) (p. 295)

Technology
  transfer (p. 312)
Transfer pricing (p. 316)
Transplants (p. 305)
Vertical integration (p. 296)

STUDY QUESTIONS

1. Multinational enterprises may diversify their operations along vertical, horizontal, and conglomerate lines within the host and source countries. Distinguish among these diversification approaches.

2. What are the major foreign industries in which U.S. businesses have chosen to place direct investments? What are the major industries in the

United States in which foreigners place direct investments?

3. Why is it that the rate of return on U.S. direct investments in the developing nations often exceeds the rate of return on its investments in industrial nations?

4. What are the most important motives behind an enterprise's decision to undertake foreign direct investment?

5. What is meant by the term *multinational enterprise*?

6. Under what conditions would a business wish to enter foreign markets by extending licenses or franchises to local businesses to produce its goods?

7. What are the major issues involving MNEs as a source of conflict for source and host countries?

8. Is the theory of MNE essentially consistent or inconsistent with the traditional model of comparative advantage?

9. What are some examples of welfare gains and welfare losses that can result from the formation of international joint ventures among competing businesses?

10. What effects does labor migration have on the country of immigration? The country of emigration? The world as a whole?

11. Table 9.6 illustrates the revenue conditions facing ABC, Inc., and XYZ, Inc., that operate as competitors in the U.S. calculator market. Each firm realizes constant long run costs $(MC = AC)$ of $4 per unit. On graph paper, plot the enterprise demand, marginal revenue, and $MC = AC$ schedules. On the basis of this information, answer the following questions.

TABLE 9.6

Price and Marginal Revenue: Calculators

Quantity	Price ($)	Marginal Revenue ($)
0	9	—
1	8	8
2	7	6
3	6	4
4	5	2
5	4	0
6	3	−2
7	2	−4

© Cengage Learning®

a. With ABC and XYZ behaving as competitors, the equilibrium price is $____ and output is . At the equilibrium price, U.S. households attain $____ of consumer surplus, while company profits total $ ____.

b. Suppose the two organizations jointly form a new one, JV, Inc., whose calculators replace the output sold by the parent companies in the U.S. market. Assuming that JV operates as a

monopoly and its costs $(MC = AC)$ equal $4 per unit, the company's output would be____ at a price of $____, and total profit would be $____. Compared to the market equilibrium position achieved by ABC and XYZ as competitors, JV as a monopoly leads to a deadweight loss of consumer surplus equal to $____ .

c. Assume now the formation of JV yields technological advances that result in a cost per unit of only $2; sketch the new $MC = AC$ schedule in the figure. Realizing that JV results in a deadweight loss of consumer surplus, as described in part *b*, the net effect of the formation of JV on U.S. welfare is a gain/loss of $____. If JV's cost reduction was because of the wage concessions of JV's U.S. employees, the net welfare gain/ loss for the United States would equal $____. If JV's cost reductions resulted from changes in work rules leading to higher worker productivity, the net welfare gain/loss for the United States would equal $____.

12. Table 9.7 illustrates the hypothetical demand and supply schedules of labor in the United States. Assume that labor and capital are the only two factors of production. On graph paper, plot these schedules.

TABLE 9.7

Demand and Supply of Labor

Wage ($)	Quantity demanded	Quantity supplied$_0$	Quantity supplied$_1$
8	0	2	4
6	2	2	4
4	4	2	4
2	6	2	4
0	8	2	4

© Cengage Learning®

a. Without immigration, suppose the labor force in the United States is denoted by schedule S_0. The equilibrium wage rate is $____; payments to native U.S. workers total $____, while payments to U.S. capital owners equal $____.

b. Suppose immigration from Hong Kong results in an overall increase in the U.S. labor force to

S_1. Wages would rise/fall to $\_\_\_\_$, payments to native U.S. workers would total $\_\_\_\_$, and payments to Hong Kong immigrants would total $\_\_\_\_$. U.S. owners of capital would receive payments of $\_\_\_\_$.

c. Which U.S. factor of production would gain from expanded immigration? Which U.S. factor of production would likely resist policies permitting Hong Kong workers to freely migrate to the United States?

PART 2

International Monetary Relations

The Balance-of-Payments

When trade occurs between the United States and other nations, many types of financial transactions are recorded in a summary called the balance-of-payments. In this chapter, we examine the monetary aspects of international trade by considering the nature and significance of a nation's balance-of-payments.

The **balance-of-payments** is a record of the economic transactions between the residents of one country and the rest of the world. Nations keep a record of their balance-of-payments over the course of a one-year period; the United States and some other nations also keep such a record on a quarterly basis.

An *international transaction* is an exchange of goods, services, or assets between residents of one country and those of another. But what is meant by the term *resident*? Residents include businesses, individuals, and government agencies that make the country in question their legal domicile. Although a corporation is considered to be a resident of the country in which it is incorporated, its overseas branch or subsidiary is not. Military personnel, government diplomats, tourists, and workers who emigrate temporarily are considered residents of the country in which they hold citizenship.

DOUBLE ENTRY ACCOUNTING

The arrangement of international transactions into a balance-of-payments account requires that each transaction be entered as a credit or a debit. A **credit transaction** is one that results in a *receipt* of a payment from foreigners. By convention, credit items are recorded with a *plus* sign. A **debit transaction** is one that leads to a *payment* to foreigners. This distinction is clarified when we assume that transactions take place between U.S. residents and foreigners and that all payments are financed in dollars. By convention, debit items are recorded with a *minus* sign (–).

From the U.S. perspective, the following transactions are credits (+), leading to the receipt of dollars from foreigners:

- Merchandise exports
- Transportation and travel receipts

- Income received from investments abroad
- Gifts received from foreign residents
- Aid received from foreign governments
- Investments in the United States by overseas residents

Conversely, the following transactions are debits (–) from the U.S. viewpoint because they involve payments to foreigners:

- Merchandise imports
- Transportation and travel expenditures
- Income paid on the investments of foreigners
- Gifts to foreign residents
- Aid given by the U.S. government
- Overseas investment by U.S. residents

Although we speak in terms of credit and debit transactions, every international transaction involves an exchange of assets and has both a credit and a debit side. Each credit entry is balanced by a debit entry, and vice versa, so that the recording of any international transaction leads to two offsetting entries. In other words, the balance-of-payments accounts utilize a **double entry accounting** system. The following two examples illustrate the double entry technique.

Example 1

IBM sells $25 million worth of computers to a German importer. Payment is made by a bill of exchange that increases the balances of New York banks at their Bonn correspondents' bank. Because the export involves a transfer of U.S. assets abroad for which payment is to be received, it is entered in the U.S. balance-of-payments as a credit transaction. IBM's receipt of the payment held in the German bank is classified as a short-term financial movement because the financial claims of the United States against the German bank have increased. The entries on the U.S. balance-of-payments would appear as follows:

	Credits (+)	Debits (–)
Merchandise exports	$25 million	
Short-term financial movement		$25 million

Example 2

A U.S. resident who owns bonds issued by a Japanese company receives interest payments of $10,000. With payment, the balances owned by New York banks at their Tokyo affiliate are increased. The impact of this transaction on the U.S. balance-of-payments would be as follows:

	Credits (+)	Debits (–)
Income receipts	$10,000	
Short-term financial movement		$10,000

These examples illustrate how every international transaction has two equal sides, a credit and a debit. If we add up all the credits as pluses and all the debits as minuses, the net result is zero; the total credits must always equal the total debits. This result means that the *total* balance-of-payments account must always be in balance. There is no such thing as an overall balance-of-payments surplus or deficit.

Even though the entire balance-of-payments must numerically balance by definition, it does *not* necessarily follow that any single subaccount or subaccounts of the statement must balance. Total merchandise exports may or may not be in balance with total merchandise imports. When reference is made to a balance-of-payments surplus or deficit, it is particular subaccounts of the balance-of-payments that are referred to, not the overall value. A *surplus* occurs when the balance on a subaccount(s) is positive; a *deficit* occurs when the balance is negative.

BALANCE-OF-PAYMENTS STRUCTURE

Let us now consider the structure of the balance-of-payments by examining its various subaccounts.

Current Account

The **current account** of the balance-of-payments refers to the monetary value of international flows associated with transactions in goods, services, income flows, and unilateral transfers. Each of these flows will be described in turn.

Merchandise trade includes all of the goods the United States exports or imports: agricultural products, machinery, autos, petroleum, electronics, textiles, and the like. The dollar value of merchandise exports is recorded as a plus (credit) and the dollar value of merchandise imports is recorded as a minus (debit). Combining the exports and imports of goods gives the **merchandise trade balance**. When this balance is negative, the result is a merchandise trade deficit; a positive balance implies a merchandise trade surplus.

Exports and imports of *services* include a variety of items. When U.S. ships carry foreign products or foreign tourists spend money at U.S. restaurants and motels, valuable services are being provided by U.S. residents who must be compensated. Such services are considered exports and are recorded as credit items on the goods and services account. Conversely, when foreign ships carry U.S. products or when U.S. tourists spend money at hotels and restaurants abroad, then foreign residents are providing services that require compensation. Because U.S. residents are importing these services, the services are recorded as debit items. Insurance and banking services are explained in the same way. Services also include items such as transfers of goods under military programs, construction services, legal services, technical services, and the like.

To get a broader understanding of the international transactions of a country, we must add services to the merchandise trade account. This total gives the **goods and services balance**. When this balance is positive, the result is a surplus of goods and services transactions; a negative balance implies a deficit. Just what does a surplus or deficit balance appearing on the U.S. goods and services account mean? If the goods and services account shows a surplus, the United States has transferred more resources (goods and services) to foreigners than it has received from them over the period of one year. Besides measuring the value of the *net transfer of resources,* the goods and services balance also furnishes information about the status of a nation's gross domestic product (GDP). This is because the balance on the goods and services account is defined essentially the same way as the *net export of goods and services* that is part of a nation's GDP.

Recall from your macroeconomics course that GDP is equal to the value of the goods and services produced in an economy over a period of time. In an economy with trade, GDP is equal to the sum of four types of spending in the economy: consumption, gross investment, government spending, and net exports of goods and services. In effect, net exports represent the value of goods and services that are produced domestically but not included in domestic consumption.

For a nation's GDP, then, the balance on the goods and services account can be interpreted as follows. A positive balance on the account shows an excess of exports over imports, and this difference must be added to the GDP. When the account is in deficit, the excess of imports over exports must be subtracted from the GDP. If a nation's exports of goods and services equal its imports, the account will have a net imbalance of zero and not affect the status of the GDP. Therefore, depending on the relative value of exports and imports, the balance on the goods and services account contributes to the level of a nation's national product.

Broadening our balance-of-payments summary further, we must include the **income balance** that consists of *income receipts and payments*. This item refers to the net earnings (dividends and interest) on U.S. investments abroad—earnings on U.S. investments abroad less payments on foreign assets in the United States. It also includes compensation to employees.

Our balance-of-payments summary is expanded to include **unilateral transfers**. These items include transfers of goods and services (gifts in kind) or financial assets (money gifts) between the United States and the rest of the world. *Private transfer payments* refer to gifts made by individuals and nongovernmental institutions to foreigners. These might include a remittance from an immigrant living in the United States to relatives back home, a birthday present sent to a friend overseas, or a contribution by a U.S. resident to a relief fund for underdeveloped nations. *Governmental transfers* refer to gifts or grants made by one government to foreign residents or foreign governments. The U.S. government makes transfers in the form of money and capital goods to developing nations, military aid to foreign governments, and remittances such as retirement pensions to foreign workers who have moved back home. In some cases, U.S. governmental transfers represent payments associated with foreign assistance programs that can be used by foreign governments to finance trade with the United States. It should be noted that many U.S. transfer (foreign aid) programs are tied to the purchase of U.S. exports (such as military equipment or farm exports) and thus represent a subsidy to U.S. exporters. When investment income and unilateral transfers are combined with the balance on goods and services, we arrive at the current account balance. This is the broadest measure of a nation's balance-of-payments regularly quoted in the newspapers and in national television and radio news reports.

Capital and Financial Account

Capital and financial transactions in the balance-of-payments include all international purchases or sales of assets. The term *assets* is broadly defined to include items such as titles to real estate, corporate stocks and bonds, government securities, and ordinary commercial bank deposits. The **capital and financial account**[1] includes both private sector and official (central bank) transactions.

Capital transactions consist of capital transfers and the acquisition and disposal of certain nonfinancial assets. The major types of capital transfers are debt forgiveness and migrants' goods and financial assets accompanying them as they leave or enter the country. The acquisition and disposal of certain nonfinancial assets include the sales and purchases of rights to natural resources, patents, copyrights,

---

[1] Since 1999, U.S. international transactions have been classified into three groups—the current account, the capital account, and the financial account. The transactions were formerly classified into the current account and capital account. See "Upcoming Changes in the Classification of Current and Capital Transactions in the U.S. International Accounts," *Survey of Current Business*, February 1999.

TRADE CONFLICTS INTERNATIONAL PAYMENTS PROCESS

When residents in different countries contemplate selling or buying products, they must consider how payments will occur, as seen in Figure 10.1. Assume that you, as a resident of the United States, buy a TV directly from a producer in South Korea. How, when, and where will the South Korean producer obtain his *won* so that he can spend the money in South Korea?

Initially you would write a check for $300 that your U.S. bank would convert to 210,000 won (assuming an exchange rate of 700 won per dollar). When the South Korean producer receives your payment in won, he deposits the funds in his bank. The bank in South Korea holds a check from a U.S. bank that promises to pay a stipulated amount of won.

Assume that at the same time you paid for your TV, a buyer in South Korea paid a U.S. producer $300 for machinery. The flowchart illustrates the path of both transactions.

When trade is in balance, money of different countries does not actually change hands across the oceans. In this example, the value of South Korea's exports to the United States equals the value of South Korea's imports from the United States; the won that South Korean importers use to purchase dollars to pay for U.S. goods are equal to the won that South Korean exporters receive in payment for the products they ship to the United States. The dollars that would flow, in effect, from U.S. importers to U.S. exporters exhibit a similar equality.

In theory, importers in a country pay the exporters in that same country in the national currency. In reality, however, importers and exporters in a given country do not deal directly with one another; to facilitate payments, banks carry out these transactions.

FIGURE 10.1

International Payments Process

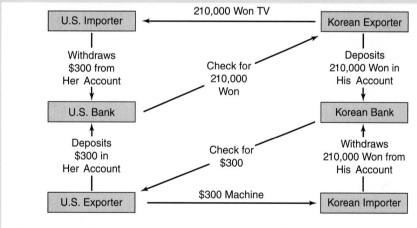

Dollars spent by U.S. importers end up as dollars received by U.S. exporters.

Won spent by Korean importers end up as won received by Korean exporters.

iStockphoto.com/photosoup

trademarks, franchises, and leases. Though conceptually important, capital transactions are generally small in U.S. accounts and thus will not be emphasized in this chapter.

The vast majority of transactions appearing in the capital and financial account come from financial transactions. The following are examples of private sector financial transactions.

Direct Investment Direct investment occurs when residents of one country acquire a controlling interest (stock ownership of ten percent or more) in a business enterprise in another country.

Securities Securities are private sector purchases of short and long-term debt securities such as Treasury bills, Treasury notes, Treasury bonds, and securities of private enterprises.

Bank Claims and Liabilities Bank claims consist of loans, overseas deposits, acceptances, foreign commercial paper, claims on affiliated banks abroad, and foreign government obligations. Bank liabilities include demand deposits and negotiable order of withdrawal (NOW) accounts, passbook savings deposits, certificates of deposit, and liabilities to affiliated banks abroad.

Capital and financial transactions are recorded in the balance-of-payments statement by applying a plus sign (credit) to capital and financial inflows and a minus sign (debit) to capital and financial outflows. For the United States, a *financial inflow* might occur under the following circumstances: (1) U.S. liabilities to foreigners rise (for example, a French resident purchases securities of IBM); (2) U.S. claims on foreigners decrease (Citibank receives repayment for a loan it made to a Mexican enterprise); (3) foreign held assets in the United States rise (Toyota builds an auto assembly plant in the United States); or (4) U.S. assets overseas decrease (Coca-Cola sells one of its Japanese bottling plants to a Japanese buyer). A *financial outflow* would imply the opposite.

The following rule may be helpful in appreciating the fundamental difference between credit and debit transactions that make up the capital and financial account. Any transaction that leads to the home country's receiving payments from foreigners can be regarded as a credit item. A capital (financial) inflow can be likened to the *export* of goods and services. Conversely, any transaction that leads to foreigners' receiving payments is considered a debit item for home countries. A capital (financial) outflow is similar in effect to the *import* of goods and services.

Official Settlements Transactions

Besides including private sector transactions, the capital and financial account includes **official settlements transactions** of the home country's central bank. Official settlements transactions refer to the movement of financial assets among official holders (for example, the U.S. Federal Reserve and the Bank of England). These financial assets fall into two categories: official reserve assets (U.S. government assets abroad) and liabilities to foreign official agencies (foreign official assets in the United States).

Official holdings of reserves are used for two purposes. First, they afford a country sufficient international liquidity to finance short run trade deficits and weather periodic currency crises. This liquidity function is usually only important to developing countries that do not have a readily convertible currency or ready access to international capital markets on favorable terms. Second, central banks sometimes buy or sell official reserve assets in private sector markets to stabilize their currencies' exchange rates. When the United States desires to support the value of the dollar in foreign exchange markets, it would sell, say, foreign currencies or gold to buy dollars; this fosters an increase in the demand for the dollar and an increase in its exchange value. Conversely, if the United States wanted to promote a weaker dollar, it would sell dollars and buy foreign currencies or gold; this would add to the supply of the dollar and cause its exchange value to decrease. In practice, the United States currently has a managed floating exchange rate that usually requires negligible foreign exchange intervention. Therefore, changes in its official reserve assets tend to be small. This topic is further discussed in Chapter 15.

Table 10.1 summarizes the **official reserve assets** position of the United States as of 2013. One such asset is the stock of gold reserves held by the U.S. government. Next are convertible currencies such as the Japanese yen that are readily acceptable as payment for international transactions and can be easily exchanged for one another. Another reserve asset is the reserve position that the United States maintains in the International Monetary Fund. Last is the special drawing right (SDR), described below.

Official settlements transactions also include liabilities to foreign official holders. These liabilities refer to foreign official holdings with U.S. commercial banks and official holdings of U.S. Treasury securities. Foreign governments often wish to hold such assets because of the interest earnings they provide. Table 10.2 illustrates the U.S. liabilities to foreign official holders as of 2013.

Special Drawing Rights

In the 1960s, countries were concerned about the adequacy of international reserves and whether the supply of reserves could increase as rapidly as the demand for them. At that time, international reserves consisted of gold, foreign currencies, and reserve positions in the International Monetary Fund. What was needed was an international reserve asset that would be acceptable to all countries and one whose supply could be expanded as the demand for reserves rose.

In 1969 a new reserve asset was created by the International Monetary Fund as a supplement to the existing reserves of member countries. Termed **special drawing rights**, this asset can be transferred among participating nations in settlement of balance-of-payments deficits or stabilization of exchange rates. If Malaysia needs to obtain British pounds to finance a deficit, it can do so by trading SDRs for pounds held by some other country that the IMF designates, say Canada. In addition to pounds, SDRs can also be exchanged for U.S. dollars, Japanese yen, and euros. The SDR is used only by governments; private parties do not hold or use them. According to IMF policy, member countries are allocated SDRs in proportion to their relative positions in the world economy. The IMF has created additional amounts of SDRs on several occasions since 1970.

The value of the SDR is defined as a basket of currencies that includes the U.S. dollar, Japanese yen, UK pound, and the euro. The weights of the currencies in the basket are based on the value of the exports of goods and services and the amount of reserves

TABLE 10.1

U.S. Reserve Assets, 2013*

Type	Amount (billions of dollars)
Gold stock**	11.0
Special drawing rights	54.9
Reserve positions in the International Monetary Fund	33.4
Convertible foreign currencies	48.3
Total	147.6

*September.
**Gold is valued at $42.22/fine troy ounce.

Source: From Board of Governors of the Federal Reserve System, available at Internet site www.federalreserve.gov.

TABLE 10.2

Selected U.S. Liabilities to Foreign Official Institutions, 2013*

	Amount (billions of dollars)
BY TYPE	
Liabilities reported by U.S. banks**	227.3
U.S. Treasury bills and certificates	372.9
U.S. Treasury bonds and notes	3,600.1
Other U.S. securities	1,388.9
Total	5,589.2
BY AREA	
Europe	856.8
Canada	32.5
Latin America/Caribbean	503.8
Asia	4,117.2
Other	78.9
Total	5,589.2

*August.
**Includes demand deposits, time deposits, bank acceptances, commercial paper, negotiable time certificates of deposit, and borrowings under repurchase agreements.

Source: From Board of Governors of the Federal Reserve System, available at Internet site www.federalreserve.gov.

denominated in the respective currencies that were held by other members of the IMF during the previous five years. As of 2014, the weights in the basket were: the U.S. dollar = 42 percent, the euro = 35 percent, the yen = 12 percent and the pound = 11 percent. The latest value of the SDR can be found on the IMF's Web site that is updated daily.

Statistical Discrepancy: Errors and Omissions

The data collection process that underlies the published balance-of-payments figures is far from perfect. The cost of collecting balance-of-payments statistics is high, and a perfectly accurate collection system would be prohibitive in cost. Government statisticians thus base their figures partly on information collected and estimates. Probably the most reliable information consists of merchandise trade data that are collected mainly from customs records. Capital and financial account information is derived from reports by financial institutions indicating changes in their liabilities and claims to foreigners; these data are not matched with specific current account transactions. Because statisticians do not have a system whereby they can simultaneously record the credit and debit side of each transaction, such information for any particular transaction tends to come from different sources. Large numbers of transactions fail to get recorded.

When statisticians sum the credits and debits, it is not surprising when the two totals do not match. Because total debits must equal total credits in principle, statisticians insert a *residual* to make them equal. This correcting entry is known as **statistical discrepancy**, or errors and omissions. In the balance-of-payments statement, statistical discrepancy is treated as part of the capital and financial account because short-term financial transactions are generally the most frequent source of error.

U.S. BALANCE-OF-PAYMENTS

The method the U.S. Department of Commerce uses in presenting balance-of-payments statistics is shown in Table 10.3. This format groups specific transactions together along functional lines to provide analysts with information about the impact of international transactions on the domestic economy. The *partial balances* published on a regular basis include the merchandise trade balance, the balance on goods and services, the current account balance, and information about capital and financial transactions.

The *merchandise trade balance*, commonly referred to as the **trade balance** by the news media, is derived by computing the net exports in the merchandise accounts. Owing to its narrow focus on traded goods, the merchandise trade balance offers limited policy insight. The popularity of the merchandise trade balance is largely because of its availability on a monthly basis. Merchandise trade data can rapidly be gathered and reported whereas measuring trade in services requires time consuming questionnaires.

As seen in Table 10.3, the United States had a merchandise trade deficit of –$738.4 billion in 2011, resulting from the difference between U.S. merchandise exports ($1,497.4 billion) and U.S. merchandise imports (–$2,235.8 billion). Recall that exports are recorded with a plus sign and imports are recorded with a minus sign. The United States was a net importer of merchandise in 2011. Table 10.4 shows that the United States has consistently faced merchandise trade deficits in recent decades. This situation contrasts with the 1950s and 1960s when merchandise trade surpluses were common for the United States.

Trade deficits generally are not popular with domestic residents and policymakers because they tend to exert adverse consequences on the home nation's terms-of-trade and employment levels, as well as on the stability of the international money markets. For the United States, economists' concerns over persistent trade deficits have often

TABLE 10.3

U.S. Balance-of-Payments, 2011 (billions of dollars)

Current Account		Capital and Financial Account	
Merchandise trade balance	–738.4	Capital account transactions, net	–1.2
Exports	1,497.4		
Imports	–2,235.8	Financial account transactions, net	556.3
		U.S.-owned assets abroad*	–483.6
Services balance	178.5	Foreign-owned assets in the U.S.	1,000.9
Travel and transportation, net	31.3	Financial derivatives, net	39.0
Military transactions, net	–11.6		
Other services, net	158.8	Statistical discrepancy	–89.2
Goods and services balance	–559.9	Balance on capital and financial account	465.9
Income receipts and payments balance	227.0		
Unilateral transfers balance	–133.0		
Current account balance	–465.9		

*Excluding financial derivatives.

Source: From U.S. Department of Commerce, *Survey of Current Business*, June 2012. See also Bureau of Economic Analysis, *U.S. International Transactions Accounts Data*, available at Internet site http://www.bea.gov/ and *Economic Report of the President*.

TABLE 10.4

U.S. Balance-of-Payments, 1980–2012 (billions of dollars)

Year	Merchandise Trade Balance	Services Balance	Goods and Services Balance	Income Receipts and Payments Balance	Unilateral Transfers Balance	Current Account Balance
1980	−25.5	6.1	−19.4	30.1	−8.3	2.4
1984	−112.5	3.3	−109.2	30.0	−20.6	−99.8
1988	−127.0	12.2	−114.8	11.6	−25.0	−128.2
1992	−96.1	55.7	−40.4	4.5	−32.0	−67.9
1996	−191.3	87.0	−104.3	17.2	−42.1	−129.2
2000	−452.2	76.5	−375.7	−14.9	−54.1	−444.7
2004	−665.4	47.8	−617.6	30.4	−80.9	−668.1
2008	−820.8	139.7	−681.1	127.6	−119.7	−673.2
2012	−735.3	195.8	−539.5	198.6	134.1	−475.0

Source: From U.S. Department of Commerce, *Survey of Current Business*, various issues.

focused on their possible effects on the terms at which the United States trades with other nations. With a trade deficit, the value of the dollar may fall in international currency markets as dollar-out payments exceed dollar-in payments. Foreign currencies would become more expensive in terms of dollars so that imports would become more costly to U.S. residents. A trade deficit that induces a decrease in the dollar's international value imposes a real cost on U.S. residents in the form of higher import costs.

Another often publicized consequence of a trade deficit is its adverse impact on employment levels in certain domestic industries such as steel or autos. A worsening trade balance may injure domestic labor, not only by the number of jobs lost to foreign workers who produce our imports but also by the employment losses due to deteriorating export sales. It is no wonder that home nation unions often raise the most vocal arguments about the evils of trade deficits for the domestic economy. Keep in mind that a nation's trade deficit that leads to decreased employment in some industries is offset by capital and financial account inflows that generate employment in other industries. Rather than determining total domestic employment, a trade deficit influences the distribution of employment among domestic industries.

Discussion of U.S. competitiveness in merchandise trade often gives the impression that the United States has consistently performed poorly relative to other industrial nations. The merchandise trade deficit is a narrow concept, because goods are only part of what the world trades. A better indication of the nation's international payments position is the *goods and services balance*. Table 10.3 shows that in 2011, the United States generated a surplus of $178.5 billion on service transactions. Combining this surplus with the merchandise trade deficit of −$738.4 billion yields a deficit on the goods and services balance of −$559.9 billion. This deficit means that the United States transferred fewer resources (goods and services) to other nations than it received from them during 2011.

In recent decades, the United States has generated a surplus in its services account, as seen in Table 10.4. The United States has been competitive in services categories such as transportation, construction, engineering, brokers' commissions, and certain health care services. The United States also has traditionally registered large net receipts from transactions involving proprietary rights—fees, royalties, and other receipts derived mostly from long established relations between U.S. based parent companies and their affiliates abroad.

Adjusting the balance on goods and services for income receipts and payments and net unilateral transfers gives the balance of the current account. As Table 10.3 shows, the United States had a *current account* deficit of –$465.9 billion in 2011. This deficit means that an excess of imports over exports—of goods, services, income flows, and unilateral transfers—resulted in decreasing net foreign investment for the United States. However, we should *not* become unduly preoccupied with the current account balance, because it ignores capital and financial account transactions. If foreigners purchase more U.S. assets in the United States (such as land, buildings, and bonds) then the United States can afford to import more goods and services from abroad. To look at one aspect of a nation's international payment position without considering the others is misleading.

Taken as a whole, U.S. international transactions always balance. This balance means that any force leading to an increase or decrease in one balance-of-payments account sets in motion a process leading to exactly offsetting changes in the balances of other accounts. As seen in Table 10.3, the United States had a current account deficit in 2011 of –$465.9 billion. Offsetting this deficit was a combined surplus of $465.9 billion in the remaining capital and financial accounts, as follows: (1) capital account transactions, net, –$1.2 billion outflow; (2) financial account transactions, net, $556.3 billion inflow; and (3) statistical discrepancy, –$89.2 billion outflow.

WHAT DOES A CURRENT ACCOUNT DEFICIT (SURPLUS) MEAN?

Concerning the balance-of-payments, the current account and the capital and financial account are not unrelated; they are essentially reflections of one another. Because the balance-of-payments is a double entry accounting system, total debits will always equal total credits. It follows that if the current account registers a *deficit* (debits outweigh credits) the capital and financial account must register a *surplus* or net capital/financial *inflow* (credits outweigh debits). Conversely, if the current account registers a *surplus*, the capital and financial account must register a *deficit* or net capital/financial *outflow*.

To better understand this concept, assume that in a particular year your spending is greater than your income. How will you finance your "deficit"? The answer is by borrowing or by selling some of your assets. You might liquidate some real assets (sell your personal computer) or perhaps some financial assets (sell a U.S. government security that you own). In like manner, when a nation experiences a current account deficit, its expenditures for foreign goods and services are greater than the income received from the international sales of its own goods and services, after making allowances for investment income flows and gifts to and from foreigners. The nation must somehow finance its current account deficit. How? The answer lies in selling assets and borrowing. In other words, a nation's current account deficit (debits outweigh credits) is offset by a net financial inflow (credits outweigh debits) in its capital and financial account.

One should not treat international capital flows as though they are passively responding to what is happening in the current account. The current account deficit, some say, is "financed" by U.S. borrowing abroad. However, international investors buy U.S. assets not for the purpose of financing the U.S. current account deficit but because they believe these are sound investments, promising a good combination of safety and return. Also, many of these investments have nothing whatsoever to do with borrowing as commonly understood, but instead involve purchases of land, businesses, and common stock in the United States.

Net Foreign Investment and the Current Account Balance

The current account balance is synonymous with **net foreign investment** in national income accounting. A *current account surplus* means an excess of exports over imports of goods, services, investment income, and unilateral transfers. This surplus permits a net receipt of financial claims for home nation residents. These funds can be used by the home nation to build its financial assets or to reduce its liabilities to the rest of the world, improving its net foreign investment position (its net worth vis-a-vis the rest of the world). The home nation experiences capital outflows and thus becomes a net *supplier* of funds (lender) to the rest of the world. Conversely, a *current account deficit* implies an excess of imports over exports of goods, services, investment income, and unilateral transfers. This deficit leads to an increase in net foreign claims on the home nation. The home nation experiences foreign capital inflows and thus becomes a net *demander* of funds from abroad, the demand being met through borrowing from other nations or liquidating foreign assets. The result is a worsening of the home nation's net foreign investment position.

The current account balance thus represents the bottom line on a nation's income statement. If it is positive, then the nation is spending less than its total income and accumulating asset claims on the rest of the world. If it is negative then domestic expenditure exceeds income and the nation borrows from the rest of the world.

The net borrowing of an economy can be expressed as the sum of the net borrowing by each of its sectors: government and the private sector including business and households. Net borrowing by government equals its budget deficit: the excess of outlays (G) over taxes (T). Private sector net borrowing equals the excess of private investment (I) over private saving (S). The net borrowing of the nation is given by the following identity:

$$
\begin{array}{ccccccc}
\text{Current Account Deficit} & = & (G - T) & + & (I & - & S) \\
\text{(net borrowing)} & & \text{Government} & & \text{Private} & & \text{Private} \\
& & \text{Deficit} & & \text{Investment} & & \text{Saving}
\end{array}
$$

An important aspect of this identity is that the current account deficit is a macroeconomic phenomenon: It reflects imbalances between government outlays and taxes as well as imbalances between private investment and saving. Any effective policy to decrease the current account deficit must ultimately reduce these discrepancies. Reducing the current account deficit requires either decreases in the government's budget deficit or increases in private saving relative to investment, or both. These options are difficult to achieve. Decreasing budget deficits may require unpopular tax hikes or government program cutbacks. Efforts to reduce investment spending would be opposed because investment is a key determinant of the nation's productivity and standard of living. Also, incentives to stimulate saving such as tax breaks, may be opposed on the grounds that they favor the rich rather than the poor.

Decreasing a current account deficit is not entirely in the hands of the home nation. For the world as a whole, the sum of all nations' current account balances must equal zero. A reduction in one nation's current account deficit must go hand in hand with a decrease in the current account surplus of the rest of the world. A complementary policy in foreign nations, especially those with large current account surpluses, can help in successful transition.

Impact of Capital Flows on the Current Account

In the preceding section we described a country's capital and financial flows as responsive to developments in the current account. The process can, and often does, work the other way around with capital and financial flows initiating changes in the current account. If foreigners want to purchase U.S. financial instruments exceeding the amount of foreign financial obligations that Americans want to hold, they must pay for the excess with shipments of foreign goods and services. A financial inflow to the United States is associated with a U.S. current account deficit.

Let us elaborate on how a U.S. current account deficit can be caused by a net financial inflow to the United States. Suppose domestic saving falls short of desired domestic investment. U.S. interest rates rise relative to interest rates abroad that attract an inflow of foreign saving to help support U.S. investment. The United States becomes a net importer of foreign saving, using the borrowed purchasing power to acquire foreign goods and services, and resulting in a like sized net inflow of goods and services—a current account deficit. But how does a financial inflow cause a current account deficit for the United States? When foreigners start purchasing more of our assets than we are purchasing of theirs, the dollar becomes more costly in the foreign exchange market (see Chapter 11). This causes U.S. goods to become more expensive to foreigners, resulting in declining exports; foreign goods become cheaper to Americans, resulting in increasing imports. The result is a rise in the current account deficit or a decline in the current account surplus as summarized in the following flowchart.

Relatively high interest rates in U.S. $\rightarrow$ Capital inflows for U.S. $\rightarrow$ Appreciation of dollar's exchange value $\rightarrow$ U.S. exports decrease/ imports increase $\rightarrow$ Current account deficit for U.S.

Economists believe that in the 1980s, a massive financial inflow caused a current account deficit for the United States. The financial inflow was the result of an increase in the U.S. interest rate relative to interest rates abroad. The higher interest rate was mainly because of the combined effects of the U.S. federal government's growing budget deficit and a decline in the private saving rate.

Instead of thinking that capital flows are financing the current account deficit, it may well be that the current account deficit is driven by capital flows: capital inflows keep the dollar stronger than it otherwise would be, tending to boost imports and suppress exports, thus leading to a current account deficit.

Is a Current Account Deficit a Problem?

Contrary to commonly held views, a current account deficit has little to do with foreign trade practices or any inherent inability of a country to sell its goods on the world market. Instead, it is because of underlying macroeconomic conditions at home requiring more imports to meet current domestic demand for goods and services than can be paid for by export sales. In effect, the domestic economy spends more than it produces and this excess of demand is met by a net inflow of foreign goods and services leading to the current account deficit. This tendency is minimized during periods of recession but expands significantly with the rising income associated with economic recovery and expansion. Current account deficits are not efficiently reversed by trade policies that attempt to alter the levels of imports or exports such as tariffs, quotas, or subsidies.

When a nation realizes a current account deficit, it experiences foreign capital inflows and becomes a net borrower of funds from the rest of the world. Is this a problem? Not necessarily. Foreign capital inflows augment domestic sources of capital that in turn keep domestic interest rates lower than they would be without foreign capital. The benefit of a current account deficit is the ability to push current spending beyond current

GLOBALIZATION THE iPHONE'S COMPLEX SUPPLY CHAIN DEPICTS LIMITATIONS OF TRADE STATISTICS

Do high technology products invented by American companies result in a trade surplus for the United States? Not necessarily. Consider the case of the iPhone.

Designed and marketed by Apple Inc. (a U.S. company), the iPhone functions as a camera phone, including visual voicemail, text messaging, a portable media player, and an Internet client, with e-mail, web browsing, and Wi-Fi connectivity. It obviously is a high technology product. However, instead of contributing to a trade surplus for the United States, the iPhone results in a bilateral trade deficit with China. This is because China ships to the United States all iPhones purchased by American consumers.

In 2009 the iPhone increased the U.S. trade deficit with China by $1.9 billion according to conventional trade statistics. How is this possible? Conventional ways of measuring trade flows do not acknowledge the intricacies of global commerce where the design, manufacturing, and assembly of goods often encompass several countries. The weakness of the conventional approach is that it considers the full value of an iPhone as a Chinese export to the United States, even though it is designed by a U.S. company and is manufactured largely from components produced in several Asian and European countries. China's only contribution to the value of an iPhone is the final step of assembling and shipping it to the United States.

As seen in Table 10.5, the entire $178.96 wholesale cost of an iPhone that was shipped to the United States in 2009, was credited to China's exports, even though the value of work performed by Chinese assemblers amounted to $6.50, or just 3.6 percent of the total. This resulted in an exaggeration of the bilateral trade deficit of the United States with China. If China was credited with producing only its portion of the value of an iPhone, its exports to the United States for the same amount of iPhones would have been a much smaller figure. This is why many economists feel that breaking down imports and exports in terms of the value added from different countries is a more accurate way of measuring trade statistics than the conventional method.

Conventional trade statistics tend to inflate bilateral trade deficits between a country used as an export processing zone by multinational firms and its destination countries. In the case of the iPhone, China only accounted for 3.6 percent of the U.S. $1.9 billion trade deficit, the remainder stemming from Japan, Germany, and other countries that produced components used to make the iPhone. By inflating the bilateral trade deficit with China, conventional trade statistics add to political tensions simmering in Washington, D.C. over what to do about China's allegedly undervalued currency and unfair trading practices.

Source: Yuqing Xing and Neal Detert, *How iPhone Widens the U.S. Trade Deficits with PRC*, Tokyo, Japan: National Graduate Institute for Policy Studies, November 2010 and Andrew Batson, "Not Really Made in China," *Wall Street Journal*, December 15, 2010, pp. B1–B2.

iStockphoto.com/photosoup

TABLE 10.5

Global Production and Manufacturing Cost of the iPhone

Of the $178.96 wholesale cost of an iPhone in 2009, components came from many countries to be assembled in China. Here's the breakdown:

Manufacturing Cost (Labor and Components)	In U.S. Dollars	Percent of Total Manufacturing Cost
Japan	60.60	33.9
Germany	30.15	16.8
South Korea	22.96	12.8
United States	10.75	6.0
China	6.50	3.6
Other	48.06	26.9
	178.96	100.0

Source: Yuqing Xing and Neal Detert, *How iPhone Widens the U.S. Trade Deficits with PRC*, National Graduate Institute for Policy Studies, Tokyo, Japan, November 2010.

production. However, the cost is the debt service that must be paid on the associated borrowing from the rest of the world.

Is it good or bad for a country to incur debt? The answer obviously depends on what the country does with the money. What matters for future incomes and living standards is whether the deficit is being used to finance more consumption or more investment. If used exclusively to finance an increase in domestic investment, the burden could be slight. We know that investment spending increases the nation's stock of capital and expands the economy's capacity to produce goods and services. The value of this extra output may be sufficient to both pay foreign creditors and also augment domestic spending. In this case, because future consumption need not fall below what it otherwise would have been, there would be no true economic burden. If, on the other hand, foreign borrowing is used to finance or increase domestic consumption (private or public) there is no boost given to future productivity. To meet debt service expense, future consumption must be reduced below what it otherwise would have been. Such a reduction represents the burden of borrowing. This is not necessarily bad; it all depends on how one values current versus future consumption.

During the 1980s when the United States realized current account deficits, the rate of domestic saving decreased relative to the rate of investment. In fact, the decline of the overall saving rate was mainly the result of a decrease of its public saving component, caused by large and persistent federal budget deficits in this period—budget deficits are in effect negative savings that subtract from the pool of savings. This negative savings indicated that the United States used foreign borrowing to increase current consumption, not productivity enhancing public investment. The U.S. current account deficits of the 1980s were greeted with concern by many economists.

In the 1990s, U.S. current account deficits were driven by increases in domestic investment. This investment boom contributed to expanding employment and output. It could not have been financed by national saving alone. Foreign lending provided the additional capital needed to finance the boom. In the absence of foreign lending, U.S. interest rates would have been higher and investment would inevitably have been constrained by the supply of domestic saving. The accumulation of capital and the growth of output and employment would all have been smaller had the United States not been able to run a current account deficit in the 1990s. Rather than choking off growth and employment, the large current account deficit allowed faster long run growth in the U.S. economy that improved economic welfare.

Business Cycles, Economic Growth, and the Current Account

How is the current account related to a country's business cycle and long run economic growth? Concerning the business cycle, *rapid* growth of production and employment is commonly associated with large or growing trade and current account *deficits*, whereas *slow* output and employment growth is associated with large or growing *surpluses*.

During a recession, both saving and investment tend to fall. Saving falls as households try to maintain their consumption patterns in the face of a temporary fall in income; investment declines because capacity utilization declines and profits fall. Because investment is highly sensitive to the need for extra capacity, it tends to drop more sharply than saving during recessions. The current account balance tends to rise. Consistent with this rise but viewed from a different angle, the trade balance typically improves during a recession because imports tend to fall with overall consumption and investment demand. The opposite occurs during periods of boom when sharp increases in investment demand typically outweigh increases in saving, producing a decline in the current account. Of course, factors other than income influence saving and investment so that the tendency of a country's current account deficit to decline in recessions is not ironclad.

The relation just described between the current account and economic performance typically holds not only on a short-term or cyclical basis, but also on a long-term basis. Often, countries enjoying *rapid* economic growth possess long run current account *deficits*, whereas those with *weaker* economic growth have long run current account *surpluses*. This relation likely derives from the fact that rapid economic growth and strong investment often go hand in hand. Where the driving force is the discovery of new natural resources, technological progress, or the implementation of economic reform, periods of rapid economic growth are likely to be periods when new investment is unusually profitable. Investment must be financed with saving, and if a country's national saving is not sufficient to finance all new profitable investment projects, the country will rely on foreign saving to finance the difference. It thus experiences a net financial inflow and a corresponding current account deficit. As long as the new investments are profitable, they will generate the extra earnings needed to repay the claims contracted to undertake them. When current account deficits reflect strong, profitable investment programs, they work to raise the rate of output and employment growth, not destroy jobs and production.

Norway provides an example of one of these productive opportunities. In the 1960s, rich petroleum deposits were discovered in the North Sea. Norway was one of the major beneficiaries of this discovery. Getting to these valuable oil and gas deposits required large and repeated investments in off shore oil platforms, transport pipelines, ships, and helicopters. Norway also had to develop knowledge of exploration and extraction to precisely locate and exploit these resources. Acquiring these items required sizable imports that created trade deficits for Norway. At the time of these discoveries, Norway lacked the equipment and expertise to take advantage of the opportunity. Although the oil revenue would eventually pay for these investments, they had to be paid in advance. Norway financed the investments by borrowing from the rest of the world. Foreign investors were happy to make these loans because Norway's capital was viewed to be more productive and earned a higher return than could be earned abroad. Once the oil came online, Norway began running persistent trade surpluses that were used to repay its original borrowing and save for a day when the petroleum reserves are exhausted. Norway's initial trade deficit was a sign of strong and continued economic growth and good things to come.

How the United States Has Borrowed at Very Low Cost

Over the past four decades, the U.S. current account has moved from a small surplus to a large deficit. This deficit is financed by either borrowing from or selling assets to foreigners. As the current account deficit has increased for the United States, the country has become a large net debtor. When a country increases its borrowing from abroad, the cost of servicing its debt is expected to increase. This is because the country must make larger payments of interest and principal to foreign lenders.

During the past two decades, there has been a paradox in U.S. international transactions: U.S. residents have consistently earned more income from their foreign investments than foreigners earn from their larger U.S. investments. The United States has been able to be a large debtor nation without bearing negative debt service cost. This paradox suggests that the U.S. current account deficits might be less burdensome than often portrayed.

What accounts for this paradox? One explanation concerns asymmetric investment returns. The United States has tended to consistently earn higher returns on its foreign investments than foreigners earn on U.S. investments. This overall rate of return advantage has generally been one to two percentage points. A main reason for this advantage is that U.S. companies take greater risks when they invest in foreign nations, such as economic and political instability. Investments that involve higher risk will not be undertaken unless they offer the potential for higher rewards. Conversely, because the United States is generally considered as a safe haven for investment, foreign investors are more likely to buy U.S. assets that offer low return and low risk.

This paradox provides an explanation of why the massive foreign borrowing by the United States has been relatively painless in the past two decades. Future borrowing prospects may not be as favorable. Skeptics fear that if global interest rates rise, the United States will have to pay higher rates to attract foreign investment, thus increasing U.S. interest payments to foreigners. These payments could swing the U.S. investment income balance from surplus to deficit and cause U.S. debt service costs to become burdensome. As this costs grows, the U.S. current account deficit and its consequences could increasingly become matters of concern for economic policy makers.[2]

Do Current Account Deficits Cost Americans Jobs?

When reading newspapers, one may get the impression that increasing trade (current account) deficits drag down the U.S. economy or at least stall economic growth. Why? Rising imports can decrease domestic employment and overall growth by subtracting from demand for domestically produced goods and services. Every cell phone, radio, or shirt that we import represents one fewer cell phone, radio, or shirt that could have been produced in the United States, resulting in the layoff of American workers who were previously employed producing those items.

Although export and import trends raise concerns about U.S. job losses, economists at the Federal Reserve Bank of New York and the Cato Institute have found that employment statistics do not bear out the relation between a rising current account deficit and lower employment.[3] Why?

A current account deficit may hurt employment in particular firms and industries as workers are displaced by increased imports. At the economy wide level, however, the current account deficit is matched by an equal inflow of foreign funds that finances employment sustaining investment spending that would not otherwise occur. A region of the United States that would benefit from the foreign purchase of American grown corn would presumably benefit as much, if not more, were the Japanese to invest in an auto plant in the United States. Foreign purchases of U.S. Treasury securities decrease long-term interest rates, helping to stimulate the U.S. economy. Foreign purchases of U.S. stock and real estate place dollars in the hands of those Americans who are selling the assets that in turn entice them to spend more freely on domestically produced goods. Whether dollars flow into the United States to purchase our goods or to purchase our assets, economic activity is promoted. The foreign purchase of American assets can stimulate the U.S. economy just as well as the export of goods and services.

When viewed as the net inflow of foreign investment, the current account deficit produces jobs for the economy: both from the direct effects of higher employment in

---

[2]Juann Hung and Angelo Mascaro, *Why Does U.S. Investment Abroad Earn Higher Returns Than Foreign Investment in the United States?* Washington, DC: Congressional Budget Office, 2005; Craig Elwell, *U.S. External Debt: How Has the United States Borrowed Without Cost?* Washington, DC: Congressional Research Service, 2006; and William Cline, *The United States as a Debtor Nation*, Washington, DC: Institute for International Economics, 2005.

[3]Matthew Higgins and Thomas Klitgaard, "Viewing the Current Account Deficit as a Capital Inflow," *Current Issues and Economics and Finance*, Federal Reserve Bank of New York, December 1999 and Daniel Griswold, *The Trade-Balance Creed: Debunking the Belief that Imports and Trade Deficits Are a Drag on Growth*, Washington DC: The Cato Institute, April 11, 2011.

investment oriented industries and from the indirect effects of higher investment spending on economy wide employment. Viewing the current account deficit as a net inflow of foreign investment helps to dispel misconceptions about the adverse consequences of economic globalization on the domestic job market.

Although this analysis indicates that current account deficits do not cause a net loss of output or jobs in the overall economy, they tend to change the composition of output and employment. Evidence suggests that over the past three decades, persistent current account deficits have likely caused a reduction in the size of the U.S. manufacturing sector while output and employment in the economy's service sector have increased.

Can the United States Continue to Run Current Account Deficits Indefinitely?

The United States has benefitted from a surplus of saving over investment in many areas of the world that has provided a supply of funds. This surplus of saving has been available to the United States because foreigners have remained willing to loan that saving to the United States in the form of acquiring U.S. assets such as Treasury securities that have accommodated the current account deficits. During the 1990s and the first decade of the 2000s, the United States experienced a decline in its rate of savings and an increase in the rate of domestic investment. The large increase in the U.S. current account deficit would not have been possible without the accommodating inflows of foreign capital coming from nations with high savings rates such as Japan and China, as seen in Table 10.6.

China is a major supplier of capital to the United States. This is partly because of China's exchange rate policy of keeping the value of its *yuan* low (cheap) so as to export goods to the United States and thus create jobs for its workers (see Chapter 15). In order to offset a rise in the value of the yuan against the dollar, the central bank of China has purchased dollars with yuan. Rather than hold dollars that earn no interest, China's central bank has converted much of its dollar holdings into U.S. securities that pay interest. This situation has put the United States in a unique position to benefit from the willingness of China to finance its current account deficit. The United States can "print money" that the Chinese hold in order to finance its excess spending.

TABLE 10.6

Foreign Holders of U.S. Securities as of 2012*

Country	Billions of Dollars	Percent of World Total
Japan	1,835	13.8
China	1,592	12.0
Cayman Islands	1,031	7.8
United Kingdom	1,008	7.6
Luxembourg	837	6.3
Canada	635	4.8
Switzerland	566	4.3
Middle East oil exporters	489	3.7

*June.

Source: U.S. Treasury Department, *Report on Foreign Portfolio Holdings of U.S. Securities as of June 30, 2012*, April 30, 2013.

The buildup of China's dollar reserves helps support the U.S. stock and bond markets and permits the U.S. government to incur expenditure increases and tax reductions without increases in domestic U.S. interest rates that would otherwise take place. Some analysts are concerned that at some point Chinese investors may view the increasing level of U.S. foreign debt as unsustainable or more risky and suddenly shift their capital elsewhere. They also express concern that the United States will become more politically reliant on China who might use its large holdings of U.S. securities as leverage against policies it opposes.

Can the United States run current account deficits indefinitely and rely on inflows of foreign capital? Since the current account deficit arises mainly because foreigners desire to purchase American assets, there is no economic reason why it cannot continue indefinitely. As long as the investment opportunities are large enough to provide foreign investors with competitive rates of return, they will be happy to continue supplying funds to the United States. There is no reason why the process cannot continue indefinitely: no automatic forces will cause either a current account deficit or a current account surplus to reverse.

United States history illustrates this point. From 1820 to 1875, the United States ran current account deficits almost continuously. At this time, the United States was a relatively poor (by European standards) but rapidly growing country. Foreign investment helped foster that growth. This situation changed after World War I. The United States was richer and investment opportunities were more limited. Current account surpluses were present almost continuously between 1920 and 1970. During the last 40 years, the situation has again reversed. The current account deficits of the United States are underlain by its system of secure property rights, a stable political and monetary environment, and a rapidly growing labor force (compared with Japan and Europe), that make the United States an attractive place to invest. Moreover, the U.S. saving rate is low compared to its major trading partners. The U.S. current account deficit reflects this combination of factors and it is likely to continue as long as they are present. Simply put, the U.S. current account deficit has reflected a surplus of good investment opportunities in the United States and a deficit of growth prospects elsewhere in the world.

Some economists think that because of spreading globalization, the pool of savings offered to the United States by world financial markets is deeper and more liquid than ever. This pool allows foreign investors to continue furnishing the United States with the money it needs without demanding higher interest rates in return. Presumably, a current account deficit of six percent or more of GDP would not have been readily fundable several decades ago. The ability to move so much of world saving to the United States in response to relative rates of return would have been hindered by a far lower degree of international financial interdependence. In recent years, the increasing integration of financial markets has created an expanding class of foreigners who are willing and able to invest in the United States.

The consequence of a current account deficit is a growing foreign ownership of the capital stock of the United States and a rising fraction of U.S. income that must be diverted overseas in the form of interest and dividends to foreigners. A serious problem could emerge if foreigners lose confidence in the ability of the United States to generate the resources necessary to repay the funds borrowed from abroad. As a result, suppose that foreigners decide to reduce the fraction of their saving that they send to the United States. The initial effect could be both a sudden and large decline in the value of the dollar as the supply of dollars increases on the foreign exchange market and a sudden and large increase in U.S. interest rates as an important source of saving was withdrawn from financial markets. Large increases in interest rates could cause problems for the U.S. economy as they reduce the market value of debt securities, causing prices on the stock market to decline, and raising questions about the solvency of various debtors. Whether the United States can sustain its current account deficit over the foreseeable future depends on whether foreigners are willing to increase their investments in U.S. assets. The current account deficit puts the economic fortunes of the United States partially in the hands of foreign investors.

The economy's ability to cope with big current account deficits depends on continued improvements in efficiency and technology. If the economy becomes more productive, then its real wealth may grow fast enough to cover its debt. Optimists note that robust increases in U.S. productivity in recent years have made its current account deficits affordable. If productivity growth stalls, the economy's ability to cope with current account deficits will deteriorate.

Although the appropriate level of the U.S. current account deficit is difficult to assess, at least two principles are relevant should it prove necessary to reduce the deficit. First, the United States has an interest in policies that stimulate foreign growth, because it is better to reduce the current account deficit through faster growth abroad than through slower growth at home. A recession at home would obviously be a highly undesirable means of reducing the deficit. Second, any reductions in the deficit are better achieved through increased national saving than through reduced domestic investment. If there are attractive investment opportunities in the United States, we are better off borrowing from abroad to finance these opportunities than forgoing them. On the other hand, incomes in this country would be even higher in the future if these investments were financed through higher national saving. Increases in national saving allow interest rates to remain lower than they would otherwise be. Lower interest rates lead to higher domestic investment that in turn boosts demand for equipment and construction. For any given level of investment, increased saving also results in higher net exports that would again increase employment in these sectors.

Shrinking the U.S. current account deficit can be difficult. The economies of foreign nations may not be strong enough to absorb additional American exports and Americans may be reluctant to curb their appetite for foreign goods. The U.S. government has shown a bias toward deficit spending. Turning around a deficit is associated with a sizable fall in the exchange rate and a decrease in output in the adjusting country, topics that will be discussed in subsequent chapters.

BALANCE OF INTERNATIONAL INDEBTEDNESS

A main feature of the U.S. balance-of-payments is that it measures the economic transactions of the United States over a period of one year or one quarter; but at any particular moment, a nation will have a fixed stock of assets and liabilities against the rest of the world. The statement that summarizes this situation is known as the **balance of international indebtedness**. It is a record of the international position of the United States at a particular time (year-end data).

The U.S. balance of international indebtedness indicates the accumulated value of U.S.; owned assets abroad as opposed to foreign owned assets in the United States. These assets include such financial assets as corporate stocks and bonds, government securities, and direct investment in businesses and real estate. The value of these assets can change as a result of purchases and sales of new or existing assets, changes in the value of assets that arise through appreciation/depreciation or inflation, and so on. The United States is considered a **net creditor** to the rest of the world when the accumulated value of U.S. owned assets abroad exceeds the value of foreign owned assets in the United States.

TABLE 10.7

International Investment Position of the U.S. at Year-End (billions of dollars)

Type of Investment*	1995	2000	2012
U.S. owned assets abroad			
U.S. government assets	257	214	666
U.S. private assets	3,149	5,954	20,971
Total	3,406	6,168	21,637
Foreign owned assets in the United States			
Foreign official assets	672	922	5,692
Foreign private assets	3,234	7,088	19,810
Total	3,906	8,010	25,502
Net international investment position	−500	−1,842	−3,865
Relative share: U.S. net international investment position/U.S. gross domestic product	6%	15%	25%

*At current cost.

Source: From U.S. Department of Commerce, Bureau of Economic Analysis, *The International Investment Position of the United States at Year End*, available at http://www.bea.gov. See also U.S. Department of Commerce, *Survey of Current Business*, various June and July issues.

When the reverse occurs, the United States assumes a **net debtor** position. Table 10.7 shows the international investment position of the United States for various years.

Of what use is the balance of international indebtedness? Perhaps the greatest significance is that it breaks down international investment holdings into several categories so that policy implications can be drawn from each separate category about the *liquidity status* of the nation. For the short-term investment position, the strategic factor is the amount of short-term liabilities (bank deposits and government securities) held by foreigners. This is because these holdings potentially can be withdrawn at short notice, resulting in a disruption of domestic financial markets. The balance of official monetary holdings is also significant. Assume that this balance is negative from the U.S. viewpoint. Should foreign monetary authorities decide to liquidate their holdings of U.S. government securities and have them converted into official reserve assets, the financial strength of the dollar would be reduced. As for a nation's long-term investment position, it is of less importance for the U.S. liquidity position because long-term investments generally respond to basic economic trends and are not subject to erratic withdrawals.

United States as a Debtor Nation

In the early stages of its industrial development, the United States was a net international debtor. Relying heavily on foreign funds, the United States built up its industries by mortgaging part of its wealth to foreigners. After World War I, the United States became a net international creditor. By 1987 the United States had become a net international debtor and it has continued to maintain that position, as shown in Table 10.7.

How did this turnabout occur so rapidly? The reason was that foreign investors placed more funds in the United States than U.S. residents invested abroad. The United States was considered attractive to investors from other countries because of its rapid economic recovery from the recession of the early 1980s, its political stability, and its relatively high interest rates. American investments overseas fell because of the sluggish loan demand in Europe, the desire by commercial banks to reduce their overseas

TRADE CONFLICTS GLOBAL IMBALANCES

If you considered the world economy as a whole in 2014, you would see that it was out of balance. Advanced countries such as the United States have tended to consume more, save less, rely on fiscal deficits, and attain large current account deficits. The trading partners of the United States, some of whom are poor, have loaned the United States, a prosperous country, the funds necessary to finance the imbalance. Conversely, emerging world countries such as China have tended to consume less, save more, have undervalued currencies, and realize large current account surpluses. Capital has flowed from fast growing emerging countries, where returns on investment are presumably high, to mature wealthy countries. Is this situation sustainable or desirable? Should the rest of the world rely on U.S. consumers as a source of demand for their exports?

Although it is difficult to predict how these trends will play out, most economists maintain that rebalancing the world economy is desirable. They note that advanced countries should consume less, save more, become more fiscally disciplined, and decrease current account deficits. Emerging countries should allow the exchange values of their currencies to rise (appreciate), consume more, save less, decrease current account surpluses, and continue investing, with some of the capital provided by outsiders. If major governments of the world work together to rebalance and coordinate their fiscal, monetary, trade, and foreign exchange policies, the adjustment process can be gradual and not disruptive to the global economy.

Such a policy adjustment is not easy to accomplish. Politicians in advanced countries must respond to the preferences of voters who often don't understand how the world economy operates and who desire policies

that entail fiscal deficits. They often want governments to spend more money on social programs—in the United States, for example, on Medicare and Social Security—without raising taxes to finance the extra spending. The usual response by advanced country governments to such demands is to run larger deficits and borrow more money. Yet many advanced country governments have been rapidly depleting their borrowing capacity and some nations, such as Greece, Portugal, Ireland, and Spain, have experienced fiscal crises. In the future, major countries might lack the ability or willingness to rescue highly indebted governments. Debt restructuring and defaults would become inevitable at that point.

Emerging nations have different concerns. Usually they have low debt-to-GDP ratios, maintain large currency reserves, continue to attain current account surpluses, and provide more capital to advanced countries than they receive. Their economies are founded upon undervalued currencies, low-cost labor, high savings rates, exports, and investment in infrastructure. These countries are apprehensive about growing too rapidly or allowing too great a volume of capital inflows that can promote asset bubbles. They are also skeptical of anything that would limit their growth, given the rising expectations of their populations.

Both sides, of course, need to modify their behavior. If they do not, the capital markets may discipline governments if the imbalances, particularly the fiscal deficits of advanced countries, continue to grow.

Source: Jane Sneddon Little, editor, *Global Imbalances and the Evolving World Economy*, Boston, Massachusetts: Federal Reserve Bank of Boston, 2008; Lowell Bryan, "Globalization's Critical Imbalances," *McKinsey Quarterly*, Boston, Massachusetts: McKinsey & Co., June 2010, pp. 57–68; and John Williamson, *Getting Surplus Countries to Adjust*, Policy Brief, Peterson Institute for International Economics, January 2011.

exposure as a reaction to the debt repayment problems of Latin American countries, and the decreases in credit demand by oil importing developing nations as the result of declining oil prices. Of the foreign investment funds in the United States, less than one-fourth went to direct ownership of U.S. real estate and business. Most of the funds were in financial assets such as bank deposits, stocks, and bonds.

For the typical U.S. resident, the transition from net creditor to net debtor went unnoticed. However, the net debtor status of the United States raised an issue of propriety. To many observers, it seemed inappropriate for the United States, one of the richest nations in the world, to be borrowing on a massive scale from the rest of the world.

THE DOLLAR AS THE WORLD'S RESERVE CURRENCY

Before we end our discussion of the balance-of-payments, let us consider the U.S. dollar as an international currency.

The dollar is the main reserve currency in the world today. Dollars are used throughout the world as a medium of exchange, unit of account, and store of value, and many nations keep wealth in dollar denominated assets such as U.S. Treasury securities. Almost two-thirds of the world's official foreign exchange reserves are held in dollars, while more than four-fifths of daily foreign exchange trades involve dollars. The euro, the second most important reserve currency, lags far behind the dollar, followed by the British pound and Japanese yen. The dollar's popularity is supported by a strong and sophisticated U.S. economy and its safe haven attractiveness for international investors. The widening trade deficits and expanding foreign debt that the United States has incurred in recent decades have weakened the prestige of the dollar.

As more people have used dollars in international transactions in the post–World War II era, the efficiencies in using dollars in exchange increased, solidifying the dollar's place as the world's premier currency. Some have compared the dollar's popularity to that of the Microsoft Windows operating system. Computer users may feel that substitute software is easier to use, but the convenience of being able to transfer files around the world to anyone using Microsoft enhances the system's popularity. In the dollar's case, widespread use of the dollar makes dealing in the currency easier and less expensive than any other: The more countries that transact in dollars, the cheaper it is for them all to transact in dollars. Any one country would hesitate to stop dealing in dollars, even if it desired to use a different currency unless it knew that other countries would do the same. This reluctance may be a key reason why the dollar is so difficult to displace as the world's main reserve currency.

Benefits to the United States

The United States realizes substantial benefits from the dollar serving as the main reserve currency of the world. First, Americans can purchase products at a marginally cheaper rate than other nations that must exchange their currency with each purchase and pay a transaction cost. Also, Americans can borrow at lower interest rates for homes and automobiles and the U.S. government can finance larger deficits longer and at lower interest rates. The United States can issue debt (securities) in its own currency, thus pushing exchange rate risk onto foreign lenders. This risk means that foreigners face the possibility that a fall in the dollar's exchange value could wipe out the returns on their investments in the United States.

For example, if a Chinese investor realizes a return of five percent on his or her holdings of U.S. Treasury securities, and if the dollar depreciates five percent against China's yuan, the investor would realize no gain. With holdings of dollar denominated assets of about $1 trillion dollars in 2009, China has been especially concerned about the possibility of losing purchasing power in the event of substantial dollar depreciation.

In spite of the appeal of the dollar, there is increasing concern about its continuing role as the world's main reserve currency. Countries such as China fear that the United States is digging a hole with an economy based on huge deficits and massive borrowing that cloud the dollar's future. They worry about the volatility of the dollar and the destabilizing effect it can have on international trade and finance. Critics claim that a credit based reserve currency such as the dollar is inherently risky, facilitates global imbalances, and promotes the spread of financial crises. As a result, they argue that the dollar should no longer serve as the world's reserve currency.

Before the dollar is displaced as a reserve currency, there must be a new contender for the throne. It is not the British pound whose best days are in the past nor the Chinese yuan whose reserve currency status is years in the future, if it ever occurs. As for the euro, the improved liquidity and breadth of Europe's financial markets have eroded some of the advantages that historically supported the preeminence of the dollar as a reserve currency. The recent financial problems plaguing Europe have weakened the status of the euro. Although Japan and Switzerland have strong institutions and financial markets, they have actively pushed down the value of their currencies in recent years, making them unappealing as stores of value. Thus, the dollar has kept its place as the dominant reserve currency, supported by the edge that U.S. financial markets still have over other markets in terms of size, credit quality, and liquidity, as well as inertia in the use of international currencies. The dollar has been regarded as a safe and secure place to park money in spite of the recent economic and political problems that have plagued the United States.

A New Reserve Currency?

In 2009, officials at the central bank of China proposed an overhaul of the international monetary system in which the SDR would eventually replace the dollar as the world's main reserve currency. Their goal was to adopt a reserve currency that is disconnected from a single country (the United States) and would remain stable in the long run, lessening the financial risks caused by the volatility of the dollar. To accomplish this objective, the Chinese advocated a new world reserve currency based on a basket of currencies instead of just the dollar. This currency basket would be fulfilled by the SDR whose value is currently based on the euro, yen, pound, and dollar in accordance with the relative importance of each currency in international trade and finance. China proposed that the size of the currency basket be expanded to include all major currencies such as the Chinese yuan and the Russian ruble. The SDR would be managed by the International Monetary Fund.

Several steps would have to be taken to broaden the SDR's use so it could fulfill IMF member countries' demands for a reserve currency. A settlement system between the SDR and other currencies would have to be established so the SDR would be widely accepted in world trade and financial transactions. Currently, the SDR is only used as a unit of account by the IMF and other international organizations. Also, the SDR would have to be actively promoted for use in trade, commodities pricing, investment, and corporate bookkeeping. Moreover, financial assets (securities) that are denominated in SDRs would have to be created to increase the attractiveness of the SDR. Achieving these results would require a significant amount of time.

Proponents maintain that allowing the SDR to serve as the world's reserve currency would provide several benefits. For the Chinese, it would cushion any depreciation in the dollar's exchange value because the dollar would only be a portion of a basket of several currencies. This would help stabilize the value of China's holdings of U.S. Treasury securities. Also, a basket reserve currency would help support aggregate demand in the world by decreasing the fear of currency volatility. Such fear served as a motivation for countries like China to save large amounts of reserves to guard against losses because of international currency volatility. Moreover, the economic welfare of the world should not depend on the behavior of a single currency, namely the dollar. Currency risk would be diversified through a basket reserve unit, thus enhancing stability and confidence throughout the world. Also, there is the issue of equity. Because the dollar is the main reserve currency where investors flee to safety during economic strife, the United States can attract the savings of other countries even when the interest rates it pays are low.

There are potential pitfalls of using the SDR as a reserve currency. One problem is that the SDR is backed by nothing other than the good faith and credit of the IMF; that is, the IMF produces nothing to support the value of the SDR. In contrast, the dollar is backed by the goods and services produced by Americans and their willingness to exchange those goods and services for dollars. Who would determine the "right price" of the SDR; the IMF? Would the IMF succumb to political pressure to change the SDR's currency weightings in favor of particular nations? The use of the SDR would add another step to each international transaction, as buyers and sellers would have to convert their local currency into SDRs. This conversion would increase the cost of doing business for companies, investors, and so on.

For the United States, a loss in its reserve currency position would entail several costs. First, Americans would have to pay more for imported goods as the dollar depreciates when foreigners no longer buy dollars as they previously did they did when the dollar served as the reserve currency. Interest rates on both private and governmental debt would increase. The increased private cost of borrowing could result in weaker consumption, decreased investment, and slower growth. The economic supremacy of the United States would be lessened if the dollar lost is reserve currency position. The United States has expressed strong reservations concerning the proposal to replace the dollar with the SDR as the reserve currency.

Adopting the SDR as a reserve currency might be technically possible and it could occur if the United States followed persistently bad economic policy in the form of deficit spending, high inflation, and currency depreciation. If foreigners expect that the costs of holding dollars (in terms of lost purchasing power) exceeded the benefits of transacting in dollars, they might opt for an alternative reserve currency. Replacing the dollar with the SDR as the reserve currency will likely not occur soon because people still realize sizable efficiencies from conducting international transactions in dollars. Until the SDR matches these benefits, it will not replace the dollar as the world's premier currency.

SUMMARY

1. The balance-of-payments is a record of a nation's economic transactions with all other nations for a given year. A credit transaction is one that results in a receipt of payments from foreigners, whereas a debit transaction leads to a payment abroad. Owing to double entry bookkeeping, a nation's balance-of-payments will always balance.

2. From a functional viewpoint, the balance-of-payments identifies economic transactions as (a) current account transactions and (b) capital and financial account transactions.

3. The balance on goods and services is important to policymakers because it indicates the net transfer of real resources overseas. It also measures the extent to which a nation's exports and imports are part of its gross national product.

4. The capital and financial account of the balance-of-payments shows the international movement of loans, investments, and the like. Capital and financial inflows (outflows) are analogous to exports (imports) of goods and services because they result in the receipt (payment) of funds from (to) other nations.

5. Official reserves consist of a nation's financial assets: (a) monetary gold holdings, (b) convertible currencies, (c) special drawing rights, and (d) drawing positions on the International Monetary Fund.

6. The current method employed by the Department of Commerce in presenting the U.S. international payments position makes use of a functional format emphasizing the following *partial* balances: (a) merchandise trade balance, (b) balance on goods and services, and (c) current account balance.

7. Because the balance-of-payments is a double entry accounting system, total debits will always equal total credits. It follows that if the current account registers a deficit (surplus), the capital and financial account must register a surplus (deficit), or net capital/financial inflow (outflow). If a country realizes a deficit (surplus) in its current account, it becomes a net demander (supplier) of funds from (to) the rest of the world.

8. Concerning the business cycle, rapid growth of production and employment is commonly associated with large or growing trade and current account deficits, whereas slow output and employment growth is associated with large or growing current account surpluses.

9. The international investment position of the United States at a particular time is measured by the balance of international indebtedness. Unlike the balance-of-payments that is a flow concept (over a period of time), the balance of international indebtedness is a stock concept (at a single point in time).

KEY CONCEPTS AND TERMS

Balance of international indebtedness (p. 348)
Balance-of-payments (p. 329)
Capital and financial account (p. 332)
Credit transaction (p. 329)
Current account (p. 331)
Debit transaction (p. 329)

Double entry accounting (p. 330)
Goods and services balance (p. 331)
Income balance (p. 332)
Merchandise trade balance (p. 332)
Net creditor (p. 348)
Net debtor (p. 349)
Net foreign investment (p. 340)
Official reserve assets (p. 335)

Official settlements transactions (p. 334)
Special drawing rights (p. 335)
Statistical discrepancy (p. 336)
Trade balance (p. 337)
Unilateral transfers (p. 332)

STUDY QUESTIONS

1. What is meant by the balance-of-payments?
2. What economic transactions give rise to the receipt of dollars from foreigners? What transactions give rise to payments to foreigners?
3. Why does the balance-of-payments statement "balance"?
4. From a functional viewpoint, a nation's balance-of-payments can be grouped into several categories. What are these categories?
5. What financial assets are categorized as official reserve assets for the United States?
6. What is the meaning of a surplus (deficit) on the (a) merchandise trade balance, (b) goods and services balance, and (c) current account balance?
7. Why has the goods and services balance sometimes shown a surplus while the merchandise trade balance shows a deficit?
8. What does the balance of international indebtedness measure? How does this statement differ from the balance-of-payments?
9. Indicate whether each of the following items represents a debit or a credit on the U.S. balance-of-payments:
   a. A U.S. importer purchases a shipload of French wine.
   b. A Japanese automobile firm builds an assembly plant in Kentucky.
   c. A British manufacturer exports machinery to Taiwan on a U.S. vessel.
   d. A U.S. college student spends a year studying in Switzerland.
   e. American charities donate food to people in drought plagued Africa.
   f. Japanese investors collect interest income on their holdings of U.S. government securities.

g. A German resident sends money to her relatives in the United States.

h. Lloyds of London sells an insurance policy to a U.S. business firm.

i. A Swiss resident receives dividends on her IBM stock.

10. Table 10.8 summarizes hypothetical transactions, in billions of U.S. dollars, that took place during a given year.

TABLE 10.8

International Transactions of the United States (billions of dollars)

Travel and transportation receipts, net	25
Merchandise imports	450
Unilateral transfers, net	−20
Allocation of SDRs	15
Receipts on U.S. investments abroad	20
Statistical discrepancy	40
Compensation of employees	−5
Changes in U.S. assets abroad, net	−150
Merchandise exports	375
Other services, net	35
Payments on foreign investments in the United States	−10

© Cengage Learning®

a. Calculate the U.S. merchandise trade, services, goods and services, income, unilateral transfers, and current account balances.

b. Which of these balances pertains to the net foreign investment position of the United States? How would you describe that position?

11. Given the hypothetical items shown in Table 10.9, determine the international investment position of the United States. Is the United States a net creditor nation or a net debtor nation?

TABLE 10.9

International Investment Position of the United State (billions of dollars)

Foreign official assets in the United States	25
Other foreign assets in the United States	225
U.S. government assets abroad	150
U.S. private assets abroad	75

© Cengage Learning®

Foreign Exchange

Among the factors that make international economics a distinct subject is the existence of different national monetary units of account. In the United States, prices and money are measured in terms of the dollar. The *peso* represents Mexico's unit of account, whereas the *franc* and *yen* signify the units of account of Switzerland and Japan, respectively.

A typical international transaction requires two distinct purchases. First, the foreign currency is bought; second, the foreign currency is used to facilitate the international transaction. Before French importers can purchase commodities from U.S. exporters, they must first purchase dollars to meet their international obligation. Some institutional arrangements are required that provide an efficient mechanism whereby monetary claims can be settled with a minimum of inconvenience to both parties. Such a mechanism exists in the form of the foreign exchange market.[1]

In this chapter, we will examine the nature and operation of this market.

FOREIGN EXCHANGE MARKET

The **foreign exchange market** refers to the organizational setting within which individuals, businesses, governments, and banks buy and sell foreign currencies and other debt instruments.[2] Only a small fraction of daily transactions in foreign exchange actually involve the trading of currency. Most foreign exchange transactions involve the transfer of electronic balances between commercial banks or foreign exchange dealers. Major U.S. banks such as JPMorgan Chase or Bank of America maintain inventories of foreign exchange in the form of foreign denominated deposits held in their branches or

---

[1]This chapter considers the foreign exchange market in the absence of government restrictions. In practice, foreign exchange markets for many currencies are controlled by governments; therefore, the range of foreign exchange activities discussed in this chapter are not all possible.

[2]This section draws from Sam Cross, *The Foreign Exchange Market in the United States*, Federal Reserve Bank of New York, 1998.

correspondent banks in foreign cities. Americans can obtain this foreign exchange from hometown banks that purchase it from Bank of America.

The foreign exchange market is by far the largest and most liquid market in the world. The estimated worldwide amount of foreign exchange transactions is about $4 trillion a day. Individual trades of $200 to $500 million are not uncommon. Quoted prices change as often as 20 times a minute. It has been estimated that the world's most active exchange rates can change up to 18,000 times during a single day.

The foreign exchange market is dominated by four currencies: the U.S. dollar, the euro, the Japanese yen, and the British pound. Not all currencies are traded on the foreign exchange market. Currencies that are not traded are avoided for reasons ranging from political instability to economic uncertainty. Sometimes a country's currency is not exchanged for the simple reason that the country produces very few products of interest to other countries.

Unlike stock or commodity exchanges, the foreign exchange market is not an organized structure. It has no centralized meeting place and no formal requirements for participation. Nor is the foreign exchange market limited to any one country. For any currency, such as the U.S. dollar, the foreign exchange market consists of all locations where dollars are exchanged for other national currencies. Three of the largest foreign exchange markets in the world are located in London, New York, and Tokyo; they handle the majority of all foreign exchange transactions. A dozen or so other market centers also exist around the world such as Paris and Zurich. Because foreign exchange dealers are in constant telephone and computer contact, the market is competitive; it functions no differently than if it were a centralized market.

The foreign exchange market opens on Monday morning in Hong Kong, which is Sunday evening in New York. As the day progresses, markets open in Tokyo, Frankfurt, London, New York, Chicago, San Francisco, and elsewhere. As the West Coast markets of the United States close, Hong Kong is only one hour away from opening for Tuesday business. Indeed, the foreign exchange market is a round-the-clock operation.

A typical foreign exchange market functions at three levels: in transactions between commercial banks and their commercial customers who are the ultimate demanders and suppliers of foreign exchange; in the domestic interbank market conducted through brokers; and in active trading in foreign exchange with banks overseas.

Exporters, importers, investors, and tourists buy and sell foreign exchange from and to commercial banks rather than each other. Consider the import of German autos by a U.S. dealer. The dealer is billed for each car it imports at the rate of 50,000 euros per car. The U.S. dealer cannot write a check for this amount because it does not have a checking account denominated in euros. Instead, the dealer goes to the foreign exchange department of, say, Bank of America to arrange payment. If the exchange rate is 1.1 euros = $1, the auto dealer writes a check to Bank of America for $45,454.55 (50,000 euros/1.1 euros = $45,454.55) per car. Bank of America will then pay the German manufacturer 50,000 euros per car in Germany. Bank of America is able to do this because it has a checking deposit in euros at its branch in Bonn.

The major banks that trade foreign exchange generally do not deal directly with one another but instead use the services of *foreign exchange brokers*. The purpose of a broker is to permit the trading banks to maintain desired foreign exchange balances. If at a particular moment a bank does not have the proper foreign exchange balances, it can turn to a broker to buy additional foreign currency or sell the surplus. Brokers thus provide a wholesale, interbank market in which trading banks can buy and sell foreign exchange. Brokers are paid a commission for their services by the selling bank.

The third tier of the foreign exchange market consists of the transactions between the trading banks and their overseas branches or foreign correspondents. Although several dozen U.S. banks trade in foreign exchange, it is the major New York banks that usually carry out transactions with foreign banks. Inland trading banks meet their foreign exchange needs by maintaining correspondent relations with the New York banks. Trading with foreign banks permits the matching of supply and demand of foreign exchange in the New York market. These international transactions are carried out primarily by telephone and computers.

Commercial and financial transactions in the foreign exchange market represent large nominal amounts; they are small in comparison to the amounts based on speculation. By far, most of currency trading is based on speculation in which traders purchase and sell for short-term gains based on minute-to-minute, hour-to-hour, and day-to-day price fluctuations. Estimates are that speculation accounts for about 90 percent of the daily trading activity in the foreign exchange market.

Until the 1980s, most foreign exchange trading was done over the phone. However, most foreign exchange trading is now executed electronically. Trading occurs through computer terminals at thousands of locations worldwide. When making a currency trade, a trader will key an order into his or her computer terminal, indicating the amount of a currency, the price, and an instruction to buy or sell. If the order can be filled from other orders outstanding, and it is the best price available in the system from other traders, the deal will be made. If a new order cannot be matched with outstanding orders, the new order will be entered into the system and traders in the system from other banks will have access to it. Another trader may accept the order by pressing a "buy" or "sell" button and a transmit button. Proponents of electronic trading note that there are benefits from the certainty and clarity of trade execution. This is unlike trading via telephone, where conflicts between traders sometimes occur about the supposedly agreed upon currency prices.

Prior to 2000, companies that needed hard currency on a daily basis to meet foreign payrolls or to convert sales in foreign currencies into U.S. dollars traditionally dealt with traders at major banks such as JP Morgan Chase. This required corporate customers to work the phones, talking to traders at several banks at once to get the right quotation. There was little head-to-head competition among the banks, and corporate clients were looking for alternatives. All of this changed when start-up Currenex, Inc. built an online marketplace where banks could compete to offer foreign currency exchange service to companies. The concept was embraced by major banks as well as corporate clients such as The Home Depot. Being online makes the currency trading process more transparent. Corporate clients can see multiple quotes instantly and shop for the best deal.

TYPES OF FOREIGN EXCHANGE TRANSACTIONS

When conducting purchases and sales of foreign currencies, banks promise to pay a stipulated amount of currency to another bank or customer at an agreed upon date. Banks typically engage in three types of foreign exchange transactions: spot, forward, and swap.

A **spot transaction** is where you can make an outright purchase or sale of a currency *now*, as in "on the spot." A spot deal will settle (in other words, the physical exchange of currencies takes place) two working days after the deal is struck. The two-day period is known as *immediate delivery*. By convention, the settlement date is the second business day after the date the transaction is agreed to by the two traders. The two-day period provides ample time for the two parties to confirm the agreement and arrange the clearing and necessary debiting and crediting of bank accounts in various international locations. The spot exchange rate is at or close to the current market rate because the transaction occurs in real time and not at some point in the future.

Here's how a spot transaction works:

- A trader calls another trader and asks for the price of a currency, say the euro. This call expresses only a potential interest in a deal, without the caller indicating whether he or she wants to buy or sell.
- The second trader provides the first trader with prices for both buying and selling.
- When the traders agree to do business, one will send euros and the other will send, say dollars. By convention, the payment is actually made two days later.

Spot dealing has the advantage of being the simplest way to meet your foreign currency requirements, but it also carries with it the greatest risk of exchange rate fluctuations, because there is no certainty of the rate until the transaction is made. Exchange rate fluctuations can effectively increase or decrease prices and can be a financial planning ordeal for companies and individuals.

In many cases, a business or financial institution knows it will be receiving or paying an amount of foreign currency on a specific date in the future. In August a U.S. importer may arrange for a special Christmas season shipment of Japanese radios to arrive in October. The agreement with the Japanese manufacturer may call for payment in yen on October 20. To guard against the possibility of the yen's becoming more expensive in terms of the dollar, the importer might contract with a bank to buy yen at a stipulated price, but not actually receive them until October 20 when they are needed. When the contract matures, the U.S. importer pays for the yen with a known amount of dollars. This is known as a **forward transaction**. A forward transaction will protect you against unfavorable movements in the exchange rate, but will not allow gains to be made should the exchange rate move in your favor in the period between entering the contract and final settlement of the currency.

Forward transactions differ from spot transactions in that their maturity date is more than two business days in the future. A forward exchange contract's maturity date can be a few months or even years in the future. The exchange rate is fixed when the contract is initially made. No money necessarily changes hands until the transaction actually takes place, although dealers may require some customers to provide collateral in advance. Notice that in a forward transaction, the buyer and seller are locked into a contract at a fixed price that cannot be affected by any changes in market exchange rates. This tool allows the market participants to plan more safely, since they know in advance what their foreign exchange will cost. It also allows them to avoid an immediate outlay of cash.

Trading foreign currencies among banks and companies also involves swap transactions. A **currency swap** is the conversion of one currency to another currency at one point in time, with an agreement to convert it to the original currency at a specified time in the future. The rates of both exchanges are agreed to in advance. Here's how a swap transaction works:

- Suppose a U.S. company needs 15 million Swiss francs for a three-month investment in Switzerland.
- It may agree to a rate of 1.5 francs to a dollar and swap $10 million with a company willing to swap 15 million francs for three months.

TABLE 11.1

Global Distribution of Foreign Exchange Transactions, 2013

AVERAGE DAILY VOLUME (BILLIONS OF DOLLARS)

Foreign Exchange Instrument	Amount	Percent
Foreign exchange swaps	$2,282	42.7
Spot transactions	2,046	38.3
Forward transactions	680	12.7
Foreign-exchange options	337	6.3
Total	5,345	100.0

Source: From Federal Reserve Bank of New York, 2013, *Triennial Central Bank Survey of Foreign Exchange and Derivatives Market*, available at http://www.newyorkfed.org/. See also Bank for International Settlements, *Triennial Central Bank Survey of Foreign Exchange and Derivatives Market.*

• After three months, the U.S. company returns the 15 million francs to the other company and gets back $10 million, with adjustments made for interest rate differentials.

The key aspect is that the two banks arrange the swap as a single transaction in which they agree to pay and receive stipulated amounts of currencies at specified rates. Swaps provide an efficient mechanism through which traders can meet their foreign exchange needs over a period of time. Traders are able to use a currency for a period in exchange for another currency that is not needed during that time.

Table 11.1 illustrates the distribution of foreign exchange transactions by U.S. banking institutions, by transaction type. Foreign exchange swaps and spot market transactions are the two most important types of foreign exchange transactions.

INTERBANK TRADING

In the foreign exchange market, currencies are actively traded around the clock and throughout the world. Banks are linked by telecommunications equipment that permits instantaneous communication. A relatively small number of money center banks carry out most of the foreign exchange transactions in the United States. Virtually all the big New York banks have active currency trading operations, as do their counterparts in London, Tokyo, Hong Kong, Frankfurt, and other financial centers. Large banks in cities such as Los Angeles, Chicago, San Francisco, and Detroit also have active currency trading operations. For most U.S. banks, currency transactions are not a large part of their business; these banks have ties to correspondent banks in New York and elsewhere to conduct currency transactions.

All these banks are prepared to purchase or sell foreign currencies to facilitate speculation for their own accounts and provide trading services for their customers such as corporations, government agencies, and wealthy private individuals. Bank purchases from and sales to their customers are classified as *retail transactions* when the amount involved is less than 1 million currency units. *Wholesale transactions* involving more than 1 million currency units generally occur between banks or with large corporate customers.

An international community of about 400 banks constitutes the daily currency exchanges for buyers and sellers worldwide. A bank's foreign exchange dealers are in constant contact with other dealers to buy and sell currencies. In most large banks, dealers specialize in one or more foreign currencies. The chief dealer establishes the overall trading policy and direction of trading trying to service the foreign exchange needs of the bank's customers and make a profit for the bank. Currency trading is conducted on a 24-hour basis, and exchange rates may fluctuate at any moment. Bank dealers must be light sleepers, ready to react to a nighttime phone call that indicates exchange rates are moving sharply in foreign markets. Banks often allow senior dealers to conduct exchange trading at home in response to such developments.

With the latest electronic equipment, currency exchanges are negotiated on computer terminals; a push of a button confirms a trade. Dealers use electronic trading boards such as Reuters Dealing and EBS that permit them to instantly register transactions and verify their bank's positions. Besides trading currencies during daytime hours, major banks have established night trading desks to capitalize on foreign exchange fluctuations during the evening and to accommodate corporate requests for currency trades. In the interbank market, currencies are traded in amounts involving at least 1 million units of a specific foreign currency. Table 11.2 lists leading banks that trade in the foreign exchange market.

How do banks such as Bank of America earn profits in foreign exchange transactions in the interbank market? They quote both a bid and an offer rate to other banks. The **bid rate** refers to the price that the bank is willing to pay for a unit of foreign currency; the **offer rate** is the price at which the bank is willing to sell a unit of foreign currency. The difference between the bid and the offer rate is the **spread** that varies by the size of the transaction and the liquidity of the currencies being traded. At any given time, a bank's bid quote for a foreign currency will be less than its offer quote. The spread is intended to cover the bank's costs of implementing the exchange of currencies. The large trading banks are prepared to "make a market" in a currency by providing bid and offer rates on request. The use of bid and offer rates allows banks to make profits on foreign exchange transactions in the spot and forward market.

Foreign exchange dealers who simultaneously purchase and sell foreign currency earn the spread as profit. Citibank might quote bid and offer rates for the Swiss franc at

TABLE 11.2

Top Ten Banks by Share of Foreign Exchange Market, 2013

Bank	Share of Foreign-Exchange Market
Deutsche Bank	15.2%
Citigroup	14.9
Barclays Capital	10.2
UBS	10.1
HSBC	6.9
JPMorgan	6.1
RBS	5.6
Credit Suisse	3.7
Morgan Stanley	3.2

Source: From "Foreign Exchange Survey," *Euromoney*, 2013, available at www.euromoney.com.

$0.5851/$0.5854. The bid rate is $0.5851 per franc. At this price, Citibank would be prepared to buy 1 million francs for $585,100. The offer rate is $0.5854 per franc. Citibank would be willing to sell 1 million francs for $585,400. If Citibank is able to simultaneously buy and sell 1 million francs, it will earn $300 on the transaction. This profit equals the spread ($0.0003) multiplied by the amount of the transaction (1 million francs).

Besides earning profits from a currency's bid/offer spread, foreign exchange dealers attempt to profit by anticipating correctly the future direction of currency movements. Suppose a Citibank dealer expects the Japanese yen to *appreciate* (strengthen) against the U.S. dollar. The dealer will likely *raise* both bid and offer rates, attempting to persuade other dealers to sell yen to Citibank and dissuade other dealers from purchasing yen from Citibank. The bank dealer thus purchases more yen than are sold. If the yen appreciates against the dollar as predicted, the Citibank dealer can sell the yen at a higher rate and earn a profit. Conversely, should the Citibank dealer anticipate that the yen is about to *depreciate* (weaken) against the dollar, the dealer will *lower* the bid and offer rates. Such action encourages sales and discourages purchases; the dealer thus sells more yen than are bought. If the yen depreciates as expected, the dealer can purchase yen back at a lower price to make a profit.

If exchange rates move in the desired direction, foreign exchange traders earn profits. Losses accrue if exchange rates move in the opposite, unexpected direction. To limit possible losses on exchange market transactions, banks impose financial restrictions on their dealers' trading volume. Dealers are subject to *position limits* that stipulate the amount of buying and selling that can be conducted in a given currency. Although banks maintain formal restrictions, they have sometimes absorbed substantial losses from unauthorized trading activity beyond position limits. Because foreign exchange departments are considered by bank management to be profit centers, dealers feel pressure to generate an acceptable rate of return on the bank's funds invested in this operation.

When a bank sells foreign currency to its business and household customers, it charges a "retail" exchange rate. This rate is based on the interbank (wholesale) rate that the bank pays when it buys foreign currency plus a markup that compensates the bank for the services it provides. This markup depends on the size of the currency transaction, the market volatility, and the currency pairs.

READING FOREIGN EXCHANGE QUOTATIONS

Most daily newspapers publish foreign exchange rates for major currencies. The **exchange rate** is the price of one currency in terms of another—the number of dollars required to purchase 1 British pound (£). In shorthand notation, ER = $/£, where ER is the exchange rate. If ER = 2, then purchasing £1 will require $2 (2/1 = 2). It is also possible to define the exchange rate as the number of units of foreign currency required to purchase one unit of domestic currency, or ER' = £/$. In our example, ER' = 0.5 ($\frac{1}{2}$ = 0.5), which implies that it requires £0.5 to buy $1. Of course, ER' is the reciprocal of ER (ER' = 1/ER).

Table 11.3 shows the exchange rates listed for October 29–30, 2013. In columns 2 and 3 of the table, the selling prices of foreign currencies are listed in dollars (USD). The columns state how many dollars are required to purchase one unit of a given foreign currency. The quote for the Argentinean peso for Wednesday (October 30) was 0.1693.

TABLE 11.3

Foreign Exchange Quotations

Exchange Rates   October 29–30, 2013*

The foreign exchange rates below apply to trading among banks in amounts of $1 million and more, as quoted at 4:00 p.m. Eastern Time by Reuters and other sources. Retail transactions provide fewer units of foreign currency per dollar

Country/currency	In USD		Per USD	
	Wed.	Tues.	Wed.	Tues.
Americas				
Argentina peso	.1693	.1698	5.9053	5.8901
Brazil real	.4565	.4581	2.1905	2.1828
Canada dollar	.9542	.9552	1.0480	1.0469
Chile peso	.001965	.001966	508.80	508.60
Colombia peso	.0005310	.0005310	1883.24	1883.24
Ecuador U.S. dollar	1	1	1	1
Mexico peso	.0773	.0774	12.9344	12.9187
Peru new sol	.3625	.3631	2.759	2.754
Uruguay peso	.04630	.04643	21.5975	21.5375
Venezuela bolivar	.157480	.157480	6.3500	6.3500
Asia-Pacific				
Australian dollar	.9484	.9480	1.0544	1.0548
1-month forward	.9465	.9462	1.0565	1.0568
3-months forward	.9426	.9423	1.0609	1.0612
6-months forward	.9373	.9369	1.0669	1.0673
China yuan	.1641	.1642	6.0946	6.0896
Hong Kong dollar	.1290	.1290	7.7534	7.7534
India rupee	.01630	.01627	61.340	61.455
Indonesia rupiah	.0000917	.0000921	10901	10855
Japan yen	.010151	.010184	98.52	98.19
1-month forward	.010152	.010186	98.50	98.18
3-months forward	.010157	.010190	98.46	98.13
6-months forward	.010163	.010197	98.40	98.07
Malaysia ringgit	.3176	.3177	3.1484	3.1474
New Zealand dollar	.8267	.8258	1.2096	1.2110
Pakistan rupee	.00940	.00939	106.395	106.550

Country/currency	In USD		Per USD	
	Wed.	Tues.	Wed.	Tues.
Philippines peso	.0232	.0232	43.103	43.103
Singapore dollar	.8067	.8058	1.2396	1.2411
South Korea won	.0009439	.0009417	1059.40	1061.88
Taiwan dollar	.03399	.03394	29.421	29.465
Thailand baht	.03215	.03219	31.106	31.064
Vietman dong	.00004738	.00004738	21105	21105
Europe				
Czech Rep. koruna	.05340	.05333	18.726	18.751
Denmark krone	.1842	.1843	5.4299	5.4262
Euro area euro	1.3736	1.3746	.7280	.7275
Hungary forint	.004673	.004676	214.00	213.86
Norway krone	.1696	.1695	5.8977	5.8987
Poland zloty	.3285	.3283	3.0443	3.0460
Russia ruble	.03125	.03114	32.001	32.112
Sweden krona	.1564	.1567	6.3934	6.3826
Switzerland franc	1.1121	1.1125	.8992	.8989
1-month forward	1.1124	1.1127	.8990	.8987
3-months forward	1.1130	1.1133	.8985	.8982
6-months forward	1.1139	1.1143	.8978	.8975
Turkey lira	.5013	.5021	1.9948	1.9917
UK pound	1.6039	1.6047	.6235	.6232
1-month forward	1.6036	1.6043	.6236	.6233
3-months forward	1.6028	1.6035	.6239	.6236
6-months forward	1.6017	1.6024	.6243	.6241
Middle East/Africa				
Bahrain dinar	2.6530	2.6528	.3769	.3770
Egypt pound	.1452	.1452	6.8880	6.8880
Israel shekel	.2841	.2845	3.5196	3.5151
Jordan dinar	1.4119	1.4139	.7083	.7073
Kuwait dinar	3.5499	3.5499	.2817	.2817
Lebanon pound	.0006636	.0006639	1506.90	1506.35
Saudi Arabia riyal	.2666	.2666	3.7503	3.7503
South Africa rand	.1005	.1011	9.9457	9.8920
UAE dirham	.2723	.2723	3.6724	3.6724

*Tuesday, October 29, 2013; Wednesday, October 30, 2013.

Source: From Reuters, *Currency Calculator*, available at http://www.reuters.com. See also Federal Reserve Bank of New York, *Foreign Exchange Rates*, available at http://www.newyorkfed.org/.

This rate means that $0.1693 was required to purchase 1 peso. Columns 4 and 5 (USD) show the foreign exchange rates from the opposite perspective, telling how many units of a foreign currency are required to buy a U.S. dollar. Again referring to Wednesday, it would take 5.9053 Argentinean pesos to purchase 1 U.S. dollar.

The term *exchange rate* in the table's heading refers to the price at which a bank will sell foreign exchange in amounts of $1 million or more to another bank. The table's heading also states at what time during the day the quotation was made (4:00 P.M. Eastern time) because currency prices fluctuate throughout the day in response to changing supply and demand conditions. Retail foreign exchange transactions, in amounts under $1 million, carry an additional service charge and are thus made at a different exchange rate.

How much does a consumer typically pay for smaller amounts of foreign currency in a retail setting? These retail rates add commissions of 1 to 10 percent, or more. For example:

- Automated teller machines (ATMs) typically add 2 percent and additional service charges in many parts of the world.
- Credit cards typically add 3 percent for the major currencies and more for other currencies.
- Foreign exchange kiosks and banks often add 4 percent when you convert hard cash for the major currencies, and more for other currencies.

An exchange rate determined by free market forces can and does change frequently. When the dollar price of pounds increases, for example, from $2 = £1 to $2.10 = £1, the dollar has *depreciated* relative to the pound. Currency **depreciation** means that it takes more units of a nation's currency to purchase a unit of some foreign currency. Conversely, when the dollar price of pounds decreases, say, from $2 = £1 to $1.90 = £1, the value of the dollar has *appreciated* relative to the pound. Currency **appreciation** means that it takes fewer units of a nation's currency to purchase a unit of some foreign currency.

In Table 11.3, look at the relation between columns 2 and 3 (USD). Going forward in time from Tuesday (October 29) to Wednesday (October 30) we see that the U.S. dollar cost of an Australian dollar increased from $0.9480 U.S. to $0.9484 U.S.; the U.S. dollar thus depreciated against the Australian dollar, and conversely, the Australian dollar appreciated against the U.S. dollar. To verify this conclusion, refer to columns 4 and 5 of the table (USD). Going forward in time from Tuesday to Wednesday, we see that the Australian dollar cost of the U.S. dollar decreased from 1.0548 Australian dollars = $1 U.S. to 1.0544 Australian dollars = $1 U.S. In similar fashion, we see that from Tuesday to Wednesday the U.S. dollar appreciated against Mexico's peso from $0.0774 = 1 peso to $0.0773 = 1 peso; the peso thus depreciated against the dollar, from 12.9187 pesos = $1 to 12.9344 pesos = $1.

Most tables of exchange rate quotations express currency values relative to the U.S. dollar, regardless of the country where the quote is provided. Yet in many instances, the U.S. dollar is not part of a foreign exchange transaction. In such cases, the people involved need to obtain an exchange quote between two non-dollar currencies. As an example, if a British importer needs francs to purchase Swiss watches, the exchange rate of interest is the Swiss franc relative to the British pound. The exchange rate between any two currencies (such as the franc and the pound) can be derived from the rates of these two currencies in terms of a third currency (the dollar). The resulting rate is called the **cross exchange rate**.

Referring again to Table 11.3, we see as of Wednesday, the dollar cost of the U.K. pound is $1.6039 and the dollar cost of the Swiss franc is $1.1121. We can then calculate the value of the U.K. pound relative to the Swiss franc as follows:

$$\frac{\$ \text{ Value of U.K. Pound}}{\$ \text{ Value of Swiss Franc}} = \frac{\$1.6039}{\$1.1121} = 1.4422$$

Each U.K. pound buys about 1.44 Swiss francs; this is the cross exchange rate between the pound and the franc. In similar fashion, cross exchange rates can be calculated between any two non-dollar currencies in Table 11.3. The *NASDAQ Currency Converter* carries out such calculations for you. It can be found at www.nasdaq.com/aspx/currency-converter.aspx/.

In 2013, Japanese automakers found that their vehicles became more affordable for consumers worldwide. Why? The exchange value of the yen was falling. Consider the case of Toyota Motor Corporation.

During 2012–2013, the yen steadily fell against the U.S. dollar as Sinzo Abe, Japan's prime minister, advocated for the decline to improve his automakers' competitiveness in global markets. In 2012, the dollar bought fewer than 80 yen while in 2013 it bought about 100 yen. When Toyota sold a Camry in the United States for $30,000 in 2012, those dollars were converted into about 2.4 million yen ($30,000 × 80¥ = 2,400,0000¥). In 2013, Toyota received about 3 million yen from such a sale ($30,000 × 100¥ = 3,000,000¥). This amounted to a 25 percent increase in the amount of yen received. That helps explain why Toyota, the world's top selling automaker, more than doubled its profit during 2012–2013. According to analysts at Morgan Stanley, Toyota receives roughly $2,000 more per vehicle when the yen depreciates from 78 to 100 yen per dollar.

The currency slide gave Toyota and other Japanese automakers a financial gain on every car that they could use to reduce prices, boost ads, and improve products, all helping boost U.S. auto sales as the economy strengthened from the Great Recession of 2007–2009.

In 2013, Toyota exported nearly twice as many cars from Japan as Honda Motor Company and Nissan Motor Company, and benefitted more than its domestic rivals from the yen's depreciation. However, Toyota officials acknowledged that the currency windfall was temporary, and said it would continue to increase productivity, decrease costs, and improve product quality to increase sales to lessen its vulnerability to currency fluctuations.

Source: Morgan Stanley, *100 Yen: Global Auto Implications*, April 18, 2013; Kiroko Tabuchi, "Toyota Bounces Back with Help from Eager American Buyers and a Weak Yen," *The New York Times*, May 8, 2013; "Toyota Ups Profit Forecast on Yen Fall," *The Japan Times News*, August 2, 2013; Yoshio Takahashi, "Toyota's Net Soars 70 Percent as Yen Falls," *The Wall Street Journal*, November 7, 2013; Daniel Inman, "Japan's Signals Sink the Yen," *The Wall Street Journal*, November 15, 2013.

FORWARD AND FUTURES MARKETS

Foreign exchange can be bought and sold for delivery immediately (**spot market**) or for future delivery (**forward market**). Forward contracts are normally made by those who will receive or make payment in foreign exchange in the weeks or months ahead. As seen in Table 11.3, the New York foreign exchange market is a spot market for most currencies of the world. Regular forward markets exist only for the more widely traded currencies. Exporters and importers, whose foreign exchange receipts and payments are in the future, are the primary participants in the forward market. The forward quotations for currencies such as the U.K. pound, Canadian dollar, Japanese yen, and Swiss franc are for delivery one month, three months, or six months from the date indicated in the table's caption (October 30, 2013).

Trading in foreign exchange can also be done in the **futures market**. In this market, contracting parties agree to future exchanges of currencies and set applicable exchange rates in advance. The futures market is distinguished from the forward market in that only a limited number of leading currencies are traded; trading takes place in standardized contract amounts and in a specific geographic location. Table 11.4 summarizes the major differences between the forward market and the futures market.

One such futures market is the **International Monetary Market (IMM)** of the Chicago Mercantile Exchange. Founded in 1972, the IMM is an extension of the commodity futures markets in which specific quantities of wheat, corn, and other commodities are

TABLE 11.4

Forward Contract versus Futures Contract

	Forward Contract	**Futures Contract**
Issuer	Commercial bank	International Monetary Market (IMM) of the Chicago Mercantile Exchange and other foreign exchanges such as the Tokyo International Financial Futures Exchange
Trading	"Over the counter" by telephone	On the IMM's market floor
Contract size	Tailored to the needs of the exporter/importer/investor; no set size	Standardized in round lots
Date of delivery	Negotiable	Only on particular dates
Contract costs	Based on the bid/offer spread	Brokerage fees for sell and buy orders
Settlement	On expiration date only, at prearranged price	Profits or losses paid daily at close of trading

© Cengage Learning®

TABLE 11.5

Foreign Currency Futures, October 30, 2013

	Open	High	Low	Settle	Change	Open Interest
JAPAN YEN (CME)—12.5 million yen; $ per 100 yen						
Dec'13	1.0247	1.0264	1.0228	1.0240	–.0034	150,637
Mar'14	1.0253	1.0281	1.0236	1.0247	–.0034	1,131

Source: From Chicago Mercantile Exchange, International Monetary Market, available at http://www.cme.com/trading.

bought and sold for future delivery at specific dates. The IMM provides trading facilities for the purchase and sale for future delivery of financial instruments (such as foreign currencies) and precious metals (such as gold). The IMM is especially popular with smaller banks and companies. Also, the IMM is one of the few places where individuals can speculate on changes in exchange rates.

Foreign exchange trading on the IMM is limited to major currencies. Contracts are set for delivery on the third Wednesday of March, June, September, and December. Price quotations are in terms of U.S. dollars per unit of foreign currency, but futures contracts are for a fixed amount (for example, 62,500 U.K. pounds).

Here is how to read the IMM's futures prices as listed in Table 11.5.[3] The *size of each contract* is shown on the same line as the currency's name and country. A contract for Japanese yen covers the right to purchase 12.5 million yen. Moving to the right of the size of the contract, we see the expression *$ per 100 yen*. The first column of the table shows the **maturity months** of the contract; using June as an example, the remaining columns yield the following information:

Open refers to the price at which the yen was first sold when the IMM opened on the morning of October 30, 2013. Depending on overnight events in the world, the opening price may not be identical to the closing price from the previous trading day. Because prices are expressed in terms of dollars per 100 yen, the 1.0247 implies that

[3]This section is adapted from R. Wurman and others, *The Wall Street Journal: Guide to Understanding Money and Markets* (New York: Simon and Schuster, Inc., 1990).

yen opened for sale at $1.0247 per 100 yen. Multiply this price by the size of a contract and you've calculated the full value of one contract at the open of trading for that day: ($1.0247 × 12.5 million)/100 yen = $128,087.50.

The *high, low,* and *settle* columns indicate the contract's highest, lowest, and closing prices for the day. Viewed together, these figures provide an indication of how volatile the market for the yen was during the day. After opening at $1.0247 per 100 yen, yen for December delivery never sold for more than $1.0264 per 100 yen and never for less than $1.0228 per 100 yen; trading finally settled, or ended, at $1.0240 per 100 yen. Multiplying the size of the yen contract times the yen's settlement price gives the full value of a yen contract at the closing of the trading day: ($1.0240 × 12.5 million)/100 yen = $128,000.

Change compares today's closing price with the closing price as listed in the previous day's paper. A plus (+) sign means prices ended higher; a minus (−) means prices ended lower. In the yen's case, the yen for December delivery settled $0.0034 per 100 yen lower than it did the previous trading day.

Open interest refers to the total number of contracts outstanding; that is, those that have not been canceled by offsetting trades. It shows how much interest there is in trading a particular contract.

FOREIGN CURRENCY OPTIONS

During the 1980s, a new feature of the foreign exchange market was developed: the option market. An **option** is simply an agreement between a holder (buyer) and a writer (seller) that gives the holder the *right*, but not the obligation, to buy or sell financial instruments at any time through a specified date. Although the holder is not obligated to buy or sell currency, the writer is obligated to fulfill a transaction. Having a throwaway feature, options are a unique type of financial contract in that you only use the contract if you want to do so. By contrast, forward contracts *obligate* a person to carry out a transaction at a specified price, even if the market has changed and the person would rather not.

Foreign currency options provide an options holder the right to buy or sell a fixed amount of foreign currency at a prearranged price within a few days or a couple of years. The options holder can choose the exchange rate he or she wants to guarantee, as well as the length of the contract. Foreign currency options have been used by companies seeking to hedge against exchange rate risk as well as by speculators in foreign currencies.

There are two types of foreign currency options. A **call option** gives the holder the right to *buy* foreign currency at a specified price, whereas a **put option** gives the holder the right to *sell* foreign currency at a specified price. The price at which the option can be exercised (the price at which the foreign currency is bought or sold) is called the **strike price**. The holder of a foreign currency option has the right to exercise the contract but may choose not to do so if it turns out to be unprofitable. The writer of the options contract (Bank of America, Citibank, and Merrill Lynch) must deliver the foreign currency if called on by a call holder or must buy foreign currency if it is put to them by a put holder. For this obligation, the writer of the options contract receives a *premium*, or fee (option price). Financial institutions have been willing to write foreign currency options because they generate substantial premium income (the fee income on a $5 million deal can run to $100,000 or more). Writing currency options is a risky business because the writer takes chances on tricky pricing. Foreign currency options are traded in a variety of currencies in Europe and the United States. *The Wall Street Journal* publishes daily listings of foreign currency options contracts. It is left for more advanced textbooks to discuss the mechanics of trading foreign currency options.

To see how exporters can use foreign currency options to cope with exchange rate risk, consider the case of Boeing that submits a bid for the sale of jet planes to an airline company in Japan. Boeing must deal not only with the uncertainty of winning the bid but also with exchange rate risk. If Boeing wins the bid, it will receive yen in the future. But what if the yen depreciates in the interim, from, 115 yen = \$1 to 120 yen = \$1? Boeing's yen holdings would convert into fewer dollars, eroding the profitability of the jet sale. Because Boeing wants to sell yen in exchange for dollars, it can offset this exchange market risk by purchasing put options that give the company the right to sell yen for dollars at a specified price. Having obtained a put option, if Boeing wins the bid it has limited the exchange rate risk. On the other hand, if the bid is lost, Boeing's losses are limited to the cost of the option. Foreign currency options provide a worst case rate of exchange for companies conducting international business. The maximum amount the company can lose by covering its exchange rate risk is the amount of the option price.

EXCHANGE RATE DETERMINATION

What determines the equilibrium exchange rate in a free market? Let us consider the exchange rate from the perspective of the United States—in dollars per unit of foreign currency. Like other prices, the exchange rate in a free market is determined by both supply and demand conditions.

Demand for Foreign Exchange

A nation's *demand for foreign exchange* is a derived demand; driven by foreigner demand for domestic goods and assets such as bank accounts, stocks, bonds, and real property. It corresponds to the *debit* items on a country's balance of payments. The U.S. demand for pounds may stem from its desire to import British goods and services, to make investments in Britain, or to make transfer payments to residents in Britain.

Like most demand schedules, the U.S. demand for pounds varies inversely with its price; that is, fewer pounds are demanded at higher prices than at lower prices. This relation is depicted by line D_0 in Figure 11.1. As the dollar depreciates against the pound (the dollar price of the pound rises), British goods and services become more expensive to U.S. importers. This is because more dollars are required to purchase each pound needed to finance the import purchases. The higher exchange rate reduces the number of imports bought, lowering the number of pounds demanded by U.S. residents. In like manner, an appreciation of the U.S. dollar relative to the pound would be expected to induce larger import purchases and more pounds demanded by U.S. residents.

Supply of Foreign Exchange

The *supply of foreign exchange* refers to the amount of foreign exchange that will be offered to the market at various exchange rates, all other factors held constant. The supply of pounds, for example, is generated by the desire of British residents and businesses to import U.S. goods and services, lend funds and make investments in the United States, repay debts owed to U.S. lenders, and extend transfer payments to U.S. residents. In each of these cases, the British offer pounds in the foreign exchange market to obtain the dollars they need to make payments to U.S. residents. Note that the supply of pounds results from transactions that appear on the *credit* side of the U.S. balance of

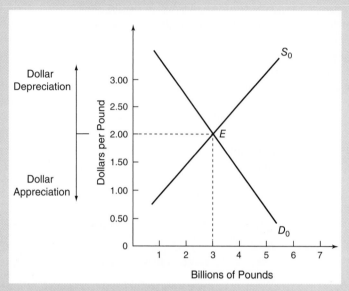

FIGURE 11.1

Exchange Rate Determination

The equilibrium exchange rate is established at the point of intersection of the supply and demand schedules of foreign exchange. The demand for foreign exchange corresponds to the debit items on a nation's balance-of-payments statement; the supply of foreign exchange corresponds to the credit items.

payments; one can make a connection between the balance of payments and the foreign exchange market.

The supply of pounds is denoted by schedule S_0 in Figure 11.1. The schedule represents the number of pounds offered by the British to obtain dollars with which to buy U.S. goods, services, and assets. It is depicted in the figure as a positive function of the U.S. exchange rate. As the dollar depreciates against the pound (dollar price of the pound rises), the British will be inclined to buy more U.S. goods. The reason, of course, is that at higher dollar prices of pounds, the British can get more U.S. dollars and hence more U.S. goods per British pound. American goods become cheaper to the British who are induced to purchase additional quantities. As a result, more pounds are offered in the foreign exchange market to buy dollars to pay U.S. exporters.

Equilibrium Rate of Exchange

As long as monetary authorities do not attempt to stabilize exchange rates or moderate their movements, the *equilibrium exchange rate* is determined by the market forces of supply and demand. In Figure 11.1, exchange market equilibrium occurs at point *E*, where S_0 and D_0 intersect. Three billion pounds will be traded at a price of $2 per pound. The foreign exchange market is precisely cleared, leaving neither an excess supply nor an excess demand for pounds.

Given the supply and demand schedules of Figure 11.1, there is no reason for the exchange rate to deviate from the equilibrium level. But in practice, it is unlikely that the equilibrium exchange rate will remain long at the existing level. This is because the forces that underlie the location of the supply and demand schedules tend to change over

TABLE 11.6

Advantages and Disadvantages of a Strengthening and Weakening Dollar

STRENGTHENING (APPRECIATING) DOLLAR

Advantages	Disadvantages
1. U.S. consumers see lower prices on foreign compete in foreign markets.	1. U.S. exporting firms find it harder to goods.
2. Lower prices on foreign goods help keep U.S. inflation low.	2. U.S. firms in import-competing markets find it harder to compete with lower priced foreign goods.
3. U.S. consumers benefit when they travel to foreign countries	3. Foreign tourists find it more expensive to visit the United States.

WEAKENING (DEPRECIATING) DOLLAR

Advantages	Disadvantages
1. U.S. exporting firms find it easier to sell goods foreign markets.	1. U.S. consumers face higher prices on foreign goods.
2. Firms in the United States have less competitive pressure to keep prices low.	2. Higher prices on foreign goods contribute to higher inflation in the United States.
3. More foreign tourists can afford to visit the United States.	3. U.S. consumers find traveling abroad more costly.

© Cengage Learning®

time, causing shifts in the schedules. Should the *demand* for pounds shift *rightward* (an increase in demand), the dollar will *depreciate* against the pound; *leftward* shifts in the demand for pounds (a decrease in demand) cause the dollar to *appreciate*. Conversely, a *rightward* shift in the *supply* of pounds (increase in supply) causes the dollar to *appreciate* against the pound; a *leftward* shift in the supply of pounds (decrease in supply) results in a *depreciation* of the dollar. The effects of an appreciating and depreciating dollar are summarized in Table 11.6.

INDEXES OF THE FOREIGN-EXCHANGE VALUE OF THE DOLLAR: NOMINAL AND REAL EXCHANGE RATES

Since 1973, the value of the U.S. dollar in terms of foreign currencies has changed daily. In this environment of market determined exchange rates, measuring the international value of the dollar is a confusing task. Financial pages of newspapers may be headlining a *depreciation* of the dollar relative to some currencies, while at the same time reporting its *appreciation* relative to others. Such events may leave the general public confused as to the actual value of the dollar.

Suppose the U.S. dollar appreciates ten percent relative to the yen and depreciates five percent against the pound. The change in the dollar's exchange value is some weighted average of the changes in these two bilateral exchange rates. Throughout the day, the value of the dollar may change relative to the values of any number of currencies under market determined exchange rates. Direct comparison of the dollar's exchange rate over time thus requires a *weighted average* of all the bilateral changes. This average is referred to as the dollar's **exchange rate index**; it is also known as the **effective exchange rate** or the **trade-weighted dollar**.

The exchange rate index is a weighted average of the exchange rates between the domestic currency and the nation's most important trading partners, with weights given by relative importance of the nation's trade with each of these trade partners. One popular index of exchange rates is the so called "major currency index," that is constructed by the U.S. Federal Reserve Board of Governors. This index reflects the impact of changes in the dollar's exchange rate on U.S. exports and imports with seven major trading partners of the United States. The base period of the index is March 1973.

Table 11.7 illustrates the **nominal exchange rate index** of the U.S. dollar. This is the average value of the dollar not adjusted for changes in price levels in the United States and its trading partners. An *increase* in the nominal exchange rate index (from year to year) indicates a dollar *appreciation* relative to the currencies of the other nations in the index and a *loss* of competitiveness for the United States. Conversely, a *decrease* in the nominal exchange rate implies dollar *depreciation* relative to the other currencies in the index and an *improvement* in U.S. international competitiveness. The nominal exchange rate index is based on **nominal exchange rates** that do not reflect changes in price levels in trading partners.

A problem arises when interpreting changes in the nominal exchange rate index when prices are not constant. When the prices of goods and services are changing in either the United States or a partner country (or both), one does not know the change in the relative price of foreign goods and services by simply looking at changes in the nominal exchange rate and failing to consider the new level of prices within both countries. If the dollar appreciated against the peso by five percent, we would expect that, other things constant, U.S. goods would be five percent less competitive against Mexican goods in world markets than was previously the case. Suppose that at the same time, the dollar appreciated; U.S. goods prices increased more rapidly than Mexican goods prices. In this situation, the decrease in U.S. competitiveness against Mexican goods would be more than five percent, and the nominal five percent exchange rate change would be misleading. Overall international competitiveness of U.S. manufactured goods depends not on the behavior of nominal exchange rates, but on movements in nominal exchange rates relative to prices.

TABLE 11.7

Exchange Rate Indexes of the U.S. Dollar (March 1973 = 100)*

Year	Nominal Exchange Rate Index	Real Exchange Rate Index
1973 (March)	100.0	100.0
1980	87.4	91.3
1984	138.3	117.7
1988	92.7	83.5
1992	86.6	81.8
1996	87.4	85.3
2000	98.3	103.1
2004	85.4	90.6
2008	80.7	88.5
2012	73.6	82.8
2013 (October)	75.2	85.2

*The "major currency index" includes the currencies of the United States, Canada, Euro area, Japan, United Kingdom, Switzerland, Australia, and Sweden.

Source: From Federal Reserve, *Foreign Exchange Rates*, available at http://www.federalreserve.gov/releases/H10/Summary/.

As a result, economists calculate the **real exchange rate** that embodies the changes in prices in the countries in the calculation. The real exchange rate is the nominal exchange rate adjusted for relative price levels. To calculate the real exchange rate, we use the following formula:

$$\text{Real Exchange Rate} = \text{Nominal Exchange Rate} \times \frac{\text{Foreign country's price level}}{(\text{Home country's price level})}$$

where both the nominal exchange rate and real exchange rate are measured in units of domestic currency per unit of foreign currency.

To illustrate, suppose that in 2013 the nominal exchange rate for the United States and Europe is \$0.90 per euro; by 2014 the nominal exchange rate falls to \$0.80 per euro. This is an 11 percent appreciation of the dollar against the euro $(\$0.90 - \$0.80)/\$0.90 = 0.11$ leading one to expect a substantial drop in competitiveness of U.S. goods relative to European goods. To calculate the real exchange rate, we must look at prices. Let us assume that the base year is 2013, at which consumer prices are set equal to 100. By 2014, U.S. consumer prices increase to a level of 108 while European consumer prices increase to a level of 102. The real exchange rate would then be calculated as follows:

$$\text{Real Exchange Rate}_{2014} = (\$0.80 \times \$1.02/\$1.08) = \$0.756 \text{ per euro}$$

In this example, the real exchange rate indicates that U.S. goods are *less* competitive on international markets than would be suggested by the nominal exchange rate. This result occurs because the dollar appreciates in nominal terms *and* U.S. prices increase *more* rapidly than European prices. In real terms, the dollar appreciates not by 11 percent (as with the nominal exchange rate) but by 16 percent $(\$0.90 - \$0.756)/\$0.90 = 0.16$ for variations in the exchange rate to have an effect on the composition of U.S. output, output growth, employment, and trade there must be a change in the real exchange rate. The change in the nominal exchange rate must alter the amount of goods and services that the dollar buys in foreign countries. Real exchange rates offer such a comparison and provide a better gauge of international competitiveness than nominal exchange rates.

In addition to constructing a nominal exchange rate index, economists construct a real exchange rate index for a broad sample of U.S. trading partners. Table 11.7 also shows the **real exchange rate index** of the U.S. dollar. This is the average value of the dollar based on real exchange rates. The index is constructed so an appreciation of the dollar corresponds to higher index values. The importance that monetary authorities attach to the real exchange rate index stems from economic theory that states a rise in the real exchange rate will tend to reduce the international competitiveness of U.S. firms; conversely, a fall in the real exchange rate tends to increase the international competitiveness of U.S. firms.[4]

ARBITRAGE

We have seen how the supply and demand for foreign exchange can set the market exchange rate. This analysis was from the perspective of the U.S. (New York) foreign exchange market. But what about the relation between the exchange rate in the U.S. market and that in other nations? When restrictions do not modify the ability of the foreign exchange market to operate efficiently, normal market forces result in a consistent relation among the market exchange rates of all currencies. That is to say, if £1 = \$2 in

---

[4]For discussions of the nominal and real exchange rate indexes see "New Summary Measures of the Foreign Exchange Value of the Dollar," *Federal Reserve Bulletin*, October 1998, pp. 811–818 and "Real Exchange Rate Indexes for the Canadian Dollar," *Bank of Canada Review*, Autumn, 1999, pp. 19–28.

New York, then $1 = £0.5 in London. The prices for the same currency in different world locations will be identical.

The factor underlying the consistency of the exchange rates is called **exchange arbitrage**. Exchange arbitrage refers to the *simultaneous* purchase and sale of a currency in different foreign exchange markets in order to profit from exchange rate differentials in the two locations. This process brings about an identical price for the same currency in different locations and thus results in one market.

Suppose that the dollar/pound exchange rate is £1 = $2 in New York but £1 = $2.01 in London. Foreign exchange traders would find it profitable to purchase pounds in New York at $2 per pound and immediately resell them in London for $2.01. A profit of 1 cent would be made on each pound sold, less the cost of the bank transfer and the interest charge on the money tied up during the arbitrage process. This return may appear to be insignificant, but on a $1 million arbitrage transaction it would generate a profit of approximately $5,000—not bad for a few minutes' work! As the demand for pounds increases in New York, the dollar price per pound will rise above $2; as the supply of pounds increases in London, the dollar price per pound will fall below $2.01. This arbitrage process will continue until the exchange rate between the dollar and the pound in New York is approximately the same as it is in London. Arbitrage between the two currencies thus unifies the foreign exchange markets.

The preceding example illustrates **two-point arbitrage** in which two currencies are traded between two financial centers. A more intricate form of arbitrage involving three currencies and three financial centers is known as **three-point arbitrage**, or triangular arbitrage. Three-point arbitrage involves switching funds among three currencies in order to profit from exchange rate inconsistencies, as seen in the following example.

Consider three currencies—the U.S. dollar, the Swiss franc, and the British pound, all of which are traded in New York, Geneva, and London. Assume the rates of exchange that prevail in all three financial centers are as follows: £1 = $1.50; £1 = 4 francs; and 1 franc = $0.50. Because the same exchange rates (prices) prevail in all three financial centers, two-point arbitrage is not profitable. However, these quoted exchange rates are mutually inconsistent. Thus, an arbitrager with $1.5 million could make a profit as follows:

1. Sell $1.5 million for £1 million.
2. Simultaneously, sell £1 million for 4 million francs.
3. At the same time, sell 4 million francs for $2 million.

The arbitrager has just made a risk free profit of $500,000 ($2 million − $1.5 million) before transaction costs!

These transactions tend to cause shifts in all three exchange rates that bring them into proper alignment and eliminate the profitability of arbitrage. From a practical standpoint, opportunities for such profitable currency arbitrage have decreased in recent years, given the large number of currency traders—aided by sophisticated computer information systems—that monitor currency quotes in all financial markets. The result of this activity is that currency exchange rates tend to be consistent throughout the world, with only minimal deviations due to transaction costs.

THE FORWARD MARKET

Foreign exchange markets, as we have seen, may be spot or forward. In the *spot market*, currencies are bought and sold for immediate delivery (generally, two business days after the conclusion of the deal). In the *forward market*, currencies are bought and sold now for future delivery, typically one month, three months, or six months from the date of the transaction. The exchange rate is agreed on at the time of the contract but payment is not made until the future delivery actually takes place. Currency dealers may require some customers to provide collateral in advance to ensure that they fulfill their obligation with the dealer. Only the most widely traded currencies are included in the regular forward market, but individual forward contracts can be negotiated for most national currencies. Forward contracts are generally valued at $1 million and more and used by only large businesses. Forward contracts are not generally used by small businesses and consumers.

Banks such as Citibank and Bank of America buy foreign exchange forward agreements from some customers and sell foreign exchange forward agreements to others. Banks provide this service to earn profits. Rather than charging a commission on their currency transactions, banks profit by buying a foreign currency at a lower price (bid price) and selling the foreign currency at a slightly higher price (offer price). For example, Bank of America may set up a contract with Walmart where it will sell the company euros 180 days from now at $1.20 per euro. This represents the bank's offer rate. As the same time, the bank may have set up a contract with Boeing to buy euros 180 days from now at $1.19 per euro. The bid/offer spread is thus $0.01 per euro. The spread is intended to cover the bank's costs involved in accommodating requests to exchange currencies, as well as a profit margin.

The spread between bid and offer rates for a currency is based on the breadth and depth of the market for that currency as well as the currency's volatility. For widely traded currencies, such as the euro and yen, the spread tends to be a smaller amount; less traded currencies, such as the South Korean *won* and the Brazilian *real*, have higher spreads. Moreover, when the exchange values of currencies are fluctuating substantially, spreads tend to widen.

The Forward Rate

The rate of exchange used in the settlement of forward transactions is called the **forward rate**. This rate is quoted in the same way as the spot rate: the price of one currency in terms of another currency. Table 11.8 provides examples of forward rates as of October 29–30, 2013. Under the Wednesday (October 30) quotations, the selling price of one-month forward U.K. pounds is $1.6036 per pound; the selling price of three-month forward pounds is $1.6028 per pound, and for six-month forward pounds it is $1.6017 per pound.

It is customary for a currency's forward rate to be stated in relation to its spot rate. When a foreign currency is worth more (more expensive) in the forward market than in the spot market, it is said to be at a **premium**; conversely, when the currency is worth less (less expensive) in the forward market than in the spot market, it is said to be at a **discount**. The per annum percentage premium (discount) in forward quotations is computed by the following formula:

$$\text{Premium (discount)} = \frac{\text{Forward Rate} - \text{Spot Rate}}{\text{Spot Rate}} \times \frac{12}{\text{No. of Months Forward}}$$

If the result is a negative forward premium, it means the currency is at a forward discount.

According to Table 11.8, on Wednesday the one-month forward British pound was selling at $1.6036, whereas the spot price of the pound was $1.6039. Because the forward price of the pound was less than the spot price, the pound was at a one-month forward discount of $0.0003, or at a 0.2 percent forward discount per annum against the dollar:

$$\text{Premium} = \frac{\$1.6036 - \$1.6039}{\$1.6039} \times \frac{12}{1} = -0.0022$$

Note that if the forward price of the pound is greater than the spot price, the pound is at a forward premium and a positive sign would appear in front of the forward premium per annum against the dollar.

TABLE 11.8

Forward Exchange Rates: Selected Examples

Exchange Rates   **October 29–30, 2013**

The foreign exchange rates below apply to trading among banks in amounts of $1 million and more, as quoted at 4:00 p.m. Eastern Time by Reuters and other sources. Retail transactions provide fewer units of foreign currency per dollar

Country/currency	In USD		Per USD	
	Wed.	Tues.	Wed.	Tues.
Japan yen	.010151	.010184	98.52	98.19
1-month forward	.010152	.010186	98.50	98.18
3-months forward	.010157	.010190	98.46	98.13
6-months forward	.010163	.010197	98.40	98.07
UK pound	1.6039	1.6047	.6235	.6232
1-month forward	1.6036	1.6043	.6236	.6233
3-months forward	1.6028	1.6035	.6239	.6236
6-months forward	1.6017	1.6024	.6243	.6241

Source: Data taken from Table 11.3 of this chapter.

Relation between the Forward Rate and Spot Rate

Referring to Table 11.8, we see that the one-month forward price of the Swiss franc is higher than the spot price; the same applies to the three-month forward price and the six-month forward price. Does this mean that traders in the market expect the spot price for the franc to increase in the future? That is a logical guess, but expectations have little to do with the relation between the forward rate and the spot rate. This relation is purely a mathematically driven calculation.

The forward rate is based on the prevailing spot rate plus (or minus) a premium (or discount) that is determined by the interest rate differential on comparable securities between the two countries involved. If interest rates in the UK are *higher* than those of the United States, the pound shows a forward *discount* that means the forward rate is less than the spot rate. Conversely; when the UK's interest rates are *lower* than those of the United States, the pound shows a forward *premium* that means the forward rate is higher than the spot rate.

To illustrate, suppose that the interest rate on 3-month Treasury bills is 2 percent in the United States and 6 percent in the UK; thus there is a 4 percent interest rate differential in favor of the UK. Also assume that both the spot rate and forward rate between the dollar and the pound are identical at $2 = 1 pound. In this situation, U.S. investors will buy pounds with dollars at the prevailing spot rate and use the pounds to purchase UK Treasury bills. To ensure that they do not lose money when pounds are converted into dollars when the Treasury bills reach maturity, they will obtain a 3-month forward contract that allows pounds to be sold for dollars at a guaranteed forward rate. When the investors buy pounds with dollars in the spot market, and sell pounds for dollars in the forward market, their actions will drive up the price of the pound in the spot market and drive down of the price of the pound in the forward market; thus, the pound moves to a discount in the forward market. The relative gains from interest rate differentials tend to be offset by losses on the foreign exchange conversions, reducing or eliminating the incentive to invest in UK Treasury bills.[5] The flowchart below illustrates this process.

To profit from relatively high interest rates in the UK, U.S. investors will	➔➔	Buy pounds with dollars in the spot market	➔➔	Spot price of the pound rises, say, to $2.01 per pound	➔➔	Pound moves to a discount in the forward market and the relative gains from investing in UK Treasury bills decrease
		Sell pounds for dollars in the forward market		Forward price of pound falls, say, to $1.99 per pound		

This is why currencies of countries whose interest rates are relatively high tend to sell at a forward discount relative to the spot rate, and currencies of countries where interest rates are relatively low will tend to sell at a forward premium relative to the spot rate.

International differences in interest rates do exert a major influence on the relation between the spot and forward rates. But on any particular day, one would hardly expect the spread on short-term interest rates between financial centers to precisely equal the discount or premium on foreign exchange, for several reasons. First, changes in interest rate differentials do not always induce an immediate investor response necessary to eliminate the investment profits. Second, investors sometimes transfer funds on an uncovered basis; such transfers do not have an effect on the forward rate. Third, factors such as governmental exchange controls and speculation may weaken the connection between the interest rate differential and the spot and forward rates.

Managing Your Foreign Exchange Risk: Forward Foreign Exchange Contract

Although spot transactions are popular, they leave the currency buyer exposed to potentially dangerous financial risks. Exchange rate fluctuations can effectively increase or decrease prices and can be a financial planning nightmare for companies and individuals. To illustrate exchange risks in spot transactions, assume a U.S. company orders machine tools from a company in Germany.

- The tools will be ready in six months and will cost 10 million euro.
- At the time of the order, the euro is trading at $1.40 per euro.
- The U.S. company budgets $14 million to be paid (in euro) when it receives the tools (10,000,000 euro @ $1.40 per euro = $14,000,000).

There is no guarantee that the rate will remain the same six months later. Suppose the rate increases to $1.60 per euro. The cost in U.S. dollars would increase by $2 million (10,000,000 euro @ $1.60 per euro = $16,000,000). Conversely, if the rate decreases to $1.20 per euro, the cost in U.S. dollars would decrease by $2 million (10,000,000 euro @ $1.20 per euro = $12,000,000).

How can firms and individuals insulate themselves from volatile currency values? They can enter the forward market and engage in **hedging**, the process of avoiding or covering a foreign exchange risk. Consider the following examples of hedging.

---

[5]According to the theory of interest rate parity, this process will continue until the interest rate differential between the two countries will be exactly offset by a 2 percent forward discount of the pound. When this occurs, the U.S. investors have no incentive to invest in the UK. It is left for more advanced textbooks to explain this point.

Case 1

A U.S. importer hedges against the dollar *depreciation*. Assume Macys owes 1 million francs to a Swiss watch manufacturer in three-month's time. During this period, Macys is in an exposed or *uncovered* position. Macys bears the risk that the dollar price of the franc might rise in three months (the dollar might depreciate against the franc) say, from $0.60 to $0.70 per franc; if so, purchasing 1 million francs would require an extra $100,000.

To cover itself against this risk, Macy's could immediately buy 1 million francs in the spot market, but this would immobilize its funds for three months. Alternatively, Macys could contract to purchase 1 million francs in the forward market, at today's forward rate for delivery in three months. In three months, Macys would purchase francs with dollars at the contracted price and use the francs to pay the Swiss exporter. Macys has thus hedged against the possibility that francs will be more expensive than anticipated in three months. Hedging in the forward market does not require Macys to tie up its own funds when it purchases the forward contract. The contract is an obligation that can affect the company's credit. Macys' bank will want to be sure that it has an adequate balance or credit line so that it will be able to pay the necessary amount in three months. Macys will not be able to benefit if the exchange rate moves in its favor as it has entered into a binding forward contract that it is obliged to fulfill.

Case 2

A U.S. exporter hedges against a dollar *appreciation*. Assume that Microsoft Corporation anticipates receiving 1 million francs in three months from its exports of computer software to a Swiss retailer. During this period, Microsoft is in an *uncovered* position. If the dollar price of the franc falls (the dollar appreciates against the franc) say, from $0.50 to $0.40 per franc, Microsoft's receipts will be worth $100,000 less when the 1 million francs are converted into dollars (1 million francs @ $0.50 per franc equals $500,000; 1 million francs @ $0.40 per franc equals $400,000).

To avoid this foreign exchange risk, Microsoft can contract to sell its expected franc receipts in the forward market at today's forward rate. By locking into a set forward exchange rate, Microsoft is guaranteed that the value of its franc receipts will be maintained in terms of the dollar, even if the value of the franc should happen to fall.

The forward market eliminates the uncertainty of fluctuating spot rates from international transactions. Exporters can hedge against the possibility that the domestic currency will appreciate against the foreign currency, and importers can hedge against the possibility that the domestic currency will depreciate against the foreign currency. Hedging is not limited to exporters and importers. It applies to anyone who is obligated to make a foreign currency payment or who will enjoy foreign currency receipts at a future time. International investors, also make use of the forward market for hedging purposes.

As our examples indicate, importers and exporters participate in the forward market to avoid the risk of fluctuations in foreign exchange rates. Because they make forward transactions mainly through commercial banks, the foreign exchange risk is transferred to those banks. Commercial banks can minimize foreign exchange risk by matching forward purchases from exporters with forward sales to importers. Because the supply of and demand for forward currency transactions by exporters and importers usually do not coincide, the banks may assume some of the risk.

Suppose that on a given day, a commercial bank's forward purchases do not match its forward sales for a given currency. The bank may then seek out other banks in the market that have offsetting positions. Thus, if Bank of America has an excess of 50-million euro in forward purchases over forward sales during the day, it will attempt to find another bank (or banks) that has an excess of forward sales over purchases. These banks can then enter forward contracts among themselves to eliminate any residual exchange risk that might exist.

How Markel, Volkswagen, and Nintendo Manage Foreign Exchange Risk

To corporate giants such as General Electric and Ford Motor Company, currency fluctuations are a fact of life for global production. But for tiny companies such as Markel Corporation, swings in the world currency market have major implications for its bottom line.[6] Markel Corporation is a family owned tubing maker located in Pennsylvania. Its tubing and insulated lead wires are used in the appliance, automotive, and water purification industries. About 40 percent of Markel's products are exported, mostly to Europe.

To shield itself from fluctuations in exchange rates, Markel purchases forward contracts through PNC Financial Services Group in Pittsburgh. Markel promises the bank, say, 50,000 euros in three months and the bank guarantees a certain number of dollars no matter what happens to the exchange rate. When Markel's financial officers think the dollar is about to appreciate against the euro, they might hedge their entire expected euro revenue stream with a forward contract. When CFOs think the dollar is going to depreciate, they will hedge perhaps half and take a chance that they will make more dollars by remaining exposed to currency fluctuations.

However, CFOs don't always guess right. In 2003, for example, Markel had to provide PNC with 50,000 euros from a contract the company purchased three months earlier. The bank paid $1.05 per euro, or $52,500. Had Markel waited, it could have sold at the going rate, $1.08, and made an additional $1,500.

Another example of hedging against foreign exchange rate fluctuations is provided by Volkswagen, a German auto company. In 2005, Volkswagen announced that it was going to increase its hedging of foreign exchange risk. Volkswagen was exposed to foreign exchange risk because most of its operating costs, especially its labor costs, were denominated in euros, while a substantial share of its revenues were denominated in U.S. dollars. Volkswagen paid its workers in euros and received dollars for the cars it sold in the United States.

Between 2002 and 2004, the euro appreciated considerably relative to the dollar. More dollars were required in order to purchase each euro. Since Volkswagen was unable or unwilling to change the price of cars sold in the United States enough to offset this swing in the exchange rate, the company's dollar revenues from sales in the United States lost substantial value in terms of euros. With costs holding steady and revenues falling, Volkswagen's profits on U.S. operations were reduced by an unfavorable change in the exchange rate between the euro and the dollar.

To avoid similar losses in the future, the company chose to combat the appreciating euro by increasing its hedging of foreign exchange risk. Between 2004 and 2005, Volkswagen more than doubled its use of a variety of currency market contracts. In essence, this hedging strategy involved buying forward contracts for euros at a predetermined rate so that if the euro were to appreciate relative to the dollar and cause an unexpected reduction in dollar revenue, the company would receive an offsetting profit from its forward contract. If the euro were to depreciate and cause an unexpected increase in dollar revenue, the company would incur an offsetting loss from its foreign currency position. In this way, Volkswagen was able to shield its revenue flow from foreign exchange volatility for the duration of its futures contracts.[7]

A different foreign currency strategy comes from Nintendo Co., the producer of Super Mario, the DS hand held game system, and the like. In 2010, Nintendo's earnings took a

---

[6]Drawn from "Ship Those Boxes: Check the Euro," *The Wall Street Journal*, February 7, 2003, p. C1.

[7]"Hedging against Foreign-Exchange Rate Fluctuations," *Economic Report of the President*, 2007, p. 154.

nosedive from the appreciating yen. Unlike other Japanese companies, decreased exports were not the main cause of Nintendo's problems. The bigger issue was its $7 billion holdings of cash in foreign currencies, mostly the U.S. dollar; this stash represented about 70 percent of Nintendo's total cash holdings. Although Nintendo used forward contracts to hedge some of the risk of an appreciating yen, it made as many overseas payments as possible with dollars rather than converting them into yen and suffer losses. Because the company had to make some payments in yen, such as taxes, it had to ensure that it would always have sufficient yen to cover those payments. Nintendo occasionally converted some of its foreign cash into yen, whenever exchange rates were favorable. Nintendo justified its foreign currency strategy as a way to take advantage of higher interest rates overseas while saving on the costs required for exchanging foreign currencies.

Does Foreign Currency Hedging Pay Off?

How much a company uses hedging depends on the type of business and how predictable its foreign exchange exposures are. Many businesses that conduct transactions abroad generally try to eliminate half of their currency risk. Companies with narrow profit margins, like commodities and agriculture, may hedge four-fifths of their known foreign exchange requirements. However, when currencies are dramatically fluctuating, a prudent hedging policy can become too expensive for many companies. Even the wisest corporate treasurer tends to avoid purely speculative trades on currencies just to increase profits; that is an easy way to lose money with disastrous bets.

Some companies do not hedge at all either because they cannot determine how much money will be coming in from abroad, or because they have a deliberate strategy of allowing currencies to balance each other out around the world. As a firm that realizes more than half of its sales in profits in foreign currencies, Minnesota Mining & Manufacturing Co. (3M) is sensitive to fluctuations in exchange rates. As the dollar appreciates against other currencies, 3M's profits decline; as the dollar depreciates, its profits increase. When currency markets go wild like they did during 1997–1998 when Asian currencies and the Russian ruble crashed relative to the dollar, deciding whether or not to hedge is a crucial business decision. Yet 3M didn't use hedges such as the forward market or currency options market to guard against currency fluctuations.[8]

In 1998, the producer of Scotch Tape and Post-Its announced that the appreciating dollar had cost the firm $330 million in profits and $1.8 billion in revenue during the previous three years. 3M's no-hedging policy made investors nervous. Was 3M unwise in not hedging its currency risk? Not according to many analysts and other big firms that chose to hedge very little, if at all. Firms ranging from ExxonMobil to Deere to Kodak have maintained that currency fluctuations improve profits as often as they hurt them. Although an appreciation of the dollar would detract from their profits, the dollar depreciation would add to them. As a result, hedging isn't necessary, because the ups and down of currencies even out over the long run.

The standard argument for hedging is increased stability of cash flows and earnings. Surveys of Corporate America's largest companies have found that one-third of them do some kind of foreign currency hedging. Drug giant Merck and Co. hedges some of its foreign cash flows using the currency options market to sell the currencies for dollars at fixed rates. Merck maintains that it can protect against adverse currency moves by exercising its options or enjoy favorable moves by not exercising them. Either way, the firm aims to guarantee that cash flow from foreign sales remains stable so that it can

---

[8]"Perils of the Hedge Highwire," *Business Week*, October 26, 1998, pp. 74–76.

sustain research spending in years when a strong dollar trims foreign earnings. According to Merck's chief financial officer, the firm pays money for insurance to dampen volatility from unknown events.

Yet many well established companies see no need to pay for protection against currency risk. Instead, they often choose to cover the risks out of their own deep pockets. According to 3M officials, if you consider the cost of hedging over the entire cycle, the drain on your earnings is very high for purchasing that insurance. Foreign currency hedging eats into profits. A simple forward contract that locks in an exchange rate costs up to half a percentage point per year of the revenue being hedged. Other techniques such as currency options are more costly. What's more, fluctuations in a firm's business can detract from the effectiveness of foreign currency hedging.

TRADE CONFLICTS CURRENCY RISK AND THE HAZARDS OF INVESTING ABROAD

For an American investor, betting on foreign securities (stocks or bonds) involves additional risks beyond the risks of investing in U.S. securities. These risks include political uncertainty, different financial and accounting standards, different regulatory environments, and different economic factors in countries other than the United States. Currency fluctuations are another risk of investing in foreign securities.

When investors purchase shares in an international securities fund, they gamble on the companies that the fund holds, its performance record, and its management style. They also wager on the local currencies that the foreign securities are denominated in, whether the fund uses currency hedges, and if they want a hedged fund. Some investors do not want to bear the risk of exchange rate fluctuations in addition to equity risk, and they wish to hedge their currency exposure back into dollars. Others see changing exchange rates as a welcome form of diversification. If returns on foreign securities and exchange rate changes both fare well, total returns increase. However, investors can lose money during a period when both perform poorly.

International investors who hedge generally use currency forwards. These are contracts between two parties to buy or sell an amount of currency at a specified future time at a price agreed upon today. The cost of hedging varies over different time periods and with different currencies. That's because it is basically determined by the discrepancy between interest rates in the United States and those in other countries. For large institutional investors, such as an investment company, using forwards is generally economical. Among major currencies such as the dollar and yen, the forward market is highly liquid and spreads tend to be thin. Hedging more exotic currencies, such as the Russian ruble or Indian rupee, costs a little more. The main disadvantage of hedging is the opportunity cost of not profiting from favorable fluctuations in exchange rates. This is why most international securities funds do not hedge their currency exposure, and others hedge only a portion of it. Managers of Oakmark Funds, an international stock fund, hedge only when they have sizable exposure to a currency that they estimate to be at least 20 percent overvalued relative to the dollar.

To provide diversification for its investors, Tweedy, Browne Co., a New York based investment company, provides two international funds. Introduced in 1993, Tweedy's Global Value Fund uses currency hedges to protect its investors from currency risk. After learning that some of its investors liked the fund's approach to stock selection, but not its hedging policy, Tweedy introduced its Global Value Fund II in 2009. This fund has the same portfolio of stocks as the Global Value Fund, but does not hedge. This allows investors the opportunity to profit from favorable fluctuations in exchange rates in addition to favorable movements in stock prices. Investors bear the risk of losing money if adverse fluctuations in exchange rates or stock prices occur.

Source: Annelena Lobb, "Making Sense of Currency Effects," *The Wall Street Journal*, October 4, 2010, p. R10 and *Global Value Fund* and *Global Value Fund II*, available at www.tweedy.com.

iStockphoto.com/photosoup

INTEREST ARBITRAGE, CURRENCY RISK, AND HEDGING

Investors make their financial decisions by comparing the rates of return of foreign investment with those of domestic investment. If rates of return from foreign investment are larger, they will desire to shift their funds abroad. **Interest arbitrage** refers to the process of moving funds into foreign currencies to take advantage of higher investment returns abroad. However, investors face the possibilities of unpredictable losses or gains when the returns from a foreign investment are converted from the foreign currency into the domestic currency. This form of risk is called **currency risk**.

An American who purchases stock in BASF, a German chemical company, will have to buy and sell the stock using the euro. If the euro value of the stock increases by 4 percent, but the euro depreciates against the dollar by 7 percent, the investor will realize a net loss in terms of total returns when selling the stock and converting back to U.S. dollars. The investor can reduce currency risk by using hedges and other techniques designed to offset any currency related losses. In practice, creating a hedge against a currency can be quite expensive and complicated and not all investors will choose to adopt this technique, as discussed below.

Uncovered Interest Arbitrage

Uncovered interest arbitrage occurs when an investor does not obtain exchange market cover (hedge) to protect investment proceeds from foreign currency fluctuations. This practice would likely occur if the cost of a hedge against a currency was very expensive. Also, during stable economic times, currencies tend to trade with relatively low volatility, making hedges somewhat unnecessary.

Suppose the interest rate on three-month Treasury bills is six percent (per annum) in New York and ten percent (per annum) in London, and the current spot rate is $2 per pound. A U.S. investor would seek to profit from this opportunity by exchanging dollars for pounds at the rate of $2 per pound and using these pounds to purchase three-month British Treasury bills in London. The investor would earn four percent more per year, or one percent more for the three months, than if the same dollars had been used to buy three-month Treasury bills in New York. These results are summarized in Table 11.9.

It is *not* necessarily true that our U.S. investor realizes an extra one percent rate of return (per three months) by moving funds to London. This amount will be realized only if the exchange value of the pound remains constant over the investment period. If the pound *depreciates* against the dollar, the investor makes *less*; if the pound *appreciates* against the dollar, the investor makes *more*.

Suppose our investor earns an extra one percent by purchasing three-month British Treasury bills rather than U.S. Treasury bills. Over the same period, suppose the dollar price of the pound falls from $2.00 to $1.99 (the pound *depreciates* against the dollar). When the proceeds are converted back into dollars, the investor *loses*

TABLE 11.9

Uncovered Interest Arbitrage: An Example

	Rate per Year	Rate per 3 Months
U.K. 3-month Treasury bill interest rate	10%	2.5%
U.S. 3-month Treasury bill interest rate	6%	1.5%
Uncovered interest differential favoring the U.K.	4%	1.0%

0.5 percent—($2 − $1.99)/$2 = 0.005. The investor earns only 0.5 percent more (1 percent − 0.5 percent) than if the funds had been placed in U.S. Treasury bills. The reader can verify that if the dollar price of the pound fell from $2 to $1.98 over the investment period, the U.S. investor would earn nothing extra by investing in British Treasury bills.

Alternatively, suppose that over the three-month period the pound rises from $2 to $2.02, a one percent *appreciation* against the dollar. This time, in addition to the extra one percent return on British Treasury bills, our investor realizes a return of one percent from the appreciation of the pound. The reason? When the investor bought pounds to finance his or her purchase of British Treasury bills, the investor paid $2 per pound; when the investor converted his or her investment proceeds back into dollars, the investor received $2.02 per pound—($2.02 − $2)/$2 = 0.01. Because the pound's appreciation adds to his or her investment's profitability, the investor earns 2 percent more than if the investor had purchased U.S. Treasury bills.

In summary, a U.S. investor's extra rate of return on an investment in the United Kingdom as compared to the United States, equals the interest rate differential adjusted for any change in the value of the pound, as follows:

$$\text{Extra Return} = (\text{U.K. Interest Rate} - \text{U.S. Interest Rate}) \\ - \text{Percent Depreciation of the Pound}$$

or

$$\text{Extra Return} = (\text{U.K. Interest Rate} - \text{U.S. Interest Rate}) \\ + \text{Percent Appreciation of the Pound}$$

Covered Interest Arbitrage (Reducing Currency Risk)

Investing funds in a foreign country involves an exchange rate risk. If economic times are quite unstable, currencies tend to trade with relatively high volatility. Hedging against exchange rate fluctuations may be viewed as beneficial, a practice known as covered interest arbitrate.

Covered interest arbitrage involves two basic steps. First, an investor exchanges domestic currency for foreign currency at the current spot rate, and uses the foreign currency to finance a foreign investment. At the same time, the investor contracts in the forward market to sell the amount of the foreign currency that will be received as the proceeds from the investment, with a delivery date to coincide with the maturity of the investment. It pays for the investor to make the foreign investment if the positive interest rate differential in favor of the foreign investment more than offsets the cost of obtaining the forward cover.

Suppose the interest rate on three-month Treasury bills is 12 percent (per annum) in London and 8 percent (per annum) in New York; the interest differential in favor of London is 4 percent per annum, or 1 percent for the three months. Suppose also that the current spot rate for the pound is $2, while the three-month forward pound sells for $1.99. This means that the three-month forward pound is at a 0.5 percent *discount*—($1.99 − $2)/$2 = −0.005.

By purchasing three-month Treasury bills in London, a U.S. investor could earn one percent more for the three months than if he bought three-month Treasury bills in New York. To eliminate the uncertainty over how many dollars will be received when the pounds are reconverted into dollars the investor sells enough pounds on the three-month forward market to coincide with the anticipated proceeds of the investment. The cost of the forward cover equals the difference between the

TABLE 11.10

Covered Interest Arbitrage: An Example

	Rate per Year	Rate per 3 Months
U.K. 3-month Treasury bill interest rate	12%	3%
U.S. 3-month Treasury bill interest rate	8%	2%
Uncovered interest-rate differential favoring the U.K.	4%	1%
Forward discount on the 3-month pound		−0.5%
Covered interest-rate differential favoring the U.K.		0.5%

© Cengage Learning*

spot rate and the contracted three-month forward rate; this difference is the discount on the forward pound, or 0.5 percent. Subtracting this 0.5 percent from the interest rate differential of one percent, the investor is able to realize a net rate of return that is 0.5 percent higher than if he or she had bought U.S. Treasury bills. These results are summarized in Table 11.10.

This investment opportunity will not last long because the profitability will soon disappear when other U.S. investors make the same investment. As many investors purchase spot pounds, the spot rate will rise. Concurrently, the sale of forward pounds will push the forward rate downward. The result is a *widening* of the discount on the forward pounds that means the cost of covering the exchange rate risk increases. This process tends to continue until the forward discount on the pound widens to 1 percent, at which point the extra profitability of the foreign investment vanishes. The spot rate of the pound might increase from \$2 to \$2.005 per pound and the price of the three-month forward pound might decrease from \$1.99 to \$1.985 per pound; the forward discount on the pound is 1 percent—$(\$1.985 − \$2.005)/\$2 = −0.01$. This offsets the extra one percent return that can be made by investing in British Treasury bills than U.S. Treasury bills.

FOREIGN EXCHANGE MARKET SPECULATION

Besides being used for the financing of commercial transactions and investments, the foreign exchange market is also used for exchange rate speculation. **Speculation** is the attempt to profit by trading on expectations about prices in the future. Some speculators are traders acting for financial institutions or firms; others are individuals. In either case, speculators buy currencies that they expect to go up in value and sell currencies that they expect to go down in value. In the foreign exchange market, speculators dominate: close to 90 percent of daily trading volume is speculative in nature.

Note the difference between arbitrage and speculation. With arbitrage, a currency trader *simultaneously* buys a currency at a low price and sells that currency at a high price, making a riskless profit. A speculator's goal is to buy a currency at one moment (such as today) and sell that currency at a higher price in the future (such as tomorrow). Speculation implies the deliberate assumption of exchange risk: if the price of the currency falls between today and tomorrow, the speculator loses money. An exchange market speculator deliberately assumes foreign exchange risk on the expectation of profiting from future changes in the spot exchange rate. Speculators assume risk by taking positions in the spot market, forward market, futures market, or options market.

Long and Short Positions

We generally associate making profits in the foreign exchange market by initially buying a currency at a low price then selling it at a higher price later on; "buy low and sell high."

This is what you are doing when you are in a **long position**: realize gains from an expected *appreciation* of a currency.

You can also make a profit by being in a **short position** in which you initially sell currency (that you do not own) at a high price then buy it back later on at a low price; "sell high and buy low." You attempt to realize profits from an expected *depreciation* of a currency.

Suppose you want to trade with the U.S. dollar and the euro. Assume that the current exchange rate is 1 euro = $1.25 ($1 = 0.80 euros). Also, assume that you borrow 1million euros from your currency broker and sell this sum to obtain $1,250,000 (1,000,000 × $1.25 = $1,250,000). Suppose the next day the euro's exchange value depreciates to 1 euro = $1.20 ($1 = 0.83 euros). You sell your $1,250,000 and get 1,037,500 euros ($1,250,000 × 0.83 = 1,037,500). You repay your loan for 1 million euros and keep 37,500 euros as profit (minus fees). In the manner, you profit from a depreciation of the euro. The flowchart below illustrates this process.

Borrow 1 million euros from a broker. Use that sum to buy $1.25 million at today's exchange rate of $1.25 = 1 euro.	→	Assume that the euro depreciates tomorrow to $1.20 = 1 euro. Sell $1.25 million 1,037,500 euros.	→	Repay the 1 million euro loan from the broker and keep 37,500 euros as profit.

Let us now consider two examples of foreign exchange speculation.

Andy Krieger Shorts The New Zealand Dollar

One of the greatest currency trades ever made was made in 1987 by 32-year-old Andy Krieger, a currency trader at Bankers Trust Company in New York. Krieger was one of the most aggressive dealers in the world with full approval of his bank. While most of the bank's currency traders had an upper dealing limit of $50 million, Krieger's limit was about $700 million, a quarter of the bank's capital at the time. By using foreign currency options, Krieger could greatly leverage his exposure: $100,000 of currency options would buy control of $30 to $40 million in actual currency. In 1987 Krieger did this to launch a speculative attack on the New Zealand dollar.

Krieger was watching the currencies that were appreciating against the dollar following the October 19, 1987 crash in the stock markets around the world. As investors and companies rushed out of the U.S. dollar and into currencies that suffered less damage in the market crash, there were bound to be some currencies that would become overvalued, resulting in a good opportunity for speculative profit. Believing that the New Zealand dollar was overvalued, Krieger bet on its fall, selling hundreds of millions of New Zealand dollars at a time and pushing its value down five percent in a day. Krieger's profited by re-buying New Zealand dollars when its price bottomed out at 59 cents. Krieger profited from a decline in the value of the New Zealand dollar between the sale and the repurchase because he paid less to buy the dollars than he received on selling them. Krieger resigned from Bankers Trust the following year, apparently unhappy about his employers who had paid him a mere $3 million for his efforts that had netted the bank a profit of more than $300 million from the raid on the New Zealand dollar.

George Soros Shorts the Yen

George Soros is a famous currency speculator who has made billions of dollars betting against currencies that he thinks will be worth less in the future (depreciate) compared to another currency. Although not all of Soros' currency bets have been successful, one profitable bet occurred during 2012–2013, as explained below.

In December 2012 Shinzo Abe was elected to become the prime minister of Japan. Abe immediately announced his desire to adopt an expansionary monetary policy amid a sluggish economy; Increase the money supply that results in decreasing interest rates and an increase in domestic spending. A side effect of falling interest rates is a depreciation of the yen as investors are not as inclined to place funds in yen-denominated assets.

With expectations of a future depreciation of the yen, Soros felt that the time was right to make big bets against it. He adopted short positions on the yen to take advantage of its anticipated lower future price. Analysts estimated that Soros made close to $1 billion profit during November 2012–February 2013 from his bet against the yen.

Betting against the yen is not for the timid. Prior to 2012–2013, Japan had failed for years to lower its currency and stimulate its economy. Many speculators who adopted short positions on the yen lost huge sums when the currency strengthened.

People's Bank of China Widens Trading Band to Punish Currency Speculators

In 2014, the People's Bank of China (the central bank) became increasingly concerned about speculators betting on expected gains in the yuan's exchange value. By purchasing yuan at a relatively low price and selling yuan at a later date as the currency appreciated, speculators could pull profits out of the market. Why did this present a problem for China? As speculators bought yuan, money flowed into China that inflated prices for assets such as property, because the real estate sector was a favorite destination of speculative capital inflows. Heavy inflows of money from abroad added to the risks of China's banking system and made the economy more vulnerable to financial shocks.

To reduce the amount of money flowing into China, the People's Bank of China sought to remove the notion that speculators had a "one-way bet" on the yuan; that is, the yuan would necessarily appreciate against the U.S. dollar. This was accomplished in two ways. First, the central bank instructed large state owned Chinese banks to aggressively purchase dollars with yuan, driving the yuan's value downward against the dollar. Next, the central bank widened the currency's trading band against the dollar. Thus, the yuan could fluctuate as much as 2 percent on either side of its daily peg against the dollar that is set by the central bank. Previously, the central bank allowed currency traders to push the yuan's daily value 1 percent in either direction of parity. Widening the trading band expanded two-way volatility in the yuan's exchange value and provided greater risk for those considering speculating on the future value of the yuan. Easy currency bets were becoming harder as the yuan's trading band doubled. These actions helped reduce the money inflows into China.

Observers saw China's move to double the yuan's trading bandwidth as an important step in establishing a market based exchange rate system in which the yuan would move up and down just like any other currency.

Stabilizing and Destabilizing Speculation

Currency speculation can exert either a stabilizing or a destabilizing influence on the foreign exchange market. **Stabilizing speculation** goes against market forces by *moderating* or *reversing* a rise or fall in a currency's exchange rate. It would occur when a speculator buys foreign currency with domestic currency when the domestic price of the foreign currency falls, or depreciates. The hope is that the domestic price of the foreign currency will soon increase, leading to a profit. Such purchases increase the demand for the foreign currency that moderates its depreciation. Stabilizing speculation performs a useful function for bankers and businesspeople who desire stable exchange rates.

Destabilizing speculation goes with market forces by *reinforcing* fluctuations in a currency's exchange rate. It can occur when a speculator sells a foreign currency when it depreciates on the expectation that it will depreciate further in the future. Such sales depress the foreign currency's value. Destabilizing speculation can disrupt international transactions in several ways. Because of the uncertainty of financing exports and imports, the cost of hedging may become so high that international trade is impeded. What is more, unstable exchange rates may disrupt international investment activity. This is because the cost of obtaining forward cover for international capital transactions may rise significantly as foreign exchange risk intensifies.

To lessen the amount of destabilizing speculation, some government officials propose government regulation of foreign currency markets. If foreign currency markets are to be regulated by government, will such intervention be superior to the outcome that occurs in an unregulated market? Will government be able to identify better than markets what the "correct" exchange rate is? Many analysts contend that government would make even bigger mistakes. Markets are better than government in admitting their mistakes and reversing out of them. That is because, unlike governments, markets have no pride. Destabilizing speculation will be further discussed in Chapter 15. More can be learned about the techniques of foreign exchange market speculation in *Exploring Further 11.1* that can be found at www.cengage.com/economics/Carbaugh.

FOREIGN EXCHANGE TRADING AS A CAREER

As you complete this international economics course and approach graduating from your college or university, you might consider becoming a foreign exchange trader. You could gain employment from a bank or company dealing in foreign exchange or you might operate independently as a day trader.

Foreign Exchange Traders Hired by Commercial Banks, Companies, and Central Banks

Foreign exchange traders are hired by commercial banks, such as JP Morgan Chase and Bank of America that make profits by trading and selling exchange from and to each other. Big companies, who have need of foreign currency in the way of doing trade, also hire currency traders. Other employers of currency traders are central banks such as the Federal Reserve, who participate in the foreign exchange market to influence the value of their currencies.

A foreign exchange trader studies the various factors that affect local economies and rates of exchange then takes advantage of any misvaluations of currencies by buying and selling in different foreign exchange markets. Only those who are comfortable with a high degree of risk and uncertainty should look into this profession as a career. One decision can make you win or lose. Confidence along with guts are the core qualities required for foreign exchange trading.

A foreign exchange trader has to handle accounts, study various reports generated on each working day, and have an update of the leading economies around the world. Most of a foreign exchange trader's time is spent talking over the phone or working on a computer. The mode of communication in foreign exchange trading has to be extremely swift. Sharp reasoning skills are required to make fast decisions. Economics and mathematics majors have a distinct advantage in applying for positions as a foreign exchange trader. Accounting background is also helpful in keeping track of positions and profit and losses throughout frantic days. A bachelor's degree is required. Few people leave to get an advanced degree in this field.

Early in a foreign exchange trader's career, the trader typically specializes by following one currency and the underlying economy of that currency. As traders gain experience and become confident in handling more than one currency, they can specialize in groups of geographically related countries, such as those who transact in Pacific Rim currencies.

Foreign exchange traders enjoy the adrenaline rush of participating in a hectic market. A trader must be on his toes every minute of the working day because any event around the world can influence the value of a currency and create an opportunity for profit. Most foreign exchange traders report that they were exhausted at day's end. A primer on foreign exchange trading is contained in *Exploring Further 11.2* that can be found at www.cengage.com/economics/Carbaugh.

TRADE CONFLICTS HOW TO PLAY THE FALLING (RISING) DOLLAR

When the dollar is expected to depreciate, U.S. investors may look to foreign markets for big returns. Why? A declining dollar makes foreign denominated financial instruments worth more in dollar terms. Those in the business emphasize that trading currency is "speculation," not investing. If the dollar rebounds, any foreign denominated investment would provide lower returns. Big losses can easily occur if your bet is wrong.

The most direct way to play an anticipated drop in the dollar would be to stroll down to Bank of America and purchase $10,000 of euros, put the bills in your safe deposit box, and convert the currency to dollars in, say, six months. However, it's not an especially efficient way to do the job because of transaction costs.

Another way is to purchase bonds denominated in a foreign currency. A U.S. investor who anticipates that the yen's exchange value will significantly appreciate in the near future might purchase bonds issued by the Japanese government or corporations and expressed in yen. These bonds can be purchased from brokerage firms such as Charles Schwab and J.P. Morgan Chase & Co. The bonds are paid for in yen that are purchased by converting dollars into yen at the prevailing spot rate. If the yen goes up, the speculator gets not only the accrued interest from the bond but also its appreciated value in dollars. The catch is, in all likelihood, others have the same expectations. The overall demand for the bonds may be sufficient to force up the bond price, resulting in a lower interest rate. For the investor to win, the yen's appreciation must exceed the loss of interest income. In many cases, the exchange rate changes are not large enough to make such investments worthwhile. Besides investing in a particular foreign bond, one can invest in a foreign bond mutual fund, provided by brokerage firms

like Merrill Lynch. Although you can own a foreign bond fund with as little as $2,500, you generally must pony up $100,000 or more to own bonds directly.

Rather than investing in foreign bonds, some investors choose to purchase stocks of foreign corporations, denominated in foreign currencies. The investor in this case is trying to predict the trend of not only the foreign currency but also its stock market. The investor must be highly knowledgeable about both financial and economic affairs in the foreign country. Instead of purchasing individual stocks, an investor could put money in a foreign stock mutual fund.

For investors who expect that the spot rate of a foreign currency will soon rise, the answer lies in a savings account denominated in a foreign currency. A U.S. investor may contact a major Citibank or a U.S. branch of a foreign bank and take out an interest bearing certificate of deposit expressed in a foreign currency. An advantage of such a savings account is that the investor is guaranteed a fixed interest rate. An investor who has guessed correctly also enjoys the gains stemming from the foreign currency's appreciation. The investor must be aware of the possibility that governments might tax or shut off such deposits or interfere with the investor's freedom to hold another nation's currency.

Finally, you can play the falling dollar by putting your money into a variety of currency derivatives, all of which are risky. You can trade futures contracts at the Chicago Mercantile Exchange or trade currency directly by opening an account at a firm that specializes in that businesses, such as Saxo Bank (Danish) or CMC (British). The minimum lot is often $10,000, and you can leverage up to 95 percent. Thus, for a $100,000 trade, the typical size, you'd have to put only $5,000 down. For an appreciating dollar, the techniques of currency speculation would be the opposite.

Currency Markets Draw Day Traders

For decades, foreign currency trading was practiced only by the biggest banks and firms like Deutsche Bank and General Electric. Then individual investors in Europe and Asia began trading currencies to pull speculative profits out of the market. By the first decade of the 2000s, many Americans were choosing to participate in this game of electronic poker. These traders range from rock stars and professional athletes to police officers, lawyers, doctors, and teachers.

Consider the case of Marc Coppola, the brother of actor Nicolas Cage and nephew of movie director Francis Ford Coppola. In 2005 he was reported to have won $1,400 on a $60,000 bet that the euro would appreciate against the dollar. Then he changed direction and gambled $40,000 that the euro would depreciate. When it dropped from $1.31 to $1.30, he cashed in half of his bet then soon cashed in the remainder. Coppola noted that he was too cautious: He feared that the euro's exchange value would suddenly reverse its direction, and exited the trade too soon. Coppola wished he had ridden the euro down to an exchange value of about $1.20, realizing additional speculative profits.

The foreign exchange market has become a speculative arena for individual traders. They establish online trading accounts that, like the foreign exchange market itself, operate 24 hours a day. Gain Capital Group, FX Solutions, Interbank FX, and Forex Capital Markets (FXCM) are some of the more popular firms that provide such accounts. To open an account, speculators need as little as $250 and they can borrow up to 400 times the value of the account, although 15 to 20 times leverage is more common.

Here's how it works. A ratio of 400-to-1 means a speculator can put up, say, $5,000 (referred to as the margin) to place a $2 million bet that the dollar will depreciate against the euro. The difference between the margin and the value of the bet is the leverage. The bet would win 200 for every 0.01 percentage point that the dollar depreciates against the euro. If the dollar fell by 1 percent against the euro, the $2 million bet wins $20,000. However, losses can be large if the bet goes wrong.

Compared to other investment opportunities, foreign exchange trading offers several advantages. The around-the-clock market allows speculators to place bets whenever they want, not just between 9:30 A.M. and 4:00 P.M. Eastern time as with the U.S. stock market. Because transaction costs are smaller, currencies are also less expensive to trade than stocks. Trading is easier because only six pairs of currency (the dollar versus euro) account for about 90 percent of trading volume compared with thousands of stocks. Unlike stocks, there cannot be a bear market in foreign exchange: because currencies are valued relative to one another; when some currencies depreciate others appreciate. Also, foreign exchange trading may be less risky than investing in stocks because currencies often move in multiyear cycles, making it simpler to identify a trend.

However, professional traders caution against amateurs speculating in foreign currencies. They estimate that only 15 percent of day traders realize profits. Although the financial leverage that can be obtained by using an online account can help generate large profits if a speculator guesses correctly, it can result in huge losses if they guess wrong. Currency speculation is a risky business. It is recommended that you do not bet next semester's tuition on a possible depreciation or appreciation of the dollar.[9]

---

[9]"Currency Markets Draw Speculation, Fraud," *The Wall Street Journal*, July 26, 2005, p. C1 and "Young Traders Run Currency Markets," *The Wall Street Journal*, November 5, 1987, p. A26.

SUMMARY

1. The foreign exchange market provides the institutional framework within which individuals, businesses, and financial institutions purchase and sell foreign exchange. Three of the world's largest foreign exchange markets are located in New York, Tokyo, and London.

2. The exchange rate is the price of one unit of foreign currency in terms of the domestic currency. From a U.S. viewpoint, the exchange rate might refer to the number of dollars necessary to buy a Swiss franc. The dollar depreciation (appreciation) is an increase (decrease) in the number of dollars required to buy a unit of foreign exchange.

3. In the foreign exchange market, currencies are traded around the clock and throughout the world. Most foreign exchange trading is in the interbank market. Banks typically engage in three types of foreign exchange transactions: spot, forward, and swap.

4. The equilibrium rate of exchange in a free market is determined by the intersection of the supply and demand schedules of foreign exchange. These schedules are derived from the credit and debit items in a nation's balance of payments.

5. Exchange arbitrage permits the rates of exchange in different parts of the world to be kept the same. This is achieved by selling a currency when its price is high and purchasing when the price is low.

6. Foreign traders and investors often deal in the forward market for protection from possible exchange rate fluctuations. However, speculators also buy and sell currencies in the futures markets in anticipation of sizable profits. In general, interest arbitrage determines the relation between the spot rate and the forward rate.

7. Speculation in the foreign exchange markets may be either stabilizing or destabilizing in nature.

KEY CONCEPTS AND TERMS

Appreciation (p. 365)
Bid rate (p. 362)
Call option (p. 368)
Covered interest
  arbitrage (p. 383)
Cross exchange rate (p. 365)
Currency risk (p. 382)
Currency swap (p. 360)
Depreciation (p. 365)
Destabilizing speculation (p. 387)
Discount (p. 375)
Effective exchange rate (p. 371)
Exchange arbitrage (p. 374)
Exchange rate (p. 363)
Exchange rate index (p. 371)
Foreign currency options (p. 368)

Foreign exchange market (p. 357)
Forward market (p. 366)
Forward rate (p. 375)
Forward transaction (p. 360)
Futures market (p. 366)
Hedging (p. 377)
Interest arbitrage (p. 382)
International Monetary Market
  (IMM) (p. 366)
Maturity months (p. 367)
Nominal exchange-rate
  index (p. 372)
Nominal exchange rate (p. 372)
Offer rate (p. 362)
Option (p. 368)
Premium (p. 375)

Put option (p. 368)
Real exchange rate (p. 373)
Real exchange rate
  index (p. 373)
Speculation (p. 384)
Spot market (p. 366)
Spot transaction (p. 359)
Spread (p. 362)
Stabilizing speculation (p. 386)
Strike price (p. 368)
Three-point arbitrage (p. 374)
Trade-weighted dollar (p. 371)
Two-point arbitrage (p. 374)
Uncovered interest
  arbitrage (p. 382)

STUDY QUESTIONS

1. What is meant by the foreign exchange market? Where is it located?

2. What is meant by the forward market? How does it differ from the spot market?

3. The supply and demand for foreign exchange are considered to be derived schedules. Explain.

4. Explain why exchange rate quotations stated in different financial centers tend to be consistent with one another.

5. Who are the participants in the forward exchange market? What advantages does this market afford these participants?

6. What explains the relationship between the spot rate and the forward rate?

7. What is the strategy of speculating in the forward market? In what other ways can one speculate on exchange rate changes?

8. Distinguish between stabilizing speculation and destabilizing speculation.

9. If the exchange rate changes from $1.70 = £1 to $1.68 = £1, what does this mean for the dollar? For the pound? What if the exchange rate changes from $1.70 = £1 to $1.72 = £1?

10. Suppose $1.69 = £1 in New York and $1.71 = £1 in London. How can foreign exchange arbitragers profit from these exchange rates? Explain how foreign exchange arbitrage results in the same dollar/pound exchange rate in New York and London.

11. Table 11.11 shows supply and demand schedules for the British pound. Assume that exchange rates are flexible.

TABLE 11.11

Supply and Demand of British Pounds

Quantity of Pounds Supplied	Dollars per Pound	Quantity of Pounds Demanded
50	$2.50	10
40	2.00	20
30	1.50	30
20	1.00	40
10	0.50	50

© Cengage Learning®

a. The equilibrium exchange rate equals _____. At this exchange rate, how many pounds will be purchased, and at what cost in terms of dollars?

b. Suppose the exchange rate is $2 per pound. At this exchange rate, there is an excess (supply/demand) of pounds. This imbalance causes (an increase/a decrease) in the dollar price of the pound, which leads to (a/an) _____ in the quantity of pounds supplied and (a/an) _____ in the quantity of pounds demanded.

c. Suppose the exchange rate is $1 per pound. At this exchange rate, there is an excess (supply/demand) for pounds. This imbalance causes (an increase/a decrease) in the price of the pound that leads to (a/an) _____ in the quantity of pounds supplied and (a/an) _____ in the quantity of pounds demanded.

12. Suppose the spot rate of the pound today is $1.70 and the three-month forward rate is $1.75.

a. How can a U.S. importer who has to pay 20,000 pounds in three months hedge the foreign exchange risk?

b. What occurs if the U.S. importer does not hedge and the spot rate of the pound in three months is $1.80?

13. Suppose the interest rate (on an annual basis) on three-month Treasury bills is 10 percent in London and 6 percent in New York, and the spot rate of the pound is $2.

a. How can a U.S. investor profit from uncovered interest arbitrage?

b. If the price of the three-month forward pound is $1.99, will a U.S. investor benefit from covered interest arbitrage? If so, by how much?

14. Table 11.12 gives hypothetical dollar/franc exchange values for Wednesday, May 5, 2008.

TABLE 11.12

Dollar/Franc Exchange Values

	IN U.S. $		CURRENCY PER U.S. $	
	Wed.	Tues.	Wed.	Tues.
Switzerland (franc)	.5851	.5846		
30-Day Forward	.5853	.5848		
90-Day Forward	.5854	.5849		
180-Day Forward	.5851	.5847		

© Cengage Learning®

a. Fill in the last two columns of the table with the reciprocal price of the dollar in terms of the franc.

b. On Wednesday, the spot price of the two currencies was _____ dollars per franc, or _____ francs per dollar.

c. From Tuesday to Wednesday, in the spot market the dollar (appreciated/depreciated) against the franc; the franc (appreciated/depreciated) against the dollar.

d. In Wednesday's spot market, the cost of buying 100 francs was _____ dollars; the cost of buying 100 dollars was _____ francs.

e. On Wednesday, the 30-day forward franc was at a (premium/discount) of _____ dollars, which equaled _____ percent on an annual basis. What about the 90-day forward franc?

15. Assume a speculator anticipates that the spot rate of the franc in three months will be lower than today's three-month forward rate of the franc, $0.50 = 1$ franc.

a. How can this speculator use $1 million to speculate in the forward market?

b. What occurs if the franc's spot rate in three months is $0.40? $0.60? $0.50?

16. You are given the following spot exchange rates: $1 = 3$ francs, $1 = 4$ schillings, and 1 franc = 2 schillings. Ignoring transaction costs, how much profit could a person make via three-point arbitrage?

EXPLORING FURTHER

The techniques of foreign exchange market speculation are contained in *Exploring Further 11.1* that can be found at **www.cengage.com/economics/Carbaugh.**

Exchange Rate Determination

Since the introduction of market determined exchange rates by the major industrial nations in the 1970s, notable shifts in exchange rates have been observed. Although changes in long run exchange rates have tended to undergo relatively gradual shifts, if we examine shorter intervals we see that the exchange rate is volatile. Exchange rates can fluctuate by several percentage points even during a single day. This chapter seeks to explain the forces that underlie fluctuations of exchange rates under a system of market determined (floating) exchange rates.

WHAT DETERMINES EXCHANGE RATES?

We have learned that foreign exchange markets are highly competitive by nature. Large numbers of sellers and buyers meet in these markets that are located in the major cities of the world and connected electronically to form one worldwide market. Participants in the foreign exchange market have excellent up-to-the-minute information about the exchange rates between any two currencies. As a result, currency values are determined by the unregulated forces of supply and demand as long as central banks do not attempt to stabilize them. The supplies and demands for a currency come from private individuals, corporations, banks, and government agencies other than central banks. In a free market, the equilibrium exchange rate occurs at the point the quantity demanded of a foreign currency equals the quantity of that currency supplied.

To say that supply and demand determine exchange rates in a free market is at once to say everything and to say nothing. If we are to understand why some currencies depreciate and others appreciate, we must investigate the factors that cause the supply and demand schedules of currencies to change. These factors include **market fundamentals** (economic variables) such as productivity, inflation rates, real interest rates, consumer preferences, and government trade policy. They also include **market expectations** such as news about future market fundamentals and traders' opinions about future exchange rates.[1]

Because economists believe that the determinants of exchange rate fluctuations are rather different in the short run (a few weeks or even days), medium run (several months), and long run (one, two, or even five years), we will consider these time frames when analyzing exchange rates. In the *short run*, foreign exchange transactions are dominated by transfers of assets (bank accounts, government securities) that respond to differences in real interest rates and to shifting expectations of future exchange rates; such transactions have a major influence on short run exchange rates. Over the *medium run*, exchange rates are governed by cyclical factors such as cyclical fluctuations in economic activity. Over the *long run*, foreign exchange transactions are dominated by flows of goods, services, and investment capital that respond to forces such as inflation rates, investment profitability, consumer tastes, productivity, and government trade policy. Because these factors tend to change slowly, their impact on the exchange rate occurs over the long run.

Note that day-to-day influences on foreign exchange rates can cause the rate to move in the opposite direction from that indicated by longer term fundamentals. Although today's exchange rate may be out of line with long-term fundamentals, this should not be construed as implying that it is necessarily inconsistent with short-term determinants—for example, interest rate differentials that are among the relevant fundamentals at the short end of the time dimension.

Figure 12.1 highlights the framework in which exchange rates are determined.[2] The figure views exchange rates as simultaneously determined by long run structural, medium run cyclical, and short run speculative forces. The figure illustrates the idea that there exists some equilibrium level or path to which a currency will eventually gravitate. This path serves as a long run magnet or anchor; it ensures that exchange rates will not fluctuate aimlessly without limit but rather will tend to gravitate over time toward the long run equilibrium path.

Medium run cyclical forces can induce fluctuations of a currency above and below its long run equilibrium path. Fundamental forces serve to push a currency toward its long run equilibrium path. Note that medium run cyclical fluctuations from a currency's long run equilibrium path can be large at times if economic disturbances induce significant changes in either trade flows or capital movements.

Longer run structural forces and medium run cyclical forces interact to establish a currency's equilibrium path. Exchange rates may sometimes move away from this path if short run forces (changing market expectations) induce fluctuations in exchange rates beyond those based on fundamental factors. Although such overshooting behavior can persist for significant periods, fundamental forces generally push the currency back into its long run equilibrium path.

Unfortunately, predicting exchange rate movements is a difficult job. That is because economic forces affect exchange rates through a variety of channels—some may induce negative impacts on a currency's value, others may exert positive impacts. Some of those channels may be more important in determining short run

---

[1]This approach to exchange rate determination is known as the balance-of-payments approach. It emphasizes the flow of goods, services, and investment funds and their impact on foreign exchange transactions and exchange rates. The approach predicts that exchange rate depreciation (appreciation) tends to occur for a nation that spends more (less) abroad in combined purchases and investments than it acquires from abroad over a sustained period of time.

[2]This figure and its analysis are adapted from Michael Rosenberg, *Currency Forecasting* (Homewood, IL: Richard D. Irwin, 1996), pp. 3–5.

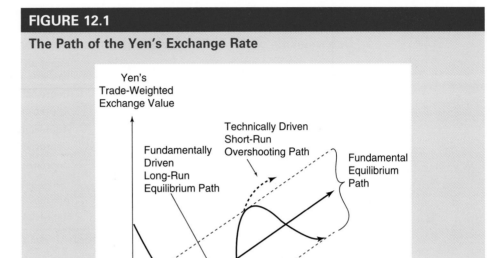

FIGURE 12.1

The Path of the Yen's Exchange Rate

This figure views the exchange value of a nation's currency as being determined by long run structural, medium run cyclical, and short run speculative forces.

© Cengage Learning®

tendencies, whereas other channels may be more important in explaining the long run trend that a currency follows.

To simplify our analysis of exchange rates, we divide it into two parts. First, we consider how exchange rates are determined in the long run. We use our knowledge of the long run determinants of the exchange rate to help us understand how they are determined in the short run.

To gain a better understanding of these determinants, you can refer to the "Forex View" column that appears daily in the *The Wall Street Journal*; it is usually located in the third section, "Money and Investing." The column typically discusses factors causing fluctuations in the dollar's exchange value.

DETERMINING LONG RUN EXCHANGE RATES

Changes in the long run value of the exchange rate are due to reactions of traders in the foreign exchange market to changes in four key factors: relative price levels, relative productivity levels, consumer preferences for domestic or foreign goods, and trade barriers. Note that these factors underlie trade in domestic and foreign goods and thus changes in the demand for exports and imports. Table 12.1 summarizes the effects of these factors.

TABLE 12.1

Determinants of the Dollar's Exchange Rate in the Long Run

Factor*	Change	Effect on the Dollar's Exchange Rate
U.S. price level	Increase	Depreciation
	Decrease	Appreciation
U.S. productivity	Increase	Appreciation
	Decrease	Depreciation
U.S. preferences	Increase	Depreciation
	Decrease	Appreciation
U.S. trade barriers	Increase	Appreciation
	Decrease	Depreciation

*Relative to other countries. The analysis for a change in one determinant assumes that the other determinants are unchanged.

© Cengage Learning®

To illustrate the effects of these factors, refer to Figure 12.2 that shows the demand and supply schedules for pounds. Initially, the equilibrium exchange rate is $1.50 per pound. We will examine each factor by itself, assuming that all other factors remain constant.

Relative Price Levels

Referring to Figure 12.2(*a*), suppose the domestic price level increases rapidly in the United States and remains constant in the United Kingdom. This causes U.S. consumers to desire relatively low priced UK goods. The demand for pounds increases to D_1 in the figure. Conversely, as the UK consumers purchase less relatively high priced U.S. goods, the supply of pounds decreases to S_1. The increase in the demand for pounds and the decrease in the supply of pounds result in a depreciation of the dollar to $1.60 per pound. This analysis suggests that an increase in the U.S. price level relative to price levels in other countries causes the dollar to depreciate in the long run.

Relative Productivity Levels

Productivity growth measures the increase in a country's output for a given level of input. If one country becomes more productive than other countries, it can produce goods more cheaply than its foreign competitors can. If productivity gains are passed forward to domestic and foreign buyers in the form of lower prices, the nation's exports tend to increase and imports tend to decrease.

Referring to Figure 12.2(b), suppose U.S. productivity growth is faster than the United Kingdom's. As U.S. goods become relatively less expensive, the UK demands more U.S. goods that results in an increase in the supply of pounds to S_2. Also, Americans demand fewer UK goods that become relatively more expensive, causing the demand for pounds to decrease to D_2. Therefore, the dollar appreciates to $1.40 per pound. In the long run, as a country becomes more productive relative to other countries, its currency appreciates.

Preferences for Domestic or Foreign Goods

Referring to Figure 12.2(c), suppose that U.S. consumers develop stronger preferences for UK manufactured goods such as automobiles and CD players. The stronger demand for UK goods results in Americans demanding more pounds to purchase these goods. As the

FIGURE 12.2

Market Fundamentals that Affect the Dollar's Exchange Rate in the Long Run

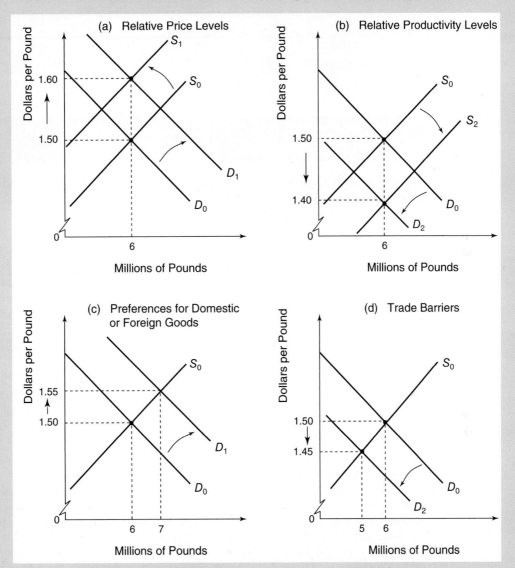

In the long run, the exchange rate between the dollar and the pound reflects relative price levels, relative productivity levels, preferences for domestic or foreign goods, and trade barriers.

demand for pounds rises to D_1, the dollar depreciates to $1.55 per pound. Conversely, if UK consumers demanded additional American computer software, machinery, and apples, the dollar would tend to appreciate against the pound. We conclude that an increased demand for a country's exports causes its currency to appreciate in the long run; conversely, increased demand for imports results in a depreciation in the domestic currency.

Trade Barriers

Barriers to free trade also affect exchange rates. Suppose that the U.S. government imposes tariffs on British steel. By making steel imports more expensive than domestically produced steel, the tariff discourages Americans from purchasing UK steel. In Figure 12.2(d), this tariff causes the demand for pounds to decrease to D_2 that result in an appreciation of the dollar to $1.45 per pound. Trade barriers such as tariffs and quotas cause a currency appreciation in the long run for the country imposing the barriers.

INFLATION RATES, PURCHASING-POWER-PARITY, AND LONG RUN EXCHANGE RATES

The determinants discussed earlier are helpful in understanding the long run behavior of exchange rates. Let us now focus on the Purchasing-Power-Parity approach and see how it builds on the relative price determinant of long run exchange rates.

Law of One Price

The simplest concept of Purchasing-Power-Parity is the **law of one price**. It asserts that identical goods should be sold everywhere at the same price when converted to a common currency, assuming that it is costless to ship the good between nations, there are no barriers to trade, and markets are competitive. It rests on the assumption that sellers will seek out the highest possible prices and buyers the lowest ones. Any differences that arise are quickly eliminated by arbitrage, the simultaneous buying at a low price and selling at a higher one.

The law of one price holds reasonably well for globally tradable commodities such as oil, metals, chemicals, and some agricultural crops. The law does not appear to apply well to non-tradable goods and services such as cab rides, housing, and personal services like haircuts. These products are largely insulated from global competition, and their prices can vary from place to place.

Before the costs of a good in different nations can be compared, its price must first be converted into a common currency. Once converted at the going market exchange rate, the price of an identical good from any two nations should be identical. After converting francs into dollars, machine tools purchased in Switzerland should cost the same as identical machine tools bought in the United States. This means that the purchasing power of the franc and the dollar is at parity and the law of one price prevails.

In theory, the pursuit of profits tends to equalize the price of an identical product in different nations. Assume that machine tools bought in Switzerland are cheaper than the same machine tools bought in the United States, after converting francs into dollars. Swiss exporters could realize a profit by purchasing machine tools in Switzerland at a low price and selling them in the United States at a high price. Such transactions would force prices up in Switzerland and force prices down in the United States until the price of the machine tools would eventually become equal in both nations, whether prices are expressed in francs or dollars. As a result, the law of one price would prevail.

Although the law of one price seems reasonable enough, a look at actual examples show why a single price might not apply in practice. First, it might not make much sense to buy cheap machine tools in Switzerland and ship them to the United States. It might cost too much to achieve the relatively more expensive prices after shipping the cheaper tools to the United States, setting up distribution networks to sell them, and so forth. These transaction costs might mean that price differences between the tools can persist. Similarly, the existence of U.S. tariffs on imported machine tools might drive a wedge between the prices of the tools in the United States and Switzerland.

Burgeromics: The "Big Mac" Index and the Law of One Price

The Big Mac hamburger sandwich sold by McDonalds provides an example of the law of one price.

Big Macs are sold in more than 40 countries and have only negligible differences in the recipe. This hamburger sandwich comes close to being an "identical good" that applies to the law of one price. Other global products could be used as a prop in this exercise, such as Coca-Cola or Starbucks coffee, but over the years the Big Mac Index has been a quick guide to prices in many countries.

Since 1986, the *Economist* magazine each year publishes the Big Mac Index that is nothing more than an attempt to measure the true equilibrium value of a currency based on one product, a Big Mac. According to the law of one price, a Big Mac should cost the same in a given currency wherever it is purchased in the world, suggesting that the prevailing market exchange rate is the true equilibrium rate. Does this always occur?

The Big Mac Index suggests that the market exchange rate between the dollar and the yen is in equilibrium when it equates the prices of Big Macs in the United States and Japan. Big Macs would thus cost the same in each country when the prices are converted to the dollar. If Big Macs do not cost the same, the law of one price breaks down. The yen is said to be overvalued or undervalued compared to the dollar. In this manner, the Big Mac Index can be used to determine the extent to which the market exchange rate differs from the true equilibrium exchange rate.

Table 12.2 shows what a Big Mac cost in different countries as of 2013. It turns out that in all of the countries surveyed, the dollar price of the Big Mac was different from the U.S. level, thus violating the law of one price. In the table, the U.S. equivalent prices denote which currencies are overvalued and which are undervalued relative to the dollar. In the United States, a Big Mac cost $4.20. In Switzerland, the dollar equivalent price of

TABLE 12.2

Big Mac Index

THE PRICE OF A BIG MAC, 2013
BIG MAC PRICES

Country/Currency	In Local Currency	In U.S. Dollars*	Local Currency Overvaluation (+), Undervaluation (−) (percent)
United States (dollar)	$ 4.20	$4.20	—
Venezuela (bolivar)	30.00	6.99	+66.4
Switzerland (franc)	6.50	6.81	+62.1
Sweden (krona)	41.0	5.91	+40.7
Euro Area (euro)	3.49	4.43	+5.5
New Zealand (dollar)	5.10	4.05	−3.6
Mexico (peso)	37.00	2.70	−35.7
Taiwan (dollar)	75.00	2.50	−40.5
India (rupee)	84.00	1.62	−61.4

*At market exchange rate, 2013. The price of each country is based on the average of four cities.

Source: From "Big Mac Currencies," *The Economist*, available at http://www.economist.com.

a Big Mac was $6.81. Compared to the dollar, the Swiss franc was *overvalued* by 62 percent ($6.81/$4.20 = 1.62). However, the Big Mac was a bargain in India where the U.S. dollar equivalent price was $1.62; the Indian rupee was *undervalued* by about 61 percent ($1.62/$4.20 = 0.39).

Our Big Mac index shows that its prices were out of alignment with each other as of 2013. In theory, an arbitrageur could purchase Big Macs for the equivalent of $2.70 in Mexico, whose peso was undervalued against the U.S. dollar, and sell them in Switzerland for $6.81, where the franc was overvalued against the U.S. dollar. This pursuit of profits would push prices up in Mexico and down in Switzerland until the price of Big Macs eventually equalized in the two countries. In practice, such arbitrage trading would not result in price equalization. Big Mac prices show that the law of one price does not hold across countries.

Why do Big Mac prices vary from one nation to another, even when adjusted for exchange rates? One reason is the cost of moving goods across borders. The Big Mac itself is not tradable, but many of its ingredients are. Transportation costs for frozen beef patties, cooking oil, sesame seed buns and other tradable Big Mac ingredients can create price gaps across countries. The costs imposed by tariffs and other trade barriers can contribute to price disparities between countries because they drive a wedge between these prices. Finally, income disparities help explain why the Big Mac sells at different prices in different countries: Prices tend to be higher in rich countries where people have greater ability to pay higher prices.

To be sure, the Big Mac Index is primitive and has many flaws. However, it is widely understood by non-economists and serves as an approximation of which currencies are too weak or strong, and by how much. Although the Big Mac Index was originally developed for fun, it has turned out to be a surprisingly useful predictor for exchange rate movements. It appears that those who were initially dubious of the validity of the Big Mac Index now realize that it might be something useful on which to chew.

Purchasing-Power-Parity

A prominent theory of how exchange rates move is the **purchasing-power-parity theory**. It says that exchange rates adjust to make goods and services cost the same everywhere and thus it is an application of the law of one price.

Our analysis of exchange rates begins by using the law of one price for a single good—steel, as shown in Table 12.3. Assume that the yen price of Japanese steel is 50,000 yen per ton and the dollar price of American steel is $500 per ton. Therefore, the law of one price says that the exchange rate between the yen and the dollar is 100 yen per dollar (50,000 yen/ton/$500/ton = 100 yen/$) to ensure that price is the same in both countries. Suppose that the yen price of Japanese steel increases ten percent, to

TABLE 12.3

The Law of One Price Applied to a Single Product—Steel
According to the law of one price, if the yen price of steel increases by 10 percent and the dollar price of steel remains constant, the yen will depreciate by 10 percent against the dollar to ensure that price is the same in both countries.

Yen Price of a Ton of Steel	Dollar Price of a Ton of Steel	Exchange Rate: Yen per dollar
50,000 yen	$500	100
55,000	500	110

GLOBALIZATION INFLATION DIFFERENTIALS
AND THE EXCHANGE RATE

The Purchasing-Power-Parity theory helps explain the behavior of a currency's exchange value. According to this theory, changes in relative national price levels determine changes in exchange rates over the long run. A currency is expected to depreciate by an amount equal to the excess of domestic inflation over foreign inflation; it appreciates by an amount equal to the excess of foreign inflation over domestic inflation.

Figure 12.3 shows the relation between inflation and the exchange rate for selected countries. The horizontal axis shows the country's average inflation minus the U.S. average inflation during the 1960–1997 period. The vertical axis shows the average percentage change in a country's exchange rate (foreign currency per dollar) over that period. Consistent with the predictions of the Purchasing-Power-Parity theory, the figure shows that countries with relatively low inflation rates tend to have appreciating currencies, and countries with relatively high inflation tend to have depreciating currencies.

Source: From International Monetary Fund, *IMF Financial Statistics*; various issues.

FIGURE 12.3

Inflation Differentials and the Dollar's Exchange Value

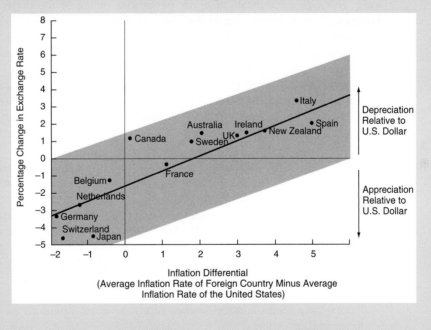

55,000 yen per ton, and the dollar price of American steel remains constant at $500 per ton. According to the law of one price, the exchange rate must increase to 110 yen per dollar (55,000 yen/ton/$500/ton = 110 yen/$), a ten percent depreciation of the yen. Applying the law of one price to the prices of steel in Japan and the United States, we conclude that if the Japanese price level increases by ten percent relative to the American price level, the yen will depreciate by ten percent against the dollar.

Although the law of one price can be applied to one good, economists are interested in how exchange rates are determined by looking at the prices of many goods, as measured by a nation's consumer price index or producer price index. The Purchasing-Power-Parity theory provides a generalized explanation of exchange rates based on the prices of many goods. Therefore, the Purchasing-Power-Parity theory is simply the application of the law of one price to national price levels.

According to the Purchasing-Power-Parity theory, what is important are relative inflationary differences between one economy and the next. If the rate of inflation is much higher in one country, its money has lost purchasing power over domestic goods. We would expect that currency to depreciate to restore parity with prices of goods abroad (the depreciation would make imported goods more expensive to domestic consumers while making domestic exports less expensive to foreigners). Thus, exports and imports of goods and services (trade flows) constitute the mechanism that makes a currency depreciate or appreciate, according to the Purchasing-Power-Parity theory.

Going one step further, the Purchasing-Power-Parity theory suggests that the *changes* in relative national price levels determine *changes* in exchange rates over the long run. The theory predicts that the foreign exchange value of a currency tends to appreciate or depreciate at a rate equal to the difference between foreign and domestic inflation.[3]

Suppose we compare the consumer price indexes of the United States and Switzerland and find that U.S. inflation exceeds Switzerland's inflation by four percentage points per year. This difference means that the purchasing power of the dollar falls relative to the franc. The exchange value of the dollar against the franc should therefore depreciate 4 percent per year, according to the Purchasing-Power-Parity theory. Conversely, the U.S. dollar should appreciate against the franc if U.S. inflation is less than Switzerland's inflation.

The Purchasing-Power-Parity theory can be used to predict long run exchange rates. We'll consider an example using the price indexes (P) of the United States and Switzerland. Letting 0 be the base period and 1 represent period 1 the Purchasing-Power-Parity theory is given in symbols as follows:

$$S_1 = S_0 \frac{P_{US1}/P_{US0}}{P_{S1}/P_{S0}}$$

where S_0 equals the equilibrium exchange rate existing in the base period and S_1 equals the estimated target at which the actual rate should be in the future.

Let the price indexes of the United States and Switzerland and the equilibrium exchange rate be as follows:

$$P_{US0} = 100 \quad P_{S0} = 100 \quad S_0 = \$0.50$$
$$P_{US1} = 200 \quad P_{S1} = 100$$

Putting these figures into the previous equation, we can determine the new equilibrium exchange rate for period 1:

$$S_1 = \$0.50 \left(\frac{200/100}{100/100} \right) = \$0.50 \ (2) = \$1.00$$

Between one period and the next, the U.S. inflation rate rose 100 percent, whereas Switzerland's inflation rate remained unchanged. Maintaining Purchasing-Power-Parity between the dollar and the franc requires the dollar to depreciate against the franc by

---

[3]This chapter presents the so called *relative version* of the Purchasing-Power-Parity theory that addresses changes in prices and exchange rates over a period of time. Another variant is the *absolute version* that states the equilibrium exchange rate will equal the ratio of domestic to foreign prices of an appropriate market basket of goods and services at a given point in time.

an amount equal to the difference in the percentage rates of inflation in the United States and Switzerland. The dollar must depreciate by 100 percent, from $0.50 per franc to $1 per franc, to maintain its Purchasing-Power-Parity. If the example assumed instead that Switzerland's inflation rate doubled while the U.S. inflation rate remained unchanged, the dollar would appreciate to a level of $0.25 per franc, according to the Purchasing-Power-Parity theory.

Although the Purchasing-Power-Parity theory can be helpful in forecasting appropriate levels to which currency values should be adjusted, it is not an infallible guide to exchange rate determination. For instance, the theory overlooks the fact that exchange rate movements may be influenced by investment flows. The theory also faces the problems of choosing the appropriate price index to be used in price calculations (consumer prices or producer prices) and of determining the equilibrium period to use as a base. Government policy may interfere with the operation of the theory by implementing trade restrictions that disrupt the flow of exports and imports among nations.

The predictive power of the Purchasing-Power-Parity theory is most evident in the long run. From 1973 to 2003, the UK price level increased about 99 percent relative to the U.S. price level as shown in Figure 12.4. As the Purchasing-Power-Parity theory forecasts, the pound depreciated against the dollar by about 73 percent during this period, although this amount is less than the 99 percent increase forecasted by the theory. The figure shows that the Purchasing-Power-Parity theory has negligible predictive power in the short run. From 1985 to 1988, the British price level increased relative to the U.S. price level. Rather than depreciating, as the Purchasing-Power-Parity theory predicts, the pound actually appreciated against the dollar. The Purchasing-Power-Parity theory is most appropriate for **forecasting exchange rates** in the long run; in the short run it is a poor forecaster.

FIGURE 12.4

Purchasing-Power-Parity: United States–United Kingdom, 1973–2011

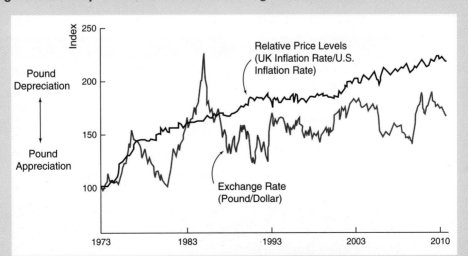

This figure suggests that the predictive power of the Purchasing-Power-Parity theory is most evident in the long run. In the short run, the theory has negligible predictive power.

Source: *Economic Report of the President* and *National Statistics Online*, available at http://www.statistics.gov.uk/.

© Cengage Learning®

DETERMINING SHORT RUN EXCHANGE RATES: THE ASSET MARKET APPROACH

We have seen that exchange rate fluctuations in the long run stem from volatility in market fundamentals including relative price levels (purchasing-power-parity), relative productivity levels, preferences for domestic or foreign goods, and trade barriers. However, fluctuations in exchange rates are sometimes too large and too sudden to be explained solely by such factors. Exchange rates can change by two percentage points or more in a single day. But variations in the determinants usually do not occur frequently or significantly enough to fully account for such exchange rate irascibility. Therefore, to understand why exchange rates can fluctuate sharply in a particular day or week, we must consider other factors besides relative price level behavior, productivity trends, preferences, and trade barriers. We need to develop a framework that can demonstrate why exchange rates fluctuate in the short run.

To understand short run exchange rate behavior, it is important to recognize that foreign exchange market activity is dominated by investors in assets such as Treasury securities, corporate bonds, bank accounts, stocks, and real property. Today, only about two percent of all foreign exchange transactions are related to the financing of exports and imports. This relation suggests that about 98 percent of foreign exchange transactions are attributable to assets being traded in global markets. Because these markets are connected by sophisticated telecommunication systems and trading occurs on a 24-hour basis, investors in financial assets can trade rapidly and modify their outlooks of currency values almost instantaneously. Over short periods such as a month, decisions to hold domestic or foreign assets play a much greater role in exchange rate determination than the demand for imports and exports does.

According to the **asset market approach**, investors consider two key factors when deciding between domestic and foreign investments: relative levels of interest rates and expected changes in the exchange rate itself over the term of the investment. These factors, account for fluctuations in exchange rates that we observe in the short run. Table 12.4 summarizes the effects of these factors.

TABLE 12.4

Determinants of the Dollar's Exchange Rate against the Pound in the Short Run

Change in Determinant*	Repositioning of International Financial Investment	Effect on Dollar's Exchange Rate
U.S. Interest Rate		
Increase	Toward dollar denominated assets	Appreciates
Decrease	Toward pound denominated	Depreciates
British Interest Rate		
Increase	Toward pound denominated assets	Depreciates
Decrease	Toward dollar denominated assets	Appreciates
Expected Future Change in the Dollar's Exchange Rate		
Appreciate	Toward dollar denominated assets	Appreciates
Depreciate	Toward pound denominated assets	Depreciates

*The analysis for a change in one determinant assumes that the other determinants are unchanged.

© Cengage Learning®

Relative Levels of Interest Rates

The level of the **nominal** (money) **interest rate** is a first approximation of the rate of return on assets that can be earned in a particular country. Differences in the level of nominal interest rates between economies are likely to affect international investment flows, as investors seek the highest rate of return.

When interest rates in the United States are significantly higher than interest rates abroad, the foreign demand for U.S. securities and bank accounts will increase, that increases the demand for the dollars needed to buy those assets, thus causing the dollar to appreciate relative to foreign currencies. In contrast, if interest rates in the United States are on average lower than interest rates abroad, the demand for foreign securities and bank accounts strengthens and the demand for U.S. securities and bank accounts weakens. This weakness will cause the demand for foreign currencies needed to buy foreign assets to increase and the demand for the dollar to decrease, resulting in a depreciation of the dollar relative to foreign currencies.

To illustrate the effects of relative interest rates as a determinant of exchange rates, refer to Figure 12.5; it shows the demand and supply schedules for pounds. Initially, the equilibrium exchange rate is $1.50 per pound. Referring to Figure 12.5(a), assume that an expansionary monetary policy of the U.S. Federal Reserve results in a fall in interest rates to three percent, while interest rates in the United Kingdom are at six percent. U.S. investors will be attracted to the relatively high interest rates in the United Kingdom and will demand more pounds to buy UK Treasury bills. The demand for pounds rises to D_1 in the figure. Concurrently, the UK investors will find investing in the United States less attractive than before, so fewer pounds will be offered to buy dollars for purchases of U.S. securities. The supply of pounds decreases to S_1 in the figure. The combined effect of these two shifts is to cause the dollar to depreciate to

FIGURE 12.5

Factors Affecting the Dollar's Exchange Rate in the Short Run

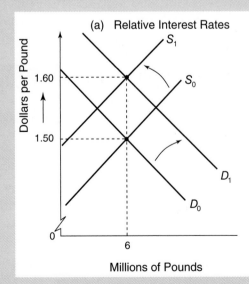
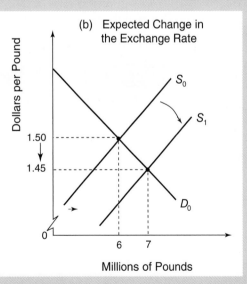

In the short run, the exchange rate between the dollar and the pound reflects relative interest rates and expected changes in the exchange rate.

$1.60 per pound. Alternatively, if interest rates were lower in the United Kingdom than in the United States, the dollar would appreciate against the pound as Americans made fewer investments in the United Kingdom and the UK investors made more investments in the United States.

Things may not always be so simple concerning the relation between interest rates, investment flows, and exchange rates. It is important to distinguish between the nominal interest rate and the **real interest rate** (the nominal interest rate minus the inflation rate).

$$\text{Real Interest rate} = \text{Nominal Interest Rate} - \text{Inflation Rate}$$

For international investors, it is the relative changes in the real interest rate that matter.

If a rise in the nominal interest rate in the United States is accompanied by an equal rise in the U.S. inflation rate, the real interest rate remains constant. In this case, higher nominal interest rates do not make dollar denominated securities more attractive to UK investors. This is because rising U.S. inflation will encourage U.S. buyers to seek out low priced UK goods that will increase the demand for pounds and cause the dollar to depreciate. British investors will expect the exchange rate of the dollar in terms of the pound, to depreciate along with the declining purchasing power of the dollar. The higher nominal return on U.S. securities will be offset by the expectation of a lower future exchange rate, leaving the motivation for increased UK investment in the United States unaffected. Only if higher nominal interest rates in the United States signal an increase in the real interest rate will the dollar appreciate; if they signal rising inflationary expectations and a falling real interest rate, the dollar will depreciate. Table 12.5 provides examples of short-term real interest rates for various nations.

Movements in real interest rates help explain the behavior of the dollar during 1974–2006, as seen in Figure 12.6. In the late 1970s, real interest rates in the United States were at low levels, as was the trade-weighted value of the dollar. By the early 1980s, U.S. real interest rates were increasing. This movement attracted investment funds to the United States that caused the dollar's exchange value to rise. After 1985, U.S. real interest rates declined and the dollar's value weakened. The positive relation between the real interest rate and the dollar's exchange rate broke down after 1995: while

TABLE 12.5

Short-Term Nominal and Real Interest Rates, 2012

Country	Nominal Interest Rate* (Percent)	Inflation Rate** (Percent)	Real Interest Rate (Percent)
Brazil	7.1	5.8	1.3
Japan	0.9	−0.1	1.0
Mexico	4.2	3.4	0.8
New Zealand	2.5	1.7	0.8
Argentina	10.4	10.3	0.1
Germany	1.6	2.0	−0.4
India	9.0	11.2	−2.2

*Rates are for 3-month treasury bills.
**Measured by the Consumer Price Index.

Source: From *International Financial Statistics*, December, 2013 and World Bank, *Data and Statistics*, available at www.data.worldbank.org.

FIGURE 12.6

Interest Rate Differentials and Exchange Rates

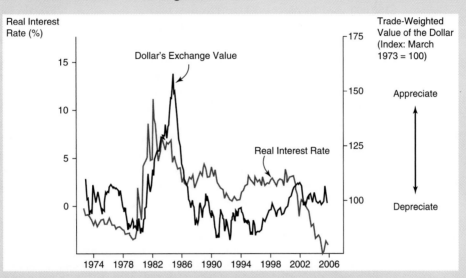

An increase in the U.S. real interest rate increases the expected return on dollar assets, such as Treasury bills and certificates of deposit. This encourages flows of foreign investment into the United States, thus causing the dollar's exchange value to appreciate. Conversely, a decrease in the U.S. real interest rate reduces the expected profitability on dollar assets, which promotes a depreciation of the dollar's exchange value.

© Cengage Learning®

U.S. real interest rates remained unchanged, the dollar appreciated. This appreciation was because of a booming U.S. stock market in the late 1990s that attracted foreign investment inflows and pushed up the dollar's exchange value, even though U.S. real interest rates remained constant. Following 2002, the U.S. real interest rate declined and the dollar's exchange value depreciated at the same time, repeating the experience of the late 1980s. We expect to see appreciating currencies in countries whose real interest rates are higher than abroad because these countries will attract investment funds from all over the world. Countries that experience relatively low real interest rates tend to find their currencies depreciating.

Expected Change in the Exchange Rate

Differences in interest rates may not be all investors need to know to guide their decisions. They must also consider that the return actually realized from an investment is paid out over some future period. This time frame means that the realized value of that future payment can be altered by changes in the exchange rate itself over the term of the investment. Investors must think about possible gains or losses on foreign currency transactions in addition to interest rates on assets.

Expectations about the future path of the exchange rate itself will figure prominently in the investor's calculation of what he or she will actually earn from a foreign investment denominated in another currency. Even a high interest rate would not be attractive if one expects the denominating currency to depreciate at a similar or greater rate and erase all economic gain. Conversely, if the denominating currency is expected to appreciate, the realized gain would be greater than what the interest rate alone would suggest, and the asset appears more lucrative.

Suppose that UK investors expect the dollar to appreciate against the pound during the next three months, from $1.50 per pound to $1.45 per pound. Given today's exchange rate of $1.50 per pound, the investors could spend 100,000 pounds and buy $150,000 used to purchase U.S. Treasury bills of this value. When the bills mature in three months, the investors could cash out the bills and receive $150,000 (plus the interest on the bills), convert these dollars into pounds at the exchange rate of $1.45 per pound, receive 103,448 pounds ($150,000/$1.45/pound = 103,448 pounds), and realize a gain of 3,448 pounds. The gain on the bills would be greater than what the interest rate alone would suggest, making the bills appear more lucrative. This would enhance the incentive of UK investors to invest in the United States.

Figure 12.5(b) (see page 405) illustrates the effects of investor expectations of changes in exchange rates over the term of an investment. Assume that the equilibrium exchange rate is initially $1.50 per pound. Suppose that UK investors expect that in three months the exchange value of the dollar will appreciate against the pound. By investing in three-month U.S. Treasury bills, UK investors can anticipate a foreign currency gain: today, selling pounds for dollars when dollars are relatively cheap, and, in three months, purchasing pounds with dollars when dollars are more valuable (pounds are cheap). The expectation of foreign currency gain will make U.S. Treasury bills seem more attractive and the UK investors will purchase more of them. In the figure, the supply of pounds in the foreign exchange market shifts rightward from S_0 to S_1 and the dollar appreciates to $1.45 per pound today. In this way, future expectations of an appreciation of the dollar can be self fulfilling for today's value of the dollar.

Referring to the previous example, UK investors expect that the dollar will appreciate against the pound in three months. What triggers these expectations? The answer lays in the long run determinants of exchange rates discussed earlier in this chapter. The dollar will be expected to appreciate if there are expectations that the U.S. price level will decrease relative to the UK price level, U.S. productivity will increase relative to UK productivity, U.S. tariffs will increase, the U.S. demand for imports will decrease, or the UK demand for U.S. exports will increase. Given anticipated gains resulting from an appreciating dollar, UK investment will flow to the United States that causes an increase in today's value of the dollar in terms of the pound, as shown in the following flowchart:

| Long run determinants of the dollar's exchange rate | → | Expected appreciation of the dollar in three months | → | Expected foreign exchange gain for UK investors | → | British investment flows to the United States today | → | The dollar appreciates against the pound today |

Any long run factor that causes the expected future value of the dollar to appreciate will cause the dollar to appreciate today.

Diversification, Safe Havens, and Investment Flows

Although relative levels of interest rates between countries and expected changes in exchange rates tend to be strong forces directing investment flows among economies, other factors can also affect these flows. The size of the stock of assets denominated in a particular currency in investor portfolios can induce a change in investor preferences. Why? Investors know that it is prudent to have an appropriate degree of *diversification* across asset types, including the currencies in which they are denominated. Even though

GLOBALIZATION INTERNATIONAL COMPARISONS OF GDP: PURCHASING-POWER-PARITY

When economists calculate a country's gross domestic product (GDP), they add up the market values of the goods and services its economy produces and get a total—in dollars for the United States and yuan for China. To compare countries' GDPs, there are two methods to convert each country's output into dollars.

The simplest way to do this is to use market exchange rates. In 2010, China produced 39,800 billion yuan of goods and services. Using the market exchange rate of 6.77 yuan to the dollar, China's GDP equaled $5,879 billion (39,800 billion yuan/$6.77 per yuan = $5,879 billion). However, that number is too low. For one thing, many goods in developing economies such as China are much cheaper than they are in countries like the United States. China has held its yuan at a rate to keep it less expensive than the dollar. As a result, it is cheaper to produce goods in China that also makes consumer items cheaper to buy. Therefore, it is not fair to compare China's output in dollar terms without taking its cheaper currency into account.

One problem with simply using market exchange rates to convert China's GDP into dollars is that not all goods and services are bought and sold in a world market. Haircuts and plumbing services do not get exchanged across countries. If all goods and services were traded in world markets without any frictions, such as tariffs or transport costs, prices would be the same everywhere after correcting for the exchange rate. In practice, many goods and services are not traded. As a result, using market exchange rates to convert China's GDP from yuan into dollars can give a misleading result: exchange rates *overstate* the size of economies with relatively high price levels and *understate* the size of economies with relatively low price levels. Exchange rates are often subject to sizable fluctuations. This fluctuation means that countries may appear to become suddenly "richer" or "poorer" even though in reality there has been little or no change in the relative volume of goods and services produced.

Purchasing-power-parity addresses these problems by taking into account the relative cost of living and the inflation rates of different countries, rather than just a comparison of GDPs based on market exchange rates. Therefore, GDPs of countries converted into a common currency using purchasing–power–parities are valued at a uniform price level and thus reflect only differences in the volumes of goods and services produced in countries.

Today, organizations such as the World Bank, International Monetary Fund, and Central Intelligence Agency accept the Purchasing-Power-Parity method as a more realistic method of making international comparisons of GDPs than the market exchange rate method. They present international statistics on each country's GDP relative to every other's based on purchasing-power-parity relative to the U.S. dollar. Referring to Table 12.6, notice that in 2012 China had the second largest GDP in the world ($8,227 billion) when measured at market exchange rates; when measured at Purchasing-Power-Parity, China's GDP equaled $12,471 billion.

Source: Organization for Economic Cooperation and Development, "International Comparisons of GDP," *PPP Methodological Manual*, Paris, France, June 30, 2005, Chapter 1.

TABLE 12.6

Comparing GDPs Internationally, 2012: Top 8 Countries (Billions of Dollars)

Country	GDP Based on Purchasing-Power-Parity	Country	GDP Based on Market Exchange Rate
United States	$15,685	United States	$15,685
China	12,471	China	8,227
India	4,793	Japan	5,960
Japan	4,487	Germany	3,399
Russian Federation	3,373	France	2,613
Germany	3,349	United Kingdom	2,435
Brazil	2,366	Brazil	2,253
United Kingdom	2,333	India	1,842

Source: World Bank, *Data and Statistics*, available at www.data.worldbank.org/. See also Central Intelligence Agency, *CIA World Factbook* and International Monetary Fund, *World Economic Outlook Database*.

dollar denominated Treasury securities may provide a high relative return, if the accumulation has been large, at some point foreign investors, considering both risk and reward, will decide that their portfolio's share of U.S. securities is large enough. To improve the diversity of their portfolios, investors will slow or halt their purchases of U.S. securities.

There is also likely to be a significant *safe-haven* effect behind some investment flows. Some investors may be willing to sacrifice a significant amount of return if an economy offers them an especially low risk repository for their funds. In recent decades, the United States, with a long history of stable government, steady economic growth, and large and efficient financial markets, can be expected to draw foreign investment for this reason.

Since the launch of the euro in the early 2000s, there have been concerns about profligacy of the members of the European Monetary Union. The main worry was that free spending countries like Italy might spend and borrow excessively and pass the costs of the bill for a bail out to their frugal brethren such as Germany. By 2010 Greece was on the verge of default and other countries like Portugal, Spain, Ireland, and Italy faced serious fiscal imbalances. Increasingly, investors became nervous about the stability of the euro zone. As a result, they sold large amounts of euros and purchased U.S. dollars that resulted in a sizable depreciation of the euro against the dollar. The investors apparently viewed the U.S. economy to be a safe haven in terms of economic stability relative to that of the euro zone economies.

In this chapter, we have learned about the determinants of exchange rates. To see how these determinants play out on a daily basis, refer to *Currency Trading*, found in the *Money and Investing* section (section C) of *The Wall Street Journal*. You will learn about trends in currency exchange values and the factors contributing to currency depreciation and appreciation. It is a great way to apply to the real world what you have learned in this chapter.

EXCHANGE RATE OVERSHOOTING

Changes in expected future values of market fundamentals contribute to exchange rate volatility in the short run. Announcements by the Federal Reserve of changes in monetary growth targets or by the president and Congress of changes in tax or spending programs cause changes in expectations of future exchange rates that can lead to immediate changes in equilibrium exchange rates. In this manner, frequent changes in policy contribute to volatile exchange rates in a system of market determined exchange rates.

The volatility of exchange rates is further intensified by the phenomenon of **overshooting**. An exchange rate is said to overshoot when its short run response (depreciation or appreciation) to a change in market fundamentals is *greater* than its long run response. Changes in market fundamentals thus exert a disproportionately large *short run* impact on exchange rates. Exchange rate overshooting is an important phenomenon because it helps explain why exchange rates depreciate or appreciate so sharply from day to day.

Exchange rate overshooting can be explained by the tendency of elasticities to be smaller in the short run than in the long run. Referring to Figure 12.7, the short run supply schedule and demand schedule of the UK pound are denoted by S_0 and D_0, respectively, and the equilibrium exchange rate is $2 per pound. If the demand for pounds increases to D_1, the dollar depreciates to $2.20 per pound in the short run. However, because of the dollar depreciation, the UK price of U.S. exports decreases, the quantity of U.S. exports demanded increases, and thus the quantity of pounds supplied increases. The longer the time period, the greater the rise in the quantity of exports is likely to be, and the greater

FIGURE 12.7

Short Run/Long Run Equilibrium Exchange Rates: Overshooting

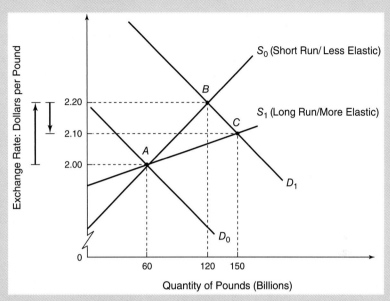

Given the short run supply of pounds (S_0), if the demand for pounds increases from D_0 to D_1, then the dollar depreciates from $2 per pound to a short run equilibrium of $2.20 per pound. In the long run, the supply of pounds is more elastic (S_1), and the equilibrium exchange rate is lower, at $2.10 per pound. Because of the difference in these elasticities, the short-run depreciation of the dollar overshoots its long run depreciation.

the rise in the quantity of pounds supplied. The long run supply schedule of pounds is thus more elastic than the short run supply schedule, as shown by S_1 in the figure. Following the increase in the demand for pounds to D_1, the long run equilibrium exchange rate is $2.10 per pound, as compared to the short run equilibrium exchange rate of $2.20 per pound. Because of differences in these elasticities, the dollar's depreciation in the short run overshoots its long run depreciation.

Overshooting can also be explained by the fact that exchange rates tend to be more flexible than many other prices. Many prices are written into long-term contracts (workers' wages) and do not respond immediately to changes in market fundamentals. Exchange rates tend to be highly sensitive to current demand and supply conditions. Exchange rates often depreciate or appreciate more in the short run than in the long run so as to compensate for other prices that are slower to adjust to their long run equilibrium levels. As the general price level slowly gravitates to its new equilibrium level, the amount of exchange rate overshooting dissipates, and the exchange rate moves toward its long run equilibrium level.

FORECASTING FOREIGN EXCHANGE RATES

Previous sections of this chapter have examined various factors that determine exchange rate movements. Even a clear understanding of how factors influence exchange rates does not guarantee that we can forecast how exchange rates will change. Not only do exchange rate determinants often point in the opposite direction, but predicting how these determinants will change is also difficult. Forecasting exchange rates is tricky, especially in the short run.

Nevertheless, exchange rate forecasts are necessary for exporters, importers, investors, bankers, and foreign exchange dealers. Corporations often have for brief periods large amounts of cash used to make bank deposits in various currencies. Choosing a currency in which to make deposits requires some idea of what the currency's exchange rate will be in the future. Long-term corporate planning, especially concerning decisions about foreign investment, necessitates an awareness of where exchange rates will move over an extended time period—hence the need for long-term forecasts. For multinational enterprises, short-term forecasting tends to be more widespread than long-term forecasting. Most corporations revise their currency forecasts at least every quarter.

The need of business and investors for exchange rate forecasts has resulted in the emergence of consulting firms, including Global Insights and Goldman Sachs. In addition, large banks such as JP Morgan Chase and Bank of America provide free currency forecasts to corporate clients. Customers of consulting firms often pay fees ranging up to $100,000 per year or more for expert opinions. Consulting firms provide forecast services ranging from video screens to "listening post" interviews with forecast service employees who provide their predictions of exchange rate movements and respond to specific questions from the client.

Most exchange rate forecasting methods use accepted economic relations to formulate a model that is then refined through statistical analysis of past data. The forecasts generated by the models are usually tempered by the additional insights or reasoning of the forecaster before being offered to the final user.

In the current system of market determined exchange rates, currency values fluctuate almost instantaneously in response to new information regarding changes in interest rates, inflation rates, money supplies, trade balances, and the like. To successfully forecast exchange rate movements, it is necessary to estimate the future values of these economic variables and determine the relation between them and future exchange rates. However, even the most sophisticated analysis can be rendered worthless by unexpected changes in government policy, market psychology, and so forth. Indeed, people who deal in the currency markets on a daily basis have come to feel that market psychology is a dominant influence on future exchange rates.

Despite these problems, exchange rate forecasters are currently in demand. Their forecasting approaches are classified as judgmental, technical, or fundamental. A Citigroup Inc. survey of about 3,000 foreign exchange traders in 2010 found that 53 percent of traders employ a combination of fundamental and technical strategies, 36 percent use a technical strategy, and only 11 percent use a strictly fundamental strategy tempered by judgmental analysis.[4] Table 12.7 provides examples of exchange rate forecasting organizations and their methods.

Judgmental Forecasts

Judgmental forecasts are sometimes known as *subjective* or *common sense models*. They require the gathering of a wide array of political and economic data and the interpretation of these data in terms of the timing, direction, and magnitude of exchange rate changes. Judgmental forecasters formulate projections based on a thorough examination of individual nations. They consider economic indicators, such as inflation rates and

---

[4]CitiFx Pro, *Survey of Forex Traders*, New York, November 2010.

TABLE 12.7

Exchange Rate Forecasters

Forecasting Organization	Methodology	Horizon
Global Insights	Econometric	24 months
JP Morgan Chase	Judgmental Econometric	Under 12 months Over 12 months
Bank of America	Econometric Technical	Over 12 months Under 12 months
Goldman Sachs	Technical Econometric	Under 12 months Over 12 months
UBS Global Asset Management	Judgmental Econometric	8 months 12 months

Source: Data collected by author.

trade data; political factors, such as a future national election; technical factors, such as potential intervention by a central bank in the foreign exchange market; and psychological factors that relate to one's "feel for the market."

Technical Forecasts

Technical analysis involves the use of historical exchange rate data to estimate future values. This approach is technical in that it extrapolates from past exchange-rate trends and then projects them into the future to generate forecasts, while ignoring economic and political determinants of exchange rate movements. Technical analysts look for specific exchange rate patterns. Once the beginning of a particular pattern has been determined, it automatically implies what the short run behavior of the exchange rate will be. Therefore, the technological approach is founded on the idea that history repeats itself.

Technical analysis encompasses a variety of charting techniques involving a currency's price, cycles, or volatility. A common starting point for technical analysis is a chart that plots a trading period's opening, high, low, and closing prices. These charts most often plot one trading day's range of prices, but also are created on a weekly, monthly, and yearly basis. Traders watch for new highs and lows, broken trend lines, and patterns that are thought to predict price targets and movement.

To illustrate technical analysis, assume you have formed an opinion about the yen's exchange value against the dollar based on your analysis of economic fundamentals. Now you want to look at what the markets can tell you; you're looking for price trends and you can use charts to do it. As shown in Figure 12.8 you might want to look at the relative highs and lows of the yen for the past several months; the trend lines in the figure connect the higher highs and the lower lows for the yen. If the yen's exchange rate moves substantially above or below the trend lines, it might signal that a trend is changing. Changes in trends help you decide when to purchase or sell yen in the foreign exchange market.

Because technical analysis follows the market closely, it is used to forecast exchange rate movements in the short run. However, determining an exchange rate pattern is useful only as long as the market continues to consistently follow that pattern. However, no pattern can be relied on to continue more than a few days, or perhaps weeks. A client must therefore respond quickly to a technical recommendation to buy or sell a currency. Clients require immediate communication of technical recommendations, so as to make timely financial decisions.

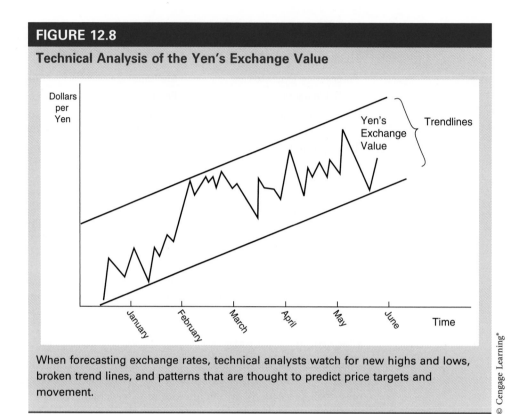

FIGURE 12.8

Technical Analysis of the Yen's Exchange Value

When forecasting exchange rates, technical analysts watch for new highs and lows, broken trend lines, and patterns that are thought to predict price targets and movement.

© Cengage Learning®

Although fundamental based models can often provide only a long-term forecast of exchange rate movements, technical analysis is the main method of analyzing shorter term movements in an exchange rate. The results of technical analysis are used to predict the market direction of an exchange rate and to generate signals to a currency trader regarding when to buy or sell a currency. It is not surprising that most foreign exchange dealers use some technical model input to help them formulate a trading strategy for currencies, especially for intra-day and one week horizons.

Fundamental Analysis

Fundamental analysis is the opposite of technical analysis. It involves consideration of economic variables that are likely to affect the supply and demand of a currency and its exchange value. Fundamental analysis uses computer based econometric models that are statistical estimations of economic theories. To generate forecasts, econometricians develop models for individual nations that attempt to incorporate the fundamental variables that underlie exchange rate movements: interest rates, balance of trade, productivity, inflation rates, and the like. If you take an econometric course at your university, you might consider preparing an exchange rate forecast as your class project. *Exploring Further 12.1* gives you an idea of the types of variables you might include in your econometric model. It can be found at www.cengage.com/economics/Carbaugh.

However, econometric models used to forecast exchange rates face limitations. They often rely on predictions of key economic variables, such as inflation rates or

TRADE CONFLICTS COMMERCIAL MEXICANA GETS BURNED BY SPECULATION

Although speculators like George Soros can pull huge profits out of the foreign exchange market, sometimes their currency bets backfire. Consider the case of Controladora Comercial Mexicana SAB (Comercial Mexicana) the owner of supermarkets and Costco stores in Mexico.

One day in October 2008, Comercial Mexicana was prospering as Mexico's third largest retailer and a competitor of discount giant Walmart. A few days later, the family owned chain went bankrupt, decimated by foreign currency losses that resulted in the firm losing almost half its value. Why did this occur?

Comercial Mexicana and other Mexican firms made bad bets using currency contracts obtained from big banks such as J.P. Morgan Chase & Co, that were linked to the dollar/peso exchange rate. Their bets were based on expectations of a stronger peso. However, the world credit crisis of 2008 threw the peso into a tailspin. Mexico's central bank, seeing the risk to its economy, sold billions of dollars from its reserves to purchase the weakening peso and thus prop up its value. The central bank burned through about 13 percent of its international currency reserves in this strategy that turned out to be futile: Mexico's peso plummeted 24 percent in October of 2008 as risk averse investors yanked money from the country.

Under the currency deal, J.P. Morgan Chase & Co. offered Comercial Mexicana financing and currency trades at favorable rates. But there was a hitch. If the dollar strengthened (the peso depreciated) beyond a certain threshold, then the firm would have to sell dollars at a loss. In some cases, the contracts had triggers that doubled the number of dollars the firm sold.

When Comercial Mexicana purchased the currency contracts, the deals were initially profitable. But soon things deteriorated as investors panicked over the global financial crisis and began pulling money out of Mexico. As the peso depreciated, Comercial Mexicana encountered losses of $1.4 billion. Being unable to pay its debt, the firm filed for bankruptcy.

Rather than sticking to its business of selling tomatoes and digital cameras to Mexican shoppers, Comercial Mexicana tried to make money on the dollar/peso exchange rate. However, the firm was unprepared for the destabilizing effects of the global financial crisis of 2008.

Source: William Freebairn, "Comercial Mexicana Drops 44 Percent After Saying Debt Rose," Bloomberg.com, October 24, 2008; "Big Currency Bets Backfire," *The Wall Street Journal*, October 22, 2008, p. A1; "Comercial Mexicana Crisis in 2008," *Explorado Mexico*; Carlos Omar Trejo-Pech, Susan White, and Magdy Noguera, *Financial Distress at Commercial Mexicana, 2008–2011*, Robert H. Smith School of Business, University of Maryland, 2011.

interest rates, and obtaining reliable information can be difficult. Moreover, there are always factors affecting exchange rates that cannot easily be quantified (such as intervention by a country's central bank in currency markets). Also, the precise timing of a factor's effect on a currency's exchange rate may be unclear. Inflation rate changes may not have their full impact on a currency's value until three or six months in the future. Econometric models are best suited for forecasting long run trends in the movement of an exchange rate. However, they do not generally provide foreign currency traders precise price information regarding when to purchase or sell a particular currency. Thus, currency traders generally prefer technical analysis to fundamental analysis when forming a trading strategy. In spite of the appeal of technical analysis, most forecasters tend to use a combination of fundamental, technical, and judgmental analysis, with the emphasis on each shifting as conditions change. They form a general view about whether a particular currency is over or undervalued in a longer term sense. Within that framework, they assess all current economic forecasts, news events, political developments, statistical releases, rumors, and changes in sentiment, while also carefully studying the charts and technical analysis.

SUMMARY

1. In a free market, exchange rates are determined by market fundamentals and market expectations. The former includes real interest rates, consumer preferences for domestic or foreign products, productivity, investment profitability, product availability, monetary and fiscal policy, and government trade policy. Economists generally agree that the major determinants of exchange rate fluctuations are different in the long run than in the short run.

2. The determinants of long run exchange rates differ from the determinants of short run exchange rates. In the long run, exchange rates are determined by four key factors: relative price levels, relative productivity levels, consumer preferences for domestic or foreign goods, and trade barriers. These factors underlie trade in domestic and foreign goods and thus changes in the demand for exports and imports.

3. In the long run, a nation's currency tends to appreciate when the nation has relatively low levels of inflation, relatively high levels of productivity, relatively strong demand for its export products, and relatively high barriers to trade.

4. According to the Purchasing-Power-Parity theory, changes in relative national price levels determine changes in exchange rates over the long run. A currency maintains its Purchasing-Power-Parity if it depreciates (appreciates) by an amount equal to the excess of domestic (foreign) inflation over foreign (domestic) inflation.

5. Over short periods of time, decisions to hold domestic or foreign financial assets play a much greater role in exchange rate determination than the demand for imports and exports does. According to the asset market approach to exchange rate determination, investors consider two key factors when deciding between domestic and foreign investments: relative interest rates and expected changes in exchange rates. Changes in these factors, in turn, account for fluctuations in exchange rates that we observe in the short run.

6. Short-term interest rate differentials between any two nations are important determinants of international investment flows and short-term exchange rates. A nation that has relatively high (low) interest rates tends to find its currency's exchange value appreciating (depreciating) in the short run.

7. In the short run, market expectations also influence exchange rate movements. Future expectations of rapid domestic economic growth, falling domestic interest rates, and high domestic inflation rates tend to cause the domestic currency to depreciate.

8. Exchange rate volatility is intensified by the phenomenon of overshooting. An exchange rate is said to overshoot when its short run response to a change in market fundamentals is greater than its long run response.

9. Currency forecasters use several methods to predict future exchange rate movements: (a) judgmental forecasts, (b) technical analysis, and (c) fundamental analysis.

KEY CONCEPTS AND TERMS

Asset market approach (p. 404)
Forecasting exchange
  rates (p. 403)
Fundamental analysis (p. 414)
Judgmental forecasts (p. 412)

Law of one price (p. 398)
Market expectations (p. 394)
Market fundamentals (p. 393)
Nominal interest
  rate (p. 405)

Overshooting (p. 410)
Purchasing-power-parity
  theory (p. 400)
Real interest rate (p. 406)
Technical analysis (p. 413)

STUDY QUESTIONS

1. In a free market, what factors underlie currency exchange values? Which factors best apply to long and short run exchange rates?

2. Why are international investors especially concerned about the real interest rate as opposed to the nominal rate?

3. What predictions does the Purchasing-Power-Parity theory make concerning the impact of domestic inflation on the home country's exchange rate? What are some limitations of the Purchasing-Power-Parity theory?

4. If a currency becomes overvalued in the foreign exchange market, what will be the likely impact on the home country's trade balance? What if the home currency becomes undervalued?

5. Identify the factors that account for changes in a currency's value over the long run.

6. What factors underlie changes in a currency's value in the short run?

7. Explain how the following factors affect the dollar's exchange rate under a system of market determined exchange rates: (a) a rise in the U.S. price level, with the foreign price level held constant; (b) tariffs and quotas placed on U.S. imports; (c) increased demand for U.S. exports and decreased U.S. demand for imports; (d) rising productivity in the United States relative to other countries; (e) rising real interest rates overseas, relative to U.S. rates; (f) an increase in U.S. money growth; and (g) an increase in U.S. money demand.

8. What is meant by exchange rate overshooting? Why does it occur?

9. What methods do currency forecasters use to predict future changes in exchange rates?

10. Assuming market determined exchange rates, use supply and demand schedules for pounds to analyze the effect on the exchange rate (dollars per pound) between the U.S. dollar and the UK pound under each of the following circumstances:
    a. Voter polls suggest that the UK's conservative government will be replaced by radicals who pledge to nationalize all foreign owned assets.
    b. Both the UK and U.S. economies slide into recession, but the UK recession is less severe than the U.S. recession.
    c. The Federal Reserve adopts a tight monetary policy that dramatically increases U.S. interest rates.
    d. Britain's oil production in the North Sea decreases, and exports to the United States fall.
    e. The United States unilaterally reduces tariffs on UK products.

f. Britain encounters severe inflation, while price stability exists in the United States.
    g. Fears of terrorism reduce U.S. tourism in the United Kingdom.
    h. The British government invites U.S. firms to invest in British oil fields.
    i. The rate of productivity growth in Britain decreases sharply.
    j. An economic boom occurs in the United Kingdom that induces the UK consumers to purchase more U.S. made autos, trucks, and computers.
    k. Ten-percent inflation occurs in both the United Kingdom and the United States.

11. Explain why you agree or disagree with each of the following statements:
    a. "A nation's currency will depreciate if its inflation rate is less than that of its trading partners."
    b. "A nation whose interest rate falls more rapidly than that of other nations can expect the exchange value of its currency to depreciate."
    c. "A nation that experiences higher growth rates in productivity than its trading partners can expect the exchange value of its currency to appreciate."

12. The appreciation in the dollar's exchange value from 1980 to 1985 made U.S. products (less/more) expensive and foreign products (less/more) expensive, (decreased, increased) U.S. imports, and (decreased, increased) U.S. exports.

13. Suppose the dollar/franc exchange rate equals $0.50 per franc. According to the Purchasing-Power-Parity theory, what will happen to the dollar's exchange value under each of the following circumstances?
    a. The U.S. price level increases by 10 percent and the price level in Switzerland stays constant.
    b. The U.S. price level increases by 10 percent and the price level in Switzerland increases by 20 percent.
    c. The U.S. price level decreases by 10 percent and the price level in Switzerland increases by 5 percent.
    d. The U.S. price level decreases by 10 percent and the price level in Switzerland decreases by 15 percent.

14. Suppose that the nominal interest rate on three month Treasury bills is 8 percent in the United

States and 6 percent in the United Kingdom, and the rate of inflation is 10 percent in the United States and 4 percent in the United Kingdom.

a. What is the real interest rate in each nation?

b. In which direction would international investment flow in response to these real interest rates?

c. What impact would these investment flows have on the dollar's exchange value?

EXPLORING FURTHER

The use of regression analysis in exchange rate forecasting is contained in *Exploring Further 12.1* that can be found at **www.cengage.com/economics/Carbaugh**.

Mechanisms of International Adjustment

In Chapter 10 we learned about the meaning of the balance-of-payments. Recall that, owing to double entry bookkeeping, total inpayments (credits) always equal total outpayments (debits) when all balance-of-payments accounts are considered. A deficit refers to an excess of outpayments over inpayments for selected accounts grouped along functional lines. A current account deficit suggests an excess of imports over exports of goods, services, income flows, and unilateral transfers. A current account surplus implies the opposite.

A nation finances or covers a current account deficit out of its international reserves or by attracting investment (such as purchases of factories) or borrowing from other nations. The capacity of a deficit nation to cover the excess of outpayments over inpayments is limited by its stocks of international reserves and the willingness of other nations to invest in, or lend to, the deficit nation. For a surplus nation, once it believes its stocks of international reserves or overseas investments are adequate—although history shows that this belief may be a long time in coming—it will be reluctant to run prolonged surpluses. In general, the incentive for reducing a current account surplus is not as direct and immediate as that for reducing a current account deficit.

The **adjustment mechanism** works for the return to equilibrium after the initial equilibrium has been disrupted. The process of current account adjustment takes two different forms. First, under certain conditions, there are adjustment factors that automatically promote equilibrium. Second, should the automatic adjustments be unable to restore equilibrium, discretionary government policies may be adopted to achieve this objective.

This chapter emphasizes the **automatic adjustment** of the current account that occurs under a fixed exchange rate system.[1] The adjustment variables that we will emphasize include prices and income. The influence of interest rates on a country's capital and financial account will also be discussed. Subsequent chapters discuss the adjustment

---

[1] Under a fixed exchange rate system, the supply of and demand for foreign exchange reflect credit and debit transactions in the balance-of-payments. However, these forces of supply and demand are not permitted to determine the exchange rate. Instead, government officials peg, or fix, the exchange rate at a stipulated level by intervening in the foreign exchange markets to purchase and sell currencies. This topic is examined further in the next chapter.

mechanism under flexible exchange rates and the role of government policy in promoting current account adjustment.

Although the various automatic adjustment approaches have their contemporary advocates, each was formulated during a particular period and reflects a different philosophical climate. The idea that the current account can be adjusted by prices stemmed from the *classical* economic thinking of the 1800s and early 1900s. The classical approach was geared toward the existing gold standard associated with fixed exchange rates. That income changes could promote current account adjustments reflected the *Keynesian* theory of income determination that grew out of the Great Depression of the 1930s.

PRICE ADJUSTMENTS

The original theory of current account adjustment is credited to David Hume (1711–1776), the English philosopher and economist.[2] Hume's theory rose from his concern with the prevailing mercantilist view that advocated government controls to ensure a continuous current account surplus. According to Hume, this strategy was self defeating over the long run because a nation's current account tends to move toward equilibrium *automatically*. Hume's theory stresses the role that adjustments in national *price levels* play in promoting current account equilibrium.

Gold Standard

The classical **gold standard** that existed from the late 1800s to the early 1900s was characterized by three conditions. First, each member nation's money supply consisted of gold or paper money backed by gold. Second, each member nation defined the official price of gold in terms of its national currency and was prepared to buy and sell gold at that price. Third, free import and export of gold were permitted by member nations. Under these conditions, a nation's money supply was directly tied to its current account. A nation with a current account surplus would acquire gold, directly expanding its money supply. Conversely, the money supply of a deficit nation would decline as the result of a gold outflow.

The current account can also be tied directly to a nation's money supply under a modified gold standard, requiring that the nation's stock of money be fractionally backed by gold at a constant ratio. It would also apply to a fixed exchange rate system in which a current account disequilibrium is financed by some acceptable international reserve asset, assuming that a constant ratio between the nation's international reserves and its money supply are maintained.

Quantity Theory of Money

The essence of the classical **price adjustment mechanism** is embodied in the **quantity theory of money**. Consider the following *equation of exchange*:

$$MV = PQ$$

where M refers to a nation's money supply. The V refers to the velocity of money—that is, the number of times per year the average currency unit is spent on final goods. The expression MV corresponds to the aggregate demand, or total monetary expenditures on

---

[2]David Hume, "Of the Balance of Trade." Reprinted in Richard N. Cooper, ed., *International Finance: Selected Readings* (Harmondsworth, England: Penguin Books, 1969), Chapter 1.

final goods. Alternatively, the monetary expenditures on any year's output can be interpreted as the physical volume of all final goods produced (Q) multiplied by the average price that each of the final goods is sold (P). As a result, $MV = PQ$.

This equation is an identity. It says that total monetary expenditures on final goods equals the monetary value of the final goods sold; the amount spent on final goods equals the amount received from selling them.

Classical economists made two additional assumptions. First, they took the volume of the final output (Q) to be fixed at the full employment level in the long run. Second, they assumed that the velocity of money (V) was constant, depending on institutional, structural, and physical factors that rarely changed. With V and Q relatively stable, a change in M must induce a *direct and proportionate change* in P. The model linking changes in M to changes in P became known as the quantity theory of money.

Current Account Adjustment

The preceding analysis showed how, under the classical gold standard, the current account is linked to a nation's money supply that is linked to its domestic price level. Let us consider how the price level is linked to the current account.

Suppose under the classical gold standard, a nation realized a current account deficit. The deficit nation would experience a gold outflow that would reduce its money supply and thus its price level. The nation's international competitiveness would be enhanced, so that its exports would rise and its imports fall. This process would continue until its price level had fallen to the point where current account equilibrium was restored. Conversely, a nation with a current account surplus would realize gold inflows and an increase in its money supply. This process would continue until its price level had risen to the point where current account equilibrium was restored. Thus, the opposite price adjustment process would occur at the same time in each trading partner.

The price adjustment mechanism as devised by Hume illustrated the impossibility of the mercantilist notion of maintaining a continuous current account surplus. The linkages (current account—money supply—price level—current account) demonstrated to Hume that, over time, current account equilibrium tends to be achieved automatically.

With the advent of Hume's price adjustment mechanism, classical economists had a powerful and influential theory. It was not until the Keynesian revolution in economic thinking during the 1930s that this theory was effectively challenged. Even today, the price adjustment mechanism is a hotly debated issue. A brief discussion of some of the major criticisms against the price adjustment mechanism is in order.

The classical linkage between changes in a nation's gold supply and changes in its money supply no longer holds. Central bankers can easily offset a gold outflow (or inflow) by adopting an expansionary (or contractionary) monetary policy. The experience of the gold standard of the late 1800s and early 1900s indicates that these offsetting monetary policies often occurred. The classical view that full employment always exists has also been challenged. When an economy is far below its full employment level, there is a smaller chance that prices in general will rise in response to an increase in the money supply than if the economy is at full employment. It has also been pointed out that in a modern industrial world, prices and wages are inflexible in a downward direction. If prices are inflexible downward, then changes in M will affect not P but rather Q. A deficit nation's falling money supply will bring about a fall in output and employment. Furthermore, the stability and predictability of V have been questioned. Should a gold inflow that results in an increase in M be offset by a decline in V, total spending (MV) and PQ would remain unchanged.

These issues are part of the current debate over the price adjustment mechanism's relevance. They have caused sufficient doubts among economists to warrant a search for additional adjustment explanations. The most notable include the effect of interest rate changes on capital movements and the effect of changing incomes on trade flows.

FINANCIAL FLOWS AND INTEREST RATE DIFFERENTIALS

Although the classical economists emphasized the price adjustment mechanism's impact on a country's current account, they were aware of the impact of changes in interest rates on international investment (capital) movements. With national financial systems greatly interdependent today, it is recognized that interest rate fluctuations can induce significant changes in a nation's capital and financial account, as discussed in Chapter 10.

Recall that capital and financial transactions include all international purchases or sales of assets such as real estate, corporate stocks and bonds, commercial bank deposits, and government securities. The vast majority of transactions appearing in the capital and financial account come from financial transactions. The most important factor that causes financial assets to move across national borders is interest rates in domestic and foreign markets. However, other factors are important such as investment profitability, national tax policies, and political stability.

Figure 13.1 shows the hypothetical capital and financial account schedules for the United States. Capital and financial account *surpluses* and *deficits* are measured on the vertical axis. In particular, financial flows between the United States and the rest of the world are assumed to respond to *interest rate differentials* between the two areas (U.S. interest rate minus foreign interest rate) for a particular set of economic conditions in the United States and abroad.

Referring to schedule CFA_0, the U.S. capital and financial account is in *balance* at point A where the U.S. interest rate is equal to that abroad. Should the United States reduce its monetary growth, the scarcity of money would tend to raise interest rates in the United States compared with the rest of the world. Suppose U.S. interest rates rise one percent above those overseas. Investors seeing higher U.S. interest rates will tend to sell foreign securities to purchase U.S. securities that offer a higher yield. The one percent interest rate differential leads to *net financial inflows* of $5 billion for the United States that thus moves to point B on schedule CFA_0. Conversely, should foreign interest rates rise above those in the United States, the United States will face *net financial outflows* as investors sell U.S. securities to purchase foreign securities offering a higher yield.

Figure 13.1 assumes that interest rate differentials are the basic determinant of financial flows for the United States. Movements along schedule CFA_0 are caused by changes in the interest rate in the United States relative to that in the rest of the world. However, certain determinants other than interest rate differentials might cause the United States to import (or export) more or less assets at each possible interest rate differential and thereby change the location of schedule CFA_0.

To illustrate, assume that the United States is located along schedule CFA_0 at point A. Assume that rising U.S. income leads to higher sales and increased profits. Direct investment (in an auto assembly plant, for example) becomes more profitable in the United States. Nations such as Japan will invest more in their U.S. subsidiaries, whereas General Motors will invest less overseas. The higher profitability of direct investment leads to a greater flow of funds into the United States at each possible interest rate differential and an upward shift in the schedule to CFA_1.

FIGURE 13.1

Capital and Financial Account Schedule for the United States

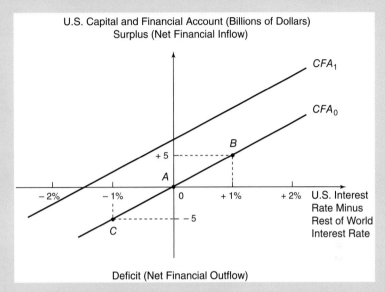

Interest rate differentials between the United States and the rest of the world induce movements along the U.S. capital and financial account schedule. Relatively high (low) U.S. interest rates trigger net financial inflows (outflows) and an upward (downward) movement along the capital and financial account schedule. The schedule shifts upward/downward in response to changes in non-interest rate determinants such as investment profitability, tax policies, and political stability.

Suppose the U.S. government levies an *interest equalization tax* as it did from 1964 to 1974. This tax was intended to reverse the large financial outflows that the United States faced when European interest rates exceeded those in the United States. By taxing U.S. investors on dividend and interest income from foreign securities, the tax reduced the net profitability (the after-tax yield) of foreign securities. At the same time, the U.S. government enacted a foreign credit restraint program that placed direct restrictions on foreign lending by U.S. banks and financial institutions and later on foreign lending of nonfinancial corporations. By discouraging flows of funds from the United States to Europe, these policies resulted in an upward shift in the U.S. capital and financial account schedule in Figure 13.1, suggesting fewer funds would flow out of the United States in response to higher interest rates overseas.

INCOME ADJUSTMENTS

When the classical economists considered mechanisms of international adjustment, they emphasized automatic price changes to promote adjustments in a nation's current account. A weakness of the classical economists was that they neglected the role of income adjustments on the current account. John Maynard Keynes addressed this weakness by formulating his **income adjustment mechanism** in the 1930s.[3] This theory focuses on automatic changes in income to bring about adjustment in a nation's current account.

Keynes asserted that under a system of fixed exchange rates, the influence of income changes in nations with current account surpluses and deficits would help restore equilibrium automatically. Given a persistent current account surplus, a nation will experience rising income and its imports will increase. Conversely, a current account deficit nation will experience a fall in income resulting in a decline in imports. These effects of income changes on import levels will reverse the disequilibrium in the current account. The income adjustment mechanism is more fully discussed in *Exploring Further 13.1* that can be found at www.cengage.com/economics/Carbaugh.

The preceding income adjustment analysis needs to be modified to include the impact that changes in domestic expenditures and income levels have on foreign economies. This process is referred to as the **foreign repercussion effect**.

Assume a two-country world, the United States and Canada, in which there initially exists current account equilibrium. Owing to changing consumer preferences, suppose the United States faces an autonomous increase in imports from Canada. This increase results in an increase in Canada's exports. The result is a decrease in U.S. income and an increase in Canada's income. The fall in U.S. income induces a fall in the level of U.S. imports (and a fall in Canada's exports). At the same time, the rise in Canada's income induces a rise in Canada's imports (and a rise in U.S. exports). This feedback process is repeated again and again.

The consequence of this process is that both the rise in income of the surplus nation (Canada) and the fall in income of the deficit nation (United States) are dampened. This is because the autonomous increase in U.S. imports (and Canadian exports) will cause the U.S. income to decrease as imports are substituted for home produced goods. The decline in U.S. income will generate a reduction in its imports. Because U.S. imports are Canada's exports, the rise in Canada's income will be moderated. From the perspective of the United States, the decline in its income will be cushioned by an increase in exports to Canada stemming from a rise in Canada's income.

The importance of the foreign repercussion effect depends in part on the economic size of a country as far as international trade is concerned. A small nation that increases its imports from a large nation will have little impact on the large nation's income level. But for major trading nations, the foreign repercussion effect is likely to be significant and must be taken into account when the income adjustment mechanism is being considered.

DISADVANTAGES OF AUTOMATIC ADJUSTMENT MECHANISMS

The preceding sections have considered automatic balance-of-payments adjustment mechanisms under a system of fixed exchange rates. According to the classical economists, automatic price changes promote adjustment in the current account. Keynesian theory emphasized another adjustment process; the effect of changes in national income on a nation's current account.

Although elements of price and income adjustments may operate in the real world, these adjustment mechanisms have a major shortcoming. An efficient adjustment mechanism requires central bankers to forgo their use of monetary policy to promote the goal

---

[3]John Maynard Keynes, *The General Theory of Employment, Interest, and Money* (London: Macmillan, 1936).

of full employment without inflation; each nation must be willing to accept inflation or recession when current account adjustment requires it. Take the case of a nation that faces a current account deficit caused by an autonomous increase in imports or decrease in exports. For income adjustments to reverse the deficit, monetary authorities must permit domestic income to decrease and not undertake policies to offset its decline. The opposite applies equally to a nation with a current account surplus. Modern nations are reluctant to make significant internal sacrifices for the sake of external equilibrium. The result is the reliance on an automatic payments adjustment process tends to be politically unacceptable.

MONETARY ADJUSTMENTS

The previous sections examined how changes in national price, interest rate, and income levels serve as international adjustment mechanisms. During the 1960s, a new theory emerged, called the *monetary approach to the balance-of-payments*.[4] The central notion of the monetary approach is that the balance-of-payments is affected by discrepancies between the amount of money people desire to hold and the amount supplied by the central bank. If Americans demand more money than is being supplied by the Federal Reserve, then the excess demand for money will be fulfilled by inflows of money from another country, say China. Conversely, if the Federal Reserve is supplying more money than demanded, the excess supply of money is eliminated by outflows of money to China. Therefore, the monetary approach focuses attention on the determinants of money demand and money supply and their impact on the balance-of-payments. It is left for more advanced textbooks to consider the monetary approach to the balance-of-payments.

SUMMARY

1. Because persistent current account disequilibrium—whether surplus or deficit—tends to have adverse economic consequences, there exists a need for adjustment.

2. Current account adjustment can be classified as automatic or discretionary. Under a system of fixed exchange rates, automatic adjustments can occur through variations in prices and incomes. The demand for and supply of money can also influence the payments position of a country.

3. David Hume's theory provided an explanation of the automatic adjustment process that occurred under the gold standard. Starting from a condition of current account balance, any surplus or deficit would automatically be eliminated by changes in domestic price levels. Hume's theory relied heavily on the quantity theory of money.

4. With the advent of Keynesian economics during the 1930s, greater emphasis was put on the income effects of trade in explaining adjustment.

5. The foreign repercussion effect refers to a situation in which a change in one nation's macroeconomic variables relative to another nation will induce a chain reaction in both nations' economies.

[4]The monetary approach to the balance-of-payments developed its intellectual background at the University of Chicago. It originated with Robert Mundell, *International Economics* (New York: Macmillan, 1968) and Harry Johnson, "The Monetary Approach to Balance-of-Payments Theory," *Journal of Financial and Quantitative Analysis*, March 1972.

6. An automatic current account adjustment mechanism has several disadvantages. Nations must be willing to accept adverse changes in the domestic economy when required for current account adjustment. Policymakers must forgo using discretionary economic policy to promote domestic equilibrium.

KEY CONCEPTS AND TERMS

Adjustment mechanism (p. 419)
Automatic adjustment (p. 419)
Foreign repercussion effect (p. 424)

Gold standard (p. 420)
Income adjustment
    mechanism (p. 424)

Price adjustment
    mechanism (p. 420)
Quantity theory of money (p. 420)

STUDY QUESTIONS

1. What is meant by the term *mechanisms of international adjustment*? Why does a deficit nation have an incentive to undergo adjustment? What about a surplus nation?
2. Under a fixed exchange rate system, what automatic adjustments promote current account equilibrium?
3. What is meant by the quantity theory of money? How did it relate to the classical price adjustment mechanism?
4. How do adjustments in domestic interest rates help affect international investment flows?
5. Keynesian theory suggests that under a system of fixed exchange rates, the influence of income changes in surplus and deficit nations helps promote current account equilibrium. Explain.
6. When analyzing the income adjustment mechanism, one must account for the foreign repercussion effect. Explain.
7. What are some major disadvantages of the automatic adjustment mechanism under a system of fixed exchange rates?

EXPLORING FURTHER

For a more comprehensive discussion of the income adjustment mechanism, go to *Exploring Further 13.1* that can be found at **www.cengage.com/economics/Carbaugh**.

Exchange Rate Adjustments and the Balance-of-Payments

CHAPTER

14

The previous chapter demonstrated that disequilibrium in the balance of trade tends to be reversed by automatic adjustments in prices, interest rates, and incomes. However, if these adjustments are allowed to operate, reversing trade imbalances may come at the expense of domestic recession or price inflation. The cure may be perceived as worse than the disease.

Instead of relying on adjustments in prices, interest rates, and incomes to counteract trade imbalances, governments permit alterations in exchange rates. By adopting a floating exchange rate system, a nation permits its currency to depreciate or appreciate in a free market in response to shifts in either the demand for or supply of the currency.

Under a fixed exchange rate system, rates are set by the government in the short run. However, if the official exchange rate becomes overvalued over a period of time, a government may initiate policies to *devalue* its currency. Currency devaluation causes a depreciation of a currency's exchange value; it is initiated by government policy rather than by the free market forces of supply and demand. When a nation's currency is undervalued, it may be *revalued* by the government; this policy causes the currency's exchange value to appreciate. Currency devaluation and revaluation will be discussed further in the next chapter.

In this chapter, we examine the impact of exchange rate adjustments on the balance of trade. We will learn under what conditions currency depreciation (appreciation) will improve (worsen) a nation's trade position.

EFFECTS OF EXCHANGE RATE CHANGES ON COSTS AND PRICES

Industries that compete with foreign producers or rely on imported inputs in production can be noticeably affected by exchange rate fluctuations. Changing exchange rates influence the international competitiveness of a nation's industries through their influence on relative costs. How do exchange rate fluctuations affect relative costs? The answer depends on the extent to which a firm's costs are denominated in terms of the home currency or foreign currency.

427

Case 1: No Foreign Sourcing—All Costs Are Denominated in Dollars

Table 14.1 illustrates the hypothetical production costs of Nucor, a U.S. steel manufacturer. Assume that in its production of steel, Nucor uses U.S. labor, coal, iron, and other inputs whose costs are denominated in dollars. In period 1, the exchange value of the dollar is assumed to be $0.50 per Swiss franc (2 francs per dollar). Assume that the firm's cost of producing a ton of steel is $500, which is equivalent to 1,000 francs at this exchange rate.

Suppose that in period 2 because of changing market conditions, the dollar's exchange value *appreciates* from $0.50 per franc to $0.25 per franc, a 100 percent appreciation (the franc depreciates from 2 to 4 francs per dollar). With the dollar appreciation, Nucor's labor, iron, coal, and other input costs remain constant in dollar terms. In terms of the franc, these costs rise from 1,000 francs to 2,000 francs per ton, a 100 percent increase. The 100 percent dollar appreciation induces a 100 percent increase in Nucor's franc-denominated production cost. The international competitiveness of Nucor is thus reduced.

This example assumes that all of a firm's inputs are acquired domestically and their costs are denominated in the domestic currency. In many industries, some of a firm's inputs are purchased in foreign markets (foreign sourcing) and these input costs are denominated in a foreign currency. What impact does a change in the home currency's exchange value have on a firm's costs in this situation?

Case 2: Foreign Sourcing—Some Costs Denominated in Dollars and Some Costs Denominated in Francs

Table 14.2 again illustrates the hypothetical production costs of Nucor whose costs of labor, iron, coal, and certain other inputs are assumed to be denominated in dollars. Suppose Nucor acquires scrap iron from Swiss suppliers (foreign sourcing) and these costs are denominated in francs. Once again, assume the dollar's exchange value appreciates from $0.50 per franc to $0.25 per franc. As before, the cost in francs of Nucor's labor, iron, coal, and certain other inputs rise by 100 percent following the dollar appreciation; however, the franc cost of scrap iron remains constant. As can be seen in the table, Nucor's franc cost per ton of steel rises from 1,000 francs to 1,640 francs—an increase of only 64 percent. Thus, the dollar appreciation worsens Nucor's international competitiveness, but not as much as in the previous example.

TABLE 14.1

Effects of a Dollar Appreciation on a U.S. Steel Firm's Production Costs When All Costs are Dollar-Denominated

| | COST OF PRODUCING A TON OF STEEL | | | |
| | PERIOD 1 $0.50 PER FRANC (2 FRANCS = $1) | | PERIOD 2 $0.25 PER FRANC (4 FRANCS = $1) | |
	Dollar Cost	**Franc Equivalent**	**Dollar Cost**	**Franc Equivalent**
Labor	$160	320 francs	$160	640 francs
Materials (iron/coal)	300	600	300	1,200
Other costs (energy)	40	80	40	160
Total	$500	1,000 francs	$500	2,000 francs
Percentage change	—	—	—	100 %

© Cengage Learning®

TABLE 14.2

Effects of a Dollar Appreciation on a U.S. Steel Firm's Production Costs When Some Costs are Dollar Denominated and Other Costs are Franc Denominated

	COST OF PRODUCING A TON OF STEEL			
	PERIOD 1 $0.50 PER FRANC (2 FRANCS = $1)		PERIOD 2 $0.25 PER FRANC (4 FRANCS = $1)	
	Dollar Cost	Franc Equivalent	Dollar Cost	Franc Equivalent
Labor	$160	320 francs	$160	640 francs
Materials $ denominated (iron/coal)	120	240	120	480
Franc denominated (scrap iron)	180	360	90	360
Total	300	600	210	840
Other costs (energy)	40	80	40	160
Total cost	$500	1,000 francs	$410	1,640 francs
Percentage change	—	—	–18%	+64%

© Cengage Learning®

In addition to influencing Nucor's franc-denominated cost of steel, a dollar appreciation affects a firm's dollar cost when franc-denominated inputs are involved. Because scrap iron costs are denominated in francs, they remain at 360 francs after the dollar appreciation; the dollar-equivalent scrap iron cost falls from $180 to $90. Because the costs of Nucor's other inputs are denominated in dollars and do not change following the dollar appreciation, the firm's total dollar cost falls from $500 to $410 per ton—a decrease of 18 percent. This cost reduction offsets some of the cost disadvantage that Nucor incurs relative to Swiss exporters as a result of the dollar appreciation (franc depreciation).

The preceding examples suggest the following generalization: as franc-denominated costs become a larger portion of Nucor's total costs, a dollar appreciation (depreciation) leads to a smaller increase (decrease) in the franc cost of Nucor steel and a larger decrease (increase) in the dollar cost of Nucor steel compared to the cost changes that occur when all input costs are dollar-denominated. As franc-denominated costs become a smaller portion of total costs, the opposite conclusions apply. These conclusions have been especially significant for the world trading system during the 1980s to 2000s as industries—for example, autos and computers—have become increasingly internationalized and use increasing amounts of imported inputs in the production process.

Changes in relative costs because of exchange rate fluctuations also influence relative prices and the volume of goods traded among nations. By increasing U.S. production costs, a dollar *appreciation* tends to *raise* U.S. export prices in foreign currency terms that induce a decrease in the quantity of U.S. goods sold abroad; similarly, the dollar appreciation leads to an increase in U.S. imports. By decreasing U.S. production costs, dollar *depreciation* tends to *lower* U.S. export prices in foreign currency terms that induce an increase in the quantity of U.S. goods sold abroad; similarly, the dollar depreciation leads to a decrease in U.S. imports.

Several factors govern the extent by which exchange rate movements lead to relative price changes among nations. Some U.S. exporters may be able to offset the price increasing effects of an appreciation in the dollar's exchange value by reducing profit margins to maintain competitiveness. Perceptions concerning long-term trends in exchange rates also promote price rigidity: U.S. exporters may be less willing to raise prices if the dollar's appreciation is viewed as temporary. The extent that industries implement pricing strategies depends significantly on the substitutability of their product: the greater the degree of product differentiation (as in quality or service) the greater control producers can exercise over prices; the pricing policies of such producers are somewhat insulated from exchange rate movements.

Is there any way that companies can offset the impact of currency swings on their competitiveness? Suppose the exchange value of the Japanese yen appreciates against other currencies that cause Japanese goods to become less competitive in world markets. To insulate themselves from the squeeze on profits caused by the rising yen, Japanese companies could move production to affiliates located in countries whose currencies have depreciated against the yen. This strategy would be most likely to occur if the yen's appreciation is sizable and is regarded as being permanent. Even if the yen's appreciation is not permanent, shifting production offshore can reduce the uncertainties associated with currency swings. Japanese companies have resorted to offshore production to protect themselves from an appreciating yen.

COST CUTTING STRATEGIES OF MANUFACTURERS IN RESPONSE TO CURRENCY APPRECIATION

For years manufacturers have watched with dismay as the home currency surges to new heights, making it harder for them to wring profits out of exports. This situation tests their ingenuity to become more efficient in order to remain competitive on world markets. Let us consider how Japanese and American manufacturers responded to appreciations of their home currencies.

Appreciation of the Yen: Japanese Manufacturers

From 1990 to 1996, the value of the Japanese yen relative to the U.S. dollar increased by almost 40 percent. In other words, if the yen and dollar prices in the two nations had remained unchanged, Japanese products in 1996 would have been roughly 40 percent more expensive, compared with U.S. products, than they were in 1990. How did Japanese manufacturers respond to a development that could have had disastrous consequences for their competitiveness in world markets?

Japanese firms remained competitive by using the yen's strength to cheaply establish integrated manufacturing bases in the United States and in dollar-linked Asia. This strategy allowed Japanese firms to play both sides of the fluctuations in the yen/dollar exchange rate: using cheaper dollar denominated parts and materials to offset higher yen related costs. While they maintained their U.S. markets, many Japanese companies also used the strong yen to purchase cheaper components from around the world and ship them home for assembly. That action provided a competitive edge in Japan for these firms.

Consider the Japanese electronics manufacturer Hitachi whose TV sets were a global production effort in the mid-1990s, as shown in Figure 14.1. The small tubes that projected information onto Hitachi TV screens came from a subsidiary in South Carolina, while the TV chassis and circuitry were manufactured by an affiliate in Malaysia. From Japan came only computer chips and lenses that amounted to 30 percent of the value of the parts used. By sourcing TV production in countries whose currencies had fallen against the yen, Hitachi was able to hold down the dollar price of its TV sets despite the rising yen.

FIGURE 14.1

How Hitachi Coped with the Yen's Appreciation

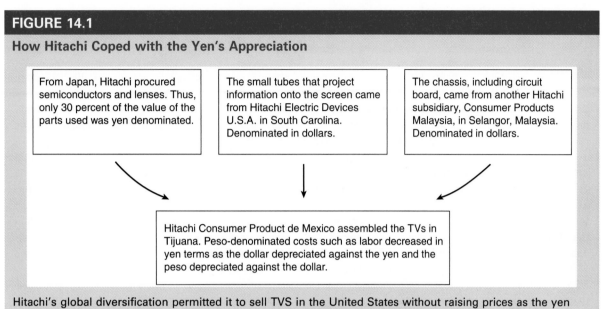

From Japan, Hitachi procured semiconductors and lenses. Thus, only 30 percent of the value of the parts used was yen denominated.

The small tubes that project information onto the screen came from Hitachi Electric Devices U.S.A. in South Carolina. Denominated in dollars.

The chassis, including circuit board, came from another Hitachi subsidiary, Consumer Products Malaysia, in Selangor, Malaysia. Denominated in dollars.

Hitachi Consumer Product de Mexico assembled the TVs in Tijuana. Peso-denominated costs such as labor decreased in yen terms as the dollar depreciated against the yen and the peso depreciated against the dollar.

Hitachi's global diversification permitted it to sell TVS in the United States without raising prices as the yen appreciated against the dollar.

To limit their vulnerability to a rising yen, Japanese exporters also shifted production from commodity type goods to high value products. The demand for commodities—for example, metals and textiles—is quite sensitive to price changes because these goods are largely indistinguishable except by price. Customers could easily switch to non-Japanese suppliers if an increase in the yen shoved the dollar price of Japanese exports higher. In contrast, more sophisticated, high value products—such as transportation equipment and electrical machinery—are less sensitive to price increases. For these goods, factors such as embedded advanced technology and high quality standards work to neutralize the effect on demand if prices are driven up by an appreciating yen. Shifting production from commodity type products to high value products from 1990 to 1996 enhanced the competitiveness of Japanese firms.

Consider the Japanese auto industry. To offset the rising yen, Japanese automakers cut the yen prices of their autos and thus realized falling unit-profit margins. They also reduced manufacturing costs by increasing worker productivity, importing materials and parts whose prices were denominated in currencies that had depreciated against the yen, and outsourcing larger amounts of a vehicle's production to transplant factories in countries whose currencies had depreciated against the yen.

In 1994, Toyota Motor Corporation announced that its competitiveness had been eroded by as much as 20 percent as a result of the yen's appreciation. Toyota therefore convinced its subcontractors to cut part prices by 15 percent over three years. By using common parts in various vehicles and shortening the time needed to design, test, and commercialize automobiles, Toyota was also able to cut costs. Moreover, Toyota pressured Japanese steelmakers to produce less costly galvanized sheet steel for use in its vehicles. Toyota reintroduced less expensive models with fewer options in an effort to reduce costs and prices and thus recapture sales in the midsize family car segment of the market.

Foreign made parts, once rejected by Japanese automakers as inferior to domestically produced parts, became much less alien to them in the 1990s. Foreign parts steadily made their way into Japanese autos, helped by both the strong yen and Japanese

TRADE CONFLICTS JAPANESE FIRMS SEND WORK ABROAD AS RISING YEN MAKES THEIR PRODUCTS LESS COMPETITIVE

Facing an appreciating yen in recent years, Japanese exporters have realized that it makes their goods more costly and less competitive in foreign markets. How can they protect their profits? By moving production to the United States and other nations and decreasing the amount of money they convert from dollars to yen.

During 2010–2011 Japanese businesses ranging from auto makers to electronics companies were transferring more of their manufacturing abroad, because the appreciating yen fostered a major restructuring of Japan's economy. Toyota Motor Corp. produced about 57 percent of its output abroad during this period, up from 48 percent in 2005. The world's leading auto manufacturer said it would begin producing its popular Prius at a plant near Bangkok, making it the first time its flagship hybrid would be mass produced outside Japan. Also, rival Nissan Motor Co. manufactured

about 71 percent of its cars abroad in 2010–2011, compared with 66 percent in 2009. Japanese business leaders said their companies had to adapt to the rising yen by sourcing more and more products outside Japan in order to compete.

Moving production to the United States and other countries can help Japanese producers escape much of the dollar/yen problem and sell their products to foreigners. This production move contributes to the excess capacity of manufacturing plants in Japan and results in job losses for Japanese workers. A continually strong yen can promote a hollowing out of Japan's economy as some have feared.

Source: "Japan Firms Send Work Overseas," *The Wall Street Journal*, October 25, 2010, p. B1 and "Japanese Firms Practice Yen Damage Control," *The Wall Street Journal*, September 26, 2003, p. A7, Mike Ramsey and Neal Boudette, "Honda Revs Up Outside Japan," *The Wall Street Journal*, December 21, 2011, p. A1.

automakers' urgency to slash costs. Moreover, Japanese auto parts makers set up manufacturing operations in Southeast Asia and South America to cut costs; these parts were then exported to Japan for assembly into autos.

Appreciation of the Dollar: U.S. Manufacturers

From 1996 to 2002, U.S. manufacturers were alarmed as the dollar appreciated by 22 percent on average against the currencies of major U.S. trading partners. This appreciation resulted in U.S. manufacturers seeking ways to tap overseas markets and defend their home turf.

Consider American Feed Co., a Napoleon, Ohio company that makes machinery used in auto plants. In 2001, the firm reached a deal with a similar manufacturing company in Spain. Both companies produce machines that car factories use to unroll giant coils of steel and feed them through presses to make parts. According to the pact, when orders come in, management of the two companies meet to decide which plant should make which parts, in essence dividing the work to keep both factories operating. As a result, American Feed can share in the benefits of having a European production base without having to take on the risks of building its own factory there. The company redesigned its machines to make them more efficient and less expensive to build. These efforts cut about 20 percent off the machines' production costs.

Sipco Molding Technologies, a Meadville, Pennsylvania tool and die maker also had to cut costs to survive the dollar's appreciation. For years, Sipco had a partnership with an Austrian company that designed a special line of tools that Sipco once built in the United States. Because of the strong dollar, the Austrian company assumed the responsibility of designing and making the tools while Sipco simply resold them. Although these efforts helped the firm cut costs, it resulted in a loss of jobs for 30 percent of its employees.

WILL CURRENCY DEPRECIATION REDUCE A TRADE DEFICIT? THE ELASTICITY APPROACH

We have seen that currency depreciation tends to improve a nation's competitiveness by reducing its costs and prices while currency appreciation implies the opposite. Under what circumstances will currency depreciation reduce a trade deficit?

Several aspects of currency depreciation must be considered and each of them will be dealt with in a separate section. The **elasticity approach** emphasizes the relative *price effects* of depreciation and suggests that depreciation works best when demand elasticity is high. The **absorption approach** deals with the *income effects* of depreciation; the implication is that a decrease in domestic expenditure relative to income must occur for depreciation to promote trade equilibrium. The **monetary approach** stresses the effects depreciation has on the *purchasing power of money* and the resulting impact on domestic expenditure levels. Let us begin by considering the elasticity approach.

Currency depreciation affects a country's balance of trade through changes in the relative prices of goods and services internationally. A trade deficit nation may be able to reverse its imbalance by lowering its relative prices, so that exports increase and imports decrease. The nation can lower its relative prices by permitting its exchange rate to depreciate in a free market or by formally devaluing its currency under a system of fixed exchange rates. The ultimate outcome of currency depreciation depends on the price elasticity of demand for a nation's imports and the price elasticity of demand for its exports.

Recall that *elasticity of demand* refers to the responsiveness of buyers to changes in price. Elasticity indicates the percentage change in the quantity demanded stemming from a one percent change in price. Mathematically, elasticity is the ratio of the percentage change in the quantity demanded to the percentage change in price. This ratio can be symbolized as follows:

$$\text{Elasticity} = (\Delta Q/Q) \div (\Delta P/P)$$

The elasticity coefficient is stated numerically without regard to the algebraic sign. If the preceding ratio exceeds 1, a given percentage change in price results in a larger percentage change in quantity demanded; this is referred to as *elastic* demand. If the ratio is less than 1, demand is said to be *inelastic* because the percentage change in quantity demanded is less than the percentage change in price. A ratio precisely equal to 1 denotes *unitary elastic* demand, meaning the percentage change in quantity demanded just matches the percentage change in price.

Next, we investigate the effects of currency depreciation on a nation's balance of trade–that is, the value of its exports minus imports. Suppose the UK pound depreciates by ten percent against the dollar. Whether the UK trade balance will be improved depends on what happens to the dollar in payments for the United Kingdom's exports as opposed to the dollar outpayments for its imports. This balance depends whether the U.S. demand for UK exports is elastic or inelastic and whether the UK demand for imports is elastic or inelastic.

Depending on the size of the demand, elasticities for UK exports and imports, the United Kingdom's trade balance may improve, worsen, or remain unchanged in response to the pound depreciation. The general rule that determines the actual outcome is the so called **Marshall–Lerner condition**. The Marshall–Lerner condition states: (1) Depreciation will *improve* the trade balance if the currency depreciating nation's demand elasticity for imports plus the foreign demand elasticity for the nation's exports exceeds 1.0. (2) If the sum of the demand elasticities is less than 1.0, depreciation will *worsen* the trade balance. (3) The trade balance will be *neither helped nor hurt* if the sum of the demand elasticities equals 1.0. The Marshall–Lerner condition may be stated in terms of the currency of either the nation undergoing depreciation or its trading partner. Our discussion is confined to the currency of the currency depreciating country, the United Kingdom.

Case 1: Improved trade balance   Table 14.3 illustrates the effect of a depreciation of the pound on the UK trade balance. Referring to Table 14.3(*a*), assume the UK demand elasticity for imports equals 2.5 and the U.S. demand elasticity for UK exports equals 1.5; the sum of the elasticities is 4.0. Suppose the pound depreciates by ten percent against the dollar. An assessment of the overall impact of the depreciation on the United Kingdom's payments position requires identification of the depreciation's impact on import expenditures and export receipts.

If prices of imports remain constant in terms of foreign currency, then depreciation increases the home currency price of goods imported. Because of the depreciation, the pound price of UK imports rises ten percent. UK consumers would be expected to reduce their purchases from abroad. Given an import demand elasticity of 2.5, the depreciation triggers a 25 percent decline in the quantity of imports demanded. The ten percent price increase in conjunction with a 25 percent quantity reduction results in approximately a fifteen percent decrease in UK out payments in pounds. This cutback in import purchases actually reduces import expenditures that reduce the UK deficit.

How about UK export receipts? The pound price of the exports remains constant but after depreciation of the pound, consumers in the United States find UK exports costing ten percent less in terms of dollars. Given a U.S. demand elasticity of 1.5 for UK exports, the ten percent UK depreciation will stimulate foreign sales by fifteen percent so that export receipts in pounds will increase by approximately fifteen percent. This increase strengthens the UK payments position. The fifteen percent reduction in import expenditures coupled with a fifteen percent rise in export receipts means that the pound depreciation will reduce the UK payments deficit. *With the sum of the elasticities exceeding 1, the depreciation strengthens the United Kingdom's trade position.*

TABLE 14.3

Effect of Pound Depreciation on the Trade Balance of the United Kingdom

(A) IMPROVED TRADE BALANCE

Sector	Pound Price (%)	Quantity Demanded (%)	Net Effect (in pounds)
Import	+10	−25	−15% outpayments
Export	0	+15	+15% inpayments

Assumptions:

UK demand elasticity for imports = 2.5

Demand elasticity for UK exports = 1.5 sum = 4.0

Pound depreciation = 10%

(B) WORSENED TRADE BALANCE

Sector	Change in Pound Price (%)	Change in Quantity Demanded (%)	Net Effect (in pounds)
Import	+10	−2	+8% outpayments
Export	0	+1	+1% inpayments

Assumptions:

UK demand elasticity for imports = 0.2

Demand elasticity for UK exports = 0.1 sum = 0.3

Pound depreciation = 10%

Case 2: Worsened trade balance   In Table 14.3(*b*), the UK demand elasticity for imports is 0.2 and the U.S. demand elasticity for UK exports is 0.1; the sum of the elasticities is 0.3. The ten percent pound depreciation raises the pound price of imports by ten percent, inducing a two percent reduction in the quantity of imports demanded. In contrast to the previous case, under relatively inelastic conditions the depreciation contributes to an *increase* rather than a decrease, in import expenditures of eight percent. As before, the pound price of UK exports is unaffected by the depreciation, whereas the dollar price of exports falls ten percent. American purchases from abroad increase by one percent, resulting in an increase in pound receipts of about one percent. With expenditures on imports rising eight percent while export receipts increase only one percent, the UK deficit will tend to *worsen*. As stated in the Marshall–Lerner condition, *if the sum of the elasticities is less than 1.0, currency depreciation will cause deterioration in a nation's trade position.* The reader is left to verify that a nation's trade balance remains unaffected by depreciation if the sum of the demand elasticities equals 1.0.

Although the Marshall–Lerner condition provides a general rule as to when currency depreciation will be successful in restoring payments equilibrium, it depends on some simplifying assumptions. For one, it is assumed a nation's trade balance is in equilibrium when the depreciation occurs. If there is initially a large trade deficit with imports exceeding exports, then a depreciation might cause import expenditures to change more than export receipts, even though the sum of the demand elasticities exceeds 1.0. The analysis also assumes no change in the sellers' prices in their own currency. This may not always be true. To protect their competitive position, foreign sellers may lower their prices in response to a depreciation of the home country's currency; domestic sellers may raise home currency prices so the depreciation effects are not fully transmitted into lower foreign exchange prices for their goods. Neither of these assumptions invalidates the Marshall–Lerner condition's spirit that suggests currency depreciations work best when demand elasticities are high.

The Marshall–Lerner condition illustrates the price effects of currency depreciation on the home country's trade balance. The extent that price changes affect the volume of goods traded depends on the elasticity of demand for imports and exports. If the elasticities were known in advance, it would be possible to determine the proper exchange rate policy to restore payments equilibrium. Table 14.4 shows estimated price elasticities of demand for total imports and exports by country.

TABLE 14.4

Long Run Price Elasticities of Demand for Total Imports and Exports of Selected Countries

Country	Import Price Elasticity	Export Price Elasticity	Sum of Import and Export Elasticities
Canada	0.9	0.9	1.8
France	0.4	0.2	0.6
Germany	0.1	0.3	0.4
Italy	0.4	0.9	1.3
Japan	0.3	0.1	0.4
United Kingdom	0.6	1.6	1.2
United States	0.3	1.5	1.8

Source: From Peter Hooper, Karen Johnson, and Jaime Marquez, "Trade Elasticities for the G-7 Countries," *Princeton Studies in International Economics*, No. 87, August 2000, p. 9.

J–CURVE EFFECT: TIME PATH OF DEPRECIATION

Empirical estimates of price elasticities in international trade suggest that according to the Marshall–Lerner condition, currency depreciation will often improve a nation's trade balance. However, a problem in measuring world price elasticities is there tends to be a *time lag* between changes in exchange rates and their ultimate effect on real trade. One popular description of the time path of trade flows is the so called **J–curve effect**. This view suggests that in the short run, currency depreciation will lead to a worsening of a nation's trade balance. As time passes, the trade balance will likely improve. This is because it takes time for new information about the price effects of depreciation to be disseminated throughout the economy and for economic units to adjust their behavior accordingly.

Currency depreciation affects a nation's trade balance through its net impact on export receipts and import expenditures. Export receipts and import expenditures are calculated by multiplying the commodity's per-unit price times the quantity being demanded. Figure 14.2 illustrates the process that depreciation influences export receipts and import expenditures.

The immediate effect of depreciation is a change in relative prices. If a nation's currency depreciates ten percent, it means import prices initially increase ten percent in terms of the home currency. The quantity of imports demanded will then fall according to home demand elasticities. At the same time, exporters will initially receive ten percent more in home currency for each unit of foreign currency they earn. This means they can become more competitive and lower their export prices measured in terms of foreign currencies. Export sales will then rise in accordance with foreign demand elasticities. The problem with this process is that for depreciation to take effect, time is required for the pricing mechanism to induce changes in the volume of exports and imports.

The time path of the response of trade flows to a currency's depreciation can be described in terms of the J–curve effect, so called because the trade balance continues to get worse for awhile after depreciation (sliding down the hook of the J) and then gets better (moving up the stem of the J). This effect occurs because the initial effect of

FIGURE 14.2

Depreciation Flowchart

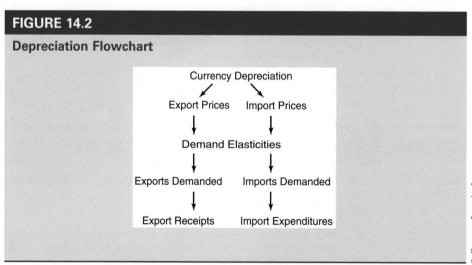

depreciation is an increase in import expenditures: the home currency price of imports has risen, but the volume is unchanged owing to prior commitments. As time passes, the quantity adjustment effect becomes relevant: import volume is depressed whereas exports become more attractive to foreign buyers.

Advocates of the J–curve effect cite the experience of the U.S. balance of trade during the 1980s and 1990s. As seen in Figure 14.3, between 1980 and 1987 the U.S. trade deficit expanded at a rapid rate. The deficit decreased substantially between 1988 and 1991. The rapid increase in the trade deficit that took place during the early 1980s occurred mainly because of the appreciation of the dollar at the time t resulted in a steady increase in imports and a drop in U.S. exports. The depreciation of the dollar that began in 1985 led to a boom in exports in 1988 and a drop in the trade deficit through 1991.

What factors might explain the time lags in a currency depreciation adjustment process? The types of lags that may occur between changes in relative prices and the quantities of goods traded include the following:

- *Recognition lags* of changing competitive conditions
- *Decision lags* in forming new business connections and placing new orders
- *Delivery lags* between the time new orders are placed and their impact on trade and payment flows is felt

FIGURE 14.3

Time Path of U.S. Balance of Trade in Billions of Dollars, in Response to Dollar Appreciation and Depreciation

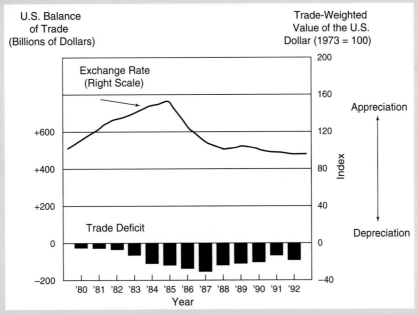

Between 1980 and 1987, the U.S. merchandise trade deficit expanded at a rapid rate. The trade deficit decreased substantially between 1988 and 1991. The rapid increase in the trade deficit that took place during the early 1980s occurred mainly because of the appreciation of the dollar at the time that resulted in a steady increase in imports and a drop in U.S. exports. The depreciation of the dollar that began in 1985 led to a boom in exports in 1988 and a drop in the trade deficit through 1991.

- *Replacement lags* in using up inventories and wearing out existing machinery before placing new orders
- *Production lags* involved in increasing the output of commodities for which demand has increased

Empirical evidence suggests that the trade balance effects of currency depreciation do not materialize until years afterward. Adjustment lags may be four years or more, although the major portion of adjustment takes place in about two years.[1]

EXCHANGE RATE PASS-THROUGH

The J–curve analysis assumes that a given change in the exchange rate brings about a proportionate change in import prices. In practice, this relation may be less than proportionate; weakening the influence of a change in the exchange rate on the volume of trade.

The extent to which changing currency values lead to changes in import and export prices is known as **exchange rate pass-through**. Pass-through is important because buyers have incentives to alter their purchases of foreign goods only to the extent that the prices of these goods change in terms of their domestic currency following a change in the exchange rate. This change depends in part on the willingness of exporters to permit the change in the exchange rate to affect the prices they charge for their goods measured in terms of the buyer's currency.

Assume Toyota of Japan exports autos to the United States and the prices of Toyota are fixed in terms of the yen. Suppose the dollar's value depreciates ten percent relative to the yen. Assuming no offsetting actions by Toyota, U.S. import prices will rise ten percent because ten percent more dollars are needed to purchase the yen than are used to pay for the import purchases. Complete pass-through thus exists: import prices in dollars rise by the full proportion of the dollar depreciation.

To illustrate the calculation of complete currency pass-through, assume that Caterpillar charges $50,000 for a tractor exported to Japan. If the exchange rate is 150 yen per U.S. dollar, the price paid by the Japanese buyer will be 7,500,000 yen. Assuming the dollar price of the tractor remains constant, a ten percent appreciation in the dollar's exchange value will increase the tractor's yen price ten percent, to 8,250,000 yen ($165 \times 50,000 = 8,250,000$). Conversely, if the dollar depreciates by ten percent, the yen price of the tractor will fall by ten percent, to 6,750,000 yen. So long as Caterpillar keeps the dollar price of its tractor constant, changes in the dollar's exchange rate will be fully reflected in changes in the foreign currency price of exports. The ratio of changes in the foreign currency price to changes in the exchange rate will be 100 percent, implying complete currency pass-through.

Partial Exchange Rate Pass-Through

Although complete exchange rate pass-through is a possibility, in practice the relation tends to be partial. Table 14.5 presents estimates of average exchange rate pass-through rates for the United States and other advanced countries over the 1975–2003 period. The exchange rate pass-through for the United States over this period was 0.42. This rate means that a 1 percent change in the dollar's exchange rate produced a 0.42 percent change in U.S. import prices. Because the percentage change in import prices was less

---

[1]Helen Junz and Rudolf R. Rhomberg, "Price Competitiveness in Export Trade among Industrial Countries," *American Economic Review*, May 1973, pp. 412–419.

TABLE 14.5

Exchange Rate Pass-Through into Import Prices after One Year

Country	Pass Through Rate (For every 1 percent a currency depreciates/ appreciates the price of imports for the country increases/decreases by)*
OECD** average	0.64%
United States	0.42
Euro area	0.81
Japan	0.57–1.0
Other advanced countries	0.60

*Estimates are based on data from 1973 to 2003.

**The organization for Economic Cooperation and Development consists of Australia, Austria, Belgium, Canada, Czech Republic, Denmark, Finland, France, Germany, Greece, Hungary, Iceland, Ireland, Italy, Republic of Korea, Japan, Luxembourg, Mexico, the Netherlands, New Zealand, Norway, Poland, Portugal, Spain, Sweden, Switzerland, Turkey, the UK, and the United States.

Source: Jose Campa and Linda Goldberg, "Exchange Rate Pass-Through Into Import Prices," *Review of Economics and Statistics*, November 2005, pp. 984–985 and Hamid Faruquee, "Exchange Rate Pass-Through in the Euro Area," *IMF Staff Papers*, April 2006, pp. 63–88.

than the percentage change in the exchange rate, exchange rate pass-through was "partial" for the United States. Similar conclusions apply to other countries included in the table. When exchange rate pass-through is partial at home and abroad, the effect of changes in the exchange rate on trade volume is lessened, as it forestalls movement in relative trade prices.

Why does exchange rate pass-through tend to be partial? The answer appears to lie in invoicing practices, market share considerations, and distribution costs.[2]

Invoice Practices Businesses involved in international trade can select the currency they want to use to express the price of their exports. They can invoice their exports in their own home currency or in the currency of their customers. Evidence on import and export invoicing in recent years reveals that the dollar is the dominant currency of invoicing across non-European countries, as shown in Table 14.6. For example, 93 percent of U.S. imports and 99 percent of U.S. exports were priced in dollars during the first decade of the 2000s.

The dominant use of dollars in invoicing U.S. trade helps explain the partial pass-through of changes in the dollar's exchange rate to U.S. import prices. When foreign producers invoice their exports to the United States in dollars, the price of these goods remains fixed in terms of the dollar if the dollar depreciates against other currencies. The exchange rate movements affect only the foreign producers' profits and will not increase the dollar price paid by U.S. importers. After a time foreign producers may choose to adjust their prices in response to the exchange rate.

Market Share Considerations Another factor that contributes to partial exchange rate pass-through for a period following a dollar depreciation is the desire of foreign producers to preserve market share for goods sold in the United States. In practice, many goods and services are produced in imperfectly competitive markets. In terms of prices for these goods, firms are able to make a profit margin over costs. Firms may choose not to pass on the full change in costs brought about by changing exchange rates and instead

---

[2]This section is drawn from Linda Goldberg and Elanor Wiske Dillon, "Why a Dollar Depreciation May Not Close the U.S. Trade Deficit," *Current Issues in Economics and Finance*, Federal Reserve Bank of New York, June 2007.

TABLE 14.6

Use of the U.S. Dollar in Export and Import Invoicing, 2002–2004

Country	Dollar Share in Export Financing	Dollar Share in Import Financing	U.S. Share in Exports
United States	99.8%	92.8%	—
Japan	48.0	68.7	24.8
South Korea	83.2	79.6	17.0
Malaysia	90.0	90.0	20.5
Thailand	84.4	76.0	17.0
Australia	69.6	50.5	8.1
United Kingdom	26.0	37.0	15.5
Euro area	30.4	38.0	14.2
EU Accession countries*	17.5	23.9	3.2

*Bulgaria, Czech Republic, Estonia, Hungary, and Poland.

Source: Linda Goldberg and Cedric Tille, "The International Role of the Dollar and Trade Balance Adjustment." *The Group of Thirty Occasional Paper No. 71*, 2006 and Annette Kamps, "The Determinants of Currency Invoicing in International Trade," *European Central Bank Working Paper No. 665*, August 2006.

elect to change their profit margins, thus reducing the sensitivity of consumer prices to the exchange rate. Exporters to the United States may accept a lower profit margin when their currency appreciates in order to keep their dollar prices constant against American competitors. This is especially pertinent for the United States that has a large market and where imports command a lower share of consumption than they do in smaller markets. Because American consumers can generally substitute domestic goods for imports, foreign exporters are reluctant to pass all of the exchange rate movement into prices because of fear of losing market share. Relatively strong domestic competition for imported goods in the United States tends to lessen the extent of exchange rate pass-through into import prices.

Kellwood Co., a major U.S. marketer of garments such as Calvin Klein, noted that some of its Asian suppliers such as sewing factories and fabric mills inquired about increasing their prices as the dollar depreciated against their currencies in the first decade of the 2000s. These suppliers knew that if they increased their prices, Kellwood could purchase inputs from other competing suppliers. To maintain Kellwood as a customer, these suppliers cut their profit margins and refrained from raising their prices, allowing Kellwood's prices on Calvin Klein garments to remain unchanged.

Distribution Costs Thus far we have considered the transmission of exchange rates into the prices of imports arriving at a country's borders. However, other costs occur between the time a good arrives at the border and the time it is sold to the consumer. These are the distribution costs of the imported good to the final consumer that include transportation, marketing, wholesaling, and retailing costs. In 1996, a Barbie doll shipped from China to the United States cost $2, and it sold for $10. The manufacturer, Mattel, earned about $1 profit on this doll. The remaining $7 represented payments for transportation in the United States and other marketing and distribution costs. For the United States, distribution costs average about 40 percent of overall U.S. consumer prices.[3] Because domestic distribution services are not traded internationally their costs are not affected by fluctuations in the dollar's exchange rate. As distribution costs become a large

---

[3]Sidney S. Alexander, "Effects of a Devaluation on a Trade Balance," *IMF Staff Papers*, April 1952, pp. 263–278.

TRADE CONFLICTS DOES CURRENCY DEPRECIATION GIVE WEAK COUNTRIES A WAY OUT OF CRISIS?

Does currency depreciation give a deficit country with chronically uncompetitive businesses and inflexible labor markets a way out of its problems? In 2012 this question was raised for weak members of the eurozone, such as Greece, who pondered whether to exit this common currency system. Greece especially felt handicapped by Germany whose rising exports resulted in an appreciation of the euro, and this disrupted the prices and costs in other parts of the zone. If Greece was to drop out of the eurozone the exchange value of its new currency (the drachma) would likely undergo a sizable depreciation. Wouldn't this foster renewed competitiveness for Greek producers?

Some analysts maintain that currency depreciation can provide relief to weak countries because it results in falling export prices for their producers. Currency depreciation increases the price of imports, providing import-competing producers an edge in their home market.

However, there is a catch. Currency depreciation works to the extent that it does not result in demands by domestic workers for wage increases, even though a depreciating currency increases the price of imports. An individual worker may not realize that currency depreciation erodes the purchasing power of wages as inflation ensues. Workers belonging to powerful labor unions are generally aware of this phenomena. As a result, union contracts often include protections against inflation. To the extent that unions attain higher wages during eras of currency depreciation, the resulting wage inflation detracts from increased competitiveness caused by depreciation. Currency depreciation provides no simple solution for a country's lack of competitiveness.

iStockphoto.com/photosoup

percentage of the consumer price, the sensitivity of the consumer price to exchange rate fluctuations is reduced. The effects of exchange rate pass-through are more fully discussed in *Exploring Further 14.1* that can be found at www.cengage.com/economics/Carbaugh.

THE ABSORPTION APPROACH TO CURRENCY DEPRECIATION

According to the elasticities approach, currency depreciation offers a price incentive to reduce imports and increase exports. Even if elasticity conditions are favorable, whether the home country's trade balance will actually improve may depend on how the economy reacts to the depreciation. The absorption approach[4] provides insights into this question by considering the impact of depreciation on the spending behavior of the domestic economy and the influence of domestic spending on the trade balance.

The absorption approach starts with the idea that the value of total domestic output (Y) equals the level of total spending. Total spending consists of consumption (c), investment (I), government expenditures (G), and net exports ($X - M$). This relation can be written as follows:

$$Y = C + I + G + (X - M)$$

The absorption approach then consolidates $C + I + G$ into a single term A that is referred to as absorption, and designates net exports ($X - M$) as B. Total domestic output equals the sum of absorption plus net exports:

$$Y = A + B$$

---

[4]See Donald S. Kemp, "A Monetary View of the Balance-of-Payments," *Review*, Federal Reserve Bank of St. Louis, April 1975, pp. 14–22; and Thomas M. Humphrey, "The Monetary Approach to Exchange Rates: Its Historical Evolution and Role in Policy Debates," *Economic Review*, Federal Reserve Bank of Richmond, July–August 1978, pp. 2–9.

This can be rewritten as follows:

$$B = Y - A$$

This expression suggests that the balance of trade (B) equals the difference between total domestic output (Y) and the level of absorption (A). If national output exceeds domestic absorption, the economy's trade balance will be positive. Conversely, a negative trade balance suggests that an economy is spending beyond its ability to produce.

The absorption approach predicts that currency depreciation will improve an economy's trade balance only if national output rises relative to absorption. This relation means that a country must increase its total output, reduce its absorption, or do some combination of the two. The following examples illustrate these possibilities.

Assume that an economy faces *unemployment* as well as a *trade deficit*. With the economy operating below maximum capacity, the price incentives of depreciation would tend to direct idle resources into the production of goods for export, in addition to diverting spending away from imports to domestically produced substitutes. The impact of the depreciation is to expand domestic output as well as to improve the trade balance. It is no wonder that policymakers tend to view currency depreciation as an effective tool when an economy faces unemployment with a trade deficit.

However, in the case of an economy operating at *full employment*, no unutilized resources are available for additional production. National output is at a fixed level. The only way that currency depreciation can improve the trade balance is for the economy to somehow cut domestic absorption, freeing resources needed to produce additional export goods and import substitutes. Domestic policy makers could decrease absorption by adopting restrictive fiscal and monetary policies in the face of higher prices resulting from the depreciation. This decrease would result in sacrifice on the part of those who bear the burden of such measures. Currency depreciation may be considered inappropriate when an economy is operating at maximum capacity.

The absorption approach goes beyond the elasticity approach that views the economy's trade balance as distinct from the rest of the economy. Instead, currency depreciation is viewed in relation to the economy's utilization of its resources and level of production. The two approaches are complementary.

THE MONETARY APPROACH TO CURRENCY DEPRECIATION

A survey of the traditional approaches to currency depreciation reveals a major shortcoming. According to the elasticities and absorption approaches, monetary consequences are not associated with balance-of-payments adjustment; or to the extent that such consequences exist, they can be neutralized by domestic monetary authorities. The elasticities and absorption approaches apply only to the trade account of the balance-of-payments, neglecting the implications of capital movements. The *monetary approach* to depreciation addresses this shortcoming.[5] According to the monetary approach; currency depreciation may induce a *temporary* improvement in a nation's balance-of-payments position. Assume that equilibrium initially exists in the home country's money market. A depreciation of the home currency would increase the price level—that is, the domestic currency prices of potential imports and exports. This increase would increase the demand for money because larger amounts of money are needed for transactions. If that increased demand is not fulfilled

---

[5]Giovanni Olivei, "Exchange Rates and the Prices of Manufacturing Products Imported into the United States," *New England Economic Review*, First Quarter 2002, pp. 4–6.

from domestic sources, an inflow of money from overseas occurs. This inflow results in a balance-of-payments surplus and a rise in international reserves. The surplus does not last forever. By adding to the international component of the home country money supply, the currency depreciation leads to an increase in spending (absorption) that reduces the surplus. The surplus eventually disappears when equilibrium is restored in the home country's money market. The effects of depreciation on real economic variables are temporary. *Over the long run, currency depreciation merely raises the domestic price level.*

SUMMARY

1. Currency depreciation (devaluation) may affect a nation's trade position through its impact on relative prices, incomes, and the purchasing power of money balances.

2. When all of a firm's inputs are acquired domestically and their costs are denominated in the domestic currency, an appreciation in the domestic currency's exchange value tends to increase the firm's costs by the same proportion, in terms of the foreign currency. Conversely, a depreciation of the domestic currency's exchange value tends to reduce the firm's costs by the same proportion in terms of the foreign currency.

3. Manufacturers often obtain inputs from abroad (foreign sourcing) whose costs are denominated in terms of a foreign currency. As foreign currency denominated costs become a larger portion of a producer's total costs, an appreciation of the domestic currency's exchange value leads to a smaller increase in the foreign currency cost of the firm's output and a larger decrease in the domestic cost of the firm's output—compared to the cost changes that occur when all input costs are denominated in the domestic currency. The opposite applies for currency depreciation.

4. By increasing (decreasing) relative U.S. production costs, a dollar appreciation (depreciation) tends to raise (lower) U.S. export prices in terms of a foreign currency that induces a decrease (increase) in the quantity of U.S. goods sold abroad; similarly, a dollar appreciation (depreciation) tends to raise (lower) the amount of U.S. imports.

5. According to the elasticities approach, currency depreciation leads to the greatest improvement in a country's trade position when demand elasticities are high. Recent empirical studies indicate that the

estimated demand elasticities for most nations are quite high.

6. The time path of currency depreciation can be explained in terms of the J–curve effect. According to this concept, the response of trade flows to changes in relative prices increases with the passage of time. Currency depreciation tends to worsen a country's trade balance in the short run, only to be followed by an improvement in the long run (assuming favorable elasticities).

7. The extent that exchange rate changes lead to changes in import prices and export prices is known as the pass-through relation. Complete (partial) pass-through occurs when a change in the exchange rate brings about a proportionate (less than proportionate) change in export prices and import prices. Empirical evidence suggests that pass-through tends to be partial rather than complete. Partial pass-through is explained by currency invoicing, market share strategies, and sizable distribution costs.

8. The absorption approach emphasizes the income effects of currency depreciation. According to this view, a depreciation may initially stimulate a nation's exports and production of import-competing goods. But this stimulus will promote excess domestic spending unless real output can be expanded or domestic absorption reduced. The result would be a return to a payments deficit.

9. The monetary approach to depreciation emphasizes the effect that depreciation has on the purchasing power of money balances and the resulting impacts on domestic expenditures and import levels. According to the monetary approach, the influence of currency depreciation on real output is temporary; over the long run, depreciation merely raises the domestic price level.

KEY CONCEPTS AND TERMS

Absorption approach (p. 433)

Elasticity approach (p. 433)

Exchange rate pass-through (p. 438)

J–curve effect (p. 436)

Marshall–Lerner condition (p. 433)

Monetary approach (p. 433)

STUDY QUESTIONS

1. How does a currency depreciation affect a nation's balance of trade?

2. Three major approaches to analyzing the economic impact of currency depreciation are (a) the elasticities approach, (b) the absorption approach, and (c) the monetary approach. Distinguish among the three.

3. What is meant by the Marshall–Lerner condition? Do recent empirical studies suggest that world elasticity conditions are sufficiently high to permit successful depreciations?

4. How does the J–curve effect relate to the time path of currency depreciation?

5. What implications does currency pass-through have for a nation whose currency depreciates?

6. According to the absorption approach, does it make any difference whether a nation's currency depreciates when the economy is operating at less than full capacity versus at full capacity?

7. How can currency depreciation induced changes in household money balances promote payments equilibrium?

8. Suppose ABC Inc., a U.S. auto manufacturer, obtains all of its auto components in the United States and that its costs are denominated in dollars. Assume the dollar's exchange value appreciates by 50 percent against the Mexican peso. What impact does the dollar appreciation have on the firm's international competitiveness? What about a dollar depreciation?

9. Suppose ABC Inc., a U.S. auto manufacturer, obtains some of its auto components in Mexico and that the costs of these components are denominated in pesos; the costs of the remaining components are denominated in dollars. Assume the dollar's exchange value appreciates by 50 percent against the peso. Compared to your answer in study question 8, what impact will the dollar appreciation have on the firm's international competitiveness? What about a dollar depreciation?

10. Assume the United States exports 1,000 computers costing $3,000 each and imports 150 UK autos at a price of £10,000 each. Assume that the dollar/pound exchange rate is $2 per pound.

    a. Calculate in dollar terms, the U.S. export receipts, import payments, and trade balance prior to a depreciation of the dollar's exchange value.

    b. Suppose the dollar's exchange value depreciates by 10 percent. Assuming that the price elasticity of demand for U.S. exports equals 3.0 and the price elasticity of demand for U.S. imports equals 2.0, does the dollar depreciation improve or worsen the U.S. trade balance? Why?

    c. Now assume that the price elasticity of demand for U.S. exports equals 0.3 and the price elasticity of demand for U.S. imports equals 0.2. Does this change the outcome? Why?

EXPLORING FURTHER

The effects of exchange rate pass-through are more fully discussed in *Exploring Further 14.1* that can be found at **www.cengage.com/economics/Carbaugh**.

Exchange Rate Systems and Currency Crises

Previous chapters have discussed the determination of exchange rates and their effects on the balance-of-payments. This chapter surveys the exchange rate practices that are currently being used. The discussion focuses on the nature and operation of actual exchange rate systems and identifies economic factors that influence the choice of alternative exchange rate systems. The chapter also discusses the operation and effects of currency crises.

EXCHANGE RATE PRACTICES

In choosing an exchange rate system, a nation must decide whether to allow its currency to be determined by market forces (floating rate) or to be fixed (pegged) against some standard of value. If a nation adopts a floating rate, it must decide whether to float independently, float in unison with a group of other currencies, or crawl according to a predetermined formula such as relative inflation rates. The decision to anchor a currency includes the options of anchoring to a single currency, a basket of currencies, or gold. Since 1971, the technique of expressing official exchange rates in terms of gold has not been used; gold has been phased out of the international monetary system. The role of gold in the international monetary system will be further discussed in Chapter 17.

Members of the International Monetary Fund (IMF) have been free to follow any exchange rate policy that conforms to three principles: exchange rates should not be manipulated to prevent effective balance-of-payments adjustments or gain unfair competitive advantage over other members. Members should act to counter short-term disorderly conditions in exchange markets. When members intervene in exchange markets, they should take into account the interests of other members. Table 15.1 summarizes the exchange rate practices used by IMF member countries.

What characteristics make a country more suited for fixed rather than flexible exchange rates? Among these characteristics is the size of the nation, openness to trade,

TABLE 15.1

Exchange Rate Arrangements of IMF Members, 2012

Exchange Arrangement	Number of Countries
Exchange arrangements with no separate legal tender*	13
Currency board arrangements	12
Conventional pegged (fixed) exchange rates	59
Pegged exchange rates within horizontal bands	1
Crawling pegged (band) exchange rates	16
Managed floating exchange rates	44
Independently floating exchange rates	43
	188

*The currency of another country circulates as the sole legal tender, or the member belongs to a monetary or currency union in which the same legal tender is shared by the members of the union.

Source: International Monetary Fund, *Annual Report on Exchange Arrangements and Exchange Restrictions*, 2012. See also International Monetary Fund, *Classification of Exchange Rate Arrangements and Monetary Policy Frameworks*, available at http://www.imf.org/.

TABLE 15.2

Choosing an Exchange Rate System

Characteristics of Economy	Implication for the Desired Degree of Exchange Rate Flexibility
Size and openness of the economy	If trade is a large share of national output, then the costs of currency fluctuations can be high. This suggests that small, open economies may best be served by fixed exchange rates.
Inflation rate	If a country has much higher inflation than its trading partners, its exchange rate needs to be flexible to prevent its goods from becoming uncompetitive in world markets. If inflation differentials are more modest, a fixed rate is less troublesome.
Labor market flexibility	The more rigid wages are, the greater the need for a flexible exchange rate to help the economy respond to an external shock.
Degree of financial development	In developing countries with immature financial markets, a freely floating exchange rate may not be sensible because a small number of foreign exchange trades can cause big swings in currencies.
Credibility of policymakers	The weaker the reputation of the central bank, the stronger the case for pegging the exchange rate to build confidence that inflation will be controlled.
Capital mobility	The more open an economy to international capital, the harder it is to sustain a fixed rate.

© Cengage Learning®

the degree of labor mobility, and the availability of fiscal policy to cushion downturns. Table 15.2 summarizes the usage of these factors. The important point is that no single currency system is right for all countries or at all times. The choice of an exchange rate system should depend on the particular circumstances facing the country in question.

CHOOSING AN EXCHANGE RATE SYSTEM: CONSTRAINTS IMPOSED BY FREE CAPITAL FLOWS

The choice of an exchange rate system depends on many variables including the freedom of capital to flow into and out of a country. One consequence of allowing free capital flows is it constrains a country's choice of an exchange rate system and its ability to operate an independent monetary policy. For reasons related to the tendency for capital to flow where returns are the highest, a country can maintain only two of the following three policies—free capital flows, a fixed exchange rate, and an independent monetary policy. This tendency is illustrated in Figure 15.1. Countries must choose to be on one side of the triangle, adopting the policies at each end, but forgoing the policy on the opposite corner. Economists refer to this restriction as the **impossible trinity**.[1]

The easiest way to understand this restriction is through specific examples. The United States allows free capital flows and has an independent monetary policy, but it has a flexible exchange rate. To combat inflation, suppose the Federal Reserve increases its target interest rate relative to foreign interest rates, inducing capital to flow into the United States. By increasing the demand for dollars relative to other currencies, these capital inflows cause the dollar to appreciate against other currencies. Conversely, if the Federal Reserve reduces its target interest rate, net capital outflows would decrease the demand for dollars causing the dollar to depreciate against other currencies. Therefore, the United States, by not having a fixed exchange rate, can maintain both an independent monetary policy and free capital flows.

FIGURE 15.1

The Impossible Trinity

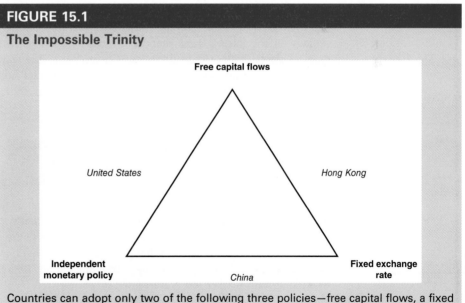

Countries can adopt only two of the following three policies—free capital flows, a fixed exchange rate, and an independent monetary policy.

© Cengage Learning®

---

[1]See Robert Mundell, "The Appropriate Use of Monetary and Fiscal Policy for Internal and External Stability," *IMF Staff Papers*, March 1962 and "Capital Mobility and Stabilization Policy under Fixed and Flexible Exchange Rates," *Canadian Journal of Economics*, November 1963.

In contrast, Hong Kong essentially fixes the value of its currency to the U.S. dollar and allows free capital flows. The trade-off is that Hong Kong sacrifices the ability to use monetary policy to influence domestic interest rates. Unlike the United States, Hong Kong cannot decrease interest rates to stimulate a weak economy. If Hong Kong's interest rates were to diverge from world rates, capital would flow into or out of the Hong Kong economy as in the U.S. case above. Under a flexible exchange rate, these flows would cause the exchange value of the Hong Kong dollar to change relative to that of other currencies. Under a fixed exchange rate, the monetary authority must offset these capital flows by purchasing domestic or foreign currency in order to keep the supply and demand for its currency fixed and the exchange rate constant. Hong Kong loses the ability to have an independent monetary policy if it allows free capital flows and maintains a fixed exchange rate.

Similar to the case of Hong Kong, until 2005 China tied its exchange rate to the U.S. dollar. China could conduct an independent monetary policy because it sets restrictions on capital flows. In China's case, world and domestic interest rates could differ because controls on the transfer of funds into and out of the country limited the resulting changes in the money supply and the corresponding pressures on the exchange rate. As these three examples show, if a country chooses to allow capital to flow freely, it must also choose between having an independent monetary policy or a fixed exchange rate.

How does a country decide whether to give up a fixed exchange rate, an independent monetary policy, or free capital movements? The answer largely depends on global economic trends. The post-World War II era saw substantial integration of markets and increasing international trade. Countries such as the United States wanted to facilitate this increase in trade by eliminating the risk of exchange rate fluctuations. In 1944, representatives from major industrial countries designed and implemented a plan that encouraged fixed exchange rates for the dollar and other currencies while maintaining independent monetary policies. Just as with the systems described above, something had to be given up—the free movement of capital flows. Participating countries imposed ceilings on the interest rates that banks could offer depositors and restrictions on the types of assets that banks could invest. Governments intervened in financial markets to direct capital toward strategic domestic sectors. Although none of these controls alone prevented international capital flows, in combination they allowed governments to reduce the amount of international capital transactions.[2]

FIXED EXCHANGE RATE SYSTEM

Few nations have allowed their currencies' exchange values to be determined solely by the forces of supply and demand in a free market. Until the industrialized nations adopted managed floating exchange rates in the 1970s, the practice generally was to maintain a pattern of **fixed exchange rates** among national currencies. Changes in national exchange rates presumably were initiated by domestic monetary authorities when long-term market forces warranted it.

Use of Fixed Exchange Rates

Fixed exchange rates tend to be used primarily by small, developing nations whose currencies are anchored to a **key currency** such as the U.S. dollar. A key currency is

---

[2]See *Economic Report of the President*, 2004, Chapters 13–14.

widely traded on world money markets, demonstrated relatively stable values over time, and been widely accepted as a means of international settlement. Table 15.3 identifies the major key currencies of the world. Instead of anchoring the value of the domestic currency to another currency, a country could fix its currency's value to a commodity such as gold, a key feature of the gold standard described in Chapter 17.

One reason why developing nations choose to anchor their currencies to a key currency is that it is used as a means of international settlement. Consider a Norwegian importer who wants to purchase Argentinean beef over the next year. If the Argentine exporter is unsure of what the Norwegian *krone* will purchase in one year, he might reject the krone in settlement. Similarly, the Norwegian importer might doubt the value of Argentina's peso. One solution is for the contract to be written in terms of a key currency. Generally speaking, smaller nations with relatively undiversified economies and large foreign trade sectors have been inclined to anchor their currencies to one of the key currencies.

Maintaining an anchor to a key currency provides several benefits for developing nations. First, the prices of the traded products of many developing nations are determined primarily in the markets of industrialized nations such as the United States; by anchoring to the dollar, these nations can stabilize the domestic currency prices of their imports and exports. Second, many nations with high inflation have anchored to the dollar (the United States has relatively low inflation) in order to exert restraint on domestic policies and reduce inflation. By making the commitment to stabilize their exchange rates against the dollar, governments hope to convince their citizens they are willing to adopt the responsible monetary policies necessary to achieve low inflation. Anchoring the exchange rate may lessen inflationary expectations, leading to lower interest rates, a lessening of the loss of output due to disinflation, and moderation of price pressures.

In maintaining fixed exchange rates, nations must decide whether to anchor their currencies to another currency or a currency basket. Anchoring to a *single currency* is generally done by developing nations whose trade and financial relations are mainly with a single industrial country partner. Therefore, the developing country anchors its currency to the currency of its dominant trading partner.

Developing nations with more than one major trading partner often anchor their currencies to a group or *basket of currencies*. The basket is composed of prescribed

---

TABLE 15.3

Key Currencies: Currency Composition of Official Foreign Exchange Reserves of the Member Countries of the International Monetary Fund, 2013

Key Currency	Composition of Official Foreign Exchange Reserves
U.S. Dollar	62%
Euro	24
British Pound	4
Japanese Yen	4
Canadian Dollar	2
Australian Dollar	1
Other	3
	100

Source: From *Currency Composition of Official Foreign Exchange Reserves* (COFER), International Monetary Fund, 2013, available at www.imf.org.

quantities of foreign currencies in proportion to the amount of trade done with the nation anchoring its currency. Once the basket has been selected, the currency value of the nation is computed using the exchange rates of the foreign currencies in the basket. Anchoring the domestic currency value of the basket enables a nation to average out fluctuations in export or import prices caused by exchange rate movements. The effects of exchange rate changes on the domestic economy are thus reduced. Rather than constructing their own currency basket, some nations anchor the value of their currencies to the **special drawing right (SDR)**, a basket of four currencies established by the IMF, as discussed in Chapter 17.

Par Value and Official Exchange Rate

Under a fixed exchange rate system, governments have assigned their currencies a **par value** in terms of gold or other key currencies. By comparing the par values of two currencies we can determine their **official exchange rate**. Under the gold standard, the official exchange rate between the U.S. dollar and the UK pound was $2.80 = £1 as long as the United States bought and sold gold at a fixed price of $35 per ounce and the United Kingdom bought and sold gold at £12.50 per ounce ($35.00/£12.50 = $2.80 per pound). The major industrial nations set their currencies' par values in terms of gold until gold was phased out of the international monetary system in the early 1970s.

Rather than defining the par value of a currency in terms of a commodity, countries may anchor their currencies against another key currency. Developing nations often set the values of their currencies to that of a large, low inflation country like the United States. The monetary authority of Bolivia may define its official exchange rate as 20 pesos per dollar.

Exchange Rate Stabilization

We have learned that a first requirement for a nation adopting a fixed exchange rate system is to define the official exchange rate of its currency. The next step is to set up an **exchange stabilization fund** to defend the official rate. Through purchases and sales of foreign currencies, the exchange stabilization fund attempts to ensure that the market exchange rate does not move above or below the official exchange rate.

In Figure 15.2, assume that the market exchange rate equals $2.80 per pound, seen at the intersection of the demand and supply schedules of UK pounds, D_0 and S_0. Also assume that the official exchange rate is defined as $2.80 per pound. Now suppose that rising interest rates in the United Kingdom cause U.S. investors to demand additional pounds to finance the purchase of UK securities; let the demand for pounds rise from D_0 to D_1 in Figure 15.2(a). Under free market conditions, the dollar would depreciate from $2.80 per pound to $2.90 per pound. But under a fixed exchange rate system, the monetary authority will attempt to defend the official rate of $2.80 per pound. At this rate, there exists an excess demand for pounds equal to £40 billion; this means that the United Kingdom faces an excess supply of dollars in the same amount. To keep the market exchange rate from depreciating beyond $2.80 per pound, the U.S. exchange stabilization fund would purchase the excess supply of dollars with pounds. The supply of pounds thus rises from S_0 to S_1, resulting in a stabilization of the market exchange rate at $2.80 per pound.

Conversely, suppose that increased prosperity in the United Kingdom leads to rising imports from the United States; the supply of pounds increases from S_0 to S_1 in Figure 15.2(b). At the official exchange rate of $2.80 per pound, there exists an excess supply of pounds equal to £40 billion. To keep the dollar from appreciating against the pound, the U.S. stabilization fund would purchase the excess supply of pounds with dollars. The

FIGURE 15.2

Exchange Rate Stabilization under a Fixed Exchange Rate System

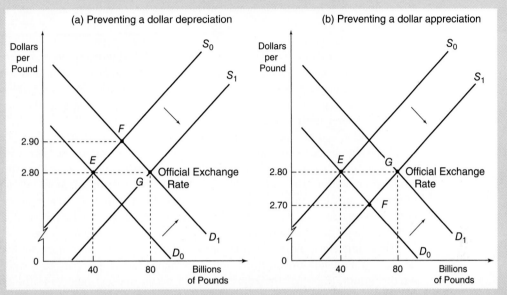

To defend the official exchange rate of $2.80 per pound, the central bank must supply all of the nation's currency that is demanded at the official rate and demand all of the nation's currency that is supplied to it at the official rate. To prevent a dollar depreciation, the central bank must purchase the excess supply of dollars with an equivalent amount of pounds. To prevent a dollar appreciation, the central bank must purchase the excess supply of pounds with an equivalent amount of dollars.

© Cengage Learning®

demand for pounds thus increases from D_0 to D_1, resulting in a stabilization of the market exchange rate at $2.80 per pound.

This example illustrates how an exchange stabilization fund undertakes its pegging operations to offset short-term fluctuations in the market exchange rate. Over the long run, the official exchange rate and the market exchange rate may move apart, reflecting changes in fundamental economic conditions—income levels, tastes and preferences, and technological factors. In the case of a **fundamental disequilibrium**, the cost of defending the existing official rate may become prohibitive.

Consider the case of a deficit nation that finds its currency weakening. Maintaining the official rate may require the exchange stabilization fund to purchase sizable quantities of its currency with foreign currencies or other reserve assets. These purchases may impose a severe drain on the deficit nation's stock of international reserves. Although the deficit nation may be able to borrow reserves from other nations or from the IMF to continue the defense of its exchange rate, such borrowing privileges are generally of limited magnitude. At the same time, the deficit nation will be undergoing internal adjustments to curb the disequilibrium. These measures will likely be aimed at controlling inflationary pressures and raising interest rates to promote capital inflows and discourage imports. If the imbalance is persistent, the deficit nation may view such internal adjustments as too costly in terms of falling income and employment levels. Rather than continually resorting to such measures, the deficit nation may decide the reversal of the disequilibrium calls for an adjustment in the exchange rate itself. Under a system of fixed exchange rates, a chronic imbalance may be counteracted by a currency devaluation or revaluation.

Devaluation and Revaluation

Under a fixed exchange rate system, a nation's monetary authority may decide to pursue a balance-of-payments equilibrium by devaluing or revaluing its currency. The purpose of **devaluation** is to cause the home currency's exchange value to *depreciate*, thus counteracting a payments *deficit*. The purpose of currency **revaluation** is to cause the home currency's exchange value to *appreciate*, counteracting a payments *surplus*.

The terms *devaluation* and *revaluation* refer to a legal redefinition of a currency's par value under a system of fixed exchange rates. The terms *depreciation* and *appreciation* refer to the actual impact on the market exchange rate caused by a redefinition of a par value or to changes in an exchange rate stemming from changes in the supply of or demand for foreign exchange.

Devaluation and revaluation policies work on relative prices to divert domestic and foreign expenditures between domestic and foreign goods. By raising the home price of the foreign currency, devaluation makes the home country's exports cheaper to foreigners in terms of the foreign currency, while making the home country's imports more expensive in terms of the home currency. Expenditures are diverted from foreign to home goods as home exports rise and imports fall. Revaluation discourages the home country's exports and encourages its imports, diverting expenditures from home goods to foreign goods.

Before implementing a devaluation or revaluation, the monetary authority must decide (1) if an adjustment in the official exchange rate is necessary to correct payment disequilibrium, (2) when the adjustment will occur, and (3) how large the adjustment should be. Exchange rate decisions of government officials may be incorrect—that is, ill timed and of improper magnitude.

In making the decision to undergo a devaluation or revaluation, monetary authorities generally attempt to hide behind a veil of secrecy. Just hours before the decision is to become effective, public denials of any such policies by official government representatives are common. This is to discourage currency speculators who try to profit by shifting funds from a currency falling in value to one rising in value. Given the destabilizing impact that massive speculation can exert on financial markets, it is hard to criticize monetary authorities for being secretive in their actions. The need for devaluation tends to be obvious to outsiders as well as to government officials and in the past has nearly always resulted in heavy speculative pressures. Table 15.5 summarizes the advantages and disadvantages of fixed exchange rates.

Bretton Woods System of Fixed Exchange Rates

An example of fixed exchange rates is the **Bretton Woods system**. In 1944, delegates from 44 member nations of the United Nations met at Bretton Woods, New Hampshire to create a new international monetary system. Members were aware of the unsatisfactory monetary experience of the 1930s during which the international gold standard collapsed as the result of the economic and financial crises of the Great Depression and nations experimented unsuccessfully with floating exchange rates and exchange controls. The delegates wanted to establish international monetary order and avoid the instability and nationalistic practices that had been in effect until 1944.

The international monetary system that was created became known as the Bretton Woods system. The founders felt that neither completely fixed exchange rates nor floating rates were optimal; instead they adopted a kind of semi fixed exchange rate system known as **adjustable pegged exchange rates**. The Bretton Woods system lasted from 1946 until 1973.

The main feature of the adjustable pegged system was that currencies were tied to each other to provide stable exchange rates for commercial and financial transactions.

When the balance-of-payments moved away from its long run equilibrium position, a nation could re-peg its exchange rate via devaluation or revaluation policies. Member nations agreed in principle to defend existing par values as long as possible in times of balance-of-payments disequilibrium. They were expected to use fiscal and monetary policies first to correct payments imbalances. But if reversing a persistent payments imbalance meant severe disruption to the domestic economy in terms of inflation or unemployment, member nations could correct this *fundamental disequilibrium* by re-pegging their currencies up to ten percent without permission from the IMF and by greater than ten percent with the fund's permission.

Under the Bretton Woods system, each member nation set the par value of its currency in terms of gold or, alternatively, the gold content of the U.S. dollar in 1944. Market exchange rates were almost fixed, being kept within a band of one percent on either side of parity for a total spread of two percent. National exchange stabilization funds were used to maintain the band limits. In 1971, the exchange support margins were widened to 2.25 percent on either side of parity to eliminate payments imbalances by setting in motion corrective trade and capital movements. Devaluations or revaluations could be used to adjust the par value of a currency when it became overvalued or undervalued.

Although adjustable pegged rates are intended to promote a viable balance-of-payments adjustment mechanism, they have been plagued with operational problems. In the Bretton Woods system, adjustments in prices and incomes often conflicted with domestic stabilization objectives. Currency devaluation was considered undesirable because it seemed to indicate a failure of domestic policies and a loss of international prestige. Conversely, revaluations were unacceptable to exporters whose livelihoods were vulnerable to such policies. Re-pegging exchange rates only as a last resort often meant that when adjustments did occur, they were sizable. Adjustable pegged rates posed difficulties in estimating the equilibrium rate to which a currency should be re-pegged. Once the market exchange rate reached the margin of the permissible band around parity, it became a rigid fixed rate that presented speculators with a one-way bet. Given persistent weakening pressure at the band's outer limit, speculators had the incentive to move out of a weakening currency that was expected to depreciate further in value as the result of official devaluation.

These problems reached a climax in the early 1970s. Faced with continuing and growing balance-of-payments deficits, the United States suspended the dollar's convertibility into gold in August 1971. This suspension terminated the U.S. commitment to exchange gold for dollars at $35 per ounce—a commitment that existed for 37 years. This policy abolished the tie between gold and the international value of the dollar, thus floating the dollar and permitting its exchange rate to be set by market forces. The floating of the dollar terminated U.S. support of the Bretton Woods system of fixed exchange rates and led to the demise of that system.

FLOATING EXCHANGE RATES

Instead of adopting fixed exchange rates, some nations allow their currencies to float in the foreign exchange market. By **floating** (or flexible) **exchange rates** we mean currency prices that are established daily in the foreign exchange market, without restrictions imposed by government policy on the extent that the prices can move. With floating rates there is an equilibrium exchange rate that equates the demand for and supply of the home currency. Changes in the exchange rate will ideally correct a payments imbalance by bringing about shifts in imports and exports of goods, services, and short-term capital movements. The exchange rate depends on relative productivity levels, interest rates, inflation rates, and other factors discussed in Chapter 12.

Unlike fixed exchange rates, floating exchange rates are not characterized by par values and official exchange rates; they are determined by market supply and demand conditions rather than central bankers. Although floating rates do not have an exchange stabilization fund to maintain existing rates, it does not necessarily follow that floating rates must fluctuate erratically. They will do so if the underlying market forces become unstable. Because there is no exchange stabilization fund under floating rates, any holdings of international reserves serve as working balances rather than to maintain a given exchange rate for any currency.

Achieving Market Equilibrium

How do floating exchange rates promote payments equilibrium for a nation? Consider Figure 15.3 that illustrates the foreign exchange market in Swiss francs in the United States. The intersection of supply schedule S_0 and demand schedule D_0 determines the equilibrium exchange rate of $0.50 per franc.

Referring to Figure 15.3(a), suppose a rise in real income causes U.S. residents to demand more Swiss cheese and watches, and therefore more francs; let the demand for francs rise from D_0 to D_1. Initially the market is in disequilibrium because the quantity of francs demanded (60 francs) exceeds the quantity supplied (40 francs) at the exchange rate of $0.50 per franc. The excess demand for francs leads to an increase in the exchange rate from $0.50 to $0.55 per franc; the dollar falls in value or depreciates

FIGURE 15.3

Market Adjustment under Floating Exchange Rates

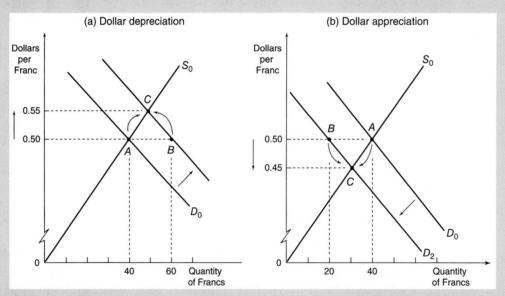

Under a floating exchange rate system, continuous changes in currency values restore payments equilibrium at which the quantity supplied and quantity demanded of a currency are equal. Starting at equilibrium point *A*, an increase in the demand for francs leads to a depreciation of the dollar against the franc; conversely, a decrease in the demand for francs leads to an appreciation of the dollar against the franc.

© Cengage Learning®

against the franc, while the franc rises in value, or appreciates against the dollar. The higher value of the franc prompts Swiss residents to increase the quantity of francs supplied on the foreign exchange market to purchase more U.S. goods that are now cheaper in terms of the franc. At the same time, it dampens U.S. demand for more expensive Swiss goods. Market equilibrium is restored at the exchange rate of $0.55 per franc when the quantities of francs supplied and demanded are equal.

Suppose instead that real income in the United States falls, causing U.S. residents to demand less Swiss cheese and watches and fewer francs. In Figure 15.3(b), let the demand for francs fall from D_0 to D_2. The market is initially in disequilibrium because the quantity of francs supplied (40 francs) exceeds the quantity demanded (20 francs) at the exchange rate of $0.50 per franc. The excess supply of francs causes the exchange rate to fall from $0.50 to $0.45 per franc; the dollar appreciates against the franc while the franc depreciates against the dollar. Market equilibrium is restored at the exchange rate of $0.45 per franc, when the quantities of francs supplied and demanded are equal.

This example illustrates one argument in favor of floating rates: when the exchange rate is permitted to adjust freely in response to market forces, market equilibrium will be established at a point where the quantities of foreign exchange supplied and demanded are equal. If the exchange rate promotes market equilibrium, monetary authorities will not need international reserves for the purpose of intervening in the market to maintain exchange rates at their par value. Presumably, these resources can be used more productively elsewhere in the economy.

Trade Restrictions, Jobs, and Floating Exchange Rates

During economic downturns, labor unions often lobby for import restrictions in order to save jobs for domestic workers. Do import restrictions lead to increasing total employment in the economy?

As long as the United States maintains a floating exchange rate, the implementation of import restrictions to help one industry will gradually shift jobs from other industries in the economy to the protected industry with no significant impact on aggregate employment. Short run employment gains in the protected industry will be offset by long run employment losses in other industries.

Suppose the United States increases tariffs on autos imported from Japan. This policy would reduce auto imports causing a decrease in the U.S. demand for yen to pay for imported vehicles. With floating exchange rates, the yen would depreciate against the dollar (the dollar would appreciate against the yen) until balance in international transactions is attained. The change in the exchange rate would encourage Americans to purchase more goods from Japan and the Japanese to purchase fewer goods from the United States. Sales and jobs would be lost in other U.S. industries. Trade restrictions result in a zero-sum game within the United States. Job increases in Detroit are offset by job decreases in Los Angeles and Portland, with exchange rate changes imposing costs on unprotected workers in the U.S. economy.

Arguments for and against Floating Rates

One advantage claimed for floating rates is their simplicity. Floating rates allegedly respond quickly to changing supply and demand conditions, clearing the market of shortages or surpluses of a given currency. Instead of having formal rules of conduct among central bankers governing exchange rate movements, floating rates are market determined. They operate under simplified institutional arrangements that are relatively easy to enact.

TABLE 15.4

Advantages and Disadvantages of Fixed Exchange Rates and Floating Exchange Rates

	Advantages	Disadvantages
Fixed exchange rates	Simplicity and clarity of exchange rate target Automatic rule for the conduct of monetary policy Keeps inflation under control	Loss of independent monetary policy Vulnerable to speculative attacks
Floating exchange rates	Continuous adjustment in the balance of payments Operate under simplified institutional arrangements Allow governments to set independent monetary and fiscal policies	Conducive to price inflation Disorderly exchange markets can disrupt trade and investment patterns Encourage reckless financial policies on the part of government

© Cengage Learning®

Because floating rates fluctuate throughout the day, they permit continuous adjustment in the balance-of-payments. The adverse effects of prolonged disequilibrium that occur under fixed exchange rates are minimized under floating rates. It is also argued that floating rates partially insulate the home economy from external forces. This insulation means that governments will not have to restore payments equilibrium through painful inflationary or deflationary adjustment policies. Switching to floating rates frees a nation from having to adopt policies that perpetuate domestic disequilibrium as the price of maintaining a satisfactory balance-of-payments position. Nations have greater freedom to pursue policies that promote domestic balance than they do under fixed exchange rates.

Although there are strong arguments in favor of floating exchange rates, this system is often considered of limited usefulness for bankers and businesspeople. Critics of floating rates maintain that an unregulated market may lead to wide fluctuations in currency values, discouraging foreign trade and investment. Although traders and investors may be able to hedge exchange rate risk by dealing in the forward market, the cost of hedging may become prohibitively high.

Floating rates are supposed to allow governments to set independent monetary and fiscal policies. This flexibility may cause another sort of problem: *inflationary bias*. Under a system of floating rates, monetary authorities may lack the financial discipline required by a fixed exchange rate system. Suppose a nation faces relatively high rates of inflation compared with the rest of the world. This domestic inflation will have no negative impact on the nation's trade balance under floating rates because its currency will automatically depreciate in the exchange market. However, a protracted depreciation of the currency would result in persistently increasing import prices and a rising price level, making inflation self perpetuating and the depreciation continuous. Because there is greater freedom for domestic financial management under floating rates, there may be less resistance to overspending and to its subsequent pressure on wages and prices. Table 15.4 summarizes the advantages and disadvantages of floating exchange rates.

MANAGED FLOATING RATES

The adoption of managed floating exchange rates by the United States and other industrial nations in 1973 followed the breakdown of the international monetary system based on fixed rates. Before the 1970s, only a handful of economists gave serious consideration to a general system of floating rates. Because of defects in the decision making process caused by procedural difficulties and political biases, adjustments of par values under the Bretton Woods system were often delayed and discontinuous. It was recognized that exchange rates should be adjusted more promptly and in small but continuous amounts in response to evolving market forces. In 1973, a **managed floating system** was adopted, under which informal guidelines were established by the IMF for coordination of national exchange rate policies.

The motivation for the formulation of guidelines for floating arose from two concerns. The first was that nations might intervene in the exchange markets to avoid exchange rate alterations that would weaken their competitive position. When the United States suspended its gold convertibility pledge and allowed its overvalued dollar to float in the exchange markets, it hoped that a free market adjustment would result in a depreciation of the dollar against other, undervalued currencies. Rather than permitting a **clean float** (a market solution) to occur, foreign central banks refused to permit the dollar depreciation by intervening in the exchange market. The United States considered this a **dirty float** because the free market forces of supply and demand were not allowed to achieve their equilibrating role. A second motivation for guidelines was the concern that floats, over time, might lead to disorderly markets with erratic fluctuations in exchange rates. Such destabilizing activity could create an uncertain business climate and reduce the level of world trade.

Under managed floating, a nation can alter the degree that it intervenes in the foreign exchange market. Heavier intervention moves the nation nearer to a fixed exchange rate status, whereas less intervention moves the nation nearer to a floating exchange rate status. Concerning day-to-day and week-to-week exchange rate movements, a main objective of the floating guidelines has been to prevent the emergence of erratic fluctuations. Member nations should intervene in the foreign exchange market as necessary to prevent sharp and disruptive exchange rate fluctuations. Such a policy is known as **leaning against the wind**—intervening to reduce short-term fluctuations in exchange rates without attempting to adhere to any particular rate over the long run. Members should also not act aggressively with respect to their currency exchange rates; they should not enhance the value when it is appreciating or depress the value when it is depreciating.

Under the managed float, some nations choose **target exchange rates** and intervene to support them. Target exchange rates are intended to reflect long-term economic forces that underlie exchange rate movements. One way for managed floaters to estimate a target exchange rate is to follow statistical indicators that respond to the same economic forces as the exchange rate trend. When the values of indicators change, the exchange rate target can be adjusted accordingly. Among these indicators are rates of inflation in different nations, levels of official foreign reserves, and persistent imbalances in international payments accounts. In practice, defining a target exchange rate can be difficult in a market based on volatile economic conditions.

Managed Floating Rates in the Short Run and Long Run

Managed floating exchange rates attempt to combine market determined exchange rates with foreign exchange market intervention in order to take advantage of the best features of floating exchange rates and fixed exchange rates. Under a managed float, market intervention is used to stabilize exchange rates in the short run; in the long run, a managed float allows market forces to determine exchange rates.

Figure 15.4 illustrates the theory of a managed float in a two-country framework; Switzerland and the United States. The supply and demand schedules for francs are denoted by S_0 and D_0; the equilibrium exchange rate, that the quantity of francs supplied equals the quantity demanded, is $0.50 per franc.

FIGURE 15.4

Managed Floating Exchange Rates

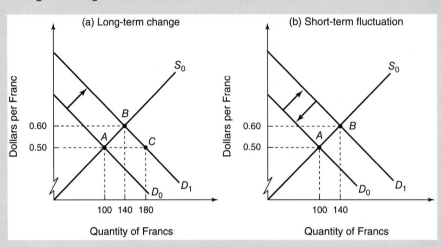

Under this system, central bank intervention is used to stabilize exchange rates in the short run; in the long run, market forces are permitted to determine exchange rates.

Suppose there occurs a permanent increase in U.S. real income as a result of U.S. residents demanding additional francs to purchase more Swiss chocolate. Let the demand for francs rise from D_0 to D_1, as shown in Figure 15.4(a). Because this increase in demand is the result of long run market forces, a managed float permits supply and demand conditions to determine the exchange rate. With the increase in demand for francs, the quantity of francs demanded (180 francs) exceeds the quantity supplied (100 francs) at the exchange rate of $0.50 per franc. The excess demand results in a rise in the exchange rate to $0.60 per franc, when the quantity of francs supplied and the quantity demanded are equal. In this manner, long run movements in exchange rates are determined by the supply and demand for various currencies.

Figure 15.4(b) illustrates the case of a short-term increase in the demand for francs. Suppose U.S. investors demand additional francs to finance purchases of Swiss securities that pay relatively high interest rates; let the demand for francs rise from D_0 to D_1. In a few weeks, assume Swiss interest rates fall, causing the U.S. demand for francs to revert to its original level, D_0. Under floating rates, the dollar price of the franc would rise from $0.50 per franc to $0.60 per franc and then fall back to $0.50 per franc. This type of exchange rate irascibility is widely considered to be a disadvantage of floating rates because it leads to uncertainty regarding the profitability of international trade and financial transactions; the pattern of trade and finance may be disrupted.

Under managed floating rates, the response to this temporary disturbance is exchange rate intervention by the Federal Reserve to keep the exchange rate at its long-term equilibrium level of $0.50 per franc. During the time period when demand is at D_1, the central bank will sell francs to meet the excess demand. As soon as the disturbance is over and demand reverts back to D_0, exchange market intervention will no longer be needed. Central bank intervention is used to offset temporary fluctuations in exchange rates that contribute to uncertainty in carrying out transactions in international trade and finance.

Since the advent of managed floating rates in 1973, the frequency and size of U.S. foreign exchange interventions have varied. Intervention was substantial from 1977 to

1979 when the dollar's exchange value was considered to be unacceptably low. American stabilization operations were minimal during the Reagan administration's first term, consistent with its goal of limiting government interference in markets; they were directed at offsetting short run market disruptions. Intervention was again substantial in 1985, when the dollar's exchange value was deemed unacceptably high, hurting the competitiveness of U.S. producers. The most extensive U.S. intervention operations took place after the Louvre Accord of 1987 when the major industrial nations reached informal understandings about the limits of tolerance for exchange rate fluctuations.

Exchange Rate Stabilization and Monetary Policy

We have seen how central banks can buy and sell foreign currencies to stabilize their values under a system of managed floating exchange rates. Another stabilization technique involves a nation's *monetary policy*. As we shall see, stabilizing a currency's exchange value requires the central bank to adopt (1) an *expansionary* monetary policy to offset currency *appreciation*, and (2) a *contractionary* monetary policy to offset currency *depreciation*.

Figure 15.5 illustrates the foreign exchange market for the United States. Assume the supply schedule of UK pounds is denoted by S_0 and the demand schedule of pounds is denoted by D_0. The equilibrium exchange rate, when the quantity of pounds supplied and the quantity demanded are equalized, is $2 per pound.

Suppose that as a result of production shutdowns in the United Kingdom caused by labor strikes, U.S. residents purchase fewer UK products and demand fewer pounds. Let the demand for pounds decrease from D_0 to D_1 in Figure 15.5(a). In the absence of

---

FIGURE 15.5

Exchange Rate Stabilization and Monetary Policy

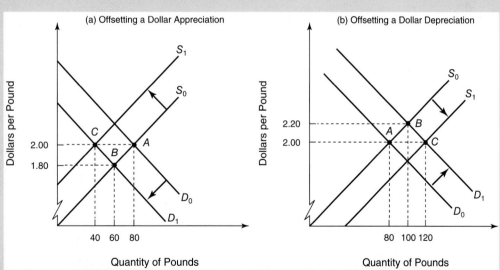

In the absence of international policy coordination, stabilizing a currency's exchange value requires a central bank to initiate (a) an expansionary monetary policy to offset an appreciation of its currency, and (b) a contractionary monetary policy to offset a depreciation of its currency.

central bank intervention, the dollar price of the pound falls from $2 to $1.80 so the dollar appreciates against the pound.

To offset the appreciation of the dollar, the Federal Reserve can increase the supply of money in the United States that will decrease domestic interest rates in the short run. The reduced interest rates will cause the foreign demand for U.S. securities to decline. Fewer pounds will be supplied to the foreign exchange market to buy dollars to purchase U.S. securities. As the supply of pounds shifts leftward to S_1, the dollar's exchange value reverts to $2 per pound. In this manner, the expansionary monetary policy has offset the dollar's appreciation.

Referring now to Figure 15.5(b), suppose a temporary surge in UK interest rates causes U.S. investors to demand additional pounds to purchase additional UK securities. Let the demand for pounds rise from D_0 to D_1. In the absence of central bank intervention, the dollar's exchange value would rise from $2 to $2.20 per pound; the dollar has depreciated against the pound.

To offset this dollar depreciation, the Federal Reserve can decrease the supply of money in the United States that will increase domestic interest rates and attract UK investment. More pounds will be supplied to the foreign exchange market to purchase dollars to buy U.S. securities. As the supply of pounds increases from S_0 to S_1, the dollar's exchange value reverts to $2 per pound. The contractionary monetary policy helps offset the dollar depreciation.

These examples illustrate how domestic monetary policies can be used to stabilize currency values. Such policies are not without costs, as seen in the following example.

Suppose the U.S. government increases federal spending without a corresponding increase in taxes. To finance the resulting budget deficit, assume the government borrows funds from the money market that raises domestic interest rates. High U.S. interest rates enhance the attractiveness of dollar denominated securities, leading to increased foreign purchases of these assets, an increased demand for dollars, and an appreciation in the dollar's exchange value. The appreciating dollar makes U.S. goods more expensive overseas and foreign goods less expensive in the United States, causing the U.S. trade account to fall into deficit.

Now assume the Federal Reserve intervenes and adopts an expansionary monetary policy. The resulting increase in the supply of money dampens the rise in U.S. interest rates and the dollar's appreciation. By restraining the increase in the dollar's exchange value, the expansionary monetary policy enhances the competitiveness of U.S. businesses and keeps the U.S. trade account in balance.

However, the favorable effects of the expansionary monetary policy on the domestic economy are temporary. When pursued indefinitely (over the long run), a policy of increasing the domestic money supply leads to a *weakening* in the U.S. trade position because the monetary expansion required to offset the dollar's appreciation eventually promotes higher prices in the United States. The higher prices of domestic goods offset the benefits of U.S. competitiveness that initially occur under the monetary expansion. American spending eventually shifts back to foreign products and away from domestically produced goods causing the U.S. trade account to fall into deficit.

This example shows how monetary policy can be used to stabilize the dollar's exchange value in the short run. When monetary expansion occurs on a sustained, long run basis, it brings with it eventual price increases that nullify the initial gains in domestic competitiveness. The long run effectiveness of using monetary policy to stabilize the dollar's exchange value is limited because the increase in the money supply to offset the dollar's appreciation does not permanently correct the underlying cause of the trade deficit—the increase in domestic spending.

Attempting to stabilize both the domestic economy and the dollar's exchange value can be difficult for the Federal Reserve. In early 1995the dollar was taking a nosedive against the yen and the U.S. economy showed signs of slowing. To boost the dollar's exchange value would have required the Federal Reserve to adopt a restrictive monetary policy that would have led to higher interest rates and net investment inflows. Further increases in domestic interest rates would heighten the danger that the U.S. economy would be pushed into a recession by the next year. The Federal Reserve had to choose between supporting domestic economic expansion or the dollar's exchange value. In this case, the Federal Reserve adopted a policy of lower interest rates, appearing to respond to U.S. domestic needs.

Is Exchange Rate Stabilization Effective?

Many governments have intervened in foreign exchange markets to try to dampen volatility and slow or reverse currency movements.[3] Their concern is that excessive short-term volatility and longer term swings in exchange rates that "overshoot" values justified by fundamental conditions may hurt their economies, particularly sectors heavily involved in international trade. The foreign exchange market can be volatile. One euro cost about $1.15 in January 1999, then dropped to $0.85 by the end of 2000, only to climb to over $1.18 in June 2003. Over this same period, one U.S. dollar bought as much as 133 yen and as little as 102 yen, a 30 percent fluctuation. Many other currencies have also experienced large price swings in recent years.

Many central banks intervene in foreign exchange markets. The largest player is Japan. Between 1991 and 2000, the Bank of Japan bought U.S. dollars on 168 occasions for a cumulative amount of $304 billion and sold U.S. dollars on 33 occasions for a cumulative amount of $38 billion. A typical case: On April 3, 2000 the Bank of Japan purchased $13.2 billion in the foreign exchange market in an attempt to stop the more than four percent depreciation of the dollar against the yen that had occurred during the previous week. Japan's intervention magnitudes dwarf all other countries' official intervention in the foreign exchange market. It exceeded U.S. intervention in the 1991–2000 period by a factor of more than 30. However, compared to overall market transactions in the foreign exchange market, the magnitude of Japan's interventions has been quite small.

Not surprisingly, intervention supported by central bank interest rate changes tends to have an even larger impact on exchange rates than intervention alone. Cases where intervention was coordinated between two central banks such as the Federal Reserve and the Bank of Japan, had a larger impact on exchange rates than unilateral foreign exchange operations. Episodes of coordinated intervention are rather rare.

Academic researchers have often questioned the usefulness of official foreign exchange intervention. Proponents of foreign exchange intervention note that it may be useful when the exchange rate is under speculative attack—when a change in the exchange rate is not justified by fundamentals. It may also be helpful in coordinating private sector expectations. Recent research provides some support for the short run effectiveness of intervention. This should not be interpreted as a rationale for intervention as a longer term management tool.[4]

---

[3]This section is drawn from Michael Hutchinson, "Is Official Foreign Exchange Intervention Effective?" *Economic Letter*, Federal Reserve Bank of San Francisco, July 18, 2003.

[4]Michael Hutchinson, "Intervention and Exchange Rate Stabilization Policy in Developing Countries," *International Finance 6*, 2003, pp. 41–59.

THE CRAWLING PEG

Instead of adopting fixed or floating rates, why not try a compromise approach—the **crawling peg**. This system has been used by nations including Bolivia, Brazil, Costa Rica, Nicaragua, Solomon Islands, and Peru. The crawling peg system means that a nation makes small, frequent changes in the par value of its currency to correct a balance-of-payments disequilibrium. Deficit and surplus nations both keep adjusting until the desired exchange rate level is attained. The term *crawling peg* implies that par value changes are implemented in a large number of small steps, making the process of exchange rate adjustment continuous for all practical purposes. The peg crawls from one par value to another.

The crawling peg mechanism has been used primarily by nations having high inflation rates. Some developing nations, mostly South American, have recognized that a pegging system can operate in an inflationary environment only if there is provision for frequent changes in the par values. Associating national inflation rates with international competitiveness, these nations have generally used price indicators as a basis for adjusting crawling pegged rates. In these nations, the primary concern is the criterion that governs exchange rate movements, rather than the currency or basket of currencies against which the peg is defined.

The crawling peg differs from the system of adjustable pegged rates. Under the adjustable peg, currencies are tied to a par value that changes infrequently (perhaps once every several years) but suddenly, usually in large jumps. The idea behind the crawling peg is that a nation can make small, frequent changes in par values, perhaps several times a year so they creep along slowly in response to evolving market conditions.

Supporters of the crawling peg argue that the system combines the flexibility of floating rates with the stability usually associated with fixed rates. They contend that a system providing continuous, steady adjustments is more responsive to changing competitive conditions and avoids a main problem of adjustable pegged rates—that changes in par values are frequently wide of the mark. Moreover, small, frequent changes in par values made at random intervals frustrate speculators with their irregularity.

In recent years, the crawling peg formula has been used by developing nations facing rapid and persistent inflation. The IMF has generally contended that such a system would not be in the best interests of nations such as the United States or Germany that bear the responsibility for international currency levels. The IMF has felt that it would be hard to apply such a system to the industrialized nations whose currencies serve as a source of international liquidity. Although even the most ardent proponents of the crawling peg admit that the time for its widespread adoption has not yet come, the debate over its potential merits is bound to continue.

CURRENCY MANIPULATION AND CURRENCY WARS

During the 2000s, accusations of currency manipulation have become widespread among world leaders. The United States has accused Japan and China of keeping the exchange values of their currencies artificially low in order to boost international competitiveness and trade surpluses. These countries have retorted that the United States has been doing the same thing.

Currency manipulation is the purchase or the sale of a currency on the exchange market by the fiscal authority or the monetary authority, in order to influence the value of that currency. By selling yen and buying dollar denominated Treasury securities, Japan can depreciate its yen against the dollar. Why? The sale of yen drives its price downward and the purchase of the dollar drives its price upward—thus, the yen depreciates against the dollar. For the United States, a depreciating yen means that Japanese goods are artificially cheaper in the United States and American goods are more expensive in Japan than they should be. U.S. exports to Japan decrease and U.S. imports from Japan increase. The lower value of the yen means that it is cheaper to hire Japanese workers and encourages American factories to move to Japan. This is bad for you if you work on a factory line in the United States and are trying to sell goods to Japan. A weak currency cheapens the price of a country's exports, making them more attractive to international buyers by undercutting competitors. This provides export driven economies a leg up on their global competitors.

During 2003–2004, the Bank of Japan intervened over a 15 month period in the yen/dollar currency market by creating 35 trillion yen. This currency was used to purchase 320 billion dollars that was then invested in U.S. Treasury securities. This increased the supply of yen and depreciated the yen's exchange value against the dollar that increased Japan's exports and helped lift the country out of a deflationary period.

During the early 2000s, many countries sought depreciation, or at least non-appreciation, of their currencies to strengthen their economies and create jobs. The list of currency manipulators has included countries such as China, Japan, Switzerland, South Korea, Hong Kong, Singapore, Malaysia, and Taiwan. Most of the remaining intervention has come from major oil exporting countries.

Artificially lowering a country's exchange rate can make its exports cheaper and fosters growth internally. That only causes problems for other countries because one currency can fall only if another rises. This imbalance could spark a currency war—a destabilizing battle where countries compete against one another to get the lowest exchange rate. This is what occurred in the 1930s with disastrous consequences. As countries abandoned the Gold Standard during the Great Depression, they used currency depreciations (devaluations) to stimulate their economies. Since this effectively pushed unemployment overseas, trading partners quickly retaliated with their own depreciations, resulting in a currency war, a collapse in international trade, and a contraction of the global economy.

The U.S. government has complained about being the victim of deliberate currency manipulation by its trading partners, especially China, who are trying to steal demand away from their American competitors. Bills in Congress have been proposed (though not passed) that would place sanctions on currency manipulators. Countervailing currency intervention could be enacted so that the United States would buy the currencies of currency manipulators in sufficient amounts to offset the impact on its own exchange rate. Another possible sanction is retaliatory tariffs that are placed on the exports of currency manipulating countries.

However, other countries complain about the currency policy of the United States, as seen in Federal Reserve's stimulation of the American economy during the Great Recession of 2007–2009 and its aftermath. The primary purpose of the Fed's policy has been to grow the U.S. economy via an increase in the money supply, a reduction in the interest rate, and increases in investment spending. The policy also has caused the dollar's exchange value to depreciate. How? As the Fed reduces the domestic interest rate, foreign investment in the United States contracts, the demand for the dollar declines, and the dollar's exchange value falls. The lower exchange rate is the byproduct of the expansionary monetary policy.

It is a tough call on what is and isn't an unacceptable currency policy. One is an economy in which the central bank increases the money supply to foster economic growth (think of the United States where the lower exchange rate is the byproduct of the expansionary monetary policy). The other is an economy in which the central bank actively intervenes in foreign exchange markets to depreciate its currency, boost exports, and steal demand from other countries (think of China where the lower exchange rate is the primary policy objective). Although we might judge the U.S. tactic to be acceptable and the Chinese tactic to be unacceptable, countries on the receiving end of currency manipulation understandably don't much care about the underlying motive; all they see is that their currency is appreciating and their exports and economic growth are threatened. However, the rationale matters. The world has suffered from inadequate aggregate demand and high unemployment in recent years. Worries about government debt burdens have led to reluctance to pursue expansionary fiscal policy (tax reductions and government spending increases) in the United States and Europe. Thus, there is more reliance on monetary policy.

In the next section, we will consider the currency manipulation conflict between the United States and China.

Is China a Currency Manipulator?

Trade tensions between the United States and China have run high during the 2000s. In 2009, U.S. Treasury Secretary Timothy Geithner restated a long held American accusation that China's desire to manipulate its currency hurts the U.S. economy. He noted that to prevent the yuan from appreciating, the People's Bank of China has massively intervened by selling yuan and purchasing dollar denominated assets such as U.S. Treasury securities.

As the argument goes, China's currency policy has resulted in its yuan being significantly undervalued relative to the dollar, giving the Chinese an unfair competitive advantage. An undervalued yuan makes U.S. exports to China more expensive than they would be if exchange rates were determined by market forces. This undervaluation harms U.S. production and employment in manufacturing industries such as textiles, apparel, and furniture that have to compete against artificially low-cost goods from China. An undervalued yuan also makes Chinese goods cheaper for American consumers, encouraging them to import more goods from China. As a result, China takes jobs away from Americans. If the dollar–yuan exchange rate was set by market forces instead of being manipulated by the People's Bank of China, the yuan would appreciate sharply, increasing the price of Chinese exports and taking pressure off U.S. manufacturing industries. China's huge trade surplus with the United States and its large accumulation of dollar reserves are cited as evidence that China has manipulated the value of its currency relative to the dollar for competitive advantage. For the sake of stability in the economies of the United States and China, and also the global economy, action needs to be taken to allow market forces to determine the dollar–yuan exchange rate.

Other analysts contend that there is little or no connection between the yuan and the health of U.S. manufacturing. They note that the transition away from manufacturing in the United States is a long run trend that goes far beyond competition from Chinese exports. Jobs have been slashed because technological improvements have made each worker more productive. If the United States wants to make its workers more competitive with those in China, it should reform its educational system rather than rely on illusory gains from changes in exchange rates.

There is a good economic rationale for China's desire to maintain a stable value against the dollar. As long as this fixed rate is credible, it serves as an effective monetary anchor for China's internal price level. After inflation skyrocketed to more than 20 percent per year during 1993–1995, the fixed rate anchor helped China regain price level stability.

China's currency intervention yields positive results for the U.S. economy. China has maintained large investments in U.S. debt that helps keep U.S. interest rates low, allowing American firms to make investments that would be unattractive at a higher cost of borrowing. Such investments increase the amount of capital available and increase the size of the economy. An undervalued yuan also promotes a lower inflation rate in the United States. China argues that its currency peg policy is not intended to favor exports over imports, but rather to foster economic stability. Chinese officials note that many developing countries, including China, tie their currencies to the dollar at a fixed rate to promote economic stability. Chinese leaders fear that abandoning the peg could induce an economic crisis in China and especially damage its export sectors at a time when painful economic reforms, such as shutting down inefficient state owned businesses and restructuring the banking system are being implemented. Chinese officials view economic stability as crucial to maintaining political stability. They are concerned that an appreciating yuan would reduce employment and decrease wages in several industries and thus cause worker unrest.

Rather than relying on an appreciation of the yuan to reduce China's trade surplus, why not rely on higher wage growth in China? In the long run, exchange rate appreciation and money wage growth are substitutes. By 2011, China was beginning to experience labor shortages as older workers retired and the supply of younger workers was diminishing because of the country's one-child policy. Restrictions on the migration of people from inland farms to coastal cities where factories are clustered, have also contributed to labor scarcities. Pressuring China to appreciate its yuan may backfire. If Chinese employers fear that the yuan will appreciate in the future that reduces their international competitiveness, then they become reluctant to grant large wage increases in the present. At the writing of this text in 2014, it remains to be seen how the U.S.–China currency conflict will play out.

CURRENCY CRISES

A shortcoming of the international monetary system is that major currency crises have been a common occurrence in recent years. A **currency crisis** also called a **speculative attack**, is a situation in which a weak currency experiences heavy selling pressure. There are several possible indications of selling pressure. One is sizable losses in the foreign reserves held by a country's central bank. Another is depreciating exchange rates in the forward market where buyers and sellers promise to exchange currency at some future date rather than immediately. In extreme cases where inflation is running rampant, selling pressure consists of widespread flight out of domestic currency into foreign currency or into goods that people think will retain value, such as gold or real estate. Experience shows that currency crises can decrease the growth of a country's gross domestic product by six percent or more. That is like losing one or two years of economic growth in most countries. Table 15.5 provides examples of currency crises.

A currency crisis ends when selling pressure stops. One way to end pressure is to devalue; establish a new exchange rate at a sufficiently depreciated level. Mexico's central bank might stop exchanging pesos for dollars at the previous rate of 10 pesos per dollar and set a new level of 20 pesos per dollar. Another way to end selling pressure is to adopt a floating exchange rate. Floating permits the exchange rate to "find its own level," that is

TRADE CONFLICTS   THE GLOBAL FINANCIAL CRISIS OF 2007–2009

Economic crises tend to occur sporadically virtually every decade and in various countries ranging from Sweden to Argentina, from Russia to Korea, and from Japan to the United States. Each crisis is unique, yet each bears some resemblance to others. In general, economic crises have been caused by factors such as an overshooting of markets, excessive leveraging of debt, credit booms, miscalculations of risk, rapid outflows of capital from a country, and unsustainable macroeconomic policies.

Concerning the global economic crisis of 2007–2009, what began as a bursting of the U.S. housing market bubble and an increase in foreclosures ballooned into a global financial and economic crisis. Some of the largest and most venerable banks, investment houses, and insurance companies either declared bankruptcy or had to be rescued financially. In the automobile industry, General Motors and Chrysler declared bankruptcy and were nationalized by the U.S. government. Many blamed the United States for the crisis and saw it as an example of the excesses of a country that did not practice sound principles of finance.

The global economic crisis brought home an important point: the United States is a major center of the financial world. Regional financial crises, such as the Asian financial crisis of 1997–1998, can occur without seriously infecting the rest of the global financial system. When the U.S. financial system stumbles, it tends to bring major parts of the rest of the world down with it. The reason is that the United States is the main guarantor of the international financial system, the provider of dollars widely used as currency reserves and as an international medium of exchange, and a contributor to much of the financial capital that sloshes around the world seeking higher yields. The rest of the world may not appreciate it, but a financial crisis in the United States often takes on a global aspect.

The financial crisis that began in the United States quickly spread to other industrial countries and also to emerging market and developing economies. Investors pulled capital from countries, even those with small levels of perceived risk, and caused values of stocks and domestic currencies to plunge. Slumping exports

and commodity prices added to the woes, pushing economies world-wide into either recession or into a period of slow economic growth. As economies throughout the world deteriorated, it became clear that the United States and other countries could not export their way out of recession: there was no major economy that could play the role of an economic engine to pull other countries out of their economic doldrums.

The global crisis played out at two levels. The first was among the industrialized nations of the world where most of the losses from subprime mortgage debt, excessive leveraging of investments and inadequate capital backing financial institutions have occurred. The second level of the crisis was among emerging market and other economies who were innocent bystanders to the crisis but who had weak economies that could be whipsawed by activities in global markets. These nations had insufficient sources of capital and had to turn to help from the International Monetary Fund, World Bank, and capital surplus nations such as Japan.

To cope with the global financial crisis, the United States and other countries attempted to control the contagion, minimize losses to society, restore confidence in financial institutions and instruments, and lubricate the wheels of the economy in order for it to return to full operation. To achieve these goals, countries such as the United States, China, South Korea, Spain, Sweden, and Germany enacted a variety of measures such as:

- Injecting capital through loans or stock purchases to prevent bankruptcy of financial institutions.
- Increasing deposit insurance limits in order to limit withdrawals from banks.
- Purchasing toxic debt of financial institutions on the verge of failure so that they would start lending again.
- Coordinating interest rate reductions by central banks to inject liquidity into the economy.
- Enacting stimulative fiscal policies to bolster sagging aggregate demand.

At the G–20 Summit on Financial Markets and the World Economy in November of 2008, participating countries generally recognized that economic crisis

iStockphoto.com/photosoup

(continued)

(continued)

was not merely an aberration that could be fixed by tweaking the system: there appeared to be no international mechanism capable of coping with and preventing global crises from erupting. The countries concluded that major changes are needed in the global financial system to reduce risk, provide oversight, and to establish an early warning system of impending financial crises. Needed reforms will be successful only if they are grounded in a commitment to free market principles. The extent to which the United States and other countries are willing to alter their financial systems remains to be seen.

Source: Dick Nanto, *The Global Financial Crisis: Analysis and Policy Implications*, April 3, 2009, Congressional Research Service, U.S. Library of Congress, Washington, DC: U.S.Government Printing Office.

TABLE 15.5

Examples of Currency Crisis

- **Mexico, December 1994–1995**. Mexico's central bank maintained the value of the peso within a band that depreciated four percent a year against the U.S. dollar. In order to reduce interest rates on its debt, the Mexican government in April 1994 began issuing debt linked to the dollar. The amount of this debt soon exceeded the central bank's falling foreign exchange reserves. Unrest in the province of Chiapas led to a speculative attack on the peso. Although the government devalued the peso by 15 percent by widening the band, the crisis continued. The government then let the peso float; it depreciated from 3.46 per dollar before the crisis to more than 7 per dollar. To end the crisis, Mexico received pledges for $49 billion in loans from the U.S. government and the IMF. Mexico's economy suffered a depression and banking problem that led to government rescues.

- **Russia, 1998**. The Russian government was paying high interest rates on its short-term debt. Falling prices for oil, a major export, and a weak economy also contributed to speculative attacks against the ruble that had an official crawling band with the U.S. dollar. Although the IMF approved loans for Russia of about $11 billion and the Russian government widened the band for the ruble by 35 percent, the crisis continued. This crisis led to the floating of the ruble and its depreciation against the dollar by about 20 percent. Russia then went into recession and experienced a burst of inflation. Many banks became insolvent. The government defaulted on its ruble denominated debt and imposed a moratorium on private sector payments of foreign debt.

- **Turkey, 2001**. The Turkish *lira* had an IMF–designed official crawling peg against the U.S. dollar. In November 2000, rumors about a criminal investigation into ten government run banks led to a speculative attack on the lira. Interbank interest rates rose to 2,000 percent. The central bank then intervened. Eight banks became insolvent and were taken over by the government. The central bank's intervention had violated Turkey's agreement with the IMF, yet the IMF lent Turkey $10 billion. In February 2001, a public dispute between the president and prime minister caused investors to lose confidence in the stability of Turkey's coalition government. Interbank interest rates rose to 7,500 percent. Thus, the government let the lira float. The lira depreciated from 668,000 per dollar before the crisis to 1.6 million per dollar by October 2001. The economy of Turkey stagnated and inflation skyrocketed to 60 percent.

Source: From Kurt Schuler, *Why Currency Crises Happen*, Joint Economic Committee, U.S. Congress, January 2002.

almost always depreciated compared to the previous pegged rate. Devaluation and allowing depreciation make foreign currency and foreign goods more costly in terms of domestic currency that tends to decrease demand for foreign currency, ending the imbalance that triggered selling pressure. In some cases, especially when confidence in the currency is low, the crisis continues and further rounds of devaluation or depreciation occur.

Currency crises that end in devaluations or accelerated depreciations are sometimes called **currency crashes**. Not all crises end in crashes. A way of trying to end the selling pressure of a crisis without suffering a crash is to impose restrictions on the ability of people to buy and sell foreign currency. These controls create profit opportunities for people who discover how to evade them, so over time controls lose effectiveness unless enforced by an intrusive bureaucracy. Another way to end selling pressure is to obtain a loan to bolster the foreign reserves of the monetary authority. Countries that wish to bolster their foreign reserves often ask the IMF for loans. Although the loan can help temporarily, it may just delay rather than end selling pressure. The final way to end selling pressure is to restore confidence in the existing exchange rate, such as announcing appropriate and credible changes in monetary policy.

Sources of Currency Crises

Why do currency crises occur?[5] A popular explanation is that big currency speculators instigate the crises for their own profit. The world's best known currency speculator, George Soros, made $2 billion in 1992 by speculating against European currencies. Speculation can also result in substantial losses. George Soros retired in 2000 after suffering the effects of losing almost $2 billion as the result of unsuccessful speculations. Currency speculation is not just an activity of big speculators. Millions of ordinary people also speculate in the form of holding foreign currency in their wallets, under their mattresses, and the like. Millions of small speculators can move markets like the big speculators do. Currency crises are not simply caused by big currency speculators who appear out of nowhere. There must be an underlying reason for a currency crisis to occur.

One source for a currency crisis is budget deficits financed by inflation. If the government cannot easily finance its budget deficits by raising taxes or borrowing, it may pressure the central bank to finance them by creating money. Creating money can increase the supply of money faster than demand is growing causing inflation. Budget deficits financed by inflation seemed to capture the essentials of many currency crises up through the 1980s. By the 1990s, however, this explanation appeared to be lacking. During the currency crises in Europe in 1992–1993, budget deficits in most adversely affected countries were small and sustainable. Most East Asian countries affected by the currency crisis of 1997–1998 were running budget surpluses and realizing strong economic growth. Economists have looked for other explanations for currency crises.

Currency crises may also be caused by weak financial systems. Weak banks can trigger speculative attacks if people think the central bank will rescue the banks even at the cost of spending much of its foreign reserves to do so. The explicit or implicit promise to rescue the banks is a form of moral hazard—a situation in which people do not pay the full cost of their own mistakes. As people become apprehensive about the future value of the local currency, they sell it to obtain more stable foreign currencies.

Some of the major currency crises of the last 20 years have occurred in countries that had recently deregulated their financial systems. Many governments formerly used financial regulations to channel investment into politically favored outlets. In return, they restricted competition among banks, life insurance companies, and the like. Profits from restricted competition subsidized unprofitable government directed investments. Deregulation altered the picture by reducing the government direction of investments and allowing more competition among institutions. Governments failed to ensure that in the new environment of greater freedom to reap the rewards of success, financial institutions also bore greater responsibility for failure. Financial institutions made mistakes in the unfamiliar environment of deregulation, failed, and were rescued at public expense. This rescue resulted in public fears about the future value of the local currency and the selling of it to obtain more stable foreign currencies.

A weak economy can trigger a currency crisis by creating doubt about the determination of the government and the central bank to continue with the current monetary policy if weakness continues. A weak economy is characterized by falling GDP growth

---

[5]Kurt Schuler, *Why Currency Crises Happen*, Joint Economic Committee, U.S. Congress, January 2002.

per person, a rising unemployment rate, a falling stock market, and falling export growth. If the public expects the central bank to increase the money supply to stimulate the economy, it may become apprehensive about the future value of the local currency and begin selling it on currency markets.

Political factors can also cause currency crises. Developing countries have historically been more prone to currency crises than developed countries because they tend to have a weaker rule of law, governments more prone to being overthrown by force, central banks that are not politically independent, and other characteristics that create political uncertainty about monetary policy.

External factors can be another source for a currency crisis. An increase in interest rates in major international currencies can trigger a currency crisis if a central bank resists increasing the interest rate it charges. Funds may flow out of the local currency into foreign currency, decreasing the central bank's reserves to unacceptably low levels and therefore putting pressure on the government to devalue its currency if the currency is pegged. Moreover, a big external shock that disrupts the economy, such as war or a spike in the price of imported oil can likewise trigger a currency crisis. External shocks have been key features in many currency crises historically.

The choice of an exchange rate system also affects whether and how currency crises occur. In recent years, fixing the value of the domestic currency to that of a large, low inflation country has become popular. Fixing the value helps keep inflation under control by linking the inflation rate for internationally traded goods to that found in the anchor country. Prior to 2002, the exchange rate for the Argentine peso was pegged at one peso per U.S. dollar. Therefore, a bushel of corn sold on the world market at $4 had its price set at 4 pesos. If the public expects this exchange rate to be unchangeable, then the fixed rate has the extra advantage of anchoring inflation expectations for Argentina to the inflation rate in the United States, a relatively low inflation country.

Despite the advantage of promoting relatively low inflation, a fixed exchange rate system makes countries vulnerable to speculative attacks on their currencies. Recall that preservation of fixed exchange rates requires the government to purchase or sell domestic currency for foreign currency at the target rate of exchange. This requirement forces the central bank to maintain a sufficient quantity of international reserves in order to fulfill the demand by the public to sell domestic currency for foreign currency at the fixed exchange rate. If the public thinks that the central bank's supply of international reserves has decreased to the level where the ability to fulfill the demand to sell domestic currency for foreign currency at a fixed exchange rate is doubted, then a devaluation of the domestic currency is anticipated. This anticipation can result in a speculative attack on the central bank's remaining holdings of international reserves. The attack consists of huge sales of domestic currency for foreign currency so that the decrease in international reserves is expedited, and devaluation results from the decline in reserves. It is no wonder that the most important recent currency crises have happened to countries having fixed exchange rates but demonstrating a lack of political will to correct previous economic problems.

Next, we will examine how the speculative attacks on East Asian currencies contributed to a major currency crisis.

Speculators Attack East Asian Currencies

After more than a decade of maintaining the Thai *baht's* peg to the U.S. dollar, Thai authorities abandoned the peg in July 1997.[6] By October, market forces had led the baht to depreciate by 60 percent against the dollar. The depreciation triggered a wave

---

[6]Ramon Moreno, "Lessons from Thailand," *Economic Letter*, Federal Reserve Bank of San Francisco, November 7, 1997.

of speculation against other Southeast Asian currencies. Over the same period, the Indonesian *rupiah*, Malaysia *ringgit*, Philippine peso, and South Korean won abandoned links to the dollar and depreciated 47, 35, 34, and 16 percent respectively. This episode reopened one of the oldest debates in economics: whether a currency should have a fixed or floating exchange rate. Consider the case of Thailand.

Although Thailand was widely regarded as one of Southeast Asia's outstanding performers throughout the 1980s and 1990s; it relied heavily on inflows of short-term foreign capital, attracted both by the stable baht and by Thai interest rates that were much higher than comparable interest rates elsewhere. The capital inflow supported a broad based economic boom that was especially visible in the real estate market.

However, by 1996 Thailand's economic boom had fizzled. As a result, both local and foreign investors grew nervous and began withdrawing funds from Thailand's financial system that put downward pressure on the baht. However, the Thai government resisted the depreciation pressure by purchasing baht with dollars in the foreign exchange market and also raising interest rates that increased the attractiveness of the baht. The purchases of the baht greatly depleted Thailand's reserves of hard currency. Raising interest rates adversely affected an already weak financial sector by dampening economic activity. These factors ultimately contributed to the abandonment of the baht's link to the dollar.

Although Thailand and other Southeast Asian countries abandoned fixed exchange rates in 1997, some economists questioned whether such a policy would be in their best interest in the long run. Their reasoning was that these economies were relatively small and wide open to international trade and investment flows. Inflation rates were modest by the standards of a developing country and labor markets were relatively flexible. Floating exchange rates were probably not the best long run option. These economists maintained that unless the Southeast Asian governments anchored their currencies to something, their currencies might drift into a vicious cycle of depreciation and higher inflation. There was certainly a concern that central banks in the region lacked the credibility to enforce tough monetary policies without the external constraint of a fixed exchange rate. Neither fixed exchange rates nor floating exchange rates offer a magical solution. What really makes a difference to a country's prospects is the quality of its overall economic policies.

CAPITAL CONTROLS

Because capital flows have often been an important element in currency crises, controls on capital movements have been established to support fixed exchange rates and thus avoid speculative attacks on currencies. **Capital controls**, also known as **exchange controls**, are government imposed barriers to foreign savers investing in domestic assets (government securities, stock, or bank deposits) or to domestic savers investing in foreign assets. At one extreme, a government may seek to gain control over its payments position by directly circumventing market forces through the imposition of direct controls on international transactions. A government that has a virtual monopoly over foreign exchange dealings may require that all foreign exchange earnings be turned over to authorized dealers. The government then allocates foreign exchange among domestic traders and investors at government set prices.

The advantage of such a system is that the government can influence its payments position by regulating the amount of foreign exchange allocated to imports or capital outflows, limiting the extent of these transactions. Capital controls also permit the government to encourage or discourage certain transactions by offering different rates for foreign currency for different purposes. Capital controls can give domestic monetary and fiscal policies greater freedom in their stabilization roles. By controlling the balance-of-payments through capital controls, a government can pursue its domestic economic policies without fear of balance-of-payments repercussions.

Speculative attacks in Mexico and East Asia were fueled in part by large changes in capital outflows and inflows. As a result, some economists and politicians argued for restrictions on capital mobility in developing countries. Malaysian Prime Minister Mahathir imposed limits on capital outflows in 1998 to help his economy regain financial stability.

Although restrictions on capital outflows may seem attractive, they suffer from several problems. Evidence suggests that capital outflows may further increase after the controls are implemented because confidence in the government is weakened. Restrictions on capital outflows often result in evasion, as government officials get paid to ignore domestic residents who shift funds overseas. Capital controls may provide government officials the false sense of security that they do not have to reform their financial systems to ameliorate the crisis.

Although economists are generally dubious of controls on capital outflows, controls on capital inflows often receive more support. Supporters contend that if speculative capital cannot enter a country, then it cannot suddenly leave and create a crisis. They note that the financial crisis in East Asia in 1997–1998 illustrated how capital inflows can result in a lending boom, excessive risk taking by domestic banks, and ultimately financial collapse. Restrictions on the inflow of capital are problematic because they can prevent funds that would be used to finance productive investment opportunities from entering a country. Limits on capital inflows are seldom effective because the private sector finds ways to evade them and move funds into the country.[7]

Should Foreign Exchange Transactions be Taxed?

The 1997–1998 financial crises in East Asia in which several nations were forced to abandon their fixed exchange rate regimes, produced demands for more stability and government regulation in the foreign exchange markets. Market volatility was blamed for much of the trouble sweeping the region.

Economists generally argue that the free market is the best device for determining how money should be invested. Global capital markets provide needy countries with funds to grow while permitting foreign investors to diversify their portfolios. If capital is allowed to flow freely, they contend markets will reward countries that pursue sound economic policies and pressure the rest to do the same. Most countries welcome and even encourage capital inflows such as foreign direct investment in factories and businesses that represent long lasting commitments. Some have become skeptical of financial instruments such as stocks and bonds, bank deposits, and short-term debt securities that can be pulled out of a country with a stroke of a computer key. That's what occurred in East Asia in 1997, in Mexico in 1994 and 1995, and in the United Kingdom and Italy in 1992 and 1993.

To prevent international financial crises, several notable economists have called for sand to be thrown in the wheels of international finance by imposing a tax on foreign exchange transactions. The idea is that a tax would increase the cost of these transactions that would discourage massive responses to minor changes in information about the economic situation and dampen volatility in exchange rates. Proponents argue that such a tax would give traders an incentive to look at long-term economic trends, not short-term hunches when buying and selling foreign exchange and securities. Traders would pay a

---

[7]Sebastian Edwards, "How Effective Are Capital Controls?" *Journal of Economic Perspective*, Winter 2000, Vol. 13, No. 4, pp. 65–84.

small tax, say, 0.1 percent for every transaction, so they would not buy or sell unless expected returns justified the additional expense. Fewer transactions suggest less volatility and more stable exchange rates.

Proponents of a tax may well contend that they are not trying to interfere with free markets, but only to prevent excess volatility. We do not know how much volatility is excessive or irrational. It's true that economists cannot explain all exchange rate volatility in terms of changes in the economic fundamentals of nations, but it does not follow from this that we should seek to regulate such fluctuations. Indeed, some of the volatility may be produced by uncertainty about government policies.

There are other drawbacks to the idea of taxing foreign exchange transactions. Such a tax could impose a burden on countries that are quite rationally borrowing overseas. By raising the cost of capital for these countries, it would discourage investment and hinder their development. A tax on foreign exchange transactions would be difficult to implement. Foreign exchange trading can be conducted almost anywhere in the world, and a universal agreement to impose such a tax seems extremely unlikely. Those countries that refused to implement the tax would become centers for foreign exchange trading.

INCREASING THE CREDIBILITY OF FIXED EXCHANGE RATES

As we have learned, when speculators feel that a central bank is unable to defend the exchange rate for a weakening currency, they will sell the local currency to obtain more stable foreign currencies. Are there ways to convince speculators that the exchange rate is unchangeable? Currency boards and dollarization are explicitly intended to maintain fixed exchange rates and thus prevent currency crises.

Currency Board

A **currency board** is a monetary authority that issues notes and coins convertible into a foreign anchor currency at a *fixed* exchange rate. The anchor currency is a currency chosen for its expected stability and international acceptability. For most currency boards, the U.S. dollar or the UK pound has been the anchor currency. A few currency boards have used gold as the anchor. Usually the fixed exchange rate is set by law, making changes to the exchange rate costly for governments. Currency boards offer the strongest form of a fixed exchange rate that is possible short of full currency union.

The commitment to exchange domestic currency for foreign currency at a fixed exchange rate requires the currency board have sufficient foreign exchange to honor this commitment. This condition means that its holdings of foreign exchange must at least equal 100 percent of its notes and coins in circulation as set by law. A currency board can operate in place of a central bank or as a parallel issuer alongside an existing central bank. Usually a currency board takes over the role of a central bank in strengthening the currency of a developing country.

By design, a currency board has no discretionary powers. Its operations are completely passive and automatic. The sole function of a currency board is to exchange its notes and coins for the anchor at a fixed rate. Unlike a central bank, a currency board does not lend to the domestic government, domestic companies, or domestic banks. In a currency board system, the government can finance its spending only by taxing or borrowing, not by printing money and creating inflation. This limitation results from the stipulation that the backing of the domestic currency must be at least 100 percent.

A country that adopts a currency board puts its monetary policy on autopilot. It is as if the chairman of the board of governors of the Federal Reserve System were replaced by a personal computer. When the anchor currency flows in, the board issues more domestic currency and interest rates fall; when the anchor currency flows out, interest rates rise. The government sits back and watches, even if interest rates skyrocket and a recession ensues.

Many economists maintain that, especially in the developing world, central banks are incapable of retaining nonpolitical independence and instill less confidence than is necessary for the smooth functioning of a monetary system. They are answerable to the prerogatives of populism or dictatorship and are at the beck and call of political changes. The bottom line is that central banks should not be given the onerous responsibility of maintaining the value of currencies. This job should be left to an independent body whose sole mandate is to issue currency against a strict and unalterable set of guidelines that require a fixed amount of foreign exchange or gold to be deposited for each unit of domestic currency issued.

Currency boards can confer considerable credibility on fixed exchange rate regimes. The most vital contribution a currency board can make to exchange rate stability is by imposing discipline on the process of money creation. This discipline results in the greater stability of domestic prices that in turn, stabilizes the value of the domestic currency. In short, the major benefits of the currency board system are as follows:

- Making a nation's currency and exchange rate regimes more rule bound and predictable
- Placing an upper bound on the nation's base money supply
- Arresting any tendencies in an economy toward inflation
- Forcing the government to restrict its borrowing to what foreign and domestic lenders are willing to lend it at market interest rates
- Engendering confidence in the soundness of the nation's money, assuring citizens and foreign investors that the domestic currency can always be exchanged for some other strong currency
- Creating confidence and promoting trade, investment, and economic growth

Proponents cite Hong Kong as a country that has benefited from a currency board. In the early 1980s, Hong Kong had a floating exchange rate. The immediate cause of Hong Kong's economic problems was uncertainty about its political future. In 1982, the United Kingdom and China began talks about the fate of Hong Kong when the United Kingdom's lease on the territory expired in 1997. Fear that China would abandon Hong Kong's capitalist system sent Hong Kong's stock market down by 50 percent. Hong Kong's real estate market weakened also, and small banks with heavy exposure in real estate suffered runs. The result was a 16 percent depreciation in the Hong Kong dollar against the U.S. dollar. With this loss of confidence, many merchants refused to accept Hong Kong dollars and quoted prices in U.S. dollars instead. Panic buying of vegetable oil, rice, and other staples emptied merchants' shelves.

In 1983, the government of Hong Kong ended its economic crises by announcing that Hong Kong would adopt a currency board system. It pegged its exchange rate at HK\$7.8 = US \$1. The currency reform immediately reversed the loss of confidence about Hong Kong's economy despite continuing troubles in the U.K.–China discussions. A stable currency provided the basis for Hong Kong to continue its rapid economic growth.

By maintaining a legal commitment to exchange domestic currency for a foreign currency at a fixed exchange rate, and a commitment to issue currency only if it is backed by foreign reserves, a currency board can be a good way to restore confidence in a country gripped by economic chaos. Although a currency board cannot solve all of a country's economic problems, it may achieve more financial credibility than a domestic central bank.

Although currency boards help discipline government spending, thereby reducing a major source of inflation in developing countries, there are concerns about currency boards. Perhaps the most common objection is that a currency board prevents a country from pursuing a discretionary monetary policy and thus reduces its economic independence. It is sometimes said that a currency board system is susceptible to financial panics because it lacks a lender of last resort. Another objection is that a currency board system creates a colonial relation with the anchor currency. Critics cite the experiences of British colonies that operated under currency board systems in the early 1900s.

It is possible for a nation's monetary system to be orderly and disciplined under either a currency board or a central banking system. Neither system by itself guarantees either order or discipline. The effectiveness of both systems depends on other factors such as fiscal discipline and a sound banking system. In other words, it is a whole network of responsible and mutually supporting policies and institutions that make for sound money and stable exchange rates. No monetary regime, however well conceived, can bear the entire burden alone.

For Argentina, No Panacea in a Currency Board

For much of the post–World War II era, when the financial press focused on Argentina, it was to highlight bouts of high inflation and failed stabilization efforts. Hyperinflation was rampant in the 1970s and 1980s, and prices increased by more than 1,000 percent in both 1989 and 1990.

In 1991, to tame its tendency to finance public spending by printing pesos, Argentina introduced convertibility of its peso into dollars at a fixed one-to-one exchange rate. To control the issuance of money, the Argentines abandoned their central bank based monetary regime that they felt lacked credibility, and established a currency board. Under this arrangement, currency could be issued only if the currency board had an equivalent amount of dollars.

The fixed exchange rate and the currency board were designed to ensure that Argentina would have a low inflation rate, one similar to that in the United States. At first, this program appeared to work: by 1995, prices were rising at less than two percent per year.

During the late 1990s, the Argentine economy was hit with four external shocks: the appreciation of the dollar that had the same negative effect on Argentine export and import competing industries that it had on similar industries in the United States; rising U.S. interest rates that spilled over into the Argentine economy, resulting in a decrease in spending on capital goods; falling commodity prices on world markets that significantly harmed Argentina's commodity exporting industries; and the depreciation of Brazil's *real* that made Brazil's goods relatively cheaper in Argentina and Argentina's goods relatively more expensive in Brazil. These external shocks had a major deflationary effect on the Argentine economy, resulting in falling output and rising unemployment.

Argentina dealt with its problems by spending much more than it collected in taxes to bolster its economy. To finance its budget deficits, Argentina borrowed dollars on the international market. When further borrowing became impossible in 2001, Argentina defaulted, ended convertibility of pesos into dollars, and froze most deposits at banks. Violence and other protests erupted as Argentineans voiced their displeasure with politicians.

Some economists have questioned whether the establishment of a currency board was a mistake for Argentina. They note that although Argentina tied itself to the American currency area as if it were Utah or Massachusetts, it did not benefit from adjustment mechanisms that enable the American currency area to work smoothly in the face of negative external shocks. When unemployment rose in Argentina, its people could not move to the United States where jobs were relatively plentiful. Federal Reserve policy was geared to the conditions of the United States rather than to Argentina. The U.S. Congress did not target American fiscal policy on problem areas in Argentina. As a result, the negative shocks to the Argentine economy were dealt with by wage and price deflation. It was a consequence of having fixed its currency rigidly to the dollar.

Dollarization

Instead of using a currency board to maintain fixed exchange rates, why not "dollarize" an economy? **Dollarization** occurs when residents of, say, Ecuador, use the U.S. dollar alongside or instead of the *sucre*. Partial dollarization occurs when Ecuadoreans hold dollar denominated bank deposits or Federal Reserve notes to protect against high inflation in the sucre. Partial dollarization has existed for years in many Latin American and Caribbean countries where the United States is a major trading partner and a major source of foreign investment.

Full dollarization means the elimination of the Ecuadorean sucre and its complete replacement with the U.S. dollar. The monetary base of Ecuador that initially consisted entirely of sucre denominated currency would be converted into U.S. Federal Reserve notes. To replace its currency, Ecuador would sell foreign reserves (mostly U.S. Treasury securities) to buy dollars and exchange all outstanding sucre notes for dollar notes. The U.S. dollar would be the sole legal tender and sole unit of account in Ecuador. Full dollarization has occurred in the U.S. Virgin Islands, the Marshall Islands, Puerto Rico, Guam, Ecuador, and other Latin American countries.

Full dollarization is rare today because of the symbolism countries attach to a national currency and the political impact of a perceived loss of sovereignty associated with the adoption of another country's unit of account and currency. When it does occur it is principally implemented by small countries or territories that are closely associated politically, geographically, and/or through extensive economic and trade ties with the country whose currency is adopted.

Why Dollarize?   Why would a small country want to dollarize its economy? Benefits to the dollarizing country include the credibility and policy discipline that is derived from the implicit irrevocability of dollarization. Behind this lies the promise of lower interest and inflation rates, greater financial stability, and increased economic activity. Countries with a history of high inflation and financial instability often find the potential offered by dollarization to be quite attractive. Dollarization is considered to be one way of avoiding the capital outflows that often precede or accompany an embattled currency situation.

A major benefit of dollarization is the decrease in transaction costs as a result of a common currency. The elimination of currency risk and hedging allows for more trade and more investment within the unified currency zone to occur. Another benefit is in the area of inflation. The choice of another currency necessarily means that the rate of inflation in the dollarized economy will be tied to that of the issuing country. To the extent that a more accepted, stable, recognized currency is chosen, lower inflation now and in the future can be expected to result from dollarization. Greater openness results from a system where exchange controls are unnecessary and balance-of-payments crises are minimized. Dollarization will not assure an absence of balance-of-payments difficulties, but it does ensure such crises will be handled in a way that forces a government to deal with events in an open manner, rather than by printing money and contributing to inflation.

Effects of Dollarization   A convenient way to think about any country that plans to adopt the dollar as its official currency is to treat it as one would treat any of the 50 states in the United States. In discussions about monetary policy in the United States, it is assumed that the Federal Reserve conducts monetary policy with reference to national economic conditions rather than the economic conditions in an individual state or region, even though economic conditions are not uniform throughout the country. The reason for this is that monetary policy works through interest rates on credit markets that are national in scope. Monetary policy cannot be tailored to deal with business conditions in an individual state or region that is different from the national economy. When Ecuador dollarized its economy, it essentially accepted the monetary policy of the Federal Reserve.

With dollarization in Ecuador, U.S. monetary policy would presumably be carried out as it is now. If Ecuadorean business cycles do not coincide with those in the United States, Ecuador cannot count on the Federal Reserve to come to its rescue, just as any state in the United States cannot count on the Federal Reserve to rescue them. This limitation may be a major downside for the Ecuadoreans. Despite this, Ecuador might still be better off without the supposed safety valve of an independent monetary policy.

Another limitation facing the Ecuadoreans is that the Federal Reserve is not their lender of last resort as it is for Americans. If the U.S. financial system should come under stress, the Federal Reserve could use its various monetary powers to aid these institutions and contain possible failures. Without the consent of the U.S. Congress, the Federal Reserve could not perform this function for Ecuador or for any other country that decided to adopt the dollar officially as its currency.

A third limitation arising from the adoption of the dollar as the official currency is that Ecuador could no longer get any **seigniorage** from its monetary system. This cost for Ecuador stems from the loss of the foreign reserves (mainly U.S. Treasury securities) that it can sell in exchange for dollars. These reserves bear interest and, therefore, are a source of income for Ecuador. This income is called seigniorage. Once Ecuador's reserves are replaced by dollar bills, this source of income disappears.

With dollarization, Ecuador enjoys the same freedom that the 50 states in the United States enjoy as to how to spend its tax dollars. Ecuador state expenditures for education, police protection, social insurance, and the like are not affected by its use of the U.S. dollar. Ecuador can establish its own tariffs, subsidies, and other trade policies. Ecuador's sovereignty is not compromised in these areas. There would be an overall constraint on Ecuadorean fiscal policy: Ecuador does not have the recourse of printing more sucre to finance budget deficits and thus has to exercise caution in its spending policies.

Official dollarization of Ecuador's economy also has implications for the United States. First, when Ecuadoreans acquire dollars they surrender goods and services to Americans. For each dollar sent abroad, Americans enjoy a one-time increase in the amount of goods and services they are able to consume. Second, by opting to hold dollars rather than the interest bearing debt of the United States, the United States, in effect, gets an interest free loan from Ecuador. The interest that does not have to be paid is a measure of seigniorage that accrues on an annual basis to the United States. On the other hand, use of U.S. currency abroad might hinder the formulation and execution of monetary policy by the Federal Reserve. By making Ecuador more dependent on U.S. monetary policy, dollarization could result in more pressure on the Federal Reserve to conduct policy according to the interests of Ecuador rather than those of the United States.

SUMMARY

1. Most nations maintain neither completely fixed nor floating exchange rates. Contemporary exchange rate systems generally embody some features of each of these standards.

2. Small, developing nations often anchor their currencies to a single currency or a currency basket. Anchoring to a single currency is generally used by small nations whose trade and financial relations are mainly with a single trading partner. Small nations with more than one major trading partner often anchor their currencies to a basket of currencies.

3. The special drawing right is a currency basket composed of the four key currencies of IMF members. The basket valuation technique attempts to make the SDR's value more stable than the foreign currency value of any single currency in the basket. Developing nations often choose to anchor their exchange rates to the SDR.

4. Under a fixed exchange rate system, a government defines the official exchange rate for its currency. It then establishes an exchange stabilization fund that buys and sells foreign currencies to prevent the market exchange rate from moving above or below the official rate. Nations may officially devalue/revalue their currencies to restore trade equilibrium.

5. With floating exchange rates, market forces of supply and demand determine currency values. Among the major arguments for floating rates are (a) simplicity, (b) continuous adjustment, (c) independent domestic policies, and (d) reduced need for international reserves. Arguments against floating rates stress (a) disorderly exchange markets, (b) reckless financial policies on the part of governments, and (c) conduciveness to price inflation.

6. With the breakdown of the Bretton Woods system of fixed exchange rates, major industrial nations adopted a system of managed floating exchange rates. Under this system, central bank intervention in the foreign exchange market is intended to prevent disorderly market conditions in the short run. In the long run, exchange rates are permitted to float in accordance with changing supply and demand.

7. To offset a depreciation in the home currency's exchange value, a central bank can (a) use its international reserves to purchase quantities of that currency on the foreign exchange market; or (b) initiate a contractionary monetary policy that leads to higher domestic interest rates, increased investment inflows, and increased demand for the home currency. To offset an appreciation in the home currency's exchange value, a central bank can sell additional quantities of its currency on the foreign exchange market or initiate an expansionary monetary policy.

8. Under a crawling-peg exchange rate system, a nation makes frequent devaluations (or revaluations) of its currency to restore payments balance. Developing nations suffering from high inflation rates have been major users of this mechanism.

9. A currency crisis, also called a *speculative attack*, is a situation in which a weak currency experiences heavy selling pressure. Among the causes of currency crises are budget deficits financed by inflation, weak financial systems, political uncertainty, and changes in interest rates on world markets. Although a fixed exchange rate system has the advantage of promoting low inflation, it is especially vulnerable to speculative attacks.

10. Capital controls are sometimes used by governments in an attempt to support fixed exchange rates and prevent speculative attacks on currencies. Capital controls are hindered by the private sector's finding ways to evade them and move funds into or out of a country.

11. Currency boards and dollarization are explicitly intended to maintain fixed exchange rates and prevent currency crises. A currency board is a monetary authority that issues notes and coins convertible into a foreign currency at a fixed exchange rate. The most vital contribution a currency board can make to exchange rate stability is to impose discipline on the process of money creation. This discipline results in greater stability in domestic prices that in turn, stabilizes the value of the domestic currency. Dollarization occurs when residents of a country use the U.S. dollar alongside or instead of their own currency. Dollarization is seen as a way to protect a country's growth and prosperity from bouts of inflation, currency depreciation, and speculative attacks against the local currency.

KEY CONCEPTS AND TERMS

Adjustable pegged exchange rates (p. 452)
Bretton Woods system (p. 452)
Capital controls (p. 470)
Clean float (p. 457)
Crawling peg (p. 462)
Currency board (p. 472)
Currency crashes (p. 467)
Currency crisis (p. 465)
Devaluation (p. 452)

Dirty float (p. 457)
Dollarization (p. 475)
Exchange controls (p. 470)
Exchange stabilization fund (p. 450)
Fixed exchange rates (p. 448)
Floating exchange rates (p. 453)
Fundamental disequilibrium (p. 451)
Impossible trinity (p. 447)

Key currency (p. 448)
Leaning against the wind (p. 457)
Managed floating system (p. 457)
Official exchange rate (p. 450)
Par value (p. 450)
Revaluation (p. 452)
Seigniorage (p. 476)
Special drawing right (SDR) (p. 450)
Speculative attack (p. 465)
Target exchange rates (p. 457)

STUDY QUESTIONS

1. What factors underlie a nation's decision to adopt floating exchange rates or fixed exchange rates?
2. How do managed floating exchange rates operate? Why were they adopted by the industrialized nations in 1973?
3. Why do some developing countries adopt currency boards? Why do others dollarize their monetary systems?
4. Discuss the philosophy and operation of the Bretton Woods system of adjustable pegged exchange rates.
5. Why do nations use a crawling peg exchange rate system?
6. What is the purpose of capital controls?
7. What factors contribute to currency crises?
8. Why do small nations adopt currency baskets against which they peg their exchange rates?
9. What advantage does the SDR offer to small nations seeking to peg their exchange rates?
10. Present the case for and the case against a system of floating exchange rates.
11. What techniques can a central bank use to stabilize the exchange value of its currency?
12. What is the purpose of a currency devaluation? What about a currency revaluation?

Macroeconomic Policy in an Open Economy

Since the Great Depression of the 1930s, governments have actively pursued the goal of a fully employed economy with price stability. They have used fiscal and monetary policies to achieve this goal. A nation that has a closed economy (one that is not exposed to international trade and financial flows) could use these policies in view of its own goals. With an open economy, the nation finds that the success of these policies depends on factors such as its exports and imports of goods and services, the international mobility of financial capital, and the flexibility of its exchange rate. These factors can support or detract from the ability of monetary and fiscal policy to achieve full employment with price stability.

This chapter considers macroeconomic policy in an open economy. The chapter first examines the way in which monetary and fiscal policy are supposed to operate in a closed economy. The chapter then describes the effect of an open economy on monetary and fiscal policy.

ECONOMIC OBJECTIVES OF NATIONS

What are the objectives of macroeconomic policy? Known as **internal balance**, this goal has two dimensions: a fully employed economy and no inflation—or more realistically, a reasonable amount of inflation. Nations traditionally have considered internal balance to be of primary importance and formulated economic policies to attain this goal. Policy-makers are also aware of a nation's current account position. A nation is said to be in **external balance** when it realizes neither deficits nor surpluses in its current account. An economy realizes **overall balance** when it attains internal balance and external balance.

Besides pursuing internal and external balance, nations have other economic goals such as long run economic growth and a reasonably equitable distribution of national income. Although these and other commitments may influence macroeconomic policy, the discussion in this chapter is confined to the pursuit of internal and external balance.

POLICY INSTRUMENTS

To attain external and internal balance, policymakers enact expenditure changing policies, expenditure switching policies, and direct controls.

Expenditure changing policies alter the level of total spending (aggregate demand) for goods and services, including those produced domestically and those imported. They include **fiscal policy** that refers to changes in government spending and taxes, and **monetary policy** that refers to changes in the money supply and interest rates by a nation's central bank (such as the Federal Reserve). Depending on the direction of change, expenditure changing policies are either expenditure increasing or reducing.

Expenditure switching policies modify the direction of demand, shifting it between domestic output and imports. Under a system of fixed exchange rates, a nation with a trade deficit could devalue its currency to increase the international competitiveness of its firms, thus diverting spending from foreign produced goods to domestically produced goods. To increase its competitiveness under a managed floating exchange rate system, a nation could purchase other currencies with its currency causing its currency's exchange value to depreciate. The success of these policies in promoting trade balance largely depends on switching demand in the proper direction and amount, as well as on the capacity of the home economy to meet the additional demand by supplying more goods.

Direct controls consist of government restrictions on the market economy. They are selective expenditure switching policies whose objective is to control particular items in the current account. Direct controls such as tariffs are levied on imports in an attempt to switch domestic spending away from foreign produced goods to domestically produced goods. Direct controls may also be used to restrain capital outflows or to stimulate capital inflows.

The formation of macroeconomic policy is subject to constraints that involve considerations of fairness and equity. Policymakers are aware of the needs of groups they represent such as labor and business, especially when pursuing conflicting economic objectives. To what extent should the domestic interest rate rise in order to eliminate a deficit in the capital account? The outcry of adversely affected groups within the nation that suffer from a high interest rate, may be more than sufficient to convince policymakers not to pursue capital account balance. Reflecting perceptions of fairness and equity, policy formation tends to be characterized by negotiation and compromise.

AGGREGATE DEMAND AND AGGREGATE SUPPLY: A BRIEF REVIEW

In your principles of macroeconomics course, you learned about a model that can be used to analyze the output and price level of an economy in the short run. This model is called the aggregate demand–aggregate supply model. Using the framework of Figure 16.1, let us review the main characteristics of this model as applied to Canada.

In Figure 16.1, the aggregate demand curve (*AD*) shows the level of real output (real gross domestic product) that Canadians will purchase at alternative price levels during a given year. Aggregate demand consists of spending by domestic consumers, businesses, government, and foreign buyers (net exports). As the price level falls, the quantity of real output demanded increases.

FIGURE 16.1

Macroeconomic Equilibrium: the Aggregate Demand–Aggregate Supply Model

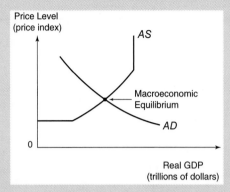

The economy is in equilibrium where the aggregate demand curve intersects the aggregate supply curve. This intersection determines the equilibrium price level and output for the economy. Increases (decreases) in aggregate demand or aggregate supply result in rightward (leftward) shifts in these curves.

Figure 16.1 also shows the economy's aggregate supply curve (*AS*). This curve shows the relation between the level of prices and amount of real output that will be produced by the economy during a given year. The aggregate supply curve is generally upward sloping because per-unit production costs, and therefore the prices that firms must receive, increase as real output increases.[1] The economy is in equilibrium when aggregate demand equals aggregate supply. This is where the two lines intersect in the figure.

An increase (decrease) in aggregate demand is depicted by a rightward (leftward) shift in the aggregate demand curve. Shifts in aggregate demand are caused by changes in the determinants of aggregate demand: consumption, investment, government purchases, or net exports. Similarly, an increase (decrease) in aggregate supply is depicted by a rightward (leftward) shift in the aggregate supply curve. Shifts in the aggregate supply curve occur in response to changes in the price of resources, technology, business expectations, and the like. Next we will use the aggregate demand–aggregate supply framework to analyze the effects of fiscal and monetary policy.

MONETARY AND FISCAL POLICY IN A CLOSED ECONOMY

Monetary policy and fiscal policy are the main macroeconomic tools by which government can influence the performance of an economy. If aggregate output is too low and unemployment is too high, the traditional policy solution is for government to increase

---

[1]The aggregate supply curve actually has three distinct regions. First, when the economy is in deep recession or depression, the aggregate supply curve is horizontal. Because excess capacity in the economy places no upward pressure on prices, changes in aggregate demand cause changes in real output, but no change in the price level. Second, as the economy approaches full employment, scarcities in resource markets develop. Increasing aggregate demand places upward pressure on resource prices, bidding up unit production costs and causing the aggregate supply curve to slope upward: more output is produced only at a higher price level. Finally, the aggregate supply curve becomes vertical when the economy is at full employment.

aggregate demand for real output through expansionary monetary or fiscal policies. This results in an increase in the country's real GDP. Conversely, if inflation is troublesome, it's source tends to be a level of aggregate demand that exceeds the rate of output that can be supported by the economy's resources at constant prices. The solution in this situation is for the government to reduce the level of aggregate demand through contractionary monetary or fiscal policy. As the aggregate demand curve decreases, the upward pressure on prices caused by excess aggregate demand is softened and inflation moderates.

Figure 16.2(a) illustrates the effects of an expansionary monetary or fiscal policy in a closed Canadian economy. For simplicity, let us assume that Canada's aggregate supply curve is horizontal until the full employment level of real GDP is attained at $800 trillion; at this point, the aggregate supply curve becomes vertical. Also assume that the economy's equilibrium real GDP equals $500 trillion, shown by the intersection of AD_0 and AS_0. The economy suffers from recession because its equilibrium output lies below the full employment level. To combat the recession, assume an expansionary monetary or fiscal policy is implemented that increases aggregate demand to AD_1. Equilibrium real GDP would increase from $500 trillion to $700 trillion and unemployment would decline in the economy.

To expand aggregate demand, the Bank of Canada (as well as central banks of other countries) would usually increase the money supply through purchasing securities in the open market.[2] Increasing the money supply reduces the interest rate within the country and this increases consumption and investment spending. The resulting increase in aggregate demand generates a multiple increase in real GDP.[3] To offset inflation, the Bank of Canada would decrease the money supply by selling securities in the open market, and the interest rate would rise. The increase in the interest rate reduces consumption and investment spending, thus decreasing aggregate demand. This decrease lowers any excess demand pressure on prices.

Instead of using monetary policy to stabilize the economy, Canada could use fiscal policy that operates either through changes in government spending or taxes. Because government spending is a component of aggregate demand, the Canadian government can directly affect aggregate demand by altering its own spending. To combat recession, the government could increase its spending to raise aggregate demand that results in a multiple increase in equilibrium real GDP. Instead, the government could combat recession by lowering income taxes that would increase the amount of disposable income in the hands of households. This increase results in a rise in consumption spending, an increase in aggregate demand, and a multiple increase in equilibrium real GDP. A contractionary fiscal policy works in the opposite direction.

---

[2]Open market operations are the most important monetary tool of the Federal Reserve (Fed). They consist of the purchase or sale of securities by the Fed; this transaction is made with a bank or some other business or individual. Open market purchases result in an increase in bank reserves and the money supply. Open market sales cause bank reserves and the money supply to decrease. Other tools of monetary policy include changes in the discount rate, the interest rate that the Federal Reserve charges banks to borrow reserves, and changes in the required reserve ratio, the percentage of their deposits that banks are required to hold as reserves.

[3]Fiscal and monetary policies are based on the multiplier effect. According to this principle, changes in aggregate demand are multiplied into larger changes in equilibrium output and income. This process results from households receiving income and then spending it, which generates income for others, and so on.

FIGURE 16.2

Effect of an Expansionary Monetary or Fiscal Policy on Equilibrium Real GDP

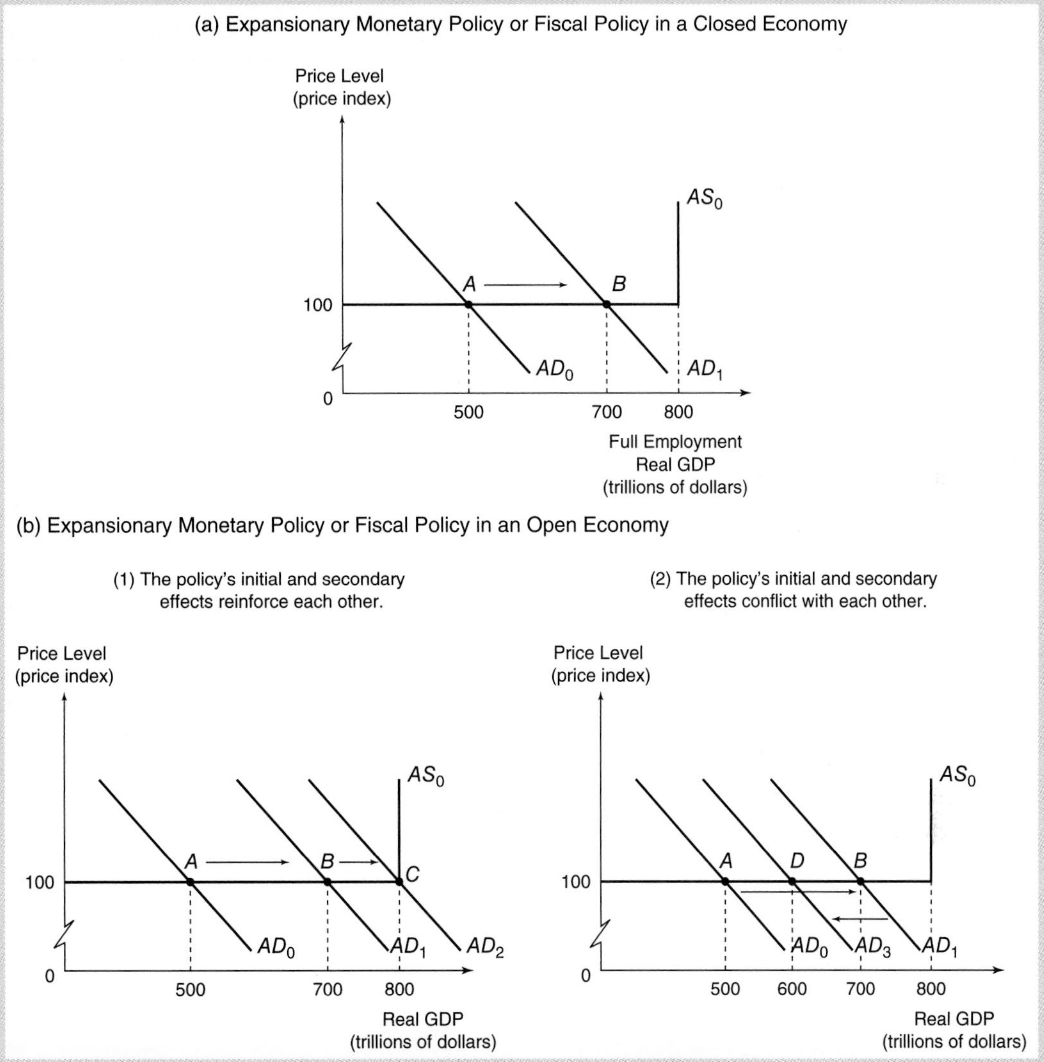

(a) Expansionary Monetary Policy or Fiscal Policy in a Closed Economy

(b) Expansionary Monetary Policy or Fiscal Policy in an Open Economy

(1) The policy's initial and secondary effects reinforce each other.

(2) The policy's initial and secondary effects conflict with each other.

(a) Expansionary Monetary or Fiscal Policy in a Closed Economy (b) Expansionary Monetary Policy or Fiscal Policy in an Open Economy (1) The policy's initial and secondary effects reinforce each other. (2) The policy's initial and secondary effects conflict with each other.

© Cengage Learning®

MONETARY AND FISCAL POLICY IN AN OPEN ECONOMY

The previous section examined how monetary policy and fiscal policy can be used as economic stabilization tools in a closed economy. Next we consider the effects of these policies in an open economy. The key question is whether an expansionary monetary policy or fiscal policy in an open economy is more or less effective in increasing real GDP than it is in a closed economy.[4]

The answer to this question is influenced by a country's decision to adopt a system of fixed or floating exchange rates, as discussed below. In practice, many countries maintain neither rigidly fixed exchange rates nor freely floating exchange rates. Rather, they maintain managed floating exchange rates in which a central bank buys or sells currencies in an attempt to prevent exchange rate movements from becoming disorderly. Heavier exchange rate intervention moves a country closer to our fixed exchange rate conclusion for monetary and fiscal policy; less intervention moves a country closer to our floating exchange rate conclusion.

Our conclusions depend on the expansionary or contractionary effects that monetary policy or fiscal policy has on aggregate demand. In a closed economy, an expansionary monetary or fiscal policy has a single effect on aggregate demand: it causes aggregate demand to expand by increasing domestic consumption, investment, or government spending. In an open economy, the policy has a second effect on aggregate demand: it causes aggregate demand to increase or decrease by changing net exports and other determinants of aggregate demand. If the initial and secondary effects of the policy result in increases in aggregate demand, the expansionary effect of the policy is strengthened. If the initial and secondary effects have conflicting impacts on aggregate demand, the expansionary effect of the policy is weakened. The examples below clarify this point.

Let us begin by assuming the mobility of international investment (capital) is high for Canada. This high mobility suggests that a small change in the relative interest rate across nations induces a large international flow of investment. This assumption is consistent with investment movements among many nations such as the United States, Japan, and Germany, and the conclusions of many analysts that investment mobility increases as national financial markets become globalized.

Effect of Fiscal and Monetary Policy under Fixed Exchange Rates

Consider first the effects of an expansionary fiscal policy or monetary policy under a system of fixed exchange rates. The conclusion that emerges from our discussion is that an expansionary fiscal policy is more successful in stimulating the economy, and an expansionary monetary policy is less successful, than they are in a closed economy. This conclusion is summarized in Table 16.1.[5]

TABLE 16.1

The Effectiveness of Monetary and Fiscal Policy in Promoting Internal Balance for an Economy with a High Degree of Capital Mobility

Exchange-Rate Regime	Monetary Policy	Fiscal Policy
Floating exchange rates	Strengthened	Weakened
Fixed exchange rates	Weakened	Strengthened

© Cengage Learning®

---

[4]This chapter considers solely the effects of expansionary monetary and fiscal policy. A contractionary monetary and fiscal policy tends to have the opposite effects.

[5]This analysis originated with R. Mundell, "The Appropriate Use of Monetary and Fiscal Policy for Internal and External Stability," *IMF Staff Papers*, March 1961, pp. 70–77 and J. M. Flemming, "Domestic Financial Policies Under Fixed and Under Flexible Exchange Rates," *IMF Staff Papers*, 1962, pp. 369–379.

Fiscal Policy is Strengthened Under Fixed Exchange Rates. Referring to Figure 16.2(b-1), assume that Canada operates under a fixed exchange rate system and its government initially has a balanced budget in which government spending equals government taxes. To combat a recession, suppose the government adopts an expansionary fiscal policy, say, an increase in its spending on goods and services. The initial effect of a rise in government spending is to increase aggregate demand from AD_0 to AD_1, the same amount that occurs in our example of expansionary fiscal policy in a closed economy. This increase causes equilibrium real GDP to expand from $500 trillion to $700 trillion.

The second effect of the expansionary fiscal policy is that increased spending causes the Canadian government's budget to go into deficit. As the government demands more money to finance its excess spending, the domestic interest rate rises. A higher interest rate attracts an inflow of investment from foreigners that results in an increased demand for Canadian dollars in the foreign exchange market. The dollar's exchange rate is under pressure to appreciate. Appreciation cannot occur because Canada has a fixed exchange rate system. To prevent its dollar from appreciating, the Canadian government must intervene in the foreign exchange market and purchase foreign currency with dollars. This purchase results in an increase in the domestic money supply. The effect of the rise in the money supply is to increase the amount of loanable funds available in the economy. As these funds are channeled into domestic spending, aggregate demand increases again, from AD_1 to AD_2 and equilibrium real GDP increases to $800 trillion.

Because the initial and secondary effects of the expansionary fiscal policy reinforce each other, real GDP increases by a greater amount than in the example of expansionary fiscal policy in a closed economy. The effect of an expansionary fiscal policy is more pronounced in an economy with capital mobility and fixed exchange rates than it is in a closed economy.

Monetary Policy is Weakened Under Fixed Exchange Rates. Contrast this outcome with monetary policy. As we will learn, in an open economy with capital mobility and fixed exchange rates, an expansionary monetary policy is less effective in increasing real GDP than it is in a closed economy.

Referring to Figure 16.2(b-2) again, assume that Canada suffers from recession. To combat the recession, suppose the Bank of Canada implements an expansionary monetary policy. The initial effect of the monetary expansion is to reduce the domestic interest rate, resulting in increased consumption and investment that expand aggregate demand from AD_0 to AD_1. This expansion causes equilibrium real GDP to rise from $500 trillion to $700 trillion.

The second effect of the monetary expansion is that a lower Canadian interest rate discourages foreign investors from placing their funds in Canadian capital markets. As the demand for Canadian dollars decreases, its exchange value is under pressure to depreciate. To maintain a fixed exchange rate, the Bank of Canada intervenes in the foreign exchange market and purchases dollars with foreign currency. This purchase causes the domestic money supply to decrease as well as the availability of loanable funds in the economy. The resulting decrease in domestic spending leads to a decrease in aggregate demand from AD_1 to AD_3 that causes equilibrium real GDP to decline from $700 trillion to $600 trillion. This contraction in aggregate demand counteracts the initial expansion that was intended to stimulate the economy. An expansionary monetary policy is weakened when its initial and secondary effects conflict with each other. Under a system of fixed exchange rates and capital mobility, monetary policy is less effective in stimulating the economy than it is in a closed economy.

Effect of Fiscal and Monetary Policy Under Floating Exchange Rates

We will now modify our example by replacing Canada's fixed exchange rate system with a system of floating exchange rates. The conclusion that emerges from this discussion is that with high capital mobility and floating exchange rates, an expansionary monetary policy is more successful in stimulating the economy, and an expansionary fiscal policy is less successful than they are in a closed economy.

Monetary Policy is Strengthened Under Floating Exchange Rates. Again assume that Canada suffers from recession. To stimulate its economy, suppose the Bank of Canada adopts an expansionary monetary policy. As in a closed economy, an increase in the supply of money results in a lower domestic interest rate that initially generates more spending on consumption and investment and causes aggregate demand to increase. Referring to Figure 16.2(b-1), as aggregate demand increases from AD_0 to AD_1, equilibrium real GDP rises from $500 trillion to $700 trillion.

The second effect of the expansionary monetary policy is that because investment is highly mobile between countries, the decreasing Canadian interest rate induces investors to place their funds in foreign capital markets. As Canadian investors sell dollars to purchase foreign currency used to facilitate foreign investments, the dollar depreciates. This depreciation results in an increase in exports, a decrease in imports, and an improvement in Canada's current account. The improving current account provides an extra boost to aggregate demand that expands from AD_1 to AD_2. This expansion causes equilibrium real GDP to increase from $700 trillion to $800 trillion.

Because the initial and secondary effects of the expansionary monetary policy are complementary, the policy is strengthened by increasing Canada's output and employment. In an economy with capital mobility and floating exchange rates, an expansionary monetary policy is more effective in stimulating the economy than it is in a closed economy.

Fiscal Policy is Weakened Under Floating Exchange Rates The result is different if the Canadian government uses fiscal policy to combat recession. Referring to Figure 16.2(b-2), the initial effect of a rise in government spending is to increase aggregate demand from AD_0 to AD_2 that causes equilibrium real GDP to increase from $500 trillion to $700 trillion. As the increased government spending causes the government's budget to go into deficit, the Canadian interest rate rises. A higher interest rate causes an inflow of investment from foreigners, that result in an increase in the demand for Canadian dollars in the foreign exchange market. The exchange value of the dollar thus appreciates which results in falling exports, rising imports, and a deterioration of Canada's current account. As the current account worsens, aggregate demand decreases from AD_2 to AD_3 and equilibrium real GDP contracts from $700 trillion to $600 trillion. Because the initial and secondary effects of the fiscal policy are conflicting, the policy's expansionary effect is weakened. Therefore, an expansionary fiscal policy in an economy with capital mobility and floating exchange rates is less effective in stimulating the economy than it is in a closed economy.

MACROECONOMIC STABILITY AND THE CURRENT ACCOUNT: POLICY AGREEMENT VERSUS POLICY CONFLICT

So far we have assumed that the goal of fiscal and monetary policy is to promote internal balance in Canada—that is, full employment without inflation. Besides desiring internal balance, suppose that Canadians want their economy to achieve current account

TRADE CONFLICTS MONETARY AND FISCAL POLICY RESPOND TO FINANCIAL TURMOIL IN THE ECONOMY

Following six consecutive years of expansion, the U.S. economy peaked in December, 2007, beginning a recession that continued throughout 2008 and 2009. This was triggered by breakdowns in key credit markets that posed great risk to the financial system and the broader economy.

The Federal Reserve responded with unprecedented measures to unclog credit markets and free up the financial flows vital to a well functioning economy. Besides lowering the federal funds rate target to virtually zero, the Federal Reserve expanded its role as lender of last resort by providing credit to banks and other financial institutions as well as businesses that were unable to secure adequate credit accommodations from banking institutions.

To provide additional stimulus to the weakening economy, the U.S. government enacted the Economic Stimulus Act of 2008. The Act was designed to provide temporary (one-time) tax rebates to those lower and middle income individuals and households who would immediately spend it. About $113 billion was dispensed, that amounted to about 0.8 percent of GDP. The government hoped the tax rebates would burn such a hole in peoples' pockets that they would not be able to resist spending it, therefore adding to aggregate demand. This optimism was unwarranted. It turned out that only 10–20 percent of the tax rebate dollars were spent: most of the money went into household saving or for paying down past debt such as credit card bills, neither of which directly expanded the economy.

When Barack Obama became president in 2009, he inherited an economy that was falling deeper into recession. Obama noted that decreases in consumption and investment spending continued to drag the economy downward. The result was a fiscal stimulus program of $789 billion, the most expansive unleashing of the government's fiscal firepower in the face of a recession since World War II. The stimulus included $507 billion in spending programs and $282 billion in tax relief, designed to increase aggregate demand: if more goods and services are being bought, whether cement for a new highway or groceries paid for with a household tax cut, there is less chance of decreasing demand resulting in companies laying off workers that would result in greater declines in demand and a deeper downturn.

iStockphoto.com/photosoup

(external) balance whereby its exports equal its imports. This balance suggests that Canada prefers to "finance its own way" in international trade by earning from its exports an amount of money necessary to pay for its imports. Will Canadian policymakers be able to achieve both internal and external balance at the same time or will conflict develop between these two objectives?

Again let's assume that the Canadian economy suffers from recession. Suppose Canada's current account realizes a deficit in which imports exceed exports so that Canada is a net borrowing country from the rest of the world. Given a system of floating exchange rates, recall that an expansionary monetary policy for Canada results in a depreciation of its dollar and therefore an increase in its exports and a decrease in its imports. This rise in net exports serves to reduce the deficit in Canada's current account. The conclusion is that an expansionary monetary policy that is appropriate for combating Canada's recession is also compatible with the objective of reducing Canada's current account deficit. A single economic policy promotes overall balance for Canada.

Instead let's assume that Canada suffers from inflation and a current account deficit. When adopting a contractionary monetary policy to combat inflation, the Bank of Canada causes the domestic interest rate to increase which results in an appreciation of its dollar. This appreciation results in a fall in Canada's exports, a rise in its imports, and a larger current account deficit. The conclusion is that Canada's contractionary monetary policy to combat inflation conflicts with its objective of promoting balance in its current account. Policy conflict prevails for the monetary policy. If Canada initially had a current account surplus, an expansionary monetary policy would help reduce it.

When Canada finds itself in a policy conflict zone, monetary policy (or fiscal policy) alone will not restore both internal and external balance. A combination of policies is needed. Suppose that Canada experiences recession with a current account deficit. An expansionary monetary policy to combat recession might be accompanied by tariffs or quotas to reduce imports and improve the current account. Each economic objective is matched with an appropriate policy instrument so that both objectives can be attained at the same time. It is left for more advanced texts to further analyze this topic.

INFLATION WITH UNEMPLOYMENT

This analysis so far has looked at the economy under special circumstances. It has been assumed that as the economy advances to full employment, domestic prices remain unchanged until full employment is reached. Once the nation's capacity to produce has been achieved, further increases in aggregate demand pull prices upward. This type of inflation is known as **demand-pull inflation**. Under these conditions, internal balance (full employment with stable prices) can be viewed as a single target that requires but one policy instrument: a reduction in aggregate demand via monetary policy or fiscal policy.

A more troublesome problem is the appropriate policy to implement when a nation experiences *inflation with unemployment*. Here the problem is that internal balance cannot be achieved just by manipulating aggregate demand. To decrease inflation, a reduction in aggregate demand is required; to decrease unemployment, an expansion in aggregate demand is required. The objectives of full employment and stable prices cannot be considered as one and the same target; they are two independent targets, requiring two distinct policy instruments.

Achieving overall balance involves three separate targets: current account equilibrium, full employment, and price stability. To ensure all three objectives can be achieved simultaneously, monetary and fiscal policy may not be enough; direct controls may also be needed.

Inflation with unemployment has been a problem for the United States. In 1971 the U.S. economy experienced inflation with recession and a current account deficit. Increasing aggregate demand to achieve full employment would presumably intensify inflationary pressures. The president implemented a comprehensive system of **wage and price controls** to remove the inflationary constraint. Later the same year, the United States entered into exchange rate realignments that resulted in a depreciation of the dollar's exchange value by 12 percent against the trade-weighted value of other major currencies. The dollar depreciation was intended to help the United States reverse its current account deficit. It was the president's view that the internal and external problems of the United States could not be eliminated through expenditure changing policies alone.

INTERNATIONAL ECONOMIC POLICY COORDINATION

Policymakers have long been aware that the welfare of their economies is linked to that of the world economy. Because of the international mobility of goods, services, capital, and labor, economic policies of one nation have spillover effects on others. Recognizing

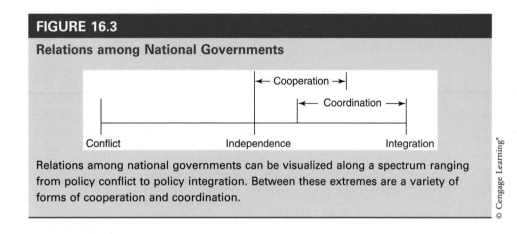

FIGURE 16.3

Relations among National Governments

Relations among national governments can be visualized along a spectrum ranging from policy conflict to policy integration. Between these extremes are a variety of forms of cooperation and coordination.

© Cengage Learning®

these spillover effects, governments have often made attempts to coordinate their economic policies.

Economic relations among nations can be visualized along a spectrum, illustrated in Figure 16.3, ranging from open *conflict* to *integration*, where nations implement policies jointly in a supranational forum to which they have ceded a large degree of authority, such as the European Union. At the spectrum's midpoint lies policy *independence*: nations take the actions of other nations as a given; they do not attempt to influence those actions or be influenced by them. Between independence and integration lie various forms of policy coordination and cooperation.

Cooperative policy making can take many forms, but in general it occurs whenever officials from different nations meet to evaluate world economic conditions. During these meetings, policy makers may present briefings on their individual economies and discuss current policies. Such meetings represent a simple form of cooperation. A more involved format might consist of economists' studies on a particular subject, combined with an in-depth discussion of possible solutions. True policy coordination goes beyond these two forms of cooperation; policy coordination is a formal agreement among nations to initiate particular policies.

International economic policy coordination is the attempt to significantly modify national policies—monetary policy, fiscal policy, exchange rate policy—in recognition of international economic interdependence. Policy coordination does not necessarily imply that nations give precedence to international concerns over domestic concerns. It does recognize, however, that the policies of one nation can spill over to influence the objectives of others; nations should therefore communicate with one another and attempt to coordinate their policies to take these linkages into account. Presumably, they will be better off than if they had acted independently.

To facilitate policy coordination, economic officials of the major governments talk with one another frequently in the context of the International Monetary Fund and the Organization for Economic Cooperation and Development. Also, central bank senior officials meet monthly at the Bank for International Settlements.

Policy Coordination in Theory

If economic policies in each of two nations affect the other, then the case for policy coordination would appear to be obvious. Policy coordination is considered important in the modern world because economic disruptions are transmitted rapidly from one nation to another. Without policy coordination, national economic policies can destabilize other economies. The logic of policy coordination is illustrated in the following basketball spectator problem.

Suppose you are attending a professional basketball game between the Los Angeles Lakers and the Chicago Bulls. If everyone is sitting, someone who stands has a superior view. Spectators usually can see well if everyone sits or if everyone stands. Sitting in seats is more comfortable than standing. When there is no cooperation, everyone stands; each spectator does what is best for her or himself given the actions of other spectators. If all spectators sit, someone, taking what the others will do as a given, will stand. If all spectators are standing, then it is best to remain standing. With spectator cooperation, the solution is for everyone to sit. The problem is that each spectator may be tempted to get a better view by standing. The cooperative solution will not be attained, without an outright agreement on coordination—in this situation, everyone remains seated.

Consider the following economic example. Suppose the world consists of just two nations, Germany and Japan. Although these nations trade goods with each other, they desire to pursue their own domestic economic priorities. Germany wants to avoid trade deficits with Japan while achieving full employment for its economy; Japan desires full employment for its economy while avoiding trade deficits with Germany. Assume that both nations achieve balanced trade with each other, but each nation's economy operates below full employment. Germany and Japan contemplate enacting expansionary government spending policies that would stimulate demand, output, and employment. Each nation rejects the idea, recognizing the policy's adverse impact on the trade balance. Germany and Japan realize that bolstering domestic income to increase jobs has the side effect of stimulating the demand for imports, thus pushing the trade account into deficit.

The preceding situation is favorable for successful policy coordination. If Germany and Japan agree to simultaneously expand their government spending, then output, employment, and incomes will rise concurrently. While higher German income promotes increased imports from Japan, higher Japanese income promotes increased imports from Germany. An appropriate increase in government spending results in each nation's increased demand for imports being offset by an increased demand for exports that leads to balanced trade between Germany and Japan. In our example of mutual implementation of expansionary fiscal policies, policy coordination permits each nation to achieve full employment and balanced trade.

This is an optimistic portrayal of international economic policy coordination. The synchronization of policies appears simple because there are only two economies and two objectives. In the real world, policy coordination generally involves many countries and diverse objectives, such as low inflation, high employment, economic growth, and trade balance.

If the benefits of international economic policy coordination are really so obvious, it may seem odd that agreements do not occur more often than they do. Several obstacles hinder successful policy coordination. Even if national economic objectives are harmonious, there is no guarantee that governments can design and implement coordinated policies. Policymakers in the real world do not always have sufficient information to understand the nature of the economic problem or how their policies will affect economies. Implementing appropriate policies when governments disagree about economic fundamentals is difficult for several reasons.

- Some nations give higher priority to price stability, for instance, or to full employment, than others.
- Some nations have a stronger legislature, or weaker trade unions, than others.

- The party pendulums in different nations, for example, shift with elections occurring in different years.
- One nation may experience economic recession while another nation experiences rapid inflation.

Although the theoretical advantages of international economic policy coordination are clearly established, attempts to quantify their gains are rare. Skeptics point out that in practice the gains from policy coordination are smaller than what is often suggested. Let us consider some examples of international economic policy coordination.

Does Policy Coordination Work?

Does coordination of economic policies improve the performance of nations? Proponents of policy coordination cite the examples of the Plaza Agreement of 1985 and the Louvre Accord of 1987.

The deterioration of the U.S. trade balance was a disturbing feature of the economic recovery of the United States in the early 1980s. This deterioration was influenced by a dramatic appreciation of the dollar that overwhelmed the other determinants of international cost competitiveness. Between 1980 and 1985, the dollar's appreciation boosted the ratio of U.S. unit labor costs to foreign unit labor costs by 39 percent, detracting from the international competitiveness of U.S. manufacturers. American net exports of goods and services declined, resulting in large trade deficits. As the U.S. economic recovery slowed, protectionist pressures increased in Congress.

Fearing a disaster in the world trading system, government officials of the **Group of Five (G–5)** nations—the United States, Japan, Germany, Great Britain, and France—met at New York's Plaza Hotel in 1985. There was widespread agreement that the dollar was overvalued and that the twin U.S. deficits (trade and federal budget) were too large. Each country made specific pledges on macroeconomic policy and also agreed to initiate coordinated sales of the dollar to shove its exchange value downward. By 1986, the dollar had dramatically depreciated, especially against the German mark and the Japanese yen.

However, the sharp decline in the dollar's exchange value set off a new concern: an uncontrolled dollar plunge. So in 1987 another round of policy coordination occurred to put the brakes on the dollar's decline. The G–5 financial ministers met in Paris and agreed in the Louvre Accord to pursue intervention policies curbing the pace of the dollar's depreciation, to be accompanied by other macroeconomic adjustments.

Although the episodes of the Plaza Agreement and Louvre Accord point to the success of policy coordination, by the first decade of the 2000s government officials were showing less enthusiasm for it. They felt that coordinating policy had become much more difficult because of the way policy is made, especially given the rise of independent central banks. Back in the 1980s, the governments of Japan and Germany could dictate what their central banks would do. Since that time the Bank of Japan and the European Central Bank have become more independent and see themselves as protectors of discipline against high spending government officials. That role makes domestic fiscal and monetary coordination difficult and international efforts to coordinate policies even more difficult. The huge growth in global financial markets has made currency intervention much less effective.

TRADE CONFLICTS DOES CROWDING OCCUR IN AN OPEN ECONOMY?

In your principles of macroeconomics course, you learned about "crowding out" in the domestic economy. Crowding out refers to private consumption or investment spending decreasing as a result of increased government expenditures and the subsequent budget deficits. The source of the decline in private spending is higher interest rates caused by budget deficits.

Suppose that the government enacts an expansionary fiscal policy, say, an increase in defense spending. The policy must be financed either by increased taxes or through the borrowing of funds to permit the enlarged federal deficit. If the government borrows funds, the total demand for funds will increase as the government competes with the private sector to borrow the available supply of funds. The additional government borrowing increases the total demand for funds and pushes up interest rates. Because of higher interest rates, businesses will delay or cancel purchases of machinery and equipment, residential housing construction will be postponed, and consumers will refrain from buying interest sensitive goods, such as major appliances and automobiles. The higher interest rates caused by government borrowing squeeze out private sector borrowing. Crowding out lessens the effectiveness of an expansionary fiscal policy.

Although economists tend to accept the logic of the crowding out argument, they recognize that government deficits don't necessarily squeeze out private spending. In recessions, the main problem is that people are not spending all of the available funds. Typically, consumers are saving more than businesses intend to invest. Such a shortage of spending is the main motivation for increased government spending. In this recessionary situation, deficit financed government spending doesn't crowd out private spending.

The extent of crowding out tends also to be lessened in an open economy with capital flows. This is because inflows of capital from abroad tend to keep interest rates lower than they otherwise would be. The government can borrow more money without forcing up interest rates that crowd private borrowers out of the market.

The experience of the United States during the first decade of the 2000s casts doubt on the crowding out hypothesis. In spite of growing federal budget deficits, interest rates remained low in the United States as foreigners were content to purchase huge amounts of securities issued by the government. Analysts noted that if not for the inflow of foreign capital, U.S. interest rates would be up about 1.5 percentage points higher. Skeptics noted that the free spending policy would eventually have to cease if foreigners begin to doubt the ability of the United States to repay its debt with sound currency. This doubt would cause foreign investors to demand higher interest rates if they were to keep lending the United States the money it needs, or they might simply stop lending to the United States, thus making the crowding out more likely.

An example of unsuccessful international policy coordination occurred in 2000. At that time, the **Group of Seven (G–7)** industrial nations—the United States, Canada, Japan, the United Kingdom, Germany, France, and Italy—launched coordinated purchases of the euro to boost its value. Although the euro was launched in 1999, at an exchange value of $1.17 per euro, by mid-2000 its value had dropped to $0.84 per euro. Many economists feared that continued speculative attacks against the euro might result in a free fall of its value that could destabilize the international financial system. To prevent this from happening, the G–7 nations enacted a coordinated intervention by purchasing euros with their currencies in the foreign exchange market. The added demand for the euro helped boost its value to more than $0.88 per euro. The success of the intervention was short lived. Within two weeks following the intervention, the euro's value slid to an all time low. Most economists considered the coordinated intervention to be a failure.

SUMMARY

1. International economic policy refers to various government activities that influence trade patterns among nations, including (a) monetary and fiscal policies, (b) exchange rate adjustments, (c) tariff and nontariff trade barriers, (d) foreign exchange controls and investment controls, and (e) export promotion measures.

2. Since the 1930s, nations have actively pursued internal balance (full employment without inflation) as a primary economic objective. Nations also consider external balance (current account equilibrium) as an economic objective. A nation realizes overall balance when it attains both internal and external balance.

3. To achieve overall balance, nations implement expenditure changing policies (monetary and fiscal policies), expenditure switching policies (exchange rate adjustments), and direct controls (price and wage controls).

4. For an open economy with a fixed exchange rate system and high capital mobility, fiscal policy is more successful, and monetary policy is less successful, in promoting internal balance than it is in a closed economy. If the open economy has a floating exchange rate system, monetary policy is more successful, and fiscal policy is less successful,

in promoting internal balance than they are for a closed economy.

5. When a nation experiences inflation with unemployment, achieving overall balance involves three separate targets: Current account equilibrium, full employment, and price stability. Three policy instruments may be needed to achieve these targets.

6. International economic policy coordination is the attempt to significantly modify national policies in recognition of international economic interdependence. Nations regularly consult with each other in the context of the International Monetary Fund, Organization for Economic Cooperation and Development, Bank for International Settlements, and Group of Seven. The Plaza Agreement and Louvre Accord are examples of international economic policy coordination.

7. Several problems confront international economic policy coordination: (a) different national economic objectives, (b) different national institutions, (c) different national political climates, and (d) different phases in the business cycle. There is no guarantee that governments can design and implement policies that are capable of achieving the intended results.

KEY CONCEPTS AND TERMS

Demand-pull inflation (p. 488)
Direct controls (p. 480)
Expenditure changing
  policies (p. 480)
Expenditure switching
  policies (p. 480)

External balance (p. 479)
Fiscal policy (p. 480)
Group of Five (G–5)
  (p. 491)
Group of Seven (G–7) (p. 492)
Internal balance (p. 479)

International economic policy
  coordination (p. 489)
Monetary policy (p. 480)
Overall balance (p. 479)
Wage and price
  controls (p. 488)

STUDY QUESTIONS

1. Distinguish among external balance, internal balance, and overall balance.
2. What are the most important instruments of international economic policy?
3. What is meant by the terms *expenditure changing policy* and *expenditure switching policy*? Give some examples of each.
4. What institutional constraints bear on the formation of economic policies?
5. Under a system of fixed exchange rates and high capital mobility, is monetary policy or fiscal policy better suited for promoting internal balance? Why?
6. What is meant by the terms *policy agreement* and *policy conflict*?
7. What are some obstacles to successful international economic policy coordination?

International Banking: Reserves, Debt, and Risk

The world's banking system plays a vital role in facilitating international transactions and maintaining economic prosperity. Commercial banks such as Citicorp help finance trade and investment and provide loans to international borrowers. Central banks such as the Federal Reserve serve as a lender of last resort to commercial banks and sometimes intervene in foreign currency markets to stabilize currency values. Also, the International Monetary Fund (IMF) serves as a lender to nations having deficits in their balance-of-payments. This chapter concentrates on the role that banks play in world financial markets, the risks associated with international banking, and strategies employed to deal with these risks.

We'll begin with an investigation of the nature of international reserves and their importance for the world financial system. This is followed by a discussion of banks as international lenders and the problems associated with international debt.

NATURE OF INTERNATIONAL RESERVES

The need for a central bank such as the Bank of England for international reserves is similar to an individual's desire to hold cash balances (currency and checkable deposits). At both levels, monetary reserves are intended to bridge the gap between monetary receipts and monetary payments.

Suppose that an individual receives income in equal installments every minute of the day and those expenditures for goods and services are likewise evenly spaced over time. The individual will require only a minimum cash reserve to finance purchases because no significant imbalances between cash receipts and cash disbursements will arise. In reality, however, individuals purchase goods and services on a fairly regular basis from day to day, but receive paychecks only at weekly or longer intervals. A certain amount of cash is therefore required to finance the discrepancy that arises between monetary receipts and payments.

When an individual initially receives a paycheck, cash balances are high. But as time progresses, these holdings of cash may fall to virtually zero just before the next paycheck is received. Individuals are concerned with the amount of cash balances that, on average, are necessary to keep them going until the next paycheck arrives.

Although individuals desire cash balances primarily to fill the gap between monetary receipts and payments, this desire is influenced by a number of other factors. The need for cash balances may become more acute if the absolute dollar volume of transactions increases because larger imbalances may result between receipts and payments. Conversely, to the extent that individuals can finance their transactions on credit, they require less cash in hand.

Just as an individual desires to hold cash balances, national governments have a need for **international reserves**. The chief purpose of international reserves is to enable nations to finance disequilibrium in their balance-of-payments positions. When a nation finds its monetary receipts falling short of its monetary payments, the deficit is settled with international reserves. Eventually, the deficit must be eliminated, because central banks tend to have limited stocks of reserves.

From a policy perspective, the advantage of international reserves is that they enable nations to sustain *temporary* balance-of-payments deficits until acceptable adjustment measures can operate to correct the disequilibrium. Holdings of international reserves facilitate effective policy formation because corrective adjustment measures need not be implemented prematurely. Should a deficit nation possess abundant stocks of reserve balances, it may be able to resist unpopular adjustment measures, making eventual adjustments even more troublesome.

DEMAND FOR INTERNATIONAL RESERVES

When a nation's international monetary payments exceed its international monetary receipts, some means of settlement is required to finance its payments deficit. Settlement ultimately consists of transfers of international reserves among nations. Both the magnitude and the longevity of a balance-of-payments deficit that can be sustained in the absence of equilibrating adjustments are limited by a nation's stock of international reserves.

On a global basis, the **demand for international reserves** depends on two related factors: the monetary value of international transactions and the disequilibrium that can arise in balance-of-payments positions. The demand for international reserves is also contingent on such things as the speed and strength of the balance-of-payments adjustment mechanism and the overall institutional framework of the world economy.

Exchange Rate Flexibility

One determinant of the demand for international reserves is the *degree of exchange rate flexibility* in the international monetary system. This is because exchange rate flexibility in part underlies the efficiency of the balance-of-payments adjustment process.

Figure 17.1 represents the exchange market position of the United States in trade with the United Kingdom. Starting at equilibrium point E, suppose that an increase in imports increases the U.S. demand for pounds from D_0 to D_1. The prevailing exchange rate system will determine the quantity of international reserves needed to bridge the gap between the number of pounds demanded and the number supplied.

If exchange rates are fixed or pegged by the monetary authorities, international reserves play a crucial role in the exchange rate stabilization process. In Figure 17.1, suppose the exchange rate is pegged at \$2 per pound. Given a rise in the demand for pounds from D_0 to D_1, the United States would face an excess demand for pounds equal to £100 at the pegged rate. If the U.S. dollar is not to depreciate beyond the pegged

FIGURE 17.1

The Demand for International Reserves and Exchange Rate Flexibility

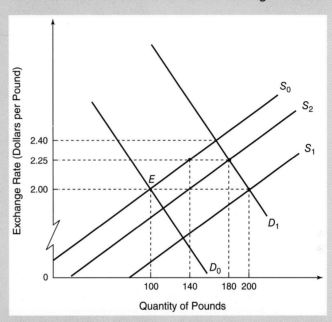

When exchange rates are fixed (pegged) by monetary authorities, international reserves are necessary for the financing of payments imbalances and the stabilization of exchange rates. With floating exchange rates, payments imbalances tend to be corrected by market-induced fluctuations in the exchange rate; the need for exchange rate stabilization and international reserves then disappears.

© Cengage Learning®

rate, the monetary authorities—that is, the Federal Reserve— must enter the market to supply pounds in exchange for dollars, in the amount necessary to eliminate the disequilibrium. In the figure, the pegged rate of $2 per pound can be maintained if the monetary authorities supply £100 on the market. Coupled with the existing supply schedule S_0, the added supply will result in a new supply schedule at S_1. Market equilibrium is restored at the pegged rate.

Rather than operating under a rigidly pegged system, suppose a nation makes an agreement to foster some automatic adjustments by allowing market rates to float within a narrow band around the official exchange rate. This limited exchange rate flexibility would be aimed at correcting minor payments imbalances, whereas large and persistent disequilibrium would require other adjustment measures.

Referring to Figure 17.1, assume that the U.S. official exchange rate is $2 per pound, but with a band of permissible exchange rate fluctuations whose upper limit is set at $2.25 per pound. Given a rise in the U.S. demand for pounds, the value of the dollar will begin to decline. Once the exchange rate depreciates to $2.25 per pound, domestic monetary authorities will need to supply £40 on the market to defend the band's outer limit. This supply will have the effect of shifting the market supply schedule from S_0 to S_2. Under a system of limited exchange rate flexibility, then, movements in the exchange rate serve to reduce the payments disequilibrium. Smaller amounts of international reserves are required for exchange rate stabilization purposes under this system than if exchange rates are rigidly fixed.

A fundamental purpose of international reserves is to facilitate government intervention in exchange markets to stabilize currency values. The more active a government's stabilization activities, the greater the need for reserves. Most exchange rate standards today involve some stabilization operations and require international reserves. If exchange rates were allowed to float freely without government interference, theoretically there would be no need for reserves. This is because a floating rate would serve to eliminate an incipient payments imbalance, negating the need for stabilization operations. Referring again to Figure 17.1, suppose the exchange market is initially in equilibrium at a rate of $2 per pound. Given an increase in the demand for foreign exchange from D_0 to D_1, the home currency would begin to depreciate. It would continue to weaken until it reached an exchange value of $2.50 per pound, at which point market equilibrium would be restored. The need for international reserves would be nonexistent under freely floating rates.

Other Determinants

The lesson of the previous section is that changes in the degree of exchange rate flexibility are inversely related to changes in the quantity of international reserves demanded. A monetary system characterized by more rapid and flexible exchange rate adjustments requires smaller reserves and vice versa.

In addition to the degree of exchange rate flexibility, several other factors underlie the demand for international reserves, including (1) automatic adjustment mechanisms that respond to payments disequilibrium, (2) economic policies used to bring about payments equilibrium, and (3) the international coordination of economic policies.

Our earlier analysis has shown that adjustment mechanisms involving prices, interest rates, incomes, and monetary flows automatically tend to correct balance-of-payments disequilibrium. A payments deficit or surplus initiates changes in each of these variables. The more efficient each of these adjustment mechanisms is the smaller and more short lived market imbalances will be and the fewer reserves will be needed. The demand for international reserves therefore tends to be smaller with speedier and more complete automatic adjustment mechanisms.

The demand for international reserves is also influenced by the choice and effectiveness of government policies adopted to correct payments imbalances. Unlike automatic adjustment mechanisms that rely on the free market to identify industries and labor groups that must bear the adjustment burden, the use of government policies involves political decisions. All else being equal, the greater a nation's propensity to apply commercial policies (including tariffs, quotas, and subsidies) to key sectors, the less will be its need for international reserves. This lower need assumes, of course, that the policies are effective in reducing payments disequilibrium. Because of uncertainties about the nature and timing of payments disturbances, nations are often slow to initiate such trade policies and find they require international reserves to weather periods of payments disequilibrium.

The international coordination of economic policies is another determinant of the demand for international reserves. A primary goal of economic cooperation among finance ministers is to reduce the frequency and extent of payments imbalances and hence the demand for international reserves. Since the end of World War II, nations have moved toward the harmonization of national economic objectives by establishing programs through such organizations as the IMF Fund and the Organization for Economic Cooperation and Development. Another example of international economic organization has been the European Union, whose goal is to achieve a common macroeconomic policy and full monetary union. By reducing the intensity of disturbances to payments balance, such policy coordination reduces the need for international reserves.

Other factors influence the demand for international reserves. The quantity demanded is positively related to the level of world prices and income. One would expect rising price levels to inflate the market value of international transactions and to increase the potential demand for reserves. The need for reserves would also tend to rise with the level of global income and trade activity.

Central banks need international reserves to cover possible or expected excess payments to other nations at some future time. The quantity of international reserves demanded is directly related to the size and duration of these payment gaps. If a nation with a payments deficit is willing and able to initiate quick actions to increase receipts or decrease payments, the amount of reserves required will be relatively small. Conversely, the demand for reserves will be relatively large if nations initiate no actions to correct payments imbalances or adopt policies that prolong such disequilibrium.

SUPPLY OF INTERNATIONAL RESERVES

The analysis so far has emphasized the demand for international reserves. But what about the **supply of international reserves**?

The total supply of international reserves consists of two distinct categories: *owned reserves* and *borrowed reserves*. Reserve assets such as gold, acceptable foreign currencies, and special drawing rights (SDRs) are generally considered to be directly owned by the holding nations. But if nations with payments deficits find their stocks of owned reserves falling to unacceptably low levels, they may be able to borrow international reserves as a cushioning device. Lenders may be foreign nations with excess reserves, foreign financial institutions, or international agencies such as the IMF.

FOREIGN CURRENCIES

International reserves are a means of payment used in financing foreign transactions. One such asset is holdings of *national currencies* (foreign exchange). The largest share of international reserves today consists of holdings of national currencies.

Over the course of the 1800s–1900s, two national currencies in particular have gained prominence as means of financing international transactions. These currencies, the U.S. dollar and the UK pound have been considered *reserve currencies* (or *key currencies*), because trading nations have traditionally been willing to hold them as international reserve assets. Since World War II, the U.S. dollar has been the dominant reserve currency. Other reserve currencies are the Japanese yen and a few other currencies that are acceptable in payment for international transactions.

The role of the pound as a reserve currency is largely because of circumstances of the late 1800s and early 1900s. Not only did Britain (now the United Kingdom) at that time play a dominant role in world trade, but the efficiency of London as an international money market was also widely recognized. This was the golden age of the gold standard and the pound was freely convertible into gold. Traders and investors felt confident in financing their transactions with pounds. With the demise of the gold standard and the onset of the Great Depression during the 1930s, Britain's commercial and financial status began to deteriorate and the pound lost some of its international luster. Today, the pound still serves as an important international reserve asset but it is no longer the most prestigious reserve currency.

The emergence of the U.S. dollar as a reserve currency stems from a different set of circumstances. Emerging from World War II, the U.S. economy was not only unharmed but actually stronger. Because of the vast inflows of gold into the United States during the 1930s and 1940s, the dollar was in a better position than the pound to assume the role of a reserve currency.

The mechanism that supplied the world with dollar balances was the balance-of-payments deficits of the United States. These deficits stemmed largely from U.S. foreign aid granted to Europe immediately after World War II, as well as from the flow of private investment funds abroad from U.S. residents. The early 1950s were characterized as a *dollar shortage era*, when the massive development programs of the European nations resulted in an excess demand for the dollars used to finance such efforts. As the United States began to run modest payments deficits during the early 1950s, the dollar outflow was appreciated by the recipient nations.

By the late 1950s, the U.S. payments deficits had become larger. As foreign nations began to accumulate larger dollar balances than they were accustomed to, the dollar shortage era gave way to a *dollar glut*. Throughout the 1960s, the United States continued to provide reserves to the world through its payments deficits. The persistently weak position of the U.S. balance-of-payments increasingly led foreigners to question the soundness of the dollar as a reserve currency. By 1970, the amount of dollar liabilities in the hands of foreigners was several times as large as U.S. reserve assets. Lack of confidence in the soundness of the dollar inspired several European nations to exercise their rights to demand that the U.S. Treasury convert their dollar holdings into gold that in turn led the United States to suspend its gold convertibility pledge to the rest of the world in 1971.

Using the dollar as a reserve currency meant that the supply of international reserves varied with the payments position of the United States. During the 1960s, this situation gave rise to the so called **liquidity problem**. To preserve confidence in the dollar as a reserve currency, the United States had to strengthen its payments position by eliminating its deficits. But correction of the U.S. deficits would mean elimination of additional dollars as a source of reserves for the international monetary system. The creation in 1970 of SDRs as reserve assets and their subsequent allocations have been intended as a solution for this problem.

GOLD

The historical importance of gold as an international reserve asset should not be under-emphasized. At one time, gold served as the key monetary asset of the international payments mechanism; it also constituted the basis of the money supplies of many nations.

As an international money, gold fulfilled several important functions. Under the historic **gold standard**, gold served directly as an international means of payments. It also provided a unit of account against which commodity prices as well as the parities of national currencies were quoted. Although gold holdings do not yield interest income, gold has generally served as a viable store of value despite inflation, wars, and revolutions. Perhaps the greatest advantage of gold as a monetary asset is its overall acceptability, especially when compared with other forms of international monies.

Today, the role of gold as an international reserve asset has declined. Over the past 30 years, gold has fallen from nearly 70 percent to less than three percent of world reserves. Private individuals rarely use gold as a medium of payment and virtually never as a unit of account. Nor do central banks currently use gold as an official unit of account for stating the parities of national currencies. The monetary role of gold is currently recognized by only a few nations, mostly in the Middle East. In most nations outside the United States, private residents have long been able to buy and sell gold as they would any other commodity. On December 31, 1974, the U.S. government revoked a 41-year ban on U.S. citizens' ownership of gold. The monetary role of gold today is only that of a glittering ghost haunting efforts to reform the international monetary system.

International Gold Standard

Under the international gold standard whose golden age was about 1880 to 1914, the values of most national currencies were anchored in gold. Gold coins circulated within these countries as well as across national boundaries as generally accepted means of payment. Monetary authorities were concerned about maintaining the public's confidence in the paper currencies that supplemented gold's role as money. To maintain the integrity of paper currencies, governments agreed to convert them into gold at a fixed rate. This requirement was supposed to prevent monetary authorities from producing excessive amounts of paper money. The so called *discipline* of the gold standard was achieved by having the money supply bear a fixed relation to the monetary stock of gold. Given the cost of producing gold relative to the cost of other commodities, a monetary price of gold could be established to produce growth in monetary gold—and thus in the money supply—at a rate that corresponded to the growth in real national output.

Over the course of the gold standard's era, the importance of gold began to decline, whereas both paper money and demand deposits showed marked increases. From 1815 to 1913, gold as a share of the aggregate money supply of the United States, France, and Britain fell from about 33 to 10 percent. At the same time, the proportion of bank deposits skyrocketed from a modest 6 percent to about 68 percent. By 1913, paper monies plus demand deposits accounted for approximately 90 percent of the U.S. money supply.

After World War I, popular sentiment favored a return to the discipline of the gold standard, in part because of the inflation that gripped many economies during the war years. The United States was the first to return to the gold standard, followed by several European nations. Efforts to restore the prewar gold standard ended in complete collapse during the 1930s. In response to the economic strains of the Great Depression, nations one by one announced that they could no longer maintain the gold standard.

In the United States, the Great Depression brought an important modification of the gold standard. In 1934, the Gold Reserve Act gave the U.S. government title to all monetary gold and required citizens to turn in their private holdings to the U.S. Treasury. This was done to end the pressure on U.S. commercial banks to convert their liabilities into gold. The U.S. dollar was also devalued in 1934, when the official price of gold was raised from $20.67 to $35 per ounce. The dollar devaluation was not specifically aimed at defending the U.S. trade balance. The rationale was that a rise in the domestic price of gold would encourage gold production, adding to the money supply and the level of economic activity. The Great Depression would be solved! In retrospect, the devaluation may have had some minor economic effects, but there is no indication that it did anything to lift the economy out of its depressed condition.

Gold Exchange Standard

Emerging from the discussions among the world powers during World War II was a new international monetary organization, the International Monetary Fund. A main objective of the IMF was to reestablish a system of fixed exchange rates, with gold serving as the primary reserve asset. Gold became an international unit of account when member nations officially agreed to state the par values of their currencies in terms of gold or, alternatively, the gold content of the U.S. dollar.

The post-World War II international monetary system as formulated by the fund nations was nominally a **gold exchange standard**. The idea was to economize on monetary gold stocks as international reserves, because they could not expand as fast as international trade was growing. This growth required the United States that emerged from the war with a dominant economy in terms of productive capacity and national wealth, to assume the role of world banker. The dollar was to become the chief reserve currency of the international monetary system. The coexistence of both dollars and gold as international reserve assets led to this system's being dubbed the *dollar-gold system*.

As a world banker, the United States assumed responsibility for buying and selling gold at a fixed price to foreign official holders of dollars. The dollar was the only currency that was made convertible into gold; other national currencies were pegged to the dollar. The dollar was therefore regarded as a reserve currency that was as good as gold because it was thought that the dollar would retain its value relative to other currencies and remain convertible into gold.

As long as the monetary gold stocks of the United States were large relative to outstanding dollar liabilities abroad, confidence in the dollar as a viable reserve currency remained intact. Immediately following World War II, the U.S. monetary gold stocks peaked at $24 billion, about two-thirds of the world total. But as time passed, the amount of foreign dollar holdings increased significantly because of the U.S. payments deficits, whereas the U.S. monetary gold stock dwindled as some of the dollars were turned back to the U.S. Treasury for gold. By 1965, the total supply of foreign held dollars exceeded the U.S. stock of monetary gold. With the United States unable to redeem all outstanding dollars for gold at $35 per ounce, its ability as a world banker to deliver on demand was questioned.

These circumstances led to speculation that the United States might attempt to solve its gold shortage problem by devaluing the dollar. By increasing the official price of gold, dollar devaluation would lead to a rise in the value of U.S. monetary gold stocks. To prevent speculative profits from any rise in the official price of gold, the United States along with several other nations in 1968 established a *two-tier gold system*. This system consisted of an *official tier*, in which central banks could buy and sell gold for monetary purposes at the official price of $35 per ounce, and a *private market*, where gold as a commodity could be traded at the free market price. By separating the official gold market from the private gold market, the two-tier system was a step toward the complete demonetization of gold.

Demonetization of Gold

The formation of the two-tier gold system was a remedy that could only delay the inevitable collapse of the gold exchange standard. By 1971, the U.S. stock of monetary gold had declined to $11 billion, only a fraction of U.S. dollar liabilities to foreign central banks. The U.S. balance-of-payments position was also deteriorating. In August 1971, President Richard Nixon announced that the United States was suspending its commitment to buy and sell gold at $35 per ounce. The closing of the gold window to foreign official holders brought an end to the gold exchange standard, and the last functional link between the dollar and monetary gold was severed.

It took several years for the world's monetary authorities to formalize the **demonetization of gold** as an international reserve asset. On January 1, 1975, the official price of gold was abolished as the unit of account for the international monetary system. National monetary authorities could enter into gold transactions at market determined prices, and the use of gold was terminated by the IMF. It was agreed that one-sixth of the fund's gold would be auctioned at prevailing prices and the profits distributed to the developing nations.

As for the United States, the 41-year ban on gold ownership for U.S. residents was ended on January 1, 1975. Within a few weeks, the U.S. Treasury was auctioning a portion of its gold on the commodity markets. These actions were a signal by the United States that it would treat gold in the same way that it treats any other commodity.

Should the United States Return to the Gold Standard?

When the United States left the gold standard, it moved to a fiat currency standard in which dollar bills circulate as legal tender and they are not redeemable into gold. Instead, the only thing that gives fiat money value is its relative scarcity and the faith placed in it by the people that use it. Critics are concerned that in a fiat monetary system, there is no restraint on the amount of money that can be created. They fear that government can incur large budget deficits and federal borrowings that are financed through the printing of paper currency. This process can result in the inflation of prices and the loss of purchasing power of money.

If the United States returned to a gold standard, its government would be limited in its ability to inflate prices through excessive issuance of paper currency. This is because the dollar would be backed by a specified amount of gold: for example, $1 would be worth 1/100 of an ounce of gold. The government can only print as much money as the United States has gold. This discourages inflation that is too much money chasing too few goods. It also discourages government budget deficits and debt that cannot exceed the supply of gold. This is why former U.S. Federal Reserve Chairman Alan Greenspan and U.S. Congressman Ron Paul have argued for the reinstatement of the gold standard.

Returning to the gold standard would present problems for the U.S. economy. It would limit the government's ability to manage the economy. The Federal Reserve would no longer be able to increase the money supply during recession or decreasing the money supply during inflation, because the money supply would have to remain constant. Yet this is why many propose a return to the gold standard. The United States could not unilaterally adopt a gold standard if other countries didn't: if it did, everyone in the world could demand that the United States replace their dollars with gold. The United States does not possess enough gold, at current rates, to pay off the portion of its debt owed to foreign investors. These problems and others have resulted in the U.S. government's lack of enthusiasm about returning to a gold standard.

SPECIAL DRAWING RIGHTS

The liquidity and confidence problems of the gold exchange standard that resulted from reliance on the dollar and gold as international monies led in 1970 to the creation by the IMF of a new reserve asset, termed **special drawing rights**. The objective was to introduce into the payments mechanism a new type of international money, in addition to the dollar and gold that could be transferred among participating nations in settlement of payments deficits. With the IMF managing the stock of SDRs, world reserves would presumably grow in line with world commerce.

Under the Bretton Woods system of fixed exchange rates, a participating country needed official reserves—government or central bank holdings of gold and widely accepted foreign currencies—that could be used to purchase the domestic currency in world foreign exchange markets, as required to maintain its exchange rate. The international supply of two key reserve assets—gold and the U.S. dollar—proved inadequate for supporting the expansion of world trade and financial development that was occurring. The international community decided to create a new international reserve asset under the auspices of the IMF. By the early 1970s, the Bretton Woods system had collapsed and the major currencies shifted to a floating exchange rate regime. The growth in international capital markets facilitated borrowing by creditworthy governments. Both of these developments lessened the need for SDRs.

Today, the SDR has only limited use as a reserve asset, and its main function is to serve as the unit of account of the IMF and some other international organizations. Some of the IMF's member nations peg their currency values to the SDR. Rather than being an international currency, the SDR is a potential claim on the freely usable currencies of IMF members. Holders of SDRs can obtain these currencies in exchange for their SDRs.

FACILITIES FOR BORROWING RESERVES

The discussion so far has considered the different types of *owned reserves*—national currencies, gold, and SDRs. Various facilities for *borrowing reserves* have also been implemented for nations with weak balance-of-payments positions. Borrowed reserves do not eliminate the need for owned reserves, but they do add to the flexibility of the international monetary system by increasing the time available for nations to correct payments disequilibrium. Let's examine the major forms of international credit.

IMF Drawings

One of the original purposes of the IMF was to help member nations finance balance-of-payments deficits. The fund has furnished a pool of revolving credit for nations in need of reserves. Temporary loans of foreign currency are made to deficit nations that are expected to repay them within a stipulated time frame. The transactions by which the fund makes foreign currency loans available are called **IMF drawings**.

Deficit nations do not borrow from the fund. Instead, they purchase with their own currency the foreign currency required to help finance deficits. When the nation's balance-of-payments position improves, it is expected to reverse the transaction and make repayment by repurchasing its currency from the fund. The fund currently allows members to purchase other currencies at their own option up to the first 50 percent of their fund quotas that are based on the nation's economic size. Special permission must be granted by the fund if a nation is to purchase foreign currencies in excess of this figure. The fund extends such permission once it is convinced that the deficit nation has enacted reasonable measures to restore payments equilibrium.

Since the early 1950s, the fund has also fostered liberal exchange rate policies by entering into *standby arrangements* with interested member nations. These agreements guarantee that a member nation may draw specified amounts of foreign currencies from the fund over given time periods. The advantage is that participating nations can count on credit from the fund should it be needed. It also saves the drawing nation from administrative time delays when the loans are actually made.

General Arrangements to Borrow

During the early 1960s, the question was raised whether the IMF had sufficient amounts of foreign currencies to meet the exchange stabilization needs of its deficit member nations. Owing to the possibility that large drawings by major nations might exhaust the fund's stocks of foreign currencies, the **General Arrangements to Borrow** were initiated in 1962. Ten leading industrial nations, called the Group of Ten, originally agreed to lend the fund up to a maximum of $6 billion. In 1964, the Group of Ten expanded when Switzerland joined the group. By serving as an intermediary and guarantor, the fund could use these reserves to offer compensatory financial assistance to one or more of the participating nations. Such credit arrangements were expected to be used only when the deficit nation's borrowing needs exceeded the amount of assistance that could be provided under the fund's own drawing facilities.

The General Arrangements to Borrow do *not* provide a permanent increase in the supply of world reserves once the loans are repaid and world reserves revert back to their original levels. However, these arrangements have made world reserves more flexible and adaptable to the needs of deficit nations.

Swap Arrangements

During the early 1960s, a wave of speculative attacks occurred against the U.S. dollar, based on expectations that it would be devalued in terms of other currencies. To help offset the flow of short-term capital out of the dollar into stronger foreign currencies, the U.S. Federal Reserve agreed with several central banks in 1962 to initiate reciprocal currency arrangements, commonly referred to as **swap arrangements**. Today, the swap network on which the United States depends to finance its interventions in the foreign exchange market includes the central banks of Canada and Mexico.[1]

Swap arrangements are bilateral agreements between central banks. Each government provides an exchange, or swap of currencies to help finance temporary payments disequilibrium. If Mexico is short of dollars, it can ask the Federal Reserve to supply them in exchange for pesos. A drawing on the swap network is usually initiated by telephone, followed by an exchange of wire messages specifying terms and conditions. The actual swap is in the form of a foreign exchange contract calling for the sale of dollars by the Federal Reserve for the currency of a foreign central bank. The nation requesting the swap is expected to use the funds to help ease its payments deficits and discourage speculative capital outflows. Swaps are to be repaid (reversed) within a stipulated period of time, normally within 3 to 12 months.

INTERNATIONAL LENDING RISK

In many respects, the principles that apply to international lending are similar to those of domestic lending: the lender needs to determine the credit risk of whether the borrower will default. When making international loans, bankers face two additional risks: country risk and currency risk.

Credit risk is financial and refers to the probability that part or all of the interest or principal of a loan will not be repaid. The larger the potential for default on a loan, the higher the interest rate that the bank must charge the borrower.

Assessing credit risk on international loans tends to be more difficult than on domestic loans. American banks are often less familiar with foreign business practices and economic conditions than those in the United States. Obtaining reliable information to

---

[1]Because of the formation of the European Central Bank and in light of 15 years of disuse, the bilateral swap arrangements of the Federal Reserve with many European central banks, such as Austria, Germany, and Belgium, were jointly deemed no longer necessary in view of the well established, present day arrangements for international monetary cooperation. Accordingly, the respective parties to the arrangements mutually agreed to allow them to lapse in 1998.

evaluate foreign credit risk can be time consuming and costly. Many U.S. banks confine their international lending to major multinational corporations and financial institutions. To attract lending by U.S. banks, a foreign government may provide assurances against default by a local private borrower, thus reducing the credit risk of the loan.

Country risk is political and is closely related to political developments in a country, especially the government's views concerning international investments and loans. Some governments encourage the inflow of foreign funds to foster domestic economic development. Fearing loss of national sovereignty, other governments may discourage such inflows by enacting additional taxes, profit restrictions, and wage/price controls that can hinder the ability of local borrowers to repay loans. In the extreme, foreign governments can expropriate the assets of foreign investors or make foreign loan repayments illegal.

Currency risk is economic and is associated with currency depreciations and appreciations as well as exchange controls. Some loans by U.S. banks are denominated in foreign currency instead of dollars. If the currency in which the loan is made depreciates against the dollar during the period of the loan, the repayment will be worth fewer dollars. If the foreign currency has a well developed forward market, the loan may be hedged. But many foreign currencies, especially of the developing nations, do not have such markets, and loans denominated in these currencies cannot always be hedged to decrease this type of currency risk. Another type of currency risk arises from exchange controls that are common in developing nations. Exchange controls restrict the movement of funds across national borders or limit a currency's convertibility into dollars for repayment, thus adding to the risk of international lenders.

When lending overseas, bankers must evaluate credit risk, country risk, and currency risk. Evaluating risks in foreign lending often results in detailed analyses, compiled by a bank's research department, that are based on a nation's financial, economic, and political conditions. When international lenders consider detailed analyses to be too expensive, they often use reports and statistical indicators to help them determine the risk of lending.

THE PROBLEM OF INTERNATIONAL DEBT

Much concern has been voiced over the volume of international lending in recent years. At times, the concern has been that international lending was insufficient. Such was the case after the oil shocks in 1974–1975 and 1979–1980, when it was feared that some oil importing developing nations might not be able to obtain loans to finance trade deficits resulting from the huge increases in the price of oil. It so happened that many oil importing nations were able to borrow dollars from commercial banks. They paid the dollars to OPEC nations that re-deposited the money in commercial banks, which then re-lent the money to oil importers, and so on. In the 1970s, the banks were part of the solution; if they had not lent large sums to the developing nations, the oil shocks would have done far more damage to the world economy.

By the 1980s, however, commercial banks were viewed as part of an international debt problem because they had lent so much to developing nations. Flush with OPEC money after the oil price increases of the 1970s, the banks actively sought borrowers and had no trouble finding them among the developing nations. Some nations borrowed to prop up consumption because their living standards were already low and hard hit by oil price hikes. Most nations borrowed to avoid cuts in development programs and to invest in energy projects. It was generally recognized that banks were successful in recycling their

OPEC deposits to developing nations following the first round of oil price hikes in 1974 and 1975. The international lending mechanism encountered increasing difficulties beginning with the global recession of the early 1980s. In particular, some developing nations were unable to pay their external debts on schedule.

Another indicator of debt burden is the **debt service/export ratio** that refers to scheduled interest and principal payments as a percentage of export earnings. The debt service/export ratio permits one to focus on two key indicators of whether a reduction in the debt burden is possible in the short run: the interest rate that the nation pays on its external debt and the growth in its exports of goods and services. All else being constant, a rise in the interest rate increases the debt service/export ratio, while a rise in exports decreases the ratio. It is a well known rule of international finance that a nation's debt burden rises if the interest rate on the debt exceeds the rate of growth of exports.

Dealing with Debt Servicing Difficulties

A nation may experience debt servicing problems for a number of reasons: it may have pursued improper macroeconomic policies that contribute to large balance-of-payments deficits; it may have borrowed excessively or on unfavorable terms; or it may have been affected by adverse economic events that it could not control.

Several options are available to a nation facing debt servicing difficulties. First, it can cease repayments on its debt. Such an action, however, undermines confidence in the nation, making it difficult (if not impossible) for it to borrow in the future. The nation might be declared in default, in which case its assets (such as ships and aircraft) might be confiscated and sold to discharge the debt. As a group, however, developing nations in debt may have considerable leverage in winning concessions from their lenders.

A second option is for the nation to try to service its debt at all costs. To do so may require the restriction of other foreign exchange expenditures, a step that may be viewed as socially unacceptable.

Also, a nation may seek debt rescheduling that generally involves stretching out the original payment schedule of the debt. There is a cost because the debtor nation must pay interest on the amount outstanding until the debt has been repaid.

When a nation faces debt servicing problems, its creditors seek to reduce their exposure by collecting all interest and principal payments as they come due, while granting no new credit. There is an old adage that goes as follows: When a man owes a bank $1,000, the bank owns him; but when a man owes the bank $1 million, he owns the bank. Banks with large amounts of international loans find it in their best interest to help the debtor recover financially. To deal with debt servicing problems, debtor nations and their creditors generally attempt to negotiate rescheduling agreements. Creditors agree to lengthen the time period for repayment of the principal and sometimes part of the interest on existing loans. Banks have little option but to accommodate demands for debt rescheduling because they do not want the debtor to officially default on the loan. With default, the bank's assets become nonperforming and subject to markdowns by government regulators. These actions could lead to possible withdrawals of deposits and bank insolvency.

Besides rescheduling debt with commercial banks, developing nations may obtain emergency loans from the IMF. The IMF provides loans to nations experiencing balance-of-payments difficulties provided that the borrowers initiate programs to correct these difficulties. By insisting on **conditionality**, the IMF asks borrowers to adopt austerity programs to shore up economies and put muddled finances in order. Such measures have resulted in the slashing of public expenditures, private consumption, and in some cases, capital investment. Borrowers must also cut imports and expand exports. The IMF views austerity programs as a necessity because with a sovereign debtor, there is no other way to make it pay back its loans. The IMF faces a difficult situation in deciding how tough to get with borrowers. If it goes soft and offers money on easier terms, it sets a precedent for other debtor nations. If it miscalculates and requires excessive austerity measures, it risks triggering political turmoil and possibly a declaration of default.

The IMF has been criticized, notably by developing nations, for demanding austerity policies that excessively emphasize short-term improvements in the balance-of-payments rather than fostering long run economic growth. Developing nations also contend that the IMF austerity programs promote downward pressure on economic activity in nations that are already exposed to recessionary forces. The crucial issue faced by the IMF is how to resolve the economic problems of the debtor nations in a manner most advantageous to them, their creditors, and the world as a whole. The mutually advantageous solution is one that enables these nations to achieve sustainable, noninflationary economic growth, thus assuring creditors of repayment and benefiting the world economy through expansion of trade and economic activity.

REDUCING BANK EXPOSURE TO DEVELOPING NATION DEBT

When developing nations cannot meet their debt obligations to foreign banks, the stability of the international financial system is threatened. Banks may react to this threat by increasing their capital base, setting aside reserves to cover losses, and reducing new loans to debtor nations.

Banks have additional means to improve their financial position. One method is to liquidate developing nation debt by engaging in outright *loan sales* to other banks in the secondary market. If there occurs an unexpected increase in the default risk of such loans, their market value will be less than their face value. The selling bank thus absorbs costs because its loans must be sold at a discount. Following the sale, the bank must adjust its balance sheet to take account of any previously unrecorded difference between the face value of the loans and their market value. Many small and medium sized U.S. banks, eager to dump their bad loans in the 1980s, were willing to sell them in the secondary market at discounts as high as 70 percent, or 30 cents on the dollar. Many banks could not afford such huge discounts. Even worse, if the banks all rushed to sell bad loans at once, prices would fall further. Sales of loans in the secondary market were often viewed as a last resort measure.

Another debt reduction technique is the *debt buyback*, in which the government of the debtor nation buys the loans from the commercial bank at a discount. Banks have also engaged in *debt-for-debt swaps* in which a bank exchanges its loans for securities issued by the debtor nation's government at a lower interest rate or discount.

Cutting losses on developing nation loans has sometimes involved banks in **debt/equity swaps**. Under this approach, a commercial bank sells its loans at a discount to the developing nation government for local currency that it then uses to finance an equity investment in the debtor nation.

To see how a debt/equity swap works, suppose that Brazil owes Manufacturers Hanover Trust (of New York) $1 billion. Manufacturers Hanover decides to swap some of the debt for ownership shares in Companhia Suzano del Papel e Celulose, a pulp and paper company. Here is what occurs:

- Manufacturers Hanover takes $115 million in Brazilian government guaranteed loans to a Brazilian broker. The broker takes the loans to the Brazilian central bank's monthly debt auction, where they are valued at an average of 87 cents on the dollar.
- Through the broker, Manufacturers Hanover exchanges the loans at the central bank for $100 million worth of Brazilian *cruzados*. The broker is paid a commission, and the central bank retires the loans.
- With its cruzados, Manufacturers Hanover purchases 12 percent of Suzano's stock, and Suzano uses the bank's funds to increase capacity and exports.

Although debt/equity swaps enhance a bank's chances of selling developing nation debt, they do not necessarily decrease its risk. Some equity investments in developing nations may be just as risky as the loans that were swapped for local factories or land. Banks that acquire an equity interest in developing nation assets may not have the knowledge to manage those assets. Debtor nations also worry that debt/equity swaps will allow major companies to fall into foreign hands.

DEBT REDUCTION AND DEBT FORGIVENESS

Another method of coping with developing nation debt involves programs enacted for debt reduction and debt forgiveness. **Debt reduction** refers to any voluntary scheme that lessens the burden on the debtor nation to service its external debt. Debt reduction is accomplished through two main approaches. The first is the use of negotiated modifications in the terms and conditions of the contracted debt, such as debt rescheduling, retiming of interest payments, and improved borrowing terms. Debt reduction may also be achieved through measures such as debt/equity swaps and debt buybacks. The purpose of debt reduction is to foster comprehensive policies for economic growth by easing the ability of the debtor nation to service its debt, thus freeing resources that will be used for investment.

Some proponents of debt relief maintain that the lending nations should permit **debt forgiveness**. Debt forgiveness refers to any arrangement that reduces the value of contractual obligations of the debtor nation; it includes schemes such as markdowns or write offs of developing nation debt or the abrogation of existing obligations to pay interest.

Debt forgiveness advocates maintain that the most heavily indebted developing nations are unable to service their external debt and maintain an acceptable rate of per capita income growth because their debt burden is overwhelming. They contend that if some of this debt were forgiven, a debtor nation could use the freed up foreign exchange resources to increase its imports and invest domestically, thus increasing domestic economic growth rates. The release of the limitation on foreign exchange would provide the debtor nation additional incentive to invest because it would not have to share as much of the benefits of its increased growth and investment with its creditors in the form of interest payments. Debt forgiveness would allow the debtor nation to service its debt more easily; this would reduce the debt load burden of a debtor nation and could potentially lead to greater inflows of foreign investment.

Debt forgiveness critics question whether the amount of debt is a major limitation on developing nation growth and whether that growth would in fact resume if a large portion of that debt were forgiven. They contend that nations such as Indonesia and South Korea have experienced large amounts of external debt relative to national output but have not faced debt servicing problems. Also, debt forgiveness does not guarantee that the freed up foreign exchange resources will be used productively—that is, invested in sectors that will ultimately generate additional foreign exchange.

THE EURODOLLAR MARKET

One of the most widely misunderstood topics in international finance is the nature and operation of the **eurodollar market**, also called the eurocurrency market. This market operates as a financial intermediary, bringing together lenders and borrowers. Originally, eurodollars were held almost exclusively in Europe, and thus the name eurodollars. Most of these deposits are still held by commercial banks in London, Paris, and other European cities; but they also are held in such places as the Bahamas, Bahrain, Hong Kong, Japan, Panama, and Singapore. Regardless of where they are held, such deposits are referred to as eurodollars. The size of the eurodollar market has increased from about $1 billion in the 1950s to more than $5 trillion in the first decade of the 2000s.

Eurodollars are bank deposit liabilities, such as time deposits, denominated in U.S. dollars and other foreign currencies in banks outside the United States, including foreign branches of U.S. banks. Transactions in dollars constitute about three-fourths of the volume of transactions. Eurodollar deposits in turn may be re-deposited in other foreign banks, lent to business enterprises, invested, or retained to improve reserves or overall liquidity. The average deposit is in the millions and has a maturity of less than six months. The eurodollar market is out of reach for all but the most wealthy. The only way for most individuals to invest in this market is indirectly through a money market fund.

Eurodollar deposits are practically free of regulation by the host country, including U.S. regulatory agencies. They are not subject to the reserve requirements mandated by the Federal Reserve and to fees of the Federal Deposit Insurance Corporation. Because eurodollars are subject to less regulation than similar deposits within the United States, banks issuing eurodollar deposits can operate on narrower margins or spreads between dollar borrowing and lending rates than can domestic U.S. banks. This gives eurodollar deposits a competitive advantage relative to deposits issued by domestic U.S. banks. Thus, banks issuing eurodollar deposits can compete effectively with domestic U.S. banks for loans and deposits.

The eurodollar market has grown rapidly since the 1950s, due in part to the U.S. banking regulations that prevented U.S. banks from paying competitive interest rates on savings accounts (Regulation Q) and have increased the costs of lending for U.S. banks. Also continuing deficits in the U.S. current account have increased the dollar holdings for foreigners, as did the sharp increase in oil prices that resulted in enormous wealth in the oil exporting countries. These factors, combined with the relative freedom allowed foreign currency banking in many countries, resulted in the rapid growth of the market.

As a type of international money, eurodollars increase the efficiency of international trade and finance. They provide an internationally accepted medium of exchange, store of value, and standard of value. Because eurodollars eliminate the risks and costs associated with converting from one currency to another, they permit savers to search the world more easily for the highest returns and borrowers to scan out the lowest cost of funds. Thus, they are a link among various regional capital markets, helping to create a worldwide market for capital.[2]

---

[2] See Charles J. Woelfel, "Eurodollars," *Encyclopedia of Banking and Finance*, 10th edition, London, UK: Fitzroy Dearborn Publishers, 1995.

SUMMARY

1. The purpose of international reserves is to permit nations to bridge the gap between monetary receipts and payments. Deficit nations can use international reserves to buy time in order to postpone adjustment measures.
2. The demand for international reserves depends on two major factors: (a) the monetary value of international transactions and (b) the size and duration of the balance-of-payments disequilibrium.
3. The need for international reserves tends to become less acute under a system of floating exchange rates than under a system of fixed rates. The more efficient the international adjustment mechanism and the greater the extent of international policy coordination, the smaller the need for international reserves.
4. The supply of international reserves consists of owned and borrowed reserves. Among the major sources of reserves are (a) foreign currencies, (b) monetary gold stocks, (c) special drawing rights, (d) IMF drawing positions, (e) the General Arrangements to Borrow, and (f) swap arrangements.
5. When making international loans, bankers face credit risk, country risk, and currency risk.
6. Among the indicators used to analyze a nation's external debt position are its debt-to-export ratio and debt service/export ratio.
7. A nation experiencing debt servicing difficulties has several options: (a) cease repayment on its debt, (b) service its debt at all costs, or (c) reschedule its debt. Debt rescheduling has been widely used by borrowing nations in recent years.
8. A bank can reduce its exposure to developing nation debt through outright loan sales in the secondary market, debt buybacks, debt-for-debt swaps, and debt/equity swaps.
9. Eurodollars are deposits, denominated and payable in dollars and other foreign currencies, in banks outside the United States. The eurodollar market operates as a financial intermediary, bringing together lenders and borrowers.

KEY CONCEPTS AND TERMS

Conditionality (p. 507)
Country risk (p. 506)
Credit risk (p. 505)
Currency risk (p. 506)
Debt/equity swap (p. 508)
Debt forgiveness (p. 509)
Debt reduction (p. 509)
Debt service/export ratio (p. 507)
Demand for international reserves (p. 496)
Demonetization of gold (p. 502)
Eurodollar market (p. 510)
General Arrangements to Borrow (p. 504)
Gold exchange standard (p. 502)
Gold standard (p. 500)
IMF drawings (p. 504)
International reserves (p. 496)
Liquidity problem (p. 500)
Supply of international reserves (p. 499)
Swap arrangements (p. 505)

STUDY QUESTIONS

1. A nation's need for international reserves is similar to an individual's desire to hold cash balances. Explain.
2. What are the major factors that determine a nation's demand for international reserves?
3. The total supply of international reserves consists of two categories: (a) owned reserves and (b) borrowed reserves. What do these categories include?

4. In terms of volume, which component of world reserves is currently most important? Which is currently least important?

5. What is meant by a reserve currency? Historically, which currencies have assumed this role?

6. What is the current role of gold in the international monetary system?

7. What advantages does a gold exchange standard have over a pure gold standard?

8. What are special drawing rights? Why were they created? How is their value determined?

9. What facilities exist for trading nations that wish to borrow international reserves?

10. What caused the international debt problem of the developing nations in the 1980s? Why did this debt problem threaten the stability of the international banking system?

11. What is a eurodollar? How did the eurodollar market develop?

12. What risks do bankers assume when making loans to foreign borrowers?

13. Distinguish between debt-to-export ratio and debt service/export ratio.

14. What options are available to a nation experiencing debt servicing difficulties? What limitations apply to each option?

15. What methods do banks use to reduce their exposure to developing nation debt?

16. How can debt/equity swaps help banks reduce losses on developing nation loans?

Glossary

A

Absolute quota   A physical restriction on the quantity of goods that can be imported during a specific time period.

Absorption approach   An approach to currency depreciation that deals with the income effects of depreciation; a decrease in domestic expenditures relative to income must occur for depreciation to promote payments equilibrium, according to the absorption approach

Adjustable pegged exchange rates   A system of semifixed exchange rates where it is understood that the par value of the currency will be changed occasionally in response to changing economic conditions

Adjustment mechanism   A mechanism that works to return a balance of payments to equilibrium after the initial equilibrium has been disrupted; the process takes two different forms: automatic (economic processes) and discretionary (government policies)

Ad valorem tariff   A tariff expressed as a fixed percentage of the value of the imported product

Advanced nations   Includes those of North America and Western Europe, plus Australia, New Zealand, and Japan

Agglomeration economies   A rich country specializes in manufacturing niches and gains productivity through groups of firms clustered together, some producing the same product and others connected by vertical linkages

Antidumping duty   A duty levied against commodities a home nation believes are being dumped into its markets from abroad

Appreciation   (as applied to currency markets) When, over a period of time, it takes fewer units of a nation's currency to purchase one unit of a foreign currency

Asset market approach   A method of determining short-term exchange rates where investors consider two key factors when deciding between domestic and foreign investments; relative levels of interest rates and expected changes in the exchange rate itself over the term of the investment

Autarky   A case of national self-sufficiency or absence of trade

Automatic adjustment   (of the balance-of-payments process) A mechanism that works to return a balance of payments to equilibrium automatically through the adjustments in economic variables

B

Balance of international indebtedness   A statement that summarizes a country's stock of assets and liabilities against the rest of the world at a fixed point in time

Balance-of-payments   A record of the flow of economic transactions between the residents of one country and the rest of the world

Basis for trade   Why nations export and import certain products

Beggar-thy-neighbor policy The practice of imposing protectionist policies to achieve gains from trade at the expense of other nations

Benelux A customs union formed in 1948 that includes Belgium, the Netherlands, and Luxembourg

Bid rate The price that the bank is willing to pay for a unit of foreign currency

Bonded warehouse A storage facility operated under the lock and key of (in the case of the United States) the U.S. Customs Service

Brain drain Emigration of highly educated and skilled people from developing nations to industrial nations

Bretton Woods system A new international monetary system created in 1944 by delegates from 44 member nations of the United Nations that met at Bretton Woods, New Hampshire

Buffer stock Supplies of a commodity financed and held by a producers' association; used to limit commodity price swings

Buy-national policies When a home nation's government, through explicit laws, openly discriminates against foreign suppliers in its purchasing decisions

C

Call option Gives the holder the right to buy foreign currency at a specified price

Capital and financial account The net result of both private sector and official capital and financial transactions

Capital controls Government imposed barriers to foreign savers investing in domestic assets or to domestic savers investing in foreign assets; also known as *exchange controls*

Capital/labor ratio A country's ratio of capital inputs to labor inputs

Cartel A group of firms or nations that attempts to support prices higher than would exist under more competitive conditions

Clean float When free-market forces of supply and demand are allowed to determine the exchange value of a currency

Commodity Credit Corporation (CCC) A government owned corporation administered by the U.S. Department of Agriculture

Commodity terms of trade Measures the relation between the prices a nation gets for its exports and the prices it pays for its imports

Common agricultural policy Members of the European Union agree to maintain identical governmental agricultural policies to support farmers

Common market A group of trading nations that permits the free movement of goods and services among member nations, the initiation of common external trade restrictions against non-members, and the free movement of factors of production across national borders within the economic bloc

Complete specialization A situation in which a country produces only one good

Compound tariff A tariff that is a combination of a specific tariff and an ad valorem tariff

Conditionality The standards imposed by the IMF on borrowing countries to qualify for a loan that can include requirements that the borrowers initiate programs to correct economic difficulties, adopt austerity programs to shore up their economies, and put their muddled finances in order

Conglomerate integration In the case of an MNE, diversification into nonrelated markets

Constant opportunity costs A constant rate of sacrifice of one good for another as a nation slides along its production possibilities schedule

Consumer surplus The difference between the amount that buyers would be willing and able to pay for a good and the actual amount they do pay

Consumption effect A trade restriction's loss of welfare that occurs because of increased prices and lower consumption

Consumption gains Post-trade consumption points outside a nation's production possibilities schedule

Convergence criteria Economic standards required of all nations in a monetary union; in the instance of the Maastricht Treaty, these standards included price stability, low long-term interest rates, stable exchange rates, and sound public finances

Corporate average fuel economy standards (CAFÉ) Fuel economy standards imposed by the U.S. government on automobile manufacturers

Cost-based definition of dumping A method of calculating the fair market value of a product in dumping cases; the U.S. Commerce Department "constructs" fair market value equal to the sum of (1) the cost of manufacturing the merchandise, (2) general expenses, (3) profit on home-market sales, and (4) the cost of packaging the merchandise for shipment to the United States

Cost-insurance-freight (CIF) valuation When ad valorem tariffs are levied as a percentage of the imported commodity's total value as it arrives at its final destination

Countervailing duty A levy imposed by importing countries to counteract foreign export subsidies; the size of the duty is limited to the amount of the export subsidy

Country risk Risk associated with political developments in a country, especially the government's views concerning international investments and loans

Country risk analysis A process that multinational corporations and banks carry out to help them decide whether to do business abroad

Covered interest arbitrage The process of moving funds into foreign currencies to take advantage of higher investment yields abroad while avoiding exchange rate risk

Crawling peg A system in which a nation makes small, frequent changes in the par value of its currency to correct balance-of-payments disequilibriums

Credit risk The probability that part or all of the interest or principal of a loan will not be repaid

Credit transaction A balance of payments transaction that results in a receipt of a payment from foreigners

Cross exchange rate The resulting rate derived when the exchange rate between any two currencies can be derived from the rates of these two currencies in terms of a third currency

Currency board A monetary authority that issues notes and coins convertible into a foreign anchor currency at a fixed exchange rate

Currency crashes Financial crises that often end in currency devaluations or accelerated depreciations

Currency crisis A situation in which a weak currency experiences heavy selling pressure, also called a *speculative attack*

Currency risk Investment risk associated with currency depreciations and appreciations as well as exchange controls

Currency swap The conversion of one currency to another currency at one point in time, with an agreement to reconvert it to the original currency at a specified time in the future

Current account The net value of monetary flows associated with transactions in goods and services, investment income, employee compensation, and unilateral transfers

Customs union An agreement among two or more trading partners to remove all tariff and nontariff trade barriers among themselves; each member nation imposes identical trade restrictions against nonparticipants

Customs valuation The process of determining the value of an imported product

D

Deadweight loss The net loss of economic benefits to a domestic economy because of the protective and consumption effect of a trade barrier

Debit transaction A balance of payments transaction that leads to a payment to foreigners

Debt/equity swap When a commercial bank sells its loans at a discount to the debtor-nation's government for local currency that it then uses to finance an equity investment in the debtor nation

Debt forgiveness Any arrangement that reduces the value of contractual obligations of the debtor nation

Debt reduction Any voluntary scheme that lessens the burden on the debtor nation to service its external debt

Debt service/export ratio The scheduled interest and principal payments as a percentage of export earnings

Demand for international reserves The requirement for international reserves; depends on two related factors: (1) the monetary value of international transactions and (2) the disequilibrium that can arise in balance-of-payments positions; the requirements for international reserves include assets such as key foreign currencies, special drawing rights, and drawing rights at the International Monetary Fund

Demand-pull inflation When a nation's capacity to produce has been achieved, and further increases in aggregate demand pull prices upward

Demonetization of gold   Occurred in the 1970s when the official price of gold was abolished as the unit of account for the international monetary system

Depreciation   (as applies to currency markets) When, over a period of time, it takes more units of a nation's currency to purchase one unit of a foreign currency

Destabilizing speculation   Occurs when speculators expect a current trend in exchange rates to continue and their transactions accelerate the rise or fall of the target currency's value

Devaluation   An official change in a currency's par value, that causes the currency's exchange value to depreciate

Developing nations   Most nations in Africa, Asia, Latin America, and the Middle East

Direct controls   Consist of government restrictions on the market economy

Dirty float   A condition under a managed floating system when free-market forces of supply and demand are not allowed to achieve their equilibrating role; countries may manage their exchange rates to improve the competitiveness of their producers

Discount   The valuation of a currency when it is worth less in the forward market than in the spot market

Doha Round   The most recent round of multilateral trade negotiations under the World Trade Organization

Dollarization   Occurs when residents of a foreign country use the U.S. dollar alongside or instead of their domestic currency

Domestic content requirements   Requirements that stipulate the minimum percentage of a product's total value that must be produced domestically if the product is to qualify for zero tariff rates

Domestic production subsidy   A subsidy that is sometimes granted to producers of import-competing goods

Domestic revenue effect   The amount of tariff revenue shifted from domestic consumers to the tariff-levying government

Double entry accounting   A system of accounting in which each credit entry is balanced by a debit entry, and vice versa, so that the recording of any transaction leads to two offsetting entries

Dumping   When foreign buyers are charged lower prices than domestic buyers for an identical product after allowing for transportation costs and tariff duties

Dynamic comparative advantage   A changing pattern in comparative advantage; governments can establish policies to promote opportunities for changes in comparative advantage over time

Dynamic effects of economic integration   Effects that relate to member nations' long-term rates of growth, that includes economies of scale, greater competition, and investment stimulus

Dynamic gains from international trade   The effect of trade on the country's growth rate and thus on the volume of additional resources made available to, or utilized by, the trading country

E

Economic integration   A process of eliminating restrictions on international trade, payments, and factor mobility

Economic interdependence   All aspects of a nation's economy are linked to the economies of its trading partners

Economic sanctions   Government mandated limitations placed on customary trade or financial relations among nations

Economic union   Where national, social, taxation, and fiscal policies are harmonized and administered by a supranational institution

Economies of scale   When increasing all inputs by the same proportion results in a greater proportion of total output

Effective exchange rate   A weighted average of the exchange rates between a domestic currency and that nation's most important trading partners, with weights given by relative importance of the nation's trade with each trade partner

Effective tariff rate   Measures the total increase in domestic production that a tariff makes possible, compared to free trade

Elasticity approach   An approach to currency depreciation that emphasizes the relative price effects of depreciation and suggests that depreciation works best when demand elasticities for a nation's imports and exports are high

Escape clause   Allows the president to temporarily terminate or make modifications in trade concessions granted foreign nations and to temporarily levy restrictions on surging imports

Euro   The official currency of the EMU

Eurodollar market   A market that operates as a financial intermediary, bringing together lenders and borrowers; also called the Eurocurrency market

European Monetary Union (EMU)   The countries of Europe that in 1999 abolished their national currencies and central banks and replaced them with the euro and the European Central Bank

European Union (EU)   A trading bloc that replaced the European Community following ratification of the Maastricht Treaty by the 12 member countries of the European Community

Exchange arbitrage   The simultaneous purchase and sale of a currency in different foreign exchange markets in order to profit from exchange rate differentials in the two locations

Exchange controls   Government imposed barriers to foreign savers investing in domestic assets (e.g., government securities, stock, or bank deposits) or to domestic savers investing in foreign assets

Exchange rate   The price of one currency in terms of another

Exchange rate pass-through   The extent to which changing currency values lead to changes in import and export prices

Exchange rate index   A weighted average of the exchange rates between a domestic currency and that nation's most important trading partners, with weights given by relative importance of the nation's trade with each trade partner

Exchange stabilization fund   A government entity that attempts to ensure that the market exchange rate does not move above or below the official exchange rate through purchases and sales of foreign currencies

Exit barriers   Cost conditions that make lengthy industry exit a rational response by companies

Expenditure changing policies   Policies that alter the level of aggregate demand for goods and services, including those produced domestically and those imported

Expenditure switching policies   Policies that modify the direction of demand, shifting it between domestic output and imports

Export controls   Enacted to stabilize export revenues, these measures offset a decrease in the market demand for the primary commodity by assigning cutbacks in the market supply

Export quotas   Limitations on export sales administered by one or more exporting nations or industries

Export subsidy   A subsidy paid to exporters so they can sell goods abroad at the lower world price but still receive the higher support price

Export-Import Bank (Eximbank)   An independent agency of the U.S. government established to encourage the exports of U.S. businesses

Export led growth   Involves promoting economic growth through the export of manufactured goods—trade controls are either nonexistent or very low, in the sense that any disincentives to export resulting from import barriers are counterbalanced by export subsidies

Export oriented policy   See export led growth

External balance   When a nation realizes neither balance-of-payments deficits nor balance-of-payments surpluses

External economies of scale   Cost reductions for a firm that occur as the output of the industry increases

F

Factor-endowment theory   Asserts that a country exports those goods that use its abundant factor more intensively

Factor-price equalization   Free trade's tendency to cause cheap factors of production to become more expensive, and the expensive factors of production to become cheaper

Fast track authority   Devised in 1974, this provision commits the U.S. Congress to consider trade agreements without amendment; in return, the president must adhere to a specified timetable and several other procedures

Fiscal policy   Refers to changes in government spending and taxes

Fixed exchange rates A system used primarily by small developing nations whose currencies are anchored to a key currency, such as the U.S. dollar

Floating exchange rates When a nation allows its currency to fluctuate according to the free market forces of supply and demand

Flying geese pattern of economic growth Where countries gradually move up in technological development by following in the pattern of countries ahead of them in the development process

Forecasting exchange rates Attempts to predict future rates of exchange

Foreign direct investment Foreign acquisition of a controlling interest in an overseas company or facility

Foreign repercussion effect The impact that changes in domestic expenditures and income levels have on foreign economies; a rise in domestic income stimulates imports, causing a foreign expansion that in turn raises demand for domestic exports

Foreign currency options Provide an options holder the right to buy or sell a fixed amount of foreign currency at a prearranged price, within a few days or several years

Foreign exchange market The organizational setting within which individuals, businesses, governments, and banks buy and sell foreign currencies and other debt instruments

Foreign-trade zone (FTZ) Special zones that enlarge the benefits of a bonded warehouse by eliminating the restrictive aspects of customs surveillance and by offering more suitable manufacturing facilities; FTZs are intended to stimulate international trade, attract industry, and create jobs by providing an area that gives users tariff and tax breaks

Forward market Where foreign exchange can be traded for future delivery

Forward rate The rate of exchange used in the settlement of forward transactions

Forward transaction An outright purchase and sale of foreign currency at a fixed exchange rate but with payment or delivery of the foreign currency at a future date

Free trade A system of open markets between countries in which nations concentrate their production on goods they can make most cheaply, with all the consequent benefits of the division of labor

Free trade area An association of trading nations whose members agree to remove all tariff and nontariff barriers among themselves

Free-on-board (FOB) valuation When a tariff is applied to a product's value as it leaves the exporting country

Free-trade argument If each nation produces what it does best and permits trade, over the long-term each party will enjoy lower prices and higher levels of output, income, and consumption than could be achieved in isolation

Free-trade-biased sector Generally comprises exporting companies, their workers, and their suppliers; it also consists of consumers, including wholesalers and retail merchants of imported goods

Fundamental analysis The opposite of technical analysis; involves consideration of economic variables that are likely to affect a currency's value

Fundamental disequilibrium When the official exchange rate and the market exchange rate may move apart, reflecting changes in fundamental economic conditions—income levels, tastes and preferences, and technological factors

Futures market A market in which contracting parties agree to future exchanges of currencies and set applicable exchange rates in advance; distinguished from the forward market in that only a limited number of leading currencies are traded; trading takes place in standardized contract amounts and in a specific geographic location

G

Gains from international trade Gains trading partners simultaneously enjoy due to specialization and the division of labor

General Agreement on Tariffs and Trade (GATT) Signed in 1947, GATT was crafted as an agreement among contracting parties, the member nations, to decrease trade barriers and place all nations on an equal footing in trading relations; GATT was never intended to become an organization; instead it was a set of bilateral agreements among countries around the world to reduce trade barriers

General Arrangements to Borrow Initiated in 1962, 10 leading industrial nations, called the Group of Ten, originally agreed to lend the fund up to a maximum of

$6 billion; in 1964, the Group of Ten expanded when Switzerland joined the group. By serving as an intermediary and guarantor, the fund could use these reserves to offer compensatory financial assistance to one or more of the participating nations

Generalized system of preferences (GSP)   A system in which industrialized nations attempt to promote economic development in developing countries through lower tariffs and increased trade rather than foreign aid

Global quota   A technique permitting a specified number of goods to be imported each year, but does not specify where the product is shipped from or who is permitted to import

Globalization   The process of greater interdependence among countries and their citizens

Gold exchange standard   A system of fixed exchange rates, with gold serving as the primary reserve asset; member nations officially agreed to state the par values of their currencies in terms of gold or, alternatively, the gold content of the U.S. dollar

Gold standard   A monetary system in which each member nation's money supply consisted of gold or paper money backed by gold, where each member nation defined the official price of gold in terms of its national currency and was prepared to buy and sell gold at that price. Free import and export of gold was permitted by member nations

Goods and services balance   The result of combining the balance of trade in services and the merchandise trade balance

Group of Five (G–5)   Five industrial nations—the United States, Japan, Germany, the United Kingdom, and France—that sent officials to a world trade meeting at New York's Plaza Hotel in 1985 to try to correct the overvalued dollar and the twin U.S. deficits

Group of Seven (G–7)   Seven industrial nations—the United states, Canada, Japan, the United Kingdom, Germany, France, and Italy—that launched coordinated purchases of the euro to boost its value

Guest workers   Foreign workers, when needed, allowed to immigrate on a temporary basis

H

Heckscher–Ohlin theory   Differences in relative factor endowments among nations that underlie the basis for trade

Hedging   The process of avoiding or covering a foreign exchange risk

Home market effect   Countries will specialize in products for which there is large domestic demand

Horizontal integration   In the case of an MNE, occurs when a parent company producing a commodity in the source country sets up a subsidiary to produce the identical product in the host country

I

IMF drawings   The transactions by which the fund makes foreign-currency loans available

Importance of being unimportant   When one trading nation is significantly larger than the other, the larger nation attains fewer gains from trade while the smaller nation attains most of the gains from trade

Import license   Used to administer an import quota; a license specifying the volume of imports allowed

Import substitution   A policy that involves extensive use of trade barriers to protect domestic industries from import competition

Impossible trinity   A restriction whereby a country can maintain only two of the following three policies—free capital flows, a fixed exchange rate, and an independent monetary policy

Income adjustment mechanism   In 1930s, John Maynard Keynes formulated this theory that focuses on automatic changes in income to bring about adjustment in a nation's current account

Income balance   Net investment income plus net compensation of employees

Increasing opportunity costs   When each additional unit of one good produced requires the sacrifice of increasing amounts of the other good

Industrial policy   Government policy that is actively involved in creating comparative advantage

Infant-industry argument   A tariff that temporarily shields newly developing industries from foreign competition

Intellectual property rights (IPRs)   The exclusive rights to use an invention, idea, product, or process for a given time awarded to the inventor (or author) through registration with the government of that invention, idea, product, or process

Interest arbitrage   The process of moving funds into foreign currencies to take advantage of higher investment yields abroad

Inter-industry specialization   When each nation specializes in a particular industry in which it enjoys a comparative advantage

Inter-industry trade   The exchange between nations of products of different industries

Internal balance   The goal of economic stability at full employment

Internal economies of scale   Reductions in the average total cost of producing a product as a firm increases the size of its plant in the long run.

International commodity agreements (ICAs)
Agreements between leading, producing and consuming nations of commodities about matters such as stabilizing prices, assuring adequate supplies to consumers, and promoting the economic development of producers

International economic policy coordination   The attempt to coordinate national policies—monetary, fiscal, or exchange-rate policy—in recognition of international economic interdependence

International joint ventures   An example of multinational enterprise in which a business organization established by two or more companies combines their skills and assets

International Monetary Fund (IMF)   Headquartered in Washington, and consisting of 184 nations, the IMF can be thought of as a bank for the central banks of member nations

International Monetary Market (IMM)   An extension of the commodity futures markets in which specific quantities of wheat, corn, and other commodities are bought and sold for future delivery at specific dates; the IMM provides trading facilities for the purchase and sale for future delivery of financial instruments (such as foreign currencies) and precious metals (such as gold)

International reserves   Assets held to enable nations to finance disequilibrium in their balance-of-payments positions

Intra-industry specialization   The focus on the production of particular products or groups of products within a given industry

Intra-industry trade   Two-way trade in a similar commodity

J

J–curve effect   A popular description of the time path of trade flows suggesting that in the very short-term, a currency depreciation will lead to a worsening of the nation's trade balance, but as time passes, the trade balance will likely improve

Judgmental forecasts   Subjective or common-sense exchange rate forecasts based on economic, political, and other data for a country

K

Kennedy Round   Round of trade negotiations named after U.S. President John F. Kennedy between GATT members during the period 1964–1967

Key currency   A currency that is widely traded on world money markets, has demonstrated relatively stable values over time, and has been widely accepted as a means of international settlement

L

Labor mobility   A measure of how labor migration responds to wage differentials

Labor theory of value   The cost or price of a good depends exclusively upon the amount of labor required to produce it

Large nation   An importing nation that is large enough so that changes in the quantity of its imports, by means of tariff policy, influence the world price of the product

Law of comparative advantage   When each nation specializes in the production of that good in which it has a relative advantage, the total output of each good increases; thus, all countries can realize welfare gains

Law of one price   Part of the purchasing-power-parity approach to determining exchange rates, asserts that identical goods should cost the same in all nations, assuming that it is costless to ship goods between nations and there are no barriers to trade

Leaning against the wind   Intervening to reduce short-term fluctuations in exchange rates without attempting to adhere to any particular rate over the long-term

Leontief paradox   The phenomenon of exports being less capital intensive than import-competing goods

Level playing field   A condition in which domestic and foreign producers can compete on equal terms

License on demand allocation   A system in which licenses are required to import at the within-quota tariff

Liquidity problem   When a government or central bank runs short of needed international reserves

Long position   Buying a currency at a low price, then selling it at a higher price later on

M

Maastricht Treaty   Signed in 1991, this agreement set 2002 as the date for completing the process of replacing the EU countries' central banks with a European Central Bank and replacing their national currencies with a single European currency

Magnification effect   An extension of the Stolper—Samuelson theorem, that suggests that the change in the price of a resource is greater than the change in the price of the good that uses the resources relatively intensively in its production process

Managed floating system   An exchange rate system in which the rate is usually allowed to be determined by the free market forces of supply and demand, while sometimes entailing some degree of government (central bank) intervention

Margin of dumping   The amount the domestic price of a firm's product exceeds its foreign price, or the amount the foreign price of a firm's product is less than the cost of producing it

Marginal rate of transformation (MRT)   The slope of the production possibilities schedule that shows the amount of one product a nation must sacrifice to get one additional unit of the other product

Market expectations   Examples include news about future market fundamentals and traders' opinions about future exchange rates

Market fundamentals   Economic variables such as productivity, inflation rates, real interest rates, consumer preferences, and government trade policy

Marshall—Lerner condition   A general rule that states: (1) Depreciation will improve the trade balance if the currency-depreciating nation's demand elasticity for imports plus the foreign demand elasticity for the nation's exports exceeds one. (2) If the sum of the demand elasticities is less than one, depreciation will worsen the trade balance. (3) The trade balance will be neither helped nor hurt if the sum of the demand elasticities equals one

Maturity months   The months of a given year when the futures contract matures

Mercantilists   An advocate or practitioner of mercantilism; a national economic system in which a nation could regulate its domestic and international affairs so as to promote its own interests through a strong foreign trade sector

Merchandise trade balance   The result of combining the dollar value of merchandise exports recorded as a plus (credit) and the dollar value of merchandise imports recorded as a minus (debit)

Migration   Moving from one country to settle in another

Ministry of Economy, Trade and Industry (METI)   Created by the Japanese government to implement its industrial policies in manufacturing

Monetary approach   An approach to currency depreciation that stresses the effects depreciation has on the purchasing power of money and the resulting impact on domestic expenditure levels

Monetary policy   Refers to changes in the money supply by a nation's central bank

Monetary union   The unification of national monetary policies and the acceptance of a common currency administered by a supranational monetary authority

Most favored nation (MFN) clause   An agreement between two nations to apply tariffs to each other at rates as low as those applied to any other nation

Multifiber Arrangement (MFA)   A system of rules negotiated by the United States and Europe to restrict competition from developing exporting countries employing low cost labor

Multilateral contract   Contract that stipulates a minimum price at which importers will purchase guaranteed quantities from the producing nations and a maximum price at which producing nations will sell guaranteed amounts to importers

Multinational enterprise (MNE)   An enterprise that cuts across national borders and is often directed from a company planning center that is distant from the host country

N

Net creditor The status of a nation when that country's claims on foreigners exceed foreign claims on that country at a particular time

Net debtor The status of a nation when foreign claims on a country exceed that country's claims on foreigners at a particular time

Net foreign investment In national income accounting, is synonymous with the current account balance

Nominal exchange rate Exchange rate quotes published in newspapers that are not adjusted inflation rates in trading partners

Nominal exchange rate index The average value of a currency, not adjusted for changes in price levels of that country and its trading partners

Nominal interest rate The rate of return on assets that can be earned in a particular country, not adjusted for the rate of inflation

Nominal tariff rate The tariff rate published in a country's tariff schedule

Nontariff trade barriers (NTBs) Policies other than tariffs that restrict international trade

Normal trade relations The U.S. government's replacement for the term most favored nation

North American Free Trade Agreement (NAFTA) A trade agreement between Canada, Mexico, and the United States that went into effect in 1994

No-trade boundary The terms-of-trade limit at which a country will cease to export a good

O

Offer rate The price at which the bank is willing to sell a unit of foreign currency

Official exchange rate The exchange rate determined by comparing the par values of two currencies

Official reserve assets Holding key foreign currencies, special drawing rights, and reserve positions in the IMF by official monetary institutions

Official settlements transactions The movement of financial assets among official holders; these financial assets fall into two categories: official reserve assets and liabilities to foreign official agencies

Offshore assembly provision (OAP) When import duties apply only to the value added in the foreign assembly process provided that domestically made components are used by overseas companies in their assembly operations

Openness The ratio of a nation's exports and imports as a percentage of its gross domestic product (GDP)

Optimum currency area A region in which it is economically preferable to have a single official currency rather than multiple official currencies

Optimum tariff A tariff rate at which the positive difference between the gain of improving terms of trade and the loss of declining import volume is maximized

Option An agreement between a holder (buyer) and a writer (seller) that gives the holder the right, but not the obligation, to buy or sell financial instruments at any time through a specified date

Organization of Petroleum Exporting Countries (OPEC) A group of nations that sells petroleum on the world market and attempts to support prices higher than would exist under more competitive conditions to maximize member nation profits

Outer limits for the equilibrium terms of trade Defined by the domestic cost ratios of trading nations

Outsourcing When certain aspects of a product's manufacture are performed in more than one country

Overall balance When an economy attains internal and external balance

Overshooting An instance of an exchange rate's short-term response to a change in market fundamentals is greater than its long-term response

P

Par value A central value in terms of a key currency that governments participating in a fixed exchange rate system set their currencies

Partial specialization When a country specializes only partially in the production of the good in which it has a comparative advantage

Persistent dumping When a producer consistently sells products abroad at lower prices than at home

Predatory dumping   When a producer temporarily reduces the prices charged abroad to drive foreign competitors out of business

Premium   The valuation of a currency when it is worth more in the forward market than in the spot market

Price adjustment mechanism   See quantity of money theory

Price-based definition of dumping   A method of calculating fair market value in dumping cases; dumping occurs when a company sells a product in its home market at a price above that for which the same product sells in the foreign market

Price-specie-flow doctrine   David Hume's theory that a favorable trade balance was possible only in the short-term, and that over time, it would automatically be eliminated via changes in product prices

Primary products   Agricultural goods, raw materials, and fuels

Principle of absolute advantage   In a two-nation, two-product world, international specialization and trade will be beneficial when one nation has an absolute cost advantage in one good and the other nation has an absolute cost advantage in the other good

Principle of comparative advantage   Ability to produce a good or service at a lower opportunity cost than others can produce it

Producer surplus   The revenue producers receive over and above the minimum amount required to induce them to supply the good

Product life cycle theory   Many manufactured goods undergo a predictable trade cycle; during this cycle, the home country initially is an exporter, then loses its competitive advantage vis-à-vis its trading partners, and eventually may become an importer of the commodity

Production and export controls   Restrictions on output that are intended to increase the price of a product.

Production gains   Increases in production resulting from specialization in the product of comparative advantage

Production possibilities schedule   A schedule that shows various alternative combinations of two goods

that a nation can produce when all of its factor inputs are used in their most efficient manner

Protection-biased sector   Generally consists of import-competing companies, the labor unions representing workers in that industry, and the suppliers to the companies in the industry

Protective effect   A tariff's loss to the domestic economy resulting from wasted resources when less efficient domestic production is substituted for more efficient foreign production

Protective tariff   A tariff designed to insulate import-competing producers from foreign competition

Purchasing-power-parity theory   A method of determining the equilibrium exchange rate by means of the price levels and their variations in different nations

Put option   Gives the holder the right to sell foreign currency at a specified price

Q

Quantity theory of money   States that increases in the money supply lead directly to an increase in overall prices, and a shrinking money supply causes overall prices to fall

R

Real exchange rate   The nominal exchange rate adjusted for changes in relative price levels

Real exchange rate index   The average value of a currency based on real exchange rates

Real interest rate   The nominal interest rate minus the inflation rate

Reciprocal Trade Agreements Act   An act passed in Congress in 1934 that set the stage for a wave of trade liberalization through negotiating authority and generalized reductions

Redistributive effect   With a tariff, the transfer of consumer surplus in monetary terms to the domestic producers of the import-competing product

Region of mutually beneficial trade   The area that is bounded by the cost ratios of the two trading countries

Regional trading arrangement   Where member nations agree to impose lower barriers to trade within the group than to trade with nonmember nations

Revaluation An official change in a currency's par value that causes the currency's exchange value to appreciate

Revenue effect Represents the government's collections of tariff revenue; found by multiplying the number of imports times the tariff

Revenue tariff A tariff imposed for the purpose of generating tax revenues and may be placed on either exports or imports

S

Safeguards Relief provided by the escape clause to U.S. firms and workers who are substantially injured from surges in imports that are fairly traded

Scientific tariff A tariff that eliminates foreign cost advantages over domestic firms

Section 301 Section of the Trade Act of 1974 that gives the U.S. trade representative (USTR) authority, subject to the approval of the president, and means to respond to unfair trading practices by foreign nations

Seigniorage Profit from issuing money

Selective quota An import quota allocated to specific countries

Short position Sell a currency (that you don't own) at a high price then buy it back later on at a low price

Small nation A nation whose imports constitute a very small portion of the world market supply

Smoot–Hawley Act Act passed in 1930 under which U.S. average tariffs were raised to 53 percent on protected imports

Social regulation Governmental attempts to correct a variety of undesirable side effects in an economy that relate to health, safety, and the environment

Special drawing right (SDR) An artificial currency unit based on a basket of four currencies established by the IMF

Specific tariff A tariff expressed in terms of a fixed amount of money per unit of the imported product

Specific-factors theory Considers the income distribution effects of trade when factor inputs are immobile among industries in the short-term

Speculation The attempt to profit by trading on expectations about prices in the future

Speculative attack See currency crisis

Sporadic dumping (distress dumping) When a firm disposes of excess inventories on foreign markets by selling abroad at lower prices than at home

Spot market Where foreign exchange can be traded for immediate delivery

Spot transaction An outright purchase and sale of foreign currency for cash settlement not more than two business days after the date of the transaction

Spread The difference between the bid and the asking price(s)

Stabilizing speculation Occurs when speculators expect a current trend in an exchange rate's movement to change and their purchase or sale of the currency moderates movements of the exchange rate

Static effects of economic integration Includes the trade-creation effect and the trade-diversion effect

Statistical discrepancy A correcting entry inserted into the balance-of-payments statement to make the sum of the credits and debits equal

Stolper–Samuelson theorem An extension of the theory of factor-price equalization, which states that the export of the product that embodies large amounts of the relatively cheap, abundant resource makes this resource more scarce in the domestic market

Strategic trade policy The policy that government can assist domestic companies in capturing economic profits from foreign competitors

Strike price The price at which an option can be exercised

Subsidies Granted by governments to domestic producers to improve their trade competitiveness; include outright cash disbursements, tax concessions, insurance arrangements, and loans at below-market interest rates

Supply of international reserves Includes owned reserves, such as key currencies and special drawing rights, and borrowed reserves that can come from the IMF and other official arrangements or can be obtained from major commercial banks

Swap arrangements Bilateral agreements between central banks where each government provides for an exchange or swap of currencies to help finance temporary payments disequilibrium

T

Target exchange rates   Desired exchange rates for a currency set by the host country and supported by intervention

Tariff   A tax levied on a product when it crosses national boundaries

Tariff avoidance   The legal utilization of the tariff system to one's own advantage in order to reduce the amount of tariff that is payable by means that are within the law

Tariff escalation   Occurs when tariff structures of industrialized nations are characterized by rising rates that give greater protection to intermediate and finished products than to primary commodities

Tariff evasion   When individuals or firms evade tariffs by illegal means such as smuggling imported goods into a country

Tariff-rate quota   A device that allows a specified number of goods to be imported at one tariff rate (the within-quota rate), and any imports above that specified number to be imported at a higher tariff rate (the over-quota rate)

Technical analysis   A method of exchange rate forecasting that involves the use of historical exchange rate data to estimate future values

Technology transfer   The transfer to other nations of knowledge and skills applied to how goods are produced

Terms of trade   The relative prices at which two products are traded in the marketplace

Terms-of-trade effect   The tariff revenue extracted from foreign producers in the form of a lower supply price

Theory of overlapping demands   Nations with similar per capita incomes will have overlapping demand structures and will likely consume similar types of manufactured goods; wealthy nations will likely trade with other wealthy nations, and poor nations will likely trade with other poor nations

Theory of reciprocal demand   Relative demand conditions determine what the actual terms of trade will be within the outer limits of the terms of trade

Three-point arbitrage   A more intricate form of arbitrage, involving three currencies and three financial centers; also called triangular arbitrage

Tokyo Round   Round of talks between GATT members from 1973–1979, in which signatory nations agreed to tariff cuts that took the across-the-board form initiated in the Kennedy Round

Trade adjustment assistance   Government assistance granted to domestic workers displaced by increased imports

Trade balance   Derived by computing the net exports (imports) in the merchandise accounts; also called merchandise trade balance

Trade promotion authority   (also known as *fast-track authority*) devised in 1974, this provision commits the U.S. Congress to consider trade agreements without amendment; in return, the president must adhere to a specified timetable and several other procedures

Trade remedy laws   Laws designed to produce a fair trading environment for all parties engaging in international business; these laws include the escape clause, countervailing duties, antidumping duties, and unfair trading practices

Trade triangle   An area in a production possibilities diagram showing a country's exports, imports, and equilibrium terms of trade

Trade creation effect   A welfare gain resulting from increasing trade caused by the formation of a regional trade bloc

Trade diversion effect   A welfare loss resulting from the formation of a regional trade bloc; it occurs when imports from a low cost supplier outside the trade bloc are replaced by purchases from a higher cost supplier within the trade bloc

Trade-weighted dollar   A weighted average of the exchange rates between a domestic currency and the currencies of the nation's most important trading partners, with weights given by relative importance of the nation's trade with each trade partner

Trading possibilities line   A line in a production possibilities diagram representing the equilibrium terms-of-trade ratio

Transfer pricing   A technique where an MNE reports most of its profits in a low tax country, even though the profits are earned in a high tax country

Transplants   The assembly plants of Japanese companies that produce automobiles in the United States

Transportation costs   The costs of moving goods from one nation to another

Two-point arbitrage   The simultaneous purchase and sale of a currency in two foreign exchange markets in order to profit from exchange rate differentials in different locations

U

Uncovered interest arbitrage   When an investor does not obtain exchange market cover to protect investment proceeds from foreign currency fluctuations

Unilateral transfers   Include transfers of goods and services (gifts in kind) or financial assets (money gifts) between the United States and the rest of the world

Uruguay Round   Round of talks between GATT members from 1986–1993 in which across-the-board tariff cuts for industrial countries averaged 40 percent

V

Variable levies   An import tariff that increases or decreases as domestic or world prices change to guarantee that the price of the imported product after payment of duty will equal a predetermined price

Vertical integration   In the case of an MNE, occurs when the parent MNE decides to establish foreign subsidiaries to produce intermediate goods or inputs that go into the production of the finished good

W

Wage and price controls   Intervention by the government to set price and wage levels

World Bank   An international organization that provides loans to developing countries aimed toward poverty reduction and economic development

World Trade Organization (WTO)   Organization that embodies the main provisions of GATT, but its role was expanded to include a mechanism intended to improve GATT's process for resolving trade disputes among member nations

Index

The U.S. Census Bureau
http://www.census.gov/ftp/pub/foreign-trade/www
Description: Extensive, recent, and historical data on U.S. exports, imports, and trade balances with individual countries. The U.S. Census Bureau has also developed a profile of U.S. exporting companies.

The World Bank Group
http://www1.worldbank.org
Description: One of the world's largest sources of developmental assistance. This site provides economic briefs and data for countries by region.

International Trade Commission
http://www.usitc.gov/
Description: Information about U.S. tariffs as well as many documents that address contemporary issues in international economics.

Office of the United States Trade Representative (OUSTR)
http://www.ustr.gov/
Description: Reports issued by the OUSTR and related entities including the National Trade Estimate Report on Foreign Trade Barriers.

The Export-Import Bank
http://www.exim.gov/
Description: Information and services from the governmentheld corporation that encourages the sale of U.S. goods in foreign markets.

U.S. Department of Commerce/International Trade Administration
http://www.ita.doc.gov/td/industry/otea/
Description: Trade statistics for the United States by world, region, or country.

Bureau of Labor Statistics/Foreign Labor Statistics
http://www.bls.gov/home.htm
Description: Comparison of the hourly compensation of U.S. workers in manufacturing to that of workers in other countries.

CIA'sHandbook of International Economic Statistics
http://www.cia.gov
Description: Comprehensive information on most countries and territories, including geography, natural resources, demographics, government, and economic statistics.

U.S. Citizenship and Immigration Services
http://uscis.gov/graphics/
Description: Comprehensive statistics on U.S. immigration.

Bureau of Economic Analysis
http://www.bea.gov/
Description: Information on the U.S. balance of payments, U.S. exports and imports, and the international investment position of the United States.

The International Monetary Fund (IMF)
http://www.imf.org/
Description: International Monetary Fund provides loans, technical assistance, and policy guidance to developing members in order to reduce poverty, improve living standards, and safeguard the stability of the international monetary system.

Penn World Table
http://pwt.econ.upenn.edu/
Description: Provides purchasing power parity and national income accounts converted to international prices for 189 countries/territories for some or all of the years 1950-2009.

TradeStats Express
http://tse.export.gov/
Description: Provides latest annual and quarterly trade data.

Public Broadcasting Service
www.pbs.org/newshour/businessdesk/2012/01/
could-a-higher-import-tariff-phtml
Description: America's largest classroom, the nation's largest stage for the arts and a trusted window to the world.

International Trade Administration
http://trade.gov
Description: Promotes trade and investment, and ensures fair trade through the rigorous enforcement of trade laws and agreements.

Level Field Institute
www.levelfieldinstitute.org
Description: A scorecard for families and public officials.

World Intellectual Property Organization
www.wipo.int/ipstats/en
Description: Promotes innovation and creativity for the economic, social and cultural development of all countries, through a balanced and effective international intellectual property system.